THE SWEETNESS OF POWER

The Sweetness of Power

MACHIAVELLI'S
DISCOURSES

GUICCIARDINI'S
CONSIDERATIONS

TRANSLATED BY

JAMES B. ATKINSON

AND DAVID SICES

NORTHERN ILLINOIS UNIVERSITY PRESS / DeKalb

Published by the Northern Illinois University Press,

DeKalb, Illinois 60115

First published in paperback 2007.

Manufactured in the United States using

50% postconsumer-recycled, acid-free paper

Design by Julia Fauci

The Library of Congress has catalogued

the hardcover edition as follows:

Machiavelli, Niccolò, 1469–1527.

[Discorsi sopra la prima deca di Tito Livio. English]

The sweetness of power: Machiavelli's Discourses and

Guicciardini's Considerations / translated and

introduced by James B. Atkinson and David Sices.

p. cm.

Includes bibliographical references and index.

ISBN-10: 0-87580-288-5 (alk. paper)

1. Political science—Early works to 1800.

2. Livy. Ab urbe condita. I. Atkinson, James B., 1934– .

II. Sices, David. III. Guicciardini, Francesco,

1483–1540. Considerazioni intorno

ai Discorsi del Machiavelli. English. IV. Title.

JC143.M33 2002

937—dc21 2001052184

ISBN-13: 978-0-87580-618-1 (paperback : alk. paper)

ISBN-10: 0-87580-618-X (paperback : alk. paper)

To Gretchen and Jacqueline, and for "the minds of the young":

Andreas, Katrina, and Nils;

Harry, Laura, Anne, and Andrew;

and their children.

Contents

"a prudent organizer of a republic who intends to serve not himself but the common good, not his own succession but the common fatherland, must strive to be the only one in authority"

—Machiavelli, *Discourses,* 1, 9, 2.

"it is possible for the sweetness of power and the unbridled power to rule to change initial good intentions into evil ones"

—Guicciardini, *Considerations,* 1, 9, 2.

Preface

The Discourses on the First Ten Books of Titus Livy is an imposing title. Even as Renaissance titles go, it is somewhat off-putting to the modern reader. It is no wonder that it is more familiarly referred to as *The Discourses.* But even this abbreviated title has not led to its becoming a familiar work. Despite the variety of Machiavelli's writings that include plays, poetry, short stories, history, diplomatic and personal correspondence, political theory, and military tactics, most readers make up their minds about him and his influence on the history of ideas from study of *The Prince* alone. Whereas, as it has been succinctly put, his "capital book" is *The Discourses.*

Because we believe that readers are better served by having a wider range of Machiavelli's works available to them, we have cooperated on translations of his plays, his correspondence, and now *The Discourses.* For those interested particularly in Machiavelli's contributions to political theory, *The Discourses* are essential reading. This reading is no easy task, however. It is not merely the title that is daunting; the work itself is intimidating.

So the translation must first and foremost be readable. We have broken up Machiavelli's long, hypotactic sentences; the Latinate construction valued by his contemporaries often blocks the understanding of readers accustomed to modern writers' terseness. What may be lost is the subtle interaction of his syntax and thought; on the other hand, the structure of his sentences becomes more readily accessible. By following editor Giorgio Inglese's example of numbering Machiavelli's sentences, we hope to compensate for this loss, enabling the reader to see what the basic sentence looked like.

The translation of some words readily understood by sixteenth-century Italian readers presents several problems, some of which are indicated in the notes. Our greatest source of difficulty was with *virtù*. It occurs in his Dedicatory Letter (see our note to its seventh sentence), so a decision needed to be reached early. It is not that *virtù* is untranslatable, like *omertà, je ne sais quoi,* or *gemütlich*. The question is: in Machiavelli's universe of discourse, should it be considered a word or a concept? Although we most frequently believed his context suggested such synonyms as "ability," "power," or "courage," we reluctantly (and despite some disagreement) decided to leave the word in Italian. Hence the reader is warned not only of the frequency of *virtù* in Machiavelli's vocabulary, but also of its importance to his exploration of a major theme in *The Discourses:* the relationship between military and political *virtù*. The simple alternative of the English "virtue" might also have brought the reader up short and served as a reminder of the problem of translation, but we believed that to be a compromise even more confusing.

Although a readable text is the first step in encouraging readers to examine *The Discourses,* other factors also come into play. The reader needs to be aware of the historical context in which the book was written and to which it alludes. Because the history upon which it is based is also ancient history, a translation needs to clarify Rome's history, and Livy's commentary on it. Finally, because Machiavelli is aware of many other writers' ideas and reactions to these notions, the translation must alert readers to Machiavelli's debts to Greek and Roman authors ranging from Aristotle to Valerius Maximus. The notes will address both of these factors.

As the basis for our translation, we have chosen the edition, with an introduction by Gennaro Sasso and notes by Giorgio Inglese, published by Rizzoli in the series *I Classici della biblioteca universale Rizzoli,* Milan, 1984, used with their permission. (The excellent edition of *The Discourses* edited by Rinaldo Rinaldi for the Unione Tipografico-Editrice Torinese [UTET] in 1999, which has become the standard scholarly edition in Italian, appeared while our work was in progress; we have consulted its meticulous, detailed annotation and its interpretive suggestions.) Inglese's volume was based to a considerable extent on the critical edition by Guido Mazzoni and Mario Casella: *Niccolò Machiavelli, Tutte le opere storiche e letterari* (Florence: Barbèra, 1929). In his Premessa to the 1984 text, Inglese outlines the loci and reasons for his departures from the critical edition, including publishing separately Machiavelli's autograph draft of the first *Proemio,* along with its definitive version, and correcting certain "prejudices" of Mazzoni's, relative to alternative manuscript and published sources: in particular, the autograph draft of the first *Proemio* in the *Carte Machiavelli* of the National Library in Florence; the versions of Discourse 3, 6, and chapters 1, 4, and 6, of Book 1 in the Florentine Archives and the National Library (the latter in the hand of Piero Ardinghelli); the complete manuscripts of *The Discourses,* transcribed by a Florentine scribe some time between 1520 and 1520, in the British Museum (Harleian MS 3533), the basis for the Mazzoni and Casella text; and the first two published editions of *The Discourses,* one by Bernardo di Giunta in Florence, 1531, and a slightly earlier one by Antonio Blado in Rome. Inglese implies in this *Premessa* that he wishes to undertake a new critical edition of the text, based on his understanding of the interrelationships between these widely scattered source materials. In the interim, we find his argument concerning chronology and the interconnections among these various sources convincing, and for that reason accept his text as the best currently available to translators. (Those seeking more detailed information about textual sources should consult his edition, pp. 35–44.)

For our translation of Guicciardini's *Considerazioni intorno ai discorsi del Machiavelli sopra la Primi Deca di Tito Livio,* we have used the edition published in the series *Scrittori d'Italia,* Francesco Guicciardini, *Opere 7: Scritti politici e ricordi,* edited by Roberto Palmarocchi (Bari: Laterza, 1933), pp. 1–65. We thank them for their kind permission to use this text. Palmarocchi's text for these unfinished commentaries was based on the autograph manuscript in the Guicciardini Archives; Palmarocchi declared himself dissatisfied with numerous misreadings in an earlier edition done by Giuseppe Canestrini: Francesco Guicciardini, *Opere inedite. Illustrate da Giuseppe Canestrini e pubblicate per cura dei conti Piero e Luigi Guicciardini* (Florence: Barbèra, Bianchi, 1857).

Those who have preceded us in making these works available to an English-speaking audience have been consulted with respect and gratitude. The edition of *The Discourses* prepared by Leslie J. Walker, S.J., in 1950 is copiously annotated, and all subsequent readers of Machiavelli's text, no matter what their native language, rely on his commentary; in 1974 it was reprinted by Penguin with a partially revised translation by Brian Richardson, and edited by Bernard Crick. In 1965 Allan Gilbert included *The Discourses* in volume 1 of his *Machiavelli: The Chief Works and Others.* There have been two more recent editions: that done by Harvey C. Mansfield and Nathan Tarcov for the University of Chicago Press in 1996, and that done by Julia Conaway Bondanella and Peter Bondanella for the World Classic Series of Oxford University Press in 1997. In addition to Inglese's edition, two other Italian editions were particularly helpful: the 1993 edition by Gian Mario Anselmi and Carlo Varotti (prepared, with the help of Paolo Fazion and Elisabetta Menetti, for Bollati Boringhieri) in the "Le grandi opere politiche" series; and especially *Discorsi sopra la prima deca di Tito Livio seguiti dalle "Considerazioni intorno ai Discorsi del Machiavelli" di Francesco Guicciardini,* edited by Corrado Vivanti for Einaudi in 1983. (The complete references for all the books mentioned in our Preface and throughout this edition can be found in our Works Consulted section.)

The basis for our citations from Livy, as for all Greek and Roman writers, is the Loeb Classical Library editions, brought out in the United States by Harvard University Press and in England by William Heinemann, Limited. Unless otherwise noted, we have done all the translations in this volume.

Professor Maurizio Viroli of Princeton University made a number of extremely useful suggestions concerning both the translation and the critical apparatus.

Finally, we gratefully acknowledge the assistance of the staff at Baker/Berry Library of Dartmouth College, and in particular Patricia Carter of the Interlibrary Loan office, as well as the generous grant from Dartmouth College's Office of the Dean of the Faculty.

Introduction

JAMES B. ATKINSON AND DAVID SICES

Fiorenza mia . . . .
vedrai te somigliante a quella inferma
che non può trovar posa in su le piume,
ma con dar volta suo dolore scherma.
—Dante, *Purgatorio,* 6, vv. 149–151

My Florence . . . .
you will see yourself like that sick woman
who can find no rest on her feather bed,
but shields herself from pain by tossing and turning.

Dante vividly captures Florence's feverish factional strife early in the fourteenth century. If the "sick woman" was "tossing and turning" then, her "pain" had certainly not abated by the early sixteenth century. The divisions that drove Dante into exile from Florence around 1302 embittered him deeply. The vicissitudes of Florentine politics that forced both Machiavelli and Guicciardini out of active roles in government led to no less bitterness in them. Enforced idleness led all three to vent their rancor in vigorous commentary. But Machiavelli and Guicciardini each developed distinct approaches to dissecting the causes and the implications of the factional strife raging, not only in Florence, but throughout all Italy in the early 1500s.

The political circumstances and tensions that drove Machiavelli and Guicciardini from power, the former in 1512 and the latter in 1527, were not parallel. Thus each one's reflection on his past and the lessons he drew from it took different forms. Machiavelli's analysis centered on political history, to clarify how a government can achieve and maintain political success. Guicciardini's centered on narrative history, to clarify why events turned out the way they did, how human cause and effect related to historical cause and effect. Whereas Machiavelli strove to isolate how political choices and decisions influence a government, and consequently its history, Guicciardini sought to isolate the motives behind choices and decisions. We shall suggest the historical context leading to this divergence before attempting a more detailed examination of the personal reasons.

THE HISTORICAL BACKGROUND

The external historical factors that determined Machiavelli's political career began in 1494. French King Charles VIII, to assert his complicated genealogical claim to the throne of Naples, invaded Italy with the largest military force the peninsula had experienced since Hannibal's invasion in 218 B.C. To protect Florence, Piero de' Medici made a series of concessions to Charles without consulting the Florentine Signoria. The irate city expelled the Medici. In December 1494, inspired by the mixture of politics and evangelical zeal of the Dominican friar and preacher Savonarola, Florentine reformers reorganized their constitution and established a republican government. This constitution is frequently termed "democratic" because, with the Great Council, it greatly enlarged the number of people who could participate in government. Machiavelli entered this government as second chancellor of the republic and secretary of the Ten of War in 1498; he served brilliantly until 1512. He was particularly loyal to Piero Soderini, the titular head of the republic as gonfaloniere (standard-bearer) for life.

In 1512 Florence recalled the Medici, thus ending its commitment to a republican regime. The city balked at the republic's temporizing policy toward Pope Julius XII's Holy League, organized to eliminate from Italy the power and influence of France, now led by King Louis XII. Fed up with this catering to the French king, Florentines hoped a strong Medici hand at the helm would both drive the French from Italy and strengthen the city's position throughout the peninsula. The pro-Medici party cashiered Machiavelli in autumn 1512. Alleged to have been involved in a plot against the Medici, he was briefly imprisoned; the following spring he reluctantly withdrew to his farm at Sant'Andrea in Percussina, near San Casciano, about ten miles southwest of Florence. There, in what felt like exile, he wrote *The Prince.* Although his interest in Livy was long-standing, his serious thinking about *The Discourses on the First Ten Books of Titus Livy* may have begun there too. But their real inspiration was fostered by an attempt to influence a group of Florentine humanists that met at the Orti Oricellari, the gardens of the home of Cosimo Rucellai, one of the dedicatees of *The Discourses,* who hosted literary, philosophical, and political discussions for a number of years. Machiavelli may have attended a few of these as early as 1514; more likely he began frequenting them in 1515 or 1516. Most of his work on *The Discourses* was done from 1517 to 1519. Although various manuscripts circulated among his friends,[1] they were not published until 1531, four years after his death.

Coincidentally, the year 1512 marks the starting point for the historical factors that determined Guicciardini's political career. In January 1512 he left Florence as the city's ambassador to meet with Ferdinand the Catholic, king of Spain. Machiavelli may well have played a minor role on this occasion: although the Council of Eighty elected Guicciardini the previous October, his instructions were prepared and finally issued by those responsible for the republic's foreign policy, the Ten of War. Machiavelli was its secretary.[2]

Despite a considerable difference in their station and political views, the ensuing years provided several points of real, not merely conjectural, contact between the two men. Guicciardini descended from a long line of *ottimati* (the best), aristocrats who firmly believed in service to their community, embodied as much in one family among their oligarchic group, the Medici, as in the city itself. His marriage in 1508 to Maria Salviati, a daughter of Alamanno Salviati, a leader of *ottimati* opposition to Soderini's government, confirmed his allegiance to this class. It is therefore not surprising that Guicciardini's link to the Medici became politically valuable on his return to Florence from Spain in 1514.

The Medici were systematically reclaiming the upper hand. An ambitious Giovanni de' Medici had been elected Pope Leo X in 1513 and set about consolidating Medici control in two of Italy's major seats of influence. He saw to it in Florence that power rested in the hands of his brother Giuliano de Medici, known as the duke of Nemours, and his nephew Lorenzo II de' Medici; he further saw to it that his cousin Giulio was elected cardinal (Giulio was to become the hapless Pope Clement VII in 1523). In neither place did his enemies yield without a struggle, however.

Because his Medici sympathies were well known, Guicciardini spent less time in his law office and began taking an active part in Florentine politics. In 1514 and 1515 he was a member of the Eight and then the Signoria. His Medici connections led Leo X to appoint him papal governor of Modena in 1516; the following year the pope added the governship of Reggio Emilia to his responsibilities. His power increased once Clement VII became pope, appointing Guicciardini president of Romagna in 1524, and in 1526 lieutenant general of the papal armies.

But because Guicciardini's continuing rise was Medici-based, as their influence declined so did his. Partly on Guicciardini's advice, Clement joined the League of Cognac in 1526, to combat the threat to Italy represented by the Holy Roman Emperor, Charles V. The pope's vulnerability to that threat resulted a year later in the sack of Rome and imprisonment by Charles V's Spanish and German mercenaries in Clement's very own fortress, the Castel Sant' Angelo, Meanwhile, anti-Medici forces in Florence were quick to seize the opportunity to drive out the Medici and set up the short-lived Last Republic, in 1527–1530, under Niccolò Capponi, a friend of Guicciardini, and Filippo Strozzi. Guicciardini, however, thought discretion the better part of valor. In what felt like exile to him, as it had to Machiavelli fifteen years earlier, he withdrew to his country villa to polish and expand his *Ricordi,* to write his *Considerations of the* Discourses *of Machiavelli,* and to prepare his magisterial *History of Italy.*

AN EXCHANGE OF LETTERS: THE PERSONAL BACKGROUND

This significant fifteen-year period included much actual contact between Machiavelli and Guicciardini, occurring against an historical background of flux and turmoil, the ebb and flow of political fortunes. Throughout his life, Machiavelli was both a political and an economic have-not, in sharp contrast to Guicciardini, an economic and political "have." But the mutual admiration, respect, and friendship of the two reveals much about them as individuals and as thinkers, making it easier to assess why one turned to political and the other to narrative history.

The first documented interaction between them does not occur until May 1521, shortly after Machiavelli began writing a history of Florence that would take four years to complete. Cardinal Giulio de' Medici was instrumental in obtaining this commission for him, and persuading the Signoria to send him on a mission to Carpi, north of Modena. There Machiavelli was to urge the Chapter General of the Minorite Friars to split off their convents in Florentine territory from those in the wider Tuscan region, so Florentine officials could more readily keep them under surveillance. As he happened to be in Carpi, Machiavelli was also asked by the Florentine Wool Guild to prevail on the friars to have one of their best preachers address the Lenten service at the Duomo. Neither task was comparable to the diplomatic missions Machiavelli carried out for Soderini's regime, but he was anxious to be of service to Florence once again, and especially to please the cardinal.

Before reaching Carpi, he stopped off in Modena, headquarters for the governor of the Papal States in Romagna. We can only speculate about the conversation between Machiavelli and Guicciardini, but the letters they exchanged on 17 May suggest what some of the topics might have been and what characterized each man's slant. Clearly, Machiavelli unburdened himself about his tension in preparing a history of Florence for a Medici, whose family would play a major role in his chronicle but occupy a lesser position in his respect. He acknowledges to Guicciardini, a Medici partisan, that "for some time now I have never said what I believe or never believed what I said; and if indeed I do sometimes tell the truth, I hide it behind so many lies that it is hard to find."[3] Machiavelli had to be extremely confident and assured of Guicciardini's regard and approval to make such an admission: quite an achievement for a visit of less than twenty-four hours.[4] The letter also demonstrated an awareness that a champion of republican Florence could not risk picking too many bones with the Medici's role in the history of Florence. By the same token, it indicates trust that Guicciardini can relish the irony and not be offended.

Machiavelli's letter, in response to one Guicciardini had written earlier that day, proves that irony was an essential ingredient of their friendship. Guicciardini's letter begins, "It was certainly good judgment on the part of the reverend consuls of the Wool Guild to have entrusted you with the duty of selecting a preacher,"[5] evidently a standard statement of praise. But he finishes the sentence with a twist, "not otherwise than if the task had been given to Panchierotto . . . or to Ser Sano to find a beautiful and graceful wife for a friend." Guicciardini couples praise with humor: the men referred to were two well-known Florentine pederasts. In the next sentence he augments praise with respect: "I believe you will serve them according to the expectations they have of you and as is required by your honor." But then he undercuts that respect: "which would be stained if at this age you started to think about your soul, because, since you have always lived in a contrary belief, it would be attributed rather to senility than to goodness."

Owning up to skeptical antipathy toward clerics may not require much courage, let alone empathy, on the part of either, but it sets the tone for the rest of Guicciardini's letter. Machiavelli follows suit. Anticlericalism dominates their interchange; they become confederates and accomplices in plotting practical jokes on the friars. Even Guicciardini's advice to Machiavelli carries an anticlerical barb: "I remind you to take care of this matter as swiftly as possible, because in staying there long you run two risks: one, that those holy friars might pass some of their hypocrisy on to you; the other, that the air of Carpi might make you become a liar, because that has been its influence not only in the present age but also for centuries gone by. If by ill chance you were to be lodged in the house of some Carpian, your case would be without remedy." Poor Machiavelli had no alternative but "to be lodged in the house of some Carpian," yet he could relish Guicciardini's logic. In his reply, Machiavelli takes that barb and proposes that they hatch a plot, heeding the invitation in the last sentence of Guicciardini's letter to learn from the "governing bishop," Teodoro Pio: "If you have visited that governing bishop, you would have seen a fine specimen of a man, someone you could learn a thousand fine tricks from."

A friendly note dashed off to express pleasure at a few hours' conversation ought not to be mistaken for a reasoned argument about a particular issue. Nevertheless, Guicciardini's letter does offer an opportunity to characterize his approach and generalize about his mental set. His irony is rooted in prudence about a mission for "his very dear Machiavelli" that he hopes will be successful. He is confident that his irony will not detract from the practical advice he gives about assessing the circumstances and handling the negotiations that Machiavelli must conduct. He realizes that Machiavelli, to have leverage in Carpi, may have to resort to a few "tricks," but imitating those who practice them should present no problem. After all, Carpi's hypocrisy and mendacity must be confronted. They should not undermine what expediency requires, once they are understood to be givens. In short, just below his surface irony lies Guicciardini's factual judgment; hence, this is a pragmatically concrete letter.

Machiavelli's reply is not. It exposes his tendency to impose a solution on the facts, rather than allow the facts to suggest a conclusion, a habit that will ultimately spark the antagonism in Guicciardini's *Considerations* of his *Discourses.* But this does not qualify Guicciardini's delight in irony and playfulness with those facts, or belie the comradeship he felt for Machiavelli. Although signatures like "as a brother" are formulaic, one senses especially at the outset of their correspondence that their mutual respect and friendship is authentic.

Because of his lower rank, Machiavelli perhaps could not be forthcoming about this bond. The friendship in his reply is thus more sensed between the lines than expressed overtly. It can be noted in his relief at such a vivid demonstration of wit. Gratified to receive such a letter, an easygoing, relaxed Machiavelli responded by giving as good as he got. Yet there is more of interest in this letter than just wit and irony. It presents various themes that both clarify the basis for their mutual friendship and suggest what it was about Machiavelli that irritated Guicciardini.

Imagine receiving a letter that starts off: "I was sitting on the toilet when your messenger arrived, and just at that moment I was mulling over the absurdities of this world."[6] Such an arresting sentence that sets the scene in a privy, whether or not the case, is a dramatic device to catch a reader's attention. Machiavelli will capitalize on this advantage, but not before reminding Guicciardini of his loyalty to Florence: "And because never did I disappoint that republic whenever I was able to help her out—if not with deeds, then with words; if not with words, then with signs—I have no intention of disappointing her now."

That point made, Machiavelli can safely carry the dramatic theme to the point of exaggeration by overextending Guicciardini's topics. Most of his letter takes its cue from the "trick" mentioned in Guicciardini's last sentence, planning a practical joke on the friars.[7] To enlist Guicciardini's "help and advice," he admits that "in my mind I am turning over some way in which I might stir up such strife among them . . . that they might start going after one another with their wooden clogs." He reports the effect on the friars of Guicciardini's crossbowman messenger's arrival, saying "bowing down to the ground, that he had been sent expressly—and in all haste." The friars "sprang up with such bowings and such a hubbub that everything was turned topsy-turvy." Because all this is a practical joke, Machiavelli, "to heighten" his "prestige," embellishes the truth with some bogus gossip. He describes all the friars standing "around with their mouths hanging open and with their caps in hand. Even as I am writing this, I have a circle of them about me; to see me write at length, they marvel and gaze at me as at one inspired; and I, to make them marvel even more, sometimes pause writing and breathe deeply; then they absolutely begin drooling—if they knew what I am writing you, they would marvel all the more!"

He tries to get Guicciardini's cooperation: "it would not be a bad idea if you were to come here under the pretext of going on an excursion, or at least to write me suggesting some master stroke; because if every day you were to send me a servant for this express purpose, as you did today, you would accomplish several good things." Not the least of them would be causing Machiavelli's "reputation to rise among those friars in this house, once they saw the dispatches arriving thick and fast." Warming to the idea, he adds: "tomorrow I expect some advice from you about my affairs and that you will send one of your crossbowmen; let him gallop and get here covered in sweat so that this gang will be dumbfounded. By so doing you will bring me honor." In addition to seeing himself as participant in a practical joke, he hints at awareness of being the author of a dramatic story: "Were I willing to overwork my imagination, I would write you about some other matter now, but I want to hold it in reserve so that I can have it fresh tomorrow."

Skeptical anticlericalism is another theme he picks up from Guicciardini. Advised to become Teodoro Pio's apprentice in trickery, Machiavelli gives his impression of him: "To me he appeared to be an example of a man properly formed, and I think the whole corresponds to the parts and he is what he seems to be—his hump does not lie; so, had I had your letter with me, I would have made a good try at drawing a bucketful out of him." The irony here, it has been suggested, depends on Machiavelli's interpretation of the "hump." Because he believes that it is an external, physical indication of an internal, spiritual imperfection, the "properly formed" bishop is exactly "what he seems to be": a teacher capable of dispensing a "bucketful" of guile from his bag of "tricks."

Machiavelli draws again on Guicciardini's theme of anticlericalism and extends it by exaggeration: "Your Lordship knows how these friars say that when one is confirmed as being in a state of grace, the Devil no long has any power to tempt him. Well, I have no need to fear that these friars will infect me with their hypocrisy because I believe that I have been adequately confirmed." The play on "confirmed" is then pushed to the point of pride at being a nonconformist: "As for the lies of these citizens of Carpi, I can beat all of them out, because it has been a while since I have become a doctor of this art." So, with the deftness of a good storyteller, Machiavelli jerks his reader back into reality.

There is a whiplash effect to his pride at being different. He sets Guicciardini up for an assertion in his first paragraph that separates him from his contemporaries even as he reasserts themes from Guicciardini's first letter. "I was completely absorbed in imagining my style of preacher for Florence: he should be just what would please me, because I am going to be as pigheaded about this idea as I am about my other ideas." Poking fun at clerics is not yet the order of the day; instead, Machiavelli tries to convey an important point about himself as a human being and a thinker. "In truth, I know that I am at variance with the ideas of [Florence's] citizens, as I am in many other matters. They would like a preacher who would teach them the way to paradise, and I should like to find one who would teach them the way to go to the Devil." He cannot help letting his bias show: "they would like their man to be prudent, honest, and genuine, and I should like to find one who would be mad . . . wil[y] . . . and . . . hypocritical . . . because I think it would be a fine thing—something worthy of the goodness of these times—should everything we have experienced in many friars be experienced in one of them."

His rancor about the fall from power can also be felt. But once that has passed, Machiavelli can be more self-revelatory. "For I believe that the following would be the true way to go to Paradise: learn the way to Hell in order to steer clear of it." None of the classical or medieval advocacy of destroying evil for him: Machiavelli follows this idea with one to which more of his detractors should give credence. "Moreover, since I am aware how much belief there is in an evil man who hides under the cloak of religion, I can readily conjure up how much belief there would be in a good man who walks in truth, and not in pretense, tramping through the muddy footprints of Saint Francis."

This exchange of letters typifies in miniature much of their subsequent correspondence, with vivid discussion of topics like a possible presentation of Machiavelli's play *La Mandragola* (The Mandrake) during Faenza's carnival season, in 1526; Machiavelli's mistress, Barbera; Guicciardini's purchase of a country estate in the Mugello that Machiavelli examined for him and thought a waste of money; the contemporary political scene; and military matters. More immediately, it reveals something about the man who has written *The Discourses* and the one who will critique them. Machiavelli's opening salvo may well have put Guicciardini's teeth on edge. Although "Magnificent One, my most respected superior" is a perfectly normal way to address Guicciardini, Machiavelli's juxtaposing of it with the confession, or fabrication, that he was "sitting on the toilet . . . mulling over the absurdities of this world . . . completely absorbed in my imagining my style of preacher" may, from Guicciardini's point of view, have stretched the limits of decorum. He was a sober, prudent man whose convictions led him to advise, "remember: whoever steers carelessly meets a careless end. The right way is to think, to examine, and to consider every detail, even the most minute, carefully; even if we do so, it takes a lot of effort to make matters turn out well. Imagine how they fare for those who let themselves drift with the tide."[8] Machiavelli's imagination dramatically exaggerated events, situations, and people, and could represent for Guicciardini a dangerous evasion of examining "every detail, even the most minute."

Second, when it came to *The Discourses*' ideas about the glories of ancient Rome and how he set up his argument for imitating it, Machiavelli's admission of being "pigheaded" would rub Guicciardini the wrong way. In part, he objected to the failure to consider every detail carefully. More important was Guicciardini's awareness of how easily his friend's "pigheadedness" could become rigidity. This was a method of argument Guicciardini could not abide: "It is a great mistake to talk about the things of this world without distinctions and absolutely and, as it were, to play by the rules. Because of differences in circumstances, nearly all such things require distinctions and exceptions; they cannot be held to the same measure. Nor are these distinctions and exceptions discovered written down in books. They must be taught by discretion."[9]

Because Guicciardini was quick to draw subtle "distinctions" and find valid "exceptions," a third difference followed from his conviction of Machiavelli's failure to do so. Perhaps as a result of legal training, Guicciardini believed his friend set up his arguments too facilely and arbitrarily from a priori hypotheses. Because propositions that were self-evident to Machiavelli were not always so to Guicciardini, he frequently took exception to Machiavelli's argumentation in his *Considerations.*

Finally, these letters signal a basic difference in each man's writing. Machiavelli's fundamental interest was politics. He visualized the situation in Carpi as a director manufacturing an amusing stage set. It was an occasion to be dramatized, one with great potential for political drama, with entertaining political ramifications. As he sought to fit political data into a pattern of history, Guicciardini's fundamental interest was historical. For all his ironic levity about the Republic of Clogs, he believed that the situation could best be summed up in a narrative history. It is not that Guicciardini was oblivious of either the drama or the political ramifications. He would rather have isolated the elements and set them up differently. Essentially he was urging Machiavelli first to get the facts straight, then leave quickly, return to Florence, and present his report expeditiously in order to prove "good judgment"—not only Machiavelli's own but the Signoria's for sending him. That was the method Guicciardini followed when he wrote his narrative history of Italy: to exercise good judgment in selecting the facts, especially those pertinent to politics, and to present them pragmatically and rationally.

This discussion suggests why Guicciardini's *Considerations* are integral to an edition of *The Discourses.* Nonconformity is the most significant personal link between the two men. Guicciardini was aware that Machiavelli "always lived in a contrary belief." Machiavelli appreciated being valued as someone who was "at variance with the ideas of [Florence's] citizens" on "many other matters." But for Guicciardini, being "at variance" did not sanction intellectual irresponsibility.

In the final analysis, he was less upset by Machiavelli's ideas than by his presentation. One way for the modern reader to account for Machiavelli's immediate impact is to observe the interplay of his ideas with one of the best thinkers among his contemporaries. Guicciardini is more representative of the thinking of his time, especially on political concerns, so he may seem to us hard on Machiavelli. Machiavelli gets into trouble by saying things "at variance" with his times. He makes outrageous statements about power and authority, for example, that run counter to received ideas. In retrospect, Machiavelli understood the mechanisms of power, though what Guicciardini had to say about his understanding was more acceptable to his audience. Noting how Machiavelli disconcerted Guicciardini thus provides a valuable framework in which to evaluate the ideas discussed and the issues raised in *The Discourses,* as well as a better idea of the broader concerns of the Renaissance.[10]

MACHIAVELLI AND *THE DISCOURSES:* THE EFFECTS OF THE INTELLECTUAL CLIMATE

Modern readers of *The Discourses* must wear bifocals. They have to keep their eyes on two sources: ancient Rome and early sixteenth-century Florence. Just as they are for Fabrizio in *The Art of War,* Rome and the Romans for Machiavelli were "my Romans." He conceived of them as his exclusive property. But the Romans became "his" in precisely the way they became a prototype for his entire generation: a product of Renaissance humanism's belief in imitating antiquity as a guiding principle for everyday life. In the realm of art, antiquity provided classical forms to imitate for aesthetic perfection. In the realm of education, antiquity provided men and ideas to imitate for the active, the contemplative, and the social life, whether in terms of medical, agricultural, or military texts. In *The Art of War,* for example, thanks to the *Epitoma rei militari* that Vegetius probably wrote between A.D. 388 and 391, the Romans became Machiavelli's paradigm for military institutions, organization, tactics, and fortifications. In *The Discourses,* on the other hand, the Romans represent the virtues of both statecraft and civic humanism, which advocated an active role in the political process for the citizenry, and in works by Cicero, for example, taught the citizenry ways to play that role.

Yet this passion for what Machiavelli regarded as the matrix of the political process was in the service of Florentine thinkers interested in reform, to illuminate the problems they confronted. Not that they were numerous; that was one source of the despair that surfaces in *The Discourses.* Those "happy few" also needed bifocals to arrive at the proper solutions, originating solely in ancient Rome, that is, Rome as seen through Machiavelli's eyes, for his perceptions were bifocal as well. At times Machiavelli voices them so plaintively, his seems a lone voice crying in the wilderness: "For it is the duty of a good man to teach others the good that you have been unable to bring about because of the hostility of the times and of Fortune so that, once many are aware of it, some of them—more beloved of Heaven—may be able to bring it about."[11]

To appreciate the desperation of that voice as Machiavelli set out his guideposts, modern readers—even those properly bifocaled—must acknowledge the huge gap between their knowledge of ancient Rome and his. He was writing for an audience so enthralled by both the recovery of ancient texts and the opportunity to interpret them that their familiarity with the sources and events described could be counted on. That same audience, though, was imbued with a double-edged view of the Roman past epitomized in the humanists' melancholic yet exultant phrase, *quanta Roma fuit ipsa ruina docet* (how great Rome was the ruins themselves teach). The results of the *studia humanitatis,* the humanities, were fresh, challenging, and inspiring; gradually they became familiar to the educated elite. That is not the case for a modern audience. There is a daunting amount of our own kind of recovery necessary before we can hope to be on a par with the earliest readers of *The Discourses.* (We reflect such recovery in our notes.) Granted, Machiavelli's inspiration is rooted in ancient Rome and his examples are based on Greek and Roman sources. This does not mean, however, that his ideas are restricted to what they wrote or thought. Once we have recovered some of this past, we can better grasp what is new about his interpretation of the past. Guicciardini's antipathy to this slant proves that what Machiavelli wrote was new, that it challenged his contemporaries. We, too, need to accept this challenge.[12]

Humanism is a word we bandy about too easily. Yet we often lose sight of what it means about how the *studia humanitatis* were taught in the Renaissance. Because Greek texts were less available, those in Latin on grammar, rhetoric, and dialectic, as well as on moral philosophy, poetry, and history, were sought in monasteries and libraries. Before attempting large-scale interpretations of these treasures, fifteenth-century scholars studied their texts first for language and style. For example, in 1440 Lorenzo Valla published a milestone in the philological study of sources, *De falso credita et ementita Constantini donatione* (The Donation of Constantine). By comparing fourth-century vocabulary with the language of the *Donation,* he proved that this document, upon which the papacy based claims to secular power, was a forgery and could not have been written prior to the eighth century. Characteristic of early Renaissance humanists is the scholar in his study meticulously verifying the accuracy of the text he is preparing for publication. Only then could he begin proselytizing for what we have come to think of as humanism's emphasis on both the individual in a secular world and a conscious return to classical ideals and forms.

This emphasis would constitute the general understanding of the goals of Renaissance humanism, but Peter Godman argues for a more complex view of Florentine humanism in the High Renaissance, in particular during the second decade of the sixteenth century, when Machiavelli was writing *The Discourses.* He believes that the commentary on Livy is in and of itself a forceful critique of humanism as Machiavelli knew it. Thus *The Discourses* represent Machiavelli's repudiation of humanists who regarded imitation of the ancients as a means not of following them, "but of equaling and surpassing their achievements. Rather divergence than correspondence stimulated their thought on this subject, and imitation was less their goal than their point of departure. Adherence to a model, single and strict, these Florentines rejected as conservative Roman purism. Modernity was their objective, pluralism their ideal, classicism their method." As far as textual analysis was concerned, "language, as they were disposed to study it, remained ever subject to change, what they perceived when they observed a text, an event, or a plant was mutability, variety, contingency."[13]

In addition to repudiating a way of thinking, Godman sees *The Discourses* as a veiled attack on one man who embodied it: Marcello Virgilio Adriani. Born in 1464, five years before Machiavelli, and a student of Cristoforo Landino and Poliziano, he was professor of classical languages in Florence's Studio from 1497 to 1502. In January 1498 he became the head of the First Chancery, and on 19 June 1498 the Great Council appointed Machiavelli second chancellor of the republic. Unlike his subordinate, Adriani managed to hold on to his position in the chancery from 1498 until his death in 1521, that is, through the initial stages of the republic, then into the Soderini regime, and on into the restoration of the Medici in 1512. Broadly speaking, both he and Machiavelli managed their careers in the context of support for Florentine republicanism, which contemporaries frequently called a *governo libero.* But with the reinstatement of the Medici, Adriani modified his republican views; moreover, he accommodated them to a humanism that stressed the power of the word and its interpretation.[14]

Machiavelli, though, remained loyal to his republican tenets. As Maurizio Viroli defines them, they were "a commitment to the ideal of a well-ordered republic—that is, a republic which is kept in order by the rule of law and by constitutional arrangements that ensure that each component of the polity has its proper place; it is a commitment to the principles of the political and civil life . . . and to a conception of political liberty understood as an absence of personal dependence."[15] *The Discourses,* written while the Medici were ascendant, reveal his allegiance to these commitments. Moreover, they are animated by a vigorous striving to persuade the young intellectual leaders of Florence (both dedicatees of *The Discourses* were in their twenties) to follow his conviction that antiquity should be imitated only according to his understanding of imitation. In other words, they were "humanist" in intent and execution, but they modified mainstream early sixteenth-century Florentine humanism, in particular that which was expounded by Marcello Virgilio Adriani and his emulators. To characterize Machiavelli's attack on this example as antihumanist is to overstate the case. To understand the significance of *The Discourses,* nevertheless, we must first understand his objections to conventional humanism's notion of "imitating antiquity."

Embedded throughout *The Discourses* are razor-sharp distinctions, briefly, often allusively, expressed. They lift the veil on the source of his "gift," a word also used in the dedication to *The Prince*. The solidity of this gift depends on his experiences in the real world, what has happened to him in "real" history, not history mediated by interpretation. His history is often shared history; it is "actual" in that both he and his Florentine readers have recently experienced it in daily life. In the second sentence of the dedication to *The Discourses,* he writes: "In [them] I have expressed all I know and all that I have learned about the conditions of the world through long experience and constant reading." As in *The Prince,* "experience" again takes precedence over "reading." In Godman's terms, this means that *res,* the thing in itself, reality, practical knowledge, takes priority over *verba,* book learning. (It is one of the ironies surrounding Machiavelli's life that what eventually returned him to the favor and patronage of the Medici was *verba,* not *res.*)

In this context imitation results in a qualitatively different kind of knowledge—not knowledge for learning's sake alone, of value in a contemplative life. It is practical, real-world knowledge anchored in reflection on the world so as to be useful for the active life. The ones who use it effectively are "not those who are princes but those who, because of their countless good qualities, would deserve to be; not those who could heap rank, honors, and riches upon me, but those who, though unable, would like to do so. For men, were they willing to judge correctly, must value those who *are* generous, not those who *can be* generous; similarly, they must value those who *know how* to govern a kingdom, not those who, without knowledge, *can* govern."[16] This gift carried heavy responsibilities for its recipients—Zanobi Buondelmonti, Cosimo Rucellai, or even someone not from their class—whose upbringing did not assume that the student would rule merely because of his education. The ideal reader must be someone committed to reform, who knows how the Romans resolved issues of reform, and who then is willing to govern with antiquity in mind. These would be the "men" who were "willing to judge correctly." Only by them could problems in the immediate world be clarified and solutions reached.

Once he has paid his dues to the dedicatees and prepared them, or more especially, readers whom he does not know personally, for what might be new in his "gift," Machiavelli broadens his horizons and is somewhat less circumspect about his goals in the prefaces. In the draft version of the autograph manuscript he specifies that his didactic purpose is "impelled by the natural desire that has always been within me to act unhesitatingly on matters that I believe bring about the common good for everyone." This aim, resulting in "new methods and institutions," runs the risk of causing him "trouble and difficulty" "because of the invidious nature of men"; after all, "men are more prone to blame than to praise the actions of others." With an eye always to the few who may read his work with understanding, the risk is worth taking because it "may pave the way for someone else who can carry out my intention with greater *virtù,* eloquence, and judgment."[17]

This intention is nothing less than to seek "unknown seas and lands" because he has "decided to set out upon a path as yet untrodden by anyone else." The truth of this assertion alerts us to the originality of *The Discourses* in the history of political thought. But the claim was also a bold reminder to its earliest readers, and it cut two ways. On the one hand, many of them would realize that what they were reading "was not a genre to which [they] were accustomed" and that when Machiavelli was writing "the *Discorsi,* Livy had not been in vogue among Florentine humanists within recent memory." On the other hand, a few of them might realize that, in late 1498, Machiavelli's superior at the Palazzo Vecchio, Marcello Virgilio Adriani, had announced "in a programmatic speech . . . his intention to expound [Livy] in the light of republican politics—an aim that he never realized." In other words, Machiavelli was advancing where Adriani "had feared, or failed, to tread."[18] Machiavelli's untrodden path, then, suggests the high standard by which he hoped to be measured.

That standard necessarily respected antiquity for both its accomplishments and its utility in politics. "I cannot help simultaneously marveling and grieving when . . . I consider how much honor people accord to antiquity . . . and [yet] . . . I see the deeds of the greatest *virtù* that histories show us, undertaken by ancient kingdoms and republics, by kings, generals, citizens, proposers of laws, and others who have toiled for their countries, being admired rather than imitated—or, to tell the truth, they have been avoided so much by all in every slightest thing they did that no trace of that ancient *virtù* has survived." That Machiavelli's contemporaries gave short shrift to what is of most immediate interest to Machiavelli—politics—particularly irritated him. First, "in the disputes that arise between citizens in civil matters . . . [they] always have recourse to those ideas or remedies that were decided on or prescribed by the ancients." Second, "civil laws are nothing but decisions made by jurists of antiquity; arranged in order, they teach our current jurists how to judge." So, when it comes to politics: "in establishing republics, preserving states, governing kingdoms, setting up militias, and conducting warfare, judging their subjects, and extending power, not one prince or republic or commander can be found who consults antiquity for models."[19]

Once antiquity is respected, however, the bases for its relevance to contemporary life must be reevaluated. Both prefaces reaffirm the Dedicatory Letter and reiterate the need to reject accepted notions of imitation and transform the education and upbringing of those who will make new, reforming decisions about antiquity's contemporary benefits. It follows because Machiavelli believes the lesson of antiquity is ignored "not so much from the weakness into which our present religion has brought the world . . . as it does from people not having a true understanding of the histories and not extracting the meaning from them when they are read or relishing the savor they contain."[20]

Machiavelli's conviction needs to be examined more closely. It may seem merely another anticlerical barb, similar to those in his letter to Guicciardini. But in fact it betrays a much more fundamental disillusion: the two major institutions shaping his generation have combined to debase what is of the highest value. When he revised the draft preface to *The Discourses* for the printed edition, he changed "religion" to "upbringing" *(educazione),* which implies what goes on in school as well as at home. We can better apprehend this blend of religion and upbringing through the context of his belief that "peoples in ancient times" were "greater lovers of freedom" than contemporary Florentines. This results, he argues, "from the same cause that makes men less strong now. This, I believe, is the difference between our upbringing and the ancients', based on the difference between our religion and the ancients'. . . . This kind of upbringing and such false interpretations [of religion] are therefore the reason for our not seeing so many republics as there were in ancient times and, consequently, for our not seeing such love of freedom among people as existed then."[21] A strong society, measured by its love of freedom, would result from the "true understanding" of Roman history that he imparts through *The Discourses.* [22] He reinforces the sentence's urgency through the metaphorical and sensual appeal of "extracting" meaning and "relishing the savor they contain." He will help us to crack the nut of proper imitation and appreciate the delicious kernel of truth lying within.

This appeal to the senses is meant to prepare us for his polemic about the practical application of imitating antiquity. He begins, "countless people who read [these histories] take pleasure in hearing about the variety of events *[accidenti]* that they contain." Despite the wonder and "pleasure" derived from them, people never think "to imitate them, deeming imitation not only difficult but impossible—as if the heavens, the sun, the elements, and mankind had altered their movements, their order, and their power from the way they were in antiquity."[23] These are constants, from his point of view; as we shall see, they certainly are not so for Guicciardini. Their value in the present is also measured by how they can serve to predict the future: "it is easy for anyone who carefully examines past matters to foresee those in the future of any republic and to apply to them the remedies that were used by the ancients or, if they are not to be found, to devise new ones because the events *[accidenti]* are similar."[24]

This constancy means that we ignore their practical lessons at our peril: "since I wish to rescue mankind from this error, I have deemed it necessary to write concerning . . . Livy . . . whatever I shall deem necessary—according to knowledge of ancient and modern affairs—for a greater understanding." It is Machiavelli, however, who does the "deeming." What is "necessary" is contingent upon "modern affairs," a direct result of his years in the chancery. It is through those lenses that what he knows about ancient affairs is to be interpreted too. The printed text contains a slight but significant modification: "whatever I shall deem necessary—according to ancient and modern affairs—for a greater understanding." Machiavelli asserts the objectivity of knowledge gained from such "affairs," thereby rendering the experience behind them even less open to attack or contrary interpretation. Finally, he is ready to declare his normative judgment: "thus those who read these explanations of mine may more easily derive from them the utility that should be sought from the study of histories."[25] It is his explanations, grounded in his experience, that will prove truly productive in the study of history under his tutelage.[26] What in the original preface were "explanations," clarifications of his position, became "discourses" in the preface revised for the printed edition; this change gives a more explicit focus to what is about to be read. So he closes his revised preface forcefully. The word "discourse" announces Machiavelli's innovation: "'Traditional' the *Discorsi* were not; nor did there exist, in Quattro- and Cinquecento Florence, a single genre of textual interpretation that made their author's choice of form self-explanatory."[27]

One final remark about Machiavelli's intent in stressing the need for practical imitation of antiquity. It is found not in the prefaces, but in the first chapter of Book 3, where he argues that one way for a republic to endure over a long period of time is "to be frequently taken back toward its origins." This is a theme he tends to disregard in the first two books, except for 1, 37; indeed, it is not really developed in Book 3. Yet it is by no means an afterthought, especially as his own personal experiences contributed a great deal to it. Expecting his immediate audience to share his disillusionment with the factional strife in both Florence and Italy at large, he makes his case briefly and goes on to other matters. The case clarifies, though, how Machiavelli's kind of imitation can be of use to reformers. Antiquity is the best model for renewal of "a society, whether it be a religion, a kingdom, or a republic." This proposition's truth rests on his assertion that "the origins of all religions, republics, and kingdoms must have some goodness, thanks to which they regain their original prestige and expansiveness." It is in the nature of things that all societies are in jeopardy of being corrupted and losing sight of the principles that gave them their healthy start. Consequently, such societies must be *riduca al segno,* returned to their original standard, the point from which modification or deterioration began. Moreover, "because this goodness becomes corrupted over the course of time, if nothing happens to bring them back to the mark, of necessity it kills off that body."[28] The Florentine body politic has in effect been killed off, so this chapter dovetails with the argument in both prefaces. It is an urgent plea for the reformers to get to work by returning to the original principles that Machiavelli not only enunciates in this chapter, but sows the seeds for throughout *The Discourses.*[29]

A stylistic device that Machiavelli used to intensify this sense of urgency was a disconcerting shift from the impersonal pronoun *si* (one) to a second person familiar form of *tu* (you). We have retained this change, to remind the reader that he retained a habit left over from the *de regimine principe* literature that he had recently been writing in *The Prince.* He was still true to his practice of establishing a sense of intimacy so he could personalize his advice.[30] It is as if he thought of himself as addressing a ruler directly, even though ostensibly he is writing discursive, not hortatory, prose.

Once the prefaces have prepared a reform-minded audience for a humanism based on practical application of personal experience, Machiavelli then proceeds in Book 1 to write "about the decisions the Romans made concerning the city's internal affairs."[31] The obvious place to start is with a discussion of Rome's constitution. Most of Book 1 is therefore based on the first six books of Livy's history, covering the history of Rome from its founding and early kings, through the early republic, to the sack of Rome by the Gauls in 390 B.C. For Livy, that date marked the point when Rome "as if from the old roots sprang up a second time" (6.1.3). Machiavelli does not opt for a systematic commentary on Livy chapter by chapter, but rather topic by topic—always with the problems of Florence in the foreground.[32] They, not Livy's text, determine the order of comment. In the early chapters Machiavelli's distinctions among kingdoms, princedoms, republics, and tyrannies are not always clear. They can usually be clarified by locating the source of power: in one person or in a group. The decision about which is best in any given example depends on which can best guarantee the state's existence and longevity. Next, he deals with religion on the utilitarian ground that it is an instrument for governing, not a source for moral and ethical teaching. Before examining Rome under the kings, he devotes several chapters to a society's passage from slavery to freedom. Subsequently, he covers concerns such as how to initiate new forms of government, how to handle ingratitude, what to do about dictatorship. Because Rome had to confront the class conflict between patricians and plebeians, he investigates the institution of the decemvirate, a Roman magistracy of ten men from both classes responsible for ruling and sharing some power between them. Finally, he looks at what happens when the people insist on more representation in government and when they actually attain some power. He argues that the people are less likely to make egregious errors of judgment than princes (an issue fought out in the American republic's early congresses in setting up a system of checks and balances).

Once Rome is seen solidly organized, both Livy and Machiavelli turn their attention to foreign expansion. Livy does this in Book VII, and Machiavelli announces that his topic in Book 2 will be "the decisions . . . the Roman People made concerning the expansion of their empire."[33] The modern reader will probably find much of this material more interesting than that in the preceding book. Although Machiavelli's central concern is still the problems of a republic, this book covers it more concretely. He never loses sight of his conviction that a carefully organized, well-regulated republic is more efficient and more powerful than a government ruled by a prince. But it cannot exist without the efficacy and power of a citizen militia; the two are interdependent. The focus of much of this book is thus on war, colonization, colonial policy, and colonial administration. As in *The Art of War,* he examines military organization, discipline, and tactics. Finally, he addresses diplomatic issues: how Rome managed its policy toward neighboring tribes in peace and war.

For the third and final book, his intention is "to demonstrate . . . how much the actions of individual men made Rome great and produced many good effects in that city."[34] It is generally agreed that, although most of the examples come from Livy, Books II to X, this aim does not describe what Machiavelli discusses in Book 3. It does not present so carefully worked-out an argument as the preceding books; thus many readers find it a letdown. Ideas do not come across clearly, and often sentences are awkward.[35] A state's internal security is one of the book's major concerns; it leads to the sixth chapter, the longest in *The Discourses:* "On Conspiracies." A number of the exemplary actions that "produced many good effects" in Rome duplicate themes covered in the first two books. Both the men and the deeds held up to admiration exemplify the belief that Cicero expressed as "the public safety is the supreme law." Machiavelli's formulation is in the context of what counselors should advise: "where the salvation of one's country is totally at stake, no consideration of whether it is just or unjust, merciful or cruel, praiseworthy or dishonorable, should matter; rather, setting aside any other concern, one should follow absolutely the course of action that saves its life and preserves its freedom."[36] Although Cicero avoids sharply distinguishing absolute morality from pragmatic necessity, both Machiavelli and Guicciardini head in that direction, suggesting the independence of the latter from the former. Addressing the problems based on the Samnite Wars in chapter 43, Machiavelli may be seen to moderate this extreme assertion of the independence of politics from ethics. But it is the kind of remark, stated in the context of an imprecisely constructed argument, that often gets him called an apologist for tyranny. If people were more familiar with *The Discourses* in their entirety, this criticism would be made less often. In the words of Federico Chabod, Machiavelli "is not, then, primarily a logician, working from principles from which, by a continuous process of reasoning, rigorous and slavish, he deduces a complete 'system.' He is first and foremost a man of imagination, who sees *his* truth in a flash, with blinding clarity, and only afterwards trusts to reason to enable him to comment on that truth."[37]

GUICCIARDINI AND HIS *CONSIDERATIONS* OF MACHIAVELLI'S *DISCOURSES:* THE EFFECTS OF THE POLITICAL CLIMATE

Francesco Guicciardini would certainly never have let reason take a back seat to imaginative perceptions about political reality. Only after what Chabod, in his continuation of the passage quoted above, calls "immediate, intuitive visions of events and their significance" had passed the test of reason could they see the light of day in his important historical works. The *Considerations* are a far cry from his *Storia d'Italia,* but they are characteristic of the mind appearing in that magisterial work, and they illuminate aspects of the *Discourses* that might not be apparent to an audience of the twenty-first century.

The anti-Medici forces in control of Florence's Last Republic banished Guicciardini from Florence and confiscated his property in March 1530. Having burned most of the bridges by which he might reestablish connections with Florence, Guicciardini went to Rome in April 1530 in hopes of obtaining an appointment from Pope Clement VII, whom he had ably served in the past. But the Medici pope could not help him in Florence and used him for only insignificant advisory duties in Rome. Guicciardini had time on his hands and bitterness on his mind. Some relief came from two Florentine cardinals residing in Rome. The library of Cardinal Niccolò Ridolfi owned the autograph copy of the manuscript for *The Discourses,* and during the latter part of 1530 Cardinal Giovanni Gaddi was in the process of copying it for publication the following year in Rome and Florence. With his access to this manuscript, Guicciardini's relief must have been double-edged. On the one hand, the manuscript was a reminder of his dead friend's companionship and intelligence. On the other, it was a reminder of Machiavelli's political sympathies, which, especially as worked out in *The Discourses,* were shared by the people who had driven Guicciardini from Florence. But these emotions did not keep him from considering them. From the notebook in which he drafted his *Considerations,* we can tell that he intended to comment on fifty-nine of Machiavelli's one hundred forty-two chapters and prefaces. But for twenty of those chapters, the notebook provides only a blank page.[38]

It is quite possible that Guicciardini selected these specific chapters for "consideration" in order to launch a systematic attack on the republicanism Machiavelli sought to perpetuate in the examples and argument of *The Discourses.* Guicciardini probably wanted to undermine republican sentiments that "constituted a severe threat to an entire group of the Florentine ruling class of which Guicciardini was, better than anyone else, a representative."[39] But Ridolfi reminds us that we risk losing sight of Guicciardini's "affectionate acerbity" toward Machiavelli, even as we acknowledge that Guicciardini's "critical remarks, nearly all correct, rarely miss the target." And we should never lose sight of the fact that "he who knew how to see his friend's weak points with such marvelous acuity, had not observed that all those errors are merely rough stones on the surface of new roads opened up by his thought."[40]

A good view of the contrast between the two men's personalities and positions is given by Guicciardini's reaction to the preface Machiavelli wrote to Book 2 of *The Discourses.* For all Machiavelli's emphasis on pragmatic imitation of antiquity, he concedes at the outset that life in ancient Rome does not necessarily surpass the present: "men always praise ancient times and blame the present, but not always with good reason; they are so partial to things of the past that they extol not only those ages which they have known about thanks to the records left by writers but also those ages which, now that they have grown old, they remember having experienced in their youth." Then, with a telltale shift to "you," he points out what might lead contemporaries to misinterpret a past that "cannot harm you or give you reason to envy it." He is primarily interested in "matters pertaining to the life and customs of men." From a standpoint we have seen in the prefaces to Book 1, he argues that "the world has always been the same way and that there has been as much good in it as evil, but this good and this evil has varied from region to region. We can see this from what information we have about those ancient kingdoms, which differed from each other because of the difference in their customs, though the world remained the same."

Machiavelli then turns the tables on this unhistorical position and rues both the loss of Roman *virtù* and the corruption of present times: "there is nothing to redeem them from the most extreme misery, infamy, and dishonor; there is no observance in them of religion or of laws or of military tradition: they are besmirched with every kind of filth. These vices are all the more detestable because they are more prevalent among those who sit in judgment, give orders to others, and wish to be idolized." He momentarily wonders whether he might "deserve to be counted among those who are mistaken" for praising "the ancient Romans' times too much" and blaming the present. But he resolves this by asserting that "if the *virtù* that flourished then and the vice that flourishes now were not brighter than the sun, I should be more reticent in my speech for fear of falling into the very same error that I accuse some people of. But since the matter is so clear that everyone sees it, I shall be courageous and say openly what I understand about those times and our own so that the minds of the young who read my writings can avoid the latter and prepare to imitate the former whenever Fortune gives them the opportunity to do so." Following this tacit appeal to his kind of humanism and his overt melancholy about "the young's" potential to reclaim and exercise ancient Rome's republican spirit, he closes with the remarks quoted earlier: "it is the duty of a good man to teach others the good that you have been unable to bring about because of the hostility of the times and of Fortune so that, once many are aware of it, some of them—more beloved of Heaven—may be able to bring it about."[41]

In his *Consideration,* Guicciardini is quick to agree with Machiavelli's "conclusion that ancient times are often praised more than is due." But then he proceeds to eye the gist of Machiavelli's preface with the disdain he shows in his *Ricordi* for those who "bring in the Romans as evidence all the time."[42] Guicciardini's historical mind rejects the notion that "there always has been as much good in the world in one age as in another, although the places may vary." Applying "reasoning, rigorous and slavish," that Machiavelli eschews, Guicciardini focuses on Machiavelli's oversimplification. He points out how painting and sculpture, military discipline, religion and literature once flourished in Rome and how painting and sculpture, at least, are enjoying a rebirth in the present. "As a result of these variations in the arts and religion and changes in human affairs, it is no wonder that men's customs, too, have varied; they often take their impetus from an institution, from opportunity, or from necessity." He thus reminds us that Machiavelli fails to account for historical variables. So he can conclude, on the one hand, by agreeing with Machiavelli that it is valid that "ancient times are not always to be preferred to present ones," and on the other, by stating that it is invalid "to deny that one age is sometimes more corrupt or has more *virtù* than others."[43]

Generally speaking, this is the vein of most of Guicciardini's *Considerations,* although this particular one is not shaped by antirepublican sentiments. Typically, his points come with staccato abruptness, even though written in long periodic sentences. What is characteristic of Guicciardini's reaction to this preface marks the *Considerations* as a whole: he is impatient with Machiavelli's oversimplification and lack of historical discrimination. This irritation quite likely resulted from Guicciardini's having his own didactic objectives and, at this point in his life, the leisure to pursue them. These goals were as strong as Machiavelli's, but Guicciardini was just beginning to work his way toward them. He "set out to teach prudence, yet somewhere along the way he discovered that prudence is unteachable. He attempted to formulate rules, but sometime between 1512 and 1530 he perceived that the world is almost totally irregular. And yet these discoveries only reinforced the conviction that without knowledge—the careful consideration of a prudent man—our acts are blind and ultimately futile. In practice the pressure of this conflict led to an emphasis on the particular event and the individual man, on pragmatic understanding rather than theoretical speculation."[44] Guicciardini believed that Machiavelli's general rules were too facilely extracted from a cursory examination of historical examples. Based on this skepticism, Guicciardini forced himself to consider each problematic situation as a new challenge. The past could be relevant to its resolution, but history or experience was never to impinge upon fresh analysis of the givens.

Hence, a constant of the *Considerations* is Guicciardini's conviction that Machiavelli's ideas "are more easily depicted in books and in men's imaginations than carried out in fact."[45] What is interesting, given the pragmatic base of Machiavelli's humanism, is how frequently Guicciardini finds his own experience at variance with Machiavelli's. This discrepancy results in Guicciardini's leveling two major charges: (1) Machiavelli breezes through his historical examples so superficially that their truth becomes distorted or erroneous; (2) the distinctions he does make are not finely enough drawn. The result is that *The Discourses* are filled with either "imaginations" or their equivalent, "theoretical speculation." This is especially true of Machiavelli's rush to political judgment. Guicciardini is much more deliberate. Furthermore, his interest in politics and political foibles has less to do with political judgment, and more with how both these aspects influence and help establish the long line of historical judgment.[46]

For instance, Guicciardini is incredulous at Machiavelli's assertion that "the common opinion that the sinews of war are money could not be more false." For him, this is a clear example of inexperience engendering distorted ideas. He can hardly wait to proclaim the opposite, that "those who waged war had a very great need of money and that without money it was impossible to keep it going, because it is necessary not only for paying soldiers but for providing weapons, provisions, spies, ammunition, and much equipment used in warfare." To clinch his point, he juxtaposes experience with imagination, with a swipe at Machiavelli: "These things are required in such superabundance that it is impossible for those who have not experienced it to imagine it." Later, when dealing with Machiavelli's discussion of whether "indulgence is needed more than punishment," Guicciardini, who has governed Modena, Reggio, and Romagna, cannot refrain from drawing distinctions. He composes his brief fastidiously. A governor "equally seasoned" with "human kindness or graciousness" and "some degree of severity," he notes, "would be most precious and would make for a tempered harmony that is very sweet and admirable." A distinction, however, is in order: "since such seasoning is rarely or never found in any man (the order of nature being such that all our affairs have some imperfection), it appears rather that every man either has more severity than graciousness or more graciousness than severity. It is not without reason that we are unsure which is more suitable."

Further along, Guicciardini observes that "the first distinction that occurs to me is to consider the nature of those whom you control." Later, "the other distinction that occurs to me is that one must differentiate between one who rules as a prince and on his own authority and one who rules as a minister and in another's name. . . . but I would make a distinction among those who command in another's name." In accordance with his early legal training, these distinctions lead him to conclude: "since we are speaking of good and legitimate governments, it can hardly be taken for granted that where there is fear there is not also love, because severity of justice, which is what produces fear, can be only loved by those who want to live well; and vice versa, the love that arises from human kindness, from easygoingness of character, and from the inclination to do favors, accompanied by justice, as must be taken for granted in a good government, cannot help being feared."[47]

The *Considerations* show us two distinct methodologies at work, then. By reading them together we witness a fascinating struggle between two fine but distinct mentalities. As Mark Phillips puts it, "Guicciardini was helped by having a strong and clear opponent in Machiavelli. . . . it is the sense of fully worked out positions on both sides that gives this confrontation the stamp of a significant occasion. Although Guicciardini had the last word, the argument could not be anything but equal. The two antagonists articulate not just private views but two permanent positions on the uses of history, and the significance of each is enhanced by its awareness of the other."[48]

In conclusion, we acknowledge the validity of Felix Gilbert's judgments of Machiavelli and Guicciardini. Gilbert ends his chapter on Machiavelli by quoting the inscription on his tomb, completed in 1787 by the sculptor Spinazzi, in Florence's Church of Santa Croce: *tanto nomini nullum par elogium* (to so great a name no praise is equal). In contrast, Gilbert closes his chapter on Guicciardini with these words: *tanto operi nullum par elogium* (to such great works no praise is equal).[49]

NOTES

1. Some commentators argue that Guicciardini read parts of the early chapters of *The Discourses,* Book 1, with their allusions to Polybius, as early as 1521. See his letter to Machiavelli of 18 May, in which he comments: "all the very same things return; and we do not see any incident that has not been seen in other times" (*Machiavelli and His Friends,* p. 339). Later in that paragraph, his reference to the "Republic of Clogs" may indicate that he has read Machiavelli's discussion of republics in 1, 2. Guicciardini writes: "you will make use of that model for some purpose, comparing it or measuring it against some of those forms of yours." For a list of the editions used throughout this edition, consult the Works Consulted.

2. Referring to the written instructions for the mission, Ridolfi writes: "Machiavelli . . . must certainly have had a hand in the drafting of the document, and if I am not mistaken, I think I sense his presence here and there" (*Life of Francesco Guicciardini,* p. 26).

3. Letter 270, dated 17 May 1521; *Friends,* p. 337. On this point, see also a letter from Donato Giannotti, dated 30 June 1533, paraphrased in Ridolfi, *Life of Machiavelli,* pp. 198–199; *Vita 7,* p. 310.

4. Ridolfi, *Life of Machiavelli,* p. 189.

5. The quotations in this paragraph and the next are from Letter 269, dated 17 May 1521, *Friends,* p. 335.

6. The quotations in this and the next five paragraphs are from Letter 270,

Friends, pp. 336–337. For more on this exchange of letters between Machiavelli and Guicciardini, see Viroli, *Niccolò's Smile,* pp. 203–214.

7. The dramatic motif of the practical joke or *beffa* in Italian literature is explored in Celse, "La *beffa* chez Machiavel." See also Rebhorn, *Foxes and Lions,* pp. 228–249, for Machiavelli as "confidence man."

8. Guicciardini, *Ricordi,* C. 187.

9. *Ricordi,* C. 6. See below, 1, Preface A, n.9, for Guicciardini's belief that this "discretion" is shaped by "the circumstances of experience" and "a good eye."

10. So the reader will have a better sense of Guicciardini's position on specific issues, the notes to this edition contain frequent quotations from his other works, even when he does not take them up directly in a *Consideration* of one of Machiavelli's chapters. For Books 2 and 3 of *The Discourses* this is especially relevant, because Guicciardini writes fewer *Considerations* of them.

11. See below, Book 2, Preface, sentence 25. The connection between Livy, who inspired *The Discourses,* and "the hostility of the times" is reminiscent of a "familiar" letter that Petrarch addressed to Livy. Written in 1350, it epitomizes the Renaissance's yearning for the perfection of the ancients: "I could wish, were it granted from on high, that either I had happened to be of your generation, or you of ours. . . . Now it is rather time for me to thank you both for many things and expressly for often having made me forget the evils of these present times and having put me into happier ones" *(Optarem, si ex alto datum esset, vel me in tuam vel te in nostram etatem incidisse . . . . Nunc tibi potius tempus est ut gratias agam cum pro multis tum pro eo nominatim, quod oblitum sepe presentium malorum seculis me felicioribus inseris.)* Petrarca, *Le Familiari,* 24, 8; pp. 243–244.

12. When assessing Machiavelli's use of the past, what some might assert is his dependence on the past, we need to remember what Montaigne wrote some seventy years later. Because he, too, relies on antiquity, his remarks bear on his own and Machiavelli's method: "The subject, according to what it is, may reveal a man to be learned and to have a good memory, but in order to pass judgment on what qualities are most his own and most worthy, one must know what is his and what is not at all his; and in what is not his, how much is due him because of the choice, arrangement, embellishment, and style that he has produced." The answer to the query in his next sentence, "suppose he has borrowed the matter and made the form worse, as often happens?" is that neither he nor Machiavelli has done so, despite their similar preference for the relaxed, essay form. (These quotations occur toward the end of "On the Art of Discussion," *Essais,* 3, 8; a B addition.)

13. *From Poliziano to Machiavelli,* p. 268.

14. This paragraph and the next two are based on Godman's closely argued chapter, "The Shadow of the Chancery," pp. 235–291.

15. *Machiavelli,* p. 116. For the extent to which republican values are paramount to Machiavelli and the argument that persuasive rhetoric energizes his discourse, see Viroli's important studies: the essay in *Machiavelli and Republicanism* and the recent *Machiavelli.*

16. See below, Dedicatory Letter, sentences 8–9. It is clear from the Dedication and Preface that it is the young who can best appreciate his gift. The last chapter of Book 1 emphasizes youth and ends with the words "at a very early age," referring to

the youthful triumphs of several Roman leaders; see Harvey C. Mansfield, Jr., *Machiavelli's New Modes and Orders:* pp. 177–180. In *Discourses,* 1, 9, sentence 2, Machiavelli writes, "I do not want to keep the minds of those who want to hear *[intendere]* something on the subject in any more suspense. He thus raises the possibility with the word *intendere,* also meaning "to learn," that some of *The Discourses* were first heard by young members of the Orti Oricellari, whose "hearing" and "learning" would result in republican reforms for Florence.

17. See below, Preface A, sentences 1 and 2 for the quotations in this paragraph and those in the next sentence. The boast of the "untrodden" path is a *topos* sanctioned by classical writers and proudly taken up in the Renaissance; see Curtius, *European Literature and the Latin Middle Ages,* pp. 85–86.

18. Godman, pp. 263, 177, 264. He also points out that Machiavelli's familiarity with Livy goes back to his boyhood. His father "compiled an index of 'all the cities and mountains and rivers'" in a copy of *Le Deche tutte di Livio in forma* (All the decades of Livy printed) purchased in 1475: Godman, p 145, quoting Bernardo Machiavelli's *Libro di ricordi* (Florence: Le Monnier, 1954) pp. 14 and 35. We also know from these memoirs that Bernardo borrowed a copy of Justin when his son was twelve years old. A less familiar historian today than in the Renaissance, Justin composed an epitome in Latin of Pompeius Trogus, *Historiae Philippicae,* (third century A.D.). It was a common text for young people; Machiavelli draws on it on several occasions in each book of *The Discourses.*

19. See below, Preface A, sentences 3–6; for slight variations see Preface B, sentences 1–4. In Preface B, for example, he sharpens his attack on the absence of his kind of imitation by altering the phrase "being admired rather than imitated" to "being praised with wonder rather than imitated."

20. See below, Preface A, sentence 7.

21. See below, Book 2, chapter 2, sentences 25 and 36.

22. The phrase "true understanding" has antecedents in the histories written by both Livy and Polybius. The latter's writings and theories were well known in Florence. Although Machiavelli knew no Greek, the notion of *anacyclosis* in Polybius was common coin among contemporary Florentine intellectuals; see Garin, pp. 12–16. Machiavelli accepts this idea and incorporates it into his discussion; see especially Book 1, chapter 2 and note 13.

23. See below, Preface A, sentence 8. The word *accidenti* in Italian often refers to unforeseen events, usually of a disastrous nature. They are "accidents" in the philosophical sense that they reflect the "variety of incidents" or "varied events" described by Greek and Roman historians.

24. See below, Book 1, 39, sentence 2; in this connection, see also the argument of 3, 43.

25. For the quotations in this paragraph, see below, Preface A, sentence 9, and Preface B, sentence 7. Machiavelli's commitment to the practical use of antiquity began early in his career. His 1503 treatise *Del modo di trattare i popoli della Valdichiana ribellati* (On the method of dealing with the rebellious people of the Valdichiana) was predicated on the contrast between Roman and modern practice in dealing with rebellions, to the latter's disadvantage: see below, 2, 23 and notes. Three years later, in the context of "military training," he laments in his *Ghiribizzi* (Fantasies) letter to Giovan

Battista Soderini that "it is not customary to bring in the Romans as evidence" for moderns to emulate (*Friends,* p. 134).

26. In his famous letter to Vettori about the composition of *The Prince,* he justifies jotting down his interpretations by remarking, with a nod to Dante, "that no one understands anything unless he retains what he has understood" (*Friends,* p. 264). In this case his appeal is not to an ancient authority. It is Beatrice telling Dante to "open" his "mind" and "hold fast" to "what I reveal to you, for listening without retaining does not make knowledge" (*Paradiso,* 5, vv. 41–42).

27. Godman, *From Poliziano to Machiavelli,* p. 273. On the other hand, the two *"Dediche editoriali"* published by Rinaldi in the appendix to the *Discourses* (Machiavelli, *Opere,* 2: 1203–1214)—particularly Bernardo di Giunta's to Ottaviano de' Medici—make it clear that, at least in the eyes of the first editors and their patrons, one justification for publishing Machiavelli's text was that it provided "excellent precepts for political administrations and governments, on which the well-being of countries and the happy lives of peoples depend" (ibid., p. 1213), and thus came under a traditional genre.

28. For the quotations in this paragraph, see below, Book 3, 1, sentences 38, 6, and 7. Although the Preface to Book 2 also adds a significant dimension to the practical imitation of antiquity, it will be examined in the general discussion of Guicciardini's *Considerations,* paying close attention to his remarks on that preface.

29. No one can say for sure what the group of men who plotted against Cardinal Giulio de' Medici in May 1522 "learned" from Machiavelli. Several of them were among his "noontime friends" at the Rucellai Gardens, in particular Zanobi Buondelmonti. Some of the conspirators were executed; Buondelmonti escaped from Florence, was branded an outlaw, but eventually returned and was present at Machiavelli's death in 1527, the year of his own death. (Whatever influence 3, 1 may have had on the conspirators, they did not heed 3, 6.)

30. All translations of "you" in this work reflect Machiavelli's normal use of the second person singular pronoun. An example of this use of *tu,* as if it were in direct address, occurs in 1, 6, sentence 29. Guicciardini's practice is the same. Any exceptions will be pointed out in the notes.

31. See below, Book 2, Preface, sentence 26. Early in Book 1 he also defines his topic as "discussing those deeds [of the Romans] occurring at home and as a result of public decision that I deem to be worthy of lengthier comment—adding to them everything that devolved from them," Book 1, 1, sentence 22.

32. For this reason, our notes provide historical information at the point where it is relevant. But some events are suitable for more than one of his points, whether the context be Rome or Florence. There are consequently numerous cross-references and some repetition of events in the notes.

33. See below, Book 2, Preface, sentence 26.

34. See below, 3, 1, sentence 40.

35. See, for example, the argument of chapter 13 or the following quotation from Book 3, 34, sentence 25: "Since people can be mistaken about a man's reputation, judgment, and actions, evaluating them higher than in truth they are (which would not happen to a prince, because he would be told and would be warned by those who advise him), in order for the people as well not to lack such advice, good

organizers of republics have prescribed an order. When a city's highest offices, in which it might be dangerous to put incompetent men, are to be filled and the people's taste seems to be directed toward naming someone who would be incompetent, any citizen is permitted to disclose the man's flaws in meetings—and he is praised for so doing—in order that the people, not lacking his knowledge, can judge better."

36. See below, 3, 41, sentence 4, and especially note 3; the statement is based on Cicero, *Laws,* 3.8. Viroli notes that "love of country should give the strength to deliberate on the course of action which will save the life and liberty of one's country, in spite of its high moral costs; but it does not have the power to turn a tragic choice into a cheerful one," *Machiavelli,* p. 166.

37. *Machiavelli and the Renaissance,* pp. 142–143. Commenting on Book 3, chapters 41 and 42, Chabod writes: "Nothing is further from Machiavelli's mind than to undermine common morality, replacing it with a new ethic; instead, he says that in public affairs the only thing that counts is the political criterion, by which he abides; let those who wish to remain faithful to the precepts of morality concern themselves with other things, not with politics" (p. 142).

38. Ridolfi, *Life of Guicciardini,* p. 208. The twenty chapters he intended to comment on are: Book 1, chapters 17–18, 35–36; Book 2, chapters 2, 4, 16–18, 21, 32; and Book 3, chapters 6, 13, 21–22, 27, 34, 36–38; Marcel Gagneux, "Une tentative de démythification," p. 200, n.4.

39. Gagneux, "Une tentative," p. 217. Gagneux goes through Machiavelli's proposition and Guicciardini's comments on a point-by-point basis, arguing that Guicciardini was motivated by his antirepublicanism. He also points out that what Guicciardini does not discuss can be equally significant, and revelatory of his viewpoint.

40. Ridolfi, *Life of Guicciardini,* p. 207. It is possible that Guicciardini's most trenchant critique of *The Discourses* is in his earlier *Dialogo del reggimento di Firenze* (Dialogue on the Government of Florence), written in 1524. Although *reggimento* is usually translated "government," we believe that "governing" is more appropriate. Pocock suggests that it "at times reads like a series of replies to leading ideas of the *Discorsi*" (*Machiavellian Moment,* p. 186).

41. See below, Book 2, preface, sentences 1, 5, 6, 12, 16, 17, and 22–25, for the quotations in this paragraph.

42. This *ricordo* continues: "One would have to have a city with conditions like theirs and then govern it according to their example. That model is as incongruous for a city whose qualities are incongruous as it would be to expect an ass to run like a horse" (*Ricordi,* C, 110).

43. The quotations in this paragraph from Guicciardini's *Consideration* of Machiavelli's preface to Book 2 come from sentences 1, 2, 6, and 7.

44. Mark Phillips, *Francesco Guicciardini: The Historian's Craft,* p. 80.

45. Guicciardini's *Consideration* of Book, 1, 10, sentence 16.

46. Perhaps Guicciardini had Machiavelli in mind when he wrote: "There are some men, when they are writing about current events, who prophesy about the future; when well-informed men make these forecasts, they appear to be quite good to those who read them. Nevertheless, they are extremely misleading. Because, just as one conclusion depends upon the other, so if any one of them fails, then so do all the

others deduced from it; every tiny alteration in the particulars changes the conclusion. Hence, it is impossible to form a judgment about the affairs of this world from a distance; they must be judged and decided upon from day to day" (*Ricordi,* C. 114; see also C. 126, quoted in part below 1, 6, n.8).

47. The quotation in these two paragraphs come from Guicciardini's *Consideration* of Book 2, 10, sentence 1 and of Book 3, 19, sentences 1–3, 5–7.

48. Phillips, *Francesco Guicciardini: The Historian's Craft,* p. 93.

49. Gilbert, *Machiavelli and Guicciardini,* pp. 200 and 300.

Discourses

on the First Ten Books of Titus Livy

NICCOLÒ

MACHIAVELLI

Contents

BOOK THREE

Dedication

NICCOLÒ MACHIAVELLI TO ZANOBI BUONDELMONTI AND COSIMO RUCELLAI

Greetings[1]

1 I am sending you[2] a gift which, if it does not measure up to the obligations I have toward you, is certainly the finest Niccolò Machiavelli could send you.[3] 2 For in it I have expressed all I know and all that I have learned about the conditions of the world through long experience and constant reading. 3 And because neither you nor anyone else can ask more of me, you cannot complain if I have not given you more. 4 You may well lament both the inadequacy of my understanding, whenever my writings are inadequate, and the flaws in my judgment, whenever my reasoning goes astray, as often occurs. 5 If this is the case, I do not know which of us should be less obligated to the other: I to you, who have compelled me to write what I would never have written on my own, or you to me, should my writing not have satisfied you. 6 Therefore accept this gift in the way in which all things are accepted among friends: one always considers the intention of the sender more than the qualities of what is sent. 7 And you may believe that I have but one satisfaction in this gift when I think that, although I may have erred in many particulars, in this one matter alone I know I have not erred: choosing you above all others to dedicate my *Discourses* to: both because in so doing I think I have shown some gratitude for the kindnesses I have received and because I think I have avoided the common practice of authors who are always wont to dedicate their works to some prince and, blinded by ambition and greed, to praise him for all his virtuous characteristics,[4] whereas they ought to censure him for his every shameful quality. 8 Consequently, in order not to fall into this error, I have chosen not those who are princes but those who, because of their countless good qualities, would deserve to be; not those who could heap rank, honors, and riches upon me but those who, though unable, would like to do so. 9 For men, were they willing to judge correctly, must value those who *are* generous, not those who *can be* generous; similarly, they must value those who *know how* to govern a kingdom, not those who, without knowledge, *can* govern. 10 Writers have higher praise for Hiero of Syracuse as a private citizen than they do for Perseus of Macedon as a king, because all Hiero lacked to be a king was a kingdom, whereas Perseus had no royal attributes whatever except his realm.[5] 11 Rejoice then in what you yourselves have sought, good or bad; if you remain so misguided as to be happy with these views of mine, I shall not fail to pursue the rest of the History, as I promised you at the outset.[6]

Farewell.

NOTES

1. Zanobi Buondelmonti (1491–1527) was one of Machiavelli's closest friends and also one of the dedicatees of his *Life of Castruccio Castracani* (1520). Both he and Cosimo Rucellai are interlocutors in Machiavelli's humanist dialogue, *The Art of War* (1521). Buondelmonti, ardently opposed to the power and influence of the Medici in Florence, was among the leading spirits behind a series of meetings held periodically from 1512 to 1522 in the gardens of the Rucellai family. Cosimo Rucellai (1495–1519) came from a rich, influential family. His grandfather, Bernardo Rucellai, a brother-in-law of Lorenzo the Magnificent, wrote *De bello italico,* about the French invasion of Italy under Charles VIII from 1494 to 1495; it provides us with the term "balance of power," a notion governing both Italian politics in the Renaissance and Machiavelli's analysis of it. He built an imposing palace with carefully laid-out gardens where men interested in history, literature, philosophy, and politics frequently met. Machiavelli attended these meetings, probably beginning in 1515 or 1516, and tested some of the ideas in the *Discourses* during their discussions. His *Art of War* (1521) is also based on the ideas current in this cenacle; it records a dialogue alleged to have been held in 1516 at the Rucellai gardens between, among others, Buondelmonti and Cosimo Rucellai, and Machiavelli's spokesman, the military commander Fabrizio Colonna. (Scholars often refer to these gardens by their Italian name, the Orti Oricellari.)

2. Throughout his dedication Machiavelli uses the second person plural form of "you" because there are two dedicatees.

3. In the dedicatory letter to *The Prince,* Machiavelli had also drawn upon the notion of the book as a gift of his intelligence in which he describes his "knowledge of the deeds of great men, learned from wide experience of recent events and a constant reading of classical authors"; there, too, he is "unable to give . . . a greater gift than the power to understand in a moment all that I have learned and understood, with many hardships and dangers, over the course of many years" (pp. 93; 95, lines 16–19).

4. Because this sentence contrasts *virtuose qualitadi* with *vituperevole parte,* we use "virtuous characteristics" here. The word *virtù* is integral to Machiavelli's expression of his ideas, so in general (despite some disagreement) we have decided not to translate it by its numerous possibilities in English. Here, for example, Machiavelli refers to "moral excellence," a possible meaning of *virtù*. But more frequently he has in mind the qualities of *virtù* associated with our phrase "by virtue of"; namely, synonyms such as "ability," "power," "authority," "force," or "courage." When he uses the word to refer to a quality he admires in successful commanders or rulers, Machiavelli seeks to conjure up in the reader's mind an image of that person's flexibility in initiating effective, efficient, and energetic action. Moreover, the results of such deeds are rooted in a resolute assertion of that leader's will and in an ability to execute the product of that person's mental calculations.

The works of two recent commentators are worth noting. Pocock notes that "on the one hand *virtù* is that by which we innovate, and so let loose sequences of contingency beyond our prediction of control so that we become prey to *fortuna;* on the other hand, *virtù* is that internal to ourselves by which we resist *fortuna* and impose upon her patterns of order, which may even become patterns of moral order. . . . The more the individual relies upon his *virtù* the less he need rely upon his *fortuna* and—because *fortuna* is by definition unreliable—the safer he is. But if *virtù* is that by which we acquire power, the ideal type . . . is the individual who acquires it wholly by the exercise of his personal qualities and not at all as the result of contingencies and circumstances outside himself" (*Machiavellian Moment,* p. 167). Kahn notes that "the problems of political innovation in the realm of contingency . . . are rhetorical problems: problems that cannot be resolved by applying fixed moral principles on the one hand or mere force on the other. . . . Thus rhetoric is not simply an instrument of *virtù* but it is also analogous to *virtù* in the sense that both are faculties for responding to the realm of contingency or fortune; and *virtù* is rhetorical because what counts as *virtù* is produced from within a rhetorical analysis of the circumstances at hand and varies accordingly. Political innovation proves to be inseparable from rhetorical invention" (*Machiavellian Rhetoric,* p. 17).

5. Hiero (or Hieron) II, of Syracuse (c. 306–215 B.C.) was born of an ordinary family from Greek Sicily. From his position as commander in chief of the Syracusan army he went on to seize power and become the tyrant of Syracuse. He allied himself with Rome and spared his city the ravages of the First Punic War between Rome and Carthage. Machiavelli also examines his career in *The Prince,* chaps. 6 and 13. Here he is probably following the third century A.D. historian Justin, 23.4. Justin's phrase *prorsus ut nihil ei regium deesse praeter regnum videretur* from 23.4.15 is also quoted in *The Prince,* 6 (p. 151, lines 130–131). See Polybius, 1.8–9; 16. Hiero is discussed in Livy, *Ab urbe condita . . . ,* hereinafter cited simply as Livy, 22.37; 23.30; 24.4–5, 22; and 25.24. Perseus (c. 212/213–166 B.C.), the son of Philip V of Macedon, was Macedonia's final king (179–168 B.C.). At the battle of Pydna in 168 B.C. he was defeated by Paulus Aemilius, who captured the fleeing Perseus and returned him to Rome as part of his triumph; see Plutarch, *Paulus Aemilius,* 24.2.

6. Namely in the Preface to Book 1, so it would appear that the preface was written before this dedicatory letter. The phrase "at the outset" reminds us that this letter was printed at the end of Book 3 in some manuscript copies and in editions published in Florence and Rome in 1531.

BOOK *One*

Preface A[1]

1 Because of the invidious nature of men, it has always been no less dangerous to find new methods and institutions[2] than it has been to seek unknown seas and lands, since men are more prone to blame than to praise the actions of others. Nevertheless, impelled by the natural desire that has always been within me to act unhesitatingly on matters that I believe bring about the common good for everyone, I have decided to set out upon a path as yet untrodden by anyone else; although it may result in trouble and difficulty for me, it could also result in reward for me through those who graciously consider the purpose of my endeavors. 2 And if the inadequacy of my understanding, my limited experience of current matters, and my shaky knowledge of ancient ones cause my effort to be flawed and of little use, at least they will pave the way for someone else who can carry out my intention with greater *virtù,* eloquence, and judgment. If this does not result in praise for me, at least it ought not to cause me blame.

3 I cannot help simultaneously marveling and grieving when, on the one hand, I consider how much honor people accord to antiquity and how often—to pass over countless other examples—a fragment of an ancient statue has been purchased for a high price so that someone may have it on hand to adorn his house and to have it copied by those who take delight in that art and they then strive with their utmost skill to show it in all their works; and when, on the other hand, I see the deeds of the greatest *virtù* that histories show us, undertaken by ancient kingdoms and republics, by kings, generals, citizens, proposers of laws,[3] and others who have toiled for their countries, being admired rather than imitated—or, to tell the truth, they have been avoided so much by all in every slightest thing they did that no trace of that ancient *virtù* has survived. 4 All the more since I see in the disputes that arise between citizens in civil matters, or in the diseases that men contract, that they always have recourse to those ideas or remedies that were decided on or prescribed by the ancients. 5 For civil laws are nothing but decisions made by jurists of antiquity; arranged in order, they teach our current jurists how to judge. Medicine, too, is nothing but observations that the physicians of antiquity made, upon which present-day physicians base their opinions. 6 Nevertheless, in establishing[4] republics, preserving states, governing kingdoms, setting up militias and conducting warfare, judging their subjects, and extending power,[5] not one prince or republic or commander can be found who consults antiquity for models. 7 I believe this situation results not so much from the weakness into which our present religion[6] has brought the world, or from the harm wrought in many Christian regions and cities by ambition born of idleness, as it does from

people not having a true understanding of the histories[7] and not extracting the meaning from them when they are read or relishing the savor they contain. 8 Thus it comes to pass that countless people who read them take pleasure in hearing about the variety of events[8] that they contain without ever thinking to imitate them, deeming imitation not only difficult but impossible—as if the heavens, the sun, the elements, and mankind had altered their movements, their order, and their power from the way they were in antiquity.[9] 9 Therefore, because I wish to rescue mankind from this error, I have deemed it necessary to write (concerning all those books of Livy's that the evils of time have not cut off from[10] us) whatever I shall deem necessary—according to knowledge of ancient and modern affairs—for a greater understanding of it. Thus those who read these explanations of mine may more easily derive from them the utility that should be sought from the study of histories. 10 And though this task may be difficult, nevertheless—assisted by those[11] who have encouraged me to take up this burden—I think I may bear it far enough so that someone else will have but a short way to bring it to its final destination.

NOTES

1. Because the first paragraph of this preface exists in autograph form, Inglese believes Preface A is probably a draft. From the number and quality of corrections on the manuscript, it is clear that Machiavelli worked out his ideas here carefully. Because the changes provide crucial clues to Machiavelli's thinking, the reader should carefully compare the two versions. His notion of himself as explorer boldly reflects the "unknown seas and lands" that Italian and Spanish explorers had recently revealed to an excited Europe. The sense of setting out "upon a path as yet untrodden by anyone else," however, is a standard classical topos; see, for example, the announcement of Lucretius that he is the first Roman poet to write a philosophical poem in Latin, *De rerum natura,* 1.v.926: *Avia Pieridum peragro loca nullius ante trita sola* (I travel through the pathless regions of the Muses, a place untrodden by anyone before me). It is echoed in Virgil, *Georgics,* 3.291–293 and Milton, *Paradise Lost,* 1, vv. 12–16.

2. Translates *ordini.* It would be interesting to speculate about the reasons why the first two printed editions omitted this important statement of his aims in the *Discourses,* namely, finding "new methods and institutions." This discovery drives the argument throughout the *Discourses.* Thus it shifts the emphasis on an individual leader in the *Prince* to one in the *Discourses* on the founders of a state and the extent to which they must devise "institutions" for a well-ordered state. (The "founding Fathers" of America and the authors of the *Federalist Papers* were fully cognizant of the ideas expressed in the *Discourses.*) Although "orders" would appear to be the obvious translation for this word, Machiavelli uses it in a variety of contexts. One of his favorites is a discussion of the first principles a society devises to organize itself. As in 1, 9, his primary focus is the single person who does the organization, be he real or fictitious. In the plural the word *ordini* most often suggests what provides a society with "order," namely, its "laws" and its "institutions." His use of the singular *ordine* often means the single item that brings "order" to a society, its "constitution"; *ordine* in Machiavelli can also refer to the "order" induced in the "rank" or "class" in a military context.

3. Machiavelli uses *latori de leggi,* drawing on the Latin sense of a "proposer" or

"agent" of laws, as in our word "legislator." Rinaldi notes the importance of the taste for archaeology in the circle of Bernardo Rucellai, and that the interaction between statue and deeds may reflect Plato, *Laws,* 931, a–e.

4. Translates *ordinare* here; it is translated as "setting up" later in this sentence, in the context of "militias."

5. Translates *imperio,* which could also refer to the extension or expansion of an "empire."

6. Note that the phrase "our present religion" here becomes "our present upbringing" *(educazione)* in Preface B. See below 2, 2, 25–36, for a similar interplay of ideas and word choice; there Machiavelli distinguishes between the *ozio* (idleness) of his contemporaries and the *virtù* of former times; cf. his poem *Dell' Ambizione,* ll. 118–123. Also see below, 3, 27, sentences 11–12.

7. The idea of having a "true knowledge of the histories" and learning from them is reminiscent of Livy's preface 1.10. Polybius, 1.35.6–10, may also be relevant.

8. Translates *accidenti;* the word often refers to unforeseen events, usually of a disastrous nature, but here it means the "variety of incidents" or "varied events" described in books of history.

9. This sentence succinctly states one of Machiavelli's basic tenets; it is repeated below, 1, 11, 26; 1, 39, 2; the Preface to Book 2, 12; and 3, 43, 3. It can also be found in his early treatise, "Concerning the Method of Dealing with the Rebellious Peoples of the Valdichiana" (1503). See Guicciardini's important distinction on this point, *Ricordi,* C. 76 (B. 114): "Everything that has been in the past and is in the present will also be in the future; but the names and appearances will be so changed that he who does not have a good eye will not recognize them. Nor will he know what example to follow or what judgment to form on the basis of what he sees." Guicciardini's caveat is clear: "It is a great mistake to talk about the things of this world without distinctions and absolutely and, as it were, to play by the rules. Because of differences in circumstances, nearly all such things require distinctions and exceptions; they cannot be held to the same measure. Nor are these distinctions and exceptions discovered written down in books. They must be taught by discretion." This important point echoes throughout the versions of this *ricordo,* C. 6: see Q-2. 12, B. 35 and B. 121. (The *accidentale della esperienza,* the "circumstances of experience," as he says in C. 10, are a great help in shaping "discretion.") Nevertheless, the idea of history as a model teaching valuable lessons to those willing to learn can also frequently be found in Polybius, as well as in Thucydides, Diodorus Siculus, Cicero, *De oratore,* 2.36, and Lucretius, *De rerum natura.*

10. The participle *intercetti,* translated as "cut off from" here, becomes *interrotti* "torn away from" in Preface B. We know that Livy's history of Rome was written in 142 books, but what was available to Machiavelli were the first ten books and books 21 to 40 (books 41 to 45 were recovered in the year he died, 1527). Today we are not much better off: we do have the books on the Third Macedonian War (178–167 B.C.), but both he and we have little more than fragments, digests, and abbreviated summaries for all the lost books of Livy.

11. The people who joined in the discussions at the Rucellai gardens, especially the dedicatees of the *Discourses,* Zanobi Buondelmonte and Cosimo Rucellai.

Preface B[1]

1 I cannot help simultaneously marveling and grieving when, on the one hand, I consider how much honor people accord to antiquity and how often—to pass over many other examples—a fragment of an ancient statue has been purchased for a high price so that someone may have it on hand to adorn his house, to have it copied by those who take delight in that art and they then strive with their utmost skill to show it in all their works; and when, on the other hand, I see the deeds of the greatest *virtù* that histories show us, undertaken by ancient Kingdoms and Republics, by kings, generals, citizens, lawgivers[2]—and others who have toiled for their countries, being praised with wonder rather than imitated—or, to tell the truth, they have been shunned so much by everybody in every way or, rather, they are avoided so much by all in everything they did that no trace of that ancient *virtù* has survived. 2 All the more since I see in the disputes that arise between citizens in civil matters, or in the diseases that men contract, that they always have recourse to those remedies or ideas that were decided on or prescribed by the ancients. 3 For civil laws are nothing but decisions made by jurists of antiquity; arranged in order, they teach current jurists how to judge. Medicine, too, is nothing else but observations that the physicians of antiquity made, upon which present-day physicians base their opinions. 4 Nevertheless, in establishing Republics, preserving states, governing Kingdoms, establishing militias, conducting warfare, judging their subjects, and extending power, not one prince or Republic or commander or citizen can be found who consults antiquity for models. 5 I am convinced that this situation results not so much from the weakness into which our present upbringing[3] has brought the world, or from the harm that ambition born of idleness has wrought in many Christian regions and cities, as it does from people not having a true understanding of the histories and not extracting the meaning from them when they are read, or relishing the savor they contain. 6 Thus it comes to pass that countless people take pleasure while reading in hearing about the variety of events that they contain without ever thinking of imitating them, deeming imitation not only difficult but impossible—as if the heavens, the sun, the elements, and mankind had altered their movement, their order, and their power from what they were in antiquity. 7 Therefore, because I wish to rescue mankind from this error, I have deemed it necessary to write (concerning all those books of Titus Livy's that the evils of time have not cut off from us) whatever I shall deem necessary—according to ancient and modern affairs—for a greater understanding of them. Thus those who read these discourses[4] of mine may derive from them the utility that should be sought from the study of histories. 8 And though this task may be difficult, nevertheless—assisted by those who have encouraged me to take up this burden—I think I may bear it far enough so that someone else will have but a short way to bring it to its final destination.

NOTES

1. In addition to the deletion of the first paragraph of Preface A, there are some specific word changes in Preface B mentioned in the notes to Preface A.

2. The translation of Machiavelli's *datori di leggi* (givers of laws or people handing down laws) is a slight change of emphasis from his diction in Preface A.

3. Translates *educazione;* a softer, though broader, condemnation than in Preface A.

4. Machiavelli sharpens the nature of his work's scope by changing the word "explanations" to "discourses" in this version.

~ 1 ~

WHAT THE ORIGINS OF CITIES HAVE USUALLY BEEN AND WHAT WERE ROME'S ORIGINS

1 Those who read about the origin of the city of Rome, and by what lawgivers[1] it was established and how, will not be surprised that so much *virtù* should have been sustained over several centuries in that city and that eventually the empire which succeeded that republic should have arisen from it. 2 Because I want first to discuss its founding, I state that all cities are built either by men indigenous to the place where they are built or by outsiders. 3 The first case occurs when the inhabitants, scattered[2] through many small villages, do not feel they have a secure place to live in. Because of both its location and the smallness of its numbers, each cannot resist on its own the strength of those who attack them; and when the enemy comes, there is not enough time to band together for self-defense or, even if there were time enough, they would have to abandon many of their strongholds and would thus immediately become their enemies' prey. Therefore, to avoid these dangers—prompted either on their own or by someone with greater authority among them—they band together and dwell in a site they have selected that is more convenient to live in and easier to defend.

4 That was the case with Athens and Venice, among many others. 5 For just such reasons scattered inhabitants built the former under the authority of Theseus. The latter was built when many people had withdrawn into some little islands that were at the head of the Adriatic Sea so as to escape from the wars that, because of the arrival of new barbarians, broke out daily in Italy after the decline of the Roman Empire; without any particular ruler to organize them, these people began to live together under those laws that seemed most likely to sustain them.[3] 6 This turned out to be fortunate for them thanks to the long period of idleness that the site provided them since that sea had no outlets and the people who were harrying Italy did not have boats to annoy them; so even a humble origin could bring them to the grandeur which is theirs now.

7 The second case—when a city is built by foreign people—occurs from men who either are free or are dependent on others, like the colonies sent by

either a republic or a prince to ease the region's population or in defense of the recently acquired land which they want to hold onto securely and without expense: the Romans built many of these cities all over their empire.[4] Or else these cities are built by a ruler, not so he can live there but for his glory, as the city of Alexandria was for Alexander. 8 Because these cities do not have their origins in freedom, it rarely turns out that they go very far and can be numbered among the capitals of kingdoms. 9 The building of Florence was like these cities because—whether it was built by soldiers of Sulla or perchance by inhabitants from the hills of Fiesole who, growing confident from the long peace that arose in the world under Octavian, gathered together to live in the Arno plain—it was built under the Roman Empire and could not, at the outset, undertake any growth other than that granted to it by the ruler's generosity.[5]

10 The builders of cities are free when a people, either under a ruler or by its own initiative, is forced by pestilence or by famine or by war to abandon its homeland and seek a new dwelling-place for itself; these people either inhabit the cities that they find in the regions that they conquer as did Moses, or they build new ones, as Aeneas did.[6] 11 This is a case where we can discern the *virtù* of the builder and the fortune[7] of what is built; it is more or less remarkable depending upon the greater or lesser degree of *virtù* in the man responsible for the origin of the city. 12 We can recognize his *virtù* in two ways: the first is in the selection of the site, the second in the drawing up of laws.

13 Because men act either by necessity or by choice and because we find that there is greater *virtù* where choice has less influence, we must consider if it would not be better to choose barren areas for the building of cities, so men, forced to exert themselves and less imbued with idleness, would live in greater unity since they might have less cause for discord because of the barrenness of the site. Such was the case of Ragusa and many other cities built in similar locations.[8] That choice would doubtless be wiser and more practical if men were content to live on their own and were not intent on seeking to dominate others. 14 Therefore, because men can find safety only through power, it is necessary to avoid barren regions and to settle in very fertile places where, since the fertility of the site enables them to expand, they can both defend themselves from whoever attacks them and crush anyone who challenges their greatness. 15 As for any idleness that the site might occasion, the city must institute laws that impose on it those obligations that the site itself might not. It should imitate those men who were judicious and inhabited very pleasant, fertile regions—those likely to produce men idle and incapable of any activity with *virtù*—and, in order to avoid the dangers that the pleasantness of the region might have caused through idleness, those men who have imposed a requirement for training on the ones who were to become soldiers. Through such an arrangement better soldiers have developed there than in regions that were naturally rugged and unproductive. 16 Among such regions was the kingdom of Egypt where, although the land was very pleasant, the requirement imposed by its laws was so powerful that quite excellent men arose from it and, had not their names been effaced by the passage of centuries, we would see that they deserve more praise than Alexander the Great and many others

whose memories are still fresh.[9] 17 Anyone who considered the reign of the Sultan and the organization of the Mamelukes and their militia before it was crushed by the Grand Turk Selim would have noted the many drills for the soldiers and would in fact understand how much they feared the idleness to which the countryside's bounty might lead them if they had not prevented it through very strong laws.[10] 18 Therefore I say that it is a wiser choice to settle in a fertile place when that fertility is controlled within proper limits by laws.[11] 19 The architect Deinocrates came to Alexander the Great, who wanted to build a city to his own glory, and showed him that he could build it atop Mount Athos; that spot, in addition to being impregnable, could be adapted so that a human form could be given to the city—a marvelous and rare deed worthy of his greatness. 20 When Alexander asked him what its inhabitants would live on, Deinocrates replied that he had not thought about that. Alexander laughed and, forgetting the mountain, built Alexandria where the inhabitants would live willingly thanks to the richness of the land and the convenience of both the sea and the Nile.[12]

21 So anyone who studies the building of Rome, if Aeneas is considered to be its first father, will classify it among the cities built by outsiders; if it is Romulus, among the cities built by inhabitants of the area—in either case he will see that Rome had free beginnings, independent of anyone.[13] He will also see, as will be pointed out below, to what necessities the laws drawn up by Romulus, Numa, and others constrained it—so that the fertility of the site, the convenience of the sea, their frequent victories, and the greatness of the empire could not corrupt it for many centuries and preserved it full of as great *virtù* as ever embellished any city or republic.

22 Because the deeds performed by the city, which Livy celebrated, resulted from either public or private decisions, either at home or abroad, I shall begin by discussing those deeds occurring at home and as a result of public decision that I deem to be worthy of lengthier comment—adding to them everything that devolved from them. The discourses in this first book, or rather in this first part, will be limited to these items.[14]

NOTES

1. Inglese's text reads *datori di leggi,* not *latori di leggi;* see Preface A, n.3 and Preface B, n.2. There may be a reminiscence of Polybius 6.2.2–3.

2. The emphasis on scattered villages banding together for collective security exists in Aristotle, *Politics* 1.1.7; 1252b16–19, Diodorus Siculus, 1.8.5–9, and Sallust, *Bellum Catilinae* 6.1–5.

3. For the legendary founding of Athens by Theseus, see Plutarch, *Theseus,* 24–25 and Thucydides, 2.15; Machiavelli discusses the founding of Venice in A.D. 451 after the invasion of Attila and the Huns in *Florentine Histories,* 1, 29. Machiavelli's treatment of this material may be indebted to the *Decades* (1437–1442) of the humanist Flavio Biondo (1392–1463), an important early contributor to Renaissance historiography.

4. Compare the thoughts Machiavelli expresses here with those in *Prince,* 3 (pp. 109; 111, lines 98–133); *Florentine Histories,* 2 opens with the assertion that establishing colonial settlements was one of the ancients' greatest *ordini.*

5. The first alternative (about the founding of Florence occurring after the Social War, the War of the Allies [91–88 B.C.], when victorious veterans from Sulla's armies remained along the Arno River in the territory belonging to the Etruscan Faesulae) can be traced to the work of the humanist and Florentine Chancellor, Coluccio Salutati (1331–1406); see his *Invectiva* ("Response to the Invective of Antonio Loschi"). It can be found both in the *Historia florentina* 1, 1 (post 1454) by the Florentine humanist scholar Poggio Bracciolini (1380–1459) and in the *Historiae florentini populi* 1, 1, begun in 1415 by the Florentine humanist Leonardo Bruni (1370–1444). Following in Salutati's footsteps, Bruni, in both his *Laudatio Florentinae Urbis* and his *Historia,* sought to link the origin of Florence to the Roman republic, not to imperial Rome. The second alternative, with the credit going to Augustus Caesar (63 B.C.–A.D. 14), is thought to be based on the work of Poliziano (1454–1494), a Florentine poet and scholar who enjoyed the favor of Lorenzo de' Medici; see Rubinstein, "Origini di Firenze," pp. 104–107. See also the discussion in Guicciardini, *Cose Fiorentine,* 1 (p. 5), and Machiavelli, *Florentine Histories* 2, 2. For more on the Social War, see *Discourses,* 2, 4, n.6.

6. For the cities in the land of Canaan that Moses gave as their inheritance to the Reubenites and Gadites, see Numbers 32:33–42. That Rome was founded by Aeneas and his descendants Romulus and Remus forms the basis of Virgil's *Aeneid,* which appeared about thirty years before the work of Livy, who also attributes the founding to Aeneas.

7. Like *virtù,* with which it is frequently coupled, *fortuna* is a tricky word to translate. Generally speaking, we use "Fortune" when the context implies the abstract idea, inherited from Latin and medieval authors, of that powerful, pervasive, and arbitrary force that militates against a person's intelligent foresight; we use "fortune" for most other contexts in which the implication is that of "fate," "destiny," or most often "luck," when "fortune" often obviously results from the operations of "Fortune."

8. Aristotle discusses the territory of an ideal state in *Politics,* 7.5.1–4; 1326b.26–1327a10. Ragusa, the modern-day Dubrovnik in Croatia, on the Dalmatian Coast of the former Yugoslavia, was an important seaport founded by Greeks from Corinth in the seventh century. The city and its republic remained under the protection of the Byzantine Empire, Venice, Hungary, and the Ottoman Turks; it kept its status as a republic until the early nineteenth century. Concerning this sentence's argument, see Mansfield, *New Modes,* p. 31.

9. The phrase "the requirement imposed by its laws" may owe something to Diodorus Siculus 1.70–95 and Aristotle, *Politics,* 7.9.5; 1329b31. Vivanti's edition of the *Discorsi* notes that attributing these virtues to the Egyptians began with the *Timaeus* of Plato and had been recently reasserted in the works of Marsilio Ficino; Diodorus Siculus was also a source for praise of Egypt.

10. The Mamelukes were a powerful, hereditary military class that formed a virtual oligarchy ruling Egypt from 1250 to 1517. Originally descended from slaves, they eventually attained their own vested rights, most important that of electing the sultan. Rinaldi identifies "the Sultan" as al-Malik as-Sahib Ayyub (1240–1249). The Ottoman emperor, Selim I, defeated the last Mameluke sultan, Tuman Bey, in 1517 and incorporated Egypt into the Ottoman empire.

11. This assertion may owe something to Livy 1.19.4, on the policies of Numa when he first became ruler of Rome.

12. For the anecdote about Deinocrates and Mount Athos, see Vitruvius, *De architectura,* 2, preface, 2–3. Deinocrates eventually built the city of Alexandria for Alexander the Great in 322 B.C. at the mouth of the Nile. See Plutarch, *Alexander,* 26.

13. For Livy on Aeneas, see 1.1–3, and on Romulus and Remus, see 1.4–6; see also Plutarch, *Romulus,* 4. On Numa, see Livy, 1.18–21, and Plutarch, *Numa,* 3.3–7.

14. Some commentators, especially Walker, see an allusion to the structure of the *Discourses* here: that Book 1 will deal with constitutional, institutional, and legal innovations—Rome's domestic policies—begun through "public resolutions"; that Book 2 will deal with foreign policies—wars, conquests and alliances, begun through "public resolutions"; and the accomplishments of "private resolutions," namely, the deeds of great Romans. Walker also believes that a passage from the end of the preface to Polybius, 6.1.8–9 is relevant: that historians need to study not only historical causation but also, in any given situation, the advantages of choosing the better alternative. See the discussion of Polybius above in Introduction, n.22, and below, 1, 2, n.9.

~ 2 ~

HOW MANY KINDS OF REPUBLICS THERE ARE AND WHAT KIND THE ROMAN REPUBLIC WAS

1 I wish to set aside consideration of those cities that were subjected to others from the outset. I shall discuss those cities that had their origins far from any external domination but immediately governed themselves as they chose, either as republics or principalities. Just as they had different origins, so they had different laws and institutions.[1] 2 Some, either at their founding or shortly afterwards, were given laws by a single man and all at once, as Lycurgus did to the Spartans.[2] Others got them by chance at different times and as the result of circumstances, as did Rome. 3 So we can call a republic fortunate if it is granted a man so prudent that he provides it with laws so instituted that, without needing to amend them, it can live under them in security. 4 We note that Sparta obeyed its laws for more than eight hundred years[3] without corrupting them and without dangerous uprisings. On the contrary, a city that is obliged to reorganize itself on its own because it did not happen upon a prudent lawgiver is unfortunate to a certain extent. 5 And an even more unfortunate city is one that is farther removed from order: that is, a city whose institutions are completely removed from the straight path that can direct it toward a perfect and true end,[4] 6 because it is almost impossible for some event to set such cities straight. Other cities which, even though they do not have perfect institutions, have had a beginning that is good and likely to get better can become perfect through the course of events.[5] 7 But it is surely true that they will never set themselves in order without danger, because many men will never agree to a new law concerning a new order in a city unless necessity shows them the need to do so. Because such necessity cannot arise without danger, the republic can easily collapse before it is directed toward perfect order. 8 The republic of Florence is ample proof: Florence was

reorganized by the incident at Arezzo in 1502; it was disorganized by the one at Prato in 1512.[6]

9 Therefore, to discuss what the institutions of the city of Rome were and what circumstances led it to perfection, I state that some people who have written about republics say there are three sorts of states among them, which they call Princedoms, Aristocracies, and Democracies, and that those who organize a city must turn to one of them accordingly as it suits their purposes.[7] 10 Still other—and in the opinion of many, wiser—people believe that there are six types of governments: of which three are very bad and three others are good in themselves but so easily corrupted that they, too, become harmful. 11 The three good ones are those mentioned above. The bad ones are the three others, which devolve from the first three; each one so closely resembles its neighbor that it is an easy leap from one type to the other: the princedom easily becomes a tyranny, an aristocracy easily becomes an oligarchy, a democracy turns without difficulty into anarchy.[8] 12 Consequently, if the organizer of a republic establishes one of these three forms of government in a city, he sets it up for only a brief period because no remedy can prevent it from slipping into its opposite form because of the similarity that there is in this instance between virtue and vice.

13 These variations in government arise by chance among men because at the beginning of the world, when inhabitants were few, people lived for a time scattered like beasts.[9] Then, as the population increased, they gathered together and, the better to defend themselves, began to look to the strongest and bravest one among them, made him their chief, and obeyed him. 14 Thus arose an understanding of what was honest and good as distinguished from what was harmful and evil: if someone harmed his benefactor, people would feel hatred and sympathy; they blamed the ungrateful and honored those who were grateful. Aware, too, that similar harm could be inflicted upon themselves, they resorted to formulating laws and devising punishments for violators so that they could prevent such harm. From this a knowledge of justice developed. 15 Consequently, when they were obliged later to choose a prince, people no longer went for the boldest man but instead for the one who was the wisest and most just. 16 But later, when they began to make sovereignty hereditary instead of elective, the heirs quickly degenerated from their forebears[10] and, abandoning deeds of *virtù,* they thought princes had no further obligation than to surpass others in luxurious living, lascivious behavior, and every other form of licentiousness. Consequently, the prince came to be hated, and because he was hated he became afraid; fear soon turned into violence: quickly tyranny arose. 17 From this subsequently came the origins of rebellions, conspiracies[11] and plots against the princes, not carried out by timid and weak men but by those who, surpassing everyone else in generosity, magnanimity, wealth, and nobility, could not abide the prince's dishonorable way of life. 18 Under the leadership of these powerful men, therefore, the populace took up arms against the prince; once he was killed, it obeyed them as liberators. 19 Hating the title of a single chief, they formed themselves into a government; initially, bearing in mind the recent tyranny, they governed themselves in accordance with the

laws they themselves had drawn up, subordinating their own interests to the common good, and governed and protected private and public matters with the greatest diligence. 20 Later, when the administration passed to their sons, who had never known the vicissitudes of Fortune or experienced evil and who refused to be satisfied with civic equality, they turned to greed, ambition, and the seizing of women; thus, they caused the transformation of a government of Aristocrats into an oligarchy without respect for any civility. Consequently, what happened to the tyrant befell them within a short time. Disgusted with their government, the populace made itself the instrument of whoever intended to attack those governing them in any way; so someone quickly appeared who killed them with the help of the populace. 21 Then, because the memory of their former prince and the outrages committed by him was still fresh after they had overthrown the oligarchy and they did not want to restore the government of the prince, they turned to democracy and organized it in such a way that neither the powerful few nor a prince could have any power in it at all. 22 And because every form of government possesses some authority at the outset, this democratic government survived for a while—but not long, especially once the generation of men who had organized it died. Anarchy, in which neither private individuals nor public officials are feared, quickly ensued, with the result that all the people acted as they saw fit: thousands of outrages were committed daily. Hence, in order to avoid anarchy, they once more return to government by a prince, either forced by necessity or on the advice of some good man.[12] From this point one returns little by little to anarchy in the ways and for the reasons given.

23 This is the cycle through which all republics have been and are governed. But they rarely revert to the same forms of government, because hardly any republic can endure long enough to pass through these transformations often and remain standing.[13] 24 What does occur is that, while the republic is in turmoil—always lacking good advice and military strength—a better organized neighboring state will subjugate it. But if that were not so, a republic would likely experience an infinite number of cycles through these various forms of government.

25 Therefore I state that all three above-mentioned forms of government are pernicious because the duration of the three good ones is brief and the three bad ones are evil.[14] 26 So, because those who organized laws wisely have realized this defect, they have avoided each form per se and opted for a form that partakes of all three. They have felt this to be more solid and more stable, because each form keeps watch over the other in a city that has a Princely, an Aristocratic, and a Democratic government.[15]

27 Among those who have deserved the most praise for such constitutions is Lycurgus, who, by organizing the laws in Sparta so as to share power among Kings, Aristocrats, and the People, created a state that lasted more than eight hundred years, reaping the highest praise for him and peace for the city.[16] 28 The opposite result occurred when Solon established laws in Athens: he set up just a democracy there, and it was so short-lived that he saw the tyranny of Pisistratus arise before he died.[17] Although his heirs were expelled after forty

years and freedom was restored to Athens because the city resumed a democratic government following Solon's laws, democracy did not survive more than a century. For although in order to preserve democracy the city enacted many ordinances restraining the arrogance of the rich and the licentiousness of the people in general, which Solon had not considered, Athens nevertheless endured but briefly, compared with Sparta, because it did not mix in princely and aristocratic power.

29 But let us get to Rome.[18] Despite not having a Lycurgus at its founding to organize it so it could endure for a long time in freedom, nevertheless, so many events occurred because of the dissension between the Plebs and the Senate that what a lawgiver had not done came about by chance. 30 Although Rome was not endowed with Fortune's first gift, it was endowed with the second one; for its initial institutions, even though they were defective, nevertheless did not lead it away from the straight path that might bring it to perfection. 31 For Romulus and all the other kings created many good laws quite conducive to a free society. But because their purpose was to found a kingdom and not a republic, as long as Rome remained free it lacked many institutions necessary for the fostering of freedom that those kings had not provided. 32 Even though the kings lost their power for the reasons and in the way I have discussed, nevertheless, those who expelled them, because they quickly appointed two consuls to replace the king, succeeded in expelling the royal name but not royal power. Thus, since the state had Consuls and a Senate, it had a mixture of only two of the three forms of government mentioned above, that is, the princely and the aristocratic.[19] 33 There remained merely to grant a place to the popular government. Hence, when the Roman Nobility became arrogant, for reasons that I shall explain later, the people rose up against it, and the Nobles were obliged to concede a share of power to the people in order not to lose it all; on the other hand, the Senate and the Consuls held onto so much authority that they were able to keep their rank in the republic. 34 Thus were created the Tribunes of the Plebs; after they were created, the government of the republic became more stable since all three forms of government had a share in it.[20] 35 Fortune was so favorable to Rome that, even though power was transferred from the King and the Aristocrats to the People—through the same steps and for the same reasons I discussed earlier—nevertheless royal power was never entirely done away with to empower the Aristocracy or the Aristocracy's power completely reduced to empower the People. But continuing its mixed form of government, Rome created a perfect republic.[21] It attained this perfection on account of the dissension between the Plebs and the Senate, as I shall demonstrate amply in the next two chapters.

NOTES

1. The phrase "different laws and institutions" translates *diverse leggi e ordini;* the "orders" meant in *ordini* are the "arrangements" or "regulations" institutionalized through constitutional means by the polity; see below 1, 18, n. 1.

2. By tradition, Lycurgus is credited with establishing Sparta's constitution governing social and military norms in the seventh century B.C. Although Plutarch wrote

a biography of him, Lycurgus may never have actually lived; see especially *Lycurgus,* 5–6. See also Polybius, 6. 10.

3. Machiavelli has his *Art of War* spokesman, Fabrizio Colonna, use this same time frame for Sparta in Book 1. It presumably ends with the domination of Sparta by Augustus in 27 B.C. and begins with the assertion in Thucydides, 1.18.1, that Sparta's good laws and government had been in effect for four hundred years by the end of the Peloponnesian War in 404 B.C. For more on the appropriateness of Fabrizio Colonna as a spokesman, see Marcia L. Colish, "Machiavelli's Art of War: A Reconsideration."

4. The opening sentence of Aristotle's *Politics* may be relevant here; see 1.1; 1252a1–6.

5. Translates *accidenti.*

6. The "new order" that Machiavelli mentions refers to two key events in 1502 and 1512 that defined the limits both of Machiavelli's political career and that of his friend and champion, Piero Soderini. In early June 1502, Arezzo and other towns in the Val di Chiana rebelled against Florentine control, and Cesare Borgia gained control of Urbino in one day. Florence turned to Louis XII of France for help against this threat to its influence in Tuscany. Fearing Borgia's plans for territorial aggrandizement, the city hastily responded by dispatching both Piero's brother Francesco Soderini, bishop of Volterra, and Machiavelli, who wrote most of the reports to the Florentine Signoria over the bishop's signature. Meanwhile, the city's Grand Council voted to appoint a gonfalonier for life, and Piero Soderini was elected to that post. (Although Guicciardini does not refer to these events in his *Consideration* of this chapter, his *History of Florence* attributes the decision to elect a lifetime gonfalonier to the panic produced by the Arezzo revolt: "the Signoria applied itself to restore order to the city's affairs and government because disorder in them occasioned all the other disorders and confusion" [chapter 23]). Soderini's rule ended a decade later, at the same time as the city's dependence on France. Pope Julius II formed the Holy League in 1511, with Venice and the Spanish king Ferdinand the Catholic, to drive the French out of Italy and, as a corollary, to reduce Florence's power in Italy. Planning to restore the Medici as Florence's rulers so he would have a secure ally, Julius II sent Ferdinand the Catholic's trusted commander Ramón de Cardona with his army toward the city. Sacking Prato on 29 August, the army threatened to take Florence. By the thirty-first, the pro-Medici party in Florence had forced Soderini to resign; Giuliano de' Medici marched into Florence on 1 September. Some time after 16 September, Machiavelli wrote a letter to an unidentified noblewoman with a personal account of these events; see *Friends,* pp. 214–217. Before the year was out, Machiavelli was dismissed from his office as Florence's second chancellor.

7. Although Plato, *Republic,* 8 and Aristotle, *Politics,* 3.5.1–4; 1279a22–1279b10 are possible sources for the distinctions within republics, the particular discussion of Rome that follows is closer to Polybius 6.3–10. Machiavelli's terminology is *Principato, Ottimati, e Popolare.* Machiavelli's "Remarks to Be Given About the Money Bill," written in 1503, opens by noting that "every city that ever existed for any length of time was governed either by an absolute prince *[principe soluto],* by aristocrats *[ottimati],* or by a democracy *[populo].*"

8. This distinction exists in Plato, *Statesman,* 302 d–e and in the reference to Aristotle's *Politics* cited in note 7, but see also Polybius, 6.4.6.

9. For this long paragraph, see Polybius, 6.5–9; at 6.5.1, Polybius acknowledges

his debt to Plato, but see also Lucretius, *De rerum natura,* 5.925–942 and Diodorus Siculus 1.8.1–2. A comparison of the Polybius sections with the argument here is instructive in particular for what Machiavelli retains and rejects, and especially how he shapes what he uses. There was a translation of the first five books of Polybius into Latin in 1450 by Niccolò Perotti. (Originally Polybius's *Histories* numbered forty books; we have only fragments, though some are considerable, from six to forty.) In Book 6 of this history of Rome's rise to world power, Polybius develops his notion of *anacyclosis.* He maintains that Rome escaped the inevitable and destructive circular sequence of political change by developing a mixed constitution that effected a balance among the monarchy (consuls), aristocracy (senate), and people. Sasso discusses fully the idea of *anacyclosis* and Machiavelli's knowledge of Polybius in *Antichi,* 1, pp. 3–118, originally published in *Studi su Machiavelli* (Naples: Morano, 1967), pp. 161–280.

10. The immediate source for this point may be Polybius, 6.7.6., but see also Aristotle, *Politics,* 3.10.7–8; 1286b5–22. and 5.8.20–21; 1312b18–38.

11. Machiavelli devotes a long chapter to conspiracies: see below, 3, 6.

12. The reading for the text here is *costretti per necessità o per suggestione d'alcuno buono uomo, per fuggire tale licenza;* some texts read *o per fuggire tale licenza,* resulting in three alternatives instead of two for the return to a princedom.

13. This paragraph is closely related to the cyclical notion of *anacyclosis* in Polybius, 6.9.10, but see the discussion of Polybius in the Introduction, n.22. For a more absolute view of this notion, see the opening sentences of *Florentine Histories,* 5, 1: "Generally the changes that countries make go most of the time from order to disorder and then pass on again from disorder to order: nature does not allow the things of this world to stand still. Once they attain their ultimate perfection, since they have no farther to go up, they must go down; similarly, once they have gone down and, as a result of their disorders, reached their lowest point, they must necessarily go up since they cannot go down any farther. Thus it turns out that they are always going down from good to bad and going up from bad to good."

14. Contrary to his classical sources, Machiavelli considers each mode by itself to be "pernicious."

15. Although Polybius proposes the cyclical theory in 6.9.10 in 6.3.7, he acknowledges that a mixed form is the most effective. He praises Rome's achievement of a mixed form balancing the three elements. Machiavelli, however, is clearly interested in the less defined periods, those of transition from one form to another—especially in the shift from a period of control to one of relative freedom.

16. With the concentration now on a mixed form of government, Machiavelli returns to his earlier example of Lycurgus and his rule in Sparta. For the time frame involved, see note 2 to this chapter. See Polybius 6.10.1–12 and his discussion of Lycurgus; also Plutarch, *Lycurgus,* and Aristotle's discussion of him in his *Politics.*

17. Solon (c. 639–c. 559 B.C.), an Athenian statesman and lawgiver, was once thought to have established democracy in Athens. Pisistratus (c. 605–527 B.C.) became tyrant of Athens on three separate occasions; his regime and that of his descendants were overthrown by Cleisthenes, who is generally credited today with being the creator of Athenian democracy. The classical sources are Plutarch, *Solon,* 18–25; 32, and Aristotle, *Politics,* 2.9.2–6; 1273b35–1274a21.

18. Perhaps taking his cue from ideas expressed in Polybius 6.10.13–11.5, Machi-

avelli in this paragraph elaborates the reasons for Rome's success more emphatically than does Polybius.

19. The first two consuls of Rome were Lucius Junius Brutus and Lucius Tarquinius Collatinus. Livy points out in 1.8.7 that Romulus established a senate in Rome.

20. The period under discussion spans roughly fifty years, from 500 to 450 B.C.

21. Later, in 1519 or 1520, Machiavelli wrote "A Commentary on Florentine Affairs After the Death of Lorenzo de' Medici the Younger," in which he argued that "the reason that Florence has always changed her types of governments so often it that is has never been either a republic or a princedom. . . . No stable government can be devised unless it is a true princedom or a true republic, for every type of government situated between the two is inadequate. A princedom can disintegrate along only one path, that of sinking toward a republic; similarly, a republic can have only one path to dissolution, that of rising toward a princedom. The governments in between *[stati di mezzo]* have two paths: they can rise toward a princedom or sink toward a republic. Hence their instability." (text in *Guerra,* pp. 261; 266–267). These *stati di mezzo* function through a combination of self-defeating methods poorly adapted to republics and princedoms. They are clearly distinguished from the Roman mixed state *[stato misto],* which he admires, as does Guicciardini in his commentary on this discourse, for its ability to balance and harmonize the best elements in a workable arrangement.

~ 3 ~

THE EVENTS THAT LED TO THE CREATION OF TRIBUNES OF THE PEOPLE IN ROME, MAKING THE REPUBLIC MORE PERFECT

1 As is pointed out by all who discuss civil society,[1] and every history is filled with examples, anyone who sets up a republic and establishes its laws must presuppose that all men are evil and always prone to exercise the malice in their minds whenever opportunity gives them free rein.[2] And when some malice remains temporarily hidden, it results from some hidden cause that is unknown because there has been no contrary experience; but time, which is said to be the father of all truth,[3] eventually brings about its revelation.

2 After the expulsion of the Tarquins, there seemed to be very great unity in Rome between the Plebs and the Senate;[4] the Nobles seemed to have put aside their arrogance and become commoners in spirit and tolerant of anyone, no matter how lowborn.[5] 3 As long as the Tarquins were alive, this deception remained hidden and its cause was not seen, since the Nobility acted decently toward the Plebs because they feared the Tarquins and were afraid the Plebs, if ill-treated, might side with them. But as soon as the Tarquins died and the Nobles' fear had disappeared, they began spitting out all the poison against the Plebs that they had kept pent up in their hearts: they insulted them every way they could.[6] 4 This corroborates what I said above: men never do good except out of necessity; but where choice abounds and they can act as they please, suddenly everything is full of turmoil and disorder.[7] 5 That is why it is said that

hunger and poverty make men industrious and laws make them good. 6 Wherever something works well by itself without the law, the law is unnecessary; but when such sound custom fails, the law is immediately required.

7 So when the Tarquins were gone and fear of them no longer checked the Nobility, a new institution had to be thought up that would duplicate the effect the Tarquins had while they were living. 8 So, after a good deal of rioting, disorder, and danger of conflict erupted between the Plebs and the Nobility, the Romans turned to creating Tribunes for the protection of the Plebs,[8] and they were invested with such preeminence and prestige that ever after they acted as intermediaries between the Plebs and the Senate, preventing the Nobles' insolence.

NOTES

1. Translates *vivere civile* (civil life); those who "discuss" it are writers on politics.

2. This hypothetical assumption of mankind's evil nature is consonant with the discussion in *Prince,* chapters 15 and 18 (p. 257, lines 20–22; p. 281, lines 29–36 and notes).

3. A proverbial expression in the Renaissance, dating back to Roman times.

4. The traditional date of the expulsion of Tarquinius Superbus is 510 B.C. following his son Sextus Tarquinius's rape of Lucretia, the wife of Tarquinius Collatinus; see Livy, 1.58–60. He discusses the "concord" in 2.1.

5. See Livy, 2.5; 8–9.

6. See Livy, 2.21.6.

7. In 1, 1, sentence 13.

8. The traditional date is 494 B.C. See Livy, 2.7–9; 18; 23–24; and 27–32 for strife between the plebs and the nobility and 2.33.1–3 for its resolution.

~ 4 ~

THE DISCORD BETWEEN THE PLEBS AND THE ROMAN SENATE MADE THAT REPUBLIC FREE AND POWERFUL

1 I do not want to neglect discussing the conflicts that existed in Rome from the death of the Tarquins until the creation of the Tribunes, and then several matters contrary to the opinion of many who say that Rome was a contentious republic, so full of disorder that had good fortune and military *virtù* not compensated for its defects it would have been inferior to all other republics.[1] 2 I cannot deny that Fortune and the army were sources of Roman power; but it certainly seems to me that these people do not realize that where there is a good army there must be good government, and it rarely happens that there is not good fortune too.[2] 3 But let us get down to the other particulars of that city. 4 I say that those who condemn the conflicts between the Nobles and the Plebs appear to me to be blaming the very things that were the primary reason for Rome's remaining free and to be paying more attention to the shouts and cries that these conflicts aroused than to the good results they had. They do not consider that in every republic there are two opposing humors[3]—the people and the upper classes—and that all laws

made to promote freedom derive from the conflict between them. We can readily see this from what occurred in Rome: from the Tarquins to the Gracchi, a period of more than three hundred years,[4] conflicts in Rome rarely involved banishment and even more rarely bloodshed. 5 It is therefore impossible to deem those conflicts harmful or a republic divided if over so long a period and despite its dissensions it exiled no more than eight or ten citizens and executed quite few and did not even levy fines against very many. 6 Nor can a republic in which there are so many examples of *virtù* reasonably be called disorderly, since good examples derive from good upbringing, good upbringing from good laws, and good laws from the very conflicts that many people condemn indiscriminately. For anyone who studies their results closely will discover that they did not lead to any exile or violence inimical to the common good, but produced laws and institutions conducive to public freedom. 7 Some might say: these ways were extraordinary and almost brutal, for we see the people united making an outcry against the Senate, the Senate against the People, men rushing riotously through the streets, shops barred, all the Plebs fleeing Rome—all things that appall whoever only reads about them.[5] I would reply that every city must have its own ways in which people can give vent to their ambitions, especially cities that want to avail themselves of their people in significant matters.[6] Among these cities Rome possessed this way: when the people wanted to get a law promulgated, they either behaved as I have described or they refused to lend their name to going to war. So in order to placate them, it was necessary to give them some degree of satisfaction. 8 The desires of a free people are rarely detrimental to freedom because they arise from either being oppressed or fear of being oppressed. 9 When such ideas are unjustified, there exists the remedy of assemblies, so some good man emerges whose speech will show them how they have erred. And as Cicero says, the people, though they may be ignorant, are open to truth and easily yield when told the truth by someone who is worthy of trust.[7]

10 Therefore the Roman government must be blamed more sparingly and one must consider that the many good results that the republic achieved were effected by only the best causes. 11 If conflict led to the creation of the Tribunes, it deserves very high praise, because, aside from giving the people a role in administration, they were created to safeguard Roman freedom, as will be shown in the next chapter.

NOTES

1. Among the "many" were Sallust, *Bellum Catilinae (De Catilinae coniuratione)*, 10–12; *Bellum Iugurthinum*, 5; *Historiae*, 1.55, 77; 3.48; Cicero, *De republica*, 2.33, and *In Catilinam* 2.13; 3.10, and Augustine, *De civitate Dei*, 2.18–19; 3.16–17. Among the humanists preceding Machiavelli, similar sentiments can be found in Coluccio Salutati and Pier Paolo Vergerio. For more on Rome's "detractors," see Sasso, *Antichi*, 1, pp. 401–536, originally published in *Memorie dell'Accademia Nazionale dei Lincei*, ser. 8, 22 (1978): 319–418.

2. For more on Fortune and Rome's army, see below, 2, 1. The phrase "good government" translates *buono ordine;* that is, the set of institutions that foster good government. The reciprocity between good government and good armies is stated early

in *Prince,* 12 (p. 219, lines 13–16), and in the opening sentences of both his *Discorso dell'ordinare lo stato di Firenze alle armi* (Discourse on the organization of the Florentine state for arms) and his *Provvisione prima, per le fanterie, del 6 dicembre 1506* (first provision for infantry of 6 December 1506), as well the proem to *The Art of War,* published in 1521.

3. Behind this sentence stands a physiological metaphor with antecedents as diverse as Saint Paul, 1 Cor. 12:12, Xenophon, *Memorabilia,* 2.3.18, Aristotle, *Politics,* 5.2.7; 1302b34–1303a3; Polybius 6.57.1, Cicero, *De officiis,* 3.5.22, and in a speech given by Menenius Agrippa reported in one of this passage's sources, Livy 2.32.9–12 (for Shakespeare's use of the latter instance, see *Coriolanus,* 1, i, 95–163). To preserve Machiavelli's metaphor, we have translated *umori* literally, though it clearly refers to "factions" or "classes." The metaphor, common in Renaissance political thought, is rooted in a medical notion that assumes that, just as a healthy human body maintains a balance between the four humors (blood, phlegm, black bile, and yellow bile), so a healthy body politic has its factions or classes in healthy alignment. Machiavelli draws on this notion in *Prince,* 9 (p. 191, lines 9–10), and in *Florentine Histories,* 2, 12 and 3, 1; in the latter example he notes that an imbalance of "humors" is "food" for unrest in republics. For more on this topic, see Parel, *Machiavellian Cosmos,* pp. 105–112.

4. Actually from 510 to 121 B.C.

5. Rinaldi draws attention to the irony of this aside.

6. In his 1520 *Discursus florentinarum rerum post mortem iunioris Laurentii Medices* (A commentary on Florentine affairs after the death of Lorenzo de' Medici the younger), Machiavelli makes a similar point in recommending to Pope Leo X that he urge Florence to reopen the Grand Council.

7. *De amicitia,* 25.95; 26.97.

~ 5 ~

SHOULD THE GUARDING OF FREEDOM BE ENTRUSTED TO THE PEOPLE OR THE NOBLES;[1] AND WHICH HAS GREATER CAUSE TO CREATE DISTURBANCES: THOSE WHO SEEK TO ACQUIRE OR THOSE WHO SEEK TO CONSERVE?

1 The provision for guarding freedom has been one of the most necessary things done by those who have constituted a republic wisely, and freedom lasts for a longer or shorter time depending upon the way this has been disposed. 2 Because every republic has upper and lower classes, people have wondered in whose hands this guard is best placed. 3 Among the Spartans, and in our day among the Venetians, it was put in the hands of the Nobles; but among the Romans it was put in the hands of the Plebs.[2]

4 It is necessary, therefore, to examine which of those republics made a better choice. 5 If we look at the reasoning, there is something to be said for either side; but if we consider the outcome, we would choose the side of the Nobles since freedom lasted longer in Sparta and Venice than it did in Rome.

6 As to the reasoning, taking the Romans first, I state that guard of anything should be delegated to those who have the least desire to usurp it. 7 And unquestionably, if we consider the aims of the Nobles and common people, we shall see in the former a great desire to dominate and in the latter merely the desire not to be dominated, and consequently a greater will for freedom, since they can have less hope of usurping it than do the Nobles.[3] Thus if the people are charged with safeguarding a freedom, it makes sense that they will take better care of it; because they cannot seize it for themselves, they will not allow others to do so. 8 On the other hand, people who defend the Spartan and Venetian systems say that those who entrust the guard to the powerful accomplish two good things: first, they fulfill their ambition more since, having this stick in their hands, they have a greater share in the republic and greater reason to be satisfied. Second, it deprives the restless spirits among the Plebs of a kind of authority, which is the cause of endless dissension and turmoil in a republic and apt to reduce the Nobility to a desperation that with time can have bad effects. 9 They cite as an example Rome itself, where, once the Tribunes of the people got such authority into their hands, having one Plebeian Consul was not enough for them: they wanted to have both.[4] 10 After that they wanted the offices of Censor, Praetor, and every other position of power in the city.[5] Nor did this satisfy them, because in time, prompted by the same madness, they began to idolize men whom they considered likely to defeat the Nobility. This led to the power of Marius and the downfall of Rome.[6] 11 In truth, if one were to discuss both these matters properly, one might be unsure as to which alternative to choose for guarding this freedom, not knowing which kind of men is more injurious to a republic: those who seek to retain an office already gained or those who seek to gain one they do not have.

12 All in all, examining everything carefully, we will arrive at this conclusion: you have in mind either a republic that seeks to form an empire like Rome or one for which it suffices to preserve its power. 13 In the first case it has to act precisely as Rome did; in the second, it can imitate Venice or Sparta, for the reasons and in the way described in the next chapter.[7]

14 But to turn our discussion to which men are more harmful in a republic, those who seek to acquire or those who fear losing what has been acquired, I state that when Gaius Maenius was made Dictator and Marcus Folius Master of the Horse, both of them Plebeians, to investigate some conspiracies that had been made against Rome in Capua the people also gave them power to investigate any Roman who contrived through ambition and irregular means to win the consulate and other offices of the city.[8] 15 Because it seemed to the Nobility that this authority was given to the Dictator against them, they spread the word in Rome that it was not Nobles who were seeking offices through ambition and irregular means but Plebeians who, not trusting in their blood or their *virtù,* sought to win these offices by irregular means; they accused the Dictator in particular. 16 This indictment was so powerful that Maenius, after giving a speech and complaining of the slanders made against him by the Nobles, abdicated the dictatorship and submitted himself to the judgment the People might make of him. He was absolved once his case had been considered. Therefore

people argued a good deal over who was more ambitious, the person who seeks to conserve or the person who seeks to acquire, because either desire can easily cause extremely great upheavals. 17 Nevertheless, they are caused most often by those who possess something, because fear of loss generates in them the same will as there is in those who wish to acquire, for men do not believe that they possess what they have securely unless they also acquire something more. 18 Furthermore, if they possess a great deal they can effect changes with greater force and greater effect. 19 Still further, their improper and ambitious behavior kindles in the hearts of those who do not possess anything the will to possess, either to get revenge by plundering them or to get for themselves those riches and offices they see badly used by others.[9]

NOTES

1. Translates *grandi*. Machiavelli is not always consistent in the terminology he uses to describe the class division of either Roman or Florentine society. His analysis is generally predicated on the existence of three distinct classes: the upper or aristocratic class, for which he uses *grandi, nobili, ottimati, potenti,* and sometimes *gentiluomini;* a bourgeois or middle class; and a lower class, for which he uses *popolo* (as in this chapter title), *ignobili, moltitudine* (equivalent to "masses"), and *plebe*. These Italian words are sometimes used in derivative forms, e.g., *nobilità, popolari,* or *popolani*. The lack of a term for the bourgeoisie results from the fact that his analysis usually focuses on the struggle for power between the upper and lower classes, as the second part of this chapter title suggests. The upper class never exclusively comprises the nobility and the lower class never exclusively comprises the disenfranchised. In other words, in Walker's solution to this contrast, "those who seek to conserve" are the "haves" and "those who seek to acquire" are the "have-nots."

2. For the Spartans, Machiavelli may have Polybius 6.10.9 in mind; he deals with Venice at greater length in the next discourse. For Rome, see Livy, 3.53.6.

3. See *Prince,* 9 (p. 191, lines 7–16), and Aristotle, *Politics,* 6.2.3; 1318b33–40. In a letter to Vettori dated 10 August 1513, Machiavelli refers to what he believed to be a universal human trait as "the sweetness of domination." He writes: "I beg you to reflect upon human affairs as they should be given credence and upon the powers of the world—and particularly of republics—how they develop: you will realize how at first men are satisfied with being able to defend themselves and with not being dominated by others; from this point they move on to attacking others physically and seeking to dominate them" (*Friends,* pp. 250, 249).

4. The laws passed by the tribunes of the plebs Gaius Licinius and Lucius Sextius in 367 and 366 B.C. resulted in requiring at least one consul to be a plebeian; Livy discusses these issues in 6.37–42 (see specifically 6.37.11–12 and 6.42.2–3). According to Livy, 6.37.12 and 6.42.2, for both consuls to be plebs was possible then, though that did not actually happen until 172 B.C.

5. The first plebeian censor was Gaius Marcius Rutulus in 351 B.C. (Livy, 7.22.7–10), and the first plebeian praetor was Quintus Publilius Philo in 337 B.C. (Livy 8.15.9). Quintus and Gnaeus Ogulnius, in 300 B.C., proposed laws that opened the offices of augur and pontifex to the plebs (Livy, 10.6.3–11). As early as the middle of the fourth century B.C., plebeians could participate in the senate. From its creation, ple-

beians could fill the office of aedile, responsible for urban administration, public works, and games, as well as the grain supply.

6. Caius Marius (157–86 B.C.), a famous Roman general who rose through the ranks to become tribune, praetor, and consul. Constantly allied with the plebeians, he epitomized for Machiavelli a person of grave danger to a republic. His wife's nephew was Julius Caesar. The Gracchi, Marius, and Julius Caesar are the ones to whom Machiavelli attributed Rome's "downfall." See Plutarch, *Marius,* 7.9.

7. Polybius devotes an entire chapter (6.50) to arguing that Sparta under Lycurgus organized a government "amply sufficient" to do as Machiavelli says, "to preserve its power." But Polybius strongly favors Rome's organization for forming an empire. Rinaldi notes that Machiavelli's aim, to "preserve" power without seeking to expand it, shows a thematic consistency between Books 1 and 2 of the *Discourses.*

8. This incident, which occurred in 314 B.C., is based on Livy, 9.26.5–22. We have followed modern critical editions in the spelling of these two men's names; the editions available to Machiavelli spelled them "Marcus Menenius" and "Marcus Fulvius." The Master of the Horse was an assistant to the dictator. Following Martelli, *Storici antichi,* pp. 9–10, Rinaldi points out that Livy (9.26.20) says that the trial was before the consuls, and thus by saying that Maenius "submitted himself to the judgment [of] the People," Machiavelli is setting up a point that he will make later toward the end of Book 1 that the people are good guardians of freedom.

9. Because Machiavelli refers to the Gracchi at the beginning of the next discourse and Sallust, *Bellum Iugurthinum,* 41, draws a series of conclusions similar to Machiavelli's here and refers to the Gracchi at the beginning of 42, Walker suggests that the facts may be Livy's but their interpretation may be based on Sallust. See also Aristotle, *Politics,* 5.2.1–2; 1302a22–34.

~ 6 ~

WHETHER SOME FORM OF GOVERNMENT COULD HAVE BEEN DEVISED IN ROME THAT MIGHT HAVE AVOIDED HOSTILITY BETWEEN THE PEOPLE AND THE SENATE

1 We have discussed above the effects of the controversies between the People and the Senate. 2 Now, because these continued until the time of the Gracchi, when they caused the downfall of freedom, some might wish that Rome had achieved the great results it did without the existence of such hostilities within it.[1] 3 I have therefore deemed it worthwhile to consider whether a form of government could have been devised in Rome that avoided such controversies. 4 In order to examine this topic, we have to look to those republics that remained free over a long time without such hostility and uprisings and discover what their government was and whether it could have been introduced into Rome.

5 Sparta has been cited above as an example among the ancients, and Venice among the moderns. 6 Sparta created a King and a small Senate to govern itself;[2] Venice did not distinguish the government with different titles but

designated those entitled to hold office under one heading: Noblemen.[3] 7 This method owed more to chance than to its lawgivers' wisdom. Many inhabitants took refuge on the shoals where the city now stands for the reasons given above; when the population increased to such a number that they were obliged to enact laws if they wished to live together, they established a form of government. They assembled frequently in councils to deliberate about the city, and when it seemed to them that they were adequately numerous for political activity, they barred any newcomer who came to live there from participating in their government.[4] Then, in the course of time, when there were many inhabitants ineligible for a governing position, they called those who ruled Noblemen to give them status, and the rest Commoners. 8 It was possible for such a system to arise and be maintained without rebellion, because when it originated whoever then lived in Venice was included in government so no one could complain. Those who came to live in Venice later, finding the government closed and restricted, had neither cause nor opportunity to start a rebellion: 9 They had no cause because they had not been deprived of anything; they had no opportunity because those who ruled them kept them in check and did not engage them in matters that might enable them to seize power. 10 Besides, those who came later to settle in Venice were few and not so numerous as to upset the balance between the rulers and the ruled, because the number of Noblemen either equaled or exceeded them.[5] So, for these reasons, Venice was able to establish its form of government and keep it united.

11 Sparta, as I have said, was governed by a King and a restricted Senate.[6] 12 Because Sparta had a sparse population, had barred the way to anyone who might come to live there, and had received the laws of Lycurgus respectfully—and, by obeying these laws, removed every reason for rebellion—Sparta maintained her position and remained united over a long time. 13 Because Lycurgus created with his laws more equality of property and less equality of rank in Sparta; because there was equal poverty there and the common people were less ambitious, since offices in the city were extended only to a few citizens and were kept out of the hands of the common people,[7] who were never treated badly by the Nobility, and so never wanted to hold office. 14 This came from the Spartan Kings because, since they were so placed in the kingdom that they were surrounded by the Nobility, the kings had no better remedy for securely maintaining their position than keeping the common people from all harm. Consequently, the common people had no fear and did not seek power. Because they did not have power or fear, the rivalry that they might have had with the Nobility, as well as the cause for rebellion, was eliminated, and they were able to live in unity for a long time. 15 But there were two primary causes of this union: one was Sparta's sparse population, which made it possible for them to be governed by a few; second, since they excluded foreigners from their republic, they had no opportunity either to become corrupted or to grow so numerous for it to become too unwieldy for the few who did govern.

16 Therefore, considering all these things, we realize that Roman lawgivers needed to do one of two things for the city to remain peaceful like the re-

publics mentioned above: either not to use the common people for war, like the Venetians, or not to admit foreigners, like the Spartans. 17 But they did both. Consequently, they gave the common people strength, numbers, and endless opportunity for rioting. 18 But when the Roman state grew calmer, this disadvantage arose: it was also weaker because it cut off the way it arrived at the greatness which it attained, so when Rome tried to remove the causes of rioting it also removed the causes of expansion. 19 In all human affairs it may be noted, upon close examination, that one drawback can never be eliminated without another one arising.[8] 20 Therefore, if you want to make a large, armed population in order to establish a great empire, you make it so you are unable to control it as you please at a later date; if you keep it either small or unarmed in order to control it, you are unable to hold on to any territory you acquire, or the population becomes so weak that you fall prey to anyone who attacks you. 21 And therefore in all our decisions we must consider where the fewest drawbacks are and take that as our best course of action, because we can never find anything that is totally clear-cut, totally without risk. 22 Like Sparta, then, Rome could have named a ruler for life and created a small Senate; but unlike Sparta, it could not limit the number of its citizens if it wanted to establish a great empire. Consequently, as far as unity was concerned, having a king for life and only a few Senators would have been of little avail.

23 If anyone wanted, therefore, to set up a republic from scratch, he would have to consider whether, like Rome, he wanted it to expand in dominion and power or for it to remain confined within narrow borders. 24 In the first case, it is necessary to set it up like Rome and allow as best one can for riots and constant dissensions, because a republic will never expand without a large number of well-armed men or, should it expand, it can never sustain itself. 25 In the second case, you can organize it like Sparta and Venice; but, since expansion is poison to such republics, those who set them up must prohibit conquest in every possible way, because such conquest based on a weak republic is its total ruin—as it turned out in Sparta and Venice.[9] 26 After conquering almost all of Greece, Sparta proved its weak foundations on the occasion—slight in itself—of the Theban revolt instigated by Pelopidas; when the remaining cities rebelled, the republic completely collapsed.[10] 27 Similarly Venice, when it had taken over a large part of Italy, not by warfare but by money and astute conduct for the most part, and had to prove its strength, lost everything in a single battle.[11]

28 I would indeed believe that, to set up a republic which endures over a long time, the way to organize it internally should be Sparta's or Venice's: it should be located in a strong place and fortified so that no one would believe he could quickly overwhelm it; and, on the other hand, it ought not to be so large that it threatened its neighbors. And thus it could thrive for a long time. 29 For people declare war on a republic for two reasons: to master it or out of fear that you may be taken over by it.[12] 30 Both these reasons are almost entirely eliminated by the means just mentioned. For if a republic is difficult to conquer because its defense arrangements are strong, as I assume, then it will rarely, or even never, happen that someone plans a campaign against it. 31 If it remains within its borders and people see from experience that it is without

ambition, then no one will ever come and make war on the republic because he is afraid. That would be even less likely if the republic's constitution or laws prohibit expansion. 32 I have no doubt that if matters could be balanced in this way, that would bring about true political life and true peace in a city. 33 But because all human affairs are in flux and cannot remain stable, they must rise or fall, and necessity leads you to do many things that reason does not.[13] So if a republic were so constituted as to be capable of supporting itself without expansion, and necessity led it to expand, then its foundations would be undermined and make it fall more quickly. 34 In addition, should Heaven be so kindly disposed that the republic was not obliged to wage war, the result would be that idleness would render it either unmanly or divided; these two things, either in conjunction or singly, would cause its downfall.[14]

35 For this reason, because I believe it is impossible to balance this matter or to adhere strictly to this middle way, it is necessary to consider the most honorable courses in organizing a republic and to arrange them in such a way that if ever necessity induced it to expand it could keep what it had occupied. 36 And to return to the start of our discussion, I believe it is essential to follow the Roman organization, not that of other republics, because I believe it is impossible to discover a middle path between the two. Any hostilities breaking out between the people and the Senate must be accepted and considered a necessary evil in the attainment of Roman greatness. 37 For in addition to the reasons already adduced to demonstrate that the Tribunes' authority was essential to safeguarding freedom, one can easily conceive the advantage that a republic reaps from the power to bring indictments. This among others was assigned to the Tribunes, a point I shall treat in the following chapter.

NOTES

1. For the Gracchi, see Guicciardini, *Considerations,* 1, 5, n.2.

2. Machiavelli mentions this comparison in 1, 5, paragraph 2. Here he refers to the *gerusía,* or council of elders, *geronti;* there were twenty-eight of them, all aristocrats over sixty years old, presided over by two kings, not one (Plutarch, *Lycurgus,* 5–6). For the remarks on Sparta here and below, see Polybius 6.48–52.

3. Translates *gentiluomini,* literally "gentlemen"; its use here refers primarily to rank and differs from Machiavelli's use elsewhere to refer to "those who live in idleness and richly on the income from their estates, without having any responsibility for either agriculture or other work essential for living" (see below, 1, 55, sentence 17). In the context of Venice, then, Machiavelli seems to regard this class more as a force for equilibrium than he might in Florence or elsewhere. He deals with the origins of Venice in *Florentine Histories* 1, 29.

4. In order to ensure the dominance of the wealthy, there was a "closing," a *serrata,* of Venice's Great Council in 1297.

5. Historians of Venice would point out that the *gentiluomini* were about 1 or 2 percent of the Venetian populace from the fourteenth to the sixteenth century. See Sasso, *Antichi,* 3:36–46, for more on Machiavelli here and throughout the *Discourses.*

6. For the discussion of Sparta in the following paragraph, see Thuycides, 1.44; Aristotle, *Politics,* 2.6.1–23; 1269a30–1271b19, Plutarch, *Lycurgus,* 27–28, and Polybius, 6.48.2–4.

7. Machiavelli ignores the five ephors in Sparta who were public officials elected annually by the people to fulfill executive and judicial functions; they were similar to the plebeian tribunes in Rome; see Aristotle, *Politics,* 4.7.4–6; 1294b14–41.

8. For a passage expressing this idea and the conclusion arrived at several sentences later about choosing an option with the "fewest drawbacks," see the *Prince,* 21 (p. 339, lines 121–125 and note), and the end of Guicciardini, *Ricordi,* C, 126: "The nature of things in this world is such that it is almost impossible to find anything that does not contain some imperfection in all its parts. You must therefore make up your mind to take things as they are and to deem good whatever has the least evil in it."

9. Again, Aristotle, *Politics,* 2.6.10; 1270a15–40, and Polybius, 6.48–49 are relevant here.

10. In 379 B.C. the city of Thebes, led by its generals Pelopidas and Epaminondas, revolted against Spartan tyranny; with its ally, Athens, they won the battle of Leuctra in 371 B.C. and began the decline of Sparta's empire.

11. A reference to the League of Cambrai, formed in 1508 and 1509 by Louis XII of France, Holy Roman Emperor Maximilian I, Pope Julius XII, Ferdinand the Catholic of Spain, and several large Italian cities to strip Venice of her power on the mainland. Their combined forces defeated Venice at Vailà (Agnadello) on 14 May 1509; the battle is also known as the Battle of Ghiradadda, after a town on the Adda River. The loss, "where in one day's battle Venice lost what she had very laboriously acquired over the course of eight hundred years" (*Prince,* 12, p. 229, lines 143–46), evidently impressed Machiavelli greatly, because he refers to it often in much the same way; see especially *Discourses,* 3, 31 and 1, 53 and 2, 10. He expressed his "low opinion" of Venice's "much greater miracle that they acquired and retained their dominion rather than lost it" in a letter to Francesco Vettori dated 26 August 1513 (*Friends,* p. 258); especially because they did not "use the common people for war" (see sentence 16 of this chapter) but hired mercenaries.

12. See Introduction, n.30.

13. Machiavelli begins *Florentine Histories,* 5, 1 on much the same note.

14. This idea also is found in both *Florentine Histories,* 5, 1, and *Asino d' oro,* 5, vv. 94–99.

~ 7 ~

HOW ESSENTIAL INDICTMENTS ARE TO MAINTAINING FREEDOM IN A REPUBLIC

1 No more useful and necessary authority can be granted to those charged with guarding a city's freedom than that of being able to indict before the people or whatever magistrate or council citizens who act in any way against free government.[1] 2 This institution has two very useful effects for a republic. 3 The first is that citizens, out of fear of being indicted, do not attempt things against the government; if they should, they are put down immediately and unconditionally. 4 The other is that it provides a way to vent those pressures[2] that well up in cities in whatever way and against whatever citizen. When these pressures have no way to be vented normally, people resort to extraordinary measures that bring down an entire republic. 5 Therefore nothing does so

much to stabilize and strengthen a republic as to organize it in such a way that any change in those pressures that stir it up has an outlet established by law.

6 This can be shown through many examples, particularly the one cited by Livy: Coriolanus.[3] He says that the Roman Nobility was angry with the Plebs because it thought the Plebs had too much power as a result of the creation of the Tribunes who defended them. Rome, as it happens, experienced a great shortage of food and the Senate sent to Sicily for grain. Hostile to the popular faction, Coriolanus advised that the time had come for the Senate to punish the Plebs and take away the power that they had seized, to the detriment of the Nobility, by reducing the Plebeians to hunger and withholding the grain supply. When this pronouncement reached the ears of the People, they became so indignant against Coriolanus that, had the Tribunes not summoned him to appear and defend his cause, rioters would have killed him as he left the Senate. 7 About this incident we should note what I said above concerning how useful and necessary it is for republics to provide a way by law for the general population to vent its anger against an individual citizen. For when normal ways do not exist, people resort to extraordinary ones; these unquestionably produce far worse effects than do the former.

8 For if a citizen is prosecuted legally, even if he has been wronged, little or no disorder ensues in the republic, because enforcement is carried out without private or outside forces, which bring about the collapse of freedom; it is carried out rather by public forces and laws, which have specified limits and do not get carried away into something that might bring down the republic. 9 To support this opinion with examples, I think that Coriolanus will suffice among those selected from antiquity. Everyone should consider how much evil would have resulted for the Roman republic had he been slain in a riot, since an attack by private persons against private persons would have arisen from it. Such an attack engenders fear, fear seeks protection, and for protection factions are formed: from factions political parties arise in cities, from parties comes the city's downfall.[4] 10 But because the affair was handled by those who had authority over it, they managed to avoid all the ills that could have arisen had it been handled by private power.

11 In our time we have seen how much disorder was caused in the republic of Florence when the masses were unable legally to vent their feeling against one of its citizens, as happened when Francesco Valori was almost a prince of the city.[5] Because many considered him ambitious and a man who wished to rise above civil status by his boldness and spite and because there was no way in the republic to resist him except through the formation of a rival party,[6] the result was that, since he feared only illegal means, he began to gather partisans to protect him. On the other hand, those who opposed him, since they had no legal means to restrain him, turned to illegal measures until they resorted to arms. 12 And if he could have been opposed legally, his authority would have been ended with harm to him alone; but since it had to be done by illegal means, harm was done not only to him but to many other noble citizens.

13 In support of the conclusion reached above, one could cite another event that also occurred in Florence. It involved Piero Soderini and was entirely the

result of a lack of means in the republic to indict the ambition of powerful citizens.[7] 14 In a republic it is not enough to indict a powerful man before eight judges;[8] the judges must be numerous because the few always act according to their fashion. 15 So had there been such measures in the city, either the citizens would have indicted him if he behaved badly, and thus would have vented their feelings without bringing in the Spanish army, or the citizens would not have dared to act against him if he had not behaved badly, for fear that they too might be indicted. Thus on all sides the desire that caused the strife would have ceased.

16 So one may conclude the following: any time we find outside forces called in by a faction of men living in a city, we can assume that it arises from its faulty constitution, since within its walls it has no institution for venting the malicious feelings arising in men unless illegal measures are used. Adequate provision is made for this by arrangements for indictments before a large number of judges, and for prestige to be granted them. 17 These measures were so well organized in Rome that, throughout all the disputes between the Plebs and the Senate, neither the latter nor the former nor any private citizen ever made plans to go outside for foreign troops. Because a remedy existed at home, there was no need to go abroad for one. 18 Although the examples cited above are quite sufficient to prove my point, nevertheless, I should like to advance one other, recounted by Livy in his History.[9] He relates that in Clusium, in those days a most illustrious Etruscan city, a certain Lucumo raped the sister of Aruns; because the rapist was powerful, Aruns was unable to get revenge. He set off to get the Gauls, who then ruled over the region now called Lombardy, urged them to come to Clusium with an armed band, and showed them how advantageous it would be to them to avenge the insult he received. If Aruns had thought that he could get revenge through the city's institutions, he would not have sought out barbarian troops. 19 But just as indictments are useful in a republic, so slander is useless and harmful, as we shall discuss in the next chapter.

NOTES

1. See Polybius, 6.14.3–7.

2. Translates *omori;* see above, Machiavelli, 1, 4, n.3.

3. In addition to Shakespeare's play, see Livy, 2.33.5–40.14. Gnaeus Marcius Coriolanus was a patrician strongly opposed to the tribunes' power and to distributing grain from Sicily to the people during a serious famine in 491 B.C. (Machiavelli also comments on this example in *The Art of War,* 6.) Charged with tyranny, Coriolanus left Rome and led the Volscian army against it.

4. See also the second paragraph of *Florentine Histories,* 7, 1. Because of the fusion of Rome and contemporary Florence in Machiavelli's vision, factional strife is an anathema. When wealth can buy power, the citizenry is endangered. This is true of both the Roman and the Florentine republics.

5. Piero de' Medici, the leader of the ruling Medici family, was expelled from Florence, partly at Francesco Valori's instigation, because he accepted a treaty with Charles VIII, the invading king of France, which the Florentines found degrading. Valori allied himself with the *Piagnoni,* the "mourners" or "wailers," the followers of Savonarola and the dominant faction in Florence. He served as Florence's "prince" until

1498, when the city turned on Savonarola, drove his party from power, and murdered Valori. Savonarola was condemned as a heretic, hanged, and his body burned. Although Machiavelli, in his fragments entitled *Nature di huomini fiorentini,* seems to admire Valori, Guicciardini's discussion of him in *History of Florence,* chapters 14–16, is less flattering.

6. Translates *sètta,* a term with more of a religious connotation than Machiavelli's usual terms, *partigiani* and *parti* (factions and [political] parties), as at the end of the sentence above.

7. Piero Soderini (1452–1522), an example Machiavelli draws upon frequently, trusted and admired his good friend Niccolò Machiavelli. He was elected Florence's life gonfalonier in 1502 and led a popular, pro-France republican regime until he was ousted in 1512 and the Medici were returned to power. Despite the allegiance that Machiavelli felt toward him, as will be clear from other passages in the *Discourses,* (e.g., 1, 52; 3, 3; 3, 9), Machiavelli blamed the fall of the republic on Soderini's indecisiveness. Rinaldi notes that it has been suggested that Machiavelli composed Book 1, chapters 3–8 and 12–18 of the *Discourses* while Soderini was in power and with him in mind to learn from them.

8. An allusion to the body responsible for administering justice in Florence, the "Council of Eight of Guard" *(Otto di guardia e di balìa).*

9. Livy, 5.33.1–6; but Machiavelli has modified the account for his own purposes. Livy states that it was the wife, not the sister, of Aruns who was raped and that Aruns sent the Gauls some wine to persuade them to invade, rather than going to see them; Livy does point out that Lucumo was "powerful," so Aruns would have had to call in outside troops to punish him. Clusium is the modern-day Chiusi, about forty-five miles southeast of Siena, not far from Lake Trasimeno. Machiavelli uses the words *Toscana, Chiusi,* and *Franciosi* in this sentence. In seeking equivalents for such words in similar contexts throughout this translation, we attempt to regularize the text by using the English words related to the context: hence, "Etruscan," "Clusium," and "Gauls." See also Martelli, *Storici antichi,* p. 12.

~ *8* ~

SLANDER IS AS HARMFUL TO A REPUBLIC AS INDICTMENTS ARE USEFUL

1 Despite the fact that the *virtù* of Furius Camillus, when he freed Rome from the oppression of the Gauls, made every Roman citizen defer to him without thinking he lost prestige or rank by so doing, nonetheless Manlius Capitolinus could not stand to see so much honor and glory granted him, since he felt he was as deserving as Camillus as far as the safety of Rome was concerned for having saved the Capitol and that he was not inferior to him as far as military merit was concerned.[1] 2 So, filled with envy, unable to calm himself because of the other man's glory, and seeing that he could not sow discord among the Senators,[2] he turned to the Plebs, sowing various insidious notions among them. 3 And among the things he said was that the treasure they had amassed to give to the Gauls, and then not given them, had been taken over by private citizens; and if it could be recovered, it could be con-

verted to public use, relieving the Plebs of taxes or private debts. 4 These words were quite effective with the Plebs, so they started to hold meetings and stirred up many uprisings at his instigation. This displeased the Senators and seemed significant and dangerous to them, and they named a Dictator to investigate the matter and curb Manlius's rashness.[3] 5 Thereupon the Dictator immediately had him summoned, and they came and confronted one another before the public, the Dictator surrounded by the Nobles and Manlius by the Plebs. 6 Manlius was asked to tell who held this treasure he was talking about, because the Senate was as anxious as the Plebs to be informed about it. Manlius did not reply specifically but evaded the question, saying that it was not necessary to tell them what they already knew, so the Dictator had him put in prison.

7 From this example it can be observed how despicable slanders are in free cities and in every other kind of society and in order to stamp them out no appropriate measure should be spared. 8 Nor can there be a better means of eliminating them than providing many opportunities for indictments, because slander is as harmful to republics as indictments are useful. There is a difference between the two: slander needs no witnesses or any other specific proof to corroborate it, so anybody can be slandered by anyone else; but he cannot be indicted since indictments need real and circumstantial evidence indicating their truth. 9 Men are indicted before magistrates, the people, and councils; they are slandered in public squares and in loggias.[4] 10 Slander is more common where indictments are less common and where cities are less well constituted to handle it. 11 Therefore a republic's lawgiver must draw up laws so that any citizen in it can be indicted without fear or hesitation. When this is done and is carefully respected, slanderers must be severely punished; they cannot complain if they are punished, since they have places open to hear indictments against any one slandered by them in the loggias. 12 Wherever this aspect is not well regulated, great disorder always ensues, because slander annoys citizens but does not punish them. When they are annoyed, they try to retaliate out of hatred rather than fear of what has been said against them.

13 As we have said, this aspect was handled well in Rome and was always handled poorly in our city of Florence. 14 And just as this law did a great deal of good in Rome, so the lack of it has done a great deal of harm in Florence. 15 Whoever reads the histories of this city will note how many slanders have been made in every period against citizens who were engaged in its important affairs.[5] 16 People would say of one man that he had stolen money from the Commune, of another that he had not won a battle because he had been bribed, and of still another that his ambition drove him to commit this or that impropriety. 17 Thus hatred arose in every quarter, which led to disagreement: from disagreement, factions;[6] from factions, ruin. 18 But had Florence had a law to indict citizens and punish slanderers, innumerable ensuing conflicts would not have occurred. For those citizens, whether they had been condemned or acquitted, would have been unable to harm the city; far fewer would have been indicted than were slandered since, as I have pointed out, people cannot be indicted as easily as they are slandered. 19 Slander has been among the various things some citizens have used to attain greatness. Used

against the powerful who thwarted their desires, slanders accomplished a great deal for these citizens because, by siding with the people and reinforcing their poor opinion of the powerful, they made allies of them.[7]

20 And although other examples of this could be advanced, I shall settle for just one. 21 The Florentine army was encamped at Lucca, commanded by messer Giovanni Guicciardini, its commissioner.[8] 22 As a result either of his bad management or of his bad fortune, the storming of Lucca did not take place. 23 Anyhow, whatever the case was, he was blamed for it, and it was said he had been bribed by the people of Lucca. This slander, fostered by his enemies, almost drove messer Giovanni to the depths of despair. 24 And though he was willing to place himself in the hands of the Captain of the People[9] to vindicate himself, nonetheless he was never able to since there were no means to do so in the republic. 25 This aroused great indignation among the friends of messer Giovanni, who were the majority of Florence's important men,[10] and those who wanted to cause upheavals. 26 For this and similar reasons, the affair grew so that it brought about the downfall of the republic.

27 Thus Manlius Capitolinus was a slanderer, not an indicter, and the Romans in this instance showed exactly how slanderers should be punished. 28 For they must be made to become indicters, and if the indictment should prove true they should either be rewarded or not be punished; but if it should prove otherwise, punished as Manlius was.

NOTES

1. See Livy, 5.44–46; 49. Furius Camillus led an army, levied in part from among the Veians, against the invading Gauls (387–386 B.C.) and saved Rome; he is sometimes regarded as the city's second founder. Manlius Capitolinus became jealous of Camillus's success among the patricians and tried to stir up the plebeians against him. For more on Capitolinus, see note 2 to Guicciardini's *Consideration* of *Discourse,* 1, 5.

2. Translates *Padri,* from the Latin *patres conscripti;* see Livy, 6.15.9.

3. Livy makes clear in 6.11.9–10 that Aulus Cornelius Cossus was named dictator to curb Manlius Capitolinus, though the pretext was the need to fight the Volscians. For the imprisonment of Manlius, see 6.16.4.

4. Machiavelli has in mind the open market areas in Italian cities where people met to socialize and gossip; see below, 1, 47, sentences 20 and 24.

5. Perhaps Machiavelli is thinking of an incident in his own life when he had to deal with slanders directed at him; it is preserved for us in a letter from his friend, Biagio Buonaccorsi, of 28 December 1509; see *Friends,* p. 192, and note 1, p. 488.

6. Again, as in note 6 to Machiavelli's 1, 7, translates *sètte.*

7. Guicciardini, in his *Consideration* of this *Discourse,* picks up the allusion here to Cosimo de' Medici and calls it "nonsense"; Machiavelli discusses this aspect of the latter's career in the second paragraph of *Florentine Histories,* 4, 26.

8. The siege of Lucca occurred in 1430, though the war dragged on for three years; Florence, meanwhile, was in great turmoil. First Siena then Milan came to Lucca's aid; Milan forced Florence to sue for peace in 1433. During this period it was alleged that Giovanni Guicciardini (1385–1435), one of Francesco's ancestors, could have ended the war but was bribed into letting it continue. One beneficiary of this

strife was Rinaldo degli Albizzi, who came to power in 1433 and soon exiled Cosimo de' Medici. The latter was able to return the following year and take control of the city. See Machiavelli's *Florentine Histories,* 4, 22–33.

9. At various points from the thirteenth through the fifteenth centuries Florence had such officials. They were supposed to be neutral, because they were brought into the city from other parts of Italy. Citizens could bring quarrels to them for adjudication. In later times these captains often led the citizen's militia. In *Florentine Histories,* 4, 25, Machiavelli notes that although the Captain cited Guicciardini, the latter's family forced him to drop the charges.

10. They were partisans of the popular party led by Cosimo de' Medici; the "republic" that Machiavelli mentions in the next sentence is what he at one point called a "republic governed by oligarchies" (in his 1520 *Discursus florentinarum rerum post mortem iunioris Laurentii Medices* [A commentary on Florentine affairs after the death of Lorenzo de' Medici the younger]); it ruled from 1393 to 1433.

~ 9 ~

IT TAKES ONE SINGLE MAN TO ORGANIZE[1] A REPUBLIC AFRESH OR TO REFORM IT COMPLETELY, DISREGARDING ITS FORMER INSTITUTIONS

1 Perhaps it will appear to some that I have gone too far into Roman history without yet mentioning the lawgivers of the republic or the laws concerning religion or the military. 2 Therefore, because I do not want to keep the minds of those who want to hear something on the subject in any more suspense, I state that many people will probably judge it a bad precedent for the founder of a civil society[2] like Romulus to have killed his brother,[3] then allowed the death of the Sabine Titus Tatius, whom he had chosen as fellow ruler.[4] They could infer from this that ambitious citizens who desire to lead might, with the authorization of their prince, attack those who resist their authority. 3 This view would be correct were we not to consider the purpose that induced Romulus to commit such a murder.

4 This should be taken as a general rule: unless a republic or kingdom is organized by one single man, it never or only rarely happens that it will be well organized from its beginnings or completely reformed anew regardless of its old laws. It is necessary, rather, for one single man to provide the system and for any such organization to spring from his mind. 5 Therefore a prudent organizer of a republic who intends to serve not himself but the common good, not his own succession but the common fatherland, must strive to be the only one in authority. And a judicious mind will never criticize someone for any extraordinary action that he might take to organize a kingdom or constitute a republic.[5] 6 It is quite appropriate that, if his act accuses him, the consequence should excuse him; and if the consequence is good, as in the case of Romulus, it will always excuse him: for he who uses violence to destroy is to be blamed, not the one who uses it to repair. 7 He must indeed be prudent[6] and *virtuoso* to such an

extent that he does not leave the authority he has taken for himself as someone else's inheritance, because, since men are more prone to evil than to good, his successor could use for ambition what he had used for *virtù*. 8 In addition, if one man is suited for organizing, what is organized will not long endure if it is left on the shoulders of one man, but it will when it is left in the care of many and if it is the business of many to maintain it.[7] 9 Because just as many people are not suited for setting something up since they cannot recognize its good because of their diverging opinions, so they cannot agree about dropping it once they do know it. 10 That Romulus was one of those who deserve to be excused in the death of his brother and his colleague, and he did what he did for the common good and not out of his own ambition, is shown by his having immediately organized a Senate whose advice he sought and whose views he took account of in his decisions.[8] 11 If we examine carefully the authority that Romulus reserved for himself, we shall see that he reserved only that of commanding the armies once war had been decided upon and of convening the Senate. 12 This was seen later when Rome became free through the expulsion of the Tarquins and none of their old laws was modified, except that the King for life was replaced by two yearly Consuls. This attests to the city's earliest institutions' being more suited to a civil and free society than to an absolute and tyrannical one.[9]

13 Countless examples could be given in support of the foregoing, such as Moses, Lycurgus, Solon, and other founders of kingdoms and republics who, because they had assumed power for themselves, were able to formulate laws for the common good. But I shall leave them out because they are well known.

14 I shall cite a less famous example, but one worth considering for those who desire to be givers of good laws: Agis, the king of Sparta,[10] who sought to bring the Spartans within the limits set by the laws of Lycurgus. It seemed to him that his city had lost much of its former *virtù* and consequently much of its power and authority, because it had strayed in some ways from these limits. Early in his rule the Spartan Ephors murdered him as a man intent upon seizing tyranny. 15 But he was succeeded on the throne by Cleomenes, who, once he discovered some of Agis's records and writings and realized what his ideas and intentions were, conceived the same desire as Agis.[11] He realized he could not achieve this good for his country unless he became the sole authority; because of men's ambitions, it seemed to him that he could not serve the many against the will of the few. So he seized a suitable opportunity and had all the Ephors and anyone else who could oppose him slain; then he restored completely the laws of Lycurgus. 16 This decision could have reawakened Sparta and given Cleomenes the reputation that Lycurgus had, were it not for the strength of the Macedonians and the weakness of the other Greek republics. 17 But after this reorganization, he was attacked by the Macedonians and conquered, because by himself he had inferior forces and no one to seek refuge with. His project, though just and commendable, therefore remained unfinished.

18 So considering all these matters, I conclude that it is necessary to be one single man when constituting a republic and that Romulus deserves to be excused, not blamed, for the deaths of Remus and Titus Tatius.

NOTES

1. In the title and throughout this chapter, Machiavelli uses *ordini* and its derivatives to discuss those who organized the first principles of a society by establishing its laws, constitutions, and institutions governing religion and the military. We have translated these derivatives according to our understanding of the context and our belief as to the best word to clarify it. See Preface A, n.2, on *ordini*.

2. Translates *vivere civile.*

3. Livy, 1.7.1–2; Cicero, *De officiis,* 3.10. Some would trace the blame for Rome's lack of unity to its origins in fratricide; see Horace, *Epodi,* 7 and Augustine, *De Civ. D.,* 3.6; 15.5.

4. Tradition says he was the king of the Sabines at the time of the Romans' rape of the Sabine women. Machiavelli attributes more historical fact to this tradition than Livy, who writes in his Preface, 6, that the traditions associated with the founding of Rome are embellished by poetic legends *(poeticis . . . decora fabulis)* rather than based on authentic historical documents *(incorruptis rerum gestarum monumentis traduntur).* At any rate, the two ruled jointly once the two communities were united; a resentful mob killed Tatius in Lavinium. Livy, 1.14.1–3 does not specify Romulus's involvement; he merely states that Romulus took no retaliatory action.

5. This passage and its context are fundamental to any association of Machiavelli with the dictum that the end justifies the means. The evidence offered here for a phrase similar to the French *le fait accuse, l'effet excuse* is rather slim, but it is clear that he posits a theoretical difference between murder for the common good and murder committed for private reasons: the former is no precedent for the latter. This passage should be compared with *Prince,* 17–18 (pp. 268–286), and below, 3, 41, sentence 4.

6. This combination of *prudenza* and *virtù* is fundamental to Machiavelli's admiring advocacy of political flexibility. He praises the Romans for these qualities in *Prince,* 3 (p. 117, lines 205–206); in *Prince,* 7, he notes that they were significant attributes of Cesare Borgia (p. 159, lines 48–49). Because "wisdom" is an important component of Machiavelli's respect for *prudenza,* we sometimes use "wise" and "wisdom" to translate it.

7. This is the argument of the closing nine paragraphs of Machiavelli's 1520 *Discursus florentinarum rerum post mortem iunioris Laurentii Medices* (A commentary on Florentine affairs after the death of Lorenzo de' Medici the younger). See below, 1, 58, sentence 32.

8. Livy, 1.8.7.; see also Plutarch, *Romulus,* 13. For Machiavelli's use of Romulus in this chapter and throughout the *Discourses* as well as his other writings, see Sasso, *Antichi,* 1:119–166, originally published in *Cultura,* 23 (1985), pp. 7–44.

9. Livy, 2.1.1–2. In this passage Livy announces that the subject of the rest of his history will be a free Rome under a rule of law now regarded as being superior to individuals. This achievement was one that Machiavelli admired and believed Florence should emulate.

10. Agis IV, from the junior or Eurypontid royal house, ruled Sparta from about 244 to 241 B.C. See Plutarch, *Agis and Cleomenes.* For the ephors, see 1, 6, n.7, but it was the other Spartan king, Leonidas, who was responsible for murdering Agis.

11. Cleomenes III followed his father, Leonidas, onto the Spartan throne and ruled from 235 to 222. He became the "sole authority," though some would call it despotism, but the social revolution he planned fell victim to his foreign policy. When he threatened to destroy the Achaean League, he was attacked and defeated at the battle of Sellasia in 222. He did, however, seek and obtain refuge in Egypt. Plutarch mentions that it was the writings of his friend Xenares, not "Agis's records and writings," that led him to imitate Agis.

~ 10 ~

THE FOUNDERS OF A REPUBLIC OR A KINGDOM ARE WORTHY OF PRAISE, BUT THOSE OF A TYRANNY ARE WORTHY OF SHAME[1]

1 Among all men who are praised, the most highly praised are those who have been leaders and organizers of religions. 2 Next come those who have founded either republics or kingdoms. 3 After them come those who are famous as military leaders who expanded either their own realm or that of their native land. 4 To these may be added men of letters; because they are of several kinds, each of them is famous according to his merit. 5 We single out various other men, countless in number, for some measure of praise owed to their profession and occupation. 6 Detestable and despicable, on the other hand, are men who destroy religions, squander kingdoms and republics, are inimical to *virtù,* letters, and any other profession that brings utility and honor to humankind, such as the godless, the violent, the ignorant, the inept, the lazy, and the cowardly. 7 And there will never be anybody, no matter how foolish or wise, evil or good, who, were the choice between the two sorts of men put before him, would not praise what is worthy of praise and blame what is worthy of blame. 8 Nevertheless, then, almost all deceived by false good or false glory, whether willingly or unknowingly, let themselves fall into the ranks of those who deserve more blame than praise. And though able to create either a republic or a kingdom to their eternal credit, they turn to tyranny; they do not perceive in this course of action how much fame, glory, honor, security, tranquillity, with satisfied minds, they flee, or how much infamy, shame, censure, danger, and anxiety they fall into.

9 And it is impossible for men, whether private citizens living in a republic or those who have become princes through either Fortune or *virtù,*[2] if they have read history and profited from the records of the past[3] not to prefer to live in their native land as Scipios rather than Caesars (if they are private citizens) and as Agesilauses, Timoleons, and Dions[4] rather than Nabises, Phalarises, and Dionysiuses[5] (if they are princes): because they would see that the latter are exceedingly reviled and the former supremely praised. 10 They would also see

that Timoleon and the others had no less power in their native lands than did Dionysius and Phalaris in theirs but that they enjoyed far more security.

11 Nor should anyone be deceived by Caesar's glory, hearing him extolled so highly by writers, because those who praise him are seduced by his fortune and frightened by the extent of imperial power, which, ruling under his name, did not permit writers to speak freely about him. 12 But anyone who wants to know what free writers would say of him should see what they say about Catiline:[6] 13 just as a man who has committed an evil is more to be blamed[7] than one who only wanted to, so Caesar is all the more despicable. 14 One should also see the praise that writers bestow on Brutus:[8] unable to blame Caesar because of his power, they bestowed praise upon his enemy.

15 A man who has become the prince in a republic should also consider how much more praise was deserved by the emperors who lived according to the law and as good princes than by those who lived otherwise once Rome had become an empire. He will see that Titus, Nerva, Trajan, Hadrian, Antoninus [Pius], and Marcus [Aurelius] did not need praetorian soldiers or masses of legions to protect them, because their habits, the goodwill of the people, and the love of the Senate protected them.[9] 16 He will furthermore see that the eastern and western armies were not enough to save Caligula, Nero, Vitellius, and so many other wicked emperors from the enemies that their evil ways and wicked lives had made for them. 17 And if their history were considered carefully it would be very instructive to any prince by showing him the way to glory or to censure, to security or to fear. 18 Because, of the twenty-six emperors from Caesar to Maximinus, sixteen were assassinated and ten died naturally. And if among those who were slain there were a few good ones, like Galba and Pertinax, they were slain by the corruption that their predecessors had left in the soldiers; and if among those who died naturally there was a scoundrel like Severus, that resulted from his great good fortune and *virtù*, two things that attend very few men. 19 In reading this history, the prince will also see how one may establish a good reign: because all the emperors who came to power by inheritance except Titus were bad; those who did so through adoption such as the five from Nerva to Marcus [Aurelius] were all good. When the empire fell to their heirs, it went back into ruin.

20 Therefore let a prince set before himself the period from Nerva to Marcus [Aurelius], compare the preceding and subsequent periods, and then choose in which one he would prefer to have been born or to have governed. 21 Because in the periods governed by good men,[10] he will behold a secure prince surrounded by secure citizens, a world full of peace and justice, the Senate with its authority, magistrates with their honors, rich citizens enjoying their riches, nobility and *virtù* exalted; he will behold complete tranquillity and well-being and on the other hand all rancor, unruliness, corruption, and ambition extinguished. He will behold a golden age in which everyone can hold and defend whatever opinion he wants. 22 In sum, he will behold a world in triumph: the prince full of reverence and glory, his people of love and security. 23 If he then considers in detail the periods of the other emperors, he will see that they are wracked by warfare, riven by sedition, barbarous in both peace and war, had so

many princes killed by the sword, and had so many civil wars and so many foreign ones; Italy was afflicted and rife with new misfortunes,[11] its cities in ruin and ransacked. 24 He will behold Rome in ashes,[12] the Capitol ravaged by its own citizens,[13] ancient temples in desolation, ceremonies corrupted, cities full of adultery; he will see the sea full of exiles, shoals covered with blood. 25 He will behold countless acts of cruelty committed in Rome: nobility, wealth, past honors, and above all *virtù* considered as deadly sins. 26 He will behold slanders rewarded, servants bribed against their lords, freemen against their masters, and any who might lack for enemies oppressed by their friends. 27 Then he will possess the fullest knowledge of the many debts Rome, Italy, and the world owe to Caesar.

28 And beyond a doubt, if he is born of man, he will be frightened by any imitation of the evil times and inspired by a tremendous desire to emulate the good ones. 29 And if a prince truly seeks worldly glory, he ought to seek to possess a corrupted city not in order to destroy it completely like Caesar but to restore it to order like Romulus.[14] 30 And truly the heavens can bestow no greater opportunity for glory on men, and men can desire no greater one. 31 And if for a city to be well organized its ruler of necessity had to be deposed, the man who did not organize it would have some excuse so as not to lose his position; but if a ruler is able to hold onto his princedom and organize it, he deserves no excuse whatsoever. 32 In conclusion, let those on whom the heavens bestow[15] such an opportunity consider that there are two paths open to them: one makes them secure while living and gives them glory after their death; the other makes them constantly anxious while they are living and grants them everlasting infamy after their death.

NOTES

1. With the assertion in this chapter title, Machiavelli joins a long line of political theorists, from Aristotle to Machiavelli's contemporary humanists, who condemn any government that does not serve the common weal. This same criterion defines the political virtue of the categories of people he discusses in the rest of this paragraph. His contempt for Julius Caesar, expressed later in this discourse, is a typical humanist revulsion, especially strong in Florence, for the man who reduced Roman liberty and prepared the way for a series of tyrants. Renaissance humanists like Poggio Bracciolini frequently paired Caesar with Scipio (see note 4 below) as exemplars of diametrically opposed ways of political life. Plutarch, on the other hand, was kinder to Caesar; see Plutarch, *Comparison of Dion and Brutus,* 2.

2. In arguing that the survival of new princedoms depends on the *virtù* of their leader, Machiavelli says that "this transformation from being an ordinary citizen to being a prince presupposes either *virtù* or Fortune" (*Prince,* 6, p. 145, lines 22–24).

3. There is a similar turn of phrase in the context of "profiting from" the "conversations" he has had—that is, the readings he has done with the writers of antiquity—in his famous letter to Francesco Vettori of 13 December 1513 (*Friends,* p. 264). Rinaldi notes that the following comparison between Scipio and Caesar was a favorite topos of Renaissance humanists; see Curtius, *European Literature.*

4. Publius Cornelius Scipio Africanus Major (236–184/3 B.C.) defeated the Carthaginians in Spain in 206 and Hannibal at Zama in North Africa in 202 during the

Second Punic War. His popularity was so great in Rome that he could easily have seized absolute control; instead, he retired to the countryside. Scipio typified Roman *virtù* for Machiavelli, whose great admiration for Scipio is expressed in the *Prince,* where he is "unique not only in his own time but in all recorded time" (chapter 17, p. 275, lines 98–99) and in his *capitolo "Dell'ingratitudine,"* where he is a "divine man sent from heaven" (v. 77); see also below, 1, 29, sentence 21. Agesilaus was king of Sparta from 399 to 360 B.C.; he was an excellent military tactician and patriot; see Plutarch, *Agesilaus* and *Comparison of Agesilaus and Pompey.* Timoleon (died c. 334 B.C.) killed his brother to thwart the latter's plans for tyranny in Corinth. He went to Syracuse in Sicily and forced Carthage to give up most of its interests in Sicily and the tyrant Dionysius II to leave Syracuse. Timoleon ousted most of the petty tyrants from the Greek cities of Sicily and then began some democratic reforms. In Syracuse his reign saw a rise in urban prosperity and the introduction of social and political reforms, although some historians have argued that his reforms were really oligarchic in nature. Dion (c. 408–354 B.C.) ruled Syracuse with an iron hand. Though he said he wanted to install constitutional government along the lines that he learned at Plato's Academy, historians have not found concrete validation of this claim. According to Plutarch and a few of Plato's letters, some of which may be spurious, he tried to invest Dionysius II, who inherited the throne of Syracuse in 367/6 from his father, the tyrant Dionysius I, with the attributes of a philosopher king; Dion's lack of success led him to drive Dionysius II out of the city. Upon Dion's murder in 354, Dionysius II returned to Syracuse, only to be driven out by Timoleon. Plutarch wrote lives of both Timoleon and Dion; see also Diodorus, *Universal History.*

5. Nabis became tyrant of Sparta shortly after 207 B.C.; hated for his cruelty, he was assassinated in 192; see also the discussion of his career in *Prince,* 9 (p. 197, lines 96–104). Phalaris, also a cruel, autocratic tyrant, ruled Acragas, the modern Agrigento, in southwestern Sicily from about 570/65 to 554/49. Dionysius I the Elder was tyrant of Syracuse from about 405 to 367 B.C.; see the previous note.

6. Lucius Sergius Catilina was the center of many conspiracies during the closing years of the Roman republic, especially one against the senatorial oligarchy and an attempt on the life of Cicero in 63 B.C. The orations of Cicero against Catiline, *In Catilinam,* are celebrated examples of ancient rhetoric. Machiavelli believes Caesar to be the more reprehensible of the two because he achieved his goal of destroying the Roman republic, whereas Catiline failed. Roman commentators were no less horrified by him; see Sallust, *Bellum Catilinae* 15 and 22 and Plutarch, *Cicero,* 1 off.

7. Some printed versions of the texts read *biasimevole* (blameworthy) instead of *da biasimare.* For a slightly different picture of Caesar, see below, 3, 6, sentence 160 and note 67, with Inglese's observations.

8. Marcus Junius Brutus (85–42 B.C.) was a member of the conspiracy that murdered Julius Caesar in 44 B.C. The most famous "praise" occurs in Plutarch, *Brutus* and *Comparison of Dion and Brutus.* Perhaps Machiavelli remembered the maxim embodied in this sentence when he came to write his *Florentine Histories.* Unable to "blame" Cosimo de' Medici because his descendant Giulio de' Medici (Pope Clement VII) had commissioned him to write the history, Machiavelli let Rinaldo degli Albizzi say of Cosimo what Machiavelli dared not; see *Florentine Histories,* 4, 28, and the letter of Donato Giannotti to Marcantonio Michieli, dated 30 June 1533, paraphrased in Ridolfi, *Life,* pp. 198–199; *Vita* 7, p. 310.

9. This discussion of Roman emperors should be compared with that in *Prince,* 19, "How to Avoid Contempt and Hatred." In the list following, those discussed or mentioned in that chapter are indicated here by an asterisk, those who were murdered are indicated by italic type; their dates of death are in parentheses: *Caesar* (technically not an emperor [44 B.C.], Augustus (A.D. 14), Tiberius (37), *Caligula* (41), *Claudius* (54), *Nero* (68), *Galba* (69), Otho (a suicide, but Machiavelli numbers him among those murdered [69]) *Vitellius* (69), Vespasian (79), Titus (81), *Domitian* (96), Nerva (98), Trajan (117), Hadrian (138), Antoninus Pius (161), Marcus Aurelius* (180), *Commodus** (192), *Pertinax** (193), *Didius Julianus** (193), Septimius Severus* (211), *Caracalla** (217), *Macrinus** (218), *Elagabalus** (222), *Alexander Severus** (235), and *Maximinus** (238). The list of twenty-six fails to account for Lucius Verus, co-emperor with Marcus Aurelius from 161 to 169; Clodius Albinus* and Pescennius Niger,* military commanders whose legions saluted them as "Augustus"; and *Geta,* co-ruler with his brother Caracalla from 209 to 212, when Caracalla assassinated him.

10. The emperors whom Machiavelli classifies as "good" are: Galba, Titus, Nerva, Trajan, Hadrian, Antoninus Pius, Marcus Aurelius, and Pertinax. Although he fails to comment explicitly on Augustus, Tiberius, Claudius, Otho, Vespasian, and Domitian, presumably he would have excluded Claudius and Domitian from the "good" category.

11. From this point to "oppressed by their friends" at the end of sentence 26, Machiavelli paraphrases Tacitus, *Histories,* 1. 2. After this paraphrase, Rinaldi calls attention to the irony of "debts" in Machiavelli's own words in sentence 27.

12. A reference to Nero's burning of Rome in 64 A.D.

13. During the struggle between supporters of Vitellius and Vespasian for power in 69, the temple of Jupiter in the Capitol was burned.

14. In *Prince,* 6, he is listed along with Moses, Cyrus, and Theseus as one of "the most outstanding men . . . who became princes because of their *virtù* and not because of Fortune" (p. 145).

15. Inglese notes that, as in *Prince,* 6, because of what "the heavens bestow," they are synonymous with Fortune. "They particularly point up traditional implications of an astrological sort. This cultural background—in part naturalistic, in part related to hermeticism—often shines through Machiavelli's writings, without its themes ever really occupying the center of reflection" (p. 218). As another example Inglese cites Machiavelli's letter to Giovan Battista Soderini, 13–21 September 1506 (see *Friends,* pp. 134–136).

~ 11 ~

ON THE RELIGION OF THE ROMANS

1 Although Rome had Romulus as its first organizer and it must recognize its birth and upbringing as his daughter, nevertheless, since the heavens[1] deemed that Romulus's laws were inadequate for so great a power, they inspired the Roman Senate's heart to choose Numa Pompilius as Romulus's successor so that Numa might arrange the matters that Romulus had left out.[2] 2 Finding a very savage population and wanting to lead it back to civil obedience through the arts of peace, he turned to religion as an instrument absolutely

necessary for preserving society; he so constituted it that for several centuries nowhere was there greater fear of God than in that republic. This facilitated any campaigns the Senate or the great men of Rome decided to undertake.

3 If one examines the countless deeds, both of the Roman people collectively and of many individual Romans, one will see that those citizens were far more afraid to break an oath than to break the law, as they respected the power of God more than that of men: this can clearly be seen by the examples of Scipio and Manlius Torquatus. 4 For after the defeat that Hannibal inflicted on the Romans at Cannae,[3] many citizens, afraid for their native land, gathered together and agreed to abandon Italy and depart for Sicily. When Scipio heard of this, he went to see them and, naked sword in hand, compelled them to swear not to desert their native land. 5 Lucius Manlius, the father of Titus Manlius, later called Torquatus, was indicted by Marcus Pomponius, the Tribune of the Plebs; but before the day of the trial arrived, Titus went to see Marcus and, threatening to kill him if he did not swear to withdraw his indictment against his father, compelled him to take an oath. Having taken the oath out of fear, Marcus did withdraw the indictment.[4] 6 So those citizens whom neither love of their native land nor its laws kept in Italy were kept there by an oath that they were compelled to take. And a Tribune dismissed the hatred that he had for the father, the insult that the son had done him, and his honor, to obey an oath he had taken; this had no other origin than the religion that Numa had initiated in the city.[5]

7 And if we consider Roman history carefully, we can see how useful religion was in controlling the armies, inspiring the Plebs, keeping men good, and shaming the wicked.[6] 8 So if one were to argue which prince Rome was more indebted to, Romulus or Numa, I believe that Numa would rather obtain first place: where there is religion, one can easily institute arms, but where there are arms and no religion, the latter is difficult to institute. 9 It can be seen that Romulus, to establish the Senate[7] and make other civil and military institutions, did not need the authority of God, but Numa did, so he pretended to be on intimate terms with a Nymph[8] who advised him about how he was to advise the people; and this all came about because he wanted to give new and unfamiliar laws to the city and was afraid that his own authority would not suffice.

10 And in truth there has never been any giver of extraordinary laws to a people who did not have recourse to God, because they would otherwise not have been accepted and because a prudent man is aware of many benefits that are not so evident to reason by themselves that he can convince others of them. 11 Therefore wise men who want to avoid this difficulty have recourse to God. 12 Thus did Lycurgus, Solon,[9] and many others who had the same objective as they did.

13 So the Roman people, marveling at his goodness and wisdom, agreed to every decision he made. 14 It is true, of course, that the fact that those were times when religious feeling was high and the men whom Numa had to deal with were untutored made it very easy for him to carry out his projects since he could easily impress any new form on them. 15 Unquestionably anyone who wished to found a republic at present would find that easier among

mountain-dwellers, where there is no civilization, than among people accustomed to living in cities, where civilization is corrupt; and a sculptor will more easily draw a beautiful statue out of rough marble than from a piece already badly blocked out by someone else.[10]

16 All things considered, therefore, I conclude that the religion Numa established was among the primary reasons for Rome's success, because it gave rise to good institutions, good institutions make for good fortune, and from good fortune came the happy outcomes of its campaigns. 17 And just as observance of divine worship is the cause for greatness in republics, so contempt for it is the cause for their downfall. 18 Because where no fear of God exists, that kingdom either must crumble or it must be sustained by fear of a prince who compensates for the lack of religion. 19 And because princes are short-lived, the kingdom must quickly fail once his *virtù* fails. 20 Hence it follows that kingdoms dependent solely upon the *virtù* of one man do not long endure, because his *virtù* dies out with his life; it occurs rarely that his *virtù* is renewed by his successors, as Dante wisely says:[11]

> Human integrity is seldom passed down
> through the branches, and this is willed
> by Him who gives it, so that
> it may be claimed from him.

21 A republic's or a kingdom's salvation, therefore, lies not in having a prince who governs wisely while he is living, but one who organizes it in such a way that when he dies it may still be maintained. 22 And although uncouth men are more easily convinced of a new law or opinion, it is not impossible thereby to convince civilized men, who assume they are not uncouth, of it. 23 The people of Florence do not consider themselves either ignorant or uncouth; nevertheless, Fra Girolamo Savonarola convinced them that he spoke with God.[12] 24 I do not wish to judge whether or not it was true, because one must speak of so great a man with reverence; but I do say that countless people believed him without ever having seen anything unusual to make them believe him, because his life, learning, and the subject that he chose[13] were enough to make them lend him credence. 25 Therefore no one should be afraid of not being able to accomplish what has been accomplished by others: for men, as was said in our preface, have been born, have lived, and have died, always under the same organizing principles.

NOTES

1. For more on "the heavens," see above, 1, 10, n.15.

2. Although reliance on Livy is clear in this discourse, Polybius 6.56.6–8 is also relevant; Martelli, *Storici antichi*, pp. 13–14, adds Valerius Maximus, *Facta et dicta memorabilia* (Memorable Deeds and Sayings), 5.6.7. Polybius is well aware of the degree to which political solidarity and national identity are determined by Roman religion. His word is "superstition," but the practices to which Polybius draws attention are those that Machiavelli emphasizes. Livy discusses the "laws" Romulus devised in 1.8,

and Numa's religious institutions in 1.18–21. Machiavelli's *popolo ferocissimo* (very savage population) in the next sentence is based on Livy's *ferocem populum,* 1.19.2.

3. During the Second Punic War in 216 B.C.; see Livy, 22.53 for the incident discussed. Polybius, 6.56.14 praises the value of Roman oaths because they were sanctioned by a strong religious faith.

4. Livy, 7.4–5; Machiavelli omits the fact that Lucius Manlius was indicted in part because of his cruel treatment of Titus.

5. Livy believed Numa's purpose in instituting religion was to divert the people from military concerns. Furthermore, he admired the result that Numa achieved: because the people believed Rome's future was guided by divine powers, they were more likely to rely on the efficacy of their own oaths and promises and less on fear of the law and its punishments (1.21.1).

6. See Polybius 6.56.9–12; in the closing section of his final speech in Book IV of *The Art of War,* Fabrizio expresses similar thoughts (pp. 441–442). As with Numa and the water goddess, Egeria (see note 8 below), Fabrizio cites the claim of French king Charles VII that he took the advice of Joan of Arc, "a maid sent by God . . . the cause of his victory" during the Hundred Years' War.

7. Livy, 1.8.7.

8. Livy, 1.19.4–5; the water goddess or "Nymph" was named Egeria.

9. Both men claimed to have acted on favorable responses from the oracle at Delphi; see Plutarch, *Lycurgus,* 6 and *Solon,* 14.

10. Here and at the end of the previous sentence Machiavelli draws on an implied comparison between political leaders and artists: the notion of the state as a work of art. A similar expression occurs in *Prince,* 26 (p. 379, lines 77–80, and note).

11. *Purgatorio,* 7, vv. 121–123: *Rade volte discende per li rami / l'umana probitate, e questo vuole / quei che la dà, perché da lui si chiami.* Dante has *risurge,* that is, shoots up through the branches, for Machiavelli's *discende.* Machiavelli's image is based on a genealogical tree, Dante's on a growing tree. Neither *virtù* nor human integrity is inherited, because God wants mankind to understand that these come from him, not from one's bloodline.

12. He was a Dominican reforming friar so famous for his preaching that Lorenzo de' Medici brought him to Florence, where he became prior of San Marco in 1491. Machiavelli was familiar with the republican ideas expressed in his *Trattato circa el reggimento e governo della città di Firenze* (Treatise on the organization and government of Florence). He denounced Florence's licentious and luxurious extravagances, drove Piero de' Medici from power in 1494, gained political control of the city and urged the establishment of an ideal Christian state, and held a "bonfire of vanities." Pope Alexander VI finally excommunicated him; eventually he was imprisoned, tried for religious heresy and political sedition, tortured, hanged, and burned in May 1498, about a month before Machiavelli received his first political appointment. Machiavelli's most detailed discussion of Savonarola is in a letter to Ricciardo Becchi, 9 March 1498 (*Friends,* pp. 8–10). There Machiavelli writes that Savonarola proclaims "that God has told him that there was someone in Florence who sought to make himself a tyrant" and that Savonarola "acts in accordance with the times and colors his lies accordingly" (p. 10). He is also an important figure in *Prince,* 6, where he exemplifies the "unarmed prophet" who always fails, in this case because Savonarola "did not have the means to

be able to hold on firmly to those who had believed or to make the skeptics believe" (p. 151, lines 109–112). Other letters in which Machiavelli refers to Savonarola were written to Francesco Vettori, 26 August 1513 (p. 257) and to Francesco Guicciardini, 17 May 1521 (p. 336). With these commentaries as a context for reading the next sentence, it is hard not to understand that "reverence" is meant with irony. Nevertheless, Machiavelli is fully cognizant, indeed respectful, of the need for political leaders to deal adequately with such "unarmed prophets." A further irony lies in the fact that Savonarola believed his spiritual power was stronger than any temporal power extant in the Italy of 1498.

13. Savonarola preached on "subjects" or texts from the Old Testament; Machiavelli specifically refers to verses from Exodus 1:12 and 2:11–12 (in the letter to Becchi) and Ezekiel 13:10 (in the letter to Vettori).

~ 12 ~

HOW IMPORTANT IT IS TO TAKE RELIGION INTO ACCOUNT; AND SINCE, THANKS TO THE ROMAN CHURCH, ITALY HAS LACKED IT, SHE IS IN SHAMBLES

1 Princes or republics that want to stay uncorrupted must, above all else, keep the ceremonies of their religions uncorrupted, and always hold them in reverence, because there can be no greater sign of a country in shambles than seeing divine worship held in low esteem. 2 This is easy to understand once one knows the basis of the religion which men are born into, because every religion has its vital center in some one of its principal institutions. 3 The vital center of Pagan religion was based on the responses of the oracles and on the caste of diviners and haruspices;[1] all their other ceremonies, sacrifices, and rites depended on these, because they readily believed that a God who could predict your future good or ill could also grant it to you. 4 From this came temples, sacrifices, prayers, and every other type of service to worship them; hence, the oracle of Delos, the temple of Jupiter Ammon, and other celebrated oracles that filled the world with admiration and devotion.[2] 5 Later, when these oracles began to speak according to those in power and the populace discovered this duplicity, men became skeptical and ready to disrupt any good institutions. 6 The princes of a republic or a kingdom must therefore maintain the foundations of the religion that they practice; and if they do so, it will be easy for them to preserve religious belief and consequently goodness and unity in their republic. 7 And they must foster and strengthen all things that happen in its favor, even if they judge them to be false. The wiser they are and the more knowledgeable about nature, the more they must do so. 8 And because wise men have followed this system, there has arisen a belief in miracles that people revere even among false religions, because wise men promote them whatever origins they may arise from and their authority then lends credence to them in everyone's eyes. 9 There were quite a few of these miracles in Rome; one was when, as the Roman soldiers were sacking the city of

Veii, some of them entered the temple of Juno and when they approached her image and asked *"Vis venire Romam?"* some thought that she nodded, others that she said "yes."[3] 10 Because, since these men were deeply religious (as Livy shows, for they entered the temple respectfully, devout and full of reverence), they thought they heard the reply to their question that they had perhaps expected, Camillus and the rest of the city's leaders strongly fostered and strengthened this belief and credulity.[4] 11 Had this sort of religion been maintained among the early rulers of the Christian republic[5] as it was established for us by its founder,[6] Christian states and republics would be more united, far happier than they are. 12 And no greater evidence of its decline can be given than seeing how the people who are closest to the Roman church, the pinnacle of our religion, are the least religious. 13 Anyone who considered its foundations and saw how different its present customs are from them would undoubtedly conclude that either its downfall or its scourge is near.[7]

14 Because many believe that the well-being of the cities of Italy derives from the church of Rome, I wish to discuss some contrary reasons that occur to me. I shall mention two very powerful ones that to my mind are incontrovertible. 15 The first is that because of the wicked examples of the [papal] court this country has lost all piety and all religion with the countless troubles and disorders that have ensued: just as we can assume all good where religion exists, so we can assume the reverse where it does not. 16 Our first debt to the Church and the priests, therefore, is that we Italians have become irreligious and wicked. But we owe them an even greater debt, the second cause of our fall: namely, the Church has kept and continues to keep this country divided.[8] 17 Surely no country has ever been united or happy until it came entirely under the jurisdiction of one republic or one prince, as has happened in France and Spain. 18 And the reason why Italy is not in the same condition, having neither one republic nor one prince to govern it like them, is the Church alone. Although the Church has resided and held temporal power here, it has not been so powerful or of such great *virtù* as to be able to take over the rest of Italy[9] and become its prince; on the other hand, when it has feared loss of control over its temporal possessions, it has not been so weak as to be unable to call in some powerful man to defend it against anyone in Italy who had become too powerful. We have seen this from many experiences in olden times when by means of Charlemagne the Church expelled the Lombards,[10] who were already the virtual kings of all Italy; and in our day when it wrested power from the Venetians with the aid of France,[11] then expelled the French with the aid of the Swiss.[12] 19 So because the Church did not have enough power to be able to take over Italy and would not allow anyone else to take over Italy, it has been the reason why Italy has been unable to come under one leader, but has instead been under a number of princes and lords. The result has been such division and weakness that Italy has become the prey not only of powerful barbarians[13] but of any aggressor. For this we Italians are indebted to the Church and no one else. 20 And if anyone wanted to see the truth more quickly by sure experience he would have to have enough power to send the papal court, with

the power it has in Italy, off to the land of the Swiss. As far as religion and military organization are concerned, they are the only people today who live like the ancients; within a short time he would see that the evil habits of the court would create more disorder in that country than any other possible event that might occur there at any time.

NOTES

1. For "Pagan" Machiavelli uses *Gentile* (Gentile), referring to a tradition other than the Judeo-Christian. The "caste" referred to is the college of augurs, which consulted the flights of birds before rendering an opinion, and that of the haruspices, who scrutinized the internal organs of sacrificial victims (Livy, 5.21.8). The augurs date from the time of Numa, but the haruspices were a later development. Livy's Book 5 pays particularly attention to religious aspects of Roman culture.

2. Because the island of Delos was supposed to be Apollo's birthplace, there was an important sanctuary dedicated to him there; Ammon began as a Libyan deity associated with the sun, then with Zeus, and finally with Jupiter: Alexander the Great consulted the temple dedicated to him.

3. Livy, 5.22.5 reads, *Visne Romam ire, Iuno?* (Do you want to go to Rome, Juno?). The Romans conquered Veii in 396 B.C. See also Martelli, *Storici antichi,* p. 15.

4. For Furius Camillus, elected dictator expressly to conquer the Veians, see above 1, 8, n.1. The statue of Juno was brought to Rome and a temple was built to house it on the Aventine Hill in 391 B.C.

5. Translates *ne' principi della republica cristiana.* By using "among the early rulers" the translators have tried to have the best of both worlds. Most commentators believe that *principi* is Machiavelli's word for "princes" or "rulers," the plural form of *principe;* others think *principi* is the plural form of *principio,* the "beginning." In our translation the adjective "early" attempts to add this connotation to "rulers." In both the sixteenth and the twentieth centuries, however, the correct form for spelling the plural of *principio* is *principii,* not *principi.* Furthermore, Walker states, "Machiavelli never uses '*principi*' for 'beginnings'" (Machiavelli, *Discourses,* 2, 34). By using the literal translation "of the Christian republic" instead of "Christendom," we mean to call attention to the contrast with Machiavelli's preceding discussion of the Roman republic. While this contrast may be ironic, it is clearly to the detriment of Christianity, because the early rulers of Christianity, whether popes or Roman emperors, failed to maintain the spirit inherent in the original conception of Christianity. Hence, "Christian states and republics" lack unity and are unhappy in the early sixteenth century.

6. That is, Jesus Christ.

7. If we assume Machiavelli was writing this sentence at some point between 1516 and 1518, then the pope was Giovanni de' Medici, Pope Leo X. It would appear that Machiavelli's comment about "present customs" indicates the dashing of his "hope" for Leo X in the *Prince,* 11, that "he will make [the papacy] respected and very great through his goodness, his countless other qualities, and his *virtù* " (p. 217, lines 100–101). The word "scourge" translates *fragello,* or *flagello,* a "whip" in the exalted sense of a preacher like Savonarola, "the scourge of God"; that is, divine punishment. Even in 1513 Machiavelli noted that Florence was "a magnet for all the world's pitchmen," where "a friar of Saint Francis who is half hermit . . . said . . . that before much time elapses . . . there will be an

unjust pope . . . who will have false prophets with him, he will create cardinals, and he will divide the Church" (letter to Francesco Vettori, 19 December 1519; *Friends,* p. 267).

8. For the ironic emphasis on the political implications of "debt" here, see above, 1, 10, n.11. In a letter to Vettori dated 26 August 1513, Machiavelli spells out more clearly what the "debt" is: "I am ready to start weeping with you over our collapse and our servitude that, if it does not come today or tomorrow, will come in our lifetime. This will be what Italy owes to Pope Julius and all those who do not come up with a remedy for us—if a remedy can now be found" (*Friends,* p. 260).

9. A textual variant, which Rinaldi retains, reads "to occupy the tyranny of Italy," though Inglese believes that "'tyranny' has a specific meaning for Machiavelli, which here would be out of place and would break the thread of reasoning."

10. Or Longobards in 774; see *Florentine Histories,* 1, 9–11. The Lombard king was taken to France, but the Lombards themselves remained in northern Italy.

11. Pope Julius II formed the League of Cambrai, which defeated Venice at the battle of Agnadello in 1509; see above, 1, 6, n.11.

12. Julius II also formed the Holy League in 1511 to drive the French out of Italy; for its success in 1512 see above, 1, 2, n.6.

13. For Machiavelli, to be dominated by any foreigner is tantamount to being ruled by a barbarian; see the title of final chapter of the *Prince,* "An Exhortation to Seize Italy and Free Her From the Barbarians."

~ 13 ~

HOW THE ROMANS USED RELIGION TO REORGANIZE THE CITY, TO PURSUE THEIR CAMPAIGNS, AND TO STOP RIOTS

1 I do not think it is irrelevant for me to cite a few examples of the Romans' making use of religion to reorganize the city and pursue their campaigns; and although there are many of them in Livy, I nevertheless shall be satisfied with these. 2 When the Roman People elected tribunes with consular power, all Plebeians save one, plague and famine came that year and certain phenomena occurred. The Nobles used this occasion against the new election of the Tribunes, saying that the gods were angry because Rome had ill used the grandeur of her power and there was no other remedy to placate the gods than to bring the election of the Tribunes back to its proper place, at which the Plebs, terrified by this religion, elected all noble Tribunes.[1] 3 It can also be seen from the capture of the Veians' city that the commanders of the armies made use of religion to keep them prepared for a campaign. Lake Albano had risen unusually that year, and since the Roman soldiers were annoyed at the long siege and wanted to return to Rome, the Romans found that Apollo and certain other oracles announced that the city of the Veians would be captured that year if Lake Albano overflowed. That made the soldiers bear the annoyances of the siege, encouraged by the hope of capturing the city; they remained satisfied to carry out the attack, so Camillus, named Dictator, captured the city after it

had been besieged for ten years. 4 Thus, when properly used, religion was effective in both capturing that city and restoring the Tribunes' office to the Nobility; either one would have been difficult to achieve without such means.[2]

5 I do not wish to fail to cite another example in this connection. 6 Many riots had occurred in Rome because of the tribune Terentilius, who wanted to propose a certain law for reasons that will be stated later at the proper time.[3] Among the first remedies that the Nobility used for it was religion, which they employed in two ways. 7 First, they had the Sibylline books[4] consulted, with the answer that the city was in danger of losing its freedom that very year thanks to the civil insurrection, something that, even though it was discovered by the Tribunes, nevertheless inspired such terror in the hearts of the Plebs that they were discouraged from following them.[5] 8 The second way was when one Appius Herdonius, with a throng of banished men and slaves numbering four thousand, occupied the Capitol by night; consequently, people feared that if the Aequi and the Volscians, the perpetual enemies of the name of Rome, had come to Rome, they would have captured it.[6] And because the Tribunes did not let up their insistence on proposing the Terentilian law because of this, saying that this outrage was trumped up and untrue, one Publius Ruberius,[7] a citizen of dignity and authority, came forth from the Senate and, with partly friendly and partly threatening words, pointed out to them the city's danger and the untimeliness of their demands. He thus forced the Plebs to swear not to depart from the will of the consul, so the Plebs, obeying him, took back the Capitol by force. 9 But when the consul Publius Valerius died in the attack, Titus Quinctius[8] was immediately renamed consul. In order not to let the Plebs rest or give them time to think of the Terentilian law, he ordered them to go out from Rome and attack the Volscians, saying that because of the oath they had taken not to abandon the consul they were obliged to follow him. The Tribunes opposed this, claiming that the oath had been made to the late consul and not to him. 10 Nevertheless, when Livy wrote these words on behalf of the ancient religion, "but there had not yet come into being such neglect for the gods, characteristic of the present generation, nor did everybody interpret laws and oaths to suit his own purposes,"[9] he shows that the Plebs out of fear of religion were willing rather to obey the consul than to believe the Tribunes. 11 The Tribunes, frightened then lest they thus lose all their standing, agreed they would remain obedient to the consul and the Terentilian law would not be discussed for a year; and the Consuls would not be able to lead the Plebs off to war for a year.[10] 12 And thus religion enabled the Senate to overcome difficulties that it would never have overcome without it.

NOTES

1. Based on Livy, 5.13–14, "terrified by this religion" directly echoes Livy's *religione etiam attoniti* in 14.5, but see Martelli, *Storici antichi,* pp. 16–17, for discrepancies; the sole plebeian tribune actually elected was Publius Licinius Calvus. These events occurred in 399 and 400 B.C.

2. See Livy, 5.15–16, for these events occurring in 398 B.C. during a ten-year siege of Veii.

3. Below in 1, 39; for the law proposed by the plebeian tribune Gaius Terentilius Harsa

and his proposal to define and thereby restrict the powers of the consuls, see Livy, 3.9.5.

4. The Cumaean sibyl is said to have offered these books of ancient prophecies to Tarquinius Priscus; a group of priests kept them in the temple of Jupiter Optimus Maximus, the Capitol, on the summit of the Capitoline Hill in Rome.

5. See Livy, 3.10.5–7

6. For these event of 460 B.C., see Livy, 3.15–18; in 15.5 Livy specifies 2,500 men, not 4,000.

7. Machiavelli probably means Publius Valerius, mentioned below as having "died in the attack"; there is no mention of a Publius Ruberius in Livy; see Martelli, *Storici antichi,* pp. 18–19.

8. Machiavelli is actually referring to Lucius Quinctius Cincinnatus, who was named consul in 460 B.C. for the first time: he was not "renamed"; see Livy, 3.19.2.

9. Machiavelli quotes Livy in Latin for the first time from 3.20.5: *Nondum haec, quae nunc tenet saeculum, negligentia Deum venerat, nec interpretando sibi quisque iusiurandum et leges aptas faciebat.* See Mansfield, *New Modes,* p. 76.

10. Livy discusses this compromise settlement in 3.21.2.

~ 14 ~

THE ROMANS INTERPRETED OMENS ACCORDING TO NEED AND PRUDENTLY MADE A PRACTICE OF OBSERVING RELIGION, BUT THEY DID NOT OBSERVE IT IF NECESSARY; AND IF ANYONE RASHLY DISPARAGED IT THEY PUNISHED HIM

1 As was discussed above,[1] not only were auguries in large part the basis of the ancient religion of the Pagans, but they were also responsible for the Roman republic's well-being. 2 For that reason the Romans took greater care about them than about any other institution; and they consulted them for consular assemblies, for initiating campaigns, for leading forth armies, for giving battle, and for every important action whether civil or military; they would never go on an expedition unless they had convinced the soldiers that the gods promised them victory. 3 And among the other types of augurs, the Romans had in their armies some categories of divines whom they called pullarii,[2] and before they ordered doing battle with the enemy, they wanted the *pullarii* to read the omens. If the chickens pecked the food, the Romans would fight with a favorable omen; if they did not peck, they would abstain from combat. 4 Nonetheless, when reason showed them that something had to be done even if the omens were unfavorable, they did so anyway; but they twisted it with such astute terms and means that they did not seem to be acting in contempt of religion.

5 The consul Papirius used this means in a very important fight he had with the Samnites, which left them completely weakened and overcome.[3] 6 Papirius was encamped opposite the Samnites and thought he was certain of victory in the fight, and since he therefore wanted to attack, he ordered the *pullarii* to read the omens; but since the chickens did not peck and the chief *pullarius* saw

the army's great eagerness for combat as well as the feeling of victory among the commander and all the soldiers, he reported to the consul that the omens were good in order for the army not to miss an opportunity to act successfully. Papirius organized his squadrons and some of the *pullarii* told a few soldiers that the chickens had not pecked, so the soldiers told Spurius Papirius, the consul's nephew. He reported it to the consul, who immediately answered that he should make sure of his own duties: that as far as he and the army were concerned the omens were favorable and if the *pullarius* had told lies, then they would turn against him. 7 And in order for the outcome to correspond to the prediction, he ordered the legates to place the *pullarii* in the front line of the fray. 8 It so happened that, while they were attacking the enemy, a Roman soldier threw a javelin and accidentally killed the chief *pullarius;* when the consul heard of that, he said that everything was going well and with the gods' favor, because his army, with that liar's death, had purged itself of any guilt and wrath that they might have against it. 9 Thus, knowing how to accommodate his plans to the omens, he decided to go into combat without the army noticing that he had in any way disregarded the rules of their religion.

10 Appius Pulcher did the opposite in Sicily during the First Punic War: wishing to go into combat against the Carthaginian army, he had the *pullarii* read the omens; when they reported that the chickens had not pecked their food, he said, "Let's see if they would like to drink!" and had them hurled into the sea.[4] 11 Then, going to combat, he lost the battle; he was condemned in Rome for this defeat, and Papirius was honored: not so much because the latter had won and the former lost as because one had acted wisely against the omens and the other rashly. 12 And this system of consulting diviners was not intended for any other purpose than to make the soldiers go into combat confidently, and from such confidence victory almost always ensues. 13 This practice was employed not only by the Romans but by outsiders; I think I should cite an example of this in the next chapter.

NOTES

1. In 1, 12, 4.

2. Literally "poultry men," referring to a category of augurs who were members of an association of priests responsible for determining whether the gods favored a particular undertaking; they did not predict the future. After observing the chickens' behavior, they made their pronouncements. Our word "auspices" comes from the Latin *avis* (bird) plus *specere* (to look at; throughout this chapter the word "omen" translates the Italian word *auspicio* or its derivatives.

3. The following paragraph may be based on Livy, 10.39.5–41, but see also Martelli, *Storici antichi,* pp. 20–22. Lucius Papirius Cursor the Younger was consul in 293 B.C. when the battle near Aquilonia took place during the Third Samnite War (298–290 B.C.). Frequently at war with the Romans, the Samnites were a group of four tribes located at the southern end of the Apennines.

4. This was Appius Claudius Pulcher, a Roman consul whom the Carthaginians defeated in a naval battle near the port of Trapani on the northwestern tip of Sicily in 249 B.C.; see Valerius Maximus, 1.4.3, and Cicero, *De natura deorum,* 2.3.7.

~ 15 ~

THE SAMNITES RESORTED TO RELIGION AS THE ULTIMATE REMEDY FOR THEIR TROUBLED AFFAIRS

1 After the Samnites had been routed several times by the Romans, most recently in Etruria when their armies and commanders had been killed,[1] and their allies, that is, the Etruscans, Lombards, and Umbrians, had been defeated, "they were no longer able to hold out with either their own men or those from foreign tribes. Nevertheless, they would not turn their backs on warfare since they were not tired even of unsuccessfully defending their freedom; they preferred to be defeated rather than not strive for victory."[2] 2 So they resolved to make a final stand. Because the Samnites knew that if they wanted to win they had to make their soldiers' minds steadfast and there was no better means than religion to do that, they decided to repeat one of their ancient sacrifices with the aid of their priest Ovius Paccius.[3] 3 They arranged it in the following way. After they had offered a solemn sacrifice and made all the leaders of the army, surrounded by slain victims and burning altar fires, vow never to lay down their arms, they summoned the soldiers one by one. Surrounded by those altars and in the midst of several centurions[4] with naked swords in their hands, the Samnites first made their soldiers vow not to divulge anything they might see or hear; then, with horrible words and frightening cries, they made them promise the gods to be ready wherever their leaders might send them, never to flee from the fray, and to slaughter anyone they saw running away. If this promise were not kept, it would fall on the heads of their families and descendants. 4 And when some of them became terrified and were unwilling to take the oath, the centurions killed them on the spot; consequently, the other men who came next, frightened by the ferocity of this spectacle, all took the oath. 5 And in order to make this muster of forty thousand men more impressive, they clothed half[5] of them in white uniforms with crests and plumes atop their helmets; so arrayed, they took up their position near Aquilonia. 6 Papirius went to meet them; to urge on his soldiers, he said that "crests caused no wounds and the Roman javelin would penetrate their painted and gilded shields."[6] 7 And to weaken the respect that his soldiers had for the enemy because of the oath they had taken, he said that it would make them afraid, not strong, because they were simultaneously forced to fear their fellow citizens, their gods, and their enemy. 8 When the battle was joined, the Samnites were conquered because Roman *virtù* and the dread engendered by past defeats[7] exceeded any steadfastness they could have received from the *virtù* of their religion and their sworn oath. 9 Nevertheless, we can see that they thought they had no other refuge and they could try no other remedy in hopes of reviving their lost *virtù*. 10 This bears full witness to how much confidence can be gained through properly used religion. 11 And although this section should perhaps rather be included among external matters,[8] nevertheless, since it is related to one of the most important institutions of the republic of Rome, I thought it ought to be connected here, in order not to divide this topic up and have to return to it several times.

NOTES

1. At a battle near Sentinum in 295 B.C. in which the famous Samnite general Gellius Egnatius was defeated along with the Samnites' allies: the Etruscans, Lombards, and Umbrians.

2. Machiavelli quotes Livy in Latin from 10.31.14: *nec suis nec externis viribus iam stare poterant; tamen bello non abstinebant: adeo ne infeliciter quidem defensae libertatis taedebat, et vinci quam non tentare victoriam malebant.*

3. See Livy, 10.38.5–13 for the following incident; but for its use, see Martelli, *Storici antichi,* pp. 23–25.

4. Machiavelli uses Livy's word *centuriones* (10.38.8), but Livy refers to them more accurately as *armati sacerdotes* (armed priests) in 10.41.3.

5. Livy's figure is 16,000 (10.38.12).

6. For Papirius, see 1, 14, n.3; Machiavelli quotes Livy in Latin from 10.39.12: *non enim cristas vulnera facere, et picta atque aurata scuta transire romanum pilum.*

7. Echoes Livy's *vinci adsueti,* 10.41.2.

8. Machiavelli intends to deal with matters of Roman foreign policy in Book 2 of *Discourses.*

~ 16 ~

PEOPLE WHO ARE ACCUSTOMED TO LIVING UNDER A PRINCE FIND IT DIFFICULT TO HOLD ONTO THEIR FREEDOM IF THEY ARE SET FREE BY SOME EVENT

1 Countless examples that we read about in the annals of ancient history show us how difficult it is for people accustomed to living under a prince to preserve their freedom if they acquire it through some event or other,[1] as Rome did after the expulsion of the Tarquins. 2 And such difficulty is understandable: these people are like nothing but a dumb animal that, though by nature wild and free, has always been raised in captivity and bondage. If by chance it is then set free in the countryside, it falls prey to the first man who seeks to chain it up again, since it is unaccustomed to foraging and does not know the places where it may take refuge.[2]

3 The same happens to people accustomed to living under the control of others: not knowing how to discuss state defense or offensive measures and not understanding princes or being understood by them, they soon return under a yoke that is usually heavier than the one they had recently thrown off their necks. They find themselves in this kind of difficulty even if the body politic is free from corruption. 4 For a people completely permeated by corruption cannot live free at all, let alone for a short time, as I shall mention later;[3] therefore our discussion concerns those peoples in whom corruption is not widespread and in whom there is more good than rot.

5 Another difficulty is added to the above, i.e., a state that becomes free creates unfriendly, not friendly factions for itself. 6 All those who profit from a tyrannical state by feeding on the prince's wealth become factions unfriendly

to it; since their means of gain has been taken from them, they cannot live happily and are obliged every day to try and bring back tyranny in order to regain their power. 7 As I have said, it does not acquire friendly factions, because a free society grants honors and prizes for certain honest and particular reasons; aside from these, it does not reward or honor anyone. When someone has honors and benefits that he feels he deserves, he professes no indebtedness to those who reward him. 8 Furthermore, while he possesses no one realizes the common benefit derived from a free society: namely, being able to enjoy one's property freely without suspicion, not to worry about the honor of one's women or children, and not to fear for oneself, because no one will ever admit indebtedness to someone who does him no harm.

9 Thus as we have said above, a free state that has newly emerged comes to have unfriendly and not friendly factions. 10 And if it should wish to remedy the disadvantages and disorders that the above-mentioned difficulties might entail, there is no more powerful, effective, sure, or necessary remedy than murdering the sons of Brutus: as history shows, they as well as other Roman youths were induced to plot against their native land only because they could not prevail so extraordinarily under the consuls as they had under the kings; consequently, the people's freedom seemed to have become their slavery.[4] 11 And anyone who tries to govern the masses either through freedom or through a princedom and does not secure himself against those who are opposed to the new order creates a short-lived state. 12 It is true that I consider those princes unfortunate who have to take extraordinary measures in order to secure their state since they have the masses against them. Because a man who has only the few as enemies can make himself secure easily and without much disturbance,[5] but he who has the many as his enemy is never safe, and the more he uses cruelty the weaker his princedom becomes. 13 So the best remedy there is to try and win over the people.[6]

14 Although this discussion differs from what has been written above, since we are speaking here of a prince and there we were speaking of a republic, nevertheless, I wish to talk about it briefly so as not to have to return to this topic later.[7] 15 So if a prince wishes to win over a once-hostile people, speaking of those princes who have become tyrants over their native land, I say that he must first consider what the people desire. And he will always find that they desire two things: first, to get revenge on those who cause their bondage; second, to regain their freedom. 16 A prince can satisfy the first desire entirely and the second one partially. 17 There is a very specific example for the first. 18 When Clearchus, the tyrant of Heraclea, was in exile, a dispute happened to arise between the people and aristocrats of Heraclea.[8] Realizing they were weaker, the aristocrats directed their support to Clearchus; they conspired with him, set him up in Heraclea against the will of the people, and took away the people's freedom. 19 So Clearchus found himself between the arrogance of the aristocrats, whom he could neither satisfy nor correct in any way, and the rage of the people, who could not bear the loss of their freedom; he decided at once to free himself from the nuisance of the Nobles and win over the people. 20 So choosing a suitable opportunity, he hacked every one of the aristocrats to pieces, to the enormous

satisfaction of the people. 21 In this way he thus satisfied one of the desires that the people had, namely, getting revenge. 22 But as for the other desire of the people, regaining their freedom, the prince, since he is unable to satisfy them, must consider what the reasons are that make them want to be free. He will discover that a few of them want to be free in order to rule; but all the others, who are innumerable, desire freedom in order to live in security. 23 Because in all republics, no matter how they are constituted, ruling positions can be attained by forty or fifty citizens at most; since this is a small number, securing oneself against them is an easy matter, either by doing away with them or by granting them as many public offices as ought in large measure to make them happy in terms of their circumstances. 24 The others, for whom living in security is enough, are easily satisfied by creating institutions and laws that simultaneously include the prince's power and the public's security. 25 If a prince does this and the people see that he will under no circumstances break such laws, then soon they will begin to live in security and happiness. 26 As an example there is the kingdom of France, which lives in security only because its kings are constrained by countless laws guaranteeing the security of all its people.[9] 27 And those who constituted that state[10] willed that its kings might do as they pleased about military and financial matters, but they could not deal with anything else other than as the laws ordained.

28 Therefore any prince or republic that does not make itself secure at the outset of its rule must, as the Romans did, make itself secure at the first opportunity. 29 Anyone who allows that to slip by regrets too late not having done what he should have.[11] 30 Thus, because the Roman people were not yet corrupted when they regained their freedom they were able to preserve it following the deaths of the sons of Brutus and the Tarquins by all those means and institutions that have been discussed earlier. 31 But had the people been corrupted, no effective remedies for preserving it could be found either in Rome or elsewhere, as we shall show in the next chapter.

NOTES

1. Machiavelli makes a similar point in *Prince,* chapters 3, 4, 5, and 20; p. 103, lines 4–6; pp. 131, 133, lines 73–79; pp. 139, 141, lines 41–48; p. 325, lines 113–122.

2. Polybius uses a similar metaphor in 6.9.9.

3. In the next chapter; the argument in chapters 17 and 18 reinforces the important distinction between an as yet uncorrupted government and one corrupted by tyranny. Because effective leadership can shape the former, it has a much better chance of success than the latter. Behind the notion of corruption in this sentence lies the metaphor of a diseased body politic; see above, 1, 4, note 3, and below, 1, 17, note 2. For this reason *materia* is translated in this context as "body" and "body politic."

4. See Livy, 2.3–5 for these events circa 510 B.C.; the last clause of sentence 10 translates part of 2.3 (Rinaldi). As in *Prince* on several occasions and *Discourses,* 3, 3, Machiavelli uses the phrase "to murder the sons of Brutus" as shorthand for a policy he recommends to any new leader; namely, eliminate all hostility to the new government as soon as possible. It is important not to confuse this Lucius Junius Brutus with the Marcus Junius Brutus mentioned in the next discourse, who was part of the assassination plot against Julius Caesar in 44 B.C. Polybius, 6.9, may also be relevant here.

5. At the end of *Prince,* 18, Machiavelli puts this point succinctly: "The few are elbowed out of the way when the many have a base for support"; p. 285, lines 99–100.

6. On this point see *Prince,* chapter 9, paragraph 2; pp. 191, 193, 195, lines 17–57. Concerning the "subtle and complex relationship" between *Prince,* 9, and this chapter and the next two, see Sasso, *Antichi,* 2:396–423.

7. Machiavelli clearly shifts the discussion from republics to princedoms; the discussion of Rome's republican constitution is interrupted for one about how a prince must deal with "the arrogance of the aristocrats" versus "the rage of the people." Inglese points out that until here, in chapters 4 to 6 and in 17 and 18, Machiavelli's argument is more a "structural" one about what happens to political forms of rule when the "body" of society comes up against the variety of laws codified to govern it.

8. Clearchus, a student of Plato and Isocrates, seized power in the Black Sea town in 364 or 363 B.C. and was assassinated in 352 or 353 B.C. Machiavelli's account is based on Justin, 16.4–5. There is a remarkable similarity between how Clearchus treated the aristocrats and how Cesare Borgia dealt with one of his governors in Romagna, Ramiro de Lorqua. Machiavelli provides the details in *Prince,* 7 (pp. 165; 167, lines 158–178).

9. Machiavelli deals extensively with the governmental organization of France in *Prince,* 19, pp. 293, 295, lines 108–134 and below in 1, 55 and 58; see also his *Ritratto di cose di Francia* (1510).

10. Who "constituted that state" is unclear; Charlemagne would be a reasonable assumption, except that in Machiavelli's *Ritratto di cose di Francia* he seems to believe that this occurred in the middle of the fifteenth century (it could thus be Louis XI, king of France from 1461 to 1483).

11. A thought similar to Machiavelli's *capitolo,* or epigram in tercets, *"Dell'occasione."*

~ 17 ~

ONCE CORRUPTED PEOPLE HAVE ACHIEVED FREEDOM THEY HAVE THE GREATEST DIFFICULTY REMAINING FREE

1 In my opinion, either the kings had to die out in Rome or Rome, in an extremely brief period of time, had to become weak and worthless. For if we consider how corrupt the kings had become, if two or three successive reigns had gone by and the corruption that was in them had begun to spread through their members,[1] then, as the members became corrupted, it would have been forever impossible to reform it.[2] 2 But by losing the head while the torso was still intact they were able to go back easily to a free and ordered society. 3 And it must be assumed as absolutely true that a corrupted city living under a prince, even though that prince and all his descendants die out, can never become free again. On the contrary, one prince has to kill the other; without the creation of a new lord, it never rests unless the goodness, along with the *virtù,* of one man keeps it free. But such freedom will endure only as long as that man lives, as happened in Syracuse with Dion and Timoleon.[3] Their *virtù* kept the city free at different times while they were living: once they died, it returned to its former tyranny.

4 But no stronger example can be seen than that of Rome, which, after the Tarquins were expelled, was able immediately both to seize and to preserve its freedom; but after the deaths of Caesar, Caligula, and Nero, after the entire Caesarian line had died out, not only could it never keep its freedom, it was never even able to initiate it.[4] 5 There was no other cause for such differing outcomes in one and the same city than the fact that in the days of the Tarquins the Roman people were not yet corrupted but in the latter times they were highly corrupted. 6 Because earlier, all that it took to keep the people steadfast and ready to avoid kings was to make them swear that they would not agree to anyone ever reigning over Rome,[5] whereas later Brutus's power and severity plus all the eastern legions were not enough to keep them ready to preserve the freedom that he, like the first Brutus, had restored to them. 7 This came from the corruption that the Marian factions had instilled in the people; when Caesar was their leader, he was able to blind the multitude so they did not realize what a yoke it had put on its own neck.[6]

8 And though the example of Rome should supersede all others, nevertheless, in this connection I wish to cite familiar examples of people from our own day. 9 So I say that no event, no matter how serious and violent, could ever make Milan or Naples free, because their members are totally corrupt.[7] 10 This was seen after the death of Filippo Visconti, because when Milan sought to restore freedom, it was unable to and could not preserve it. 11 Rome was very fortunate, therefore, that the kings had quickly become corrupted so that they were expelled from it before their corruption had passed into the city's vital organs; this lack of corruption was the reason that the countless riots in Rome did the republic no harm but rather benefited it since men had good intentions.

12 And the following conclusion can be drawn:[8] wherever the body[9] is not corrupted, riots and other civil strife do no harm; wherever it is corrupted, well-ordered laws are of no avail unless they are promoted by someone who uses extreme force to get them observed until the body becomes good. I do not know whether this has ever occurred or whether it is possible for it to occur: because as I just finished saying, we can see that a city that has gone into decline through corruption of its body, should it ever happen to rise up again, does so as a result of the *virtù* of one man who is living then, not as a result of the *virtù* of the people at large that supports good institutions. No sooner does such a man die than it reverts to its original ways. That is what happened in Thebes, which, through the *virtù* of Epaminondas, was able to retain the form and power of a republic while he was living but reverted to its earlier disorder when he died.[10] 13 The reason is that one man cannot live long enough to have time to develop good habits in a city that has had bad ones for a long time. 14 And if one man with a very long life or two consecutive reigns of *virtù* do not set the city in order, their absence, as has been stated above, brings down the city unless it is renewed with many perils and great bloodshed. 15 Because such corruption and a lack of aptitude for living in freedom arise from inequality existing in the city, and in order to restore equality in it one must use very extraordinary means, which, as I shall point out in greater detail elsewhere,[11] few people know how or wish to use.

NOTES

1. Translates *membra,* "members" or "limbs," continuing the body politic metaphor from the previous chapter; see note 2.

2. The body politic metaphor is again operative in this discourse; see above 1, 4, n.3. Here and elsewhere (see, for example, chapter 18, n.5) it is linked to the Scholastic notion of matter and form. The social body, the people, is the material *(materia)* to be properly shaped to the form that the leader seeks to impose or create. In turn, this doctrine is rooted in the Aristotelian sense of the potential form inherent in matter, of act and potency. In other words, a perfect creation depends upon the ability of the creator (God, the leader, the sculptor) to release the potential for excellence inherent in the material being used for creation. Referring to Moses, Cyrus, Romulus, and Theseus in *Prince,* 6, Machiavelli says: "By examining their actions and lives, we realize that they received nothing else from Fortune but the opportunity which gave them the raw material *(materia)* that they could shape into whatever form pleased them" (pp. 145, 147, lines 42–46).

3. See above, chapter 10, n.4.

4. The Julian-Claudian line, referring to Julius Caesar's direct and adopted descendants, ended with Nero's death in A.D. 68.

5. See Livy, 2.1.9. As in 16, n.4, the contrast is between Lucius Junius Brutus and the later Marcus Junius Brutus. The latter, with Cassius, gathered his forces with "all the eastern legions" in Macedonia and Syria.

6. On Gaius Marius, who died in 86 B.C., see above, chapter 5, n.6. He attempted to hold on to power by allying himself with the plebeians. Julius Caesar's ties to him were attributable to family and to his policy of placating the people at all costs during his early rise to power.

7. Later, in 1, 55, Machiavelli will argue that Naples and Milan are states in which it is impossible to establish a republic because of the excessive number of "gentlemen," that is, members of a feudal nobility. Here the emphasis in on Filippo Visconti, who died in August 1447; the freedom of the "Golden Ambrosian Republic" lasted until February 1450, when Francesco Sforza, Visconti's son-in-law, seized power. See *Florentine Histories,* 6, 13, 20–24; and *Prince,* 12.

8. Walker's remarks on this "conclusion" are important (Machiavelli, *Discourses,* 2:44). He points out that this sentence contains three principles, which, though they are condensed, are basic to Machiavelli's thinking: when class conflict is managed properly, it can be to the state's advantage; the form government takes depends upon the proper human material; and one man must control the state during times of emergency. See Rinaldi, 1, pp. 530–531, n.50, on this point.

9. Translates *materia* here and throughout this paragraph; again, the sense is the social body politic.

10. See above, chapter 6, n.10, for the connection between Epaminondas, Thebes, and Pelopidas; the example is based on Polybius, 4.32–33 and 6.43.

11. The fact that "elsewhere" could be at the close of the next discourse, in Book 1, chapter 26, or most likely in 1, 55, suggests that Machiavelli never decided definitively on the order of these discourses. Machiavelli makes a similar point in *Discursus florentinarum rerum post mortem iunioris Laurentii Medices* (1520).

~ 18 ~

HOW FREE GOVERNMENT MIGHT BE PRESERVED IN CORRUPTED CITIES IF IT IS ALREADY THERE; IF NOT, HOW IT COULD BE ESTABLISHED

1 I think it is not irrelevant or contradictory to the preceding discourse to consider whether free government can be preserved in a corrupted city when there already is one or whether one can be established when there is none. 2 Concerning this I say that it is very difficult to do either; and although it is almost impossible to provide any rule for that, since it would be necessary to proceed according to the degree of corruption, nevertheless, since it is good to discuss everything, I do not want to leave this out. 3 And I shall presume an extremely corrupted city, further increasing the difficulty thereby, because no laws or institutions are adequate to stem the tide of general corruption. 4 For just as good mores need laws to preserve them, so laws need good mores if they are to be observed. 5 Furthermore, institutions and laws made at a republic's founding when men were good are no longer relevant later on when men have turned evil. 6 And if laws change according to events in a city, its institutions never or only rarely vary; this makes new laws inadequate, because the institutions, which remain stable, corrupt them.[1]

7 And in order to make this point clearer let me state that in Rome there were institutions of government, or rather of state, and then laws which, with the magistrates, held the citizens in check. 8 The state's institutions were the authority of the People, the Senate, the Tribunes, the Consuls, the way magistrates were petitioned and named, and the way laws were made. 9 These institutions varied little or not at all with events. 10 The laws that held citizens in check, such as the law against adultery, the sumptuary law, the one on ambition and many others, did change as the citizens gradually became corrupted.[2] 11 But while keeping the state's institutions, which were no longer valid in corrupt times, stable, the laws that were modified were inadequate to keep men good; but they would indeed have been of use if the institutions had been modified along with the reform of the laws.

12 The truth, that such institutions were not good in a corrupted city, can be seen expressed under two main headings: the naming of magistrates and the making of laws. 13 The Roman people granted the consulate and other principal offices of the city only to those who requested it. 14 This was a good rule at the outset, because only citizens who considered themselves worthy of them requested it; and to be turned down was ignominious, so everyone behaved well in order to be considered worthy. 15 Later, when the city became corrupted, this method became extremely harmful, because those who had the greatest power, not those with the greatest *virtù,* sought the magistracies; the powerless, though men of *virtù,* refrained from seeking out of fear. 16 This problem did not arise all at once but came gradually, as one falls into every other problem.

Because after the Romans conquered Africa and Asia and brought almost all Greece to submission, they grew sure of their freedom and thought they no longer had any enemies to fear.[3] 17 This assurance and the enemies' weakness made the Roman people, in bestowing the consular office, seek not *virtù* but graciousness, choosing for the office those who were best at getting along with men, not those who were best at defeating the enemy; afterward, from those who were the most gracious, they descended to bestowing it on those who had the most power; thus, for lack of such a rule, good men were completely excluded from office. 18 A tribune or any other citizen could set a law before the People; each citizen could speak either for or against it before it was voted on. 19 This rule was good as long as the citizens were good, since it was always good for anyone who seeks the public's benefit to be able to set it out, and it is good for each person to able to express his opinion about it so that the people, once they have heard each man speak, can then choose the best. 20 But once the citizens turned bad, such a rule became very bad, because only the powerful proposed laws, not for general freedom but for their own power, and out of fear of these men no one could speak against these laws; so the people were either deceived or forced into voting for their own downfall.[4]

21 For Rome to remain free once it was corrupted, it would therefore have had to make new institutions, just as during the course of its existence it made new laws, because different rules and ways of life have to be devised for a bad subject than for a good one: the form cannot be the same in completely opposite matter.[5] 22 But because institutions must be altered either immediately, once they are no longer found to be good, or little by little, as each one is recognized, I say that both of these things are almost impossible. 23 Any alteration that is done little by little must be done by a wise man who sees this problem from afar and in its initial stages.[6] 24 It is very easy for no one like that ever to emerge in a city. And even if one did emerge, he might never convince anyone else of what he himself understood, because men accustomed to living one way do not want to change it; all the more so if they do not see the evil face-to-face but have to have it shown them by speculation. 25 As for altering these institutions all at once when everyone recognizes that they are not good, I say that, even though everybody readily recognizes this drawback, it is hard to correct it. Because normal measures are not enough to accomplish this since the normal ways are now bad; but it is necessary to resort to extraordinary ones, such as violence and arms, and above all else to become the prince of that city and be able to control it as one sees fit. 26 Reorganizing a city for political life presupposes a good man, but becoming prince of a republic by violent means presupposes a bad one. For this reason, we find it seldom happens that a good man seeks to become a prince through evil means even though his aim be good or that an evil man, once he has become prince, seeks to do good, since it never enters his mind to use for good the power he has acquired wickedly.[7]

27 From all the things mentioned above there arises the difficulty or impossibility of preserving a republic or creating a new one in a corrupted city. 28 And even if one had to create or preserve one there, it would be necessary to direct it more toward a royal government than toward a popular one so that those men

who cannot be punished for their unruliness by laws might be checked in some other way by a quasi-royal power.[8] 29 And trying to make them become good by other means would be either a very harsh or a completely impossible undertaking, as I have said above that Cleomenes did.[9] If, to rule alone, he slaughtered the Ephors and if, for similar reasons, Romulus slaughtered his brother and the Sabine, Titus Tatius, and then they used their authority well, it must nonetheless be noted that neither of them had subjects so sullied with the kind of corruption that we are speaking of in this chapter. Therefore they were able to seek their aims, and in seeking them, to disguise them.

NOTES

1. The subsequent discussion will clarify the distinction between law and institution, but compare the discussion in chapter 2, n.1.

2. Machiavelli is referring to such laws as the *Lex Julia de adulteriis* of 18 B.C.; the sumptuary laws designed to reduce the "inequality" he mentions in the last sentence of the previous discourse, such as the *Lex Oppia,* c. 195, which Livy mentions (34.1–8), and another in 215 B.C., and the *Lex Fannia* limiting expenses on dinner parties, 161 B.C.; and the laws on the political process and electoral corruption, known as *ambitus,* such as the *Lex Poetelia* of 358 B.C. (Livy, 7.15.12) and the *Lex Cornelia Baebia de Ambitu* of 181 B.C. (Livy, 40.19.11).

3. Rome's major conquests occurred during the period from the end of the Second Punic War (201 B.C.) and the Second Macedonian War (196) to the defeat of Carthage at the end of the Third Punic War (146). With the defeat of Antiochus at the battle of Magnesia in 190, Asia Minor was in Roman hands; the defeat of Perseus at Pydna in 168 gave Rome control of Macedonia and Greece. Africa was considered Rome's after 146, and the consul Manius Aquillius brought Asia into Rome as a province after 129 B.C.

4. "Deceived or forced" *(ingannato o sforzato)* is close to Machiavelli's notion of force and fraud *(la forza, la fraude).* See especially *Prince,* 7 (p. 173, lines 270–271 and note), and later in chapter 18 (pp. 279–281, and notes). It is also close to the speech of someone attempting to stir up a crowd prior to the Ciompi Rebellion in 1378: "If you observe the way men do things, you will see that everyone who attains great riches and great power has done so by means of force or fraud; then, once men possess these things by seizing them through deception or violence, they whitewash the shocking things done in gaining them by hiding them behind a false label of profit" (*Florentine Histories,* 3.13). For more on this issue, see below, Book 2, 13, 18, and Book 3, 40. Also pertinent are Aristotle, *Politics,* 5.3.8 (1304b8–18); 5.8.22. (1313a5–10) and Cicero, *De officiis,* 1.13.41.

5. See chapter 17, n.2 for the intellectual tradition behind Machiavelli's choice of words here.

6. Foresight is an important characteristic of *uno prudente,* a prudent leader, "a wise man." Machiavelli says in *Prince,* 3 (p. 115, lines 175–195 and notes), that it characterized Roman policy.

7. Although political activity is the primary referent for "good" and "evil" here, these words suggest a moral dimension as well.

8. The perceived need for a strong leader in times of emergency is consistent in Machiavelli, though it is commonplace in "advice to prince" writings, the *de regimine*

principum tradition, from Xenophon, Plato, Aristotle, and Cicero through Aquinas, Dante, Egidio Colonna, and Marsilius of Padua into the Renaissance with writers like Philippus Beroaldus, Poggio Bracciolini, Erasmus, Thomas Elyot, and Giovanni Pontano.

9. For the examples mentioned in this sentence and the next, see the notes to chapter 9. There are some commentators who believe it was the kind of thinking at the end of this chapter that led Machiavelli to rethink his writing projects while in political exile. Preoccupied with thoughts of the kind of strong leadership necessary to guide a state moving from slavery to freedom, the general topics of the last three chapters, Machiavelli, they argue, abandoned the *Discourses,* wrote the *Prince,* and returned to the *Discourses* with a new topic, consideration of Rome's kings, which he would discuss in the next six chapters.

~ *19* ~

A WEAK RULER SUCCEEDING AN EXCELLENT ONE CAN HOLD ON, BUT A WEAK RULER WHO SUCCEEDS ANOTHER WEAK ONE CANNOT HOLD ANY KINGDOM

1 If we consider the *virtù* and procedures of Romulus, Numa, and Tullus, the first three Roman kings,[1] we can see that Rome enjoyed very great fortune in having its first king very fierce and warlike, the next peaceful and religious, and the third similar in fierceness to Romulus and fonder of war than of peace. 2 For Rome needed an organizer of civil society to emerge among her early rulers, but afterward there was an equal need for other kings to take up Romulus's *virtù* once again, otherwise the city would have become soft and a prey to its neighbors.[2] 3 It can therefore be observed that a successor who has less *virtù* than his predecessor can hold onto a government through the *virtù* that the previous ruler had and enjoy the fruits of his labors; but should it happen either that he lives a long life or that after him another does not come along to take up the *virtù* of the predecessor again, the kingdom is bound to fall. 4 Thus, conversely, if there are two rulers of great *virtù* one after another, it can often be seen that they accomplish very great things and their fame rises up to the heavens.

5 David was evidently quite a superior man in arms, learning, and judgment; and his *virtù* was so great that after he conquered and beat all his neighbors he left to his son, Solomon, a peaceful kingdom that he was able to keep by the arts of peace and not by war, and he was able to enjoy the fruits of his father's *virtù*. 6 But yet he was not able to leave it to his son, Rehoboam, who, because he was neither like his grandfather in *virtù* nor like his father in good fortune, barely managed to remain heir to the sixth part of his kingdom.[3] 7 Bayazid, the sultan of Turkey, although he was fonder of peace than of war, was able to enjoy the fruits of his father Mohammed's labors; since, like David, the latter had conquered his neighbors, he left Bayazid a stable kingdom that could easily be held with the arts of peace. 8 But if his son, Selim, the present ruler, had been like his father and not his grandfather, the kingdom would have fallen; but he can be seen to bid fair to surpass his

grandfather's glory.[4] 9 With these examples I say, therefore, that a weak prince who succeeds an excellent one can hold on but that a weak one who succeeds another weak one cannot hold any kingdom unless it was, like France, preserved by its ancient institutions. Princes who do not rely on war are weak ones.

10 I therefore conclude in this discourse that the *virtù* of Romulus was so great that it enabled Numa Pompilius to rule Rome for many years with the arts of peace; but after him came Tullus, who regained Romulus's prestige by his ferocity; after him came Ancus, so endowed by nature that he could practice peace and tolerate war.[5] 11 And at first he attempted to stick to the path of peace, but he quickly understood that his neighbors, who judged him to be soft, had little respect for him. So he realized that if he wanted to hold on to Rome he had to turn to war and be like Romulus, not Numa.

12 Let all princes who hold power take this as their example: whoever is like Numa will hold onto it or not according to how the times or Fortune turns under them;[6] but whoever is like Romulus, armed like him with wisdom and military might, will hold onto his power under any circumstances, unless some stubborn, overwhelming force robs him of it. 13 And we may certainly assume that if as its third king Rome had been granted a man who was unable to use the military to restore its prestige, then it would never, or only with very great difficulty, later have been able to gain a foothold or accomplish all it did. 14 Hence, as long as Rome lived under the kings, it ran the risk of falling under either a weak or a wicked king.

NOTES

1. Livy deals with this period in 1.4–31; specifically with Tullus Hostilius, the third king, in 1.22–31. See also Mansfield, *New Modes,* pp. 88–89.

2. Livy, 1.22.2.

3. For these biblical figures, see I Samuel, II Samuel, I Kings, I Chronicles, and II Chronicles; as for "remaining heir to the sixth part," see I Kings 12:16–19. Machiavelli praises Castruccio Castracani for pointing out that "whoever knows he is unsuited for war ought to strive to rule with the arts of peace."

4. Machiavelli refers to Bayazid, the sultan of the Ottoman Empire from 1481–1512; he was the son of Mohammed II (Mehemet), the Ottoman sultan from 1451 to 1481, who was known as the "Conqueror" because of his victory at Constantinople in 1453. Bayazid's son, Selim I, was the Ottoman sultan from 1512 to 1520. This fact may provide a *terminus a quo* and a *terminus ad quem* for the *Discourses.* Some argue that the immediacy of this passage indicates he may have been working on Book 1 in 1517.

5. Ancus Martius, Rome's fourth king; Livy mentions that his character was well balanced, with a touch of both Romulus and Numa in it (1.32.4). Machiavelli's next sentence is based on Livy, 1.32–35.

6. Later, in 3, 9, Machiavelli will again discuss the times and Fortune. The element of *virtù* is key in the wise, effective leader's ability to deal with Fortune. Although *virtù* is important here, Machiavelli's degree of emphasis on it varies from context to context; see especially his Letter to Giovan Battista Soderini of September 1506 (*Friends,* pp. 134–136 and notes), *Prince,* 25 (pp. 360–371 and notes), and below, Book 2, chapters 1, 29, and 30 (with their relevant notes).

~ 20 ~

TWO SUCCESSIVE REIGNS OF PRINCES OF *VIRTÙ* ACCOMPLISH GREAT THINGS; WELL-ORGANIZED REPUBLICS NECESSARILY HAVE SUCCESSIVE RULERS OF *VIRTÙ*, SO THEIR ACQUISITIONS AND EXPANSION ARE GREAT

1 Once Rome had expelled its kings, it avoided the dangers that, as stated above, it was prone to if either a weak or an evil king succeeded to the throne. 2 For the highest power was given to the consuls, who came to that power not by inheritance, deceit, or violent ambition, but by free suffrage, and they were always quite superior men: enjoying the fruits of their *virtù* and fortune, Rome was able little by little to arrive at its ultimate greatness in as many years as it had been under the kings.[1] 3 For we can see that two successive reigns of princes with *virtù* suffice to gain the world, as in the case of Philip of Macedon and Alexander the Great.[2] 4 All the more should a republic do so, since with its electoral procedures it has not only two successive reigns but countless princes of the greatest *virtù* succeeding one another: there will always be this kind of succession with *virtù* in any well-organized republic.

NOTES

1. According to Livy, Rome was ruled by kings for 244 years (1.60.3). Machiavelli's arithmetic has led many readers astray: 266 B.C. is a date prior to the Roman republic's pinnacle of greatness. Doubling it, we arrive at 22 B.C., when Rome had an extensive empire but had long since ceased to be a republic.

2. A reference to father and son: Philip of Macedon (382–336 B.C.) conquered Greece, Alexander the Great (356–323 B.C.) conquered the Persian Empire. Livy, 9.17–19, in chapters no longer considered a rhetorical digression, hypothesizes how Rome might have fared in a war with Alexander the Great.

~ 21 ~

HOW BLAMEWORTHY ARE A PRINCE AND A REPUBLIC THAT LACK THEIR OWN MILITARY FORCES

1 Contemporary princes and modern republics that lack their own soldiers for defense and offense ought to be ashamed of themselves[1] and, given the example of Tullus, consider that such a flaw results not from a lack of men suitable for military service but by their own fault, for not knowing how to turn their men into soldiers. 2 For when Tullus succeeded to the throne of Rome after it had been at peace for forty years, he found not one man who had ever been to war; nevertheless, when he made plans to go to war, he did not consider making use of either the Samnites, the Etruscans, or others who were accustomed to bearing arms but he decided, as a very prudent man, to

make use of his own people. 3 And such was his *virtù* that under his rule he was quickly able to make quite excellent soldiers of them.[2] 4 And it is truer than any other truth that if there are no soldiers where there are men it results from the prince's failing, not from some other failing of either location or nature.[3]

5 There is a quite recent example of this. 6 For everyone knows that a short while ago the king of England attacked the kingdom of France, and he took no other soldiers than his own people; and because his kingdom had gone more than thirty years without making war, it had neither soldiers nor a commander who had ever seen military service.[4] Nevertheless, with such men he was not afraid to attack a kingdom full of commanders and good armies, who had been continuously on active duty in the Italian wars. 7 This all resulted from the king's being a prudent man and his kingdom well organized, who does not discontinue military training in peacetime.

8 The Thebans Pelopidas and Epaminondas, when they had liberated Thebes and delivered it from its bondage to Spartan power, found themselves in a city accustomed to enslavement and amid an unmanly populace.[5] So great was their *virtù* that they did not fear to put the Thebans under arms and go with them to meet the Spartan armies in the field and defeat them; and the man who writes about this says[6] that these two leaders quickly showed that warriors were born not only in Sparta but everywhere else that men were born, as long as there was someone who knew how to train them for the military, as we can see Tullus knew how to train the Romans. 9 And this idea could not be expressed better than by Virgil, and he could not gotten closer to it in other words, than those where he says:

And Tullus will incite his idle men to arms.[7]

NOTES

1. A similar thought is expressed in similar language in the topic sentence of *Prince,* 12, a chapter of advice to a new prince concerning "various kinds of armies" and the dangers of "mercenaries."

2. Livy covers the career of Tullus Hostilius in 1.22–31.

3. Compare Machiavelli's *capitolo,* or epigram in tercets, *"Dell'ambizione,"* vv. 109–120.

4. In July 1513 Henry VIII, in league with the Holy Roman Emperor, Maximilian I, entered northeastern France and won the Battle of the Spurs on 16 August; the battle was so named because of the French army's hasty flight at Guinegate (Enguinegatie, in the Pas-de-Calais). When Machiavelli says England "had gone more than thirty years without making war," he is probably referring back to the victory of Henry Tudor, Henry VII, at the Battle of Bosworth Field in 1485, ending the War of the Roses. The English incursion into France to defend the independence of Brittany in 1491–1492 was not significant enough for Machiavelli to consider it a "war." See the letter to Vettori of 26 August 1513 (*Friends,* pp. 257–258).

5. On this example, see above 1, 6, n.10, and the battle of Leuctra in 379 B.C.; see also Sasso, *Antichi,* 2:407–408, n.41.

6. Although Machiavelli refers to Plutarch, *Pelopidas,* 17, the qualifier "as long as

there was someone who knew how to train them for the military" is Machiavelli's own judgment.

7. Quoted in Latin from the *Aeneid,* 6. vv. 813–814: *"residisque movebit / Tullus in arma viros."* Machiavelli replaces *residisque* with *desidesque;* although both words mean "idle," Inglese notes that the latter word may well come from Livy's usage working on Machiavelli's memory.

~ 22 ~

WHAT SHOULD BE NOTED IN THE CASE OF THE TRIO OF ROMAN HORATII AND THE TRIO OF ALBAN CURIATII

1 Tullus, the king of Rome, and Mettius, the king of Alba, agreed that the people whose trio of men mentioned above were victorious would be master over the others.[1] 2 All the Alban Curiatii were killed and one of the Roman Horatii survived; so Mettius, the Alban king, together with his people, became the Romans' subjects. 3 When that Horatius returned victorious to Rome, he encountered one of his sisters, betrothed to one of the three dead Curiatii, weeping for the death of her betrothed, and he slew her. 4 Consequently, that Horatius was brought to trial for this crime; after much dispute he was set free, more as a result of his father's pleas than for his own merits. 5 Three things should be noted here: first, one must never risk one's entire fortune with part of one's army; next, worthy actions never compensate for guilty ones in a well-organized city; third, that courses of action are never wise if one ought to have, or can have, doubts about their being honored. 6 Being subjugated is a matter of such consequence to a city that no one should ever believe that either of those kings or peoples would have been happy for three of their citizens to have made them subjects. This can be seen from what Mettius tried to do: although he admitted defeat and swore allegiance to Tullus immediately after the Roman's victory, nevertheless, during the first expedition that they agreed to undertake against the Veians, it can be seen he tried to deceive Tullus.[2] Mettius seemed to have realized too late the rashness of the action that he had taken. 7 And because this third topic of note has been discussed extensively, we shall speak only of the other two in the next two chapters.

NOTES

1. Livy, 1.23.4, says the Albans chose Mettius Fufetius as dictator, not king; for these events and the fight between the two sets of triplets, see Livy, 1.24–26.

2. The later deception of Mettius involved keeping his troops on the sidelines while the Romans attacked the Veians; Rome won the battle anyway and killed Mettius by tying him to two chariots driven in opposite directions so his body was pulled apart (Livy, 1.27–30). Machiavelli's neutral reaction to this punishment is not reflected in Livy, who remarks that such punishment "repudiates the laws of humanity" (1.28.11).

~ 23 ~

ONE SHOULD NEVER RISK ONE'S ENTIRE FORTUNE AND NOT ONE'S ENTIRE ARMY, SO DEFENDING PASSES IS OFTEN HARMFUL

1 It has never been deemed a wise course of action to place your entire fortune at risk and not your entire army. 2 This is done in several ways. 3 The first is to do like Tullus and Mettius when they committed their countries' entire fortune and the *virtù* of as many men as both had in their armies to the *virtù* and fortune of three of their citizens, which represented a very small fraction of each man's army. 4 And they did not realize that as a result of this course of action all the effort their predecessors had put into organizing the republic to keep it free for a long time and to make its citizens the defenders of their own freedom was almost in vain since the loss of freedom was in the power of so few. 5 Those kings could not have been more ill-advised in this matter.

6 People who plan on holding difficult positions and defending passes when the enemy is coming also almost always fall into this problem. For this decision will almost always be harmful unless you can conveniently keep your entire army in that difficult position. 7 In this case such a course of action should be taken; but if the place is rugged and you cannot keep your entire army there, it is a harmful course of action.[1] 8 I am led to believe this by the example of those who, attacked by a powerful enemy and with their region surrounded by mountains and steep places,[2] have never tried to fight the enemy up in the passes and the mountains but have gone to the other side of the mountains to encounter them; or when they did not want to do so, have waited for them within those mountains in favorable, not steep, places. 9 And the reason is the one already mentioned: since not many men can be brought in to guard mountainous places, both because they cannot live there for long and because the places are narrow and have room for very few men, it is not possible to withstand an enemy coming against you in force. And it is easy for the enemy to come in force because his intention is to pass through and not halt; it is impossible for someone to lie in wait in great numbers, since he must encamp there for a longer time, not knowing when the enemy will pass through, in places that are, as I have said, narrow and barren. 10 Thus when you lose the pass that you had expected to hold on to, and which both your people and your army had counted on, most of the time such terror seizes your people and the remainder of your troops that you are left the loser without being able to test their *virtù*. Thus you come to have lost your entire fortune with part of your army.

11 Everyone knows how hard it was for Hannibal to cross the Alps dividing Lombardy from France[3] and how hard it was for him to cross those dividing Lombardy from Tuscany;[4] nevertheless, the Romans waited for him, first along the Ticinus and then on the Arezzo plain, and they preferred to

have their army destroyed by the enemy in areas where there was some chance of winning, rather than take it up into the mountainous regions to be destroyed by the unfavorable site.

12 And anyone who reads all the histories judiciously will find that few commanders of *virtù* have attempted to hold such passes, both because of the stated reasons and because they could not all be closed, since in mountains as in open country there exist not only the customary, well-traveled routes but many others, which, though unknown to outsiders, are known to local inhabitants, with whose aid you will always be led to any spot against the will of your opponent. 13 A very recent example of this can be adduced: in 1515, when King Francis of France planned to cross into Italy to recapture the government of Lombardy, the principal argument made by those who were opposed to his campaign was that the Swiss would hold him back in the mountain passes.[5] 14 But as experience later showed, this argument of theirs turned out to be groundless: the king skirted two or three places that they were guarding and entered by another, unknown route; he was in Italy and upon them before they had realized it. 15 So they retreated into Milan in terror, and the entire population of Lombardy went over to the French, since they had been wrong in their belief that the French would be checked up in the mountains.[6]

NOTES

1. For many of the points made in this paragraph, see remarks in the *Art of War,* Books 4 and 7, as well as Machiavelli's letter to Francesco Vettori of 10 December 1514 (*Friends,* pp. 295–302 and notes).

2. Translates *luoghi alpestri;* the emphasis is on the wild, steep, precipitous nature of the terrain: alpine in that sense but not Alpine, the specific geographic designation soon to be discussed.

3. Livy, 21.32–38.

4. That is, the Apennines; see Livy 21.58. The Carthaginians defeated a Roman army under Publius Scipio at battles along the Ticinus and Trebia Rivers in 218 B.C. (Livy, 21.45–46; 54–56), and Hannibal again defeated a Roman army led by Gaius Flaminius near Lake Trasimeno "on the Arezzo plain" in 217 B.C. (Livy, 22.4–5).

5. Although Louis XII was obliged to forgo his designs on Italy, after his defeat at the Battle of Novara on 6 June 1513, Francis I sought to assert French claims to Milan; "those who were opposed to his campaign" included Pope Leo X, the king of Spain, the Holy Roman Emperor, Maximilian I, and the Swiss. Ignoring the passes held by the Swiss, Francis entered Italy with 35,000 troops through the Col d'Argentière between the Cottian and Maritime Alps; though it was hardly an "unknown route," military experts considered it too difficult for a large army to traverse. Francis drove the Swiss out of Italy after a fierce two-day battle at Marignano [Melegnano], near Milan, in September 1515. As above, 1, 19, n.4, Machiavelli's use of this "very recent example" helps us with a *terminus a quo* for this passage. Guicciardini covers these events in his *Storia d'Italia,* 12, 12–15.

6. Francesco Vettori alludes to the political situation behind these events in a letter to Machiavelli dated 3 December 1514. Because of Vettori's hint that Pope Leo X will see his analysis, Machiavelli responds with a long letter dated 10 December; see *Friends,* pp. 293–294; 295–302 (the topographical issues are discussed on p. 297).

~ 24 ~

WELL-ORGANIZED REPUBLICS ESTABLISH REWARDS AND PUNISHMENTS FOR THEIR CITIZENS AND NEVER OFFSET ONE WITH THE OTHER

1 The merits of Horatius were very great since he had defeated the Curiatii by his *virtù;* because he murdered his sister, his crime was heinous. Nevertheless, the Romans were so distressed by this murder that, despite the fact that his merits were so great and so recent, they brought him to trial for his life.[1] 2 To someone considering it superficially, this might seem to be an example of the people's ingratitude; nevertheless, anyone who examines it more closely and considers more deeply what the institutions of republics must be will blame people for acquitting him rather than for seeking to condemn him. 3 And the reason is that no well-organized republic ever canceled out its citizens' faults by their virtues. Once it has established rewards for good actions and punishments for bad ones and has rewarded someone for doing good, if that same person then does ill, it punishes him without any regard for his good actions. 4 And when these institutions are properly observed, a city remains free for a long time; otherwise, it will always soon collapse. 5 For if in addition to the glory that some outstanding service to the city brings him a citizen is given such boldness and confidence that he can do some bad action without fear of punishment, he will soon become so arrogant that all civic life will be destroyed.

6 Of course, if one wants to retain punishment for evil actions, it is necessary to keep rewards for good ones, as we can see Rome did. 7 And although a republic may be poor and able to give little, it must not refrain from giving that little: because every small gift given to someone as recompense for good actions, even if they are great, will always be considered honorable and very great by the recipient. 8 The story of Horatius Cocles is quite well known,[2] as is that of Mucius Scaevola:[3] how one held the enemy back at a bridge until it was cut down and the other burned the hand that had failed in trying to slay Porsenna, the king of the Etruscans. 9 To each of them for these outstanding actions, the people awarded two *staia* of land.[4] 10 The story of Manlius Capitolinus is also well known. 11 For having saved the Capitol from the Gauls who were encamped there he was awarded a small amount of flour by those who were besieged in it with him.[5] 12 In terms of the [economic] conditions[6] then current in Rome, that reward was considerable. It was such that later when Manlius, moved either by envy or by his evil nature, aroused sedition in Rome and sought to win over the people, no consideration whatever was given to his merits; he was hurled down from the very Capitol that he had saved earlier with so much glory to himself.

NOTES

1. Machiavelli returns here to an incident from chapter 22.

2. Livy tell this famous story of Roman virtue in 2.10–11.

3. Livy says in 2.12–13 that Porsenna spared the life of Mucius Scaevola ("the left-handed") because, when he was condemned to be burned alive for his assassination attempt, he unflinchingly held his right hand in the fire and lost the use of it.

4. Livy notes that Horatius Cocles was rewarded with a statue and "as much land as could be ploughed in a day" (2.10.12). For Livy's measure of area, Machiavelli substitutes a measure of volume, the *staio;* presumably Machiavelli is thinking of the amount of grain a specific amount of land could be expected to yield. Inglese notes that in Machiavelli's day a *staio* in Tuscany equalled the yield of about 1200 square meters, that is, roughly one-fourth of an acre. Mucius Scaevola, however, was rewarded with some land on the other side of the Tiber known as the Mucian Meadows *(Mucia Prata);* see Livy 2.13.5, and the discussion in Martelli, *Storici antichi,* p. 26.

5. See Guicciardini's *Consideration* of *Discourses,* 1, 5, n.2. The relevant chapters in Livy are 5.47 and, for the revolt and death of Manlius, 6.16–20.

6. Translates *fortuna;* Livy specifies that though the reward was small, the shortages and famine in Rome were then so great that it was a "huge token of affection" because people robbed themselves of necessities in order to honor Manlius Capitolinus (5.47.8). Machiavelli omits that Manlius also received a small portion of wine from the grateful populace.

~ 25 ~

ANYONE WHO WANTS TO REFORM AN OUTMODED GOVERNMENT IN A FREE CITY SHOULD RETAIN AT LEAST THE GHOST OF FORMER WAYS

1 Anyone who desires or wants to reform the government of a city, if it is to be acceptable and maintained to everyone's satisfaction, is forced to retain at least the ghost of its former ways so that people do not think the constitution has been altered, even if the new institutions are in fact completely different from those of the past.[1] For the majority of men cherish what seems to be as much as what is; in fact they are frequently more influenced by the way things seem to be than by the way they are.[2] 2 For this reason the Romans, who learned of this necessity from the beginnings of their free society, when they created two consuls in exchange for one king, did not let them have more than twelve lictors, in order not to surpass the number serving the kings.[3] 3 Furthermore, because Rome offered an annual sacrifice that could be made only by the king in person and because the Romans did not want their people to want for anything from the past through the absence of kings, they created someone called the "King for Sacrifices" to preside over that sacrifice and made him subordinate to the high Priest.[4] So in this way the people came to be satisfied with the sacrifice and never had cause to desire the return of the kings because of its absence. 4 And this must be observed by all those who want to eliminate a former way of life in a city and bring it to a new, free way of life: since

change disturbs men's minds, you must strive to make those changes retain as much as possible of the former ways; and if the magistrates differ in number, authority, and terms of office from the former ones, they should at least retain their names. 5 And this, as I have stated, must be observed by anyone who wishes to organize a political society, whether by way of a republic or a monarchy; but he who wishes to create an absolute power, which the authors[5] called "tyranny," must renew everything, as will be stated in the next chapter.

NOTES

1. Compare Machiavelli's remarks in *Prince,* 19, p. 313, lines 389–395.

2. Machiavelli returns to this point in *Discourses,* 1, 53. It occurs several times in the *Prince:* see the relevant passages at the end of chapters 15 and 18, p. 259, lines 56–60, and p. 285, lines 84–104.

3. Livy, 1.8.3. Romulus began the institution of the lictors to escort the king. As a sign of their authority, they carried *fasces,* bundles of rods with a protruding ax blade symbolizing life and death. These attendants were retained when consuls replaced the kings (Livy, 2.1.7–8). Our word "fascism" originates in this Latin word: the Italian nationalist party, organized in 1919 and exercising power through Mussolini from 1922, revived the symbol to represent its authority.

4. Livy discusses the *rex sacrificulus* in 2.2.1–2.

5. Translates *autori;* as in Dante, the word "author" refers to the authority of the Ancients. One obvious precedent for a discussion of tyranny would be Aristotle: see *Politics,* 3.5.5; 1279b16–20 and 4.8.1–3; 1295a1–24. See also Plato, *Republic,* 8.565e–566b; Polybius, 5.11.6; Cicero, *Republic,* 1.33; Aquinas, *On Kingship,* 1.1.11. Clearly the emphasis on tyranny is to draw attention to the fact that the ruler's self-interest, not the interests of the state, dominates a despotic tyranny. See also Sasso, *Antichi,* 2, pp. 437 ff., for Xenophon, *Hiero,* 4.11 and 7 as a source.

~ 26 ~

A NEW PRINCE IN A CITY OR A REGION[1] THAT HE HAS TAKEN MUST MAKE EVERYTHING NEW

1 If someone becomes prince either of a city or a state,[2] all the more so if his underpinnings are weak and he does not turn to civil life by way of either a monarchy or a republic, he must remake everything in the state, because that is his best prescription for holding on to the princedom since he is a new prince.[3] In cities that means making new governmental positions with new names, new powers, and new men; making the rich poor and the poor rich, as David did when he became king, "He hath filled the hungry with good things; and the rich he hath sent empty away."[4] In addition, it means building new cities, tearing down some already built, and moving inhabitants from one place to another; in sum, leaving nothing in the region intact and making certain that nothing in it—rank, office, position, or wealth—is held by anyone unless he acknowledges that he owes these thing to you.[5] He should take as

his model Philip of Macedon, Alexander's father, who by these methods became ruler of Greece from a petty king. 2 And those who write about him say that he moved men around from region to region as herdsmen move their herds.[6] 3 These are quite cruel methods, inimical to any society, not just Christian but human; any man ought to avoid them and prefer to live as a private citizen rather than as a king who causes men such ruin. Nevertheless, anyone who is unwilling to take the first path toward the good, should he wish to stay [in power], must enter on this evil path.[7] 4 But men take middle ways that are very dangerous, because they are unable to be either completely bad or completely good, as the next chapter will show through an example.[8]

NOTES

1. Translates *provincia* in this chapter.

2. Translates *stato* in an implied parallelism with *provincia* in the chapter title.

3. This point is also made in *Prince,* 6, p. 147, lines 66–72, and again in chapter 7, p. 157, lines 25–35. Contradicting what he says in the next sentence here, Machiavelli recommends in *Prince,* 9, that a new prince govern by himself and not through "governing magistrates" (p. 199, lines 120–129).

4. Quoted in Latin *(qui esurientes implevit bonis, et divites dimisit inanes)* from Mary's Magnificat, Luke 1:53. Machiavelli takes words originally referring to God and applies them to King David. They do bear a similarity, however, to David's words in Psalms 34:10 and 107:9 (Douay, 33:11; 106:9). See also Sasso, *Antichi,* 2:457–461; Mansfield, *New Modes,* pp. 99–100; and Martelli, *Storici antichi,* p. 27.

5. This may be the sentence that provokes Guicciardini's oft-quoted remark about Machiavelli in the last sentence of his *Consideration* of this chapter.

6. Although Machiavelli is referring primarily to Justin, 8.5.7, see also Polybius, 8.8–11 for his discussion of Philip of Macedon and whether he should be termed a tyrant.

7. For Machiavelli's famous distinction between "the good or bad use of ruthless measures," see *Prince,* 8, pp. 187, 189, lines 143–189.

8. For more on the "middle way," see above, 1, 6, sentence 35. Following a middle way is not actively confronting reality, a procedure that Machiavelli consistently recommends because "time does thrust everything forward and can produce good as well as bad, bad as well as good" (*Prince,* 3, p. 117, lines 206–208). See also Gilbert, "Florentine Political Assumptions."

~ 27 ~

MEN VERY RARELY KNOW HOW TO BE COMPLETELY BAD OR COMPLETELY GOOD

1 Because he had taken an oath[1] against all tyrants who ruled the Church's lands, Pope Julius II, when he went to Bologna in 1505 to expel from that state the house of Bentivoglio, which had held power in the city for a hundred years, also wanted to drive Giampaolo Baglioni out of Perugia, of which he was the tyrant.[2] 2 Arriving near Perugia with the courage and decisiveness well known to all, he did not wait to enter the city with his army to guard

him, but entered it unarmed, even though Giampaolo was inside it with many troops that he had assembled to defend himself. 3 So, borne on by that impetuousness with which he managed everything, he put himself in the hands of his enemy with merely his bodyguard; he then took Giampaolo off with him, leaving a governor in the city to administer justice[3] for the Church. 4 The pope's boldness and Giampaolo's cowardice were noted by wise men who were with the pope; they could not figure how it came about that the latter did not immediately crush his enemy, to his everlasting glory, and enrich himself with booty since accompanying the pope were all the cardinals with all their valuables. 5 And it could not be believed that Baglioni was restrained by goodness or conscience, because no pious respect could have descended into the breast of a lawless man who kept his sister for himself and had slain his cousins and nephews in order to rule. People concluded that it came about because men are not able to be honorably bad or perfectly good, and when a cunning deed has grandeur in it or is exalted to some extent, they do not know how to go about it.

6 Thus Giampaolo, who did not care if he was incestuous and publicly assassinated his relatives, was not able, or to put it better, did not dare, when he had a perfect opportunity for it, to undertake an action in which everyone would have admired his courage. It would have left an everlasting memorial for himself, since he would have been the first man to show prelates how little those who live and rule as they do are to be esteemed. He would have accomplished something whose grandeur would have overcome any opprobrium, any danger, that it might have incurred.

NOTES

1. Translates *aveva congiurato,* which could also mean "conspired."

2. In August 1506, not 1505, Julius II (Giuliano della Rovere), pope from 1503 to 1513, set out from Rome toward both Perugia, where the condottiere Giampaolo Baglioni ruled (from 1500 to 1506 and then again from 1513 to 1520), and Bologna, where the Bentivoglio family had ruled off and on since 1401 (its current ruler was Giovanni Bentivoglio). The pope may in fact have begun in 1505 his long, ultimately unsuccessful negotiations with France and also Venice to help him subdue the potentially rebellious princes of Romagna. Florence was clearly aware of the gathering storm clouds. Its Council of the Ten of War sent Machiavelli to Rome to report on the pope's activities in August 1506. Thus, he was one of the "wise men who were with the pope." His dispatches, contained in his second legation to the Court of Rome, offer an interesting commentary on the pope's machinations. The following judgment, written 13 September 1506, contradicts his remarks here about Baglioni: "Giampaolo . . . will do no evil to the man who has come to deprive him of his state . . . thanks to his good nature and human kindness" (*Legazioni e commissarie,* II, p. 980). His use of Julius II as an example is no more consistent, though Machiavelli consistently berates him for his impetuousness. In his *"Ghiribizzi"* letter to Giovan Battista Soderini, also written in September 1506, Machiavelli notes that "this pope obtains through chance—and disarmed—what ought to be difficult to attain even with organization and with weapons" (*Friends,* p. 135). See also Machiavelli's judgments in the *Prince:* on the one

hand, Julius "succeeded at all these undertakings and earned all the more praise because he did everything for the aggrandizement of the church, not for that of some individual" (11, p. 217, lines 81–84); on the other hand, he begins his analysis of Julius's career in *Prince,* 25 with the remark that he "used impetuous tactics in every one of his exploits" (p. 367, lines 91–92). As Inglese points out, "in his judgment of Della Rovere, Machiavelli alternates between recognition of his good fortune and disdain for someone who, as an 'ecclesiastical prince,' tramples on the 'laws' of politics [*Prince,* 11], claiming to be moved by a 'higher cause.' . . . One may then understand how much Machiavelli's intellectual annoyance was aggravated by his observation that the Pontiff's absurd pretension was encouraged and satisfied by his adversaries' moral and political mediocrity" (p. 240). Guicciardini recounts the pope's attack on Bologna in his *Storia d'Italia,* 7, 3; both his account and his judgments are similar to Machiavelli's.

3. Translates *ragione,* "reason."

~ 28 ~

HOW THE ROMANS WERE LESS UNGRATEFUL TOWARD THEIR CITIZENS THAN WERE THE ATHENIANS

1 Anyone who reads of the things done by republics will find in all of them some sort of ingratitude toward their citizens, but will find less of it in Rome than in Athens and perhaps any other republic. 2 And if we seek the reason for this, speaking of Rome and Athens, I believe it happened because the Romans had less reason to be suspicious of their citizens than the Athenians. 3 Because if we look at Rome from the expulsion of the kings until Sulla and Marius, freedom was never taken away by any of its citizens; so there was no great reason for it to be suspicious of them and, consequently, to offend them unintentionally.[1] 4 The opposite, however, occurred in Athens: after Pisistratus took its freedom away during its most flourishing period and under a pretense of goodness, when it once again regained its freedom and recalled both the wrongs it had received and its past servitude, it very quickly grew vindictive, not only for its citizens' faults but for any semblance of faults.[2] 5 This brought about the exile and death of many excellent men, as well as the ostracism rule and every other violence that Athens did to its aristocrats at various times.[3] 6 And what these writers say about politics[4] is quite true: that people bite back more fiercely after they have regained their freedom than when they have preserved it.[5] 7 So anyone who considers what has been said will neither accuse Athens nor praise Rome in this; rather, he will blame only necessity for the difference in the events that occurred in these cities. 8 Because if one considers things with discernment, one will see that if freedom had been taken away in Rome as in Athens Rome would not have been more merciful toward its citizens than the latter.[6] 9 We can make a very precise inference about this from what happened to Collatinus and Publius Valerius after the expulsion of the kings: the former, although he had taken part in freeing Rome, was sent into exile for no other reason than that of bearing the name of the Tarquins; the other, who had

merely created suspicion of himself by building a house on the Caelian hill, was also about to be sent into exile.[7] 10 Seeing how suspicious and severe Rome was toward these two, we may conclude that it would have acted ungratefully, like Athens, if, like Athens, it had been offended by its citizens during its early stages and before its expansion. 11 And in order not to have to go back over this question of ingratitude, I shall say what is necessary about it in the next chapter.

NOTES

1. The period in which the Roman republic, in his judgment, was not corrupt, though Machiavelli seems to have forgotten this sentence in his discussion of the Decemvirate (below, 1, 34–35; 40–45) and the tyrannical behavior of Appius; see especially 1, 40 below.

2. On Pisistratus, see 1, 2, n.17. For the "pretense of goodness," see Plutarch, *Solon,* 29.2–3. Thucydides discusses the increased sense of the "vindictive" in 3.43.

3. Ostracism was a punishment attributed to Cleisthenes: see above, 1, 2, note 17; it involved the popular assembly's voting banishment on fragments of terra-cotta called *ostrakon*.

4. Translates *civilità,* "civil life" or "society."

5. Cicero, *De officiis,* 2.7.24; Machiavelli also uses this axiom in his discussion of the final days of the duke of Athens in Florence in 1343; *Florentine Histories,* 2, 37.

6. Machiavelli repeats this idea in his *capitolo "Dell' ingratitudine,"* vv. 130–132. This entire poem is relevant to his discussion here and in the following chapters (29–32).

7. Livy discusses these events in 2.2 and again in 2.7; Collatinus and Brutus helped found the Roman republic by leading a revolt against Tarquinius Superbus. They became the first two consuls, but Brutus persuaded Collatinus to go into voluntary exile (2.2.7) because he was a Tarquin. Publius Valerius, surnamed Publicola, "the people's friend," was elected to succeed Brutus; see below, 1, 32, n.2. People believed he intended to turn the "house" into "an impregnable citadel"; it was on the Velian, not the Caelian, Hill (2.7.6).

~ 29 ~

WHICH IS MORE UNGRATEFUL, THE PEOPLE OR A PRINCE?

1 Concerning the subject mentioned above, it seems relevant to me to discuss which offers greater examples of ingratitude, the people or a prince. 2 And the better to discuss this question, I shall state that the vice of ingratitude arises from either avarice or suspicion.[1] 3 Because when either the people or a prince have sent one of their commanders out on an important mission in which the commander, if he has won, has achieved considerable glory, the prince or the people are expected to reward him in return. And if instead of a reward they are so motivated by avarice as to dishonor or offend the commander, since their desire for gain prevents them from satisfying him, then they are making an inexcusable mistake; indeed, they go down through eternity with

disgrace. 4 Yet there are many princes who commit this error; Tacitus states the reason with this maxim: "It is easier to pay back an insult than a favor, because gratitude is considered a burden and vengeance a profit."[2] 5 But when they do not reward him, or to state it better, they offend him, motivated not by avarice but by suspicion, then both the people and the prince rate some excuse.

6 And we read about a great many instances of ingratitude arising from this cause: because a commander who has conquered territory for his prince by his *virtù,* overcoming the enemy and covering himself with glory and his soldiers with riches, of necessity acquires such great prestige both with his soldiers and the enemy, as well as with the prince's own subjects, that his victory cannot taste good to the lord who has sent him. 7 And because man by nature is ambitious and suspicious and incapable of setting limits to any good Fortune, it is impossible for the suspicion that immediately arises in a prince after his commander's victory not to be increased through some arrogance of manner or speech shown by the man himself. 8 So the prince cannot think of anything but protecting himself against his commander: to do so, he considers either putting him to death or depriving him of the prestige he has earned for himself among his army or the people and showing as energetically as possible that the victory resulted not from the commander's *virtù* but from Fortune or the enemy's cowardice or the wisdom of the other leaders who were with him during the military action.

9 When Vespasian was in Judea and was proclaimed emperor by his army, Antonius Primus, who was in Illyria with another army, sided with him and came from there to Italy against Vitellius, who was ruling in Rome; with a great deal of *virtù* Antonius defeated two of Vitellius's armies and took Rome. So Mucianus, dispatched by Vespasian, found everything done and all difficulties overcome thanks to Antonius's *virtù.* 10 The reward that Antonius received for it was that Mucianus promptly stripped him of his military command and gradually deprived him of all his power in Rome. So Antonius went off to find Vespasian, who was still in Asia, and was received by him in such a manner that within a short time, deprived of all rank, he died almost in despair.[3] 11 And histories are full of such examples. 12 In our own times, everyone now living knows how energetically and with what *virtù* Gonzalo Fernández, campaigning for Ferdinand, the king of Aragon against the French in the kingdom of Naples, conquered and won the kingdom; and the reward he received for his victory was that Ferdinand left Aragon and, coming to Naples, first stripped him of his military command, then his fortresses, and after that took him back with him to Spain, where he died without honor a short while later.[4] 13 So this suspicion is so natural to princes that they cannot help it; and it is impossible for them to show gratitude toward those who have made great conquests by their victory under their banners.

14 And it is no miracle nor anything particularly remarkable if the people cannot help what a prince cannot help. 15 Because a city that lives free has two aims, one conquest, the other to remain free, it is bound to err in both these matters through excess of passion. 16 Concerning errors in conquest, they will be spoken of in their place.[5] 17 Concerning errors in remaining free,

they are, among others: offending citizens whom it should reward; being suspicious of citizens in whom it should trust. 18 Although these conditions produce great evils in a republic that has fallen into corruption and often lead it rather to tyranny, as happened in Rome when Caesar took by force what ingratitude denied him,[6] nevertheless, they are a source of great benefits in an uncorrupted republic and allow it to live free since men remain better and less ambitious because they fear punishment.

19 It is true that among all peoples that have ever held power Rome was the least ungrateful, for the reasons discussed above;[7] because one may say that there is no other example of its ingratitude than that of Scipio, since Coriolanus and Camillus were exiled because of the harm that both of them had done to the Plebs. 20 One[8] was not forgiven because he had always maintained a hostile attitude toward the people; the other was not only recalled but venerated as a prince throughout the rest of his life.[9] 21 But the ingratitude shown toward Scipio arose from a suspicion that the citizens began to feel for him that had not been felt toward the others: it arose from the greatness of the enemy that Scipio had defeated, the prestige given him by his victory in so long and perilous a war, the swiftness of that victory, and the goodwill that youth, prudence, and his other memorable qualities of *virtù* gained for him.[10] 22 These things were such that, if for nothing else, the public officials of Rome feared his authority, which wise men disliked as something to which Rome was unaccustomed. 23 And his life seemed so extraordinary that Cato Priscus, considered a holy man, was the first to oppose him and say that a city could not be called free when there was a citizen in it who was feared by the public officials. 24 So, if in this example the people of Rome accepted the opinion of Cato, they deserve the excuse that, as I have said above, is deserved by people and princes who are ungrateful out of suspicion. 25 So to conclude this discourse, I say that because this vice of ingratitude is practiced out of either avarice or suspicion, the people obviously never practice it out of avarice; they do so out of suspicion much less than princes[11] since they have less reason for suspicion, as will be stated below.[12]

NOTES

1. Machiavelli provides the same origin for ingratitude in *"Dell'ingratitudine,"* v. 25 ("the daughter of *Avarizia e di Sospetto*"). It should also be pointed out that the poem, contrary to what he says in this chapter, argues that the people provide "greater examples of ingratitude" than do princes, although vv. 166–167 say that "there are few grateful princes . . . in the world." See especially vv. 61–63 and note 11 below.

2. Quoted in Latin from Tacitus, *Histories,* 4.3.2: *[Tanto] proclivius est iniuriae quam beneficio vicem exsolvere, quia gratia oneri, ultio in questu habetur.* The context refers to the fall of Vitellius and rise of Vespasian discussed in the next paragraph.

3. In A.D. 69 the eastern legions of the Roman army in Syria, Judea, and Egypt elected Vespasian emperor, a title he retained until his death in 79. Antonius Primus was in Pannonia, an area roughly equivalent to modern-day Hungary, Slavonia, and Bosnia; though the inhabitants were considered Illyrians, Illyria was farther south in an area along the Dalmatian coast including modern-day Albania. Antonius's victories over "two of Vitellius's armies" occurred at Bedriaco in the Po River valley near

Cremona and at Terni, about sixty miles north of Rome. Except for the death of Antonius Primus, about which we know very little, the source for this material is Tacitus, *Histories,* 2.79–80, 86; 3.2–3, 15–26, 46–49, 58–63, 78; 4.39; 80; see Martelli, *Storici antichi,* pp. 28–29. In fact, Guicciardini's remarks in his *Consideration* of this material are closer to Tacitus's account than are Machiavelli's.

4. Gonzalo Fernández de Córdoba, 1435–1515, known as "The Great Captain," commanded the Spanish army in Italy from 1500 to 1507 and asserted the claims of "Ferdinand the Catholic," king of Spain from 1479 to 1516. The king arrived in Italy in October 1506 and returned home with Gonzalo in June 1507. Although Machiavelli consistently uses Gonzalo as an example of ingratitude (see *"Dell'ingratitudine,"* vv. 163–165), Guicciardini believes Gonzalo is an inappropriate example because, in fact, he did die with renown and wealth; see *Consideration* of this chapter, sentence 12, and *Storia d'Italia,* 7, 2 and 8; 12, 19.

5. In chapter 30 (the next one); see also below, 2, 3–4.

6. Machiavelli is referring to the onset of Caesar's civil war with Pompey in 49 B.C.: prior to crossing the Rubicon, he seized Ariminum, the modern-day Rimini. On the Adriatic, at the junction of the ancient Via Aemilia and Via Flaminia, it controlled access to Cisalpine Gaul, the fertile region between the Apennines and the Alps. The Rubicon enters the Adriatic about ten miles north of Rimini. For a similar statement about Caesar, see *"Dell'ingratitudine,"* vv. 151–156. Both examples are based on Plutarch, *Julius Caesar,* 29, 32, 46–47.

7. In the preceding chapter (28).

8. That is, Coriolanus; see above, 1, 7, n.3. The people believed that Coriolanus was against them because he proposed withholding their grain supply until they agreed with him; they impeached and banished him for his "ingratitude." In turn, he joined their enemies, the Volscians. See Livy, 2.33–35.

9. That is, Marcus Furius Camillus, who is sometimes regarded as the city's second founder because he led an army against the invading Gauls and saved Rome (387–386 B.C.). But earlier in his career, after his victories over the Veians, his policies and behavior caused resentment among the tribunes of the plebeians; they forced him into exile (Livy, 5.23–26; 29; 32.8–9; 46; 49). Nevertheless, when the Gauls threatened Rome in 390 B.C., he was recalled and was victorious.

10. "The greatness of the enemy" was no less than that of Hannibal at the battle of Zama in 202 B.C., for which Publius Cornelius Scipio was named "Africanus." Jealous tribunes accused him of expropriating the spoils of war, though they were primarily afraid of his popularity. Marcus Porcius Cato (234–149 B.C.), known both as "the Censor" and "the Elder," was Scipio's lifelong enemy; politically, the two sides were the aristocrats, who sided with Scipio, and the small landowners, who sided with Cato. Martelli, *Storici antichi,* p. 30, observes that the source for the indirect quotation attributed to Cato in sentence 23 has yet to be found. See Livy, 26.19 and 38.50–60. Machiavelli devotes nineteen tercets to Scipio in *"Dell'ingratitudine,"* vv. 73–129.

11. Ingratitude "triumphs in every ruler's heart, but it thrives in the hearts of the people whenever it holds sway"; *"Dell'ingratitudine,"* vv. 61–63; see note 1 to this chapter.

12. Both in the next chapter and in 1, 58.

~ 30 ~

THE MEANS A PRINCE OR A REPUBLIC SHOULD USE TO AVOID THIS VICE OF INGRATITUDE AND THE ONES COMMANDERS OR CITIZENS SHOULD USE SO AS NOT TO BE TROUBLED BY IT

1 To avoid the need to have to live under suspicion or to be ungrateful, a prince should go on campaigns in person, as the Roman emperors did at first, as the Turk does in our times, and as those who have *virtù* have done and continue to do.[1] 2 For the glory and conquest are all theirs if they win; when they are not there they do not believe they can make use of that conquest, since the glory is someone else's, unless they obliterate the other person's glory, which they were unable to win for themselves. They become ungrateful and unjust; their loss is unquestionably greater than their gain. 3 But when they remain home at their leisure and send a commander, either through negligence or lack of wisdom, I have no advice to give them except what they themselves know.

4 But I do say to the commander, since I deem that he cannot escape the pangs of ingratitude, that he should do one of two things. Either he should leave the army right after the victory and place himself in the hands of his prince,[2] avoiding any arrogant or ambitious gesture so that the latter, relieved of any suspicion, has cause either to reward him or not to harm him. Or else, if the commander does not think this should be done, he should courageously choose the opposite course and do everything possible to have the conquest thought of as his own and not that of his prince: he should make the soldiers and subjects favorable to him, form new alliances with his neighbors, seize fortresses with his men, bribe the leaders of his army, and secure himself against those he is unable to bribe. By these means he should try to punish his lord for any ingratitude that he may show him. 5 There are no other ways; but as was said above, men do not know how to be either completely wicked or completely good.[3] 6 And it always happens that commanders have no wish to leave the army right after a victory, they cannot behave modestly, and they do not know how to use violent measures that have something honorable in themselves; so, remaining ambivalent, they are crushed within their hesitation and ambivalence.

7 As for a republic that wishes to avoid this vice of ingratitude, it cannot be given the same remedy as the prince: that is, to go [in person][4] and not send someone on its campaigns, since it has to send one of its citizens. 8 The remedy I must give it is that it should hold to the same methods the Roman republic used to be less ungrateful than other republics. 9 This arose from its methods of government: since the entire city was used in wartime, both Nobles and commoners, in every age so many men of *virtù* appeared, honored with so many victories, that the people had no reason to fear any of them, because there were so many of them and each guarded one against the others. 10 And they remained so full of integrity and so scrupulous not to show any trace of ambition or cause for the people to attack them for their ambition that, if one of

them came to dictatorship, the sooner he gave it up the greater the glory he received.[5] 11 And thus, because such ways could not breed suspicion, they did not breed ingratitude. 12 So a republic that does not want to have reason to show ingratitude should govern itself like Rome, and a citizen who wants to avoid its pangs should observe the measures observed by Roman citizens.

NOTES

1. A principle enunciated in the opening words of *Prince,* 14 (p. 247, lines 1–9). See also *Prince,* 12, in the context of a prince exercising control over his army: "a prince ought personally to go and perform the duty of a general," p. 223, lines 59–61. For "the Turk," see above, 1, 19, n.4: Selim I. Rinaldi draws attention to Mansfield, *New Modes,* p. 196, for the rare moral use of "ungrateful and unjust" at the end of the next sentence.

2. Inglese notes that this point might be based on Tacitus, *Agricola,* 40.

3. Above, 1, 27, but see 1, 26, n.8, on "middle ways," none of which is recommended here.

4. Translators' emendation.

5. Lucius Quinctius Cincinnatus, the first dictator to resign his office, was the most beloved for his decision; he did so after sixteen days in office: Livy, 3.29.7. Others whom Livy mentions are Quintus Servilius Priscus, who resigned after eight days (4.47.6), and Titus Quinctius Cincinnatus, who resigned after twenty days (6.29.10). See also Livy, 23.23 (Rinaldi).

~ *31* ~

ROMAN GENERALS WERE NEVER PUNISHED EXCESSIVELY FOR MISTAKES THEY COMMITTED; NOR WERE THEY EVER PUNISHED FOR HARM TO THE REPUBLIC THAT RESULTED FROM THEIR IGNORANCE OR POOR CHOICE OF ACTIONS

1 As we discussed above,[1] not only were the Romans less ungrateful than other republics, but they were also more merciful and more cautious than any other [republic][2] in punishing their military commanders. 2 For if their mistake had been from malice, they were chastised humanely; if it was out of ignorance, not only were they not punished but they were rewarded and honored. 3 This policy was well considered by them, because they deemed that it was of such great importance for those who commanded their armies to have their minds free and untrammeled, with no other outside concerns in deciding on courses of action that they did not wish to add new difficulties and dangers to something difficult and dangerous in itself, since they thought that if they did add them no one would ever be able to act with *virtù.* 4 Take for example the army they sent to Greece against Philip of Macedon[3] or in Italy against Hannibal or the peoples they conquered earlier: the commander in charge of this expedition was anxious about all the concerns involved in those matters, which are weighty and quite important. 5 Now if to such concerns

had been added several examples of the Romans' having crucified or killed otherwise those who had lost battles, it would have been impossible amid so much mistrust for a commander to deliberate vigorously.[4] 6 Hence, deeming that the ignominy of losing was a considerable penalty for such men, they did not wish to flummox them with some other greater penalty.

7 Here is an example of a mistake not committed out of ignorance. 8 Sergius and Virginius were encamped at Veii, each in charge of part of the army: Sergius was facing the direction from which the Etruscans might come and Virginius the other way.[5] 9 It so happened that when the Faliscans and some other tribes attacked Sergius he allowed himself to be defeated and put to flight before sending for help from Virginius. 10 And on the other side, Virginius, expecting Sergius to be humiliated, was willing to see his country dishonored and the army destroyed rather than come to his aid. 11 A truly bad and noteworthy example, one promising no good for the Roman republic if either of them were not punished. 12 It is true that, whereas any other republic would have given them the death penalty, it penalized them monetarily.[6] 13 This happened not because their offenses did not deserve greater punishment but because, for the reasons already mentioned, the Romans wanted to adhere to their ancient customs in this case.

14 As for mistakes due to ignorance, there is no finer example than that of Varro, through whose rashness Hannibal defeated the Romans at Cannae, so the republic was in danger of losing its freedom.[7] Nevertheless, because it was out of ignorance and not malice, not only did the Romans not punish him but they honored him; and upon his return to Rome everyone of senatorial rank went out to greet him: since they could not thank him for the battle, they thanked him for returning to Rome and not despairing of Rome's situation. 15 When Papirius Cursor wanted to have Fabius killed for fighting with the Samnites against his orders, among the other reasons Fabius's father cited against the dictator's insistence was that the Roman people had never done on the occasion of any loss by its generals what Papirius wanted to do in victory.[8]

NOTES

1. In chapter 28.

2. Translators' emendation.

3. Philip V (238–179 B.C.), king of Macedon; specifically, the Second Macedonian War, which began in 200 and ended with his defeat at Cynoscephalae in 197. A peace treaty was agreed to in 196.

4. Polybius mentions the crucifixion of Carthaginian generals (1.11.5); this was not the Roman practice.

5. Manius Sergius and Lucius Virginius were appointed consular tribunes in 402 B.C.: see Livy, 5.8–12. Livy refers to two Etruscan tribes bordering on the Veians, the Faliscans and Capenates, in 5.8.5–6.

6. Based on Livy, 8.33.17. Rinaldi, based on Gilbert, notes that most of the chapters in this section of Machiavelli's Book 1, chapters 25 to 37, comment on the second

book of Livy; he suggests that, since this chapter refers to events in later books of Livy, it was perhaps added to the sequence at a later date.

7. Caius Terentius Varro served jointly with Lucius Aemilius Paulus as consul in 216 B.C. They commanded on alternate days; Varro rashly decided to attack Hannibal and was defeated at Cannae. Paulus was killed, but Varro regrouped the survivors and won the admiration of the Roman people (Livy, 22.61).

8. Based on Livy, 8.30–35, this illustration is from the Second Samnite War (326–304 B.C.). Quintus Fabius Maximus Rullianus was Master of the Horse under the dictator Lucius Papirius Cursor. Disobeying the latter's orders not to fight, Fabius attacked the Samnites and won the battle of Imbrinium in 325. Papirius arraigned Fabius before the Senate; the father's speech gained the son's pardon.

~ *32* ~

A REPUBLIC OR A PRINCE SHOULD NOT POSTPONE CONFERRING FAVORS ON MEN UNTIL HE NEEDS THEM

1 Admittedly, the Romans were successful in being generous to the people just as danger was imminent, when Porsenna attacked Rome to restore the Tarquins and the Senate (fearing the Plebeians might accept the kings rather than support the war) tried to make sure of them by lifting the salt excise and all other taxes, stating that the poor acted in the public behalf by feeding their children and that for this benefit the people should risk enduring siege, famine, and war.[1] But no one, trusting in this example, should postpone winning over the people until periods of danger, because what worked for the Romans will never work for him. 2 For the masses will deem they have gotten that favor not from you but from your enemies; and since they must fear that once the need is past you will take away what you have been forced to grant them, they will feel no obligation to you. 3 The reason why this course of action turned out well for the Romans was that the government was new and not yet stabilized. The people had seen that laws had already been enacted in favor of them; for example, one for appeal to the Plebs,[2] so they might believe that this favor had been granted them not so much because of the arrival of the enemy as because of the Senate's predisposition to favor them. 4 Furthermore, their memory of the kings, who had vilified and insulted them in many ways, was fresh.[3] 5 And because such causes rarely occur, such remedies will rarely turn out to be effective. 6 Therefore anyone who wields power, whether a republic or a prince, should consider beforehand what bad times may beset him and then what men he may need in those adverse times; then he should deal with them in the way he judges he would have to deal with them should any emergency arise. 7 And someone who behaves otherwise—either a prince or a republic, but especially a prince—and then believes that he will win men back to himself with favors once danger arises, is fooling himself: because he not only does not make sure of them, but he hastens his downfall.

NOTES

1. See Livy, 2.9.5–7. But Livy says that the government, rather than "lifting" the salt tax, took over its imposition (Martelli, *Storici antichi,* p. 30).

2. The law known as *provocatio* permitted an appeal to the people against sentences handed down by Roman public officials (Livy, 2.8.1–2). It was urged by Publius Valerius and was one of the reforms that won him the name Publicola, "the people's friend"; see above, 1, 28, n.7.

3. Machiavelli is probably thinking of Tarquinius Superbus, driven from power only two years prior to this law.

~ 33 ~

WHEN A PROBLEM HAS DEVELOPED EITHER WITHIN A STATE OR AGAINST IT, IT IS SAFER TO DELAY THAN TO MEET IT HEAD-ON

1 As the Roman republic grew in prestige, armed forces, and dominion, its neighbors, who had not thought at first how much harm the new republic could cause them, began too late to realize their mistake. In an attempt to remedy what they had not remedied earlier, some forty tribes banded together in a league against Rome.[1] Therefore the Romans, along with other remedies they were wont to use during pressing dangers, turned to naming a Dictator; that is, to giving one man power to make decisions without consultation and to execute his decisions without any appeal. 2 This remedy proved useful then and was the reason the Romans overcame their imminent dangers, and it also proved to be quite useful in all the events that threatened the republic at any time during the growth of its dominion.

3 The first thing to discuss about this event is how, whenever a problem arises, either within a republic or against it, from an internal or external cause, and has grown so great that it begins to alarm everyone, it is much safer to delay than to try to eliminate it. 4 For almost always those who try to reduce its strength increase it instead, and they speed up the trouble they feared from it. 5 And in a republic, events like this arise much more often from internal than from external causes. Very often either a citizen has been allowed to acquire more power than is reasonable or corruption begins to affect a law that is the vital source of freedom; and this error is allowed to persist until it is more dangerous to try to remedy it than to let it go on. 6 And it is all the more difficult to recognize these problems at their inception, because it always seems more natural for men to support things in the beginning; more than in anything else, such support can be for actions that seem in themselves to have some *virtù* and are done by young people. 7 Because if in a republic a young Noble who has in himself extraordinary *virtù* is seen to emerge, the eyes of all the citizens begin to turn toward him and they concur in honoring him without reservation. So if he has any ambition, combining the advantages given him by nature and this event, it soon gets to the point

where, when the citizens realize their mistake, they have few remedies for avoiding it. When they try to use the remedies they have, they do nothing but speed his power up.

8 Other examples of this could be cited, but I wish to give only one, concerning our own city. 9 Cosimo de' Medici, the man who initiated the greatness of the house of Medici in our city, attained such great prestige from support based on his wisdom and the other citizens' ignorance that he began to alarm the government, so the other citizens considered it dangerous to offend him and extremely dangerous to let him remain thus.[2] 10 But in those days there lived Niccolò da Uzzano, who was considered a very experienced man in civil matters. Because they had committed the first mistake of not recognizing the dangers that could stem from Cosimo's prestige, he saw to it that as long as he lived no one ever committed a second one: to try and do away with him. He deemed that such an attempt would lead to the utter downfall of their government. That actually happened after his death, since the citizens who remained did not heed his advice, rose up against Cosimo, and drove him from Florence. 11 Hence it came about that Cosimo's faction, resenting this insult, recalled him a while later and made him prince of the republic, a rank to which he would never have been able to rise without such open opposition.

12 The same thing happened in Rome with Caesar, whose *virtù* was supported by Pompey and the others; their support soon turned into fear. Cicero testifies to this, saying that Pompey began too late to fear Caesar.[3] 13 Fear made them look for remedies, and the remedies they used hastened their republic's downfall.

14 Therefore I say that because it is difficult to recognize these evils when they arise, this difficulty resulting from the way such matters fool you at the outset, to delay once they are recognized is a wiser course of action than to attack them: if one delays, either they go away by themselves or at least the evil is postponed for a longer time. 15 And in all things, princes who plan either to eliminate such evils or to oppose their force and impetus must keep their eyes open so as not to increase rather than lessen them and to drag something along with them in the belief that they are pushing it away—as it were, to drown a plant by watering it. 16 But the strength of the illness must be considered carefully: when you feel able to cure it, you must set about doing so mercilessly; otherwise, let it be and do not attempt it under any circumstances.[4] 17 Because what happened to Rome's neighbors would happen, as has been discussed above, once Rome had attained such power, it would have been healthier for her neighbors to try to appease the city and hold it back with peaceful means rather than to make Rome consider new institutions and new defenses by warlike means.[5] 18 For their banding together into a league produced nothing but a more united, more vigorous Rome, devising new methods by which it increased its power within a shorter time. 19 Among these was the creation of the Dictator, a new institution that enabled Rome not only to overcome impending dangers but also to avoid the countless ills that the republic would have encountered without this remedy.

NOTES

1. Livy, 2.18.3 mentions thirty tribes that formed the Latin League against Rome. As the threat of war with them increased, Rome turned to the institution of the dictatorship around 501 B.C. Livy names Titus Lartius as the first of these (2.18.5). See the discussion in Martelli, *Storici antichi,* pp. 31–32.

2. The following example, during a war with Lucca in 1433, is covered in *Florentine Histories,* 4, 26–33; for more on Cosimo de Medici (1389–1464), see *Florentine Histories,* 7, 4. An oligarchic group, in which Niccolò da Uzzano and Rinaldo degli Albizzi were powerful, opposed the virtual one-man control that Cosimo exercised over the city. Niccolò broke with his faction and supported Cosimo but died in 1432 before he could persuade the city not to banish him. Rinaldo quickly succeeded in persuading them to do so in October 1433. Within a year Cosimo was recalled and ruled Florence single-handedly as "prince of the republic" until his death. Rinaldi suggests that perhaps Machiavelli also had in mind a contemporary example, that of Soderini and the constant threat of a Medici return, which did occur in 1512.

3. Cicero, *Letters to His Friends,* 16.11.

4. The use of a medical metaphor to express the need for foresight is typical of the *de regimine principum* tradition; it can also be found in Cicero and Seneca. For its use in *Prince,* see 3, p. 115, lines 179–187 and notes.

5. Walker (Machiavelli, *Discourses*), 2, pp. 62–63, points out that Machiavelli seems to be referring to the events specified in note 1 to this chapter, a period when Rome had not "attained such power" that it would have been advisable for the Latin League to temporize. Walker believes that Machiavelli is confusing this situation with the Great Latin War of 340–338 B.C.; Livy, 8.1–11.

~ *34* ~

DICTATORIAL POWER DID MORE GOOD THAN HARM TO THE ROMAN REPUBLIC; THE POWERS THAT CITIZENS TAKE UPON THEMSELVES ARE DANGEROUS FOR CIVIL LIFE, NOT THOSE GIVEN THEM BY PEOPLE VOTING FREELY AND PUBLICLY

1 Some writers have condemned the Romans who found a way to create a Dictator in the city as causing Rome's tyranny with passing time. They claim that the first tyrant in the city ruled it under the title of Dictator and say that had it not been for this Caesar would not have been able to legitimate his tyranny under any public title.[1] 2 This matter was not well considered by the man who holds this opinion; and it was believed against all reason. 3 For it was not the title or the rank of Dictator that subjugated Rome but the power that citizens usurped through the length of command. Had Rome not had the title of Dictator, they would have taken another one, because power easily acquires titles, not the converse. 4 And it is apparent that as long as the Dictatorship was granted in accordance with public institutions and not by his own

power it always did the city good.[2] 5 Because republics are harmed not by power that comes by normal means but by public officials who are created and by power that is granted by extraordinary means. This is apparent from what happened in Rome over so long a period of time when no Dictator ever did anything but good for the republic.

6 There are quite obvious reasons for this. 7 First, for it to be possible for a citizen to oppress and to seize extraordinary power, he has to have many qualities that he can never have in an uncorrupted republic: he has to be very rich and have a large number of adherents and partisans, which he cannot have wherever the laws are observed. Even if he did, such men are so threatening that people voting freely do not choose them. 8 Furthermore, the Dictator was named for a limited term, not for life, and only to remove the cause for which he had been created. His power included the ability to decide on his own about the remedies for that urgent danger, to act on all matters without consultation, and to punish anyone without appeal.[3] But he could not do anything to weaken the government, as it would have been to take power away from the Senate or the People, to abolish the age-old institutions of the city, and to make new ones. 9 So, taking together the brief duration of his Dictatorship and his limited authority, with the Roman people not being corrupted, it was impossible for him to exceed his limits and harm the city. Experience shows that he was always effective.

10 And certainly, of all Rome's institutions, the Dictatorship is one that deserves to be considered and counted among the ones that led to the greatness of its power, for without such an institution cities will have difficulty getting out of extraordinary events. 11 Because a republic's customary institutions function slowly: no council or public official can run everything by itself; in many matters one needs the other. It takes time to reconcile their wills, so their remedies are very dangerous when they have to deal with something that cannot wait. 12 And that is why republics must have some such means among their institutions. The Venetian republic, which excels among modern republics, has set aside powers for a few citizens who, in times of urgent need and without broader consultation, can make decisions unanimously.[4] 13 When a republic lacks such means, it is necessary for it either to collapse in observing the constitution or to break with it in order not to collapse. 14 And in a republic nothing should ever occur that has to be dealt with by extraordinary means. 15 Because, although the extraordinary means may work well then, the example does harm nevertheless: people become accustomed to breaking laws for a good purpose and then under that pretext they are broken for ill. 16 So a republic will never be perfect unless its laws have provided for everything and supplied a remedy for any event and prescribed means for applying it. 17 And therefore I say in conclusion: those republics that in cases of urgent danger do not have recourse either to a Dictator or to some such power will always collapse under serious events.

18 Concerning this new institution, we should note how wisely the Romans provided for choosing him. 19 Creating a Dictator was embarrassing for the Consuls because they too had to submit to authority, like others, even though they had been the city's leaders. Because it was assumed that this

might cause scorn among the citizens, they decided that the power to choose him should be in the hands of the Consuls. It was thought that when events arose such that Rome needed this monarchical power they would appoint the Dictator willingly: since they themselves did it, it would cause them less pain. 20 Wounds and any other harm that a man does to himself spontaneously and by choice hurt far less than those done you by someone else. 21 Admittedly, during the final days the Romans were wont in place of the Dictator to give such power to the Consul with these words: "Let the Consul see to it that the republic does not suffer any harm."[5] 22 And, to return to our subject, I conclude that Rome's neighbors, in their attempt to conquer them, made Rome organize not only to defend itself but to attack them with greater force, greater consideration, and greater authority.

NOTES

1. Who these "writers" are is unclear. Using volume 1 of a text edited by Johann Jacob Reiske (Leipzig: Gotthard T. Georg, 1774–1777), Inglese suggests Dionysius of Halicarnassus, *Antiquitates Romanae,* 5.77, 1033–1035, but he warns that "Dionysius concludes by affirming that things are useful or harmful according to the use that is made of them." We would thus identify "the first tyrant" as Lucius Cornelius Sulla (c. 138–78 B.C.); he was appointed Dictator in 81. Livy is uncertain when a dictator was first appointed (2.18.4). Although he believes it was Titus Lartius, some authorities say Manius Valerius; this would have been around 500 B.C. during the Latin war. For more on sources for this chapter, the next one, and chapter 40, see Sasso, *Antichi,* 2:472–481.

2. Prior to Sulla there had been no Dictator for 120 years. The law provided that the consuls appoint a dictator from among their rank with approval by the Senate for a six-month period. He was given special powers for specific emergencies. Caesar, however, was appointed by a praetor, Lepidus, without Senate approval. His first term in 49 B.C. was eleven days; then in 48, after he defeated Pompey at Pharsalia, his term was a year. During each of the next three years he was made Dictator, but in 45 he was also made *imperator* for life. Because he is working up to a huge generalization at the end of this paragraph, Machiavelli's emphasis is on the constitutional nature of the Dictator. Nevertheless, as history has shown, providing for emergency powers is an important issue in any constitutional republic.

3. One of the emergency powers was that there was no right to appeal any of his decisions; see Polybius, 3.87.7–8.

4. In 1355 the Venetians definitively instituted a Council of Ten, which the doge could convene, though they first created it in 1310 to deal with the revolt of Baiamonte Tiepolo.

5. Quoted in Latin, based on Livy, 3.4.9: *"videat Consul, ne Respublica quid detrimenti capiat"* (see also 6.19.3), to indicate that the Senate, out of direst necessity, agreed to hand over absolute power, provided that doing so would in no way harm the republic. Both quotations refer to events early in Roman history, not during the "final days" of the republic. Machiavelli is probably referring to the period from about 130 B.C. on during the time of the Gracchi and the civil wars, when the Senate used the formula while providing the consuls with many repressive powers.

~ 35 ~

WHY THE CREATION OF THE DECEMVIRATE IN ROME WAS HARMFUL TO THAT REPUBLIC'S FREEDOM ALTHOUGH IT WAS DONE BY PEOPLE VOTING FREELY AND PUBLICLY

1 Over a period of time, the election of ten citizens named by the Roman people to make their laws led to their becoming tyrannical and openly usurping Roman freedom,[1] so there seems to be a contradiction to what was discussed above: namely, that power seized violently is harmful to republics, not that granted by election. 2 Hence we must consider the ways by which power is granted and the time for which it is granted. 3 And whenever unrestricted power is granted for a long time, defining a "long time" as a year or more, it will always be dangerous; its results will be either good or evil depending upon whether those to whom it is given are evil or good. 4 And if one considers the power that the Decemvirate and the Dictators had, the Decemvirate's will be seen to be greater beyond comparison. 5 Because once the Dictator was named there still remained the Tribunes, Consuls, and Senate with their powers, and the Dictator could not take them away. And even if he had been able to deprive someone of the Consulate or of the Senate, he could not abolish the senatorial rank and make new laws. 6 Thus the Senate, the Consuls, and the Tribunes, since they retained their power, came to be more or less his watchdogs and kept him from leaving the straight path. 7 But quite the opposite occurred with the creation of the Decemvirate, because the Consuls and Tribunes were abolished; they were granted power to make laws and to act in every other matter as if they were the Roman People.[2] 8 Once they found themselves alone, without Consuls, Tribunes, or any appeal to the People, and consequently that they had no one to oversee them, the Decemvirate, motivated by the ambition of Appius Claudius, were able to grow arrogant during their second year.[3] 9 And that is why it must be noted that when it was said that the power granted by people voting freely never harmed any republic it is assumed that people are never led to grant it except under specific conditions and for a specific time. But whenever people are led to grant power injudiciously and in the way the Roman People granted it to the Decemvirate, because they were either deceived or blinded otherwise, they will always experience what the Romans did. 10 This can be shown easily if we consider why the Dictators remained good and why the Decemvirate turned out badly and also if we consider what republics that have been regarded as well-organized have done to grant power for a long term, as the Spartans did to their kings and the Venetians do to their doges. For we can see in both instances that watchdogs were posted, making it so they could not misuse their power.[4] 11 And it does not matter in this case that the material was not corrupted, because absolute power corrupts material in a

very short time and makes friends and supporters for itself.[5] 12 And it does no harm for him to be poor or have no kin because riches and all other favors quickly follow after him, as we shall discuss in particular about the creation of the previously mentioned Decemvirate.[6]

NOTES

1. Livy devotes numerous chapters in Book 3 to the Decemvirs (32–54). He begins chapter 33 by announcing that their appointment in 451 B.C. was a constitutional change comparable to the expulsion of the kings; they were renewed the following year, but then they were disbanded. The Ten were a body whose judgments could not be appealed and all other public offices were suspended for a year (32.6). They promulgated a new code of laws, later known as the Laws of the Twelve Tables, Rome's earliest legal code.

2. According to Livy, the laws the tribunes made were not subject to the Decemvirate's jurisdiction (32.7).

3. Once the Decemvirs were renewed, Appius Claudius managed to get his supporters elected so as to further his autocratic plans.

4. These same two examples are part of the discussion above, 1, 5–6; see notes. Although the Spartan kings and Venetian doges were elected for life, the former had as "watchdogs" the ephors, a senate, and a second king, and the latter's were a signoria, a senate, and a grand council.

5. On Machiavelli's choice of words in this sentence, see above, 1, 17, n.2.

6. Especially below, 1, 40, but 1, 40–45 passim.

~ 36 ~

CITIZENS WHO HAVE HELD HIGHER OFFICES SHOULD NOT DISDAIN LOWER ONES

1 The Romans had named Marcus Fabius and G. Manilius as consuls and won a very glorious battle against the Veians and the Etruscans; Quintus Fabius, the consul's brother, who had been consul the year before, was killed in it.[1] 2 So we must consider how well-suited that city's institutions were for making it great and how wrong are other republics that depart from its ways. 3 For although the Romans were great lovers of glory, they did not consider it dishonorable nevertheless to obey someone now whom they had previously commanded and to find themselves serving in an army that they had once led. 4 This custom is contrary to the views, institutions, and ways of citizens in our day. In Venice there still is the error that a citizen, once he has held a high post, is ashamed to accept a lower one, and the city allows him to refuse it. 5 Even if this were honorable in private life, it is of absolutely no use in public life. 6 For a republic ought to have greater hope and confidence in a citizen who descends from a higher post to take on a lower one than in one who rises from a lower one to take on a higher one: 7 it cannot reasonably believe in him unless it sees men around him who are of such stature or *virtù* that his untested nature can be tempered by their

advice and authority. 8 Had there been in Rome the custom that exists in Venice and other modern republics and kingdoms, that anyone who had once been Consul would never again wish to go into the armies except as Consul, countless obstacles to remaining free might have resulted, because of both the mistakes that untried men would have made and the ambition that they would have been able to exercise more freely, since they would not have had men around them in whose eyes they would have feared to do wrong. Thus they would have come to be less constrained, which would have turned out to be completely to the public's disadvantage.[2]

NOTES

1. See Livy, 2.43–47. The "year before" was 481 B.C. Most authorities agree that the other consul's correct name is Gnaeus Manlius. See the discussion in Martelli, *Storici Antichi*, pp. 32–33.

2. This chapter seems to have been inspired by the seventeenth chapter of Plutarch, *Moralia, Praecepta gerendae reipublicae* (Precepts of statecraft), 17; 813c.–814c.

~ 37 ~

WHAT TURMOIL THE AGRARIAN LAW GAVE RISE TO IN ROME; AND HOW MAKING A LAW IN A REPUBLIC THAT LOOKS FAR BACK AND IS CONTRARY TO A CITY'S ANCIENT CUSTOM PRODUCES GREAT TURMOIL

1 Ancient writers had the maxim that men are wont to be distressed by evil and bored by good and that both of these two passions produce the same results.[1] 2 For whenever men cease fighting out of necessity, they fight out of ambition: it is so powerful in men's hearts that it never leaves them, no matter what position they have attained.[2] 3 The reason is that nature has created men such that they can desire all things but cannot obtain all things, so, since desire is always greater than the power to acquire, the result is discontent and dissatisfaction with what we have.[3] 4 Hence the origin of the swings in their fortune: because men in part desire to have more and in part fear the loss of what they have acquired, they become embroiled in hatred and war, which destroy one country and raise another to new heights.

5 I have written this discourse because it was not enough for the Roman Plebs to protect themselves against the Patricians by creating the Tribunes, a desire forced on them by necessity; once they attained their goal, they immediately began fighting out of ambition and trying to share public offices and property[4] with the Patricians since these are what men most prize.[5] 6 This produced the disease that led to the struggle over the Agrarian Law, which ended up by causing the republic's downfall.[6] 7 So, because well-organized republics have to keep their treasuries rich and their citizens poor, there must have been some defect in this law in the city of Rome: either it was not made in such a

way at the outset as not to need constant revision, they put off rewriting it so long that looking back caused turmoil, or, if it was drawn up well at the outset, it became corrupted later by usage. So, for whatever reason, this law was never spoken of in Rome without the city's being thrown into chaos.[7]

8 The law had two main provisions: 9 one, that no citizen could own more than so many *iugera*[8] of land; the other, that land taken from the enemy should be divided among the Roman people. 10 Thus the Patricians were injured on two counts: those who possessed more property than the law permitted (in the majority Patricians) were to be deprived of it and, since the enemies' property was divided among the Plebs, their means of growing rich was taken away.[9] 11 So, because these injuries were directed at powerful men who believed that they were defending the public interest[10] by resisting the law, whenever people were reminded of it, the entire city was thrown into chaos, as I have mentioned. The Patricians patiently and assiduously employed delaying tactics: either by assembling an army to be led outside the city gates[11] or backing another Tribune against the Tribune who proposed the law,[12] or sometimes accepting part of it, or else by sending a colony into the place where land was supposed to be distributed—this happened in the district of Antium, which occasioned a dispute about the law, so they sent into that place a colony drawn from Rome to which the district was assigned.[13] 12 Livy has a noteworthy expression for this, saying that it was hard to find anyone in Rome who would volunteer to go to the colony because the Plebs were so much more willing to wish for things in Rome than to possess them in Antium.[14] 13 This feeling about the law went on seething for a while until the Romans began to lead their armies into the remote corners of Italy or beyond its border; from that time on, it seemed to stop.[15] 14 This happened because the fields possessed by Rome's enemies became less desirable to the Plebs, since they were far from their eyes and they were in a place where they were not easy to farm. Yet the Romans were less punitive of their enemies in that way, and when they did strip a city of its surrounding districts, they set up colonies there. 15 For these reasons, consequently, the Agrarian Law remained more or less dormant up to the Gracchi. When they revived it, Roman freedom collapsed entirely because it found the power of its adversaries doubled and, because of this, so much hatred was kindled between the Plebs and the Senate that, beyond all civilized habit and custom, they resorted to arms and bloodshed.[16] 16 So, since the public magistrates could provide no remedy and none of the factions had any confidence in them any longer, private remedies were resorted to; each of the parties decided to choose a leader to defend it. 17 The Plebs got a head start in this turmoil and disorder by turning their allegiance to Marius so that they made him consul four times; meanwhile, with brief interruptions, he prolonged his consulate so he was able to make himself consul three more times.[17] 18 Because the Patricians had no remedy for this plague, they turned their backing to Sulla; making him their party's leader, they got civil wars, and, after much bloodshed and many swings of fortune, the Patricians won out.[18] 19 These feelings were revived later at the time of Caesar and Pompey, because when Caesar made himself the leader of Marius's

party and Pompey of Sulla's, Caesar emerged as the victor in the ensuing strife and became Rome's first tyrant; as a result the city was never again free.[19]

20 Such, therefore, were the beginning and the end of the Agrarian Law. 21 And although we have shown elsewhere[20] how the conflicts between the Senate and the Plebs kept Rome free because laws favoring freedom arose from them, and thus the outcome of the Agrarian Law may seem at variance with that conclusion, I state that I will not budge from that opinion because of this: the ambition of the Nobility is so great that unless a city strikes it down through various ways and means it quickly brings the city to its knees. 22 So if the conflict over agrarian law struggled three hundred years before enslaving Rome, it would perhaps have been enslaved much sooner had the Plebs not always checked the Patricians' ambition both by this law and by their other desires. 23 This also shows how much more people value material goods than public offices.[21] 24 For the Patricians in Rome always yielded these offices up to the Plebs without undue turmoil; but when material goods were involved, they were so stubborn about protecting them that the Plebs resorted to the extraordinary means discussed above to satisfy their craving.[22] 25 The Gracchi were the driving force behind this disorder; their intent should be praised more than their wisdom. 26 Because attempting to do away with a disorder that has arisen in a republic by making a law that looks far backward is an ill-considered course of action. As has been discussed at length above, it does nothing but hasten the evil that the disorder leads to; but if you employ delaying tactics, either the evil arrives more slowly or else it dies out by itself in the course of time before reaching its end.

NOTES

1. This sentence introduces a passage that distills a notion fundamental to Machiavelli's thought. He echoes a marginal notation made on a letter to Giovan Battista Soderini in September 1506, the *Ghiribizzi* letter. There he says "men tire of the good and complain about the bad" (*Friends,* p. 134). He again refers to this aphorism below in 3, 21. The "ancient writers" who are the source of this maxim remain an enigma, but see Plato, *Laws,* 3.687c; Aristotle, *Politics,* 5.10.1–6; 1316a1–1316b26; Polybius, 6.9.1–14. It should be noted that Plato's *Laws* are cited frequently in Rinaldi's edition as pertinent to Machiavelli's argument throughout the *Discourses.*

2. His *capitolo "Dell'ambizione"* makes the same point.

3. This sentence and the next continue the development of an idea basic to Machiavelli's thought; see the letter to Francesco Vettori quoted above in 1, 5, n.3. In his letter to Vettori of 10 August 1513, Machiavelli refers to what he believed a universal human trait as "the sweetness of domination" and reminds Vettori that "at first men are satisfied with being able to defend themselves and with not being dominated by others; from this point they move on to attacking others physically and seeking to dominate them" (see *Friends,* pp. 250, 249).

4. Translates *sustanze* (substances).

5. Based on Livy, 6.35.6; see also Aristotle, *Politics,* 5.2.1–6; 1302a16–1302b34.

6. The first Agrarian Law, which gave land seized at the end of war with the Hernici to the plebs, was issued by the consul Spurius Cassius in 486 B.C. (Livy,

2.41.3). Livy notes that "never, from then until now, has the question ever been brought up without leading to very serious disorders"; Machiavelli echoes this point at the end of the next sentence: "without the city's being thrown into chaos." During the republic there were some forty laws dealing with distribution of public land, with political "turmoil" a common thread when they were proposed. See the discussion in Martelli, *Storici antichi,* pp. 34–35.

7. Machiavelli's point seems to be that the state should receive the fruits of conquest and the people ought to be kept poor so that they will not strive for "property" (*sostanze,* "substances"). This point is reiterated below, 2, 19 and 3, 16; see Cato's speech in Sallust, *Catiline,* 52.22 and the "ways" of Cato in Horace, *Odes* 2.15.13–14. But Machiavelli seems to waver between the strength of men's desire for "property" and the problem of conquest leading to collapse. As Inglese asks, "How could a republic be founded on the repression of the strongest of human passions, without being transformed into an authoritarian government or even without destroying the very bases of its own power?" (Machiavelli, *Discorsi,* p. 251). For more on the question of "looking back" causing "turmoil," see *Florentine Histories,* 3.3: "one cannot make a more injurious law for a republic than one whose looking back is long-standing."

8. Refers to a Latin measure of land: a *jugerum* contained about 28,000 square feet; an acre, 43,560 square feet.

9. In the first instance Machiavelli refers to a later period, a law proposed by Gaius Licinius and Lucius Sextius in 377 B.C. that advanced the interests of the plebs at the expense of the patricians by proposing that a private citizen could hold no more than 500 *jugera* (about 300 acres) of public land (Livy, 6.35.5). The patricians fought this proposal for a decade. In the second instance, Machiavelli has in mind the first Agrarian Law; see note 6 above.

10. See for example the statements made in the speech of Appius Claudius Crassus in Livy, 6.40–41.

11. The result of such a decision was to shut off debate of a law (Livy, 3.10.3–4).

12. By exercising their veto right (Livy, 2.44.3).

13. In 467 B.C. the consuls Titus Aemilius and Quintus Fabius proposed sending colonists to newly conquered Antium, the present-day Anzio, so the interests of large landholders could be protected against the plebs' demand that the public land nearest Rome be redistributed (Livy, 3.1.5–6).

14. Livy, 3.1.7.

15. Generally speaking, the disputes over agrarian law calmed down once Rome conquered the entire peninsula toward the end of the fourth and the beginning of the third century B.C. only to resurface with Tiberius Gracchus, who was elected tribune in 133 B.C.

16. For the Gracchi, see Guicciardini's *Consideration* of 1, 5, n.2; see also Plutarch, *Tiberius and Caius Gracchus,* 8–19.

17. On Marius see above, 1, 5, n.6. The facts are that he was first elected consul in 107 B.C., then five succeeding times from 104 to 100, and finally for the seventh time in 86; for the relevance of Plutarch, *Marius* 28, see Ridley, "Roman History," p. 205.

18. Sulla (138–78 B.C.) was identified with the aristocratic faction and opposed the popular party led by Marius, who died in 85; see Guicciardini's *Consideration* of 1, 10, n.3. See also Plutarch, *Marius* and *Sulla.*

19. Pompey, identified with the aristocratic faction, was defeated by Caesar, a partisan of the popular faction, at Pharsalus and later killed in Egypt in 48 B.C. Caesar's path to the dictatorship was thus cleared. Machiavelli's contempt for Caesar is evident from 1, 10; his remarks on Caesar's tyrannical nature are similar to those in Aquinas, *On Kingship,* 4, 1.

20. Above in 1, 4.

21. To arrive at a period closer to the three hundred years specified in sentence 22, Martelli suggests that Machiavelli's dates might run from the first Agrarian Law (486 B.C.) to the period during the struggles between Marius and Sulla around 133 B.C. (*Storici antichi,* p. 36). In *Prince,* 17, Machiavelli recommends that a prince "keep his hands off the property of his subjects and citizens. . . . above all he should restrain himself from other people's property: men are quicker to forget the death of a father than the loss of an inheritance" (p. 273, lines 63–64; 67–69).

22. Machiavelli could find support in Livy, Preface, 12, that the reason for Rome's decline was that the patricians were so "stubborn" about "protecting" their "material goods. This explanation is also a constant theme in Sallust.

~ *38* ~

WEAK REPUBLICS ARE IRRESOLUTE AND CANNOT MAKE DECISIONS; IF THEY EVER DO ELECT SOME COURSE OF ACTION, IT ARISES OUT OF NECESSITY MORE THAN CHOICE

1 Because there was a very serious plague in Rome, so it seemed to the Volscians and the Aequi that the time had come for them to attack Rome, these two tribes formed an enormous army, attacked the Latins and the Hernici, and laid waste to their lands. The Latins and Hernici were forced to make this known to Rome and beg the Romans to defend them. Because the Romans were afflicted by the epidemic, the answer was that they should take their defense upon themselves with their own army because they could not defend them.[1] 2 Here we can see the Senate's magnanimity and wisdom: whatever Fortune brought it sought to take the lead in the decisions that its people had to make; and, when necessity required, the Senate was never ashamed to make a decision at variance with its policy or its previous decisions.

3 I say this because on other occasions this same Senate had forbidden those peoples to arm and defend themselves; a less prudent Senate than this one would have felt it degrading to concede such defense to them.[2] 4 But it always judged things as they should be judged and always chose the lesser evil as the better course of action.[3] It looked bad for it not to defend its subjects and, for reasons already given and for many other evident ones, it would look bad for its subjects to arm themselves without Rome. Nevertheless, realizing that because the enemy was at their doorstep they would necessarily arm themselves in any case, it took the honorable alternative. It decided that what they had to

do should be done with its authorization so they would not get into the habit of disobeying Rome out of choice, even if they were doing so out of necessity.

5 Although this course of action may seem like one that any republic ought to take, nevertheless, weak and ill-advised republics do not know how to grasp it, nor do they know how to gain glory from such necessities.[4] 6 Duke Valentino had taken Faenza and made Bologna give into his conditions.[5] 7 Then, because he wanted to return to Rome by way of Tuscany, he sent one of his men to Florence to request safe passage for himself and his army. 8 Consultation was held in Florence about how this matter should be handled, but no one ever advised granting it to him. 9 They did not follow the Roman way in this matter. The duke was very heavily armed, but the Florentines were virtually unarmed so that they could not have prevented his passage. Hence it would have been much more to Florence's glory for it to appear that the duke passed through with their permission rather than by force; for while it was entirely to Florence's shame, it might have been somewhat less so if they had handled it differently. 10 But the worst quality that republics have is irresoluteness, so whatever course of action they take, they do of necessity; and any good that happens to be done to them they do out of necessity and not out of their wisdom.[6]

11 I wish to give two other examples of this that occurred in the government[7] of our city in our time. 12 In 1500, after King Louis XII of France had recaptured Milan, he was desirous of giving back Pisa in order to get the 50,000 ducats that Florence had promised him after that restitution.[8] So he sent his armies toward Pisa under the command of Monsieur de Beaumont who, though French, was nonetheless a man whom the Florentines trusted highly. 13 The army and its commander set up camp between Cascina and Pisa in order to go and attack the city walls. While he was pausing there several days to prepare his attack, Pisan envoys came to Beaumont and offered to surrender the city to the French army on these conditions: he was to agree on the king's word not to hand Pisa over to the Florentines until four months had passed. 14 The Florentines completely rejected this offer with the result that they went into battle and came out of it with shame. 15 The only reason for rejecting this course of action was that they did not trust the king's word, even though they ill-advisedly had been forced into the king's hands despite the fact that they did not trust him. They did not realize how much better it would be for the king to give them back Pisa once he was inside it or, if he did not give it back, for him to reveal his true nature rather than for him to promise them Pisa before he had taken it and then for Florence to be obliged to pay for promises. 16 So they would have acted much more profitably had they agreed to let Beaumont take Pisa under whatever promises were given. That was the experience seen later on in 1502 when the king of France sent Monsieur Imbault to help Florence with French troops after Arezzo had rebelled.[9] Arriving near Arezzo, he promptly began to discuss a treaty with the people of Arezzo who, like the Pisans, wanted to hand their city over under certain promises. 17 This course was rejected in Florence. When Monsieur Imbault realized this, since it seemed to him that the Florentines had little understanding of the affair, he began to hold treaty discussions on his own with-

out the participation of the Commissioners. So he concluded it to his liking, and under its terms he entered Arezzo with his troops; he let the Florentines know that they were crazy and did not understand the ways of the world: if they wanted Arezzo, they should let the king know since he could give it to them much better once his troops were inside the city rather than outside. 18 In Florence there was no end to the vituperation and blame heaped on Imbault; it never ceased until people realized that if Beaumont had acted like Imbault they might have had Pisa as well as Arezzo.

19 So, to return to my subject, irresolute republics never take good actions unless they are forced to, because their weakness never lets them reach a decision where any doubt is involved. Unless some threat of violence impels them to eliminate this doubt, they always remain hesitant.

NOTES

1. Livy refers to these events of 463 B.C. in 3.6–8. The interpretation of the Senate's response to these events is Machiavelli's own; it is not found in Livy, although he does refer to the senate's "gloomy response" (3.6.5).

2. In 494 B.C.; see Livy 2.30.

3. See above, 1, 6, n.8 for a similar expression of this idea and a cross-reference to *Prince,* 21.

4. Although they are abstractions, Machiavelli holds up the "glory," honor, and prestige due Marcus Aurelius as qualities a prince should emulate because, properly used, they become concrete factors of a new prince's power (*Prince,* 19; p. 299, lines 185–188; 197–200).

5. The events referred to occurred in the spring and early summer of 1501 during the second campaign in Romagna of Duke Valentino (Cesare Borgia). Machiavelli and Guicciardini both cover this material elsewhere in their writings: the former in both *Prince,* 7 (pp. 161; 163, lines 101–118), and *Parole da dirle sopra la provisione del danaio* (Remarks to be given about the money bill) written in 1503; the latter in *Storia d'Italia,* 5, 4. Machiavelli's treatment in "Remarks" is part of a little-read treatise, yet it is extremely important for understanding his defense of freedom and appreciating his analytical powers.

6. Although he has in mind Florence's vacillation about joining the Holy League in 1512, Guicciardini expresses similar thoughts about neutrality; he argues that it is "wise for whoever is so strong that he need not fear the victor. . . . Otherwise, neutrality is foolish and injurious. . . . Neutrality undertaken out of irresolution, and not out of judgment is worst of all: namely, when you are unable to reach a decision, you act in such a way that you do not even satisfy someone who, at the moment, would be happy were you to assure him of your neutrality. Republics commit this kind of mistake more than princes do, because it results from divisions among decision makers, as one person advises one thing and another something else; there are never enough men to agree to make one view prevail. This is precisely what happened in 1512" (*Ricordi,* C. 68; see also Q2. 18 and B. 15, 16).

7. Translates *stato.*

8. Florence considered France to be strong enough to help in the city's prolonged efforts to gain control of Pisa. The two powers concluded a treaty in October 1499 by which France would send troops to help besiege Pisa in return for a cash settlement that Florence could ill afford. The Florentines "trusted" Jean de Polignac, lord of Beaumont

and Randon, "highly" because, unlike other French commanders, he had returned the fortified town of Leghorn to Florence in 1494 when Piero de' Medici handed it over to the invading French king, Charles VIII (see *Decennale* I, vv. 121–123). French and Swiss troops under Beaumont advanced on Pisa in June 1500, but Florence was in arrears with the armies' salaries. As Florence began its siege, the Swiss mercenaries mutinied because they had not been paid; Florence was therefore obliged to lift the siege "with shame." Machiavelli was personally involved in these events on two occasions. In late June and early July, the Signoria sent him, along with two commissioners, to deal with the grumbling French army about its wages; the lack of agreement led to the army's revolt. At the end of July he was sent on a legation to France to explain the defeat to Louis XII and to persuade him not to renege on his commitments to aid Florence in its war against Pisa.

9. Monsieur Imbault is Imbaud de Rivoire, lord of La Batie (Henri J. A. Rochas, ed., *Biographie du Dauphiné contenant l'histoire des hommes nés dans cette province* [Paris, 1856–1860]). Both Machiavelli and Guicciardini comment on these events: see Machiavelli's *Del modo di trattare i popoli della Valdichiana ribellati* (On the method of dealing with the rebellious populace in the Val di Chiana) and Guicciardini's *Storia d'Italia,* 5, 1; 9. Again, Machiavelli was personally involved in these events. In June 1502 Florence dispatched both Francesco Soderini, bishop of Volterra, the brother of Piero, and Machiavelli to negotiate directly with Cesare Borgia. The aim was to get Borgia to give up his attempt to seize power in Tuscany. Borgia's ally, Vitellozzo Vitelli, had taken Arezzo, a city in the Val di Chiana subject to Florence. Florence turned to its ally, again the French king Louis XII, who ordered his field commander, Imbaud de Rivoire, to attack Arezzo. Once in possession of the city, he hesitated about handing it over to Florence, whose Commissioners urged its immediate return to Florentine control. It took most of the month of August to achieve Arezzo's restoration. These negotiations also involved Machiavelli, whom Florence sent to Arezzo in the middle of the month to urge the new French commander, Monsieur de Langres, to carry out his order to return Arezzo to Florence. Because Florence did recover Arezzo, this is a less obvious example in support of Machiavelli's argument here. Monsieur de Langres is variously identified as Antoine de Torote, lord of Blacy and Langres, and Philibert de Choiseul, lord of Lanques and governor of Langres; see below, 3, 27, n.6 (Rinaldi).

~ 39 ~

THE SAME EVENTS ARE OFTEN TO BE SEEN AMONG DIFFERENT PEOPLES

1 Anyone who considers present and ancient matters readily understands that the same desires and feelings exist in all cities and all peoples and they always have. 2 So it is easy for anyone who carefully examines past matters to foresee those in the future of any republic and to apply to them the remedies that were used by the ancients or, if they are not to be found, to devise new ones because the events are similar.[1] 3 But because these considerations are neglected or not understood by those who read or, if they are understood, are not known to those who govern, the same problems always ensue in every age.

4 After 1494, when the city of Florence had lost a part of its dominions, such as Pisa and other towns,[2] it was obliged to declare war on those holding them. 5 Because the occupying forces were powerful, the result was that a good deal was spent on war fruitlessly: the result of spending was a good deal of taxes; from the taxes came endless complaints by the people. And because this war was administered by a council of ten citizens called the Ten of War, the populace gradually became resentful of it as if it were the cause of both the war and its expenses; they became convinced that if the council were eliminated the war would be too. So when it was to be reelected, they did not vote for new members and they let it expire; they transferred its duties to the Signoria.[3] 6 This decision was so harmful that not only did it not stop the war, as the populace was convinced, but once the men who administered it wisely were removed, so much disorder ensued that in addition to Pisa, Arezzo and many other places were lost. Thus the people regretted their error, and, since the cause of the disease was the fever and not the doctor, they re-elected the Council of Ten.

7 These same feelings arose in Rome against the title of the Consuls. Because when the people saw that one war led to another and they could never rest, they should have realized that it arose from the ambition of the neighbors who wished to attack them. Instead, they thought it arose from the ambition of the Nobles who, unable to punish the Plebs inside Rome because the power of the tribunes protected them, sought to take them far from Rome under the Consuls so that the Nobles could oppress them where they were completely helpless. 8 Hence they thought it necessary either to do away with the Consuls or to regulate their power so they would have no authority over the people either inside or outside Rome. 9 The first man to attempt this law was a Tribune, Terentilius; he proposed that five men should be named to investigate the Consuls' power and restrict it.[4] 10 This angered the Nobility considerably, since they felt that the grandeur of their authority had waned so completely that the Nobility no longer had any status left in the republic. 11 Nevertheless, the Tribunes were so stubborn that the title of consul died out;[5] after some other arrangements were made, they were eventually satisfied to establish Tribunes with consular power rather than Consuls: they hated their title far more than their authority. 12 So they continued for a long time until, realizing their mistake, they established the Consulate again, just as the Florentines went back to the Ten.

NOTES

1. The ideas in this first paragraph are fundamental to Machiavelli's assumption in the *Discourses* that because history repeats itself people can learn both moral and practical precepts from it; see Book 1, Preface A, n.9. Guicciardini's *Ricordi* contain conflicting ideas on this point: on the one hand he seems to agree, as in C. 76 (B. 114), quoted above, 1, Preface A, n.9; yet he is wary of judging by example: "To judge by example is extremely misleading. Unless they be similar in all respects, examples are useless, since the slightest variation in the circumstance may be the reason for the greatest divergence in the effect. When these variations are minute, discerning them requires a good and

perspicacious eye" (C. 117). And, as if annoyed at Machiavelli's constant use of Roman examples, he questions the efficacy of doing so. When, for example, the characteristics of Rome and Florence differ, any comparison is as useless as expecting "an ass to run like a horse" (C. 110); see Preface to Book 2, n.9, for more discussion of this point.

2. As a result of the campaigns of the French king, Charles VIII, in Italy.

3. Machiavelli became secretary to the *Dieci di Balìa* (the Ten of Power) in July 1498. The council was allowed to "expire" in 1499. In September 1500 it was reformed, assigned more limited powers, and renamed the *Dieci di Libertà e Pace,* the Ten of Liberty and Peace; see below, Guicciardini's *Consideration,* sentence 4. In other words, despite what Machiavelli says in this chapter, the office of the Ten was reinstated two years before the loss of Arezzo. On this issue, see Guicciardini, *History of Florence,* chapter 18. The events in Florentine history to which Machiavelli refers occurred between 1499 and 1502; see notes 8 and 9 to the previous discourse.

4. See Livy, 3.9.5, for the plebeian tribune, Caius Terentilius Arsa, and his proposal in 462 B.C. to define and thereby restrict the powers of the consuls. See the discussion in Martelli, *Storici antichi,* p. 37.

5. See Livy, 4.6.8; thus, "for a long time," almost a century, Rome had military tribunes who could come from among either the patricians or the plebs and possessed consular authority. With the Licinian Law in 367 B.C., the consulate was restored and opened to the plebs; see Livy, 6.35, 38–42.

~ 40 ~

THE ESTABLISHMENT OF THE DECEMVIRATE IN ROME AND WHAT SHOULD BE NOTED ABOUT IT, IN WHICH WILL BE CONSIDERED AMONG MANY OTHER THINGS HOW A REPUBLIC CAN BE EITHER SAVED OR CONQUERED BY SUCH AN EVENT

1 Because I wish to discuss in detail the events that occurred in Rome as a result of establishing the Decemvirate,[1] I do not believe it irrelevant first to describe everything that ensued from its establishment and then to go into the points that are noteworthy in these actions. They are many and of great import, both for those who wish to keep a republic free and for those who might plan to subjugate one. 2 For this discussion will reveal that the Senate and the Plebs made many mistakes that were prejudicial to freedom and that Appius, the head of the Decemvirs, made many mistakes that were prejudicial to the tyranny he had presumed to establish in Rome.

3 After many arguments and disputes between the People and the Nobility over ratifying new laws in Rome whereby the state's freedom might be made more stable, they agreed to send Spurius Postumius and two other citizens to Athens for examples of the laws Solon gave it so that Roman laws could be based on them.[2] 4 When these men had gone and returned, they proceeded to choose the citizens who would examine and ratify these laws; ten citizens

were chosen for a year, among whom was Appius Claudius, a shrewd and restless man. 5 So they could make these laws without any interference, all the other Roman offices, in particular the Tribunes and Consuls, were eliminated, and the right to appeal to the People was eliminated. This office thus became Rome's sole ruler. 6 Then, because of the support that the Plebs gave him, all the power of his other colleagues was delegated to Appius.[3] For he had made himself so popular through his actions that it seemed amazing how he had quite suddenly taken on a new nature and new character since he had previously been considered a harsh persecutor of the Plebs.

7 The Decemvirs behaved quite civilly, retaining only twelve lictors, who preceded the one who was presiding among them. 8 Although they had absolute power, they nevertheless, whenever they had to punish a Roman citizen for homicide, had him brought before the people and had him judged by them.[4] 9 They wrote their laws on ten tablets, and before ratifying them they put them in a public place so that everyone could read them and discuss them. That way the Decemvirs could learn whether there was any flaw in them so they could be amended before they were ratified.[5] 10 At this point Appius had a rumor spread throughout Rome[6] that if two other tablets were added to these ten they would be brought to completion; this suggestion gave the people the opportunity to rename the Decemvirs for another year. The people readily agreed to this both so that the Consuls should not be reelected and because they felt they could manage without Tribunes since, as was stated above, they themselves were judging cases.[7] 11 Once the decision was made to reelect them, all the Nobility was prompted to seek these offices. Appius was among the first; he acted so kindly toward the Plebs while asking for it that his colleagues began to be suspicious of it: "for they believed that so proud a man would not be amiable for nothing."[8] 12 Fearing to oppose him openly, they decided to do so on the sly: although he had been in office for less time than anyone,[9] they gave him power to propose the future Decemvirs to the people; they thought he would observe the conditions that the others did, not to propose oneself, since in Rome that was an unusual and shocking thing to do. 13 "But in fact he seized upon this obstacle as an opportunity,"[10] and he named himself among the first, to the surprise and annoyance of all the Nobles: he then named nine others to suit his purposes. 14 This new mandate, made for another year, began to show their error to the people and the Nobility. 15 Because Appius immediately "put an end to playing an unnatural role"[11] and began to show his innate arrogance; within a few days he infected his colleagues with his own habits. 16 To intimidate the people and the Senate, they made one hundred twenty lictors instead of twelve.[12]

17 For several days everyone shared this fear, but then the Decemvirs began to get along with the Senate and to attack the Plebs. If someone attacked by one of the Decemvirs appealed to another one, he was treated worse in the appeal than in the original decision.[13] 18 So the Plebs, realizing their mistake and filled with misgivings, began to look in the Nobles' faces "and clutch at the breath of freedom from the source by which they had so greatly feared enslavement that they had brought the republic to its current state."[14] 19 The

Nobility was pleased with their affliction "in hopes that the people themselves, troubled by current conditions, might want the Consuls back."[15] 20 When the final days of the year arrived, the two tablets of laws were completed but not published. 21 This gave the Decemvirs the opportunity to continue in office; they began to hold onto the government by violence and to make supporters for themselves of the young Nobles, to whom they gave the property of those whom they condemned:[16] "bribed with these gifts, the youths preferred license for themselves to freedom for all."[17]

22 At this point it happened that the Sabines and Volscians[18] declared war on the Romans. Fear of war made the Decemvirs see the weakness of their government, because without the Senate they could not raise troops for the war; if they convened the Senate, they thought they would lose their control. 23 However, under pressure, they adopted this latter course. When the senators came together, many of them—Valerius and Horatius in particular—spoke out against the arrogance of the Decemvirs.[19] Their power would have been done away with completely had not the Senate, out of spite toward the Plebs, wished to show its power; they thought that if the Decemvirs gave up office of their own accord that might mean that the Tribunes of the Plebs would not be reinstated.[20] 24 They therefore decided to go to war and issued forth with two armies led by some members of the Decemvirate. Appius remained to govern the city.[21] 25 That was when he fell in love with Virginia, and when he tried to take her by force, her father Virginius killed her in order to deliver her.[22] Turmoil ensued in Rome and the armies: joining with the remainder of the Roman Plebs, the armies went off to the Sacred Mount, where they stayed until the Decemvirs left office, Tribunes and Consuls were established, and Rome was restored to the form of its ancient freedom.

26 Thus we can observe from this text first of all that the problem of creating this tyranny arose in Rome for the same reasons that the majority of tyrannies arise in cities: from the people's excessive desire to be free and from the Nobles' excessive desire to command.[23] 27 Should they not agree to make a law on behalf of freedom but one or the other party throws its support to someone, that is when tyranny quickly arises. 28 The people and Nobles of Rome agreed to establish the Decemvirate and to establish it with so much power, because of a desire that each of the parties had: one to abolish the consuls, the other to abolish the tribunes. 29 Once it was established, since the Plebs felt that Appius had become popular and would strike down the Nobility, the people turned to support him. 30 Whenever the people are led to make the mistake[24] of giving someone influence so he can attack those it hates, if the person is shrewd, the result will always be that he becomes the tyrant of that city. 31 Because with the people's support he will make sure to crush the Nobility and he will never resort to oppressing the people until he has crushed it; at that point the people, realizing they are enslaved, have nowhere to take shelter.

32 This has been the method used by all those who have established tyrannies in republics. 33 And had Appius used this method, his tyranny would have taken on greater life and would not have failed so rapidly. But he did exactly the opposite, and he could not have behaved more unwisely. For

in order to hold onto tyranny, he made enemies of those who had granted it to him and who could have sustained him in it, and he made enemies[25] of those who had not taken part in giving it to him and who could not have sustained him in it. He lost those who were friendly to him and sought to make friends of those who could not be his friends. 34 For though the Nobles desire to be tyrants, the segment of the Nobility that is outside of the tyranny is always the tyrant's enemy. Because of its great ambition and greed, he can never win it over completely, since a tyrant can have neither so much wealth nor so many offices as to satisfy every one of them. 35 Thus Appius made a quite obvious mistake in abandoning the people and drawing closer to the Nobles, both for the reasons stated above and because, if one tries to hold on to something by violence, the one who constrains must be more powerful than those who are constrained.

36 From this arises the fact that those tyrants who have the populace[26] as their friends and the Nobles[27] as their enemies are more secure, because their violence is sustained by greater forces than that of those who have the people as their enemies and the Nobility as their friends.[28] 37 Because with that support one's own forces suffice for self-preservation, as they did for Nabis, the tyrant of Sparta.[29] When all Greece and the Roman people attacked him, he made sure of a few Nobles; having the people as his friends, he defended himself through them, which he could not have done had he had them as enemies. 38 In the other case, having few friends inside the city, one's own forces do not suffice and one has to seek external ones. 39 And these must be of three kinds: one, foreign bodyguards to guard your person; another, arming the rural districts to perform the duty that the Plebs would have had; the third, allying yourself with powerful neighbors for your defense. 40 Anyone who follows these methods and practices them well could save himself one way or another, even if he had the people as his enemy. 41 But Appius could not use that of winning over the countryside since it and Rome were one and the same; what he could have done, he did not know how to. So he fell at the very beginning.

42 The Senate and the people made very grave mistakes in establishing the Decemvirate. Because, although it is stated above (in the discussion of the Dictator)[30] that offices that are self-created, not those the people create, are harmful to freedom, nevertheless, when the people establish offices, they must do so in such a way as to have some concerns about becoming evil. 43 Whereas it is necessary for the people to provide a safeguard to keep the offices good, the Romans took it away by making them the sole office in Rome and eliminating all others out of the Senate's excessive desire (as we stated above) to abolish the Tribunes and the people's to abolish the Consuls. This so blinded them that they cooperated in such disorder. 44 As King Ferdinand said, men often act like some smaller birds of prey in whom the desire to pursue their victim, as nature incites them to do, is so strong that they do not sense another, larger bird hovering over them to kill them.[31]

45 One may therefore learn from this discourse, as I stated in the heading, the Roman people's mistake in seeking to preserve freedom and the mistakes of Appius in seeking to hold onto tyranny.

NOTES

1. Machiavelli alludes to this aim at the end of chapter 35.

2. The other two "citizens" were Aulus Manlius and Publius Sulpicius Camerinus; see Livy, 3.31.8. In this and the next five chapters, Machiavelli closely follows Livy's account of the Decemvirate in 3.31–58.

3. Livy, 3.33.7, for this, a translation of Livy's remarks, and the next sentence.

4. Livy, 3.33.8–10. On the lictors, see above, 1, 25, n.3.

5. Livy, 3.34.1–5.

6. Livy, 3.34.7 states merely that such was the rumor, not that Appius initiated it.

7. Machiavelli made this point in sentence 8. Livy, 3.34.8, is the basis for this sentence. Because the Decemvirs permitted the right of appeal, the plebs were even more reassured.

8. Quoted in Latin from Livy, 3.35.6, *"haud gratuitam in tanta superbia comitatem fore,"* though Machiavelli adds *"credebant enim"* (for they believed).

9. Livy, 3.35.8; "on the sly" translates Machiavelli's *arte* and Livy's *ars.*

10. Quoted in Latin with some discrepancies from Livy, 3.35.9, which reads: *"impedimentum pro occasione arripuit."* Martelli observes that all Machiavelli's citations of Livy in this chapter contain slight discrepancies, perhaps because of his working habits (*Storici antichi,* pp. 38–40).

11. Quoted inexactly in Latin from Livy, 3.36.1, which reads: *"Ille finis Appio alienae personae ferendae fuit."*

12. Based on Livy, 3.36.1–7; see Mansfield, *New Modes,* p. 128.

13. Based on Livy, 3.36.5–9.

14. Quoted in Latin from Livy, 3.37.1: *"et inde libertatis captare auram unde servitutem timendo in eum statum rem publicam adduxerant."*

15. Quoted inexactly in Latin from Livy, 3.37.3, which reads: *"ut taedio praesentium consules duo tandem et status pristinus rerum in desiderium veniant."*

16. Based on Livy, 3.37.4–8.

17. Quoted inexactly in Latin from Livy, 3.37.8, which reads: *"Hac mercede iuventus nobilis corrupta non modo non ire obviam iniuriae, sed propalam licentiam suam malle quam omnius libertatem."*

18. At 3.38.5, Livy specifies the Aequi, not the Volscians.

19. According to Livy, Lucius Valerius Potitus (3.39.2) and Marcus Horatius Barbatus (3.39.3).

20. Based on Livy, 3.41.5–6.

21. Based on Livy, 3.41.7–8.

22. This incident, along with the rest of the paragraph, is based on Livy, 3.44–54; the final clause is a close paraphrase of 3.54.7.

23. The ideas that Machiavelli develops here closely parallel the argument of *Prince,* 9, "Concerning the Civil Princedom," in which he ends the first paragraph by noting: "I submit that a man rises to this kind of princedom with the assistance of either the common people *(populo)* or the rich people *(grandi),* for these two opposing classes *(umori)* exist in every city. The civil princedom is a product of this fact: the common people want to be neither governed nor oppressed by the rich, and the rich want to govern and oppress the common people. In a city one of three consequences

results from these two conflicting desires: a princedom, freedom, or anarchy" (p. 191, lines 7–16).

24. In *Prince,* 9, this "mistake" is not beneficial to a tyrant; rather, it permits a prince to gain control: "when the common people *(populo)* realize they are unable to hold out against the rich *(grandi),* they direct their influence toward some one person and make him prince so that they can be protected by his power" (p. 193, lines 24–28).

25. Inglese alters the text, which reads *inimico* (enemy), to read *amico* (friend), saying that sense requires it; Rinaldi, however, retains *inimico,* glossing the first of the "enemies" in this sentence as the plebs and the second as the patricians.

26. Translates *l'universale.*

27. Translates *grandi.*

28. In *Prince,* 9, Machiavelli points out that "a prince can never secure himself against a hostile populace *(populo),* because they are many; he can secure himself against rich people *(grandi),* because they are few" (p. 193, lines 43–46). Over the course of Book 1, Machiavelli's ideas about "the people" have gradually been developing. They will come to the forefront later, below, 1, 57 and 1, 58; there as here the emphasis is on their power. But as he continues to think about the Decemvirate, he will note in various chapter titles "how easily men can be corrupted" (42) and "a multitude without a leader is ineffectual" (44).

29. He is referred to in chapter 10, n.5, and is considered at length in *Prince,* 9.

30. Above, chapter 34; see Sasso, *Antichi,* 2:475–481.

31. Because no positive identification of this saying has been made, recent commentators believe Machiavelli had in mind either Ferrante (Ferdinand) I, who ruled Naples from 1458 to 1494, or Ferdinand of Aragon; previously it was thought to refer to Ferdinand (Ferdinand the Catholic), king of Spain, who lived from 1452 to 1516.

~ 41 ~

TO SWITCH FROM HUMILITY TO ARROGANCE, FROM MERCY TO CRUELTY, WITHOUT RESPECT FOR THE MEAN IS UNWISE AND INEFFECTUAL

1 In addition to the other methods used poorly by Appius to preserve tyranny, switching too quickly from one trait to another was of no little importance.[1] 2 Because his stratagem of fooling the Plebs by pretending to be a man of the people was properly used,[2] as were the methods that he used to get the Decemvirate reappointed, his boldness in getting himself named against the feelings of the Nobility, and naming associates to suit his purpose. But once he had accomplished this, what was not at all properly used, as I say above, was his sudden change in character: after being a friend, to show himself an enemy of the Plebs; after being compassionate, to be arrogant; after being easygoing, to be cantankerous.[3] And he did so with such rapidity, without offering any excuse, that everybody could not help recognizing the falseness

of his spirit. 3 Because someone who has seemed good for a while and wants to become bad for his own purposes must do so with respect for the mean. He should act in such a way, according to circumstances, that before your changed character alienates your former supporters, it has provided you with so many new ones that you do not come to lessen your power. Otherwise, finding yourself exposed and friendless, you fall.

NOTES

1. Chapters 41 to 45 amount to Machiavelli's reflections on the example of Appius Claudius and the Decemvirate discussed in the previous chapter.

2. See Livy, 3.35.8.

3. See Livy, 3.56.7.

~ 42 ~

HOW EASILY MEN CAN BE CORRUPTED

1 It may also be noted in this matter of the Decemvirate how easily men are corrupted and let their nature change into something totally different, no matter how good and well-trained they are. Consider how the youths that Appius had chosen to surround himself with grew quite friendly to tyranny just for the minimal profit that they derived from it and how Quintus Fabius, though an excellent man among the second Decemvirate, was blinded by a little ambition and convinced by Appius's shrewdness, so he exchanged his good ways for quite bad ones and became like him.[1] 2 Examined carefully, this will make legislators in republics or kingdoms more ready to rein in human appetites and deprive them of any hope of being able to do wrong with impunity.

NOTES

1. Quintus Fabius Vibulanus was consul three times, in 467, 465, and 459 B.C.; Machiavelli's judgment of him, embodied in the chapter title, reflects that of Livy, 3.41.8.

~ 43 ~

THOSE WHO FIGHT FOR THEIR OWN GLORY ARE GOOD AND LOYAL SOLDIERS

1 One may also consider in connection with the discussion above how much difference there is between a happy army, which is fighting for its own glory, and one that is dissatisfied and fighting for someone else's ambition. 2 For whereas the Roman armies always used to be victorious under the Consuls, under the Decemvirs they always lost.[1] 3 From this example we may recognize reasons, in part, for the ineffectualness of mercenary soldiers, who have no other

reason to hold fast than what little pay you give them.[2] 4 This reason is not and cannot be enough to make them loyal or so friendly to you that they want to die for you. 5 Because in armies where there is no affection for the person they are fighting for, to make them his supporters, there can never be enough *virtù* for them to resist an enemy with some *virtù*. 6 And because this love and this competitiveness can arise only from your subjects, it is necessary to recruit soldiers from one's subjects if one wishes to maintain one's position, to hold on to a republic or a kingdom, as we can see all those who have achieved great advantages with their armies have done. 7 The Roman armies under the Decemvirs had as much *virtù* but did not achieve their usual results because they lacked the same attitude. 8 But as soon as the office of the Decemvirate was abolished and they began to fight as free men, the same courage came back to them; as a result their campaigns had a happy outcome in keeping with their former custom.[3]

NOTES

1. To the Sabines near Eretum and to the Aequi on Mount Algidus; Livy 3.42.3.

2. Machiavelli rails against mercenary forces throughout his works, especially below, 2, 10, *The Art of War,* and *Prince,* 12, where part of his argument is that "there is no love or reason to hold [mercenaries] on the battlefield other than their meager pay, which is not enough to make them want to die for you" (p. 221, lines 29–32).

3. In 448 B.C. "free" Romans defeated the Sabines (Livy, 3.62–63) and both the Aequi and Volscians in 448 and 446 (Livy, 3.61, 66–70).

~ 44 ~

MASSES WITHOUT A LEADER ARE INEFFECTUAL; AND HE MUST NOT FIRST THREATEN AND THEN ASK FOR POWER

1 Because of the incident of Virginia, the Roman Plebs had withdrawn with their weapons to the Sacred Mount.[1] 2 The Senate sent its envoys to ask by what authority they had deserted their commanders and withdrawn onto the Mount. 3 The Senate's authority was so greatly respected that, since there was no leader among them, nobody ventured to reply. 4 Livy says that they did not lack what to say in reply but they lacked someone to give the reply.[2] 5 This shows precisely the ineffectualness of masses without a leader. 6 Once this confusion became known to Virginius, he ordered twenty military Tribunes to be named as leaders for discussions and meetings with the Senate. 7 When they asked that Valerius and Horatius be sent so they could explain to them what they wanted, they refused to go unless the Decemvirate first stepped down from office.[3] Arriving at the Mount, where the Plebs were, they were told that what the Plebs wanted was for Tribunes of the Plebs to be appointed, for every office to have an appeal to the people, and for all of the Decemvirs to be handed over to them, because they wanted to burn them alive.

8 Valerius and Horatius praised their first two demands but blamed the third one for being wicked, saying: "you damn cruelty, yet into cruelty you

rush."[4] They advised them to drop any mention of the Decemvirs and pay attention to taking back their authority and power; then they would not lack ways of obtaining satisfaction. 9 Here we can plainly see how foolish and unwise it is to demand something and say right away: "I wish to do such and such ill with it," for one must not show one's intention, but one should seek to obtain one's desire come what may. 10 Because it is enough to ask a man for weapons without saying, "I want to kill you with them," since once you have the weapons in hand, you can satisfy your appetite.

NOTES

1. See above, 1, 40, n.22 for these events in Livy, 3.44–54; the "envoys" mentioned in the next sentence were Spurius Tarpeius, Gaius Julius, and Publius Sulpicius (3.50.15).

2. An unacknowledged quotation from Livy, 3.50.16, as is the next sentence from 3.51.1.

3. Livy, 3.50.16. Martelli reminds us that the action occurred not on the Sacred Mount but on the Aventine Hill (*Storici antichi,* p. 41).

4. Inexactly quoted in Latin from Livy 3.53.7, which reads, *"quippe qui crudelitatis odio in crudelitatem ruitis"* (out of hatred for it, you rush into cruelty).

~ 45 ~

BREAKING AN ENACTED LAW, ESPECIALLY FOR ITS AUTHOR, SETS A BAD PRECEDENT; DAILY REOPENING FRESH WOUNDS IN A CITY IS VERY HARMFUL TO THE ONE WHO GOVERNS IT

1 Once the treaty was concluded and Rome was restored to its original status, Virginius summoned Appius before the people to defend his case. 2 He appeared, accompanied by many Nobles; Virginius ordered him to be put in prison. 3 Appius began to cry out and appeal to the people; Virginius said that he was not worthy to have the right to appeal, since he had destroyed it, and to have as his defenders the people whom he had offended. 4 Appius replied that the people should not violate the right of appeal that they had been so desirous of enacting. 5 Appius was imprisoned, however, and he committed suicide before the day of the trial.[1] 6 Although the wicked life of Appius deserved the severest punishment, nevertheless, violating the law was not a civil act, all the more so when it had just been made. 7 For I do not believe there is any worse precedent to set in a republic than to make a law and then break it; all the more so when it is the one who made it who breaks it.

8 After 1494 Florence reorganized its government with the help of Friar Girolamo Savonarola, whose writings show his learning, wisdom, and the *virtù* of his mind.[2] Among the other institutions designed to protect the citizens, he had a law enacted that decisions that the Eight and the Signoria made for crimes against the state[3] could be appealed to the people (a law that he long

argued for and obtained with the greatest of difficulty). It so happened that a short while after its confirmation five citizens were condemned to death by the Signoria on behalf of the state; when they tried to appeal, they were not allowed to, and the law was not complied with.[4] 9 This damaged the friar's reputation more than any other event: because if appeal was useful, he ought to have had it complied with; if it was not useful, he should not have had it voted in. 10 And this event was noted all the more because the friar, in the many sermons that he gave after this law was broken, never either condemned or excused those who had broken it; because it proved to be to his purpose, he did not want to condemn it, yet he could not excuse it. 11 Because this revealed his ambitious and partisan spirit, it damaged his reputation and drew widespread disapproval.[5]

12 Reopening fresh grievances daily in the minds of your citizens by inflicting fresh wounds on this person or that also does a state quite a lot of harm, as occurred in Rome after the Decemvirate. 13 Each of the Decemvirs, as well as other citizens, was at various times accused and condemned, so there was extreme fear among the entire Nobility, who deemed that such condemnations would never be ended until the entire Nobility was destroyed. 14 And it would have produced a great deal of trouble in Rome had not the tribune Marcus Duillius intervened; he issued an edict that reassured all the Nobility: for a year no citizen was permitted to cite or accuse any other Roman citizen.[6] 15 Thus we can see how harmful it is to a republic or a prince to keep the minds of subjects in uncertainty and fear by continual punishments and affronts. 16 Unquestionably one cannot have a more destructive regulation, because men who begin to fear imminent evil secure themselves against danger however they can; they become bolder and less hesitant about attempting new things. 17 Therefore it is necessary either never to injure anyone or to commit the injuries all at once and then reassure men and give them reason to calm and steady their spirits.[7]

NOTES

1. Livy, 3.54–58.

2. For the expulsion of the Medici in 1494, Savonarola, and background on the republican constitution he helped to establish in Florence, see above, 1, 7, n.5 (for Valori, involved in the decision discussed in sentence 8 below) and especially, 1, 11, n.12. See Sasso, *Antichi,* 1:360–371, for evidence that Machiavelli was quite aware of Savonarola's doctrinal writings.

3. Translates *per casi di stato.* The appeal was directed to the Great Council, not exactly the "people"; to be a member of the Council one had to be an enfranchised citizen, and only a limited number of men were able to vote. "The Eight" refers to the *Otto di guardia e de balìa* (Council of Eight of Guard). See Guicciardini, *History of Florence,* chapter 12, for the appeal "to the people."

4. In 1497 Giovanni Cambi, Bernardo del Nero, Giannozzo Pucci, Niccolò Ridolfi, and Lorenzo Tornabuoni, five members of the aristocratic party, or *ottimati,* who were opposed to Savonarola and republicanism, plotted to restore Piero de' Medici to power. Francesco Valori, a leader of Savonarola's party, successfully urged

that the five be executed. These events are covered in Guicciardini, *History of Florence,* chapter 15.

5. While it is true that Savonarola never "condemned or excused" the law, he was opposed to its enactment in the first place; furthermore, in 1497 he was in exile and had been excommunicated by Pope Alexander VI, Rodrigo Borgia.

6. The first three sentences of this paragraph are based on Livy, 3.58–9.

7. At the end of his discussion of Agathocles and Oliverotto da Fermo in *Prince,* 8, Machiavelli writes: "when seizing power a conqueror ought to examine closely all the damage he must inflict, and inflict it all at once so that he is not obliged to repeat it daily. . . . Abuses ought to be inflicted all at once—the shorter savored, the less resented" (p. 187, lines 156–159; 166–167).

~ 46 ~

MEN RISE FROM ONE AMBITION TO ANOTHER; FIRST THEY TRY NOT TO BE HARMED, THEN THEY HARM OTHERS

1 Once the Roman people had regained their freedom and returned to their original status, which was even greater now since many new laws had been made to confirm their power, it seemed reasonable for Rome to calm down for a while.[1] 2 Nevertheless, experience showed the opposite, because new disorders and conflicts arose there daily. 3 And because Livy very wisely indicates the reason why this happened, it seems only fitting for me to recall his words precisely. He states[2] that either the people or the Nobility always became arrogant whenever the other gave way; when the Plebs remained quiet within their bounds, the young Nobles began to insult them, and the Tribunes could provide few remedies against this because they too were attacked. 4 The Nobility, on the other hand, even though they felt that their young men were too fierce, nevertheless did not mind if someone was going beyond bounds as long as it was their own members who were doing it and not the Plebs. 5 Thus the desire to defend freedom made each side try so to gain the upper hand that it oppressed the other. 6 And the rule in such incidents is that, while men are trying not to fear, they begin to make others fear; they inflict on others the abuses they shun for themselves: as if it were necessary either to harm or be harmed.

7 Here we can see one of the ways, among others, in which republics break up, how men rise from one ambition to another, and how much truth there is in a saying that Sallust has Caesar say: "Every bad example results from good beginnings."[3] 8 First of all, as has been stated above, the citizens in a republic who are ambitious try not to be able to be injured, not only by private citizens but also by public officials. To do this, they seek friendships; they acquire them through ostensibly honest means, either by subsidizing them with money or by defending them against the powerful. Because this seems to be an act of *virtù,* it easily deceives everyone, and hence no remedy is taken until, persevering without obstacle, he arrives at such standing that private citizens

fear him and public officials respect him. 9 When he has risen to this level, if there has been no previous opposition to his greatness, then he has achieved such a position that it is very dangerous to try and oppose him, for the reasons that I stated above[4] about the danger there is in dealing with a problem that has already increased considerably in a city. Thus the matter comes to such a pass that it is necessary either to try and do away with the man, at the risk of sudden downfall, or, if one lets him continue, to fall into obvious servitude unless death or some event sets you free. 10 For once a man has reached the above-mentioned status in which citizens and public officials are afraid of attacking him and his friends, then he does not have a difficult time getting them to judge and attack people acording to his will. 11 For this reason a republic must have the following among its institutions: to make sure its citizens cannot do evil under the guise of doing good and that their influence serves and does not harm freedom, as we shall discuss in its place.[5]

NOTES

1. Machiavelli refers to the period mentioned in chapter 40, sentence 25 above, when "Rome was restored to the form of its ancient freedom." Here the "new laws" refer to the "consular laws" that Livy discusses in 3.55, where it is clear, by the way, that it is specifically the plebs, not precisely the generality of "the Roman people," who are being discussed.

2. 3.65.7; Machiavelli's next several sentences paraphrase 3.65.8–11.

3. Quoted in Latin from Sallust, *De Catilinae coniuratione (Bellum Catilinae),* 51.27: *"Quod omnia mala exempla ex rebus bonis orta sunt";* for Machiavelli's "good beginnings," Sallust says "from good things."

4. In 1, 33.

5. In 3, 28: "Attention Must Be Paid to the Actions of Citizens because a Good Deed Often Masks the Beginnings of Tyranny"; see also Aristotle, *Politics,* 5.8.13; 1308b20–24.

~ 47 ~

EVEN THOUGH MEN MAY BE MISTAKEN IN GENERAL MATTERS, THEY ARE NOT MISTAKEN IN PARTICULARS

1 The Roman people, as has been stated above, came to detest the title of consul[1] and wanted Plebeian men to be able to be made Consuls or to have their power diminished. In order not to tarnish consular power in either way, the Nobility took a middle course and settled for naming four Tribunes with consular power who could be Plebeians as well as Nobles.[2] 2 The Plebeians were satisfied with this, since they felt the Consulship was abolished and they could have their own share in this highest of offices. 3 A noteworthy event developed from this: when it came time to elect these Tribunes, all of whom might have been Plebeians, the Roman people chose only Nobles.[3] 4 Livy says the following about this: "The result of this election showed that there is

one attitude during the struggle for freedom and honor, and another when the struggle is over and men's judgment is free from prejudice."[4] 5 If we examine how this comes about, I believe it results from the fact that men may be greatly deceived in general matters but less so in particulars.[5] 6 In general, the Roman Plebs believed that they deserved the Consulate because they played the greatest role in the city, because they bore the greatest risk in wartime, and because they provided the muscle that kept Rome free and made it powerful. 7 Because, as has been stated, they believed this desire of theirs was reasonable, they wanted to get this power one way or another. 8 But when they had to make a judgment about their men individually, they recognized their shortcomings and judged that none of them deserved what they had appeared to deserve as a whole. 9 So, being ashamed of them, they turned to those who did deserve it. 10 Amazed at this decision, Livy deservedly says the following: "where will you find such modesty, fair-mindedness, and greatness of spirit in one single person today, that an entire people possessed then?"[6]

11 To corroborate this, another noteworthy example can be cited, which occurred in Capua after Hannibal had defeated the Romans at Cannae.[7] 12 All Italy was in turmoil as a result of this defeat, and Capua was also about to riot because of the hatred that existed between the people and the Senate. At the time Pacuvius Calavius was in the highest office: he recognized the threat that the city would riot and decided to use his rank to reconcile the Plebs with the Nobility. 13 Once he thought of this, he assembled the Senate and told them of the hatred the people felt toward them and the risk that they would murder them and turn the city over to Hannibal since Rome's affairs were in a sorry state. He then added that if they were willing to let him handle the matter he would manage to bring the factions together: he wanted to lock them inside the palace and, to save them, give the people power to punish them. 14 The senators deferred to this idea and, after he shut the Senators up in the palace, he called the people to a meeting. 15 He said that the time had come when they could humble the Nobles' pride and avenge themselves for the abuses received from them since they were all locked up under his guard. But because he believed that they did not want their city to be left without a government, it was necessary, if they wanted to murder the former Senators, to appoint new ones. Consequently, he had had the names of each Senator put into a pouch and he would begin to withdraw them in their presence; he would have those drawn murdered one by one as soon as a successor had been found. 16 He began by drawing one name. When the people heard it, they let out a great roar and called the man proud, ruthless, and arrogant. When Pacuvius asked them to a name a replacement, the entire assembly fell silent; then, after a brief interval, one of the Plebs was nominated. Upon hearing his name, some began to whistle, some to laugh, some to speak ill of him one way, some another. So it continued, one after the other: all those nominated were deemed unworthy of senatorial rank. 17 So, seizing this opportunity, Pacuvius said, "Since you consider that the city is badly off without a Senate and you cannot agree as to who should replace the former Senators, I think it might do well for you all to

be reconciled; for the fear the Senators have experienced must have humbled them so much that you will now discover in them the human kindness that you have been seeking elsewhere."[8] 18 Because they agreed with this, harmony with those of senatorial rank ensued; once they were forced to get down to particulars, the error in which they had stood was revealed.

19 Furthermore, people are mistaken in general when they make judgments about things and their events; once they get to know them in their particulars, the people lose such delusion. 20 After 1494, when the princes of Florence had been driven from the city, no constituted government existed there but rather a sort of ambitious lawlessness: public affairs were going from bad to worse.[9] Many common people, seeing that the city was falling apart and not seeing any other cause for it, blamed the ambition of a few powerful people who fomented disorder in order to establish a government to their own liking and to deprive them of their freedom. These men stood around the loggias and public squares speaking ill of many citizens and threatening that were they ever members of the Signoria, they would expose their deceit and punish them. 21 It often happened that this kind of person ascended to the highest public office; when he had risen to that place and seen matters closer at hand, he realized the disorders from which they arose, the dangers impending, and the difficulty of remedying them. 22 Once he realized that the times, not men, caused this disorder, he quickly changed his mind and manner: knowledge of particulars corrected the error that he had assumed when considering them in general. 23 Hence those who had heard him speak earlier when he was a private citizen, seeing him then keep still in the highest office, believed that it resulted not from having a truer understanding of matters but rather from his having been duped and corrupted by the Nobles. 24 And because this happened to many men on many occasions, it led to a proverb among them: "these men are of one mind in the public square and another in the palace."[10]

25 Therefore if we consider everything that has been discussed, we may see that one can make the people, when they have realized that they have been mistaken by a generality, open their eyes quickly, once a way has been discovered to make them get down to particulars, as Pacuvius did in Capua and the Senate in Rome. 26 I also believe that one may conclude that a wise man must never ignore the people's judgment about particular things in the distribution of public offices and honors; for only in this are the people not wrong and if they sometimes are, it happens so rarely that a few men who might have such distributions to make will be deceived more frequently. 27 And it does not seem superfluous for me to point out in the next chapter the rule the Roman Senate followed for disabusing[11] the people in its distribution of offices.

NOTES

1. See 1, 39, sentence 11.

2. Livy, 4.6.8; in 9 he specifies that there were three tribunes, not four.

3. Livy, 4.6.11.

4. Quoted in Latin from 4.6.11, *"Eventus eorum comitiorum docuit alios animos in contentione libertatis dignitatisque, alios secundum deposita certamina in incorrupto iudico esse,"*

though Machiavelli changes Livy's *libertatis dignitatisque* (freedom and dignity) to *libertatis et honoris* (freedom and honor).

5. In a similar vein, Guicciardini writes: "The future is so deceptive and subject to so many accidents that most of the time even the wisest of men misjudge it. Were you to examine his predictions closely, particularly in their details (for general matters are often more accurately predicted), you would find little difference between them and those of men considered to be less wise. Hence to abandon a present good for fear of a future evil is, most of the time, crazy—unless the evil is quite certain and immediate or very great compared with the good. Otherwise, you lose a good thing that you could have had out of a fear that could later prove groundless" (*Ricordi,* C. 23 partially echoed in B. 96).

6. Quoted in Latin, Livy, 4.6.12, *"Hanc modestiam aequitatemque et altitudinem animi, bui nunc in uno inveneris, quae tunc populi universi fuit?"*

7. Based on Livy, 23.2–4.

8. Machiavelli contrives this speech for dramatic effect; it is not in Livy, although it is based on 23.2–4.

9. The phrase "the princes of Florence" refers to the Medici family. The Florentines were furious with Piero de' Medici for ceding territory in Tuscany to the invading French king, Charles VIII; see Guicciardini, *History of Florence,* chapter 11.

10. Machiavelli alludes to a popular Florentine proverb of his day.

11. Translates *isgannare (disingannare);* Inglese notes that the manuscript reading *ingannare,* followed in some texts, is illogical in this context. In his more recent edition, Rinaldi (1:658, n.108) uses a complex course of reasoning to justify the alternative reading, *ingannare.*

~ *48* ~

IF ONE WISHES TO KEEP AN OFFICE FROM BEING GIVEN TO A BASE OR EVIL MAN, HAVE IT SOUGHT EITHER BY SOMEONE TOO BASE AND EVIL OR BY SOMEONE TOO NOBLE AND GOOD

1 When the Senate feared that the Tribunes with consular power might be Plebeians, they had one of two possibilities: either to have the position sought by the most highly esteemed men in Rome, or else by suitable means to corrupt some base and quite dishonorable Plebeians who, mixed in with the Plebeians of better quality who would normally seek the position, would also seek it.[1] 2 This second way would make the Plebeians ashamed to offer it; the first one would make them ashamed to take it. 3 This all reconfirms the preceding discourse, where it is shown that the people, if they are mistaken in general matters, are not mistaken in particulars.

NOTES

1. See Livy, 4.56–57.

~ 49 ~

CITIES WITH FREE ORIGINS LIKE ROME HAVE DIFFICULTY FINDING LAWS TO SUSTAIN THEM, BUT FOR CITIES THAT HAVE BEEN ENSLAVED FROM THE START IT IS VIRTUALLY IMPOSSIBLE

1 The evolution of the Roman republic shows clearly how difficult it is when establishing a republic to provide all the laws that will keep it free. Despite the fact that many laws were established, first by Romulus, then by Numa, Tullius Hostilius, Servius, and finally by the ten citizens designated for that task, nevertheless in the management of the city new needs were constantly discovered and it was necessary to establish new institutions. That is what happened when they created the Censors, who were one of the provisions that helped keep Rome free as long as it did continue in freedom.[1] 2 Because when they became the arbiters of Rome's mores, they were a very potent reason why the Romans put off becoming corrupt for so long. 3 During the first stages of creating that office, they did indeed make the mistake of setting it up for five years, but this was corrected before long by the prudence of the dictator Mamercus, who by new legislation reduced the office to eighteen months.[2] The Censors who were in office took this so badly that they barred Mamercus from the Senate, something strongly criticized by both the Plebs and the Fathers. 4 Because the history does not show whether Mamercus was able to defend himself against this, it must be that either the historian is at fault or Rome's institutions were not good in this respect, because it is not good for a republic to be constituted in such a way that a citizen can be attacked without recourse for having issued a law promoting free society.

5 But returning to the beginning of this discourse, I say that the creation of this new office should make one consider that if cities that had their origins in freedom and governed themselves, like Rome, have great difficulty finding good laws to keep them free it is no wonder that cities that have been subjected since their origins find it not just difficult but impossible ever to organize themselves so they can live civilly and in peace.[3] 6 We see that this happened to the city of Florence: it was subject to the Roman Empire at its origin and always lived under the control of others, so it remained for a while in abjection without giving a thought to itself. Then, when an opportunity to breathe came, it began to formulate its own institutions; these could not be good, because they were mixed in with the older ones, which were bad. So it went along managing itself during the two hundred years for which we have trustworthy annals without ever having had a government by which it could truly be called a republic.[4] 7 The difficulties it has had have always existed in all cities with such origins. 8 Although free, public elections have often granted broad powers to a few citizens to reform it; nevertheless, they have never organized it for the common good, but always in the interests of their party.[5] The result has been not order but greater disorder in the city.

9 To get to some particular examples, I say that among the other things that the one who establishes a republic must consider into the hands of what kind of men he places authority over its citizens' life and death. 10 Rome dealt with this, because normally one could appeal to the people; if something important did occur that made it dangerous to postpone action pending appeal, they had recourse to the Dictator, who acted immediately; they never resorted to this remedy except out of necessity. 11 But Florence and the other cities that originated as it did, since they were subject, placed this power in an outsider sent by the prince to perform this duty. 12 Later, when they gained their freedom, they kept this power in an outsider whom they called a Commander.[6] This was very harmful since he could easily be corrupted by powerful citizens. 13 But later on, as this institution changed because of changes in government, they named eight citizens to carry out the duties of the Commander.[7] This institution went from bad to worse for the reasons that have been stated elsewhere: the few were always the agents of the few and the most powerful. 14 The city of Venice avoided this by having ten citizens[8] who can punish any citizen without appeal. 15 And because they would not be sufficient to punish the powerful, even though they had authority to do so, they established the Forty and, furthermore, have made it so that the Council of Pregadi, which is the Greater Council, can punish them.[9] Consequently, if there is no lack of an accuser, there is no lack of a judge to keep powerful men in check. 16 Therefore, when we see that even in Rome, whose government was constituted by itself and so many wise men, fresh reasons arose every day necessitating the creation of new institutions to foster a free society, it is no wonder if in other cities whose origins were more disordered so many difficulties arise that it is impossible for them ever to be put back in order.

NOTES

1. Livy discusses the origin of the Censors in 443 B.C. in 4.8.1–2. He notes that they were originally charged with taking the census but that they gradually acquired the power to "regulate the morals and discipline of the Romans," including the qualifications for senator.

2. Tiberius Aemilius Mamercus in 433 B.C.; see Livy, 4.23–24. But, as he is about to demonstrate, Machiavelli is examining this source in the spirit of critical inquiry characteristic of modern historians.

3. Machiavelli has adjusted the statement in the chapter's title from "virtually impossible" to "impossible."

4. These views are reflected in Machiavelli's *Florentine Histories,* 2, 2–3. There the two-hundred-year period to which he refers runs roughly from Charlemagne's reign, which lasted from 768 until 814, to 1215 and the beginning of the struggles between the Guelphs, the papal party in Florence, and the Ghibellines, who were partisans of the Holy Roman Emperor in Germany. For him "trustworthy annals" and the beginnings of a "republic" date from 1250; see sentence 12 below. See also the early part of his *Florentine Affairs after Lorenzo's Death* (1520).

5. As regards the potential divisions that "the interests of their party" entailed and the resultant "disorder," Machiavelli is more sanguine about them in the preface to

Florentine Histories than he is here; there he writes that "in [his] judgment" they provide an "example of our city's potency."

6. Translates *capitano.* The *capitano di popolo* was instituted in 1250; see *Florentine Histories,* 2, 5.

7. Machiavelli discusses "elsewhere" the body responsible for the administration of justice in Florence, the Council of Eight of Guard *(Otto di guardia e de balìa),* in chapter 7 above. See also *Florentine Histories,* 4, 29 and 5, 4.

8. Venice provided for a Council of Ten, with authority over issues of public safety, in 1310.

9. The Forty, the Quarantìa, with judicial authority similar to the Supreme Court as well as influence in fiscal matters, was instituted many years earlier in 1179. The Council of the Pregadi were *pregati* or "bidden," "requested" by the Doge to provide consultative opinions, like a senate, to the Great Council. When this body met as a committee of the whole (what Machiavelli calls *universalità* in the next chapter), it consisted of roughly fifteen thousand "gentlemen" who appointed smaller councils that governed and administrated justice. For more on Machiavelli's respectful views on Venice's governmental organization, see above, chapter 6.

~ 50 ~

NO COUNCIL OR OFFICIAL SHOULD BE ABLE TO HALT CITIES' ACTIONS

1 Titus Quinctius Cincinnatus and Gnaeus Julius Mento were consuls in Rome; because there was a rift between them, all action of the republic was halted.[1] 2 When the Senate saw this, it urged the two Consuls to name a Dictator to do what they could not do because of their disagreement. 3 But the Consuls, who disagreed on everything else, were in agreement about only this: they would not name a Dictator. 4 So because the Senate had no other recourse, it resorted to help from the Tribunes, who on the Senate's authority forced the Consuls to obey.

5 From this we should note first the usefulness of the Tribunes' office in checking the ambition that the powerful showed not only against the Plebs but also among themselves; second, a city should never organize itself so that a few people can make any of the decisions that are normally necessary for sustaining the republic. 6 For example, if you give power to a council to make a distribution of offices and perquisites or to an official to administer some undertaking, it is a good idea either to impose on him the need to do it one way or another or, should he not want to act, to set it up so that someone else can and must do it. Otherwise this institution would be flawed and dangerous, as it would have been in Rome had they not been able to use the authority of the Tribunes against the reluctance of those Consuls.

7 In the Venetian Republic, the Great Council[2] distributes offices and perquisites. 8 It sometimes happened that their general assembly, as a result of either scorn or some false conviction, did not name successors to the city's officers

and those who administered their empire abroad. 9 This caused extreme disorder, because suddenly both the conquered territories and the city itself had no legitimate judges; it was impossible to obtain anything unless the general assembly of the Great Council was either satisfied or realized its mistake. 10 This flaw would have gotten the city into a bad situation if its wise citizens had not foreseen it; taking a suitable opportunity, they made a law prohibiting any offices that are or might be within or outside the city from ever being vacated until their replacements and their successors had been named. 11 Thus the council was deprived of the possibility of halting public actions at the republic's peril.

NOTES

1. See Livy, 4.26 for these events, which occurred in 431 B.C.
2. See note 9 to Machiavelli's previous discourse.

~ 51 ~

A REPUBLIC OR A PRINCE MUST PRETEND TO DO OUT OF GENEROSITY WHAT NECESSITY OBLIGES

1 In all their actions, prudent men always take credit for themselves, even if necessity should oblige them to do so in any case. 2 The Roman Senate did practice such prudence when it decided to use the treasury to pay men who served in the army, when they had been wont to serve at their own expense.[1] 3 But the Senate saw that in this way it was unable to wage war for very long and hence that it could neither besiege cities nor lead armies far off. Because it felt it to be necessary to be able to do both these things, it decided to give the stipends, but it did so in such a way as to take credit for what necessity obliged it to. 4 This gift was so welcome to the Plebs that Rome went wild with joy, since it appeared to them to be a great favor, one they had never hoped for and would never have sought on their own. 5 Although the Tribunes strove to cancel this credit out, pointing out that it added rather than removed a burden on the Plebs (since it was necessary to levy taxes to pay this wage), nevertheless, they were unable to act as if the Plebs had not accepted it. 6 This was further increased by the Senate through the way it levied taxes: it imposed the heaviest and largest ones, and the first ones that were paid, on the Nobility.

NOTES

1. See Livy, 4.59.11 and 60 for this decision in 405 B.C., prior to Rome's campaign against the Etruscan city of Veii.

~ 52 ~

THERE IS NO SURER AND LESS DISRUPTIVE WAY TO RESTRAIN THE INSOLENCE OF A MAN WHO RISES TO POWER IN A REPUBLIC THAN PREEMPTING THE WAYS BY WHICH HE COMES TO POWER BEFORE HE DOES

1 From the preceding discourse it can be seen how much prestige the Nobility acquired with the Plebs through the gestures for their benefit that we have read about through both the institution of pay and through the means of levying taxes. 2 If the Nobility had stayed with this institution,[1] it would have been rid of all turmoil in the city and the Tribunes would have been deprived of their prestige with the Plebs, and consequently their authority. 3 In a republic, and especially in corrupt ones, there truly cannot be a better, less disruptive, or easier way to oppose any citizen's ambition than preempting the ways he is seen to be traveling to achieve the position he seeks before he does. 4 Had it been used against Cosimo de' Medici,[2] this means would have been a much better course of action for his adversaries than driving him out of Florence. For if the citizens who were his rivals had adopted his style of favoring the people, then they would have succeeded in taking out of his hands the weapons he relied on most without turmoil and violence.

5 Piero Soderini had made his reputation in the city of Florence just by favoring the populace; that gave him a reputation among the people as a lover of the city's freedom.[3] 6 Had the citizens who envied his greatness preempted before he did the ways by which he was becoming great, it truly would have been much easier, and a more honest thing, less dangerous and less harmful to the republic than trying to oppose him so that with his downfall all the rest of the republic fell.[4] 7 Because if they had taken from his hands the weapons with which he made himself powerful (as they could easily have done), they would have been able to oppose him in all the councils and in public deliberations without any suspicion and without fear. 8 And were some to reply that, if the citizens who hated Piero made a mistake in not taking over before he did the ways by which he gained his prestige with the people, Piero also made a mistake by not taking over the ways by which his opponents were making him afraid. Piero deserves forgiveness on this score: both because it would have been difficult for him to do that and because they were not honorable for him, inasmuch as the ways they took to attack him were to support the Medici; they defeated him by means of this support and in the end caused his downfall. 9 Therefore Piero could not take that course of action honorably, since he could not keep his reputation while destroying the freedom that he had been chosen to safeguard. Furthermore, because this support could not be made in secret and in an instant, it would have been very dangerous for Piero: as soon as he had shown himself to be a friend of the Medici, he would have become suspect and odious to the people.[5] The result would have been a much better opportunity for his enemies to attack him than they had previously had.

10 Therefore men must consider the drawbacks and dangers in every course of action and not take one if there is more danger than profit, even if they have been advised in a way consistent with their decision. 11 Because if they do otherwise, what happened to Cicero would happen to them in this case: by trying to decrease Mark Antony's support, he increased it.[6] 12 After the Senate had judged Mark Antony to be an enemy of the Senate and he had mustered a large army, the majority of them soldiers who had followed Caesar's party, Cicero, to get these soldiers away from him, urged the Senate to increase Octavian's prestige and send him against Mark Antony with the consuls Hirtius and Pansa. He claimed that as soon as the soldiers following Mark Antony heard the name of Octavian, Caesar's nephew, and being called Caesar, they would desert the former and side with the latter. Thus, when Mark Antony had been stripped of support, it would be easy to defeat him. 13 The affair turned out quite the opposite, because Mark Antony won Octavian over and, deserting Cicero and the Senate, sided with him. 14 This matter led to the complete destruction of the party of the Optimates.[7] 15 That was easy to foresee. People should never have believed what Cicero was convinced of; they should always have paid attention to the name[8] that had so gloriously liquidated his enemies and acquired rule over Rome for itself. And people should never have believed that they could have anything consistent with the name of freedom from either Caesar's successors or his partisans.

NOTES

1. That is, the policy of "gestures" for the plebs' "benefit"; "institution" translates *ordine.*

2. See above, 1, 33, n.2, and *Florentine Histories,* 4, 27–33. See also Mansfield, *New Modes,* pp. 152–153.

3. See above, 1, 7, n.5, and below, 3, 3, n.3.

4. The "citizens who envied [Soderini's] greatness" were an aristocratic faction, the *ottimati,* against whom Machiavelli directs his anger here, an emotion also characteristic of his *Ricordo ai Palleschi* (Memorandum to Medici supporters). One of the *ottimati* leaders was Alamanno Salviati, Francesco Guicciardini's father-in-law and the dedicatee of Machiavelli's *Decennale primo;* two other important ones were Bernardo Rucellai and Giovan Battista Ridolfi. Piero Soderini was forced to resign on 31 August 1512, and on the evening of the next day Lorenzo de' Medici, the third son of Lorenzo the Magnificent, forced into exile at the court of Urbino when his brother Piero was exiled from Florence in 1494, made his triumphal entry into Florence. See Machiavelli's immediate comments on these events in his letter to an unknown gentlewoman written some time after 16 September 1512; see *Friends,* pp. 214–217. See also Guicciardini, *Storia d'Italia,* 11, 4, and *History of Florence,* 25.

5. A succinct statement of Soderini's dilemma: since his main support lay with the popular faction, he could not be "a friend of the Medici" with their support among aristocrats. As gonfalonier he was pledged to "safeguard" the republic. Although Machiavelli often blamed Soderini for vacillation, that is not the case here in his defense of Soderini's loyalty to the republic. Guicciardini's antirepublican sentiments are clear in his assessment of Soderini: "his plan was . . . to make himself a man of the people . . . and to please the masses" (*History of Florence,* chapter 20).

6. The following is a brief summary of the events described in the rest of this paragraph. Cicero consistently opposed Julius Caesar; he supported Pompey and later Brutus and Cassius. After Caesar's assassination in 44 B.C., the senate condemned Mark Antony and, as Cicero "exhorted," ordered an army led by the consuls Aulus Hirtius and Gaius Vibius Pansa to defeat him. They did so at the battle of Mutina, near the present-day Modena, in 43, but the two consuls died. In a series of speeches late in 44 and early in 43 called the "Philippics" (after the orations of Demosthenes against Philip of Macedon for threatening Athenian liberty), Cicero urged Rome to put Octavian in charge of the army, and the senate agreed. Octavian, however, turned against the Senate, joined with Lepidus, Rome's military commander in Gaul, and became reconciled with Antony; late in 43 the three formed the second triumvirate, which ruled Rome for five years. Octavian did not object to Antony's insistence that Cicero be proscribed; soldiers eventually killed him, and Antony had him beheaded and his hands nailed to the Rostra, the speaker's platform in the Forum.

7. By using a word from contemporary Florentine politics for the aristocratic, noble party, *Ottimati,* Machiavelli indicates how much his focus is Florence even when discussing Roman history.

8. That is, they should have given more credit to the power and prestige behind the name of "Caesar," a title that Julius passed on to his adopted son, Octavian.

~ *53* ~

THE PEOPLE, DECEIVED BY A FALSE KIND OF GOOD, OFTEN DESIRE THEIR OWN RUIN; AND HIGH HOPES AND BOLD PROMISES EASILY STIR THEM

1 After the city of the Veians was conquered,[1] the Roman people came to believe that it would be useful for the city of Rome if half the Romans were to go and live in Veii; they argued that because the countryside around Veii was fertile and the city was full of buildings and close to Rome, half the Roman citizens could prosper and, because of the proximity of its location, no civic activity would be disturbed. 2 This seemed so futile and harmful to the Senate and the wisest Romans that they freely declared they would sooner suffer death than consent to such a decision. 3 Consequently, when this matter came up for discussion, the Plebs were so inflamed against the Senate they would have resorted to arms and bloodshed if the Senate had not shielded itself behind some aged and esteemed citizens; reverence for them restrained the Plebs, who did not carry their insolence any further.

4 Here two things must be observed. 5 The first is that the people, deceived by a false image of good, often desire their own ruin; if someone in whom they trust does not make them understand that this is bad and what would be good, countless dangers and injuries are brought upon republics. 6 And when fate wills that the people trust in no one, as sometimes happens, when they have been deceived by either events or men in the past, then of necessity they come to ruin. 7 In his discussion in *De monarchia,* Dante says about this that the

people often shout "Long live" their death and "Death to" their life.[2] 8 The result of this skepticism is that sometimes good decisions are not made in republics. This was stated earlier[3] about the Venetians who, when assailed by so many enemies, could not make up their minds to win over some of them by restoring what they had taken from others (which is why war had been declared and the league of princes formed against them) until their ruin occurred.

9 Therefore this distinction can be made concerning what it is easy and what it is hard to convince people of: either what you have to convince them of represents a profit or a loss at first view or else it seems a courageous or cowardly course of action. 10 And when a profit is seen in matters proposed to the people, even though a loss may lie concealed beneath them, and when they seem courageous, even though the republic's downfall may lie hidden beneath them, the masses will always be easy to convince of them. So it will always be hard to convince them to accept courses of action in which cowardice or a loss appears, even though safety and profit may lie concealed beneath them.

11 What I am saying can be corroborated by numerous examples, Roman and foreign, modern and ancient. 12 For from this stemmed the bad opinion that arose in Rome of Fabius Maximus, who was unable to convince the Roman people that it was useful for the republic to proceed slowly in its war and to resist Hannibal's attack without fighting back; the people judged this course of action cowardly and did not see the advantage there was in it and Fabius did not have arguments sufficient to prove it to them.[4] 13 But the people are so blinded by bold ideas that the Romans made the mistake of authorizing Fabius's Master of the Horse to fight, even though Fabius did not want to; because of that authorization the Roman army was on the verge of being defeated had not Fabius, in his wisdom, found a remedy.[5] Even this experience was not sufficient for the people: they then made Varro consul for no other merit of his than having promised, through all the squares and public places in Rome, to defeat Hannibal any time authorization was granted him.[6] 14 From this came the battle and the defeat of Cannae and almost the downfall of Rome.[7]

15 I wish to cite yet another Roman example on this subject. 16 Hannibal had been in Italy for eight or ten years; he had filled the entire land with slain Romans. At that point Marcus Centenius Penula, a man of quite base origin (despite his having held some rank in the army), came to the Senate; if they gave him authorization to raise a volunteer army anywhere he chose in Italy, he offered to hand Hannibal over to them in no time, captured or dead. 17 His request seemed rash to the Senate. Nevertheless, they thought that if they refused him and his request later became known to the people then turmoil, spite, and ill will against the senatorial order might result. So they agreed to his request, preferring to endanger all the men who accompanied him rather than arouse fresh anger among the people; they knew how acceptable such a course of action would be and how difficult it would be to dissuade them. 18 So he went with an undisciplined and motley crew to meet Hannibal, and no sooner did he arrive at the encounter than he was defeated and killed along with all those following him.[8]

19 In the city of Athens in Greece, Nicias, a very grave and wise man, could never convince people that going to attack Sicily was a bad idea; when they so decided, against the will of the wise men, Athens' total ruin ensued.[9] 20 When Scipio was named consul and sought the province of Africa, he promised Carthage's total ruin. When the Senate refused on the advice of Fabius Maximus, he threatened to propose it to the people, for he knew very well how much such plans please the people.[10]

21 Examples could be given in this connection from our city: as when, after defeating Bartolomeo d'Alviano at San Vincenzo, messer Ercole Bentivoglio, the commander of the Florentine troops, together with Antonio Giacomini, went to camp at Pisa.[11] The people decided on that campaign because of messer Ercole's bold promises, even though many wise citizens disapproved of it; nevertheless, they had no recourse against it since they were impelled by the general will, based on the commander's bold promises.

22 Therefore I say there is no easier way to cause the downfall of a republic in which the people hold power than to set it upon bold campaigns, because wherever the people have any influence these campaigns will always be welcomed; anyone who is of a different opinion will have no remedy for them. 23 But if this results in the city's ruin, it also and even more frequently brings about the ruin of the individual citizens put in charge of such campaigns. Because the people count on victory, when the loss comes they do not blame either Fortune or the commander's powerlessness but his wickedness and ignorance; more often than not they either put him to death or imprison or banish him, as happened to innumerable Carthaginian commanders and many Athenian ones. 24 And no victory that they may previously have achieved is of any avail to them because the present loss cancels out everything. That is what happened to our Antonio Giacomini, who failed to capture Pisa as the people had presumed and he had promised; he fell into such popular disgrace that, despite his countless good deeds in the past, his life was spared more thanks to the mercy of those in power than for any other reason protecting him among the people.[12]

NOTES

1. In 395 B.C. after a ten-year struggle; see Livy, 5.24–25.

2. Not in *De monarchia,* but in *Convivio,* 1, 11; the point is that the people frequently advocate policies that are in fact prejudicial and denounce those that might benefit them.

3. Machiavelli probably has in mind above, 1, 6, sentence 27 (see note 11 to 1, 6, for "the league of princes formed against them"), but a more explicit statement can be found below, 3, 31, sentences 13 and 14.

4. Quintus Fabius Maximus, known as *Cunctator* (the Delayer) because he sought to avoid direct engagement with Hannibal during the Second Punic War, 218–201 B.C. He was made dictator in 217.

5. Livy, 22.25–30; Marcus Minucius was the *magister equitum,* Master of the Horse.

6. Livy, 22.34–35; 38–39.

7. For more on Caius Terentius Varro and the defeat at Cannae in 216, see Livy, 22.46–49 and above, 1, 31, n.7 above.

8. Livy, 25.19, though Livy describes the centurion Penula in rather less boastful terms. Martelli believes Machiavelli's treatment is intended to make the example of Penula consonant with the chapter's title (*Storici antichi,* pp. 46–47).

9. These events involving the Athenian general Nicias (470–413 B.C.) are discussed in Thucydides, 6.8–9; see also Plutarch, *Nicias,* 12, and below, 3, 16, and note 1.

10. Livy, 28.40–45; Scipio sought to take the campaign directly to Africa in 205 B.C.

11. Alviano was one of Gonzalo Fernández de Córdoba's condottieri; he abandoned the Spanish general in the kingdom of Naples after their victory at the Battle of Garigliano and headed for central Italy, where he joined forces with other mercenary leaders. On his way to reinforce Pisa, Alviano was defeated by Bentivoglio and Giacomini at a battle on 17 August 1505 near Torre di San Vincenzo on the Tyrrhenian Sea north of Piombino. Elation at their victory led the Council of Eighty, which the popular party controlled, and the Great Council, at Soderini's urging, to order an attack on Pisa. Guicciardini echoes Machiavelli's thoughts on this unwise decision: "wise and authoritative citizens" opposed the attack, "we should have proceeded according to the opinion of the wise men, not the multitude's, which is ignorant, does not scrutinize the particulars of matters, and is willing to act on any shred of hope" (*History of Florence,* chapter 26, and *Storia d'Italia,* 6, 15). Toward the end of August, Florence sent Machiavelli to join the all-out attack on Pisa with orders for Bentivoglio and Giacomini on how to conduct the siege, which ended in failure and Giacomini's disgrace in mid-September. See Machiavelli's personal letters to him, *Friends,* pp. 113–114. (Antonio Giacomini is sometimes referred to as Antonio Tebalducci or Antonio Giacomini Tebalducci; see below, 3, 16, n. 5.)

12. Some see a hint of personal regret in this paragraph, particularly after the failure of Machiavelli's militia at the sack of Prato in 1512 and his subsequent exile.

~ 54 ~

HOW MUCH POWER A GRAVE MAN HAS TO RESTRAIN AROUSED MASSES

1 The second noteworthy thing concerning the text cited in the chapter above is that nothing is so likely to restrain aroused masses as reverence for some grave, authoritative man confronting them. It is not without reason that Virgil says:

> Then if they chance to see any man grave in his piety
> And merits, they are silent and stand with attentive ears.[1]

2 Therefore the one who is put in charge of an army or finds himself in a city where rioting occurs, must show himself before them with as much grace and dignity as he can, surrounding himself with the insignia of the rank he holds in order to make himself more respected.

3 A few years ago Florence was divided into two factions, the Frateschi and the Arrabbiati (as they were called); when armed fighting broke out, the Frateschi were beaten.[2] Among the latter was Paolantonio Soderini, a very

highly esteemed citizen in those days. During the rioting, the people went to his house under arms to loot it. His brother, messer Francesco, then bishop of Volterra and today a cardinal, by chance happened to be in the house. As soon as he heard the noise and saw the crowd, he donned his most venerable garments and over them his bishop's surplice, he confronted the armed men, and he halted them with his presence and his words. This was noted and celebrated throughout the entire city for many days.[3]

4 I therefore conclude that there is no stronger or more necessary recourse for restraining aroused masses than the presence of a man who appears, and is, worthy of respect by his presence. 5 It can therefore be seen, returning to the text already cited,[4] how stubbornly the Roman Plebs stayed with their plan to go to Veii, because they judged it useful and did not recognize how much harm lay beneath it, and how, since a great deal of turmoil arose from it, civil strife would have arisen had not the Senate restrained their fury with men who were grave and highly respected.

NOTES

1. Quoted in Latin from *Aeneid,* 1, vv. 151–152: *"Tum pietate gravem ac meritis si forte virum quem / conspexere, silent arrectisque auribus astant."*

2. The supporters of Savonarola, see above, 1, 11, nn.12 and 13, were the Frateschi (the Friar's followers); the Arrabbiati (the "rabid" or "enraged" ones) were opposed to both Savonarola and the Medici and advocated a republic along aristocratic lines for Florence. The most influential leaders of the Frateschi were Francesco Valori and Piero Soderini's brother, Paolantonio.

3. Guicciardini omits Francesco's actions in early April 1498 from his account in *History of Florence,* chapter 16.

4. Livy, 5.24–25; 51–55, cited above, 1, 53.

~ 55 ~

HOW EASY IT IS TO GOVERN AFFAIRS IN A CITY WHERE THE MASSES ARE NOT CORRUPT; EQUALITY PREVENTS ESTABLISHING A PRINCEDOM, AND WHERE THERE IS NONE A REPUBLIC CANNOT BE ESTABLISHED

1 Although there has been considerable discussion above about what is to be feared or hoped for in corrupted cities,[1] it seems nevertheless relevant to consider a decision of the Senate concerning the vow that Camillus made to give Apollo one tenth of the Veians' spoils. 2 When these spoils fell into the hands of the Roman Plebs and there was no other way to make a new accounting of it, the Senate issued an edict that everyone should show in public one-tenth of what he had looted. 3 Although this decision did not take effect, since the Senate later found other means and placated Apollo by a different way, to the satisfaction of the Plebs,[2] nevertheless, it can be seen from this

decision how much trust the Senate had in their goodness, judging that no one would fail to show exactly all the edict required him to. 4 On the other hand, it can be seen that the Plebs thought not of cheating the edict by giving less than they owed but rather of freeing themselves from it by showing open indignation. 5 This example, along with many others that have been given above,[3] shows how much goodness and religion there was in those people and how much good could be expected of them.

6 And in truth, where such goodness does not exist, no good can be expected, nor can any be expected from those regions that are seen to be corrupted in our day, as Italy is above all others.[4] 7 France and Spain also exhibit their share of corruption.[5] If we do not see so many disorders in these countries as arise every day in Italy, that derives not so much from the people's goodness, which they lack for the most part, as from their having a king who keeps them united not only through his *virtù* but through the institutions[6] of those kingdoms, which are not yet spoiled. 8 Indeed, this goodness and religion can still be seen to be great among the inhabitants of the land of Germany.[7] Consequently, many republics live free there and observe their laws in such a way that no domestic or foreign power dares seize them. 9 And to show that a healthy measure of the ancient goodness flourishes in them, I wish to give an example similar to the one mentioned above about the Senate and the Roman Plebs.

10 When the need arises for those republics to spend a sum of money for public expenses, it is customary for those officers or councils that have authority for it to levy on all the inhabitants of the city a one or two percent tax on what each of them has in cash value. 11 When such a decision has been made, each man presents himself before the collector of that tax in accordance with the city's laws; first, he takes an oath to pay the requisite amount; then he throws into a chest assigned to that purpose what he believes in conscience he ought to pay: the only witness to such payment is the one who pays. 12 From this we can imagine how much goodness and religion there still is in those men. 13 And we must assume that each one pays the right amount: because if it were not paid, the taxation would not yield the total they designated to be raised in keeping with former taxes collected; if it were not achieved, fraud would be realized, and when it was realized, some other measure than this would be taken. 14 Such goodness is all the more to be admired these days because it is more rare; indeed, it can be seen to have survived only in that land.

15 This arises from two things: one, their not having had many dealings with their neighbors, because the latter have not visited them and they have not gone to visit the others, because they have been satisfied with the goods, living on the foods, and clothing themselves with the woolens that the country provides. This has eliminated any cause for dealings and the origin of all corruption, because they have not been able to pick up either French or Spanish or Italian customs, and those nations as a whole are the source of the world's corruption.[8] 16 The other cause is that those republics, in which uncorrupted political life has been maintained, do not allow any of their citi-

zens to exist or to live in the style of gentlemen. On the contrary, they maintain complete equality among themselves, and they are very hostile to the lords and gentlemen that do exist in the land; and if by chance any fall into their hands they put them to death, as the origin of corruption and the cause of all civil strife.[9]

17 And to clarify what the name of *gentlemen* means, I shall say that we call gentlemen those who live richly in idleness and on the income from their estates without having any care for either agriculture or other work essential for living. 18 Such men are destructive to any republic and any land; but still more destructive are those who, in addition to the wealth mentioned above, have strongholds under their command and subjects who obey them.[10] 19 The kingdom of Naples, the lands of Rome,[11] Romagna, and Lombardy are full of these two kinds of men.[12] 20 From this arises the fact that no republic and no political life has ever arisen in those regions because those classes of men are completely hostile to any kind of civil society.[13] 21 It would be impossible to try and introduce a republic into lands that are constituted in such a way; but were anyone to assume the responsibility, there would be no other way to try to reorganize them than establishing a kingdom there. 22 The reason is that where the material is so corrupted that laws are not an adequate restraint, then some superior force must necessarily be instituted along with them: a royal hand that with absolute and overwhelming power can put a check on the overwhelming ambition and corruption of the powerful.[14]

23 This reason can be proved by the example of Tuscany, where we can see that three republics, Florence, Siena, and Lucca, have existed for a long time in a small area of land, and the other cities of this region have been so subject that we can see that they preserve, or they would like to preserve, their freedom with their courage and their institutions.[15] 24 This all results from there being no lords with their own strongholds in this region and no or very few gentry; but there is so much equality that civil society[16] could be easily be introduced into it by a wise man, one with knowledge of ancient forms of civil society.[17] 25 But up to the present its misfortune has been so great that it has not encountered any man who was able or knew how to do it.

26 From this discourse I therefore have drawn the following conclusions. Anyone who wants to establish a republic where there are many gentlemen cannot do so unless he first eliminates all of them. Anyone who wants to establish either a kingdom or a princedom where there is great equality will never be able to do so unless he draws out of that equality many men with ambitious and restless spirits and makes them gentlemen in fact, not in name, endowing them with strongholds and estates and supporting them with property and men so that, surrounded by them and thanks to their support, he preserves his power, and thanks to him they preserve their ambitions. The rest are obliged to bear a yoke that force and nothing but force can make them bear.[18] 27 Thus a balance is created between subjectors and subjected: men stay put, each in his own order. 28 Because transforming a land suited to be a kingdom into a republic and one suited to be a republic into a kingdom is a

matter for a man who has rare brains and power, there are many who have tried to do it and few who have been able to carry it out. 29 In part the magnitude of the deed frightens men and in part it inhibits them so much that they fail from the very start.

30 I believe that the experience of the Venetian republic, in which only those who are gentlemen can hold office, will seem contrary to this belief of mine that where there are gentlemen a republic cannot be established. 31 The answer to this is that the example is in no way opposed to this, because in that republic they are gentlemen more in name than in fact. They do not have large revenues from landed estates; their great wealth is based on trade and movable goods; furthermore, none of them possesses strongholds or has any jurisdiction over men. Rather, the term *gentleman* among them is a term of dignity and prestige, not based on any of the grounds that make people be called gentlemen in other cities. 32 Just as other republics all have their divisions under different names, so Venice is divided into gentlemen and commoners; they wish the former to hold or to be eligible to hold every office and the latter to be completely excluded from it. 33 For reasons stated elsewhere,[19] this does not lead to disorder in that city.

34 Therefore let anyone who establishes a republic do so where great equality exists or has been created.[20] On the contrary, let him establish a princedom where there great inequality exists. Otherwise he will create something that lacks balance and permanence.[21]

NOTES

1. Above in 1, 16–18; although this chapter is related to them, Machiavelli alters his point of view significantly.

2. See Livy, 5.21–25, for this incident and its ramifications.

3. In 1, 12.

4. Machiavelli berates Florence for such "corruption" in *Florentine Histories,* 7, 28.

5. Machiavelli's thoughts about Spain and the policies of Ferdinand the Catholic are pretty much restricted to his letters to Francesco Vettori, especially Letter 212, dated 29 April 1513 (*Friends,* pp. 231–236). On the other hand, for all his respect for French laws and institutions (see above, 1, 16, n.9), he still characterizes the people as "corrupted."

6. Inglese's text reads the plural form *l'ordini,* though most previous texts have the singular *l'ordine.*

7. Machiavelli's direct experience "of the land of Germany" was restricted to his visit to the Tyrol and part of Switzerland in a diplomatic mission with Vettori to the Holy Roman Emperor Maximilian; it lasted from December 1507 until June 1508. His participation led to the *Rapporto delle cose della Magna fatto questo dì 17 Giugno 1508* (Report on affairs in Germany written this day 17 June 1508); a *Discorso sopra le cose della Magna e sopra l'imperatore* (Discourse about German affairs and about the emperor), written for Florentine envoys; the *Ritratto delle cose della Magna* (Portrayal of German affairs), written after a second mission to Maximilian I; and *Prince,* 10, p. 205, lines 28–45.

8. Machiavelli has polarized this description for his own purposes; the historical truth of these observations is less important than what they reveal about his thinking.

He does, however, mention trade between Venice and German cities in *Ritratto delle cose della Magna.*

9. Relevant texts for Machiavelli's belief that equality is a necessary precondition to establishing a republican form of government are his *Florentine Affairs after Lorenzo's Death* (1520) and *Florentine Histories,* 3, 1. Machiavelli's notion of a republic is alluded to here in his phrase *il vivere politico* (political life). In turn, it is tantamount to what above, 1, 17, sentence 2, he describes as *vivere liberi e ordinati* (living in a free and ordered society) and later in this chapter, sentence 20, *civilità* (a civil society); in sentence 24 he uses both *civilità* and *uno vivere civile.*

10. The drawback that feudal societies represent is that the feudal lords with their "strongholds" constitute a kind of state that cannot be easily incorporated into a republic because of their being "hostile to any kind of civil life" *(civilità):* that is, the kind characteristic of a republic; see sentence 20 of this chapter. This notion is also present in *Prince,* 4, and *Ritratto di cose di Francia.*

11. Translates *Terra di Roma,* the "city" or "lands" of Rome; Machiavelli alludes to the territory under papal control.

12. Milan and Naples are among the places mentioned above, 1, 17, where a republic cannot thrive; see 1, 17, n.7.

13. Translates *civilità.*

14. In the final analysis, this would be the justification for a ruler as described in the *Prince.* The quasi-monarchical powers advocated above, 1, 18, sentence 28 (and see note 8), are justified there because of the people's corruption, defined as "unruliness"; the inability to subject them to laws is not the issue here, because a prince arrives at the laws in conjunction with a populace that is not corrupted. In the *capitolo "Dell'ambizione"* Machiavelli notes that ambition, defined as mankind's "natural instinct" to wish another person "ill" *(mal),* must be "reigned in by laws or greater force" (vv. 79–81).

15. Cities that Machiavelli has recently discussed, such as Arezzo in 1502 (see above, 1, 39) and Pisa (above 1, 53), which remained outside Florentine control from 1495 to 1509.

16. Translates *uno vivere civile.*

17. Translates *civilità.*

18. The argument here would appear to run counter to what Machiavelli says about "civil princedoms" in *Prince,* 9 and above, 1, 40, concerning saving or conquering a republic; in both instances the support of the people, not that of a feudal nobility, is what he recommends. The prince needs the people's support as a countervailing power to the rich and powerful, the *grandi.* See Sasso, *Antichi,* 2:435–436; 461–467.

19. See above, 1, 6, sentences 8–10.

20. As per sentence 27 above.

21. The argument of this subtle, important chapter calls for great insight on the part of those instituting a new government, such as framers of constitutions. They must ensure that their document conforms to the society for which it is devised, because the society cannot be modified easily. The founders' skill can produce a republic with "balance and permanence"; their failure can produce a tyranny "that lacks balance and permanence."

~ 56 ~

BEFORE GREAT EVENTS[1] OCCUR IN A CITY OR A REGION, THERE ARE SIGNS FORESHADOWING THEM OR MEN PROPHESYING THEM

1 How it comes about I do not know, but both ancient and modern examples show that no serious event has ever happened in a city or a land that was not foretold by either diviners or revelations or wonders or other celestial signs. 2 Not to go very far from home to prove this, everyone knows what was foretold by Fra Girolamo Savonarola[2] before King Charles VIII of France came into Italy, and moreover that throughout Tuscany people said they had heard and seen armed troops fighting together in the air above Arezzo.[3] 3 Besides this, everyone knows that before the death of Lorenzo de' Medici the elder,[4] a thunderbolt struck the cathedral at its highest point, causing very great damage to the building.[5] 4 Everyone also knows that shortly before Piero Soderini, whom the Florentine people had made gonfalonier for life, was driven out and stripped of his rank, the palace was similarly struck by lightning.[6] 5 Examples in addition to these could be cited, but I shall omit them to avoid being tedious. 6 I shall mention only the one that Livy tells of before the coming of the Gauls to Rome: how one Marcus Caedicius, a Plebeian, reported to the Senate that, as he was passing along the Via Nova in the middle of the night, he heard a louder than human voice warning him to report to the officials that the Gauls were coming to Rome.[7] 7 I believe the reason for this ought to be discussed and interpreted by someone who has knowledge of natural and supernatural things, which we do not. 8 Yet it might be, as some philosophers[8] would have it, that since the air is full of intelligences that foresee the future by means of their natural *virtù* and have pity on men, they warn them through such signs so that they can prepare for defense. 9 But however it may be, one thus sees it to be the truth, and after such events extraordinary and strange things always occur in lands.

NOTES

1. Translates *accidenti*.

2. Charles VIII was king of France from 1483 until 1498; his invasion of Italy lasted from September 1494 until October 1495. Savonarola's preachings prior to this invasion were full of dire predictions about a scourge that would cleanse Florence and save Italy from corruption.

3. See Guicciardini, *Storia d'Italia,* 1, 9.

4. Lorenzo de' Medici the Magnificent ruled Florence from 1469 until his death on 8 April 1492; he is called "the elder" to distinguish him from Lorenzo II, duke of Urbino (the man to whom *The Prince* was dedicated), who ruled Florence from 1513 to 1518.

5. Machiavelli refers to this event concerning the cathedral of Santa Maria del Fiore, which he also calls the Church of Santa Reparata (i.e., the Duomo) in *Florentine Histories,* 8, 36. Luca Landucci entered the fact in his *Diary* three days before on 5 April 1492 (pp. 52–53).

6. According to the *Diary* of Luca Landucci, the Palazzo della Signoria or Palazzo Vecchio was struck on the night of 4 November 1511 (pp. 247–248); Soderini was banished in early September 1512.

7. Based on Livy, 5.32; he says "silence of the night" (5.32.6), rather than Machiavelli's more dramatic "middle of the night" and "more distinct" rather than Machiavelli's "louder." The Gauls burned Rome in 390 B.C.

8. Cicero, *De divinatione,* 1.30.64; but similar ideas were also current in Renaissance Italy among philosophers ranging from Ficino and Pico della Mirandola to Pomponazzi. Nevertheless, Machiavelli's emphasis is on the natural, not the supernatural, *virtù* of these "signs." For more on this topic, see Niccoli, *Prophecy and People.*

~ 57 ~

TOGETHER THE PLEBS ARE BOLD; INDIVIDUALLY THEY ARE WEAK

1 After the invasion by the Gauls and the destruction of their homeland, many Romans had gone to live in Veii, contrary to the Senate's decree and order. To remedy this disorder it ordered everyone in its public edicts to return to Rome within a stated time and under stated penalties to live there.[1] 2 At first these edicts were mocked by those they were directed against; then, when the time to obey drew near, everybody did so. 3 And Livy says these words: "From being ferocious as members of the masses, each man alone grew so frightened that he became obedient."[2]

4 And truly the nature of the masses cannot be shown better than it is in this text, in this respect. 5 Because the masses are often bold in speaking out against their prince's decisions; then, when they come face-to-face with the penalty, they hasten to obey because they do not trust one another. 6 Thus we can clearly see that what people have to say about their positive or negative inclinations must not be granted much importance when you are organized in such a way as to be able to sustain them if they are well-disposed and, if they are ill-disposed, to be sure they do not harm you. 7 This applies to negative dispositions that people have arising from some other cause than the loss either of their freedom or of a beloved prince who is still living. For negative dispositions resulting from these causes are more to be feared than anything and require strong remedies to check them; other negative dispositions will be easy [to manage] as long as they do not have leaders to fall back on. 8 For on the one hand, nothing is more to be feared than the masses unleashed and leaderless; on the other hand, there is nothing weaker. For even if they chance to have weapons in hand, it will be easy to quell them as long as you have a refuge in which to flee the initial violence: once their minds have cooled off a bit and each man sees he has to go back home, they begin to fear for themselves and plan for their safety either by running away or by coming to terms. 9 Hence if the aroused masses seek to avoid these dangers, they should immediately choose one of their members as a leader to direct

them, keep them united, and plan their defense. The Roman Plebs did so when they left Rome after the death of Virginia and, for their safety, named twenty Tribunes from among themselves.[3] 10 And if they do not do this, then what Livy says in the words quoted above always come true: when they are all together, they are bold, but when each man then starts to think of his own danger, they grow cowardly and weak.

NOTES

1. See Livy, 5.49.8, and 6.4.5–6.

2. Quoted in slightly altered Latin from 6.4.5, which reads, *"ex ferocibus universis singulos, metu suo quemque, oboedientes."* Again, Martelli believes the alteration to be deliberate on Machiavelli's part to make the example fit his thesis (*Storici antichi,* p. 48).

3. For this event based on Livy, 3.50–51, see above, 1, 44, n.3.

~ 58 ~

THE MASSES ARE WISER AND MORE CONSTANT THAN A PRINCE

1 Our Livy, like all other historians, affirms that nothing is more vain and inconstant than the masses.[1] 2 In accounts of men's actions, we frequently are shown the masses to have condemned someone to death and then lamented and yearned most deeply for the same man, as we see the Roman people did with Manlius Capitolinus, whom they most deeply yearned for after condemning him to death. 3 Here are the author's words: "Shortly thereafter, when there was no longer any danger from him, longing for him took hold of the people."[2] 4 And elsewhere, when he describes the events that occurred in Syracuse after the death of Hieronymus,[3] the grandson of Hiero, he says: "This is the nature of the masses: either they bow humbly or they tyrannize arrogantly."[4] 5 I do not know whether I will be taking on an area that is harsh and full of such difficulty that I either have to abandon it to my shame or pursue it to my reproach, since I want to defend a position that, as I have said, every writer rejects. 6 But, however this may be, I do not and I never shall judge the defense of any opinion by reason without recourse to either authority or force to be a flaw.[5]

7 I say, therefore, that all men individually, and especially princes, can be accused of this flaw of which writers accuse the masses, because anyone who is not regulated by laws would make the same mistakes as the unbridled masses. 8 This can be easily realized because there are and have been many princes but few good and wise ones. I am speaking of princes who were able to break the reins that can control them; I exclude from these the kings who originated in Egypt when laws governed that land in most remote antiquity, those who originated in Sparta, or those who originate in our day in France, a kingdom that is governed more by laws than any other kingdom that we know of in our time.[6] 9 Kings who originate under such constitutions are not

to be numbered in the category in which one must consider each man's individual nature and see if it resembles that of the masses, because the comparison should be between kings controlled by laws and similarly controlled masses. One will see the same goodness in both of them. One will also see, as was the case with the Roman people, that the masses neither "tyrannize arrogantly" nor "bow humbly." For as long as the republic endured uncorrupted, the people never served humbly and never tyrannized arrogantly; rather, with their institutions and officials they held their own rank honorably. 10 When it was necessary to rise up against a powerful man, they did so, as we have seen with Manlius, the Decemvirate, and others who sought to oppress them; and when it was necessary to obey Dictators and Consuls for the public safety, they did so. 11 If "longing . . . took hold of the [Roman] people" for Manlius when he was dead, it is no wonder: the people missed his *virtù*,[7] which had been such that its memory aroused sympathy in everyone and would have had the power to work the same effect on a prince, for all writers are of the opinion that *virtù* is praised and admired even in one's enemies. 12 If Manlius had been brought back to life amid such longing, the people of Rome would have passed the same judgment upon him as they did when, after they had released him from prison, they condemned him to death a short while later;[8] nonetheless, one can see princes reputed wise who have put some person to death and then very deeply missed him: as Alexander did Clitus and other friends of his and Herod did Mariamne.[9] 13 But what our historian says about the nature of the masses he does not say of those governed by laws, like the Romans, but of unbridled ones, like the Syracusans; they made the mistakes that enraged and unbridled men make, as did Alexander the Great and Herod in the examples cited. 14 Hence the nature of the masses is no more to be blamed than that of princes, for they all err equally when they all can err without interference. 15 There are many examples of this, in addition to what I have said, both among the Roman emperors and among other tyrants and princes; as much inconstancy and fickleness can be seen in their lives as ever could be found in any masses.

16 Therefore my conclusion goes against the common opinion, which says that the people (when they are in power) are fickle, changeable, and ungrateful; I hold that these sins are not otherwise in them than they are in individual princes.[10] 17 Anyone who accuses both the people and princes might be telling the truth, but if he leaves out the princes he is wrong. For the people, if they command and are well organized, will be just as stable, wise, and grateful as a prince or better than a prince, even one who is considered wise. On the other hand, a prince uncontrolled by laws will be more ungrateful, fickle, and unwise than the people. 18 The difference in their actions arises not from a different nature (since it is the same in all men, and if there is greater good it is in the people) but from their having more or less respect for the laws under which they each live. 19 And anyone who considers the Roman people will see that for four hundred years they were hostile to the title of king and lovers of the glory and common good of their native land; he will see a great many examples given by them that attest to both these things. 20 If someone were

to cite their ingratitude toward Scipio, I answer with what was discussed at length on this matter above,[11] the people were shown to be less ungrateful than princes. 21 But as to wisdom and stability, I say that the people are wiser, more stable, and of better judgment than a prince. 22 And not without reason is the voice of the people likened to that of God,[12] because we see that popular opinion has marvelous effects in its predictions to such an extent that it seems as if it foresees their bad or good fortune through some secret *virtù*. 23 As to judging matters, when they hear two orators of equal *virtù* tending in different directions, they are very rarely seen not to take the better opinion and not to grasp the truth of what they hear. 24 And if, as was said above,[13] they err in matters that involve courage or that seem useful, a prince too also often errs in matters involving his own passions, which are more intense than those of the people. 25 They can also be seen to make far better choices in their selection of public officials than a prince; the people will never be persuaded that it is good to elect a scoundrel with corrupt habits to high office, whereas a prince can easily and in a thousand ways be so persuaded. 26 The people can be seen to begin to detest something and to persevere in that belief for many centuries, but not a prince. 27 For both these things I wish the example of the Roman people to suffice: in so many hundreds of years and in so many elections of Consuls and Tribunes, they did not hold four elections that they had to regret. 28 And, as I have said, they detested the title of king so much that no obligation to any of their citizens who tried to assume that title could save him from due punishment. 29 Furthermore, we can see cities where the people rule achieve enormous growth,[14] much greater than those always ruled by a prince,[15] as did Rome after the expulsion of the kings and Athens after it freed itself from Pisistratus.[16] 30 This can arise from nothing but governments by the people being better than governments by a prince. 31 I do not want anyone to counter my opinion with all that our historian says in the above-mentioned passage or in any other: for if we examine all the disorders of the people and all the disorders of princes, all the glories of the people and all those of princes, the people will be seen to be far superior in goodness and glory. 32 If princes are superior to the people in establishing laws, forming civil societies, establishing new statutes and institutions, the people are so superior in preserving what has been established that they unquestionably add to the glory of those who establish them.[17]

33 In short, to conclude this matter, I say that governments by princes have endured for a long time and governments by republics have endured for a long time; both of them needed to be regulated by laws: for a prince who can do as he pleases is mad; a people that can do as it pleases is unwise. 34 So if we discuss a prince obligated to the laws and a people enchained by them, more *virtù* will be seen in the people than in the prince; if we discuss both of them unregulated, we shall see fewer errors in the people than in the prince, and they are less serious and will have better remedies. 35 For licentious and rioting people can be addressed by a good man and can be easily brought back to the right way; a bad prince can be addressed by no one and the only remedy for him is the knife.[18] 36 Hence we can imagine the seriousness of each one's

disease: for if words are sufficient to cure the people's illness and the knife is needed to cure a prince's, no one will ever fail to judge that greater errors lie where the greater cure is needed. 37 When the people are indeed unleashed, the follies that they commit are not to be feared and we are not to be frightened of the present evil but rather the evil it may produce: amid such confusion a tyrant can arise. 38 But with bad princes the opposite occurs: we fear the present evil and we hope in the future, since men convince themselves that his evil life can make freedom arise. 39 Thus you[19] see the difference between them: it is equivalent to that between what is and what is to be. 40 The cruelties of the masses are against anyone they fear may seize the common wealth; those of a prince are against anyone he fears may seize his own wealth. 41 But sentiment against the people arises because anyone can speak ill of the people without fear and openly even while they are in power; a prince is always spoken of with a thousand fears and precautions. 42 Because this material draws me to it, it seems relevant to discuss in the next chapter what sorts of alliances someone else can place most trust in, those formed with a republic or those formed with a prince.

NOTES

1. Livy, 6.17.1, though it is a commonplace in classical historiography.

2. Quoted in Latin from 6.20.15: *"Populum brevi, postquam periculum ab eo nullum erat, per se ipsas recordantem virtutes desiderium eius tenuit."* Machiavelli omits *per se ipsas recordantem virtutes* (remembering only his virtuous qualities). See above, 1, 24, sentences 10–12, for Manlius Capitolinus.

3. Livy, 24.4–7; 21.

4. Quoted in Latin with slight differences from 24.25.8: *"Haec natura multitudinis est: aut humiliter servit, aut superbe dominatur."*

5. In his letter to Vettori of 29 April 1513, Machiavelli writes, " I do not want to be prompted by any authority but reason" (*Friends,* p. 233). His self-promoting stance in the previous sentence, however, calls attention both to the extent to which he diverges from accepted opinion on many political issues and to his desire to have an impact on them through his writings. Hence, as Guicciardini would be among the first to point out, Machiavelli's argument may not always be governed by "reason."

6. On Egypt and its laws, see above, 1, 1, n.10; on Sparta, see above, 1, 2, n.2 and 3; on France, see above, 1, 16, n.10.

7. Translates *le sue virtù;* we have not retained the plural in the translation.

8. See Livy, 6.14–20. Although the plebs' urgings obtained his release from prison, he was again imprisoned and condemned to death.

9. Clitus saved Alexander's life at the Battle of Granicus in 334 B.C. But at a drunken banquet in 316 he belittled Alexander, who then murdered him, much to Alexander's subsequent regret; see Diodorus Siculus, 17.21.57, and Plutarch, *Alexander,* 16; 50–52. Herod, king of Judea from 40 to 4 B.C., married Mariamne in 38; in a fit of jealousy he ordered her death then lived to regret his decision; see Josephus, *Antiquities of the Jews,* 15.7.4–7, and *History of the Jewish War,* 1.22.1–5.

10. For the following remarks, it might be interesting to compare what Machiavelli says about how he "goes against common opinion" in this and others of his

works (see above, 1, 4, sentences 7–9; above, 1, 16; and above, 1, 47, sentence 26). As for the *Prince,* he says, "people *[populi]* are fickle by nature; it is easy to persuade them of something, but it is hard to fix that persuasion in them" (chapter 6, p. 149, lines 99–101); he argues against the "trite adage" that "whoever builds upon the common people *[populo]* builds upon mud" (chapter 9, ed, cit., lines 105–106, p. 197); also "it can be said of men in general *[delli uomini si può dire generalmente]* that they are ungrateful, fickle, dissembling, hypocritical, cowardly, and greedy" (chapter 17, p. 271, lines 39–41); again, "well-organized states and wise princes have taken great pains not to distress the rich and to satisfy the people *[populo],* keeping them happy" (chapter 19, p. 293, lines 104–107). This last should be read in the context of Machiavelli's belief that a prince must effect a compromise between two competing interests because a civil princedom results from the fact that "the common people *[populo]* want to be neither governed nor oppressed by the rich *[grandi]* and the rich want to govern and oppress the common people" (chapter 9, p. 191, lines 11–14). Finally, in *Florentine Histories,* 8, 19 he says, "the mass of the people of Florence *[populo universale]* [are] subtle interpreters of all matters." But see his *Florentine Histories,* 2, 13, for a situation in which the people were "capricious" and their leaders were hesitant about making a decision.

11. See above, 1, 29.

12. The phrase *"vox populi, vox Dei"* was current in the Middle Ages.

13. Above, 1, 53.

14. Translates *augumenti.* It is not altogether clear whether the "augmentation" is external, referring to territorial expansion, or internal, referring to progress; most commentators think it refers to the former.

15. See the last sentence of 1, 55 and note. For all the attention to social context there, here, and in the next sentence, Machiavelli is stating the superiority of republics over princedoms.

16. Machiavelli will deal with this example below, 2, 2, sentence 10.

17. Above, 1, 9, sentence 8, is relevant here: "if one man is suited for organizing, what is organized will not long endure if it is left on the shoulders of one man, but it will when it is left in the care of many and when it is the business of many to maintain it."

18. Translates *il ferro,* literally "steel"; the "remedy" clearly is murder through taking matters into one's own hands. A possible medical resonance in "knife" is suggested by Machiavelli's use of it in the next sentence in the context of "illness."

19. Translates *vedete;* Machiavelli uses the second-person plural form, which can either be a simple plural for several persons or a more formal form of address for one person. His use would not deserve comment except that he normally uses *tu* for "you."

~ 59 ~

WHICH ALLIANCE OR LEAGUE OTHERS CAN TRUST IN MORE: ONE FORMED WITH A REPUBLIC OR ONE FORMED WITH A PRINCE

1 Because it is a daily occurrence for one prince to make a league and an alliance with another one or one republic with another, and also for leagues and treaties to be similarly contracted between a republic and a prince, I believe we should examine which promise is more reliable and which should be given more credence, a republic's or a prince's. 2 All things considered, I believe that in many cases they are similar but that in a few there is some discrepancy. 3 Consequently, I believe that neither a prince nor a republic will honor agreements made with you by force; I believe that if fear for their state enters into it both will break their promise and prove ungrateful to you so as not to lose it.[1] 4 Demetrius, the one who was called conqueror of cities,[2] had conferred countless benefits on the Athenians. But later, when his enemies defeated him and he sought refuge in Athens as a city friendly and obligated to him, it happened that the city would not receive him; this pained him much more than the loss of his troops and army had. 5 Pompey, after he was defeated by Caesar in Thessaly, took refuge in Egypt with Ptolemy, whose kingdom Pompey had once restored to him, yet Ptolemy had him killed.[3] 6 These things can be seen to have had the same causes;[4] nevertheless, the republic acted more humanely and caused less harm than did the prince. 7 So where there is fear, we will in fact find the same amount of good faith. 8 And whether one finds either a republic or a prince that may expect to fall because of keeping a promise to you, this too can result from similar causes. 9 As to the prince, it can very well happen that he is the friend of a powerful prince who, though up to that time he has had no opportunity to defend him, he may hope will restore him to his princedom at some future time, or else that, having been a follower and supporter of the powerful prince, he does not expect the prince's enemies to keep their promises or treaties with him. 10 The princes of the kingdom of Naples who supported the French cause were of this sort.[5] 11 And as for republics, of this kind was Saguntum in Spain, which expected to fall because of supporting the Roman cause,[6] and Florence as well, because of supporting the French cause in 1512.[7] 12 And I believe, after weighing everything, that in cases where there is imminent danger, you will find somewhat more reliability in republics than in princes. 13 Because even though republics might have the same courage and will as a prince, their being slower to react will always make them take longer in making up their minds than a prince; therefore, they take longer to break their promise than a prince does.

14 Alliances are broken for gain. 15 In this, republics are far more observant of treaties than are princes. 16 And examples could be cited of a prince breaking his promise for a very slight gain and a republic not breaking its promise

for a large profit. That was the course of action that Themistocles proposed to the Athenians.[8] In an assembly he stated that he had a proposal that would bring great profit to their native land, but he could not tell it lest it be revealed; if he revealed it, the opportunity to carry it out would be lost. 17 Hence the Athenian people chose Aristides to be informed of the matter, and then it would be decided according to his judgment. Themistocles pointed out to him that the entire Greek fleet, although it was under a treaty with Athens, was in a place where it could easily be won over or destroyed, thus making the Athenians complete masters of the region. 18 So Aristides reported to the people that Themistocles' course of action was quite effective but very dishonest; for that reason the people rejected it completely. 19 Philip of Macedon and the other princes, who sought and gained more profit by breaking promises than by any other means, would not have done so.[9]

20 Because it is a common practice, I shall not discuss the breaking of pacts through nonobservance, but I am discussing those that are broken for extraordinary reasons. As I have said above, I believe that the people make fewer errors than a prince does, and for this reason one can put more trust in them than in a prince.

NOTES

1. *Prince,* 18 considers the conditions under which "princes should keep their word."

2. Demetrius Poliorcetes (Greek for "conqueror of cities") was king of Macedonia from 294 to 288 B.C. Earlier in his career, Athens was grateful to him because he drove out the ruling tyrant, Demetrius of Phalerum, in 307. In 301 he and his father Antigonus were defeated at the battle of Ipsus by Seleucus Nicator and Lysimachus, but Athens denied his request for asylum; see Plutarch, *Demetrius.*

3. After his defeat in 48 B.C. at Pharsalus in Thessaly, Pompey sought refuge in Egypt with the son of Ptolemy XI (or XIII according to some authorities), nicknamed Auletes, the "flute player," whom Pompey had helped to keep his Egyptian throne. It was his son, Ptolemy XII (or XIV) who ordered Pompey's death; see Plutarch, *Pompey,* 76–79. Martelli also cites Caesar, *Bellum civile,* 3.103.2–5, as a source (*Storici antichi,* p. 49 n.41).

4. Namely, angering the dominant power: in one case, the enemies of Demetrius; in the other, Rome.

5. France and Spain asserted their claim to rule the kingdom of Naples. In 1503 and 1504 Gonzalo Fernández de Córdoba (see above, 1, 29, n.4) imprisoned many of the barons who supported France. When the French were soundly routed at the Battle of Garigliano in late December 1503, Gonzalo abandoned his baronial prisoners.

6. Because Saguntum (today Sagunto, north of Valencia) insisted on keeping its alliance with Rome in 219 B.C., Hannibal destroyed it the following year (Livy, 21.5–15).

7. Piero Soderini and Florence supported France against the Holy League, formed by Pope Julius II, "to liberate Italy from the barbarians," which included Spain, Venice, and Germany with the Swiss. The league had promised to restore the Medici to Florence. With their decisive victory at the Battle of Ravenna in April 1512, the League, under Ramón de Cardona, moved on Prato, near Florence, on 28 August; within two weeks the Medici were back in power.

8. Themistocles (c. 528–462 B.C.) was an Athenian statesman and general who fought Persia and Sparta. Against his rival Aristides, he advocated increasing Athenian naval power. The incident referred to occurred after the Athenian victory over the Persians at the Battle of Salamis in 480 B.C. It is discussed in both Plutarch, *Themistocles,* 20, and Cicero, *De officiis,* 3.11.49.

9. See above, 1, 26, n.6.

~ 60 ~

THE CONSULATE AND ALL OTHER OFFICES IN ROME WERE GIVEN WITHOUT REGARD TO AGE

1 We can see throughout the course of history that the Roman republic, after the Consulate was opened to the Plebs, granted it to its citizens without regard to age or birth; although regard for age never existed in Rome, they always looked for *virtù* in either young or old wherever it might be found.[1] 2 That can be seen through the example of Valerius Corvinus, who was made Consul at twenty-three; this Valerius, speaking to his soldiers, said that the Consulate was "the reward of merit, not of blood."[2] 3 Whether this matter was well considered would be open to lengthy discussion. 4 And as to birth,[3] that was granted by necessity, and the necessity that there was in Rome would exist in any city that wanted to achieve the same results as Rome did, as we have said elsewhere.[4] One cannot cause men discomfort without rewarding them, nor can men be deprived without danger of the hope of pursuing a reward. 5 And therefore it was necessary early on for the Plebs to have hope of receiving the Consulate, and for a while[5] they were satisfied with this hope without getting it; later, hope was not enough, and the result had to be achieved. 6 But a city that does not employ its Plebs in any glorious matter can treat them as it wishes, as was discussed elsewhere; but a city wishing to do what Rome did must not make such distinction.[6] 7 Granting this to be the case, there can be no objection to that of age; rather it is necessary, because if the masses have to elect a young man to a rank that needs an old man's wisdom, it is necessary for some very notable action on his part to cause him to attain that rank. 8 When a young man has such great *virtù* as to have made himself known by doing something remarkable, it would be a very harmful thing if the city were unable to avail itself of him then but had to wait until the vigor of his courage and his readiness for action grew old with him, when his native land could avail itself of them at an early age. Thus Rome availed itself of Valerius Corvinus, Scipio, Pompey, and many others who won triumphs at a very early age.[7]

NOTES

1. In 366 B.C., Gaius Licinius and Lucius Sextius were elected tribunes of the plebs. They proposed abolishing military tribunes and electing one consul from among the plebs; Livy, 6.35–42. Patrician opposition was not overcome until 377 when Lucius Sextus became the first plebeian consul (Livy, 7.1.2). Age was, in fact, a consideration,

though it was not until 180 B.C. that it became codified with the *Lex Villia Annalis* (Livy, 40.44.1, and Cicero, *De Legibus,* 3.9). Machiavelli implies that the Romans knew how to get around the consideration of age (Tacitus, *Annals,* 11.22).

2. The nickname *corvinus* refers to the story Livy tells (7.26) of the raven *(corvino)* that landed on Valerius's helmet during his hand-to-hand combat with a huge Gaul. The quotation is from Livy, 7.32.14: *"nec generis, ut ante, sed virtutis est praemium";* Machiavelli substitutes *sanguinis* (blood) for Livy's *generis* (birth).

3. Translates *sangue* here and throughout this chapter.

4. Both here and later in sentence 6 of this chapter, Machiavelli refers to his discussion at the end of 1, 6, sentences 23–24.

5. Inglese points out that, according to Livy, 6.42, the plebeians' right to the consulate coincided with the election of the first plebeian consul. Diodorus Siculus says, however, that plebeians could be consuls after the Decemvirs were abolished in 449 B.C., roughly a century before Livy's assertion. It may be that Machiavelli is confusing his sources, and is referring to what Livy says about the military tribunate (6.37.5).

6. Essentially, establishing a class distinction for holding office.

7. Livy, 7.26.12, says Valerius was twenty-three years old when he became consul; Scipio was elected aedile before he was legally of age (Livy, 25.2); a grudging Sulla allowed Pompey his first triumphal procession into Rome in his early twenties in 79 B.C. (Plutarch, *Pompey,* 13–15).

BOOK *Two*

Preface

1 Men always praise ancient times and blame the present, but not always with good reason; they are so partial to things of the past that they extol not only those ages which they have known about, thanks to the records left by writers, but also those ages which, now that they have grown old, they remember having experienced in their youth. 2 Even if their judgment is wrong, as it most often is, I am convinced that the causes leading to this error are varied. 3 The first, I believe, is that we do not know the truth about ancient matters completely; more often than not things that would reflect badly on those times are concealed and other things that may bring forth glory for them are expressed in splendid, great detail. 4 Because most writers are so respectful of the fortune of conquerors that, in order to glorify their victories, they not only exaggerate what conquerors have done with great *virtù* but also render the deeds of their enemies so illustrious that anyone born later in the two regions, whether the victorious or the vanquished one, has reason to marvel at those men and those times: he is obliged to praise and love them to the utmost. 5 Furthermore, because either fear or envy makes men hate things, the two most potent sources of hatred for the past have been eliminated: the past cannot harm you or give you reason to envy it. 6 But the reverse happens in those matters that are dealt with and are visible. Because they are not in any way concealed from your complete knowledge and, along with the good, you are aware of many other things that displease you about them, you are obliged to judge them far inferior to antiquity, even though the present may truly deserve more glory and fame than antiquity. I do not have in mind matters pertaining to the arts: they are so evident in and of themselves that the times can deprive them of or grant them very little more glory than they deserve for themselves. But I am speaking of those matters pertaining to the life and customs of men, about which such evident testimony cannot be seen.[1]

7 I therefore repeat that the above-mentioned custom of praising and blaming is real, but it is not always true that to do so is wrong. 8 Because sometimes it is necessary for people to judge correctly; for, since human affairs are always in flux, they are either rising or falling.[2] 9 We see that some distinguished man organizes a city or a region for political life and that for a while, through the *virtù* of that organizer, it keeps on steadily improving. 10 Anyone who is born in such a state, then, and praises ancient more than modern times is mistaken; his error results from the things stated above. 11 But people who are born in that city or region later, when its time has come to descend toward a worse condition, are not then mistaken.

12 And when I think how these matters go, my judgment is that the world has always been the same way and that there has been as much good in it as evil, but this good and this evil has varied from region to region. We can see this from what information we have about those ancient kingdoms, which differed from each other because of the difference in their customs, though the world remained the same.[3] 13 Only there was this difference: whereas the world had first invested its *virtù* in Assyria, it then located it in Media, later in Persia, until it came around to Italy and Rome.[4] 14 And if the Roman Empire has not been succeeded by any lasting empire that gathered together the world's *virtù,* we see, nevertheless, that this quality has been scattered among many nations where people lived with *virtù,* such as were the kingdom of the Franks, the kingdom of the Turks, that of the Sultan, and today the peoples of Germany. Even earlier there was the Saracen sect that achieved so many great things and, once it destroyed the Eastern Roman Empire, took over so much of the world.[5] 15 So, after the fall of the Romans, there has existed in all these regions and in all these sects, and in some parts of them there still exists, the *virtù* that is desired and deservedly praised. 16 Whoever is born in these regions and praises past times more than the present might be mistaken, but whoever is born in Italy or Greece and has not become either a northerner[6] in Italy or a Turk in Greece is right to blame his own times and to praise the others. For in the latter regions there is much that makes them wonderful, whereas in the former there is nothing to redeem them from the most extreme misery, infamy, and dishonor; there is no observance in them of religion, of laws, or of military tradition: they are besmirched with every kind of filth.[7] 17 These vices are all the more detestable, because they are more prevalent among those who sit in judgment, give orders to others, and wish to be idolized.

18 But to return to our discussion, I say that if men's judgment is prejudiced when judging which is better, the present or a past age about which they could not have so perfect knowledge as they have of their own times because of its distance, it ought not to prejudice old men when they judge the times of their youth and of old age, since they have known and seen them both equally. 19 That would be true if throughout their lifetime men were of the same judgment and had the same desires: but since the latter do vary, though the times do not, they cannot seem the same to men because they have different desires, pleasures, and concerns in their old age than they had in their youth. 20 Because as they grow old men lose their strength and gain in judgment and wisdom, things that seemed bearable and good to them in their youth necessarily become unbearable and bad as they grow old; and whereas they should blame their judgment for this, they blame the times instead. 21 Furthermore, human desires are insatiable, because nature has given us the ability and the will to desire everything and fortune has given us the ability to achieve but little; the result is unremitting discontent in the minds of men and disgust with the things they have. Hence men blame the present, praise the past, and desire the future, even though they are not motivated to do so by any reasonable cause.[8]

22 So I do not know whether I shall deserve to be counted among those who are mistaken if in my *Discourses* I praise the ancient Romans' times too

much and blame our own.[9] 23 And truly if the *virtù* that flourished then and the vice that flourishes now were not brighter than the sun I should be more reticent in my speech for fear of falling into the very same error that I accuse some people of. 24 But because the matter is so clear that everyone sees it, I shall be courageous and say openly what I understand about those times and our own so that the minds of the young who read my writings can avoid the latter and prepare to imitate the former whenever Fortune gives them the opportunity to do so.[10] 25 For it is the duty of a good man to teach others the good that you have been unable to bring about because of the hostility of the times and of Fortune so that once many are aware of it some of them—more beloved of Heaven—may be able to bring it about. 26 Because in the preceding book of *Discourses* I spoke about the decisions the Romans made concerning the city's internal affairs, in this one we shall speak about those the Roman people made concerning the expansion of their empire.[11]

NOTES

1. Machiavelli returns to an idea developed in his Preface A to Book 1, sentence 3.

2. For a similar expression of this idea, see 1, 6, sentence 33 and note 13. Here Machiavelli may be following Polybius, 6.51.4 and 6.57, about the pattern of ascent-summit-death in political life; if so, it is, as Inglese (based on Sasso) notes, an idea at variance with the cyclical notion of *anacyclosis* in Polybius, 6.9.10 that Machiavelli was following above, in 1, 2, sentences 13–24. See also Lactantius, *Divinae Institutiones,* 7 (Rinaldi).

3. Again, a similarity with Preface A to Book 1 (see sentence 8 and notes). Guicciardini, however, disagrees with this notion; see his *Considerations,* sentence 2. Yet see his letter to Machiavelli written 18 May 1521: "with only the faces of the men and the extrinsic colors changed, all the very same things return; and we do not see any incident that has not been seen in other times. But changing the names and forms of things means that only the prudent recognize them; therefore, history is good and useful, because it sets before you and makes you recognize and see again what you had never known or seen" (*Friends,* p. 339).

4. This kind of succession is seen in his *capitolo "Di fortuna,"* vv. 130–144, but in greater detail and without the omission of Greece. It is based on Plutarch, *Moralia, De fortuna Romanorum* (On the fortune of the Romans), 4; 317f–318a. Again, Rinaldi cites Lactantius; see *Divinae Institutiones,* 7.15. On this question, see Martelli, *Storici antichi,* pp. 50–57.

5. The "kingdom of the Franks" refers to Charlemagne, king of the Franks from 768 to 814 and emperor of the West from 800 to 814; "the kingdom of the Turks" refers to the Ottoman or Turkish Empire, founded in the late thirteenth century; that of "the Sultan" refers to the sultanate of the Mamelukes in Egypt (see 1, 1, n.10); "the peoples of Germany" include those in the cities of Switzerland and Germany; the "Saracen sect" is Islam, although it was the Ottoman Turks who destroyed "the Eastern Roman [or Byzantine] Empire."

6. Machiavelli's word is *oltramontano* (people from beyond the mountains). It usually refers to those on the northern side of the Alps, but because here the word is equated with the "Turk in Greece," a foreign power that conquered Greece, he means

all those with territorial designs on Italy: the French, Spanish, Swiss, or Germans as well as their supporters within Italy.

7. Inglese reminds us to be alert in Book 2 to a shift in Machiavelli's judgment concerning the present. In contrast to a more idealized ancient Rome, he becomes more bitter and pessimistic about his own era and consequently seems to mistrust the possibility for the corrupt present to "redeem" itself through action and *virtù*. As the next sentence shows, his main evidence is that the people in power, in government or in the Church, are vice-ridden.

8. Another concise statement of one of Machiavelli's basic assumptions about human nature; see 1, 37, sentences 3 and 4, and note 3, and his *capitolo "Dell'ambizione,"* vv. 70–81.

9. In a famous passage, undoubtedly with Machiavelli in mind, Guicciardini scorns those who "bring in the Romans as evidence all the time. One would have to have a city with conditions like theirs and then govern it according to their example. That model is as incongruous for a city whose qualities are incongruous as it would be to expect an ass to run like a horse" (*Ricordi,* C, 110). See also C, 117, quoted above, 1, 39, n.1, and the following passage, more emphatic than his *Ricordi,* from *Storia d'Italia,* 1, 14. It is in the context of what Guicciardini regarded as Piero de' Medici's mistaken judgment in following an example his father set in 1479: Lorenzo de' Medici persuaded Ferdinand of Naples to break his alliance with Pope Sixtus IV during the latter's war against Florence. Piero, in turn, decided to seek help from his former enemies against the invading French, under Charles VIII, in the fall of 1494; this error soon contributed to the expulsion of the Medici in November: "It is unquestionably very dangerous to be guided by examples unless identical qualities correspond not only in general but in every particular, unless matters are handled with identical prudence, and unless, apart from every other fundamental, one has on one's side an identical Fortune."

10. In line with his doubt that the corrupt present can "redeem" itself through action (see note 7 above), Machiavelli seems to assume that the "opportunity" to "imitate" his principles will come only at some point in the future, a position he also takes in *Art of War.* The "young who read" both that and the *Discourses* may well be those attending the discussions in the Rucellai gardens, but he is also addressing future generations of republican thinkers, those "more beloved of Heaven." The melancholy of these closing sentences may reflect Machiavelli's desperate hope that the next generation, following his teachings ("the duty of a good man to teach"), can reassert the republican values of ancient Rome in the face of a growing concentration of power among the Medici in both Florence and Rome.

11. A summary statement of the contrasting purpose of Books 1 and 2.

~ 1 ~

WHICH WAS MORE THE CAUSE OF THE EMPIRE THAT THE ROMANS ACQUIRED, *VIRTÙ* OR FORTUNE[1]?

1 Many, including Plutarch, a deeply serious writer, have held the opinion that the Roman people were favored in acquiring their empire more by Fortune than by *virtù*. 2 Among the other reasons that he cites, he says it can be shown that by their own admission the people recognized all their victories as coming from Fortune, since they built more temples to Fortuna than to any other god.[2] 3 And it appears that Livy shares this opinion, because rarely does he have any Roman speak about *virtù* without adding Fortune to it. 4 I do not wish to admit this idea, nor do I believe that it can be upheld. 5 Because if a republic can be found to have ever made the gains that Rome did, that is because there has never been a republic that was organized as Rome was to allow acquisition.[3] 6 The *virtù* of their armies caused them to acquire their empire; their rules of procedure and their own customs, provided by their first lawgiver,[4] allowed them to keep what they had acquired, as I shall relate more fully later in several discourses.

7 These writers say that never having carried on two very powerful wars at one time was due to the Fortune, not the *virtù,* of the Roman people.[5] They fought against the Latins only when they had not so much beaten the Samnites as fought in their defense;[6] they did not fight the Etruscans until they had first subjugated the Latins and almost totally weakened the Samnites by means of frequent defeats.[7] Had two of these powers combined at full strength and while they were fresh, one may easily imagine that the result unquestionably would have been the downfall of the Roman republic.[8] 8 But whatever the reason for this, Rome never had two very powerful wars at the same time; on the contrary, it always seemed as if either when one broke out, the other would subside, or when one subsided, the other would break out.

9 This can be seen easily from the order of the wars they waged: because, setting aside the ones they waged before the Gauls took Rome, we can see that while the Romans were fighting the Aequi and Volsci and as long as they remained powerful no other armies ever attacked Rome.[9] 10 When these were subdued, war broke out against the Samnites;[10] although the Latins rebelled against the Romans before that war ended, nevertheless, when that rebellion ensued the Samnites formed a league with Rome and helped the Romans subdue the Latins' arrogance.[11] 11 When they were subdued, war broke out again with Samnium.[12] 12 After the Samnite armies had been defeated in many battles, war broke out with the Etruscans.[13] 13 When that was settled, the Samnites rose up once again because of Pyrrhus's crossing into Italy.[14] 14 When he was repulsed and sent back to Greece, they started the first war with the Carthaginians,[15] and that war was scarcely finished when all the Gauls, both on this side and beyond the Alps, conspired against the Romans until they were defeated with tremendous slaughter between Populonia and Pisa, where the tower of San Vicenzo is today.[16] 15 When this war ended, they had

no wars of any significance for the space of twenty years, because the Romans fought only the Ligurians and the remaining Gauls in Lombardy.[17] 16 So matters stood until the Second Carthaginian War broke out; it kept Italy busy for sixteen years.[18] 17 When this ended with the greatest glory, the Macedonian War broke out; when it was over, the one against Antiochus and Asia began.[19] 18 After that victory no princes or republics were left in the entire world that could oppose the Roman army by themselves or united together.

19 But before that final victory, anyone who carefully considers the order of these wars and the way the Romans waged them will see a great deal of *virtù* and wisdom mingled in with Fortune. 20 Therefore, if one were to examine the cause of such Fortune, it would be easy to find. It is quite certain that once a prince or a people attain such great renown that every neighboring prince and people fears it and is afraid to attack it on their own, it will always happen that none of them will attack it unless by necessity. Consequently, it is almost as if that power has the choice to make war on whichever of its neighbors it likes and to appease the others by its diligence. 21 The neighbors are easily appeased partly out of respect for its power and partly because they are deceived by the methods that it uses to lull them to sleep. 22 The other powers that are far away and have no business with it consider the matter remote and not pertaining to them; they persist in this error until this fire is at their doorstep. Once it is there, they have no means of extinguishing it but their own armies, which are no longer adequate since it has become very powerful. 23 I will leave out how the Samnites stood by and watched the Romans conquer the Volsci and Aequi. In order not to be too wordy, I shall turn to the Carthaginians, who were a great, highly esteemed power when the Romans were fighting the Samnites and Etruscans: they already held all of Africa, Sardinia, and Sicily and had dominion over part of Spain. 24 This power of theirs, along with their borders being far from the Roman people, caused the Carthaginians never to think of attacking them or of helping the Samnites and the Etruscans. On the contrary, as people will do when things are prospering, they acted instead on Rome's behalf by allying themselves with them and seeking their friendship.[20] 25 They never noticed the mistake they had made until the Romans, having subdued all the people between themselves and the Carthaginians, began to fight with them for control over Sicily and Spain. 26 The same thing happened to the Gauls, to Philip, king of Macedon, and to Antiochus as to the Carthaginians: each believed that as long as the Roman people were busy with someone else, the latter would win and there would be time to defend himself against Rome by either peace or war. 27 Consequently, I believe that the Fortune that the Romans had in this matter would have been shared by all princes if they acted like the Romans and possessed the same *virtù*.[21]

28 In this connection, had I not spoken of it at length in my treatise *On Princedoms,* it would be good to show the method the Roman people used upon entering the territory of other peoples, because this matter is discussed at length there.[22] 29 Briefly, I shall say only this: in new territories the Romans always contrived to have some ally who would serve either as a ladder to climb or a gate to enter or as a means to hold it. So we see that they entered

Samnium by means of the Capuans,[23] Etruria by means of the Camertes,[24] Sicily by means of the Mamertines,[25] Spain by means of the Saguntines,[26] Africa by means of Masinissa,[27] Greece by means of the Aetolians,[28] Asia by means of Eumenes and other princes,[29] and Gaul by means of the Massaliotes and the Aedui.[30] 30 Thus they never lacked for such support to facilitate their undertakings both in acquiring territories and in keeping them. 31 People who observe this will see they have less need of Fortune than those who are not good observers of it. 32 In order for everyone to know better how much more their *virtù* could achieve than their fortune in acquiring their empire, we shall discuss in the next chapter what the peoples the Romans had to fight were like and how stubbornly they defended their freedom.

NOTES

1. In the *Prince* Machiavelli works out the interplay between *virtù* and Fortune in terms of the political leader; here he analyzes it as a component of the state. His verb, *acquistare,* has overtones of "to conquer"; we have retained the literal translation "to acquire," even though the verb and its forms shade over to "conquest" in many of the sentences in this and following chapters as he takes up the question of the expansion of the Roman Empire. On this fundamental question of the cause of Rome's empire and Plutarch's relevance to the issue, see Sasso, "Machiavelli e i detrattori antichi e nuovi: Per l'interpretazione di *Discorsi,* 1, 4," in *Antichi,* pp. 406–441, originally published in *Memorie dell'Accademia nazionale dei Lincei,* ser. 8, 22 (1978): 319–418; for more commentary, see Martelli, *Storici antichi,* pp. 57–70.

2. Plutarch, *Moralia, de fortuna Romanorum,* 5; 318d–319b.

3. This is the argument of 1, 6, especially sentences 23–37.

4. Romulus; see 1, 19, sentences 1–4.

5. Plutarch, *Moralia, de fortuna Romanorum,* 2; 316e–317c.

6. Livy, 7.32–37; 8.1–6.

7. Livy covers these events in Books 8 to 10.

8. Livy draws a similar conclusion in 10.45.2–3.

9. These events are covered in Livy, 6.2; 7–9; 11–12; 32 and 7.19.

10. Livy, 7.27; 29–32; the First Samnite War ran from 343 to 341 B.C.

11. Livy, 8.2; 6; 10–11; the revolt of the Latins lasted from 340 to 338 B.C.

12. Livy, 8.14; 23–25; the second Samnite war was fought from 327 to 321 and again from 316 to 304 B.C. The Third Samnite War began in 298 and ended in 290 B.C.

13. Livy refers to these events in Books 9 and 10; war with the Etruscans lasted from 310 to 300 and was finally "settled" by a treaty in 294 (Livy, 10.37). Books 1 and 2 of Polybius discuss the events that Machiavelli will allude to in sentences 13 through 15.

14. In 281 B.C. the city of Tarentum called on Pyrrhus, king of the Molossians of Epirus in northwestern Greece, to protect it against the Romans; he defeated the Romans at the battle of Heraclea [Minoa] in 280. He won his early battles at such a cost of men that the phrase "Pyrrhic victory" was coined. After losing to the Romans in 275 at Beneventum, Pyrrhus was obliged to abandon to Rome the Samnite territory he controlled.

15. The First Punic War lasted from 264 to 241 B.C.

16. The wars with the Gauls lasted from 238 to 225 B.C. with their defeat at

Telamon near Populonia on the Tyrrhenian Sea north of Piombino; see Polybius, 2.31, for his estimate that during this battle, one of the bloodiest in antiquity, forty thousand Gauls died. For Torre di San Vincenzo, see above, 1, 53, note 11.

17. Battles with the Gauls and Ligurians lasted from 224 until 222 when they, the Insubrae, and other tribes were defeated at the battle of Clastidium, the present-day Casteggio, about thirty miles west of Piacenza.

18. The Second Punic War lasted from 218 to 201 B.C.

19. The Second Macedonian War "broke out" in 200 B.C. and lasted until the defeat of Philip V of Macedon at the battle of Cynoscephalae in 196. War against Antiochus III of Syria began in 193 and ended in 188 with the peace of Apamea, though Antiochus had been defeated at the battle of Magnesia (ad Sipylum) in 190.

20. Livy, 7.27.2, refers to such a treaty in 348 B.C., though according to tradition the two signed a treaty during the first year of the republic in 509; see Polybius, 3.22.

21. Thus Fortune is less the unforeseen acting arbitrarily upon human affairs (see *Prince,* 25) than the result of wise leaders exercising their *virtù*. In the terms of the chapter's title, then, *virtù* is a "cause" of Fortune.

22. Specifically *Prince,* chapters 3, the penultimate paragraph of 4, and 5. He defines Roman policy, their "method," in chapter 3: "they sent in colonial settlements, retained the less powerful without increasing their strength, humbled the powerful, and forbade potent invaders to gain an influential grip" *Prince,* 3, (p. 113, lines 162–165). Some commentators see this sentence as important evidence for dating the composition of both the *Prince* and the *Discourses.*

23. Livy, 7.29–32; when the Samnites attacked the Sidicines, the latter called on the Capuan League for help; when the league feared being overwhelmed, it then appealed to Rome (340 B.C.). A number of the following examples will be repeated below, 2, 9.

24. Livy, 9.36; the Camertes allied themselves with the Romans against the Etruscans in 310 B.C. The modern-day descendants of the Camertes live in Camerino, a town high in the Apeninnes about midway between Perugia and the Adriatic.

25. Polybius, 1.7–12; the Mamertines were originally mercenaries hired by Agathocles (see below, 2, 12, n.3, and *Prince,* 8); in 289 B.C. they took over Messana, the modern Messina, a port city in northeast Sicily. When the Carthaginians attacked them in 264, Rome answered their call for help, thereby precipitating the First Punic War.

26. For these events occurring in 219 B.C., based on Livy, 21.5–15, see 1, 59, n.6.

27. He was the king of Numidia who, upon learning that Scipio was about to invade Africa during the Second Punic War, renounced his treaty with Carthage and sided with Rome in 204 B.C. (Livy, 28.16–30.45).

28. Rome invaded Greece after allying itself with the Aetolian League against Philip V of Macedon in 211 B.C. (Livy, 26.24). This example is also examined in *Prince,* 3.

29. Because Eumenes II, king of Pergamum, a city in the northwest of present-day Turkey, feared the imperialistic aims of Antiochus in 193 B.C., he urged the Romans to fight the Syrian king and helped the Romans at the battle of Magnesia in 190; for this aid Rome rewarded Eumenes with vast areas of Asia Minor (Livy, 35.13; 37.37–45).

30. The Massaliotes, originally Greek settlers from Phocaea, present-day Foca on the western coast of Asia Minor, established a trading center at the site of modern-day

Marseilles, France, around 600 B.C. During the Second Punic War they sided with Rome and requested Rome's help against the Ligurians to their east in 154 and again in 125 B.C. The Aedui were a tribe of northern Gaul in present-day Burgundy; because they were such staunch allies, Rome came to their aid against the Allobroges, a Celtic tribe southeast of Burgundy in Dauphiné and Savoy, in 122, the same year Rome established its first colony north of the Alps at Aquae Sextiae, present-day Aix-en-Provence. The Aedui were the first barbarians Rome accepted as kinsmen and were solidly behind Caesar during the Gallic Wars.

~ *2* ~

WHAT PEOPLES THE ROMANS HAD TO FIGHT AND HOW STUBBORNLY THEY DEFENDED THEIR FREEDOM

1 Nothing made it harder for the Romans to conquer neighboring peoples and parts of remote provinces than the love of freedom that many peoples had in those days; they defended it so stubbornly that they would never had been subjugated, save by exceptional *virtù*. 2 We know from many examples the dangers they put themselves in to keep or to recover their freedom and the revenge they took against those who had wrested it from them. 3 We also know from reading the histories what harm servitude wreaked on peoples and cities.

4 Whereas in our time there is only land that can be said to have free cities in it,[1] in ancient times there were many quite free peoples in every land. 5 In Italy, during the times that we are discussing now, we can see that, from the mountains[2] that still divide Tuscany from Lombardy all the way to the tip of Italy,[3] all peoples were free: the Etruscans, the Romans, the Samnites, and many other peoples who lived in the rest of Italy. 6 It is never reported that there was any king there, except for those who ruled in Rome and Porsenna, the king of Etruria; history does not say how his lineage died out.[4] 7 But it can indeed be seen that in the times when the Romans campaigned against Veii Etruria was free; and it so enjoyed its freedom and so hated the title of prince that, when the Veians established a king for their protection in Veii and asked them for help against the Romans, the Etruscans, after holding many meetings, decided not to aid the Veians as long as the latter were living under the king: they deemed it was wrong to defend the homeland of those who had already subjected it to someone else.[5]

8 It is an easy matter to understand how this affection for living free arises among peoples, for experience shows us that cities have never increased in either dominion or wealth except while they were free. 9 And truly it is a wonderful thing to consider how great Athens became within a century after it freed itself from the tyranny of Pisistratus.[6] 10 But above all it is quite wonderful to consider how great Rome became after it freed itself from its kings.[7] 11 The reason is easy to understand, because it is not the private good but the common good that makes cities great. 12 And without a doubt the common

good is respected only in republics, because everything that fosters it is carried out; even if it may be harmful to this or that private citizen, those whom this common good favors are so numerous that they can go ahead in opposition to the interest of those few who may be harmed by it. 13 The opposite occurs when there is a prince: most of the time what favors him harms the city and what favors the city harms him. 14 Thus, as soon as a tyranny over a free society[8] appears, the least ill that may result to those cities from it is no further progress or growth in power or wealth; but usually, or rather always, what happens is that they turn backward. 15 If destiny made a tyrant with *virtù* appear, one whose courage and military *virtù* enlarged his dominion, no good to the republic would come of it, but to him alone, because he cannot honor any of those citizens whom he tyrannizes, even if they are talented and good, since he does not want to have to be suspicious of them.[9] 16 Nor can he subject the cities that he acquires or make them tributaries of the city over which he is tyrant, because making it powerful is not in his interest; it is in his interest to keep the state disunited and to make each town and each region acknowledge him. 17 Hence he alone, not his country, profits from his acquisitions. 18 Should anyone want to confirm this opinion with innumerable other reasons, let him read the treatise that Xenophon wrote, *On Tyranny.*[10]

19 It is no wonder, therefore, that people of antiquity persecuted tyrants with such hatred, loved living free,[11] and valued the word "freedom." 20 That is what happened when Hieronymus, the grandson of Hiero of Syracuse, was killed in Syracuse. When the news of his death reached his army, which was not far from Syracuse, it first began to riot and take up arms against his murderers; but when they heard that people were proclaiming freedom in Syracuse, attracted by that word, the army calmed down completely, stifled their anger against the tyrannicides, and began to think of how a free society could be established in the city.[12] 21 It is no wonder either that peoples take extraordinary revenge against those who have wrested their freedom from them. 22 I wish to report only one of many examples: it occurred in Corcyra, a city of Greece, at the time of the Peloponnesian War.[13] The area was then divided into two factions, one of which supported the Athenians, the other the Spartans, with the result that many cities there were divided internally: one group pursued the friendship of Sparta, the other that of Athens. When it happened that the Nobles prevailed in Corcyra and deprived the people of their freedom, the populace, aided by the Athenians, recovered power; once they got their hands on all the Nobles, they incarcerated them in a prison large enough to hold them. Then, on the pretext of sending them into exile in different places, they took them out eight or ten at a time and put them to death with many examples of cruelty. 23 When those remaining realized this, they decided to escape this ignominious death as far as possible; arming themselves with whatever they could, they fought against those who wanted to enter and defended the prison entrance. So the people, hearing this disturbance, assembled in a crowd, tore open the prison's upper story, and smothered the Nobles in its rubble. 24 Many other such horrendous and noteworthy cases also occurred in Greece; so we can see the truth that freedom that has been taken

from you is avenged with more violence than freedom that someone has tried to take from you.[14]

25 Therefore, when we think of what might give rise to the peoples in ancient times being greater lovers of freedom than in ours, I believe it arises from the same cause that makes men less strong now. This, I believe, is the difference between our upbringing and the ancients', based on the difference between our religion and the ancients'. 26 Our religion, because it has shown us the truth and the true way,[15] causes us to esteem worldly honor less, whereas the Pagans,[16] esteeming it greatly and having placed their highest good in it, were fiercer in their actions. 27 We can infer this from many of their institutions, beginning with the magnificence of their sacrifices compared with the humbleness of ours, in which there is some pomp, more refined than magnificent, but no fierce or bold acts. 28 Pomp or magnificence was not absent from their ceremonies, but they were supplemented with acts of sacrifice full of bloodshed and ferocity and the slaughter of hordes of animals; this terrifying sight made men resemble it. 29 Furthermore, ancient religion exalted only men full of worldly glory, such as commanders of armies and rulers of republics. 30 Our religion has glorified humble and contemplative men more than active ones. 31 It has then placed its highest good in humility, abjection, and contempt for things human; the other religion placed it in greatness of spirit, strength of body, and all the other things capable of making men very strong. 32 And if our religion requires you to have strength within yourself, it wants you to be ready to suffer rather than do something strong. 33 This way of life, therefore, seems to have made the world weak and handed it over as prey to wicked men who can control it securely since the general run of men, in order to go to Heaven, think more of enduring their blows than of avenging them. 34 Although the world may seem to have become effeminate and Heaven unarmed, that doubtless arises more from the cowardice of men who have interpreted our religion in terms of idleness, not *virtù*. 35 For were they to consider that it allows us to exalt and defend our native land, they would see that it wishes us to love and honor it and to prepare ourselves to be such as can defend it. 36 This kind of upbringing and such false interpretations are therefore the reason for our not seeing so many republics as there were in ancient times and, consequently, for our not seeing such love of freedom among people as existed then. 37 Still, I believe that the cause of this is rather that the Roman Empire, with its armed might and its greatness, wiped out all the republics and civil societies.[17] 38 Even though the empire later fell apart, its cities have not yet been able to put themselves back together and reorganize for civil life, except in a very few places in the empire.

39 However that may have been, the Romans found in every least part of the world a league of republics very well armed and quite stubborn in defense of their freedom. 40 This shows that without rare and extreme *virtù* the Roman people would never have been able to conquer them. 41 I think the Samnites will suffice as an example of some aspects of this league. It seems remarkable, as Livy admits, that they were so powerful and their armies so

strong that they were able to resist the Romans up to the time of the consul Papirius Cursor, son of the first Papirius (a period of forty-six years), despite the many defeats, the destructions of towns, and the many disasters their land underwent.[18] Especially because that region, where there were so many cities and so many inhabitants, is now virtually uninhabited.[19] At that time it was so well organized and so strong as to be unconquerable, had it not been attacked by the Romans' *virtù*.

42 And it is easy to understand the origin of that order and the present disorder: it all comes from living in freedom then and living in servitude now. 43 Because, as I have said above,[20] all towns and countries everywhere that live in freedom make enormous gains. 44 For in them one sees larger populations, since marriage is freer and more attractive to men; each one eagerly brings into the world the children that he thinks he can provide for. He has no fear that he will be deprived of his patrimony, and he knows not merely that the children are born free and not in slavery but that they can become rulers by means of their *virtù*. 45 Wealth can be seen to multiply more greatly there, both that which comes from agriculture and that which comes from industry,[21] because everyone willingly abounds in things and seeks to acquire the goods that he thinks he can enjoy once they are acquired. 46 Consequently, by vying with one another men work toward the private and public welfare: both grow wonderfully.

47 The opposite of all these things comes about in countries that live in servitude; the harsher their servitude is, the more they decline from their accustomed well-being. 48 And of all harsh servitudes, the harshest is that subjugating you to a republic: first, because it is the longest lasting and one can have less hope of release; second, because it is the aim of a republic to make its own body grow by exhausting and weakening all the other bodies. 49 A prince who subjugates you does not do this unless, like some oriental princes, he is a barbarian who devastates the country and scatters all human civilities. 50 But if he has humane and normal principles within him he usually loves his subject cities equally and lets them keep all their industry and almost all their former institutions. 51 Thus, while they cannot grow like free cities, they do not collapse like enslaved ones either; I am referring to the servitude of cities enslaved to a foreigner, because I have spoken above about those enslaved by one of their own citizens.[22]

52 Therefore anyone who considers all that has been said will not be surprised at the power that the Samnites had while they were free or at their weakness when they later were enslaved. Livy shows this in several places, particularly in the war with Hannibal. There he shows that when the Samnites were being attacked by a legion of men in Nola they sent emissaries to beg Hannibal for help. In their address they said that they had fought the Romans for a century with their own soldiers and their own commanders, that they had held out frequently against two consular armies and two consuls, and that now they were brought so low that they could scarcely defend themselves against the little Roman legion in Nola.[23]

NOTES

1. A reference to Germany, which for Machiavelli also included Switzerland; see 1, 55, n.7.

2. Translates *alpi,* meaning here the Apennines.

3. Meaning the region of Calabria in the "toe" of the Italian "boot."

4. Porsenna is discussed in Livy, 2.9–15; in 2.9.1 he is called the "king of Clusium," one of Etruria's twelve cities; Machiavelli may have used Clusium as a metonymy for all of Etruria; the city is the modern Chiusi, at the southern end of the Val di Chiana southeast of Siena.

5. Livy, 5.1, though in sentence 3 he specifies hatred for the actual king rather than the "title of prince" or the institution of the monarchy.

6. See 1, 2, n.17, on Pisistratus; Machiavelli's "century" runs approximately from 510 to 404 B.C., from the last of the Pisistratides to the fall of Athens under Spartan domination (Herodotus, 5.78, and Thucydides, 1.17).

7. A similar expression occurs in Sallust, *Bellum Catilinae,* 7. 3.

8. Translates here and in sentence 21 *uno vivere libero.*

9. Piero Capponi's condemnation of the Medici regime in his long speech early in Book 1 of Guicciardini's *Dialogo del reggimento di Firenze* makes this same point about the Medici: "since they are suspicious of everyone, they are forced to have eyes in the back of their heads and keep under their thumbs everyone whom they consider too great or too intelligent." In his *History of Florence* Guicciardini states that suspicion was a specific shortcoming of Lorenzo de' Medici: "it was caused perhaps not so much by his nature as by his being aware that he had to keep a free city subjugated" (chapter 9).

10. Usually cited as *Hieron,* a dialogue with Hiero II of Syracuse (c. 306–215 B.C.) as interlocutor; for more on his career, see Dedicatory Letter, note 5.

11. Translates *il vivere libero.*

12. Livy, 24.4–7; 21–22.

13. That is, on the island of Corfu around 425 B.C.; based on Thucydides, 3.70–85; 4.46–48. Martelli notes some discrepancies with Thucydides (*Storici antichi,* p. 72).

14. As if offering advice, Machiavelli particularizes and personalizes the foregoing political lesson, especially since the "you" is the second-person familiar pronoun.

15. An echo of John 14:6, predicated perhaps on John 8:32, as well as Preface A, sentence 7 and note.

16. Translates *Gentili.*

17. Translates *viveri civili.*

18. Livy, 10.31; 38–42. The "period of forty-six years" is based on 10.31.10, though an approximate calculation would be fifty years; for the dates of the Samnite Wars, see 2, 1, nn.10 and 12. Papirius Cursor's son became consul in 293 B.C. See also Mansfield, *New Modes,* pp. 196–197.

19. Samnium was in south central Italy in the southern region of the Apennines. The area then occupied by the Hirpini was desperately poor in Machiavelli's day and still is now.

20. The gist of sentences 8–12 of this chapter.

21. Translates *arti*.

22. In sentence 14; but *Prince*, 9, "Concerning the Civil Princedom," is also relevant.

23. Livy, 23.41–42.

~ 3 ~

ROME BECAME A GREAT CITY BY RUINING ITS NEIGHBORING CITIES AND READILY ACCEPTING FOREIGNERS INTO PUBLIC OFFICE

1 "Rome, meanwhile, increased on the ruins of Alba."[1] 2 Those who plan on a city's becoming a great power should try with all their might to fill it with inhabitants, for without this plentiful supply of men they will never succeed in making a city great. 3 This is done in two ways: by friendship or by force.[2] 4 By friendship, through keeping roads open and safe for foreigners who might plan to come and dwell in the city so that people live there willingly; by force, through destroying nearby cities and sending their inhabitants to live in your city. 5 Rome observed this so well that in the time of its sixth king Rome had eighty thousand men living in it under arms.[3] 6 For the Romans wanted to act as a good farmer does: in order for a plant to grow and to produce and ripen its fruits, he trims the first branches it sends forth; thus, with the *virtù* remaining in the stock of the plant, with time it can grow greener and more fruitful.[4] 7 Sparta and Athens are examples demonstrating that this method of growth and of making an empire was necessary and right. Even though they were two well-armed republics organized with excellent laws, they nevertheless did not achieve the greatness of the Roman Empire; yet Rome seemed more turbulent and less well organized than they were. 8 No other reason for this can be adduced than the one already advanced: because Rome, since it had enlarged the body of its city in those two ways, could already muster eighty thousand soldiers and Sparta and Athens never exceeded twenty thousand each.[5] 9 This came about not from Rome's location being more favorable than theirs but only from a different way of doing things. 10 Because Lycurgus, the founder of the Spartan republic, considered that nothing could more easily undo his laws than mixing in new inhabitants, he did everything to avoid foreigners having dealings there; in addition to banning intermarriage, citizenship, and other dealings that bring men together, he decreed that leather coins should be spent in his republic so that nobody might be tempted to bring merchandise or any craft there. In that way, Sparta could never increase its number of inhabitants.[6] 12 And because all our actions imitate nature,[7] it is neither possible nor natural for a thin trunk to hold up a heavy branch. 12 Therefore a small republic cannot occupy cities or kingdoms that are stronger or larger than it is; and if it does occupy them, nonetheless, what happens to it is like what happens to a tree if it had a branch heavier than

its trunk: it can barely hold the branch up and the slightest wind blows it down. 13 This was seen to happen to Sparta; once it occupied all the cities of Greece, no sooner had Thebes revolted than all the other cities revolted, and the trunk remained alone without branches.[8] 14 That could not happen to Rome, which had a trunk so thick that it could easily hold up any branch. 15 Therefore this way of doing things, together with the others that will be spoken of below, made Rome great and very powerful. 16 That is what Livy shows in a few words by saying: "Rome, meanwhile, increased on the ruins of Alba."[9]

NOTES

1. Quoted in Latin from Livy, 1.30.1, which Machiavelli alters slightly both here and in sentence 16: *"Roma interim crescit Albae ruinis."* Inglese and others note that quoting Livy's text at the beginning of a chapter may give us a hint about Machiavelli's original intention: to gloss specific passages from Livy in the form of a commentary rather than to construct an elaborate essay of political theory (see below, 2, 23, and 3, 10); see also Baron, "Citizen and Author." For the belief that Venice is on Machiavelli's mind, though not overtly discussed, see Sasso, *Antichi,* 3:41–43.

2. An opposition Machiavelli makes in the second sentence of his earliest known work, *Discorso fatto al magistrato dei Dieci sopra le cose di Pisa* (Discourse made to the magistracy of the Ten on the affairs of Pisa) in 1499. Such either/or constructions typify Machiavelli's thought processes throughout his life.

3. Servius Tullius was "the sixth king"; the figure comes from Livy, 1.44.2.

4. The first of a series of agricultural images Machiavelli uses throughout the chapter to point up his argument.

5. Machiavelli refers to the time when Servius Tullius ruled, traditionally from 578 to 535 B.C. Inglese modifies here the figure of 280,000 soldiers given in some texts so as to agree with sentence 5. Scholars challenge Machiavelli's figures for Sparta and Athens; according to Thucydides, 2.31, thirteen thousand would have been the maximum number of soldiers for Athens while Herodotus, 9.28, gives ten thousand for Sparta.

6. On Lycurgus, see 1, 2, nn.2, 16, and Plutarch, *Lycurgus,* 9.2–3 and 27.6–9; on coinage, compare Seneca, *De beneficiis,* 5.14, and Polybius, 6.49. But see Martelli, *Storici antichi,* p. 73, for how Machiavelli distorts these sources.

7. A classical commonplace; Cicero, *Laws,* 1.25–29, especially 26.

8. See 1, 6, n.10.

9. See note 1 to this chapter.

~ 4 ~

REPUBLICS HAVE HAD THREE WAYS OF EXPANDING

1 Anyone who has studied ancient history finds that republics have had three ways of expanding. 2 One, observed by the ancient Etruscans, was a league comprising several republics in which none exceeds the others in either authority or rank; as they took other cities they made allies of them, similarly to the way the Swiss in our time do and as the Achaeans and the Aetolians did

in antiquity in Greece.[1] 3 Because the Romans waged many wars against the Etruscans, I shall expatiate on them in detail, the better to show the characteristics of this first way. 4 In Italy before the Roman Empire existed, the Etruscans were very powerful on sea and on land. Although there is no detailed history of their affairs, a few records and some signs of their greatness do still exist.[2] 5 We know that they sent a colony, which they called Adria, to the upper sea; it was so noble that it gave its name to the sea that Latins still call the Adriatic. 6 We also hear that their armed forces were obeyed from the Tiber as far as the foothills of the Alps that now encircle the bulk of Italy, despite the fact that the Etruscans lost their power over the territory known today as Lombardy two hundred years before the Romans had grown in great strength.[3] That land was occupied by the Gauls who, motivated either by necessity or by the sweetness of its fruits—and especially of its wine—came into Italy under their leader, Bellovesus. After defeating and chasing out the inhabitants of the region, they settled in that place, where they built many cities; they called the region Gaul from the name that they had then, and they kept it until the Romans conquered them. 7 So the Etruscans lived in that equality, and they went about expanding in the first way stated above. There were twelve cities,[4] among which were Chiusi, Veii, Arezzo, Fiesole, Volterra, and so on, which governed the Etruscan empire by a league. 8 They could not extend their expansion beyond Italy; for reasons stated below, the greater part of Italy also remained intact. 9 The second way is to make allies for oneself, but not to the extent, however, that you do not keep for yourself the position of consulship, the seat of power, and leadership of the campaigns. That was the way observed by the Romans. 10 The third way is to make subjects right off rather than allies for oneself, as the Spartans and Athenians did. 11 Of these three ways, the last is completely useless, as it was seen to be in the two republics just mentioned, which collapsed only because they had acquired a dominion that they could not keep. 12 Because to take on responsibility for governing cities by force, especially any that have been accustomed to living in freedom, is difficult and tiring.[5] 13 And if you are not armed, and heavily, you can neither command nor rule them. 14 And in order to be so, it is necessary to make allies to help you and add to the population of your city. 15 Because Sparta and Athens did neither of these, their way of doing things was completely useless. 16 And because Rome, which exemplifies the second way, did both, it thereby rose to such widespread power. 17 Because it alone lived in this way, it was also the only one to become so powerful. Throughout all of Italy it had made a great many allies which for the most part lived under equal laws with Rome; on the other hand, as has been stated above, since Rome had always reserved for itself the seat of power and the position of command, its allies, without realizing it, subjugated themselves by their own efforts and their own bloodshed. 18 The Romans began to leave Italy with their armies, to turn kingdoms into provinces, and to make subjects of people accustomed to living under kings so they were not troubled at being made subjects; because these people had Roman governors and had been defeated by armies with a Roman ensign, they did not recognize anything but Rome as their superior. As a result, Rome's allies in Italy suddenly found themselves surrounded by Roman subjects and crushed by the very great large city that Rome was. 19 When they realized the error under which they had been living, it was too late for them to remedy it: Rome had acquired such great power thanks to her foreign provinces and, because its own city was very large and heavily armed, so great was its internal strength.[6] 20 Although its allies conspired against Rome to avenge their injuries, within a short time they were the losers in the war, worsening their condition: from being allies, they too became subjects. 21 This way alone of doing things, as has been stated, was observed by the Romans; a republic that wishes to expand cannot act in any other way, because experience has not shown us any surer or truer one.

22 The above-mentioned way of leagues (in which the Etruscans, the Achaeans, and the Aetolians lived, and as the Swiss do today) is the next best one after the Romans'; because it is not possible to expand very much with it, two advantages result: one, you do not easily get yourself into wars; second, you can easily keep what little you take. 23 The reason why such a republic cannot expand is this: it is fragmented and placed in various seats; that makes it difficult to consult and make decisions. 24 It also makes them reluctant to dominate: because many communities participate in dominion, they do not value such acquisition as highly as does a single republic that hopes to enjoy it all for itself. 25 In addition, they govern themselves by council, and they have to be slower in all decision making than those who dwell within the same city-walls. 26 Experience also shows that there is a fixed limit to such a way of doing things, and we have no example showing us that it may be exceeded. This is for a league to total twelve or fourteen communities, then not to seek to go beyond that; once they have attained the level at which they think that they can defend themselves against anyone, they do not seek greater dominion, both because necessity does not compel them to have more power and because, for the reasons stated above, they do not see anything to be gained from the acquisitions.[7] 27 For they would have to do one of two things: either continue to make allies, and this large number would lead to confusion, or they would have to make subjects; but because they see problems in this and not much to be gained by holding them, they do not care to. 28 Therefore, when they have reached such a number as to think they can live securely, they resort to two measures: one is to extend patronage and offer protection and by these means extract money from all sides which can easily be distributed among themselves; the other is to wage war for others and to get payment from any prince who pays them for his campaigns, as we see the Swiss do today and as we read that the above-mentioned people did. 29 Livy gives evidence for this where he says that when Philip, the king of Macedonia, came to negotiate with Titus Quinctius Flamininus they discussed a treaty together in the presence of a Praetor of the Aetolians.[8] When the Praetor came to speak with Philip, the king reproached him with greed and bad faith, declaring that the Aetolians were not ashamed to wage war for one man and then send their soldiers into the enemy's service too so that the flags of Aetolia could frequently be seen among two opposing armies.

30 Therefore this way of doing things by leagues is known to have always been done and had the same results. 31 This way of making subjects has also always been seen to be weak and to have had little benefit; and when leagues have still exceeded their limit, they have quickly fallen. 32 And if this way of making subjects is not useful in armed republics, it is completely useless in those that are unarmed, as the republics of Italy have been in our day. 33 Hence we know that the way the Romans did things was right; this is all the more remarkable since there never was an instance of it before Rome and no one has imitated it since then. 34 As for leagues, there are only the Swiss and the Swabian league that imitate the Romans.[9] 35 And as we shall say at the conclusion of this topic, so many institutions that Rome observed, germane both to internal and foreign matters, are in our day not only not imitated but not even taken into account: some deemed untrue, some impossible, some irrelevant and not useful. Thus, remaining in this ignorance, we are prey to whoever has wanted to overrun this land. 36 Even though imitating the Romans should seem hard, imitating the ancient Etruscans ought not to seem so, especially to the Tuscans of today. 37 Because if the Etruscans, for the reason stated, were unable to form an empire like Rome's, they were able to acquire such power in Italy as that way of doing things might grant them. 38 Over a long time this way was reliable, winning very great glory of empire and arms and high praise for customs and religion.[10] 39 This power and glory were first diminished by the Gauls then destroyed by the Romans: so much so that, although two thousand years ago the power of the Etruscans was great, at present there is almost no record of it. 40 This matter has made me wonder how such oblivion comes about, and this will be discussed in the next chapter.

NOTES

1. Francesco Vettori and Machiavelli discussed Swiss policy and the precedents of the Etruscans, Aetolians, and Achaeans in an exchange of letters during August 1513: see the passages quoted in note 7 to this chapter. The Aetolian League was formed in the third century B.C. in western Greece to free its members from Macedonian control. It joined the Romans in 211 B.C. and fought with them against both the Achaean League, formed by other Greek states allied with Macedonia, and Philip V of Macedon during the First Macedonian War (215–205 B.C.).

2. The following account of the Etruscans and Gauls is based on Livy, 5.33–35, though early Florentine historiography did deal briefly with the Etruscans; see the opening passage of Leonardo Bruni, *Historiae florentini populi* (1429). The power "on sea and on land" and the "upper sea" of the next sentence translate phrases from Livy, 5.33.7.

3. A paraphrase of Livy, 5.33.5.

4. This figure corresponds to the one Livy gives in 4.23.5, but in the passage that Machiavelli seems to have in mind Livy says that there were two groups of twelve cities: one on the eastern and the other on the western side of the Apennines. Bruni, however, refers to twelve cities *(Historiae florentini populi).*

5. Machiavelli examines the Spartans and Athenians in *Prince,* 5, and points out that "whoever becomes master of, but does not destroy, a city used to living as a free

community may expect to be destroyed by it, because during an insurrection the city can always take refuge in invoking the name of freedom and its traditional institutions, which are never forgotten, whatever the course of time or whatever favors be accorded" (p. 139, lines 28–35).

6. The "foreign provinces" were Asia Minor, Greece, northern Africa, Sicily, Spain, Cisalpine Gaul, and Narbonne. For the remainder of the paragraph, Machiavelli takes his example from the Social War (War of the Allies), 91–88 B.C.; see *Discourses,* 1, 1, n.5. An Italic league formed a republic with its capital at Corfinium (present-day Corfinio) in the eastern foothills of the Apennines about forty miles southwest of Pescara. In fact, Julius Caesar, then a consul, was instrumental in passing a law granting Roman citizenship to all those who remained loyal to Rome: the *lex Iulia* in 90. Martelli argues that the Romans granted citizenship to the members of the Italic league (*Storici antichi,* p. 74).

7. The foregoing analysis reflects the exchange of letters between Machiavelli and Vettori mentioned in note 1 to this chapter. Vettori writes, "I am among those who fear the Swiss greatly, but I do not much believe they can become the next Romans . . . because if you study the *Politics* well and the republics that have existed, you will not find that a republic divided like this one [the Swiss confederation] can make its way. It seems to me that an example of this has been given by them, because when they could easily have taken all of Lombardy they did not do it, because they say it was not in their interest because, as you can see with those they have taken up till now, they have made them allies and not subjects. They do not want any more allies, because they do not want to have to divide their tribute into more shares; it is not in their interest to keep subjects, because they would have to look after them at their own expense" (*Friends,* p. 255, and notes, p. 510). Machiavelli's reply begins, "Where I think you are completely mistaken concerns the Swiss, whether or not to fear them, because I believe that we have a very great deal to fear from them. . . . I do not know what Aristotle says about confederated republics, but I certainly can say what might reasonably exist, what exists, and what has existed; I recall having read that the Etruscans held all Italy as far as the Alps until the Gauls drove them out of Lombardy. The reason why the Aetolians and Achaeans did not advance had more to do with the times than with themselves because they constantly had an extremely powerful Macedonian king on their backs who would not let them escape from the nest—and after the Macedonians came the Romans. So, rather than their constitution, it was foreign military power that prevented them from expanding. Now the Swiss do not want to create subject nations because they do not see any advantage in it for them. . . . But . . . the Swiss already have a duke of Milan [Massimiliano Sforza] and a pope [Leo X] as their Italian dependents; the Swiss have added the tribute these two pay to their revenue and will not lose it; when the time comes that one of them does miss it, the Swiss will consider it sedition and resort to their lancers. Once they have won the contest, they will think about making themselves secure; to do so, they will tighten the screws on those whom they have conquered. Thus they will gradually subjugate everything" (ed. cit., pp. 258–259, and notes, p. 511).

8. Livy, 32.32–34; the praetor mentioned was Phaeneas, who spoke as an ally of Rome at a council near Nicea in 197 B.C. after the victory of Flamininus at Elatea.

9. The Swabian League was a confederation established among princes and

cities of southern Germany in 1488. In 1499 the Swiss turned back its efforts to force them to acknowledge the sovereignty of the Holy Roman Emperor. It was disbanded in 1534.

10. Livy, 5.1.6, praises the Etruscans for being more devoted to religion than other tribes.

~ 5 ~

CHANGING RELIGIONS[1] AND LANGUAGES, TOGETHER WITH EVENTS LIKE FLOODS OR THE PLAGUE, OBLITERATE THE RECORDS OF THINGS

1 I think the philosophers who have claimed that the world is eternal[2] could be answered that if it really were so old it would be reasonable for there to be a record of more than five thousand years, even if we did not see how the records of the past are obliterated for various reasons, some of which come from men, some from heaven.[3] 2 Those that come from men are the changing of religion[4] and languages. 3 For whenever a new sect,[5] that is, a new religion, emerges, its first concern is to wipe out the old one in order to establish its reputation; when the founders of a new sect[6] happen to speak a different language, they obliterate it easily. 4 We can see this if we consider the means that Christianity used against Paganism;[7] it eliminated all the latter's institutions and ceremonies and obliterated every record of the ancient theology. 5 It is true that Christianity did not succeed in completely obliterating knowledge of what its outstanding men accomplished; this came about because it had kept the Latin language; it did that of necessity since it had to write down its new law in it. 6 Had they been able to write it down in a new language, bearing in mind the other persecutions they carried out against them, there would be no record of the past at all. 7 Anyone who reads about the means used by Saint Gregory[8] and the other heads of the Christian religion will see how persistently they tracked down every record of the past, burning the works of poets and historians, ruining images and destroying everything else that might yield some sign of antiquity. 8 So that, if they had added a new language to this persecution, in a very short time we should have seen everything forgotten. 9 We must therefore believe that what Christianity wished to do to the Pagans, the Pagans had done to the preceding sect.[9] 10 Because sects change two or three times in five or six thousand years, the record of things done before that time is lost; even if some trace of it remains, it is considered mythical and no one puts any faith in them. That is what happened to the history of Diodorus Siculus which, although it accounts for forty or fifty thousand years, is nonetheless considered to be a pack of lies, as I believe it is.[10]

11 As for the causes that come from heaven, they are those that stamp out the human race and reduce the population of part of the world to very few. 12 This results from either plague or famine or flood: the last is the most important, both because it is the most universal and because the survivors are all

uncouth mountain men who, having no knowledge of anything ancient, cannot leave it to their descendants. 13 Should there survive among them someone who had such knowledge, he conceals it and distorts it in his own way so that he can increase his prestige and renown; consequently what remains for those who follow is only what he has been willing to write down about it—nothing else. 14 I do not believe it can be doubted that these floods, plagues, and famines occur because every history is full of them, because this effect can be seen from the oblivion into which things fall, and because it seems reasonable it should be so.[11] 15 When a lot of superfluous matter has accumulated in nature as in simple bodies, it often moves by itself and produces a purge that makes for that body's health. So it is with the compound body of the human race. When every country is filled with inhabitants (so that no one can live there or go elsewhere, since every location is settled and filled up) and when human wisdom and guile have gone as far as they can go, the world must necessarily purge itself by one of the three means.[12] Thus men, having become fewer and beaten down, may live more comfortably and improve.

16 So, as we have stated above, the Etruscans were once powerful, full of religion and *virtù;* they had their customs and native language, but all of that was stamped out by the power of Rome.[13] 17 So that, as has been stated, there remains only the memory of their name.

NOTES

1. Translates *sètte,* sects, but see sentence 3 of this chapter.

2. An Aristotelian notion found in *Physics,* 8; *Metaphysics* 12.6–7, 1071b3–1073a12, and *On the Heavens,* 1.9, 279a7–279b3, which Cicero refers to in *Tusculan Disputations,* 1.28.70. The Roman Catholic Church vigorously opposed the thesis that the world is eternal; see Augustine, *City of God,* 12.10–11. Machiavelli, in fact, seems to take particular aim at this text. For a detailed discussion of the *de aeternitate mundi* question, see Sasso, *Antichi,* 1:167–399.

3. See Lucretius, *De rerum natura,* 5.324–350.

4. Translates *sètte,* sects.

5. Translates *sètta,* sect.

6. Translates *sètta,* sect.

7. Translates *la Gentile.*

8. Gregory the Great was pope from 590 to 604. These "ways" are discussed in a twelfth-century treatise on the principles of government: John of Salisbury, *Policraticus,* 2.26, and 8.19. Gregory's opposition to classical culture has often been noted; Savonarola, in a sermon on 9 February 1497, referred to his burning of Livy's *Decades* (Inglese).

9. Livy indicates that the Romans did not act this way toward Etruscan religion (5.21–22) or language and literature (9.36.3–4). See also Mansfield, *New Modes,* p. 203.

10. During the first century B.C., Diodorus Siculus wrote an unreliable universal history in Greek, the *Bibliotheca historica,* that ended with an account of Julius Caesar's Gallic Wars up to 54 B.C. In his preface, he acknowledges that he is relying on fable and tradition for events preceding the Trojan War, but his time frame is not Machiavelli's; indeed, it is unclear how Machiavelli arrived at his figures.

11. In addition to a possible allusion to Noah and his ark, the foregoing discussion owes much to classical sources: Plato, *Timaeus,* 22a–23c, and *Laws,* 676b–678c; Aristotle, *Politics,* 2.5.12; 1269a4–8, and *Metaphysics,* 12.8 1074b1–14; Polybius, 6.5.5; Lucretius, 5.338–344; Cicero, *De republica,* 6.21. Some of this material may also relate to Machiavelli's carnival song *De' romiti* (On hermits) and his letter to Guicciardini of 18 May 1521 with its offhand remark about "the deluge that is to come" (*Friends,* p. 340).

12. Inglese notes the interaction between Machiavelli's notion of necessity and the assertion that there is a conjunction between human and natural events, a belief rooted in an astrological tradition.

13. In the preceding chapter.

~ 6 ~

HOW THE ROMANS WENT ABOUT MAKING WAR

1 Having discussed how the Romans went about expansion, we shall now discuss how they went about making war; in each of their actions we shall see how wisely they differed from the method generally used by others, to clear the way to attaining supreme greatness. 2 Whoever makes war by choice, or else by ambition, is seeking to acquire and to keep what is acquired and to act in such a way that it enriches, not impoverishes, his city and his native land. 3 It is therefore necessary in both acquiring and keeping to avoid expenditures and rather to do everything to profit the public treasury. 4 Anyone who wants to do all these things must follow the Roman style and way: this was first of all to make wars, as the French say, short and heavy,[1] because by going on campaigns with large armies, the Romans dispatched all the wars that they had with the Latins, the Samnites, and the Etruscans in a very short time. 5 If we observe all those that they fought from the founding of Rome until the siege of Veii,[2] we shall see they were all dispatched, this one in six, that one in ten, this one in twenty days. 6 For this was their custom: as soon as war was declared, they marched forth with their armies against the enemy and quickly pitched battle. 7 When this was won, the enemy came to terms in order that their countryside would not be entirely laid waste, and the Romans penalized them in land; these lands they converted to private use or assigned to a colony. Situated on the conquered peoples' frontier, the colony became a guard post for Rome's borders to the profit both of the colonists, who got the fields, and Rome's public treasury, which maintained this guard without any expense.[3] 8 This way could not have been safer or stronger or more profitable. For while their enemies were not in the field, the guard post was sufficient; if they went forth in great numbers to attack the colony, the Romans again issued forth in great numbers and fought against them. Once they had pitched and won the battle, imposing even heavier terms on them, they returned home. 9 Thus little by little they came to acquire prestige among their enemies and strength in themselves.

10 They kept on using this method until they changed their way of waging war. This occurred after the siege of Veii when, in order to be able to fight a

long war, they ordered their soldiers to be paid; previously they did not pay them because, since wars were brief, it was unnecessary.[4] 11 Although the Romans provided pay and by virtue of this were able to fight longer wars and necessity kept them in encampments longer because they were fighting at a greater distance, nevertheless, they never varied either from their first principle of ending their wars quickly, depending upon the place and time, or from sending out colonies.[5] 12 The Consuls' ambition held them to their first rule, namely, making wars brief, not to mention that being their natural custom; because their term lasted a year and six months of that year were in garrison, they wanted to end the war in order to hold a triumph. 13 The Romans were held to sending out colonies by the great profit and convenience that resulted from them. 14 They did indeed change somewhat concerning spoils. They were not so generous with them as they had been at first: both because, since the soldiers had their salary, that no longer seemed so necessary to them, and because, since the spoils were much greater, they planned to swell the public treasury with them so that they were not forced to carry on campaigns through taxes levied on the city. 15 In a short time this rule made their treasury very rich. 16 These two methods, therefore, concerning both the distribution of spoils and the sending out of colonies, made Rome grow rich from war, whereas other princes and unwise republics are impoverished by it.[6] 17 And the matter went so far that a Consul did not feel he could hold a triumph if with his triumphal procession he did not bring a good deal of gold and silver and every other kind of spoils into the treasury. 18 Thus by the above-mentioned terms and by finishing wars quickly (since they were expert at wearying their enemies at length by routs, raids, and treaties made to their advantage), the Romans became richer and richer and more and more powerful.

NOTES

1. A reference to French military vocabulary current in Machiavelli's day, that a war should be *courte et grosse* (brief but intense). Italians were well aware that after the invasion of Italy by Charles VIII in 1494, military terminology—and, more significant, warfare itself—had been irrevocably altered; see Machiavelli, *Art of War.* Guicciardini concurs: "When the French came to Italy, they introduced such efficiency into war that, up to 1521, the loss of a campaign meant the loss of a state" (*Ricordi,* C 64). See also Guicciardini, *Storia d'Italia,* 1, 9 and 11, and his discussion of the battle of Fornovo, 6 July 1495, in *History of Florence,* chapter 13.

2. According to Livy, 5.22.8, this lasted "ten continuous summers and winters" from 406 to 396 B.C.

3. Relevant passages in Livy can be found in 2.31.4; 3.1.5; 10.1.1 and 10.5; for more on colonies, see note 5 below.

4. See Livy, 4.59.11, and 60, and 1, 51, above.

5. In *Prince,* 3, Machiavelli advises that when a prince "acquires states in a region where the language, customs, and institutions are heterogeneous[,] . . . [then] establishing colonial settlements in one or two places so that they may be like shackles on that state is another and better remedy, because a prince must either do that, or else garrison many cavalry and infantry units there. A prince does not spend much

on settlements, so with little or no expense he can establish and retain them" (p. 107, lines 74–76; p. 109, lines 98–104).

6. Fabrizio Colonna makes the same point in his fifth speech in Machiavelli's *Art of War,* 5; see also the opening passages of *Florentine Histories,* 6, 1.

~ 7 ~

HOW MUCH LAND THE ROMANS ALLOTTED PER COLONIST

1 I believe it is hard to find the truth about how much land the Romans distributed per colonist, because I believe they gave more or less depending on the places where they sent their colonies. 2 We may infer that in any case and in any given place the distribution was meager: first, in order to be able to send more men, since they were assigned to guarding the surrounding country; second, since they lived in poverty at home, it could not be expected that the Romans should want their men to have too great abundance abroad. 3 And Livy says that when Veii was taken they sent a colony there and distributed to each settler three and seven-twelfths *jugera* of land (which equals in our measurement . . .),[1] because, in addition to the things mentioned above, they thought that what mattered was not how much land there was but how arable it was. 4 It is indeed necessary for the entire colony to have public fields where each can graze his livestock and forests to get firewood; without these things a colony cannot be set up.

NOTES

1. Machiavelli left a blank at this point, presumably intending to do his calculations later. The relevant passage in Livy is 5.30.8, but there exists a textual variant for this passage; see also 4.47.7, for colonists being supplied with fewer *jugera.* A *jugerum* is equivalent to about five-eighths of an acre, so the amount of land concerned is roughly 2.5 acres.

~ 8 ~

WHY PEOPLE LEAVE THEIR NATIVE PLACES AND OVERRUN THE LANDS OF OTHERS

1 Because we have discussed above the way the Romans carried on war and how the Etruscans were attacked by the Gauls,[1] I do not think it is irrelevant to our subject to discuss how two kinds of war are waged. 2 One is waged out of the ambition of princes or republics seeking to extend their power, as were the wars that Alexander the Great and the Romans waged, and those waged every day by one power against another. 3 These wars are dangerous, but they do not completely drive out a country's inhabitants, because the victor is satisfied with the people's obedience; and he generally lets them live under their

own laws and always in their own houses and with their own property. 4 In the other kind of war, an entire people with all its families, driven either by famine or by war, leaves a place and goes forth to seek a new home and a new country, not to rule it, like those in the example above, but to possess it all for themselves and to drive out or kill its former inhabitants. 5 This war is extremely cruel and frightening. 6 Sallust is speaking of this kind of war at the end of the *History of the Jugurthine War* when he states that, after Jugurtha was defeated, the Romans felt the commotion of the Gallic invasion of Italy. There he says that the Roman people fought with every other nation solely about who was going to rule, but with the Gauls they were always fighting for each one's survival.[2] 7 Because it is enough for a prince or a republic attacking a country to do away only with those in command;[3] but these populations need to do away with everybody, because they want to live off of what others lived off of.

8 The Romans fought three of these extremely dangerous wars. 9 The first was when Rome was captured and occupied by the Gauls who, as was mentioned above,[4] had taken Lombardy from the Etruscans and made it their home. Livy cites two causes for this. First, as has been stated above, the sweetness of the fruits and the wine in Italy, which Gaul lacked, enticed them. Second, because the kingdom of Gaul had so increased in population that it was impossible to feed it there, the rulers in those places decided that a portion of the population must go and seek a new land. Once that decision was made, they chose Bellovesus and Segovesus, two Gallic kings, to be commanders of those who were to leave; Bellovesus came to Italy and Segovesus went to Spain.[5] 10 The occupation of Lombardy resulted from Bellovesus's incursion and from it the first war that the Gauls waged against Rome.[6] 11 The next was the one they waged after the First Carthaginian War, when they slew more than two hundred thousand Gauls between Piombino and Pisa.[7] 12 The third was when the Teutons and the Cimbri came into Italy; after they had defeated several Roman armies, Marius defeated them.[8] 13 So the Romans won these three extremely dangerous wars. 14 And it did not take less *virtù* to win them, because later, when Roman *virtù* failed and its armies lost their ancient valor, its empire was destroyed by similar peoples: the Goths, Vandals, and so on, who occupied the entire Western Empire.[9]

15 As has been mentioned above, those people leave their countries driven by necessity; the necessity arises either from famine or from a war and oppression that has been done to them in their own countries so they are forced to seek new lands. 16 These people are numerous and then they violently enter the countries of others, slaughter the inhabitants, take possession of their property, make a new kingdom, and change the region's name, as did Moses and the peoples that seized the Roman Empire. 17 For the new names existing in Italy and other countries had no origin other than having been so named by their new conquerors. That is the case of Lombardy, which was called Cisalpine Gaul; France was called Transalpine Gaul, and is now named for the Franks, because that was how the peoples who occupied it were called; Slavonia was called Illyria; Hungary, Pannonia; England, Britannia; and many other regions that have changed their names, which it would be tiresome to relate.[10]

18 Moses also called the part of Syria he occupied Judea. 19 And because I have said above that sometimes some people are driven out of their own home by war and hence are forced to seek new lands, I would like to cite the example of the Maurusians, a people formerly in Syria.[11] When they heard that the Hebrews were on their way, they believed that they could not resist them, so they thought it would be better to save themselves and leave their own country than to lose their lives too in trying to save it. Departing with their families, they set off for Africa where they settled down and drove off the inhabitants that they found in those places. 20 Thus they who had been unable to defend their own country were able to seize that of others. Procopius, who writes of the war that Belisarius waged against the Vandals who had occupied Africa, reports having read characters written on certain columns in the places where these Maurusians dwelt showing the reason for their departure from Syria; they read: "We are the Maurusians, who fled in the face of Joshua the marauder, son of Nava."[12] 21 These peoples are therefore greatly to be feared since they are driven by dire necessity; if they do not encounter good armies, they will never be withstood.

22 But when those who are forced to abandon their native land are not numerous, they are not so dangerous as those peoples whom we have discussed, for they cannot exercise such violence but must occupy a place by cunning and, once they have occupied it, stay there by means of allies and confederates. 23 We can see this was done by Aeneas, Dido, the Massaliotes, and the like, all of whom were able to stay where they settled through the consent of the neighbors.[13]

24 People leave in large numbers, and they have almost all left the regions of Scythia.[14] These are cold and poverty-stricken places where, because there were very many of them and the region's nature is unable to feed them, they are forced to leave, since there are many things to drive them out and nothing to keep them. 25 And if for the past five hundred years none of these peoples has happened to overrun any country, that has been for several reasons. 26 The first is the great evacuation that the region had during the decline of the empire, when more than thirty [different] peoples left it. 27 The second is that Germany and Hungary, which some of these tribes also left, now have reclaimed their land so that people can live there comfortably and so they are not forced to change places.[15] 28 On the other hand, since their men are very warlike, they are like a bastion to keep the Scythians, who border on them, from presuming they can defeat them or pass them by. 29 Very great movements of Tartars often occur, which are then withstood by the Hungarians and the people of Poland; they often boast that, if it were not for their arms, Italy and the Church would frequently have felt the weight of Tartar armies.[16] 30 And I would like this to suffice concerning the above-mentioned peoples.

NOTES

1. In 2, 4 and 6.

2. In the final paragraph, 114, Sallust discusses the battle of Arausio, present-day Orange, in 105 B.C. Sallust incorrectly includes the Cimbri and Teutones among the

tribes of the Gauls. Machiavelli's point may be based on a less reliable text of Sallust than those currently available.

3. When a prince conquers a people "in the same region and of the same language," then Machiavelli says that "it is very easy to hold on to them—particularly when they are not used to living as a free community. To possess them securely, it is enough to wipe out the line of princes who were reigning" (*Prince,* 3, p. 107, lines 54–60).

4. Above, 2, 4, sentence 6; Livy's account occurs in 5.33–35.

5. Livy says that Segovesus went to the Hercynian highlands in southern Germany (the Black Forest, the Hartz, and Bohemia), not Spain (5.34.4). Martelli points out that Livy specifies that these events occurred closer to 590 B.C., not, as the next sentence implies, in 390 (*Storici antichi,* p. 76).

6. In 390 B.C.

7. The First "Carthaginian" or Punic War lasted from 264–241 B.C. On the interaction between Rome and the Gauls, see above, 2, 1, n.16. At this point Machiavelli is referring to a series of Gallic Wars lasting from 226 to 222 B.C. The number of soldiers slain is too high; see Polybius, 2.31. See also Martelli, *Storici antichi,* p. 77.

8. He did so first at the battle of Aquae Sextiae, present-day Aix-en-Provence, in 102 B.C. and then in 101 at the battle of Campi Raudii, present-day Vercelli, midway between Milan and Turin.

9. The first paragraph of *Florentine Histories,* 1, 1, also traces this material.

10. On the issue of naming, see also *Florentine Histories,* 1, 5.

11. The word "Maurusians" refers to the population of Mauritania, an area covered today by Morocco and Algeria; our word "Moors" is derived from it. On the question of Syria, see Martelli, *Storici antichi,* p. 77.

12. Procopius, a sixth-century A.D. historian of Byzantine Greece, was the secretary of the Roman emperor Justinian's general Belisarius. The third and fourth book of his *De bello Vandalico* deals with the war in Africa against the Vandals, whom Belisarius conquered in 534. Machiavelli's quotation in Latin is based on 4.10.22: *"Nos Maurusii, qui fugimus a facie Iesu latronis filii Navae." "Iesu"* means both Joshua and Jesus, though it clearly refers here to Joshua, the successor of Moses and, according to the Old Testament, the son of Nun.

13. Livy describes two traditions about the landing of Aeneas on Italian shores (1.1.6–11); Justin tells of Dido's flight from Phoenicia to Carthage in Africa (18.4–5); for the Massaliotes, see above, 2, 1, n.30.

14. An area originally referred to as bounded on the west by the Carpathian Mountains in east-central Europe and on the east by the Don River in southeastern Ukraine. The remainder of this paragraph refers to the history of Eastern Europe after the fall of the Roman Empire.

15. In *Florentine Histories,* 2, 1, Machiavelli notes that "unhealthy regions become healthy because a multitude of men seize them all at once; they clean up the land by means of agriculture and they purify the air with fires, something nature could never provide."

16. The Tartars, or Tatars, were tribes from Mongolia that overran parts of Asia and eastern Europe in the thirteenth century and controlled Russia until the reign of Ivan IV, at the end of the fifteenth century.

~ 9 ~

WHAT CAUSES COMMONLY GIVE RISE TO WARS BETWEEN THE POWERFUL

1 The cause of the war that broke out between the Romans and the Samnites, who had long been in a league, is a common one that arises between all powerful princedoms.[1] 2 It either comes about by chance or is brought on by the one who desires to start a war. 3 The one between the Romans and the Samnites broke out by chance, because the Samnites did not intend to wage war against the Romans while waging one against the Sidicines and then the Campanians. 4 But when the Campanians were crushed, they appealed to Rome, contrary to the expectation of the Romans and the Samnites. Because the Campanians put themselves in the Romans' hands, they were forced to defend them as if they were their own and to take on a war which they did not feel they could avoid with honor. 5 For it certainly seemed logical to the Romans that they could not defend the Campanians as allies against their allies the Samnites, but they certainly felt it shameful not to defend them as subjects or even as tributaries, for they thought that not undertaking such a defense would stand in the way of all those who intended to come under their sway. 6 Therefore, because Rome had as its aim empire and glory, and not peace, it could not refuse this undertaking. 7 This same cause provided the basis for the first war against the Carthaginians because of the defense that the Romans undertook in Sicily of the people of Messina; this too was due to chance.[2] 8 But the second war that arose between them later was certainly not due to chance, because Hannibal, the Carthaginian general, attacked the Saguntines, allies of the Romans in Spain, not to harm them but to provoke the Roman army and have an opportunity to fight them and to pass over into Italy.

9 This way of starting new wars has always been customary between the powerful and those who have some regard for both their word and other things. 10 Because if I want to wage war against a prince and there are firm agreements between us that have been observed for a long time, rather than attack him I shall attack one of his allies with a different justification and on a different pretext. For I know full well that in attacking his ally either he will be annoyed, and I shall fulfill my aim of waging war on him; or, if he is not annoyed, he will reveal his weakness or his disloyalty by not defending one of his tributaries. 11 Either of these two things is going to detract from his reputation and make my plans easier.

12 So, with respect to starting a war, we must note both what has been said above about the surrender of the Campanians and, in addition, what remedies a city has that cannot defend itself by itself, yet still wants to defend itself against an attack has: 13 to give itself over voluntarily to the one whom you intend to get to defend you, as did the Capuans with the Romans and the Florentines with King Robert of Naples, who, although he was unwilling to defend them as allies, later defended them as subjects against the forces of Castruccio of Lucca, who was attacking them.[3]

NOTES

1. Livy, in 7.19, discusses the league, formed in 354 B.C.; the First Samnite War, which Machiavelli is about to discuss, lasted from 343 to 341 B.C. (see Livy, 7.29–32). This material is also treated above, 2, 1, sentence 10.

2. Actually at that point "the people of Messina" were the Mamertines; see above, 2, 1, n.25. Here and in the next sentence the wars "against the Carthaginians" are commonly known as the Punic Wars.

3. There are several points to be made here. First, Machiavelli's use of the advisory tone in the familiar "you" is worth noting. Second, "the Capuans" are interchangeable with "the Campanians" of the first part of the sentence because the town of Capua gave its name to the surrounding territory. Finally, Machiavelli refers to an event that occurred in 1325; for its background, see *Florentine Histories,* 2, 24–31. During the fourteenth-century struggle between the Guelphs and Ghibellines for control in Florence, the former asked Robert d'Anjou, the king of Naples, for help in 1311 against the Holy Roman Emperor, Henry VII, and the Ghibellines. There ensued a series of battles between Florence and her neighbors. In 1316 Castruccio Castracani became lord of Lucca and Pisa and persistently attacked Florentine territory. In 1325 he defeated the Florentine army at the battle of Altopascio. Again, the ruling Guelphs in Florence turned for aid to Robert of Naples. Once the city agreed to relinquish its sovereignty for ten years, the king sent the duke of Athens to govern it; in 1326 Robert replaced the duke with his son, Charles, duke of Calabria, who was able to keep Castracani at bay for several years. See also Machiavelli, *Life of Castruccio Castracani of Lucca,* less a biography than an astutely wrought literary essay written in a historical style about what it means to be a prince.

~ 10 ~

THE SINEWS OF WAR ARE NOT MONEY,[1] AS COMMON OPINION WOULD HAVE IT

1 Because anyone can start a war at will but not end it, a prince must measure his forces before undertaking a campaign and act accordingly.[2] 2 But he must be wise enough so as not to be mistaken about his forces, and he will be mistaken any time he measures them by either money, situation, or the good will of the men unless he has his own army as well. 3 Because the above-mentioned things indeed increase your forces, but they do not really give them to you, and by themselves they are nothing and are not worth anything without a loyal army. 4 For without one, money is not enough for you and the resistance of your country does not help you; men's loyalty and goodwill are short-lived, because they cannot be loyal to you if you cannot defend them. 5 Where strong defenders are lacking, every mountain, every lake, every inaccessible place becomes level. 6 Money, also, not only cannot defend you but gets you looted sooner.

7 The common opinion that the sinews of war are money could not be more false.[3] 8 Quintus Curtius Rufus states this maxim concerning the war between Antipater of Macedon and the Spartan king.[4] He relates how the king

of Sparta was forced to fight and was defeated for lack of money and how if he had postponed the engagement for several days, the news of Alexander's death would have reached Greece and he would have been the victor without fighting. 9 But because he did not have money and feared that his army would desert him for lack of it, he was forced to risk the fortunes of battle; for this reason Quintus Curtius affirms that the sinews of war are money. 10 This maxim is cited every day and followed by princes who are not sufficiently wise. 11 Relying on it, they believe that it is enough for them to possess a large treasury in order to defend themselves, and they do not think that, if a treasury were enough to conquer, Darius would have beaten Alexander[5] and the Greeks would have beaten the Romans; in our day Duke Charles would have beaten the Swiss,[6] and a few days ago the pope and the Florentines combined would have had no difficulty beating Francesco Maria, the nephew of Pope Julius II, in the war at Urbino.[7] 12 But all the above-named men were beaten by those who deem good soldiers to be the sinews of war, not money.

13 Among the other things that Croesus, the king of the Lydians, showed Solon of Athens was a limitless treasury; asked what he thought of his power, Solon answered that he did not believe him the more powerful for that: war is waged with steel, not gold; someone could come along who had more steel than he had and take it away from him.[8] 14 In addition to this, after the death of Alexander the Great, when a horde of Gauls crossed over into Greece and then into Asia, the Gauls sent emissaries to the king of Macedonia to discuss a treaty; the king, in order to show his power and to frighten them, showed them a good deal of gold and silver. 15 Whereupon the Gauls, who already decided on peace, broke it, so strong a desire grew in them to rob him of that gold; so the king was despoiled for the very thing he had accumulated for his defense.[9] 16 A few years ago the Venetians, although they still had their exchequer full of funds, lost their entire state without their money being able to defend them.[10]

17 Therefore I say that good soldiers are the sinews of war, not, as common opinion would proclaim, gold; gold does not suffice to find good soldiers, but good soldiers suffice to find gold.[11] 18 If the Romans had wanted to wage war with money rather than with steel, all the treasure in the world would not have been sufficient, given the great campaigns they undertook and the difficulties that there were in them. 19 But because they waged their wars with steel, they never suffered for a lack of gold, for those who feared them brought it right into their camps. 20 And if that Spartan king[12] for lack of money had to risk the fortunes of battle, what happened to him on account of money has often happened for different reasons, for it has been seen that if an army lacks provisions and it must either starve to death or engage in battle it always chooses to fight, since that is more honorable and Fortune may favor you in some way. 21 It has also happened frequently that when a commander sees aid coming to his enemy's army he has to fight them and risk the fortunes of battle or wait for them to be strengthened and have to fight them anyway, to his own enormous disadvantage. 22 As with Hasdrubal when he was attacked in the Marches by Claudius Nero, together with the other Roman consul, it has also been seen that when a commander must either flee or

fight he always chooses to fight, believing that he may win by this decision even if it is highly doubtful, whereas with the other he has to lose whatever happens.[13] 23 There are, therefore, many necessities that make a commander decide to fight against his will. Lack of money may sometimes be one of them, but that does not mean that money must be considered the sinews of war any more than other things that lead men to such necessities.

24 So again I repeat that not gold but good soldiers are the sinews of war. 25 Money is indeed necessary, secondarily, but it is a need that good soldiers overcome themselves, because it is as impossible for good soldiers to lack money as it is for money by itself to get good soldiers. 26 Every history shows in a thousand places that what we are saying is true, even though Pericles advised the Athenians to wage war against the entire Peloponnesus, claiming that they could win it with diligence and the power of money.[14] 27 Although the Athenians prospered for some time in that war, in the end they lost it: Sparta's leadership and good soldiers were worth more than Athenian diligence and money. 28 But Livy gives a truer witness to this opinion than anyone else. In discussing whether Alexander the Great would have beaten the Romans if he had come to Italy, he shows that three things are necessary in war: plenty of good soldiers, wise commanders, and good fortune. Analyzing whether the Romans or Alexander would have prevailed in these matters, he then draws his conclusion without ever mentioning money.[15] 29 The Capuans, when the Sidicines asked them to take up arms against the Samnites with them, must have measured their power by money and not by soldiers,[16] because once they did decide to help them, the Capuans were defeated twice and were forced to become Roman tributaries in order to save themselves.[17]

NOTES

1. Translates *I danari non sono il nervo della guerra.* Taking our cue from Cicero, *Orationes Philippicae,* 5.2.5: *"primum nervos belli,pecuniam infinitam, qua nunc eget"* (first, the sinews of war, infinite money, that he now needs) throughout this chapter we have reversed Machiavelli's elements to emphasize the metaphorical cast and made plural what he has in the singular. In a word, he is challenging the accepted notion that money is the driving force, the fuel, for making war. A good army composed of well-trained soldiers is the backbone or mainstay for waging war successfully. Gilbert notes that Machiavelli's challenge is aimed particularly at a notion prevalent in many governmental councils of the Florentine republic; see *Florentine Political Assumptions,* p. 203.

2. The following sentences are analogous to passages in the *Prince* and his discussion of what self-sufficient princedoms require: a strong military force, a strong defense system, and strong loyalty among the subjects, especially those in a nonmercenary army (chapters 10, 12–14).

3. Classical assertions can be found in authors ranging from Plutarch, *Agis and Cleomenes,* 27, to Cicero; by Machiavelli's day the expression was a commonplace in discussions of foreign and domestic policy.

4. Quintius Curtius Rufus wrote a history of Alexander the Great during the first century A.D. Modern critical editions indicate a lacuna, 6.1, at the episode that Machiavelli cites, namely, the Spartan king Agis III's rebellion against Alexander's

general, Antipater. The death of Agis in 331 B.C. occurred eight years prior to Alexander's death in 323, not "several days." See Martelli, *Storici antichi,* pp. 79–80, for how Machiavelli manipulates his sources to fit his argument.

5. Darius III ruled Persia from 336 to 330 B.C.; Rufus, 3.13, may be the source for this assertion.

6. Charles the Bold (1433–1477), duke of Burgundy; the Swiss Confederation defeated him at Grandson in March 1476 and later, in June, at Morat.

7. The expression "a few days ago" is important for establishing the chronology for the composition of the *Discourses;* Machiavelli must have written this after September 1517; see also 2, 17, n.7. The Medici pope, Leo X, who reigned from 1513 to 1521, put his nephew Lorenzo de' Medici II the Younger (the person to whom Machiavelli dedicated the *Prince*) in charge of Urbino in August 1516. The ousted duke, Francesco Maria della Rovere, recovered Urbino in February 1517 and held it until 17 September, when Francis I, king of France, and Charles V, the Holy Roman Emperor, forced him to return control of his duchy to Pope Leo. Guicciardini deals with this material in *Storia d'Italia,* 13, 1–8.

8. Croesus was the last king of Lydia, c. 560–546 B.C. The anecdote that Machiavelli mentions is found in Lucian, *Charon,* 12; but Charon's interaction with Solon, the Athenian lawgiver, is mentioned in Herodotus, 1.30–33, and followed closely in Plutarch, *Solon,* 27–28.

9. This episode is based on Justin, 25.1–2, and the Macedonian king is Antigonus II, surnamed Gonatas (c. 320–239 B.C.). Machiavelli's word is *Franciosi,* which we have translated as "Gauls," though strictly speaking the people involved were Galatians, a Celtic tribe from the Danube region, who invaded Greece in 280 B.C.

10. A reference to the battle of Vailà (Agnadello) on 14 May 1509; see above, 1, 6, n.11.

11. Toward the end of *Art of War,* 7, Fabrizio Colonna provides a series of pithy precepts for conducting war; the third from the last echoes the assertion expressed here.

12. Machiavelli returns to the example of Agis III used in sentence 8 above.

13. During the Second Punic War Hannibal's brother Hasdrubal was killed in 207 B.C. at the battle of Sena Gallica, along the Metaurus River near the modern town of Fano, by two Roman Consuls: Gaius Claudius Nero and Marcus Livius Salinator (Livy, 27.48).

14. In 432 B.C. shortly before the outbreak of the Peloponnesian War between Athens and Sparta that lasted until Sparta's victory in 404; Thucydides, 1.141–143.

15. A reference to a famous passage in which Livy argues that Alexander could never have triumphed over the Romans (Livy, 9.17–19; see especially 9.17.3–4). It is similar to a passage at the end of Machiavelli's *Discorso sopra le cose della Magna e sopra l'Imperatore* (Discourse concerning affairs in Germany and the emperor).

16. In his conclusion Livy is not so explicit as Machiavelli. Machiavelli returns to the example occurring during the First Samnite War to which he alludes in 2, 9, and again in the next chapter; see Livy, 7.29–31.

17. Because Guicciardini points it out in the first sentence of his *Consideration* of this chapter and because the focus of Book 2 is now solidly on war, it should be noted that Guicciardini is right in saying that Machiavelli was able only to "imagine" war. Machiavelli's knowledge of war ranges from his reading of Vegetius to his treatise, the *Art of War:* it is theoretical. The sixteenth-century novella writer Matteo Bandello gives

a graphic illustration of this. Out of respect for the *Art of War,* Giovanni delle Bande Nere let Machiavelli drill three thousand of his troops one sun-drenched day in 1526. Machiavelli's efforts produced total confusion, and Giovanni had to extricate both his men and an embarrassed Machiavelli. Giovanni is quoted as noting that "Niccolò knew how to write things well and [I] knew how to do them." Bandello comments: "How great the difference is between someone who knows and who has not set in operation what he knows and someone who, as well as knowing, has often rolled up his sleeves and plunged in, as we usually say, and has derived his thoughts and mental view from outward deeds" (*Le Novelle,* 1, 40; ed. Brognoligo, 2, p. 83). Bandello thus begins a literary line that includes W. Somerset Maugham's 1946 novel *Then and Now,* in which Maugham weaves the plot of Machiavelli's play *La Mandragola* into his fictional account of Machiavelli's diplomatic mission to Cesare Borgia in the fall and early winter of 1502.

~ 11 ~

IT IS NOT WISE TO ALLY ONESELF WITH A PRINCE WHOSE REPUTATION IS GREATER THAN HIS FORCES[1]

1 When Livy wanted to show the Sidicines' mistake in trusting in the Campanians' help and the Campanians' mistake in thinking they could defend them, he could not state it in more vivid words than by saying: "In their aid to the Sidicines, the Campanians brought reputation rather than soldiers for their defense."[2] 2 In this we must note that leagues made with princes who do not have either the opportunity to help you because of their distance from you or the forces to do so because of disorganization or some other reason bring more reputation than aid to those who count on them. That is what happened to the Florentines in our day when the pope and the king of Naples attacked them in 1479; being allies of the king of France, the Florentines derived "reputation rather than defense" from that alliance.[3] That is what would also happen to a prince who, trusting in Emperor Maximilian, undertook some campaign because it is one of those alliances that brings "reputation rather than defense" to the one who made it, just as this text says the alliance with the Capuans brought the Sidicines.[4]

3 So the Capuans were mistaken in this respect, because they thought they had more forces than they did. 4 Thus men's lack of wisdom sometimes makes them wish to undertake the defense of others, even when they do not know how or are unable to defend themselves. So too, when the Roman armies went forth to meet the Samnite army, the people of Taranto sent emissaries to the Roman Consul to inform him that they wanted peace between the two peoples and that they were going to wage war against whoever strayed from peace. So the Consul, laughing at this proposal, had the call to battle sounded in the presence of the emissaries and commanded his army to go and meet the enemy, showing the Tarentines with deeds and not words the answer they deserved.[5] 5 And because in the present chapter I have discussed the courses of action that princes unwisely chose in the defense of others, in the next one I want to speak about those that they choose for their own defense.

NOTES

1. The danger that such a prince represents is illustrated in a quotation from Tacitus, *Annales,* 13.19, that Machiavelli incorporates into the last paragraph of *Prince,* 13.

2. Machiavelli, returning to his example from the end of the previous chapter, quotes in Latin from Livy, 7.29.5; his text differs slightly from that in modern editions: *"Campani magis nomen ad praesidium sociorum quam vires cum attulissent."* He quotes two phrases in Latin from this passage in the next sentence; see also Martelli, *Storici antichi,* pp. 80–81.

3. Once it became clear after the Pazzi Conspiracy that Florence was ignoring the interdict that Pope Sixtus IV issued against it in 1478 for seeking to be independent, the pope entered into an alliance with Ferdinand of Aragon, king of Naples. Papal troops led by the latter's son, Alfonso, duke of Calabria, and Federico da Montefeltro, duke of Urbino, invaded Florentine territory and forced the city to ask Louis XI, the king of France, for help and Lorenzo de' Medici to go to Rome and sue for peace. This material is covered in Machiavelli, *Florentine Histories,* 8, 10–18, and Guicciardini, *History of Florence,* chapter 5.

4. A reference to Maximilian of Hapsburg, the Holy Roman Emperor from 1493 to 1519. The fact that Machiavelli is writing in the present tense suggests that this sentence was written before 1519. Machiavelli's dismissive comments about him echoes those in his analyses of German affairs in his *Rapporto* (1508), *Discorso* (1509), *Ritratto* (1512), and his letter to Vettori of 10 December, in which the emperor is described as being "unpredictable and capricious" (*Friends,* p. 301), and in *Prince,* 23 (p. 351, lines 30–45). For the interchangeability of Capuans and Campanians of sentence 2 above, see above, 2, 9, n.3.

5. The reference is to 320 B.C., during the Second Samnite War, and to the consul Papirius Cursor (Livy, 9.14). Livy does not say that the consul laughs, but rather that since the auspices were favorable, he ordered the attack because the Tarentines could see that the gods were on Rome's side.

~ 12 ~

WHETHER IT IS BETTER WHEN ONE FEARS ATTACK TO LAUNCH A WAR OR TO WAIT FOR IT

1 I have sometimes heard men quite experienced in matters of war argue, if there are two princes with almost equal forces and the bolder one has declared war on the other, which is the better course of action for the other prince: to wait for the enemy within his own borders or to go and meet him at home and attack him? I have heard reasons cited on each side. 2 Those who defend going to attack the other prince cite the advice that Croesus gave Cyrus when, on his arrival at the borders of the Massagetae to wage war against them, their queen Tomyris sent him a message asking him which of two courses of action he would choose: either to enter her kingdom, where she would await him, or to let her come and meet him.[1] 3 When the matter came up for discussion, Croesus, contrary to the opinion of others, recom-

mended going and meeting her, claiming that to defeat her far from her kingdom would not deprive her of it, because she would have time to recover; but if he defeated her within her borders, he would be able to pursue her when she fled and, by not giving her room to recover, take away her power. 4 In this connection they also cite the advice that Hannibal gave Antiochus when that king planned to wage war against the Romans. In it he shows that Rome could be defeated only in Italy, because there others could avail themselves of its arms, riches, and allies; but anyone who fought them outside of Italy and left Italy available to them left them a never-ending source to supply them with forces as needed. Hannibal concluded that Rome could sooner be taken away from the Romans than their empire and Italy sooner than their other provinces.[2] 5 They also cite Agathocles who, unable to sustain a war at home, attacked the Carthaginians who were waging war against him and forced them to sue for peace;[3] they cite Scipio who attacked Africa to get the war out of Italy.[4]

6 Those who argue the contrary say that anyone who wants to bring harm on an enemy should get him far from home. 7 On this point they cite the Athenians, who remained superior while they were waging a convenient war at home; when they departed and went to Sicily with their armies, they lost their freedom.[5] 8 They cite the poetic tales showing that Antaeus, the king of Libya, attacked by Hercules the Egyptian, was unbeatable as long as he waited for him within his kingdom's borders; but once he left them, through Hercules' shrewdness, he lost his power and his life.[6] 9 This gave rise to the fable that while Antaeus was on the ground he recovered his strength from his mother, who was the Earth; Hercules, observing this, lifted him up and kept him off the earth. 10 They also cite modern judgments. 11 Everyone knows that in his day Ferdinand, king of Naples, was considered a very wise prince.[7] Two years before his death, when it was reported that the king of France, Charles VIII, intended to come and attack him, Ferdinand, after making great preparations, fell ill. With death approaching, he left among other memoranda to his son Alfonso that he should wait for the enemy within his kingdom and not for anything in the world should he take his forces outside his country, but he should wait for him entirely within his borders. 12 Alfonso did not observe this; sending an army into Romagna, he lost it and his state without fighting.

13 Beyond what has been stated, the reasons that both sides advance are: attackers come with greater courage than those who wait, and this increases the confidence of an army; in addition, it takes many opportunities to call upon his resources away from the enemy, since he cannot call upon subjects who have been pillaged. And the ruler, since the enemy is on his soil, is obliged to be more careful about taking money from his subjects and impoverishing them so that, as Hannibal said, he comes to dry up the source that makes it possible for him to fight the war. 14 Furthermore, because the attacker's soldiers find themselves in the country of others, they are more obliged to fight, and, as we have stated several times, that necessity makes for *virtù*.

15 On the other hand, it is said that awaiting the enemy is waiting with a great advantage, because without any difficulty you can give him much

difficulty providing food and everything else that an army needs; because you have better knowledge of the country than he does, you can better hinder his plans; because you can easily muster all your forces, you can encounter him with more of them, though you cannot move them all far from home. If you are defeated, you can easily regroup, both because much of your army will escape, since they have places of refuge nearby, and because reinforcements do not have to come far so that you come to risk all your forces but not all your fortune; and if you go far away you risk all your fortune but not all your forces.[8] 16 And there have been some who, in order the better to weaken their[9] enemy, have allowed him to advance a few days into their country and seize many towns so that he weakens the enemy army by leaving garrisons in each of them and they can then fight it more easily.

17 But to state now how *I* understand this, I think a distinction must be made: either I have an armed country, as did the Romans or as the Swiss do, or I have an unarmed one, as did the Carthaginians or as the king of France and the Italians do. 18 In the latter case, the enemy must be kept off your own soil, because if your *virtù*[10] is in money, not men, any time your access to it is impeded you are done for; and nothing impedes you from it so much as war on one's own soil. 19 Some examples of this are the Carthaginians, who were able to wage war against the Romans with their revenues as long as their own soil was free; when it was under attack, they could not stand up to Agathocles. 20 The Florentines had no recourse against Castruccio, the lord of Lucca, because he was waging war against them on their own soil so that they had to put themselves in the hands of King Robert of Naples for their defense.[11] 21 But once Castruccio was dead, those same Florentines had the courage to attack the duke of Milan[12] on his own soil and manage[13] to take away his kingdom; they showed such *virtù* in distant wars but such cowardice in nearby ones.

22 But when kingdoms are armed, as was Rome and as the Swiss, they are more difficult to defeat the closer you get to them, because these bodies can assemble more forces to resist an attack than they can to attack someone else. 23 Nor does Hannibal's authority in this instance impress me, because passion and his own interest made him talk that way to Antiochus. 24 For had the Romans had those three defeats in Gaul in the same space of time that Hannibal inflicted on them in Italy,[14] they undoubtedly would have been done for: they would have not have availed themselves of the remnants of their armies as they did in Italy, they would not have found it so easy to regroup, and they could not have resisted the enemy with those forces as they were able to. 25 They have never been found to have sent forth armies exceeding 50,000 men to attack a foreign region, but to defend their own soil after the First Punic War, they put 1,800,000[15] of them in arms against the Gauls. 26 Nor could they could then have beaten the latter in Lombardy[16] as they beat them in Etruria, because against so great a number of enemies they could not have led so many forces that far away or fought them so easily. 27 The Cimbri defeated a Roman army in Germany, and the Romans had no remedy for it.[17] 28 But once they got to Italy and the Romans could assemble all their forces,

they routed them.[18] 29 The Swiss are easy to defeat away from their home soil, where they cannot send more than about thirty or forty thousand men, but to defeat them on their home soil, where they can muster one hundred thousand men, is very difficult.[19]

30 I therefore conclude once again that a prince who keeps his people armed and organized for war should always await a powerful and dangerous war at home and not go to meet it. 31 But he who has unarmed subjects and whose country is unaccustomed to war should always keep them as far from home as he can. 32 Thus both of them, each in his own way, will defend themselves best.

NOTES

1. This account is based on Herodotus, 1.205–214. Cyrus the Great (559–529 B.C.) founded the Persian Empire, and the Massagetae were a tribe in the area between the Caspian Sea and Lake Aral. See *Art of War,* 6, and Fabrizio Colonna's use of this example. Croesus (c. 560–546 B.C.) was king of Lydia.

2. After his defeat in the Second Punic War (218–201 B.C.), Hannibal sought refuge with Antiochus III, king of Syria. The latter tried unsuccessfully to carry out Hannibal's advice during the Syrian War (192–189 B.C.) The anecdote is based on Livy, 34.60.

3. See *Prince,* 8, based on Justin, 22, and Livy, 28.43. Agathocles, who exemplifies a prince who rose "to the princedom through iniquitous or nefarious means," is credited within "a brief span of time [of bringing] the Carthaginians to dire straits: they were compelled to make a pact with him, to be satisfied with possessing North Africa, and to leave Sicily to Agathocles" (*Prince,* 8, p. 177, lines 7–8; p. 179, lines 40–45).

4. See above, 1, 53, n. 10.

5. The Athenians' disastrous invasion of Sicily occurred in 415 B.C.; the destruction of their fleet in 413 paved the way for the Spartan victory in the Peloponnesian War: see Thucydides, 7.82–87.

6. In Greek mythology the legendary Libyan king Antaeus was a giant, son of Poseidon and the earth goddess Gaea. The eleventh labor of Hercules was stealing the golden apples of the Hesperides, the three daughters of Night living somewhere in the "west." Crossing north Africa, he met Antaeus who would challenge each stranger to wrestle with him; if Antaeus won, the challenger would be killed. Hercules' victory by strangling him in midair once he had lifted him off the ground, from which the giant's strength was presumably renewed (because he could draw on his mother's strength each time he was thrown down), seems to be an interpretation originating with Apollodorus, a mythographer of the second century B.C. It is unclear why Machiavelli calls Hercules "the Egyptian." True, he was in north Africa and another exploit during the same labor was the murder of an Egyptian despot named Busiris. Vivanti, in his edition of the *Discorsi,* notes a reference in the *Chronicles* by Eusebius of Caesarea for his year 3950 to the protection that "Hercules the Egyptian" provided athletes. Indeed, the Greek word for the "labors" that Hercules had to perform is *athloi,* contests undertaken for a prize, the origin of our word "athlete." Rinaldi cites as a likely source *De laboribus Herculis,* 3.27, an early Renaissance defense of poetry by the Italian humanist Coluccio Salutati (1331–1406), who was admired in Florence as

both a scholar and the advocate of an active political life devoted to civic humanism; see Baron, *Crisis.* For more on this issue, see the detailed treatment in Martelli, *Storici antichi,* pp. 81–88.

7. Ferdinand I (Ferrante I) was king of Naples from 1458 to 1494. He descended from a line of kings of Aragon who had usurped the rights of the French Anjou dynasty. One of the reasons that Charles VIII cited for his invasion of Italy in 1494 was a reassertion of this Angevin claim. Ferdinand I was followed on the throne by Alfonso II in January 1494. Later that year he ordered his son, Ferdinand II (Ferrante II), to Romagna at the head of an army that was eventually forced to retreat to Naples. Alfonso also ordered his brother, Federico, to the Ligurian Sea in command of his fleet; the French, led by Duke Louis d'Orléans, the future Louis XII, won a decisive naval battle in September 1494. Having ordered these unsuccessful campaigns and lost his people's confidence, Alfonso abdicated in favor of Ferrante II in February 1495.

8. Some of these points repeat ideas developed above in 1, 23.

9. Machiavelli uses the singular "his" here and throughout the sentence.

10. There may be some irony in Machiavelli's use of *virtù* here.

11. See above, 2, 9, n.3.

12. If Machiavelli is referring to the period following Castruccio's death (1328), then the "duke of Milan" could be Giovanni Visconti, who ruled Milan from 1351 to 1354. Inglese notes, however, that he was an archbishop and was not called "duke"; furthermore, the struggle was not "on his own soil" but rather in Tuscany. Machiavelli discusses this war at the end of *Florentine Histories,* 2, 42. Inglese has a more likely candidate: Gian Galeazzo Visconti, the first Milanese duke to be called "duke" and a leader involved in frequent skirmishes with Florence from 1385 to 1402. See Machiavelli, *Florentine Histories,* 3, 25.

13. Translates *operare,* not the *sperare* (to hope) of some printed texts.

14. Hannibal defeated the Romans four times rather than three: at two branches of the Po River (Ticinus and Trebbia) in 218 B.C., at Lake Trasimeno near Perugia in 217, and at Cannae in Apulia in 216; see Livy, 21 and 22. For Machiavelli's manipulation of his sources, see Martelli, *Storici antichi,* pp. 89–91.

15. Partly on the basis of Polybius, 2.24, discussing the forces at the battle of Telamon in 225 B.C., Inglese suggests 800,000 as a more credible figure; even that may be excessive, because the figure in Polybius is 700,000.

16. At the battle near Telamon mentioned in the previous note.

17. It is believed Machiavelli does not refer to the battle of Arausio (Orange) near Avignon in 105 B.C. but to a battle in the ancient province of Noricum in the Tyrolian region covering northeastern Italy and southern Austria (modern Styria) in 113.

18. In 101 at the battle of Campi Raudii; see above, 2, 8, n.8.

19. Probably an allusion to the Battle of Marignano in September 1515; see above, 1, 23, n.4 (though it was not an "easy" victory for the French).

~ 13 ~

ONE GETS FROM LOW TO HIGH FORTUNE MORE BY DECEIT THAN BY FORCE

1 I believe it to be quite true that seldom, if ever, does it happen that men of little fortune attain high rank without force and without deceit, provided that the rank that someone else has obtained has not been either granted him or left to him as an inheritance.[1] 2 Nor do I think it ever happens that force alone is enough, but it will indeed happen that deceit alone will be enough. One who reads the lives of Philip of Macedon, Agathocles the Sicilian, and many other like them will clearly see that from the lowest or at least from low fortune they have attained either a kingdom or very great powers.[2] 3 In his *Life of Cyrus* Xenophon shows this need to deceive, if we bear in mind that the first expedition that he had Cyrus make against the king of Armenia is full of deceit and that he has him take over his kingdom by deceit, not by force.[3] 4 Concerning such action he concludes nothing else than that it is necessary for a prince who wants to do great things to learn how to deceive. 5 In addition to him, he had Cyrus deceiving his maternal uncle, Cyaxares, king of the Medes, in several ways; he shows that Cyrus could not have attained the greatness that he did without this deceit. 6 Nor do I believe that there can ever be anyone starting out from a low degree of fortune who has attained great power by naked force and sincerity alone, but certainly by deceit alone, as Gian Galeazzo did to take the government and power over Lombardy away from his uncle, messer Bernabò.[4]

7 What princes are obliged to do during the initial stages of their rise, republics are also obliged to do, until they have grown powerful and force alone is enough. 8 Because everywhere either by chance or by choice Rome used all means necessary to achieve greatness, it did not overlook this one either. 9 It could not initially have used any greater deception than choosing the way I have discussed above of making allies for itself,[5] since under this guise it made them subjects, as the Latins and other surrounding peoples were. 10 For Rome first made use of their armies to subdue neighboring peoples and gain prestige for her government; then, once they were subdued, it grew so large that it could defeat anyone. 11 And the Latins never noticed that they were completely subjected until they saw the Samnites defeated twice and forced to sue for peace.[6] 12 Because this victory greatly enhanced the Romans' prestige among distant rulers, who thus heard the name "Rome" but did not feel its arms, it produced envy and fear in those who saw and felt its arms, among whom were the Latins.[7] 13 This envy and fear were so powerful that not only the Latins but also the Roman colonies in Latium[8] together with the Campanian states, which only recently had been defended, conspired against the name of Rome. 14 The Latins began this war in the way we have already mentioned[9] that the majority of wars begin: not by attacking the Romans but by defending the Sidicines against the Samnites, who were fighting the Sidicines with Rome's authorization.[10] 15 That it is true that the Latins arose

because they realized this deception is shown by Livy through the mouth of the Latin praetor, Annius Setinus, who said the following words in their council: "For if we can endure servitude even now under the semblance of a treaty among equals," etc.[11] 16 It may thus be seen that during the initial stages of their expansion the Romans too did not fail to use deceit; it has always been necessary for it to be used by those who want to rise from lowly beginnings to the highest ranks. As with the Romans, the more covert it is the less outrage it causes.[12]

NOTES

1. See above, 1, 18, n.4, for cross-references to the topic of force and deceit elsewhere in the *Discourses,* the *Prince,* and *Florentine Histories,* as well as Aristotle and Cicero.

2. Philip II, the father of Alexander the Great, ruled Macedon from 359 to 336 B.C. See above, 1, 26, n.6, for the basis of this reference in Justin. For Agathocles, see above, 2, 12, n.3.

3. Cyrus was the founder of the Achaemenid Persian Empire (559–529 B.C.); he subjugated the Medes in 550. Although Machiavelli cites Xenophon, *Cyropaedia,* as his source, the relevant sections (1, 5, 6; 2, 4–3, 1; 4, 1, 5; and 5, 5) do not support Machiavelli's claims; for example Xenophon says Cyrus was a vassal of Cyaxares. See also the relevant passages in Herodotus, 1.

4. Bernabò Visconti ruled Milan from 1355 to 1385, when he was imprisoned and slain by his nephew Gian Galeazzo Visconti, who called himself the "Count of *Virtù*" and made himself the first duke of Milan. Machiavelli refers to this at the end of *Florentine Histories,* 1, 27.

5. Above, 2, 4.

6. The two Samnite defeats were at Mount Gaurus and Saticula; a third defeat occurred at Suessula. These battles were fought in 343 B.C. during the First Samnite War (343–341); Livy, 7.32–33; 36–37.

7. For "distant rulers," see Livy, 7.38.2, and for "the Latins," see Livy, 8.1–6

8. Livy mentions Setia, Circeii, Signia, and Velitrae (8.3.9).

9. Above, 2, 9.

10. As above in 2, 9, sentence 3, the Sidicines were Samnites from the area around their major town, Teanum (modern-day Teano), a small town about ten miles northwest of Capua.

11. Quoted in Latin from Annius of Setina in Livy, 8.4.2: *"Nam si etiam nunc sub umbra foederis aequi servitutem pati possumus."*

12. Machiavelli's conclusion seems to be a political one, in contrast to Guicciardini's last sentence in his *Consideration,* which seems to take a moral stance. Walker makes a lengthy argument that the examples chosen from Livy by Machiavelli to prove his conclusion show, rather, that Rome was accused of deceit, not that it practiced deceit. See also the comment in the last sentence below, 3, 19, n.5.

~ 14 ~

MEN OFTEN DECEIVE THEMSELVES BY BELIEVING THAT HUMILITY CAN OVERCOME PRIDE

1 It is often seen that humility not only does not help but is harmful, especially when it is practiced toward insolent men who have conceived hatred for you out of either envy or other reasons. 2 Our historian testifies to this in the cause for war between the Romans and the Latins.[1] 3 When the Samnites complained to the Romans that the Latins had attacked them,[2] the Romans refused to prohibit the Latins from fighting such a war since they did not want to anger them; not only did this not anger the Latins but it made them more courageous against the Romans, and they revealed themselves as enemies sooner. 4 This is attested in the words spoken by the above-mentioned Latin praetor, Annius, when he stated in the same council, "By denying them soldiers, you have tried their forbearance; who can doubt that they were enraged? . . . Yet they have this pain. . . . They heard that we are equipping an army against their allies the Samnites, yet they did not move out of the city. What is the source of this great acquiescence on their part if not an awareness of both our strength and theirs?"[3] 5 This text brings out very clearly how much the Romans' forbearance increased the Latins' arrogance.[4]

6 Hence no prince should ever wish to forget his dignity nor ever relinquish anything willingly, if he wants to relinquish it honorably, except when he can or he believes he could hold on to it. For if the matter has reached the point where you cannot relinquish it in the way just mentioned, it is almost always better to let it be taken away from you by force than out of fear of force.[5] 7 Because if you relinquish it out of fear, you do so to avoid war, yet most of the time you do not avoid it. For a person to whom you have given something up with manifest cowardice will not stand pat but will want to take other things from you; he will be all the more aroused against you the less he respects you. On the other hand, you will find that your supporters are colder toward you, since they think that you are either weak or cowardly. 8 But if you mobilize your army, even though it may be inferior to his, as soon as your adversary's intent has been revealed, he will begin to respect you. The other surrounding princes also respect you more; once you are armed, someone who would never help you if you gave up will then be willing to help you.[6] 9 This applies if you have one enemy; but should you have several of them, it will always be a wise course of action to hand over some of your possessions to one of them in order to win him back to your side, even if the war has already broken out, and to dislodge him from the others allied against you.[7]

NOTES

1. Livy, 8.2.12.

2. After the defeats mentioned above, 2, 13, n.6, the Samnites allied themselves with Rome.

3. Quoted in Latin from Livy, 8.4.7–10; the translators have supplied the ellipses:

"Temptastis patientiam negando militem; quis dubitat exarisse eos . . . Pertulerunt tamen hunc dolorem. . . . exercitus nos parare adversus Samnites, foederatos suos, audierunt nec moverunt se ab urbe. Unde haec illis tanta modestia, nisis a conscientia virium et nostrarum et suarum?"

4. In this context and elsewhere, "forbearance" can sometimes convey a negative connotation of "passivity" or "inactivity." See below, 3, 3, sentence 5, and the *capitolo "Di fortuna,"* v. 87. In the context of encouraging Machiavelli in his pet project of a citizens' militia and a possible attack on Pisa, Francesco Soderini wrote on 29 May 1504: "It seems to be necessary to be patient so as not to bring pressure, but to remember it at the right time. Certainly, in states and in republics, too much patience gives courage to villains, wherever they may be found and whoever they may be" (*Friends,* p. 102).

5. Here the context is international politics, whereas the argument above, 1, 51, is more concerned with domestic situation.

6. In this context, see Machiavelli's analysis in *Prince,* 25, of Pope Julius II's campaign against Bologna in 1506; pp. 367; 369, lines 94–118. See too his analysis of the potential results of the Treaty of Madrid between Charles V and Francis I in January 1526; *Friends,* pp. 380–383.

7. Machiavelli may have in mind the situation of Venice against the League of Cambrai in 1508 and 1509; see above, 1, 6, n.11, and 1, 53, sentence 8.

~ *15* ~

WEAK STATES WILL ALWAYS BE HESITANT TO MAKE UP THEIR MINDS, AND LENGTHY DECISIONS ARE ALWAYS HARMFUL

1 On this same matter and on these same beginnings of war between the Latins and the Romans, one may observe how good it is in every consultation to come to the gist of what is to be decided and not to remain always hesitant or uncertain about the affair. 2 This is seen clearly in the consultation that the Latins held when they were thinking of distancing themselves from the Romans. Once the Romans had realized the bad mood that had affected the Latin people, in order to satisfy themselves about the matter and see whether they could win them back without recourse to arms, they let them know they should send eight citizens to Rome, because they had to consult with them.[1] 3 On hearing of this and being aware they had done many things against the Romans' will, the Latins held a council to arrange who should go to Rome and to instruct him as to what he should say. 4 While the council was engaged in this argument, Annius, their praetor, spoke these words: "It is my opinion that it is more pertinent to our general interests *for you to consider* what is to be done than what is to be said. Once our plans are clarified, it will be easy to adapt words to deeds."[2] 5 These words are doubtless quite true and should be appreciated by every prince and every republic. For where there is hesitation and uncertainty about what someone else wants to do, one does not know how to adapt one's words; but once minds have been made up and

what has to be done has been decided, it is an easy matter to find words for it. 6 I have noted this question all the more willingly for often having known such hesitation to have harmed public actions to the detriment and shame of our republic.[3] 7 In uncertain courses of action, needing courage to decide them, such hesitation will always happen to exist when it is weak men who have to discuss and decide.[4]

8 Slow and lengthy decisions are no less harmful than hesitating ones as well, especially those that have to be decided in favor of some ally, because with their slowness they help no one and one harms oneself. 9 Decisions made in this way arise either from weakness of courage and armed forces or from the ill will of those who have to decide; prompted by their own passion to try to topple the state or to fulfill some other desire of theirs, they do not allow decision making to go forward but hamper and thwart it. 10 For even though good citizens see popular fervor turning toward the harmful side, they will never hinder decision making, especially about things that cannot wait.

11 After Hieronymus, the tyrant in Syracuse, died, there was a great war between the Carthaginians and the Romans, and the Syracusans began to argue whether they should carry on an alliance with Rome or with Carthage.[5] 12 The fervor of the parties was so intense that the matter remained uncertain, so no decision was being taken. Finally Apollonides, one of the foremost Syracusans, in a speech full of wisdom[6] showed that neither those who were for joining the Romans nor those who wished to side with the Carthaginians should be blamed; but this hesitation and slowness to make a decision were indeed to be detested. He saw in such hesitation the downfall of the republic, but if a decision was made, whatever it might be, some benefit could be hoped for. 13 Nor could Livy better show the harm that remaining undecided brings in its wake than he does in this passage. 14 He demonstrates it as well in the case of the Latins, for, when they sought help from the Lavinians against the Romans, they put off deciding for so long that just as they were leaving their gates with their army to help them, news came that the Latins had been defeated.[7] 15 Whereupon their Praetor, Milionius, said: "This brief march will cost us dearly with the Roman people."[8] 16 If the Lavinians had decided earlier either to help or not to help the Latins, they would not have annoyed the Romans if they had not helped them; if they did help them and it came in time, they could have made the Latins win by the addition of their armed forces; but by putting it off they stood to lose out in any case, as it turned out. 17 And if the Florentines had paid attention to this text, they would not have had either so many setbacks or such trouble with the French as they did during King Louis XII of France's incursion into Italy against Duke Ludovico of Milan.[9] 18 When the king was making treaties for this incursion, he sought the Florentines' agreement; their ambassadors at the king's court agreed with him to remain neutral and for the king, when he entered Italy, to support the Florentines in government and take them under his protection. The king gave the city a month's time to ratify it. 19 Those who, for lack of wisdom, favored the affairs of Ludovico postponed this ratification; finally, when the king was already on the point of victory and the Florentines

wished to ratify it, the ratification was rejected, since he realized that the Florentines had entered into alliance with him under duress, not voluntarily. 20 This cost the city of Florence a great deal of money and almost brought down the government,[10] as happened to it another time later for a similar reason.[11] 21 This course of action was all the more blameworthy because it was of no use to Duke Ludovico either; if he had won, he would have shown many more signs of enmity against the Florentines than did the king. 22 Although the evil that republics derive from this weakness has been discussed above in another chapter,[12] I have nevertheless decided to repeat it, since I had the occasion once more because of a new incident, and especially since I thought it was material that has to be noted by republics like ours.

NOTES

1. Machiavelli continues to follow Livy's discussion at the beginning of Book 8; in 8.3.8, however, Livy refers to ten citizens, rather than eight.

2. Quoted in Latin from Livy, 8.4.1: *ad summam rerum nostrarum pertinere arbitror,* ut cogitetis magis *quid agendum nobis, quam quid loquendum sit.* (Machiavelli's textual addition is in italic type in the translation and in roman type in his quotation from Livy.)

3. Machiavelli discusses a specific example from 1499 later in this *Discourse;* see sentences 17–22 below. Eleven years later, when Florence was trying to avoid antagonizing both Pope Julius II and the French king, Louis XII, it sent Machiavelli to the king to explain its fence-sitting policy. Machiavelli wrote a strongly worded memorandum urging Florence to end its equivocation; see his letter from Blois dated 9 August 1510 (*Legazioni e commissarie,* 3, 1281–1285).

4. This notion is examined at greater length in *Prince,* 21; pp. 333; 335, lines 48–65.

5. Hieronymus, the grandson of Hiero II, ruled Syracuse for thirteen months in 215–214 B.C.

6. Livy, 24.28. Syracuse sided with Carthage and was defeated by the Romans in 212 B.C. As both Ridley, "Roman History," p. 208, and Martelli, *Storici antichi,* pp. 93–94, point out, Machiavelli's discussion of Apollonides' speech in Livy reverses its meaning there to prove Machiavelli's point here.

7. The Lavinians were the inhabitants of Lavinium, a town north of present-day Anzio where Aeneas was said to have landed. The phrase, "put off deciding for so long" is based on Livy, 8.11.3.

8. Based on Livy, 8.11.4, but quoted by Machiavelli in Italian.

9. Because he sought to assert French claims to the duchy of Milan, Louis XII resolved in April 1499, a year after he came to the throne, to invade Italy. By September his army, led by Gian Giacomo Trivulzio, captured Milan; Trivulzio had previously been a famous military commander employed by Duke Ludovico "Il Moro" Sforza. He went over to the French side, and Louis XII rewarded him by naming him governor of Milan. When Florence was asked to choose between "Il Moro" and Louis XII, some Florentines favored Sforza, because he had helped them in their campaign to subdue Pisa. Negotiations with Louis XII began in June (the minutes for a meeting to debate this issue on 26 June are in Machiavelli's hand) but were not concluded until 12 October. By then Louis controlled Milan, so he signed an agreement whereby he

would help Florence in its Pisa campaign and Florence would send troops and money to the king for his projected attack on Naples. See Guicciardini, *History of Florence,* chapter 18.

10. The aid Florence promised Louis hardly qualifies as a "neutral" act, but Machiavelli may have had in mind that the Florentine emissaries had secretly promised Louis that they would not interfere with his Milanese campaign. The accord provided that Florence would pay 25,000 florins, a sum previously owed to Ludovico Sforza, to Louis XII; see Guicciardini, *History of Florence,* chapter 19, and *Storia d'Italia,* 4, 11.

11. An allusion to the events of 1512 that led to the fall of the Florentine republic and the return of the Medici, for which Machiavelli blamed the temporizing policies of Piero Soderini. He blames Florence for its neutrality at this time in *Prince,* 21; p. 339, lines 114–118. See too, below, 2, 27, sentences 12–17 and notes 4–5. Guicciardini also comments on this: "The Florentines, full of mistrust, were beginning to taste the fruits of an imprudently employed policy of neutrality and to realize that it was an insufficient defense to have an abundance of justice on their side, when at the same time they lacked prudence" (*Storia d'Italia,* 11, 2). See also his *Ricordi,* C. 68, quoted above, 1, 38, n.6.

12. Above, 1, 38, three out of the four examples of which are from Florentine history.

~ 16 ~

HOW FAR THE SOLDIERS OF OUR TIMES DEPART FROM THE INSTITUTIONS OF THE ANCIENTS

1 The most important battle that the Roman people ever fought in any war with any nation was the one they fought with the Latin people during the consulate of Torquatus and Decius.[1] 2 Because all reason would dictate that, just as the Latins became subjected because they lost it, the Romans would have been subjected had they not won it. 3 Livy is of this opinion, because he gives the armies as equal in every respect: organization, *virtù,* determination, and size.[2] The only distinction he makes is that the leaders of the Roman army had greater *virtù* than those of the Latin army.[3] 4 It can also be seen that in the handling of this battle two incidents arose that had not arisen previously and that have had few examples since: namely, in order to keep the soldiers courageous and obedient to their commands and resolved to fight, one of the consuls killed himself and the other his son.[4] 5 The equality that Livy says there was between these armed forces was that, since they had campaigned together for a long time, they were alike in language, organization, and weapons, because in drawing up for battle they followed the same methods and the ranks and their leaders had the same names. 6 Because their armies and *virtù* were equal, something extraordinary had to occur to strengthen the spirit of one side and make it more determined than the other; and, as we have previously stated,[5] victory is based on such determination, because as long as it endures in the hearts of those who are fighting, armies

never turn tail. 7 And for it to endure longer in the hearts of the Romans than the Latins, in part fate and in part the Consuls' *virtù* caused Torquatus to have to kill his son and Decius himself.

8 Showing the equality of these armed forces, Livy also shows the entire organization that the Romans followed in their armies and in combat. 9 Because he explains this extensively, I shall not repeat it further; I shall discuss only what I judge noteworthy and what, because all the commanders in our day have neglected it, has caused great disorder in armies and in combat. 10 So I say that we gather from Livy's text that the Roman army had three main divisions, which can be called in Tuscan[6] three groups; they called the first *hastati,* the second *principes,* the third *triarii,* and each of these had its own cavalry. 11 In organizing for battle, they put the *hastati* in front; they placed the *principes* in second place directly behind them; in the third, still in the same file, they placed the *triari.* 12 They placed the cavalry of all these ranks to the right and the left of these three formations; the groupings of this cavalry were called *alae* from their form and placement, because they looked like two wings on that body. 13 They arranged the first group, the *hastati,* which was in front, in a close formation so it could push the enemy back and withstand them. 14 Because the second battle line, the *principes,* was not the first to fight, but was expected rather to aid the first one if it were beaten or pushed back, it was not kept in close formation; but its ranks were kept thin so that it could receive the first group into its ranks if ever it was pressed by the enemy and had to retreat without becoming disorganized.[7] 15 The ranks of the third group, the *triari,* were even thinner than the second in order to receive the first two groups, the *principes* and the *hastati,* within itself if necessary. 16 So with the groups deployed in this formation, they gave battle, and if the *hastati* were exhausted or beaten, they retreated into the thin ranks of *principes;* united all together, making one body of two groups, they rejoined the fray. 17 If these too were pushed back, exhausted, they all retreated into the thin ranks of the *triari,* and all three groups, becoming one body, renewed the fray; if they were overcome at that point because they could not regroup further, they lost the battle. 18 And because every time this last group, the *triari,* was used the army was in danger, there arose the proverb: "The matter has reached the *triari,*" which in Italian usage means "We have bet our final stake."[8]

19 Just as military commanders in our day have abandoned all the other institutions and observe no aspect of ancient discipline so they have also abandoned this one, which is of no little importance. For anyone who arranges things so that he can regroup three times during a battle has to have Fortune as his enemy three times if he is to lose, and he has to have opposing him a *virtù* that is capable of defeating him three times. 20 But anyone who stands up only against the first assault, as all Christian armies do today, can easily lose because any disorganization, any moderate *virtù,* can deprive him of victory. 21 What makes our armies incapable of recovering three times is having lost the means to receive one group within the next. 22 This comes from people organizing their battles at present according to one of two defects. Either they

put their groups shoulder-to-shoulder one alongside the other, making their battle array wide across and narrow in depth; this makes them weaker because they have little from front to rear. 23 And if ever, to make it stronger, they shorten their groups in the Roman manner, if the front line is broken, since they have no arrangement for it to be received by the second, they all become entangled and are broken up. 24 Because if the one in front is pushed back, it collides with the second one; if the second tries to move forward, the first one gets in its way; as the first collides with the second and the second with the third, so much confusion results that often the slightest incident brings down an army. 25 At the battle of Ravenna (in which Monsieur de Foix, the commander of the French troops, died), one that by the standards of our day was quite a well-fought battle, the Spanish and French armies were drawn up in one of the ways mentioned above: that is, both armies advanced with all their soldiers lined up shoulder-to-shoulder so that they each had only a front line and were much wider across than deep.[9] 26 This always happens to armies whenever they have a large battlefield, as they did at Ravenna. 27 For, knowing the disorder retreat can cause, they avoid it when they can, as has been stated, by placing their soldiers in a single line and with a broad front; but when the country limits them, they stand in the disorder mentioned above without looking for a remedy. 28 With this same disorder they ride through the enemy country, whether they are plundering or carrying out some other military maneuver. 29 At Santo Regolo, in the country around Pisa,[10] and in other places where the Pisans defeated the Florentines during the days when there was war between the Florentines and that city (because of its revolt after King Charles of France's invasion of Italy), such a collapse arose from nothing else but friendly cavalry: since it was in front and repulsed by the enemy, it crashed into the Florentine infantry and the latter broke, at which point the rest of the troops turned tail. 30 And messer Ciriaco dal Borgo, the former leader of the Florentine infantry,[11] has affirmed many times in my presence that he has never been defeated except by friendly cavalry. 31 When they are campaigning with the French, the Swiss, who are masters of modern warfare, are above all careful to position themselves on the flank so that friendly cavalry, were it to be repulsed, does not collide with them. 32 And although these things seem easy to understand and very easy to do, nevertheless, none of our contemporary military commanders has yet been found to imitate the ancient institutions and correct the modern ones. 33 Although they too have divided the army in three parts, calling one part the "vanguard," the second the "main body," and the third the "rear guard," they are used only for controlling them in their billets. But when they do use them, as we have stated above, it is rare that all these units are not made to risk the same fortune.

34 And because many people, to excuse their ignorance in these matters, claim that the violence of artillery does not allow the practice of many of the ancients' institutions in our day, I wish to discuss this subject in the next chapter and examine whether artillery prevents our being able to practice the ancients' *virtù*.

NOTES

1. The following incident is based on the discussion in Livy, 8.3–11, of the battle of Veseris at the foot of Mount Vesuvius and then at Trifanum in 340 B.C. The consuls for that year were Titus Manlius Torquatus and Publius Decius Mus.

2. Livy, 8.6.15, 8.8.2, and 8.9.3.

3. Livy, 8.10.8–9.

4. Before the battle each consul agreed, should the flanking troops of either leader give way, to sacrifice himself in order to "maintain . . . courage and obedience." Those of Decius Mus did yield; he rode into the heart of the enemy troops, an easy target. Contrary to his father's orders, the son of Manlius Torquatus engaged an enemy commander, Geminus Maecius, in single combat and was victorious. Nevertheless, because his son "stood in awe of neither consular authority nor his father's dignity" (8.7.15), Manlius ordered the lictor to tie him to a stake and bring an ax down upon his neck. Livy notes that through the ages the "orders of Manlius" became synonymous with severity (8.7.22).

5. See above, 1, 14–15; it will also be discussed in 3, 33 below.

6. Translates *toscanamente;* Machiavelli means in his "modern" Italian as opposed to Latin. He then uses three Latin terms: *hastati* (vanguard), *principes* (second line), and *triarii* (rear guard). Walker believes they are probably of Etruscan origin; they are discussed in Livy, 8.8.

7. Machiavelli here and in similar passages of his *Art of War,* Books 3 and 4, relies on the only surviving extensive discussion of Roman military organization, the *Epitoma rei militaris* in four books written at the end of the fourth century A.D. by Vegetius. Because it had the cachet of antiquity, Machiavelli was loath to challenge it. Nevertheless, if we analyze his example, it is doubtful that enemy forces would stand idly by waiting before pressing their attack on a retreating company; instead they would take the initiative.

8. Machiavelli uses a phrase from betting that means "the chips are down." His Latin reads *"res redacta est ad triarios"* and is loosely based on Livy, 8.8.11, who also cites it as a proverb. The word "Italian" translates *toscano.*

9. The Battle of Ravenna was fought on Easter Sunday, 11 April 1512, by France against the forces of the Holy League, Pope Julius II, Spain, and Venice. Although France won the battle, Louis XII decided to abandon his Italian campaign because of his heavy losses and the death of his nephew Gaston de Foix, the duke of Nemours, whom Louis had put in charge of Milan. One of the pope's commanders was Fabrizio Colonna, Machiavelli's spokesman in the *Art of War;* he led a vanguard of eight hundred men. Perhaps because Colonna led a defeated unit, Machiavelli never refers to this battle in the *Art of War.* He alludes to it only briefly in this chapter and the next. Guicciardini, on the other hand, describes Colonna's shrewd military advice and tactics as well as his bravery; *Storia d'Italia,* 10, 13,

10. Although Charles VIII invaded Italy in 1494, the reference is to a battle in May 1498 and Pisa's defeat, with the aid of Venetian forces, of the Florentine troops led by Rinuccio da Marciano. Paolo Vitelli quickly took over as condottiere in June. See *Decennale,* 1, vv. 184–186, and Guicciardini, *History of Florence,* chapter 17.

11. Periodically, Ciriacio de' Palamidessi da Borgo San Sepolcro was a Florentine infantry leader, particularly during the wars with Pisa, which lasted off and on from 1495 to 1509.

~ 17 ~

HOW HIGHLY ARTILLERY SHOULD BE REGARDED IN OUR TIMES AND WHETHER THE VIEW THAT IS GENERALLY HELD OF IT IS VALID

1 When I consider, in addition to what is mentioned above, how many pitched battles (called in our day by a French word, "days," and by the Italians "deeds of arms)"[1] were waged by the Romans at different times, I have begun to consider the general opinion of many people. This would have it that had there been artillery in those days, the Romans would not have been permitted and it would not have been so easy for them to seize provinces and make peoples tributary as they did, nor would they in any case have made such great conquests.[2] 2 They also say that men using these firearms cannot practice or demonstrate their *virtù* as they could in ancient times.[3] 3 They add a third thing: it is more difficult to engage in a battle now than it was then, and one cannot stay within the institutions of those days so that war will eventually be reduced to artillery.

4 Because I deem it not to be outside my topic to discuss the truth of these opinions, the degree to which artillery has increased or diminished the strength of armies, and whether it deprives or provides an opportunity for good commanders to show their *virtù,* I shall begin by addressing their first opinion: that the ancient Roman armies would not have made the conquests that they did had there been artillery. 5 In reply to this I say that war is waged either to defend oneself or to attack; therefore, we must first examine which of these two sorts of war artillery helps or harms the most. 6 Although there is something to be said on both sides, I believe nevertheless that artillery does incomparably more harm to those defending themselves than to those who attack.[4]

7 The reason why I say this is that the defenders are either inside a town or in the field within a palisade. 8 If they are inside a town, either it is small, as are the majority of fortresses, or it is large: in the first case, the defenders are completely lost, because an artillery attack is such that no wall exists, no matter how thick, that cannot be brought down by it within a few days; and if those inside do not have enough room to retreat into with both trenches and ramparts, they are lost. They can neither stave off the attack of an enemy who then wishes to enter through a breach in the wall, nor is any artillery they might have of use for this, because this is a maxim: where men can go headlong and en masse, artillery cannot stop them. 9 Therefore we cannot defend towns against the savagery of those from beyond the Alps; attacks by Italians are indeed withstood, since they go into battle (which, quite appropriately, Italians call a "skirmish") not en masse but in small units. 10 And those who advance with such disorder and halfheartedness toward a breach in a wall defended by artillery go toward certain death; artillery is effective against them. But when those who approach a breach packed together en masse with one man shoving the other go through anywhere, unless they are stopped by either

trenches or ramparts, artillery does not hold them back. Although some of them may die, it cannot be so many as to prevent their victory. 11 The truth of this has been learned in many successful assaults that those from beyond the Alps have made in Italy and especially from that on Brescia.[5] When the city rebelled against the French, since the fortress was still held for the king of France, the Venetians, in order to stave off an attack that could come from the latter within the town, fortified the street leading down from the fortress to the city with artillery: they posted it in front, on the flanks, and in every other promising location. 12 Monsieur de Foix paid no attention to it; instead he marched through the middle of it with his squadron, which had dismounted, and seized the city; it has not been heard that he received any significant harm from it. 13 So, as we have said, whenever the defenders of a small town find their walls torn down, if they have no place to retreat to with ramparts and trenches and they must count on artillery, they are quickly defeated.

14 If you are defending a large town and have the possibility of retreat, artillery is nevertheless incomparably more useful to those who are outside than to those inside. 15 First, because if you want artillery to damage the besiegers, you must rise above the town's level with it, for if you stay on the level, any slight embankment or rampart that the enemy builds remains secure and you can do him no harm. 16 Consequently, because you have to rise and drag yourself onto a gallery along the walls or somehow rise above the ground, you get into two difficulties. First, you cannot get artillery up there of the size and power that the one outside can bring, since large things cannot be maneuvered in tight spaces. Second, even if you could get it up there, you cannot make those ramparts dependable and secure to protect the artillery, as the besiegers can, since they are on the ground and have as much advantage and as much room as they themselves want. Hence, if the besiegers have a great deal of powerful artillery, it is impossible for those defending a town to keep artillery in elevated positions; and, as has been stated, if they have to locate it in low areas, it becomes useless for the most part. 17 So the defense of the city has to be reduced to defending it hand to hand, as was done in ancient times, and with light artillery. If light artillery offers some defensive value, there is a disadvantage that counterbalances artillery's advantage. Because now that it exists, town walls have become lowered and flattened, almost buried in trenches. So, when it comes to hand-to-hand combat, because either the walls have been breached or the trenches have been filled in, the besieged have far more disadvantages than they once had. 18 Therefore, as has been stated above, these weapons are much more useful to those besieging towns than those being besieged.

19 As for the third thing, withdrawing to a camp within a palisade in order not to fight unless it is to your convenience or advantage, I say that in this case you normally have no more recourse to keep from fighting than the ancients had; and sometimes, because of the artillery, you are at an even greater disadvantage. 20 For if the enemy comes upon you and has a slight advantage in terrain, as can easily happen, and he is on higher ground than you are, or if you have not yet constructed your embankments and sheltered yourself well with them before he arrives, then he immediately forces you out without your having any

recourse: you are obliged to leave your fortifications and meet the fray. 21 That is what happened to the Spaniards at the Battle of Ravenna;[6] because they were entrenched between the Ronco River and an embankment but had not built it high enough and the French held a slight advantage in the terrain, the artillery compelled them to leave their fortifications and meet the fray. 22 But assuming, as must usually be the case, that the campsite you have chosen is on higher ground than the others facing you and the embankments are good and secure, so thanks to the site and your other preparations the enemy does not dare attack you, then in this instance people will resort to the methods the ancients practiced whenever someone was in an impregnable position with his army: running about the country, seizing or besieging the towns friendly to you, cutting off your supplies. 23 Until some necessity will force you to move out and fight; in this, artillery is not much use, as will be stated below. 24 So, considering what kinds of wars the Romans waged and realizing that they waged almost all their wars to attack others and not to defend themselves, it will be seen, if the things mentioned above are true, that they would have had a greater advantage and would have conquered more swiftly if artillery had existed in those times.

25 As for the second point, that because of artillery men are unable to demonstrate their *virtù* as they could in antiquity, I say that whenever men have to appear in small detachments it is true that they run greater danger than back then, if they had to scale a town's walls or make attacks like that, where men were not grouped close together but had to appear individually, one at a time. 26 It is also true that commanders and leaders of armies are more exposed to mortal danger now than back then because they can be reached by artillery fire anywhere; it is of no use to be among the rearmost detachments and supplied with very strong men. 27 Nevertheless, we can see that either of these two dangers rarely does extraordinary harm, because people do not scale the walls of well-fortified towns, nor do they go and attack them with weak attacks; but if one wishes to capture them, the matter boils down to a siege, as was done in ancient times. 28 In those towns that are captured by an attack, though, the dangers are not much greater than they were then, because even in those days the defenders of towns did not lack for things to shoot; even though the attacks were not so violent, as far as slaughtering men was concerned, they had similar results. 29 As for the death of commanders and condottieri, during the past twenty-four years that there have been wars in Italy,[7] there have been fewer instances of it than there were during ten years' time in antiquity. 30 Except for Count Ludovico della Mirandola, who died at Ferrara when the Venetians attacked that state a few years ago, and the duke of Nemours, who died at Cerignola, artillery has not chanced to kill anyone, for Monsieur de Foix died by the sword at Ravenna and not by firearms.[8] 31 Consequently, if men do not show their *virtù* individually, it is not a result of artillery but of inferior organization and the weakness of their armies: since these lack *virtù* as a whole, they cannot show it in a part.

32 As for the third point they make, that one cannot fight hand to hand and that war will be conducted entirely by artillery, I say that this opinion is completely false and it will always be considered so by those who want to

employ their armies according to ancient *virtù.* 33 Whoever wants to create a good army must accustom his men by means of simulated or real exercises to come at the enemy with him wielding swords and to fight chest to chest; he has to put more trust in his infantry than in his cavalry for reasons that will be stated below.[9] 34 If he does put his trust in his infantry and in the methods already stated, artillery becomes completely useless. For when advancing on the enemy, infantry can avoid artillery strikes more easily than in antiquity they could avoid the onslaught of elephants, scythe-bearing chariots, and other unusual obstacles that the Roman infantry encountered, against which they always found a remedy. 35 And they would have found one all the more readily against artillery since the time in which artillery can harm you is shorter than that when elephants and chariots could do harm. 36 Because in the midst of the fray the latter threw you into disarray, the former interferes with you only before the fray; infantry can easily escape this interference either by advancing under the terrain's natural cover or by getting down on the ground when they fire. 37 Experience has shown that even this is not necessary, especially as a defense against heavy artillery, which cannot be regulated in such a way: either if it aims high, it misses you; or if it aims low, it falls short.[10] 38 Then, when the armies have engaged in hand-to-hand combat, it is as clear as day that neither heavy nor light artillery can harm you, because if the one who has the artillery is in front, he becomes your prisoner; if he is behind, he harms his allies more than you. On the flanks too he cannot hit you in such a way that you cannot go and get him, and the same result comes about. 39 There is not much dispute on this point: we have seen the example of the Swiss at Novara in 1513, when without artillery or cavalry they went to meet the French army, equipped with artillery inside their fortifications, and they put them to flight with having any interference from it.[11] 40 And the reason, aside from what has been said above, is that artillery, for it to work, needs to be protected by either walls, moats, or embankments; if one of these protections is missing, it is either captured or it becomes useless, as happens to it when it must be protected by men, as occurs during battles or combats. 41 It can be used on the flank only in the way that the ancients used their catapults: they set them up outside of their detachments so that they fought outside the ranks; any time they were charged by cavalry or others, their refuge was behind the legions. 42 Anyone who counts on it in any other fashion does not understand things well and trusts in something that can easily deceive him. 43 And if the Turks won victories against the Shah and the Sultan by means of artillery, that was not as a result of any other *virtù* than its unusual noise, which frightened their cavalry.[12]

44 Coming to the end of this discourse, I therefore conclude that artillery is useful to an army whenever it is mixed with ancient *virtù,* but without that, it is completely useless against an army with *virtù.*[13]

NOTES

1. Translates *Giornate [Journées]* and *fatti d'arme.*

2. In the third book of the *Art of War,* Fabrizio Colonna deals with the issue of artillery; it follows immediately on an examination of how the Romans drew up their

battle lines, the subject of chapter 16. It is interesting to note, then, that in response to a question from Luigi Alamanni toward the middle of the book, Colonna discusses at length whether the Romans would have prevailed had they had artillery against them. His response is at variance with the position Machiavelli takes here.

3. Guicciardini, *History of Florence,* chapter 11, describes the "fire and pestilence" that entered Italy with Charles VIII's invasion in 1494 and how artillery "changed the art of war." In his *Storia d'Italia,* 1, 11, he refers to "the new plague of artillery" and calls cannon a "diabolical rather than human weapon." Ariosto too laments the loss of *virtù* that firearms bring; see *Orlando Furioso,* 11, vv. 26 ff., and 9, vv. 90–91.

4. Guicciardini, on the other hand, asserts that artillery is more effective in defensive operations than in sieges (*Storia d'Italia,* 15, 6). Vivanti, in his edition of the *Discorsi,* points out that in the interval between the composition of the *Discourses* and the *Storia d'Italia* (1535–1540) significant strides had been made in the construction of fortifications.

5. A reference to an event earlier in the Holy League's war against France; see above, 2, 16, n.9. The city of Brescia in Lombardy overthrew its French occupiers on 2 and 3 February 1512, though the town's fortress remained in French hands. Gaston de Foix returned to Brescia from Bologna on 17 February and inflicted a bloody sack on the nineteenth; it is vividly described in Guicciardini, *Storia d'Italia,* 10, 10.

6. See above, 2, 16, n.9, and Guicciardini, *Storia d'Italia,* 10, 13.

7. Another indication that Machiavelli was writing this section in 1517 or 1518, since Charles VIII invaded Italy in September 1494; see above, 2, 10, n.7.

8. Ludovico Pico della Mirandola commanded the papal army and was killed in December 1509 when the Venetians attempted to recover from Ferrara some of the towns in their territory that they lost after the battle of Agnadello (Vailà); see above, 1, 6, n.11. Guicciardini discusses this incident in *Storia d'Italia,* 8, 14. Louis d'Armagnac was the duke of Nemours and Louis XII's viceroy in Naples. He was killed on 28 April 1503 at the battle of Cerignola, an important battle leading to Spanish control of Naples. Guicciardini, in *Storia d'Italia,* 10, 13, says Gaston de Foix was killed by a "lance thrust in his side" during a cavalry charge.

9. In the next chapter.

10. Inglese observes that despite the truth of this assertion Machiavelli's "cult of Antiquity" prevents him from believing that "technical progress" could come up with a solution to the problem, and thus he is far from "the spirit of Leonardo da Vinci" (p. 427).

11. With no cavalry and little artillery, the Swiss infantry, fighting for Massimiliano Sforza, the duke of Milan, beat the French under Louis de La Trémouille and Gian Giacomo Trivulzio at the Battle of Novara, a decisive one in the Holy League's fight against France, on 6 June 1513. Guicciardini, however, notes that the French had not had enough time to construct fortifications, *Storia d'Italia,* 11, 12. For Machiavelli's analysis of this battle's political implications, see his letter to Francesco Vettori, 20 June 1513 (*Friends,* pp. 237–238).

12. These allusions refer to the Turk Selim I, the sultan of Turkey from 1512 to 1520, who defeated the sophy Ismail I, the shah of Persia, at the Battle of Chaldiran with artillery in 1514, and again against the Mameluke sultans of Egypt and Syria at Aleppo in 1516, and in 1517 at Reydanieh, near Cairo.

13. In his polemic against artillery Machiavelli seems loath to renounce his Roman model. His paramount consideration is to protect the inviolability of *virtù,* so he has to hedge on an issue for which there are few Roman examples. Livy, for example, refers in passing to *tormentis machinisque,* a catapult and military equipment that discharged missiles (6.9.2). His conclusion, however, which seems outdated to us, was shared by many of his contemporaries. For more on the issue of artillery, see J. R. Hale, "Armies, Navies," and his *Artists and Warfare.*

~ 18 ~

HOW, ON THE AUTHORITY OF THE ROMANS AND THE EXAMPLE OF THE ANCIENTS' MILITIA, INFANTRY SHOULD BE VALUED MORE THAN CAVALRY

1 It can be shown clearly by many reasons and many examples how much more the Romans valued foot soldiers than those on horseback for all military actions and how they based all plans for their armies on them. Many examples show this: among others, when they fought against the Latins near Lake Regillus; there, when the Roman army had already given way, they had men on horseback get down on foot to help their men; in that way the battle started up again and victory was won.[1] 2 Here it is evident that the Romans placed more trust in them when they were on foot than in staying on horseback. 3 They used this same measure in many other engagements, and they always found it a very good remedy against their dangers.

4 This should not be countered with the opinion of Hannibal: when he saw that the Consuls had made their cavalry dismount during the battle of Cannae, he made fun of such a course of action, saying: *"Quam mallem vinctos mihi traderent equites!"* That is, "I would prefer that they were given to me in fetters."[2] 5 Even though this opinion came from the mouth of a most excellent man, nevertheless, if we are to follow authority we must believe in a Roman republic and its many quite excellent commanders rather than one lone Hannibal. 6 Even though there are evident reasons for this opinion without authorities.[3] A man on foot can go into many places that a horse cannot. He can be taught how to stay in formation and, no matter how disrupted it might be, how he may regroup; it is difficult to make horses stay in formation and impossible to regroup them once they are disrupted. 7 Besides, there are some horses—like some men—that have little spirit and others that have a lot; often it happens that a spirited horse is ridden by a cowardly man and a cowardly horse by a man with spirit. Whichever way this disparity goes, it leads to frustration and disorder. 8 Well-ordered infantry can break through cavalry easily and can be broken through by them [only] with difficulty. 9 In addition to many ancient and modern examples, the authority of those who give rules for civil matters corroborates this opinion; they show that wars began to be waged at first with cavalry because there was as yet no organization for infantry. But when it did become organized, they realized immediately how

much more useful it was than cavalry.[4] 10 This does not mean that horses are not necessary in armies, though, for scouting, for scouring and looting the countryside, for pursuing the enemy when he is in flight, and for still being in part an opposition to the adversaries' cavalry; but the foundation and sinew of an army, and what has to be valued the most, must be the infantry.

11 Among the sins of the Italian princes who have made Italy a slave to foreigners,[5] there is no greater one than having taken little account of this institution and having turned all their concern to troops on horseback. 12 This disorder arose out of the ill will of the leaders and out of the ignorance of those who held power. 13 Because when the Italian militia was turned over some twenty-five years ago to men who did not hold power but were more or less soldiers of fortune, they immediately realized that they could hold onto their prestige, since they were armed and the princes were not.[6] 14 Because they were unable to pay a large number of foot soldiers regularly and they were unable to depend upon subjects, and because small numbers would not give them any prestige, they turned to keeping cavalry. With two or three hundred cavalrymen in his pay, a condottiere would maintain his prestige, and the payroll was not so great that it could not be met by the men who held power. 15 In order for this to occur more readily, and the better to keep up their prestige, they took all esteem and prestige away from the infantry and applied it to their cavalry: this disorder increased so much that even among some of the largest armies the infantry constituted only a very small fraction.[7] 16 This custom, along with many other disorders that were mingled with it, made the Italian armies so weak that this land has been easily trampled by all the people from beyond the Alps.

17 This error of valuing cavalry more than infantry is shown more clearly by another Roman example. 18 When the Romans were encamped at Sora and a cavalry squadron rode out of the town to attack their camp, the Roman Master of Horse advanced to meet them with his cavalry.[8] When they clashed, fate dictated that the leader of each army died during the initial onslaught. The others remained leaderless even though the fray continued, so in order to facilitate the enemy's defeat, the Romans dismounted and forced the enemy cavalrymen to do the same so they could defend themselves; and by this means the Romans carried off the victory. 19 There can be no better example than this to show how much more *virtù* there is in infantry than in cavalry. For if the Consuls made the Roman cavalry dismount in other actions, it was to help out the infantry, which was in trouble and needed help; but in this instance they dismounted not to help out the infantry or to fight enemy foot soldiers but because, while fighting cavalry against cavalry, they decided that, since they could not defeat them on horseback, they could defeat them more easily by dismounting. 20 I therefore must conclude that a well-organized infantry can be defeated only with the greatest of difficulty and then only by other infantry. 21 The Romans Crassus and Mark Antony fought many battles for domination of the Parthians with very few cavalry and a large number of infantry, and they had innumerable Parthian cavalry opposing them.[9] 22 Crassus was left there dead with part of his army; Mark Antony got away by his

virtù. 23 Nevertheless, even in this Roman affliction we see how the infantry prevailed over the cavalry. Because even though they were in broad country with few mountains, even fewer rivers, far removed from the seashore and from any conveniences, nevertheless, Mark Antony, in the judgment of the Parthians themselves, got away by his great *virtù;* and never did the entire Parthian cavalry dare to test the ranks of his army. 24 Although Crassus remained there, anyone who reads about his actions attentively will see that he was tricked rather than overpowered. Never throughout all his troubles did the Parthians dare to attack him; rather, they brought him to extreme distress by constantly hounding his flanks, cutting off his supplies, and making promises they did not keep.[10]

25 I think I would have a harder time convincing people how much more powerful the infantry's *virtù* is than the cavalry's were it not for many modern examples that provide quite abundant testimony of it. 26 We have seen nine thousand Swiss at Novara, mentioned above, go and attack and defeat ten thousand cavalry and as many infantry, because the cavalry could not harm them and they had little regard for the infantry, since they were mostly troops from Gascony and poorly trained.[11] 27 Then we saw twenty-six thousand Swiss go and attack King Francis of France north of Milan; he had twenty thousand cavalry, forty thousand infantry, and a hundred wagons of artillery with him; although they did not win the battle as they had at Novara, they fought with *virtù* for two days and then, when they were defeated, half of them escaped. 28 Marcus Atilius Regulus assumed he could stand off not only cavalry but elephants with his infantry; although his plan did not succeed, it was not however because the *virtù* of his infantry was not great enough, but because he did not have sufficient confidence in them to believe he could overcome that difficulty.[12] 29 I reply, therefore, that in order to conquer a well-organized infantry, it is necessary to oppose them with infantry better organized than they are, otherwise one goes to certain defeat. 30 In the days of Filippo Visconti, the duke of Milan, about sixteen thousand Swiss descended into Lombardy. The duke, who then had Carmagnola as his commander, sent him to meet them with about a thousand cavalry and not much infantry.[13] 31 Unfamiliar with their battle-order, he went to meet them with his cavalry, assuming that he could defeat them quickly. 32 But when he found them unmovable, he retreated after losing many of his men; because he was a very able man and knew how to choose new courses of action under new circumstances, he went to meet them after getting reinforcements. Approaching them, he had all his men at arms dismount, stationed them at the head of his infantry, and went and attacked the Swiss. 33 They had no recourse because Carmagnola's men at arms, who were on foot and well armed, were able to penetrate easily among the Swiss ranks without suffering any injury: once they penetrated them, they were able to attack them easily;[14] so out of their entire number the only portion remaining alive were those spared by Carmagnola's mercy.

34 I believe that many realize the difference in *virtù* there is between these two organizations; but so great is the wretchedness of these times that

neither ancient nor modern examples nor admission of error is sufficient to make modern princes mend their ways and realize that, if they want to lend prestige to the army of a country or a state, it is necessary to revive this organization, stick by it, endow it with prestige, and give it life so that it may give both life and prestige back to the prince. 35 And just as they deviate from these ways, so they deviate from the others mentioned above; hence, as we shall discuss below, the result is that conquests bring harm, not greatness, to a state.[15]

NOTES

1. For the construction of this chapter's argument and its parodic relation to a Scholastic disputation, see below, Guicciardini's *Consideration* of 2, 12, n.1. The battle "fought against the Latins" took place near Tusculum, on the outskirts of Frascati, about sixteen miles southeast of Rome in 496 B.C. (Livy, 2.20); see the discussion in Martelli, *Storici antichi,* pp. 94–95.

2. Machiavelli rarely follows his Latin quotations with a translation into Italian. Livy's Latin, from 22.49.3, means, "How I would prefer that he give them to me in fetters." Machiavelli has added *equites,* "cavalrymen," to clarify the antecedent of "them." Hannibal lost this battle, fought in 216 B.C. For Machiavelli's use of Livy, see the discussion in Martelli, *Storici antichi,* pp. 95–96.

3. On the question of "reasons" and "authorities," see Machiavelli's letter to Vettori of 29 April 1513, analyzing the Treaty of Orthez between Ferdinand the Catholic, king of Spain, and Louis XII, king of France (*Friends,* pp. 231–236). There Machiavelli sees less equivalence between the two; he writes, " I do not want to be prompted by any authority but reason" (p. 233). Rinaldi notes that the immediate "authorities" are the writers of political theory, especially Aristotle, *Politics,* 4.13.10–11, 1297b.

4. Noting that Lucretius, 5.1297, may lie behind this sentence, Inglese points out that the progression Machiavelli follows is rooted in the shift in Greek tactics from the "aristocratic cavalry to the 'democratic' infantry of the hoplites."

5. A verbal echo of *Prince,* 12, pp. 221; 223, lines 44–48. In fact, the argument following is stated forcefully at the end of *Art of War,* Book 7, *Florentine Histories,* 5, 1, as well in *Prince,* 12, and the numerous ordinances Machiavelli wrote in setting up the Florentine citizen militia.

6. Because in *Prince,* 12, Machiavelli traces the ills of Italian towns relying on condottieri back to the fourteenth century, it seems curious that he merely goes back twenty-five years here. Inglese allows for a textual corruption, but Machiavelli may be aiming at consistency with his dates here and in sentence 29 of the previous chapter.

7. See *Prince,* 12, p. 231, lines 177–189, for a similar explanation of the condottieri's role in the decline of the infantry. It is preceded by an equally damning reference to people "from beyond the Alps," as at the end of sentence 16 here.

8. Livy, 9.21–22, during the Second Samnite War in 315 B.C. The locality is not Sora, which Livy discusses in chapter 23, but Saticola, a town on the border between Campania and Samnium near the modern S. Agata dei Goti, about thirty miles northeast of Naples, off the road to Benevento. The Master of Horse was Quintus

Aulius Cerretanus. In what follows, the verbal echoes of Livy, 9.22.10 are clear, but for Machiavelli's use (or misuse) of Livy, see the discussion in Martelli, *Storici antichi,* pp. 97–98.

9. Marcus Licinius Crassus was a member of the first triumvirate along with Julius Caesar and Pompey. He died at the battle of Carrhae in 53 B.C. while fighting the Parthians, a Scythian people who ruled Iran and Mesopotamia. Mark Antony, along with Ventidius, led a campaign against the Parthians from 39 to 38 B.C. Machiavelli follows Plutarch, *Crassus,* 19–31, and *Antony,* 37–50; "the judgement of the Parthians themselves" about Antony in the next sentence is mentioned in 49.3. Walker points out, however, that neither source asserts the superiority of infantry over cavalry.

10. Crassus was already defeated, but he was betrayed by one of his advisers, Andromachus. The idea of Crassus being "tricked rather than overpowered" *(ingannato piuttosto che sforzato)* is reminiscent of Machiavelli's force and fraud dialectic. See above, 1, 18, n.4, for numerous cross-references to the topic of force and fraud.

11. See above, 1, 23, n.5, for the Battle of Novara and the Battle of Marignano (Melegnano), referred to in the next sentence in the phrase "north of Milan," although it is actually about ten miles southeast of the city. It is also referred to in the previous chapter; see note 8. Guicciardini, *Storia d'Italia,* 11, 12, also describes the Battle of Novara. Military historians frequently dispute the size of the fighting forces that Machiavelli gives throughout his text, be the battle ancient or modern. Gascony was a region in southwestern France whose soldiers were often more boastful of their prowess than they had a right to be. Inglese notes that troops from Gascony mutinied on 7 July 1500 during Florence's unsuccessful attack on Pisa, referred to above, 1, 38, n.8.

12. Marcus Atilius Regulus was consul in 256 B.C. During the First Punic War, his victory at the naval battle of Ecnomus led to the invasion of Africa and an attack on Carthage in 255. The battle to which Machiavelli refers was fought near the city; see Polybius, 1.33–34. Machiavelli refers to it in *Art of War,* 4, as well.

13. Filippo Visconti was duke from 1412 to 1447. He hired Francesco Bussone da Carmagnola (c. 1385–1432) as his mercenary commander. Carmagnola's defeat of a Swiss army, 5 July 1422, at the battle of Arbedo, near Bellinzona, was often cited against Machiavelli because it showed that mercenaries could conquer a well-trained national force. Fabrizio Colonna comments on this victory in his fourth speech in *Art of War,* 2. Visconti suspected Carmagnola, probably correctly, of treason, so in 1425 Carmagnola accepted a Venetian offer to lead their army. In *Prince,* 12, Machiavelli examines his career with the Venetians, noting that they thought Carmagnola "possessed enormous *virtù*" (p. 227, lines 129–130).

14. In *Prince,* 26, Machiavelli comments that "the Swiss have reason to fear the infantry who meet them in battle with a resolve equal to theirs" (p. 381, lines 111–113).

15. The calm regret of this conclusion exhibits a marked difference in tone from the jeremiad of *Prince,* 26, and the anger in *Art of War* against Italian rulers who fail to attend to "the art of war."

~ 19 ~

THAT CONQUESTS BY POORLY CONSTITUTED REPUBLICS THAT DO NOT ACT IN ACCORDANCE WITH ROMAN *VIRTÙ* LEAD TO THEIR DOWNFALL, NOT THEIR RISE

1 These opinions, contrary to the truth, based on the bad examples introduced by this corrupt period of ours, are the reason men do not consider deviating from accustomed ways. 2 Who could have convinced an Italian thirty years ago that ten thousand infantrymen could attack ten thousand cavalry and as many infantry on a plain and not only fight with them but defeat them, as we saw at Novara in an example we have cited several times?[1] 3 Even though histories are full of such examples, nevertheless, they would not have believed them; if they had, they would have said that men are better armed today and that a squadron of men at arms would be fit to charge a rocky cliff, let alone an infantry corps. Thus they ruined their judgment with these false excuses. 4 And they would not have considered that Lucullus, with just a few infantrymen, defeated a hundred fifty thousand cavalrymen of Tigranes, and that among those horsemen there was a kind of cavalry very similar to our men at arms.[2] 5 Just as this fallacy has been revealed by the example of troops from beyond the Alps[3] (and we can see from this that what is recounted about infantry in the histories is true), so all the other institutions of the ancients should be believed to be true and useful. 6 Were this to be believed, republics and princes would make fewer mistakes, would be stronger in resisting an attack made against them, and would not take hope in flight; those who held political power[4] in their hands would know better how to direct it, by way either of expanding or of maintaining it. 7 And they would believe that the right way to make a republic great and to acquire power is to increase their city's population, to make allies and not subjects for themselves, to send out colonies to watch over conquered countries, to make use of plunder, to overpower the enemy with raids and battles, not sieges, to keep the public treasury rich and the private sector poor, and to maintain military exercises with the greatest care.[5]

8 Should this means of expansion not appeal to them, they would realize that conquests by any other means lead to the downfall of republics. They would put a check on all ambition, carefully regulate their city with its laws and mores, prohibit it from conquest, and consider only defending themselves and keeping their defenses well organized—as do the German republics, which have lived for some time, and continue to live, in freedom according to these ways. 9 Nevertheless, as I said before when I discussed the difference between setting up institutions to conquer and setting them up to endure,[6] it is impossible for a republic to succeed in remaining peaceful and enjoying its freedom and with close borders. If it does not disturb others, it will be disturbed; the desire and need to conquer will result from being disturbed. And if it did not have an external enemy, it would find one at home, as seems necessarily to happen to all great cities. 10 And if the republics of Germany can

live in this way and have been able to endure for some time, it is because of certain conditions that exist in that country and not elsewhere, without which they could not hold onto such a way of life.

11 The part of Germany about which I am speaking was, like France and Spain, subjugated by the Roman Empire. But later, when the empire began to decline and its title of empire was diminished in that province, the more powerful cities—according to either the emperors' cowardice or their need—began to set themselves free, ransoming themselves from the empire by reserving a small annual tax for it, so gradually all the cities that belonged directly to the emperor and were not subject to any prince ransomed themselves in this way.[7] 12 At the same time that these cities were ransoming themselves, some communities subject to the duke of Austria happened to revolt against him, among them Fribourg, the Swiss, et cetera; from the outset they prospered until they gradually expanded so much that not only have they not returned under the yoke of Austria but they are feared by all their neighbors: these are the ones that are called the Swiss.[8] 13 So this land is divided into the Swiss, the republics (which they call free towns), the princes, and the emperor. 14 And the reason why wars do not arise among so many different kinds of societies—or if they do, they do not last long—is the symbol of the emperor; although he does not have an army, he nevertheless has so much prestige among them that he is a conciliator for them: by interposing himself with his authority as a go-between, he immediately quells any trouble. 15 The greatest and longest wars that have existed there are the one that arose between the Swiss and the duke of Austria; although for many years the emperor and the duke of Austria have been the same person, even so he has not been able to overcome the boldness of the Swiss, with whom there has never been any means of agreement except by force.[9] 16 And the rest of Germany has not been much help to him: both because the communities are unwilling to attack anyone who, like themselves, wishes to live free and because their princes, in part, are unable to help him since they are poor and, in other cases, are unwilling since they envy his power. 17 Those communities, therefore, can live content with their little dominion, because thanks to the imperial authority they have no reason to wish it to be larger; they can live in unity within their walls because they have an enemy nearby who would seize the opportunity to occupy them if ever they clashed with each other. 18 If conditions in that region were different, they would have to try to expand and disrupt that tranquillity of theirs.

19 But because such conditions do not exist elsewhere, this kind of society cannot be chosen, and it is necessary either to expand by means of leagues or to expand like the Romans. 20 And anyone who acts otherwise courts death and destruction, not life, because conquests are harmful in countless ways and for many reasons. 21 For he can very easily acquire dominion and not simultaneously acquire armed forces; anyone who acquires dominion and does not simultaneously acquire armed forces must fall.[10] 22 Anyone who is impoverished by wars is unable to acquire armed forces, even if he is victorious, for he puts more into conquests than he gains from them.

That is what the Venetians and Florentines did: when one held Lombardy and the other Tuscany, they were both much weaker than they were when one was content with the sea and the other with six miles of borders.[11] 23 For everything arose from their wanting to conquer and being unable to choose the means; they deserve all the more blame for having no excuse: they saw the means that the Romans used and they could have followed their example, whereas the Romans had no example, yet by their wisdom were able to find it on their own. 24 Moreover, conquests sometimes do more than a little harm to any well-constituted republic when it conquers a city or a province full of enticements, whose mores one can catch from the commerce one has with them; that is what happened first to Rome and then to Hannibal through the conquest of Capua.[12] 25 Had Capua been farther away from the city so that the soldiers' error had not had a remedy near at hand, or had Rome been in some way corrupted, that conquest would undoubtedly have been the downfall of the Roman republic. 26 And Livy testifies to this with these words: "Even then Capua was not at all healthy for military discipline; with its means for every kind of indulgence, it turned the soldiers' captivated minds away from the memory of their native land."[13] 27 In truth, such cities or provinces take revenge on their conquerors without a fight and without bloodshed because, once they have filled them with their evil mores, they expose them to defeat by whoever attacks them. 28 And Juvenal could not have considered this topic better in his *Satires* when he says that as a result of their conquest of foreign towns, foreign mores had entered the hearts of the Romans and that in place of frugality and other outstanding *virtù,* "gluttony and dissipations settled in and avenged the conquered world."[14] 29 So if conquest could be harmful for the Romans during the period when they acted with such wisdom and *virtù,* what then will it be with those who act differently from their ways and who depend upon either mercenary or auxiliary soldiers, in addition to the other mistakes they make, which have been discussed extensively above? 30 The harm that often thus results will be mentioned in the next chapter.

NOTES

1. In the two previous chapters; again, the dating refers to a period just before the invasion of Italy in 1494 by the French under Charles VIII.

2. Lucius Licinius Lucullus defeated Tigranes, king of Armenia, at a battle near Tigranocerta, modern Silvan, in Armenia in 69 B.C. See Plutarch, *Lucullus,* 26–28; again, the figures for the size of the forces are vastly different. See Ridley, "Roman History," p. 209, and Martelli, *Storici antichi,* pp. 98–99, for commentary on the manipulation of Plutarch. See also *Art of War,* 2, where the same similarity "to our men at arms" is noted in a discussion of this battle.

3. Specifically, the Swiss.

4. Translates *uno vivere civile.*

5. These are points that Machiavelli has made above in the early chapters of Book 2; see also 1, 37, sentence 7.

6. *Discourses,* 1, 6, sentences 23–37.

7. Pope Leo III crowned Charlemagne emperor of the West at Saint Peter's on Christmas Day in A.D. 800. At his death in 814, the Carolingian Empire began to disintegrate as the western Franks (broadly speaking, France) separated from the eastern Franks, Germany. On 31 January 962, Pope John XII made a Saxon, Otto I, emperor of the political entity that came to be known as the Holy Roman Empire.

8. With a kind of constitution, the League of the Three Forest Cantons, Uri, Schwyz, and Unterwalden, was formed in 1291 for mutual defense against the Hapsburg rulers of Austria. Here and below "the duke of Austria" and "Austria" are shorthand for the Hapsburgs, who controlled the canton of Fribourg from 1277 to 1452; it joined the Helvetian Confederacy in 1481.

9. The Holy Roman Empire and the House of Hapsburg became "the same person" in 1438 when the Hapsburg duke of Austria, Albert V, was crowned Holy Roman Emperor Albert II.

10. In Machiavelli's letter to Francesco Vettori of 10 December 1514, he comments: "you must understand that frequently one acquires territory and not armed forces; and if you think it through carefully you will realize that . . . the king of France's acquisition of cities in Italy is one of territory, not armed forces. . . . France has more to fear because he has untrustworthy territories and because the Swiss, who can be prompted to act against him with money, have not been used up; once they were attacked by France, the Swiss would really be his enemy" (*Friends,* p. 296).

11. Venetian expansion onto the mainland as far west as the Ghiara d'Adda, the region between the Mincio and Adda Rivers, began in the early fourteenth century. Florence's expansion beyond her walls began in the second half of the fourteenth century when it conquered Prato, Pistoia, San Gimignano, Volterra, and Arezzo (Rinaldi). Then it took Pisa in 1406 and Livorno in 1421. They did not, however, enlist local troops to defend their newly acquired territory. Thus, starting in 1506, Machiavelli began a series of treatises advocating a citizen militia; his conviction of its numerous advantages informs the discussion in the next chapter. The fundamental argument in the *Discourses,* that a carefully organized, well-regulated republic is more effective and more powerful than a government ruled by a prince, goes hand-in-hand with his belief in the effectiveness and power of a citizen militia. One could not exist without the other.

12. Livy discusses the deleterious effects of the Romans' garrison in Capua, a city synonymous with dissipation, during the First Samnite War in 343 B.C., in 7.38–41. Similar effects on Hannibal's troops occurred during the Second Punic War in 216; see Livy, 23.18.10–16.

13. Livy, 7.38.5: *"Iam tunc minime salubris militari disciplinae Capua, instrumento omnium voluptatum, delinitos militum animos avertit a memoria patriae."*

14. From Juvenal 6.293: *"gula et luxuria incubuit, victumque ulciscitur orbem";* Machiavelli adds *gula et* to Juvenal's text.

~ 20 ~

WHAT RISK IS RUN BY A PRINCE OR A REPUBLIC USING AUXILIARY OR MERCENARY TROOPS

1 If I had not treated at length in another work of mine how ineffective mercenary and auxiliary troops are and how effective one's own are, I would expatiate much more in this discourse than I shall do; but because I have spoken of it at length elsewhere, I shall be brief on this topic.[1] 2 Because I have found such an extensive example concerning auxiliary soldiers in Livy, it has not seemed wise to me to pass it over completely, because auxiliary soldiers are those that a prince or a republic send, commanded and paid by them, to aid you. 3 As for Livy's text,[2] I say that after the Romans had defeated two Samnite armies in two different locations with their own armies,[3] which they had sent to help the Capuans, and thus delivered the Capuans from the war that the Samnites were waging against them, they wanted to return to Rome. In order that the Capuans not fall prey again to the Samnites once they were deprived of a defense garrison, the Romans left two legions in the Capuan area to defend them. 4 These legions, growing corrupt through leisure, began to take pleasure in it,[4] so, forgetting their country and reverence for the Senate, they decided to take up arms and seize control of the area that they had defended by their *virtù;* it seemed to them that the inhabitants were unworthy of possessing what they could not defend. 5 This matter, when it was discovered, was crushed and punished by the Romans, as will be shown at length when we discuss conspiracies.[5]

6 Therefore I say once again that of all the types of soldiers, auxiliaries are the most harmful, because the prince or republic that uses them as help has no authority whatever over them; only the one sending them has authority over them. 7 For auxiliary soldiers are those who are sent to you by a prince, as I have stated, under his commanders, under his banners, and paid by him, as was the army that the Romans sent to Capua. 8 When soldiers like these have won, they usually plunder both those that have hired them and those they have been hired against; they do so either because of the ill will of the prince who sends them or out of their own ambition. 9 Although the Romans had no intention of breaking the agreement and the treaties they had made with the Capuans, nevertheless, the ease with which these soldiers felt that they could conquer them was such that it was able to convince them to consider taking the Capuans' town and government away from them. 10 Many examples could be given of this, but I want this one to suffice along with that of the people of Rhegium, whose lives and city were taken from them by a legion that the Romans had placed in defense there.[6]

11 So a prince or a republic should take any other course of action rather than resort to bringing auxiliary troops into their state for defense if they have to put their trust in them totally: any agreement, any treaty, even a harsh one,[7] that they may have with the enemy will be easier on them than such a course of action. 12 And if past matters are read carefully and present ones are discussed, we shall discover for every one that has had a happy outcome countless

others have been disappointed by it. 13 A prince or an ambitious republic cannot have a better opportunity to seize a city or a province than to be requested to send their armies to its defense. 14 Therefore anyone who is so ambitious as to call for such help, not only to defend himself but to attack someone else, is seeking to acquire what he cannot hold and what can easily be taken away from him by the one who acquires it for him. 15 But men's ambition is so great that in order to satisfy an immediate desire they do not consider what evil may soon result from it.[8] 16 And examples from the ancients do not move him, either in this or in the other matters discussed, because if men were moved by those examples, they would see that the more they show generosity toward their neighbors and that they are averse to seizing them, the more they put themselves in their hands, as will be stated below through the example of the Capuans.

NOTES

1. Machiavelli refers to *Prince,* chapter 12 on mercenaries, and 13 on auxiliaries, but his scorn for these troops also permeates his *Art of War.*

2. The incidents referred to in 343–342 B.C. can be found in Livy, 7.38–41, but Livy, 7.38.4, does not specify that the nature of the legions was "defensive" (Ridley, "Roman History," p. 209). Given the details in Livy, Mansfield, *New Modes,* p. 252, notes Machiavelli's odd definition of these soldiers as "auxiliaries."

3. See *Discourses,* 2, 13, n.6.

4. The same situation is mentioned in the previous discourse; see its notes 12 and 13.

5. In *Discourses,* 3, 6, sentences 188–191.

6. In 280 B.C. the inhabitants of modern-day Reggio in Calabria asked Rome to send a garrison to protect them from Pyrrhus, the invading king of Epirus. The next year these troops took over the city and remained there until 271, when Rome sent another army to quell the rebellious troops and restore freedom to the city. See Polybius, 1.7; the incident is alluded to in speeches that Livy incorporates in 28.28 (by Scipio) and 31.31 (by a Roman spokesman).

7. Translates *ancora che dura,* which could also be read "as long as it lasts."

8. A similar notion exists in his *capitolo "Dell'ambizione,"* vv. 106–108.

~ 21 ~

THE FIRST PRAETOR THAT THE ROMANS SENT ANYWHERE WAS TO CAPUA FOUR HUNDRED YEARS AFTER THEY BEGAN TO WAGE WAR

1 We have discussed at length above how different the Romans were in their ways of acquisition from those who extend their jurisdiction nowadays and how they let the towns they did not destroy live under their own laws, even those that surrendered to them as subjects and not as allies.[1] The Roman people left behind no sign of power in them, but they did subject them to a few conditions; if these were observed, the Romans kept them in their government and dignity. 2 These ways are known to have been observed until

they went out of Italy and began to turn kingdoms and states into provinces. 3 A very clear example of this is that the first Praetor the Romans sent anywhere was to Capua.[2] They sent him not out of their own ambition but because they were asked to by the Capuans, who, since there was dissension among them, deemed it necessary to have a Roman citizen inside their city to reorganize and reunite them. 4 Inspired by this example and constrained by the same need, the people of Antium also asked for a Prefect; Livy says of this incident and this new way of ruling: "that now not only Roman arms but Roman law were becoming widespread."[3]

5 We can thus see how this procedure facilitated Roman expansion. 6 For in particular cities that are used to living in freedom or accustomed to governing themselves locally remain far more peacefully content under a power that they do not see, even if it had some weight to it, than under one that they see every day so that they seem to be reproached for their enslavement every day. 7 This also entails another advantage for the prince: since his ministers do not have the judges and magistrates who render civil or criminal justice in those cities under their control, no judgment can ever result in the prince's being blamed or disgraced; that way many causes for slander and hatred of him are eliminated. 8 And there is a recent Italian example that this is true, in addition to the ancient ones that could be cited. 9 As everyone knows, Genoa has been occupied by the French several times.[4] Each time, except at present, the king has always sent a French governor to govern it in his name. 10 Only now, not as a result of the king's choice but because necessity arranged it that way, has he let the city govern itself and with a Genoese governor. 11 And unquestionably were there anyone to ask which of these two ways provides the king with greater security in his reign over it and greater happiness for its people, unquestionably he would approve this latter way.

12 Furthermore, the more averse you appear to be to conquering them, the more readily men throw themselves into your lap; the more humanely and friendly you act toward them, the less they fear you for their freedom. 13 This friendliness and generosity made the Capuans hasten to ask the Romans for a Praetor; yet if the Romans had shown the slightest wish to send one there, they immediately would have become suspicious and would have drawn away from them. 14 But what need is there to go for examples to Capua and Rome when we have them in Florence and Tuscany? 15 Everyone knows how long since it has been that the city of Pistoia came voluntarily under Florentine rule.[5] 16 Everyone also knows how much enmity there has been between the Florentines and the people of Pisa, Lucca, and Siena; and this difference of mind did not come about because the people of Pistoia do not prize their freedom as do the others and do not consider themselves the equal of others but because the Florentines always behaved like brothers toward them and as enemies toward the others. 17 This has made the Pistoians come willingly under their control; the others have done and are still doing everything possible not to end up that way.[6] 18 Unquestionably, had the Florentines made their neighbors friendly by either leagues

or assistance and not made them hostile instead, they would by now unquestionably be the masters of Tuscany. 19 This does not mean that I deem that one should not use arms and force, but they must be kept as a last resort, when and where other ways do not suffice.

NOTES

1. See above, 2, 4, and 19.

2. According to Livy, praetors were first established in 366 B.C. (6.42.11). Lucius Furius was sent to Capua at the city's request in 317 B.C. as a remedy for its "internal discord"; but see the discussion in Martelli, *Storici antichi,* p. 100.

3. Machiavelli's text reads, *"quod iam non solum arma, sed iura romana pollebant."* It is modified from Livy, 9.20.10: *"nec arma modo sed iura etiam Romana late pollebant"* (not Roman arms alone but even Roman law began spreading far and wide). See the discussion of this modification in Martelli, *Storici antichi,* p. 101.

4. France controlled Genoa at the turn of the fifteenth century from 1396 to 1409; within Machiavelli's recent memory, however, it was in French hands from 1499 to 1506 and again from May 1507 until 1512. The doge of Genoa, Ottaviano Fregoso, turned the city over to Francis I; the French king made him governor until imperial troops restored republican government under an elected doge, Antoniotto Adorno.

5. In *Florentine Histories,* 2, 30, Machiavelli says that Florence took control of Pistoia by "negotiated treaty" in 1328. Full control came in 1331 after a series of conflicts with Castruccio Castracani, the ruler of Pisa. See also below, 2, 25, n.4.

6. Pisa's successful effort "not to end up" under Florentine control lasted from 1494 until 1509; see above 1, 38, n.8; 1, 39, nn.2, 3; and 1, 53, n.11. Siena remained independent until the rule of Cosimo de' Medici in 1555, but see *Florentine Histories,* 7, 32, for Siena's "indignation" against Florence. Lucca never did "end up that way"; see *Florentine Histories* 5, 11.

~ 22 ~

HOW WRONG MEN'S OPINIONS OFTEN ARE WHEN JUDGING IMPORTANT MATTERS

1 How wrong men's opinions often are has been and is still seen by those who happen to witness their deliberations; often, if these are not carried on by outstanding men, they are contrary to all truth. 2 Because outstanding men are considered enemies in corrupted republics (particularly in times of peace), out of envy or other reasons of ambition, people follow either what is deemed right, by general error, or what is put forward by men seeking approval rather than the common welfare. 3 Later, during times of adversity, people discover this error and, out of necessity, turn for help to those who were almost forgotten in times of peace, as we shall discuss fully in its proper place.[1] 4 Some events also occur about which men who do not have much experience of matters are mistaken, since in and of itself the event

contains enough that appears likely so that men believe the things that they are convinced of about them.

5 These things have been said because of what the Praetor, Numisius, persuaded the Latins of after they were defeated by the Romans[2] and because of what many people believed a few years ago when Francis I, the king of France, came to conquer Milan, which was defended by the Swiss.[3] 6 So I say that when Louis XII had died and François d'Angoulême, succeeding to the French throne, desired to restore to his rule the duchy of Milan, which had been seized by the Swiss a few years before with the support of Pope Julius II, he wanted to get help in Italy to facilitate his undertaking. Besides the Venetians, whom Louis had won back over, he tried the Florentines and Pope Leo X, for it seemed to him that his undertaking would be easier if he had won them over: the king of Spain's troops were in Lombardy and the emperor's forces were in Verona. 7 Pope Leo did not give in to the king's wishes but was convinced by those who were advising him (as people have said) to remain neutral,[4] since they indicated to him that in that course of action lay certain victory. For it was not in the Church's interest to have either the king or the Swiss be powerful in Italy, but in order to restore its ancient freedom it was necessary to free it from servitude to both of them. 8 Because it was impossible to defeat either of them, either singly or both together, it was necessary for one to overcome the other and then for the Church and its allies to attack the one that remained victorious. 9 It was not possible to find a better opportunity than the present, since both of them were in the field and the pope had his forces ready so as to be able to show up on the borders of Lombardy near both armies on the pretext of wanting to protect his possessions and to stay there until the battle took place. 10 Because both armies were full of *virtù,* there was reason to think that it would be bloody for both sides and would leave the victor so weakened that it would be easy for the pope to attack and defeat him. That way the pope would come to remain gloriously as master of Lombardy and power broker for all Italy. 11 How wrong this opinion was could be seen from the outcome of the affair: when the Swiss were defeated after a long battle, not only did the papal and Spanish troops not dare attack the victors but they got ready to flee. Even that would not have been of use to them had it not been for either the compassion or the indifference of the king; he did not try for a second victory but settled for making a treaty with the Church.[5]

12 With hindsight this opinion has certain reasons that seem true, but are absolutely contrary to the truth. 13 For it rarely happens that the victor loses a great number of his soldiers: the victor's are killed in the fight, not in flight; in the heat of battle, when men are face-to-face, few of them fall, especially since battles do not last very long most of the time. Even if they do and many of the victors die, the glory that is gained from victory and the terror that it entails is so great that it far exceeds the harm that he might have suffered from the death of his soldiers. 14 Consequently, an army that attacked the victor in the belief that he was weakened would find itself mistaken, unless that army was in such a condition that at any time—before or after the

victory—it could take him on. 15 In this case, depending upon its fortune and its *virtù*, it might win or lose, but the one that had fought earlier and won would have the advantage rather than the other. 16 We know this to be true from the experience of the Latins and the error that Praetor Numisius had and the harm that the people who believed him derived from it. When the Romans had defeated the Latins, he proclaimed all over the country of Latium that now was the time to attack the Romans, weakened by the battle that they had fought with them; that the Romans had been left with a victory in name only,[6] but they had suffered all the other losses as if they had been defeated; and that the slightest force that attacked them once again would be enough to finish them off. 17 So the people who believed him formed a new army and were immediately defeated; they suffered the harm that those who hold such an opinion will always suffer.[7]

NOTES

1. Below, 3, 16.

2. Lucius Numisius, from Circeii, was a praetor of the Latins during a revolt in 340 B.C.; see Livy, 8.3–11. Machiavelli referred to this earlier; see above, 2, 13, n.11, and 2, 16, n.1. After suffering defeat at Vesuvius, Numisius wrongly assumed that the Roman army was debilitated even though it had won. He urged continuation of the war and was soundly defeated at Trifanum.

3. Machiavelli has in mind 1515. Louis XII died 31 December 1514, and the duke of Angoulême, Francis I, succeeded him on 1 January 1515. He sought to restore Milan to his control since France had lost it in 1512 when the Swiss had driven the French from Lombardy. Massimiliano Sforza, the son of Ludovico il Moro, ruled Milan, but the Swiss were in fact the real power, especially after they repulsed a French invasion at the battle of Novara in June 1513 and forced France to withdraw from Italy. Leo X had become pope three months earlier, in March. During the first months of 1515, Francis I consolidated his forces by renewing the Treaty of Blois, originally signed by Louis XII, so Venice would support his designs on Italy. Meanwhile, Francis was opposed by the forces of Maximilian I, the Holy Roman Emperor, Spain under Ferdinand the Catholic, Switzerland, and Milan.

4. On 3 December 1514, Francesco Vettori wrote to Machiavelli requesting a letter with his thoughts on whether or not Pope Leo X ought to side with France, adding, "I should like you to discuss this matter in such a way as if you thought your writing was going to be seen by the pope" (*Friends*, p. 294). Machiavelli obliged with two lengthy analytical letters, dated 10 and 20 December 1514, advising Leo to back Louis XII, whose policies regarding Italy were soon to be followed by Francis I, and not remain neutral (pp. 295–305). Despite the fact that, as Vettori wrote, "both your letters concerning the question have been seen by the pope . . . [and] all were astonished at their wit and praised their judgment" (30 December 1514; p. 307), Machiavelli's advice went unheeded. See also *Prince*, 21, pp. 333; 335, lines 48–65.

5. The French entered Italy in August 1515 and drove the Swiss out of Italy at the two-day battle of Marignano on 13–14 September. On 23 October Francis I concluded a treaty with the pope; see Guicciardini, *Storia d'Italia*, 12, 16.

6. Based on Livy, 8.11.6: *"victoriaeque nomen tantum penes Romanos esse."*

7. Rinaldi calls attention to the fact that this chapter is another in a series of Machiavelli's "polemics" against commonly held beliefs; see above, Book 1, chapters 4, 53, and 58, and Book 2, chapters 10 and 19. This theme is basic to the *Prince;* in fact, most of Machiavelli's writings strive to make readers reexamine long-standing beliefs and assumptions.

~ 23 ~

HOW MUCH THE ROMANS, WHEN JUDGING THEIR SUBJECTS FOR ANY ACTION THAT NECESSITATED JUDGMENT, AVOIDED THE MIDDLE WAY

1 "The situation in Latium was now such that they were unable to tolerate either peace or war."[1]

2 Of all the unhappy states, the unhappiest is that of a prince or a republic brought to the point where it can neither accept peace nor sustain war. In this position are those who are hurt too much by the conditions of peace and if they want to wage war, on the other hand, they are obliged to give themselves as prey to those who help them or be left as prey to the enemy. 3 People get to this point through bad advice and bad courses of action, because, as has been stated above,[2] they have not evaluated their forces carefully. 4 Because a republic or prince that evaluated them properly would hardly be brought to the point the Latins were brought to: when they should not have made a treaty with the Romans, they did so, and when they should not have declared war on them, they did so; thus they managed to act in such a way that the Romans' enmity and alliance were equally harmful to them. 5 So the Latins were defeated and completely overwhelmed first by Manlius Torquatus and then by Camillus, who, after forcing them to surrender and put themselves in the Romans' hands, putting garrisons in all the towns of Latium, and taking hostages from each of them, returned to Rome and reported to the Senate that all Latium was in the hands of the Roman people.[3] 6 Because this judgment is noteworthy and deserves to heeded so princes can imitate it when such opportunities are given them, I want to quote the words that Livy put in the mouth of Camillus. They are evidence of both the way the Romans followed in expansion and how, in their governmental judgments, they always avoided the middle way and opted for extremes.[4] 7 For a government is nothing other than keeping subjects[5] in such a way that they cannot or must not hurt you;[6] this is accomplished either by making oneself completely secure against them, depriving them of any way to harm you, or by benefiting them so that it would be unreasonable for them to desire a change of fortune. 8 All of which can be understood first from Camillus's statement and then from the Senate's judgment about it. 9 His words were these:

> The immortal gods have given you such power in this matter that the decision whether Latium should exist or not is in your hands. Thus, insofar as Latium is concerned, you can assure a permanent peace for yourselves with

> either severity or pardon. Do you wish to take more cruel measures against people who have surrendered or been conquered? You may annihilate all Latium . . . do you wish, by following the example of your forefathers, to enlarge the Roman republic by accepting conquered people as citizens? The material for rising to the heights of glory is at hand. Certainly power that is obeyed gladly is by far the most solid. . . . Therefore, while the minds of these people are stunned in expectation, they must be seized first through either punishment or benefit.[7]

10 This statement was followed by the Senate's decision, and it was in accordance with the Consul's words; so, bringing before themselves town by town all the people who were of importance, the Senate either benefited or destroyed them:[8] to those benefited they granted exemptions, privileges, self-rule, and made them secure in every respect. As for the others, they demolished their towns, sent in colonies, brought them back to Rome, and dispersed them so that they could no longer harm them with arms and plots. 11 As I have said, the Romans never took a neutral course with those of importance.

12 This judgment should be imitated by princes. 13 The Florentines ought to have adhered to it when Arezzo and all of Valdichiana rebelled in 1502;[9] if they had done so, they would have secured their power and made the city of Florence very great and provided it with the lands that it lacks for subsistence. 14 But they used the middle way, which is very harmful when judging men: some of the people of Arezzo they imprisoned, others they fined; they deprived all of them of public offices and their ancient rank; and they left the city intact. 15 If some citizens advised during the deliberations that Arezzo should be destroyed, those who appeared to be wiser were answered that it would be of little honor to the republic to destroy the city, because it would appear that Florence lacked the armed forces to hold it. 16 These are the kinds of reasons that appear true but are not: by the same reasoning one would not execute a parricide or a wicked or troublesome person, since it would be shameful for the prince to indicate that he lacks the power to curb a single man. 17 People who hold opinions like that do not see that individual men and an entire city sometimes sin against a state so that, as an example to others and for his own security, a prince has no other remedy than to destroy it. 18 Honor consists in being able and knowing how to punish it, not in being able to hold it with enormous dangers, because a prince who does not punish someone who does wrong so that he cannot do any more wrong is considered either ignorant or a coward.

19 The necessity of this judgment that the Romans made is further confirmed by the sentence that they passed on the people of Privernum.[10] 20 Here we must note two things in Livy's text: first, what is said above, that subjects have to be either benefited or destroyed; the other, how fruitful greatness of spirit and speaking the truth are when expressed in the presence of prudent men. 21 The Roman Senate was assembled to judge the people of Privernum, who had rebelled and then had been brought back by force into submission to Rome. 22 The people of Privernum had sent many citizens to beg for pardon from the Senate; when they came into its presence, one of them was

asked by a senator "what punishment he thought the people of Privernum deserved."[11] 23 To which the man from Privernum replied: "what is deserved by those who consider themselves worthy of being free." 24 The Consul answered: "if we release you from your punishment, what kind of peace may we hope to have with you?" 25 To which he replied: "if you grant us a good one, then a loyal and permanent peace; if it is a bad one, it will not last long at all." 26 Upon which the wiser part of the Senate, although many grew angry at this, said "the voice of a man had been heard, one born free. Was it credible that any people or even any individual would remain in a painful condition, which he regrets, longer than necessary? A loyal peace exists where its terms are accepted willingly; loyalty could not be hoped for in a place they tried to enslave."[12] 27 And at these words they decided that the people of Privernum should be Roman citizens and they honored them with the privileges of citizenship, saying, "only those whose thoughts are exclusively about freedom are worthy of becoming Romans.[13] 28 This true and generous reply was so pleasing to those of great spirit, because any other reply would have been false and cowardly. 29 Those who believe otherwise about men, especially about those who are accustomed either to be free or to see themselves as free, are mistaken about them; under this error they choose courses of action that are not good for themselves and not apt to satisfy the others. 30 From this arise frequent rebellions and the downfall of states.

31 But to return to our discussion, I conclude both for this judgment and the one passed on the Latins: when one is to judge powerful cities, which are accustomed to living free, they must be either benefited or punished; otherwise any judgment is in vain.[14] 32 And the middle way must be avoided completely, because it is harmful, as it was to the Samnites when they had bottled the Romans up at the Caudine Forks. They refused to heed the advice of the old man who recommended that the Romans should be allowed to depart in honor or they should all be slaughtered; but choosing a middle way, the Samnites disarmed them, put them under the yoke, and let them go covered with ignominy and scorn.[15] 33 So shortly thereafter they realized to their sorrow that the old man's judgment had been right and their decision harmful, as will be discussed more fully in its place.

NOTES

1. Livy, 8.13.2: *"Iam Latio is status erat rerum, ut neque bellum neque pacem pati possent"*; Machiavelli reverses the order of war and peace. For a theory about beginning a chapter with a quotation from Livy and Machiavelli's original intention, see above, 2, 3, n.1.

2. In 2, 10, sentence 1; it has also been a tacit assumption for many of the recent chapters. The examples that follow were discussed above in chapters 4 and 13 of Book 2.

3. Manlius Torquatus defeated the Latins, led by Lucius Numisius, at Trifanum in 340 B.C.; see the previous chapter, note 2. In 338, Lucius Furius Camillus, the grandson of Marcus Furius Camillus, conquered all of Latium; see Livy, 8.13. Martelli notes (*Storici antichi,* pp. 102–103) that the Senate in the following example, used also in the 1503 treatise discussed in the next note, did the opposite of what Machiavelli asserts and discusses his modifications of Livy's text.

4. Early in his career Machiavelli wrote *Del modo di trattare i popoli della Valdichiana ribellati* (How to treat the rebellious populace of Val di Chiana). It is important as an early work revealing what became his characteristic analytical method: to compare and contrast ancient and contemporary examples in order to show what policy decisions ought to be. In this 1503 treatise, the examples are those in this discourse; see sentence 13 below. It and its version of "the words Livy put in the mouth of Camillus" form the linchpin of his early argument that "the Romans once thought that a rebellious population ought to be either helped or crushed, and that every other way was extremely dangerous." As Livy says in this context, "The Latins decided to adopt a middle course and stay in their towns so that the Romans might be provoked and have a pretext for hostilities" (8.13.3). Hence the Romans would follow a diametrically opposed policy. Avoiding such a "middle way" is strongly argued for in the *Prince* and is closely linked to Machiavelli's consistent advice to avoid neutrality; see sentence 11 below and note 4 to the preceding discourse.

5. Translates *sudditi,* normally "subjects," but here it could refer to "subjugated or subject peoples." The word *sudditi* in both Machiavelli and Guicciardini frequently retains this connotation of subjugation.

6. The opening sentence of *Prince,* 1, defines government with a similar emphasis on the authority to command as the locus of political power: "all states and all dominions that have had or now have authority over men" (p. 97, lines 1–2).

7. Livy, 8.13.14–17: *"Dii immortales ita vos potentes huius consilii fecerunt, ut, sit Latium an non sit, in vestra manu posuerint. Itaque pacem vobis, quod ad Latinos attinet, parare in perpetuum, vel saeviendo vel ignoscendo potestis. Vultis crudelius consulere in detitios victosque? licet delere omne Latium . . . Vultis exemplo majorum augere rem romanam, victos in civitatem accipiendo? materia crescendi per summam gloriam suppeditat. Certe id firmissimum imperium est, quo obedientes gaudent. . . . Illorum igitur animos, dum expectatione stupent, seu poena, seu beneficio praeoccupari opportet."*

8. Machiavelli returns to this phrase later in the chapter, sentence 20. This disjunction echoes *Prince,* 3, where Machiavelli writes that "men ought to be either pampered or destroyed: for men can avenge slight injuries, but not severe ones; hence an injury done to a man ought to be such that there is no fear of reprisal" (p. 111, lines 118–121) and sets up his judgment in the next paragraph, sentence 18.

9. In early June 1502, during Cesare Borgia's third campaign to extend his power and that of his father, Pope Alexander VI, in Romagna and central Italy, Vitellozzo Vitelli, one of Borgia's lieutenants, persuaded Arezzo to rebel against Florentine control. King Louis XII of France was also alarmed at the Borgias' grab for power in Italy, so he helped Florence subdue the revolt in August. See above, 1, 38, n.9, and Guicciardini, *History of Florence,* chapter 22.

10. Livy, 8.19–21. This rebellion began in 330 B.C. and was put down in 329; the modern name for the town is Piperno. According to Martelli, this is another example of Machiavelli's distortion of Livy (*Storici antichi,* pp. 103–104).

11. This quotation and the next three are from Livy, 8.21.2–4: *"quam poenam meritos Privernates censeret, Eam . . . quam merentur qui se libertate dignos censent. . . . Quid si poenam remittimus vobis, qualem nos pacem vobiscum habituros speremus? Si bonam dederitis . . . et fidam et perpetuam; si malam, haud diuturnam."* Machiavelli's text reads *fidelem* for *fidam* in the last quotation.

12. Quoted with slight variations from Livy, 8.21.6–7: *"dicere viri et liberi vocem auditam: an credi posse ullum populum aut hominem denique in ea condicione cuius eum paeniteat, diutius quam necesse sit mansurum. Ibi pacem esse fidam ubi voluntarii pacati sint, neque eo loco ubi servitutem esse velint, fidem sperandam esse."*

13. Livy, 8.21.9: *"eos demum qui nihil praeterquam de libertate cogitent* [Machiavelli: *cogitant*], *dignos esse qui Romani fiant."*

14. In *Prince,* 5, Machiavelli eliminates the notion of "benefit" from his argument: "Whoever becomes master of, but does not destroy, a city used to living as a free community may expect to be destroyed by it, because during an insurrection the city can always take refuge in invoking the name of freedom and its traditional institutions, which are never forgotten, whatever the course of time or whatever favors be accorded" (p. 139, lines 28–35).

15. Herrenius Pontius, the father of the Samnite general, gave this advice during the Second Samnite War, 321 B.C.; see Livy, 9.2–3 (particularly 9.3.11, where Livy writes about the *media via*). As he says in the next sentence, Machiavelli will return to this example below, 3, chapters 40–42. As Martelli points out, Herrenius Pontius is not a Roman and hence is not a good example of the assertion in this chapter's title (*Storici antichi,* p. 104).

~ 24 ~

FORTRESSES GENERALLY DO FAR MORE HARM THAN GOOD

1 To the wise men of our day it will perhaps seem to have been ill-considered for the Romans, while trying to secure themselves against the people of Latium and the city of Privernum, not to have thought of building some fortresses to act as a brake to keep them loyal, especially since there is a saying in Florence, quoted by our wise men, that Pisa and other cities like it must be held with fortresses.[1] 2 If the Romans had been like them, they truly would have thought of building them; but since they had a different *virtù,* different judgment, different power, they did not build any. 3 As long as Rome remained free and followed its institutions and constitutions with their *virtù,* it never built any to hold either cities or provinces, but it did save some of those [already] built. 4 Hence, seeing the Romans' procedures in this respect, and that of the princes in our day, I think we should consider whether it is good to build fortresses or whether they do harm or good to those who build them. 5 We must therefore consider whether fortresses are made to defend oneself against the enemy or to defend oneself against subjects. 6 In the first case they are unnecessary; in the second, harmful.

7 To begin by explaining why they are harmful in the second case, I say that when a prince or a republic fears their subjects and their rebellion such fear must first arise from hatred that their subjects bear toward them, a hatred due to their bad behavior; this bad behavior arises either from a belief that

they can be held by force or from a lack of wisdom on the part of those governing them. 8 One of the things that gives rise to the belief that they can be forced is having fortresses looming over them, because the ill treatment that is the cause of hatred arises in great part from the fortresses the prince or the republic has; if that is true, they are far more harmful than useful.[2] 9 For one thing, as has been stated, they make you act more boldly and more violently toward your subjects. Then, there is not so much security inside them as you think, since all the troops, all the violence used to restrain a people amount to nothing, with two exceptions: either for you always to have a good army to put in the field, as the Romans did, or for you to scatter, kill, disorganize, and separate them so that they cannot get together to attack you. 10 Because if you impoverish them, "weapons are left to those despoiled"[3]; if you disarm them, "rage provides weapons";[4] if you slay their heads and you continue abusing the others, the heads are born again like those of the Hydra.[5] If you build fortresses, they are useless[6] in times of peace, because they give you more courage to harm your subjects; but in times of war they are really useless, because they are attacked by both the enemy and your subjects; and it is impossible for them to offer resistance to both. 11 And if ever they were unuseful, it is in our days because of artillery; it is impossible to defend small areas into which someone cannot retreat behind ramparts against its fury, as we have discussed above.[7]

12 I am going to discuss this matter in greater detail. 13 Either you, a prince, want to hold the populace of your city in check with these fortresses or you, a prince or a republic, want to hold a city seized in war in check. 14 I am going to turn to the prince and tell him that, for the reasons stated above, such a fortress cannot be more useless for holding his citizens in check: it makes you more ready and less hesitant to oppress them; this oppression makes them so inclined toward your downfall and inflames them to the extent that the fortress, its cause, cannot then defend you. 15 So a wise and good prince, in order to remain good and not to give either cause or ambition for his sons to become wicked, will never build a fortress; so they will rely not on fortresses but on the goodwill of men. 16 And if Count Francesco Sforza, when he became duke of Milan, was considered wise and nevertheless made a fortress in Milan, I say that in this he was not wise and that the outcome demonstrated that the fortress resulted in his heirs' harm and not their security.[8] 17 Because judging that, thanks to it, they could live in security while oppressing their citizens and subjects, they did not spare any kind of violence; so, having become exceedingly hateful, they lost that state the first time an enemy attacked them. Neither did the fortress defend them nor did it prove at all useful in wartime, and in peacetime it had done them a good deal of harm. For had they not had it and, out of a lack of wisdom, sorely mistreated their citizens, they would have discovered the danger sooner and would have withdrawn from it; then they would have been able to resist the French onslaught more valiantly with friendly subjects without a fortress than with hostile subjects with a fortress. 18 These are of no use to you in any way, because they are lost either through the deceit of those guarding them, through the violence of

those attacking them, or through starvation. 19 And if you want them to be of use to you and to help you to recapture a lost state in which only the fortress is left you, you have to have an army with which you can attack the one who has driven you out. If you should have such an army, you would recapture your state in any case, even if the fortress were not there, and all the more easily for the men's being more friendly to you than they were, since you treated them badly because of [your] pride in the fortress. 20 Experience showed that this fortress in Milan was of no use to either the Sforzas or the French in adverse times; rather, it brought harm and ruin upon them all since because of it they did not think of a more honorable means to hold onto the state.

21 Federigo's son, Guidobaldo, the duke of Urbino, who was reputed such a good general in his day, when he was driven out his state by Cesare Borgia, the son of Pope Alexander VI, and later returned because of an unexpected incident, had all the fortresses that were in the province demolished, judging them to be dangerous.[9] 22 Because he was loved by his men, in respect to them he did not want fortresses; as far as his enemies were concerned, he saw that he could not defend his fortresses, since they needed an army in the field to defend them. So he decided to destroy them. 23 After Pope Julius drove the Bentivoglios out of Bologna, he built a fortress in the city and then had people killed[10] by his governor.[11] 24 So the people rebelled and he quickly lost the fortress; thus the fortress was of no use to him and did him harm, whereas, if he had behaved differently, it would have been of use to him. 25 When Niccolò da Castello, the Vitellis' father, returned to his homeland from exile, he immediately demolished two fortresses that Pope Sixtus IV had built there, judging that the people's goodwill, not a fortress, would maintain him in the state.[12]

26 But the freshest and most noteworthy, in every way, of all the other examples, and suited to showing the uselessness of building them and the usefulness of demolishing them, is that of Genoa, which occurred very recently. 27 Everyone knows how Genoa rebelled in 1507 against King Louis XII of France, who came to reconquer it personally with all his forces.[13] Once he had recaptured it, he built a fortress stronger than any other that has been heard of to the present day. Situated on top of a promontory extending into the sea that the Genoans called Codefà, it was impregnable because of its site and every other circumstance; from it he dominated the entire port and a good portion of the city of Genoa. 28 It then happened in 1512 that, when the French troops had been thrown out of Italy, Genoa rebelled despite the fortress and Ottaviano Fregoso took over its government; with great effort he captured it by means of starvation in the space of sixteen months. 29 Everyone believed, and many people advised, that he should preserve it for a refuge in any incident; but because he was very wise, knowing that it was not fortresses but men's will that kept princes in power, he tore it down. 30 Thus, without basing his power on fortresses but on his *virtù* and wisdom, he kept to it and still does. 31 Whereas it used to take only a thousand infantrymen to change the government of Genoa, his adversaries have attacked him with ten thousand and not been able to harm him.[14] 32 We see then from this example that demolishing a fortress did not harm Ottaviano and building one did not

defend the king. 33 Because when he was able to come into Italy with his army, he was able to recapture Genoa without having a fortress there; but when he was unable to come into Italy with his army, he could not hold onto Genoa even though he did have a fortress there. 34 Therefore it was an expense for the king to build it and shameful to lose it; for Ottaviano, glorious to recapture it and useful to demolish it.

35 But let us come to republics that make fortresses not in their homeland but in the towns that they conquer. 36 And if the above-mentioned example of France and Genoa were not enough to demonstrate this error, I should like Florence and Pisa to suffice. The Florentines built fortresses to hold onto the city and did not realize that if they wanted to hold onto a city that had always been hostile to the name of Florence, that had always lived in freedom, and that had freedom as a pretext for rebellion, it was necessary to observe the Roman way if they wanted to hold onto it: either make it an ally or destroy it.[15] 37 The *virtù* of fortresses was seen on the arrival of King Charles, to whom they surrendered either out of treachery by those guarding them or out of fear of greater harm; had they not existed, the Florentines would not have based their ability to hold onto Pisa on them, and the king would not have been able in this way to deprive the Florentines of the city.[16] And the ways in which it had been kept up to that time by chance would have been enough to hold onto it and probably would not have proven any worse than the fortresses.

38 I conclude therefore that a fortress is harmful to hold onto one's own homeland; to hold onto conquered towns, fortresses are useless. 39 I would only like to cite the authority of the Romans, who tore down walls and did not raise them in the towns that they wished to hold onto by force. 40 And to counter this opinion, if anyone should bring up Tarentum in ancient times, and Brescia in modern ones, places that were recovered thanks to fortresses after a revolt of their subjects, I would answer that Fabius Maximus was sent with his entire army within a year to recapture Tarentum.[17] That would have been enough to recover it even if there had been no fortress, and though Fabius did take that course, if it had not existed he would have taken another one which would have had the same result. 41 What use a fortress is I do not know if, in order to recover a town, you need a consular army and someone like Fabius Maximus as general. 42 That the Romans would in any case have taken it back can be seen from the example of Capua, where there was no fortress and they reconquered it by virtue[18] of their army.[19] 43 But let us come to Brescia. 44 I say that what happened in that revolt rarely happens: that a fortress which remains under your control when the town has revolted has a great army nearby like that of the French. For Monsieur de Foix, the king's general who was with the army in Bologna, when he heard of the loss of Brescia, started off in that direction without delay; arriving at Brescia in three days, he took it back by means of the fortress. 45 However, in order for the fortress of Brescia to be of use, it also needed someone like Monsieur de Foix and a French army to come and relieve it within three days. 46 So this example is not sufficient to refute contrary examples; for during the wars of

our time many fortresses have been taken and retaken with the same fortune that the countryside has been retaken and taken, not only in Lombardy but in Romagna, the kingdom of Naples, and all over Italy.

47 But as for constructing fortresses to defend oneself against foreign enemies, I say that they are unnecessary for people and kingdoms that have good armies and for those that do not have good armies they are useless; because good armies are sufficient to defend themselves without fortresses, fortresses cannot defend you without good armies. 48 The experience of those who have been considered to excel in both government and other matters shows us this, as do the Romans and Spartans: for if the Romans did not construct fortresses, the Spartans not only abstained from them but did not allow walls around their cities, because they wanted the individual man's *virtù* to protect them, not some other defense. 49 Which is why, when a Spartan was asked by an Athenian if the walls of Athens seemed beautiful to him, he answered: "Yes, if they were inhabited by women."[20] 50 So it would sometimes be useful, but not necessary, for any prince who has good armies to have some fortresses on his state's seacoast border to hold off the enemy for a few days until he gets organized. 51 But when a prince does not have a good army, having fortresses throughout his state or at the borders is either harmful or useless. Harmful, because he easily loses them and, once lost, they wage war on him; or else, if they were so strong that the enemy could not seize them, the enemy army leaves them behind and they come to be of no profit. For when good armies do not meet very strong resistance, they penetrate enemy lands without concern for cities or fortresses that may be left behind, as is seen in ancient histories, and as Francesco Maria was seen to do in quite recent times when he left ten enemy cities behind without any concern to attack Urbino.[21] 52 Therefore a prince who can raise a good army can do without constructing fortresses; one who does not have a good army should not construct them. 53 He should rather fortify the city in which he lives and keep it supplied and its citizens in readiness to resist an enemy attack long enough for a treaty or outside aid to free him. 54 All other plans are expensive in times of peace and useless in times of war.

55 So anyone who considers all I have said will recognize that, just as the Romans were wise in every other arrangement of theirs, so were they prudent in the judgment about the Latins and the people of Privernum: not bothering about fortresses, they protected themselves against them in ways of greater *virtù* and wisdom.

NOTES

1. Machiavelli returns to the example from the preceding chapter. In *Prince,* 20, he is equally scornful of the wisdom of this "saying" and those who blindly repeat it: "Our forefathers and those who were thought wise used to say that . . . Pisa [must be held] by fortresses. . . . In the days when Italy was relatively stable, this may have been a sound policy; but I do not believe that today it can be given as a rule" (p. 321, lines 50–57). Inglese and Rinaldi note that the scorn behind "the wise men of our day" is echoed by some of Machiavelli's contemporaries. They cite Isabella d'Este's letter to

her husband, Francesco II Gonzaga, in which she calls on "all the lords and powers in the world to care more for the hearts of their subjects than for fortresses, treasure, and men of arms" (28 February 1495).

2. Machiavelli concludes *Prince,* 20, with a more moderate position about the usefulness of fortresses, in line with the reservations in Guicciardini's *Consideration* of this chapter. But Machiavelli's final words in *Prince,* 20, are: "I disapprove of anyone who, relying upon his fortresses, considers the hatred of his people unimportant" (p. 329, lines 175–177). On 2 June 1526 Machiavelli wrote to Guicciardini that "the most detrimental initiative a republic can undertake is to construct a stronghold, or something that could be quickly fortified, within its precincts" (*Friends,* p, 390); see also end of *Florentine Histories,* 2, 34.

3. Quoted in Latin from Juvenal, *Satires,* 8.124: *"spoliatis arma supersunt."*

4. Quoted in Latin from Vergil, *Aeneid,* 1.150: *"furor arma ministrat."*

5. The word "heads" here translates *capi,* with a potential pun on the word meaning both "head" and "leader." Thus Machiavelli prepares for the image of the Hydra, a monster that grew two heads for every one that was cut off.

6. Some older texts read "useful."

7. In 2, 17, sentence 13.

8. Francesco Sforza ruled Milan from 1450 to 1466; see above, 1, 17, n.7. The Visconti fortress of Porta Giovia was destroyed in 1447, the first year of the "Golden Ambrosian Republic." Sforza had his own fortress, the Castello Sforzesco, constructed on the same site in 1450; it can still be seen in central Milan. After his death in 1466, it did not save his two sons, Galeazzo Maria and Ludovico il Moro. Galeazzo Maria was Milan's tyrannical ruler until he was killed by a conspiracy in 1477 (referred to below, 3, 6, sentence 153). His son, Gian Galeazzo, ruled Milan for three years until his uncle Ludovico wrested control from him in 1480. When Louis XII invaded Milan in 1499, Ludovico fled for his life, but the people recalled him in 1500. The French captured him during the Battle of Novara in April 1500 and he died in prison in 1510. In 1512 the French left Milan, and Ludovico's son, Massimiliano, was installed as a puppet duke until the Sforzas once more were overthrown by the "French onslaught" after the Battle of Marignano in 1515.

9. Federigo da Montefeltro was duke of Urbino from 1444 to 1482; his son, Guidobaldo, ruled until 1508. After the events discussed in note 9 of the preceding chapter and during his third campaign in Romagna, Cesare Borgia captured Urbino in late June 1502. But Guidobaldo was able to regain his city the following October because of the "unexpected incident": a revolt among Cesare's lieutenants (including Paolo Orsini, Vitellozzo Vitelli, Oliverotto da Fermo, and Giampaolo Baglioni) that Machiavelli relates in the *Descrizione del modo tenuto dal duca Valentino nello amazzare Vitellozzo Vitelli . . .* (Description of the method used by Duke Valentino in the murder of Vitellozzo Vitelli . . .). On 8 October the conspirators signed an agreement at Magione, on Lake Trasimeno, to oppose Borgia; the "Description" indicates how Borgia ruthlessly eliminated them at Senigallia during the final days of 1502. Late in October Urbino rose up in favor of Guidobaldo. Toward the end of November, after he made a realistic assessment of Cesare's military strength and the conspirators' inability to help him, Guidobaldo ordered his fortresses in Gubbio and Pergola demolished so that he could center his defense in the fortress of San Leo in Urbino; see Guicciardini, *Storia*

d'Italia, 5, 11. But events forced him to leave Urbino in December, unable to return safely until August 1503, when Cesare's power began to wane after the death of his father, Pope Alexander VI. Machiavelli refers to the destruction of the fortresses on several occasions: in his legation to Cesare Borgia, the dispatch of 23 December 1502; the letter of "fantasies" or "speculations" *(Ghiribizzi)* to Giovan Battista Soderini in 1506 (*Friends,* p. 134), where it is compared neutrally with Francesco Sforza's construction of them for safety, and Borgia's capture of Urbino is mentioned in *Art of War,* chapter 7. Here and in *Prince,* 20 the two examples are contrasted. So, because in the "Description of the method" Machiavelli writes "Guidobaldo . . . had all the fortresses in that state destroyed because, trusting in the people, he did not want the enemy to seize fortresses that he did not think he could defend and, as a result, for his enemies to hold his friends in check," some would argue that, added to Ghiglieri's handwriting analysis, this is evidence that he wrote the "Description" at some point between 1514 and 1517, not in 1503 as previously thought. That passage also correctly notes that Guidobaldo destroyed his fortresses when he was forced to flee Urbino, not, as this sentence implies, when he returned.

10. Translates *assassinare.*

11. As part of Pope Julius II's plan to rid Italy of foreign interests and control, he entered Bologna in November 1506 and forced Giovanni Bentivoglio to hand the city over to him. Julius began to build a fortress near the Porta Galliera in 1507. In 1511 the people revolted against his cruel governors, particularly Cardinal Francesco Alidosi, bishop of Pavia, who arrived in Bologna in May 1508 and took over the fortress. The Bentivoglios were restored to power shortly thereafter and had it demolished. Again, see *Prince,* 20.

12. At several points during his career, Niccolò Vitelli (1414–1486) ruled Città di Castello. He was the father of Paolo and Vitellozzo Vitelli, referred to in the notes to this and the preceding chapter; see *Florentine Histories,* 7, 31; 8, 15. Niccolò returned on this occasion in 1482 with the help of Lorenzo de' Medici (the "Magnificent"). Sixtus IV, Francesco della Rovere, was pope from 1471 to 1484; see *Florentine Histories,* 8, 27.

13. For more on the background of this situation, see above, 2, 21, n.4. *Codefà* literally means "top of the light"; Louis XII's fortress was often referred to as "the Lantern."

14. Members of rival families, the Adornos and Fieschi, attacked Fregoso in Genoa late in 1513; Guicciardini numbers the troops at 3,000, not 10,000 (*Storia d'Italia,* 11, 16). For the complicated history and the question of when Machiavelli wrote this passage, see Walker, 2, nn.9–10, pp. 132–133.

15. Again, the lines from *Prince,* 5, quoted in note 14 of the previous chapter are relevant (p. 139, lines 28–35).

16. Charles VIII invaded Italy in 1494; see above, 1, 38, n.8, for more background. Piero de' Medici's handing over the fortresses of Pisa, Pietrasanta, and Sarzana to the French in 1494 led to the ousting of the Medici from Florence in November.

17. Hannibal took Tarentum in 212 B.C. during the Second Punic War, but the Roman garrison managed to hold onto the fortress until they were liberated three years later; see Livy, 25.7–11; 26.39; 27.15–16, 20, 25. For the irony of sentence 41, see Plutarch, *Fabius Maximus,* 23. For Brescia, here and in sentences 43–47, see above, 2, 17, n.5.

18. Translates *virtù.*

19. After Hannibal captured it in 216 B.C., the Romans reconquered it in 211 after a lengthy siege; Livy, 26. 14.

20. In the *Moralia* of Plutarch there are *Apophthegmata Laconica,* "notable sayings of the Spartans"; the phrase occurs three times but never with reference to Athens. See 190A, where it is said about an unspecified city; 212E, where Agesilaus is the speaker; 215D, where Agis says it about Corinth. Martelli adds Valerius Maximus, 3.7.8, as a source and discusses the nature of Machiavelli's attributions (*Storici antichi,* pp. 105–106).

21. For Francesco Maria della Rovere and Urbino, see above, 2, 10, n.6.

~ 25 ~

ATTACKING A DIVIDED CITY IN ORDER TO CAPTURE IT THANKS TO ITS DIVISION IS A BAD POLICY

1 There was so much division between the Plebs and the Nobility in the Roman republic that the Veians, along with the Etruscans, thought they could take advantage of this division to eliminate the very name of Rome.[1] 2 They formed an army and overran the Roman countryside, so the Senate sent Gaius Manlius and Marcus Fabius against them. When they brought their army near the Veians' army, the Veians repeatedly abused and shamed the name of Rome by both attacks and insults: such was their boldness and insolence that the Romans, no longer divided, became united; going into combat, they overcame them and were victorious. 3 It can thus be seen, as we discussed above,[2] how wrong men may be in choosing their course of action; many times they think they will win something and they lose it. 4 The Veians believed by attacking the divided Romans that they would defeat them, and the attack was the cause of the latter's unity and their own downfall. 5 For most of the time the cause of division in republics is idleness and peace;[3] the cause of unity is fear and war. 6 Hence, had the Veians been wise, the more they saw Rome divided, the more they would have kept war from the Romans and sought to conquer them with the arts of peace.

7 The way is to try to become trusted by a city that is divided and, as long as they do not come to blows, negotiate between the factions as a referee. 8 If they do come to blows, give delayed support to the weaker party, both so as to keep them fighting longer and let them wear themselves out and so large forces do not make them all suspect that you want to conquer them and become their prince. 9 When this business is handled well, it will almost always manage to reach the outcome that you sought for yourself. 10 The city of Pistoia, as I have stated in another discourse[4] and in another connection, did not come under the republic of Florence by any other ruse than this. Because it was divided and the Florentines supported first one faction, then the other, through no fault of either side they brought it to such a pass that, worn out by that tumultuous way of life, it threw itself spontaneously into the arms of Florence. 11 The city of Siena never changed governments with the support of the Florentines except when their support was weak and inconsiderable.[5] 12 For when it was considerable and strong,

it made the city united in defense of the ruling government. 13 I want to add another example to the ones already mentioned. 14 Counting on their divisions, Filippo Visconti, the duke of Milan, waged war on the Florentines several times, and he always came out the loser; so he had to say, complaining of his campaigns, that the Florentines' follies had made him spend two millions' worth of gold in vain.[6]

15 As has been stated above, therefore, the Veians and the Etruscans were mistaken in this opinion and ultimately were defeated in battle by the Romans. 16 So will anyone be mistaken in the future who thinks he can conquer a people by such means and for such a cause.

NOTES

1. Based on Livy, 2.44.7; the events discussed relate to the Etruscan war, from 480 to 474 B.C., which Livy covers in chapters 44–47. Machiavelli provides more details about this war in the next discourse. The "division" resulted from a proposed measure to alter the distribution of land. In the next sentence, some texts read Gnaeus for Gaius Manlius, who is mentioned above, 1, 36, n.1.

2. In 2, 22.

3. See above, 1, 6, sentence 34 and n.14.

4. Above, 2, 21, sentences 15–16, and n.5. But see also *Florentine Histories,* 2, 16–21, in which he describes how factional strife spread even to Florence, and *Prince,* 20 (p. 321, lines 50–62), for Pistoia and factional strife. Pistoia was the subject of several early works Machiavelli wrote in 1501 and 1502: *Ragguaglio delle cose fatte dalla repubblica fiorentina per quietare le parti di Pistoia* (Report on the things done by the Florentine republic to ally the factions of Pistoia) and his *De rebus pistoriensibus* (Concerning Pistoian matters) consisting of *Sommario della città* (Summary of the city) and *Sommario del contado* (Summary of the surrounding countryside).

5. Although these two cities were frequently at loggerheads (see *Florentine Histories,* 7, 32; 8, 16), what Machiavelli is alluding to is not clear. He may have in mind an event occurring in March 1516: Pandolfo Petrucci, who ruled Siena from 1487 to 1512 and to whom Florence had sent Machiavelli as head of legations in 1501 and 1503, abdicated his rule over the city in favor of his son, Borghese, in 1512. Four years later Rafaello Petrucci, the bishop of Grosseto, was supplied with 200 lancers and 2000 infantrymen by Pope Leo X; he drove Borghese out, and the pope appointed Lorenzo de' Medici as condottiere of Siena; see Guicciardini, *Storia d'Italia,* 12, 18. (Rinaldi believes that this is the event Machiavelli had in mind.) Lorenzo, the grandson of Lorenzo the Magnificent, then became duke of Urbino in October 1516; it was to him that Machiavelli dedicated *The Prince.*

6. Filippo Visconti attacked Florence on several occasions: from 1424 until his defeat at Maclodio in October 1427; from 1430 until a peace was brokered in April 1433; from 1436 to 1440 with the Florentine victory at Anghiari—illustrated by Leonardo in a fresco for the Palazzo Vecchio in Florence, which survives only in Rubens's sketch of its center section. For more on Visconti, see also above, 2, 18, n.13. The duke began another war with Florence in 1446, but he died in August of the following year. Machiavelli points out the dangers of "counting on . . . divisions" to form policy in *Prince,* 20: "Such policies, moreover, are indicative of weakness in the prince:

a vigorous princedom never allows itself such divisiveness—divisiveness that is of value to a prince only in peacetime, since its use facilitates control over his subjects; but wartime points up the fallacy of such a policy" (pp. 321; 323, lines 73–79).

~ 26 ~

INSULTS AND ABUSE AROUSE HATRED AGAINST THOSE USING THEM WITHOUT ANY BENEFIT TO THEM

1 I believe that to refrain from either threatening or insulting anyone with words is one of the wisest things men do, because neither of them deprives your enemy of strength, but one makes him more wary and the other makes him hate you more and plan more zealously to attack you. 2 This can be seen from the example of the Veians, who were discussed in the preceding chapter. To the injury of war against the Romans they added the shame of words, from which every wise commander should make his soldiers refrain. For these are things that inflame the enemy and excite him to vengeance and, as has been stated, in no way hinder him from attacking; so they are all weapons that turn against you. 3 A notable example of this occurred in Asia, where Kavadh, the Persians' general, had been encamped for a long time at Amida and, weary of the tedium of the siege, had decided to leave.[1] As he was striking his camp, the townspeople all appeared on the walls; made arrogant by victory, they spared no kind of insult, slandering, blaming, and castigating the enemy as contemptible and craven. 4 As a result Kavadh, provoked, changed his mind; going back to the siege, his indignation at the insult was so great that within a few days he took and sacked them. 5 The same thing happened to the Veians: as has been stated, it was not enough for them to wage war on the Romans, they also slandered them with words; going right up to the camp's palisade to insult them, they provoked them much more with words than with arms. The soldiers, who had fought unwillingly before, compelled the Consuls to give battle, so the Veians bore the penalty of their own arrogance, like those mentioned above.[2]

6 Therefore good princes of armies and good governors of republics have to take every necessary step so that these insults and accusations are not made either in the city or in their armies, either among themselves or against the enemy. For when made against the enemy, the disadvantages mentioned above result, and when made among themselves the results would be worse, if they are not prevented, as wise men have always prevented them. 7 When the Roman legions left in Capua conspired against the Capuans, as will be recounted in its place,[3] this conspiracy led to sedition and was then put down by Valerius Corvinus; among the other stipulations that were made in the treaty, very grave punishment was ordered for those who might ever reproach any of those soldiers for their sedition.[4] 8 In the war against Hannibal, Tiberius Gracchus was made commander over a certain number of slaves the Romans had armed for lack of sufficient manpower; among the first things he ordered was capital punishment for whoever reproached any of

them for their slavery.[5] 9 As was stated above, the Romans considered insulting men and reproaching them for anything shameful such a harmful thing, because nothing so inflames their minds or generates greater disdain, whether it be said in truth or jest. 10 "For harsh jokes, when drawn too much from the truth, leave a bitter memory behind."[6]

NOTES

1. Kavadh was the Sassanid king of Persia from 481 to 531. To drive the Romans from Asia, he twice waged war against them: from 503, when he captured Amida in Mesopotamia, to 505; and again from 524 to 531. See Procopius, *De bello Persico,* 1.17.

2. Machiavelli continues his analysis of the events discussed in note 1 to the previous chapter, especially Livy, 2.43–45. His phrase "like those mentioned above" refers to the inhabitants of Amida.

3. In his discussion of conspiracies below, 3, chapter 6, sentences 188–191. He has already referred to this: see above, 2, 19, n.12.

4. See Livy, 7.38–42 and 41.3 for the "stipulation."

5. A reference to the situation after Rome's stinging defeat at the battle of Cannae in 216 B.C. during the Second Punic War. Tiberius Gracchus, who commanded a force of eight thousand slaves, was a great uncle of the tribune who advocated changing the Agrarian Laws: see Guicciardini's *Consideration* of Machiavelli's *Discourse,* 1, 5, n.2. See Livy 23.25, as well as 22.57, and 24.14–16, though Livy does not specify "capital punishment"; see Martelli, *Storici antichi,* p. 107.

6. Quoted in Latin: *"Nam facetiae asperae, quando nimium ex vero traxere, acrem sui memoriam relinquunt,"* adapted from a comment about Nero in Tacitus, *Annals,* 15.68: *"ille ferociam amici metuit, saepe asperis facetiis inlusus, quae ubi multul ex vero traxere, acrem sui memoriam relinquunt."*

~ 27 ~

WINNING SHOULD BE ENOUGH FOR WISE PRINCES AND REPUBLICS, BECAUSE WHEN IT IS NOT THEY USUALLY LOSE OUT[1]

1 Using disparaging words against the enemy usually arises from insolence that victory or a false hope of victory gives you; false hope makes men err not only in words but also in deeds. 2 Because whenever this hope enters men's hearts, it makes them go too far and usually lose the opportunity to gain a sure good, hoping to get an unsure better. 3 And because this is a question that deserves consideration, since men are very often mistaken about it to the harm of their state, I think I should examine it in detail, with ancient and modern examples, since it cannot be examined so clearly by reasons.

4 After he defeated the Romans at Cannae, Hannibal sent his envoys to Carthage to announce the victory and ask for aid.[2] 5 The Senate debated what should be done. 6 Hanno, an old, prudent Carthaginian citizen, advised that they should use this victory wisely to make peace with the Romans, since

they could have it on honorable terms, because they had won, and they should not expect to be able do so after a defeat. For the Carthaginians' intent ought to be to show the Romans that they were capable of fighting them, and, since they had won a victory over them, they should not seek to lose it out of hope for a greater one. 7 This course of action was not taken, but later, when the opportunity was lost, the Carthaginian Senate indeed realized that it was wise. 8 When Alexander the Great had already taken all the East, the republic of Tyre, in those days a noble and powerful city because, like Venice, it was on the water, realized Alexander's greatness.[3] They sent emissaries to tell him that they wanted to be his loyal servants and grant him whatever obedience he wanted, but that they would not accept either him or his troops inside the town. Whereupon Alexander, indignant that a city wished to close gates that all the world had opened to him, rejected them and, not accepting their conditions, went to camp there. 9 The town was on the water and very well supplied with provisions and other necessary supplies, so after four months Alexander realized that one city was taking more time from his glory than many other conquests had. He decided to try for a treaty and grant them what they had requested for themselves. 10 But the people of Tyre had become arrogant: not only would they not accept the treaty but they slaughtered those who came to discuss it. 11 Indignant at this, Alexander set to storming it with such force that he took it, demolished it, and slaughtered and enslaved its men.

12 In 1512 a Spanish army came into Florentine territory to restore the Medici in Florence and raise money from the city; they had been brought there by citizens from within who had given them hope that, as soon as they were on Florentine territory, they would take up arms in support of them.[4] But once the Spanish had come onto the plain and discovered no one, and being short of supplies, they tried for a treaty; the people of Florence, made arrogant by this, did not accept it. From this resulted the loss of Prato and the downfall of the Florentine government.

13 Therefore princes who are attacked can make no greater mistake, when the attack is done by men far more powerful than they are, than rejecting any treaty, particularly when it is offered to them. For no offer will ever be so abject that there is not somewhere within it some good for those who accept it, and there will be some part of victory for them in it. 14 Because it should have been enough for the people of Tyre that Alexander accepted conditions that he had first refused and their victory was considerable when they had made so great a man with arms in hand stoop to their wishes. 15 It should have been enough for the Florentine people too; if the Spanish army gave in to some of their wishes and did not fulfill all of its own, theirs was quite a victory. For the army's intention was to change the government in Florence, end its allegiance to France, and squeeze money out of it. 16 If the Spanish army had gotten two out of three things (that is, the last two) and one remained for the people (that is, the preservation of their government), there was within each some honor and some satisfaction.[5] 17 And the people should not have cared about those two things since they remained alive; and even if they foresaw a greater and almost certain victory, they should not have wanted to put it

in any way into the discretion of Fortune, since their last chance was at stake. No prudent man will ever risk that unless he is forced to.

18 Hannibal left Italy, where he had spent sixteen years in glory, because the Carthaginians recalled him to come to his country's aid.[6] He found Hasdrubal and Syphax defeated, and he found the kingdom of Numidia lost and Carthage pushed back within the limits of its walls, with no other recourse except him and his army. 19 Realizing that this was his country's last chance, he did not want to put it at risk until he had tried every other remedy. He was not ashamed to sue for peace, as he figured that if his country had any hope it was in that and not in war; then, when peace was denied him, he did not wish to fail to fight even if he was to lose, figuring that he might still win or, if he lost, lose gloriously. 20 And if Hannibal, who had such great *virtù* and his own army intact, first sought peace instead of battle, when he saw that, by losing, his country would become enslaved, what should another man of less *virtù* and experience than he do? 21 But men make this mistake: they do not know how to fix limits to their hopes; counting on them, without taking measure of themselves otherwise, they are overcome.

NOTES

1. To allay Florentine sentiment against heavy war levies, Giovanni di Bicci de' Medici, the first of the Medici line to acquire great wealth and political influence (1360–1429), pointed out that "he who is satisfied with half a victory will always be better off, because those who wish to triumph completely often lose out" (*Florentine Histories,* 4, 14). Compare both of these remarks with this chapter's last sentence. For the construction of this chapter's argument and its parodic relation to a Scholastic disputation, see below, Guicciardini's *Consideration* of 2, 12, n.1.

2. Based on Livy, 23.11–13; the Roman defeat at Cannae occurred in 216 B.C. Hanno was a leader of the aristocratic party in Carthage. During the Second Punic War, 218 to 201 B.C., he sought peace with Rome and opposed Hamilcar Barca and Hannibal.

3. Based on Quintus Curtius Rufus, *De rebus gestis Alexandri Magni,* 4.2–19; Plutarch, *Alexander* mentions the seven-month siege of the Phoenician city of Tyre in 332 B.C. after Alexander's decisive victory in 333 over Darius and the Persians at Issus in ancient Cilicia (near the modern city of Iskenderun in Lesser Armenia).

4. After the French victory at the Battle of Ravenna in April 1512, the tide turned as the Swiss joined Julius II's Holy League with Spain. The enemies of Florence met at Mantua in August and decided to drive Piero Soderini out of Florence and restore the Medici. Spanish forces under Ramón de Cardona, the viceroy of Naples, left Bologna and advanced toward Barberino, about fifteen miles from Florence, where "he descended from the mountains" (Guicciardini, *Storia d'Italia,* 11, 3) so that he would be "on the plain" to attack Florence. "The loss of Prato" occurred with its sack on 29 August, and Machiavelli's hand-picked militia, to his mortification, fled the city after putting up little resistance. The "downfall" of the Florentine republic and the end of Machiavelli's political career came with the surrender of Florence and the overthrow of Soderini on 31 August. Giuliano de' Medici entered Florence on the evening of the next day.

5. Guicciardini is quite emphatic on this point: "[Ramón de Cardona] sent one of his men to indicate that it was not the league's intention to change either the city's government or freedom, provided that, for Italy's security, [Soderini] be removed as gonfaloniere. The league wished that the Medici might be able to enjoy their native city, not as heads of the government, but as private citizens and, in all matters like any other citizens, to live under the laws and public officials" (*Storia d'Italia,* 11, 3).

6. Toward the end of the Second Punic War, Scipio Africanus Major drove the Carthaginians out of Spain in 206 B.C. He invaded Africa in 204 and defeated Hasdrubal, the son of a Carthaginian general named Gisco (not Hannibal's brother), and Syphax, a Numidian general and king allied with Carthage, in 203. After a short-lived armistice, fighting resumed, and the Second Punic War ended in 202 with the Battle of Zama and Scipio's defeat of Hannibal. See Livy, 30.9; 19–20; 29–31; see also Polybius, 15, 6–8. Martelli argues that the example from Livy proves the opposite of what Machiavelli asserts (*Storici antichi,* pp. 108–109).

~ 28 ~

HOW DANGEROUS IT IS FOR A REPUBLIC OR A PRINCE NOT TO AVENGE AN INSULT MADE TO THE COMMUNITY OR AN INDIVIDUAL

1 What insults can do to men can be easily recognized by what happened to the Romans when they sent the three Fabii as envoys to the Gauls who had come to attack Etruria, and specifically Clusium.[1] 2 Because the people of Clusium had sent to Rome for aid against the Gauls, the Romans sent ambassadors to the Gauls, who were to tell them in the name of the Roman people to refrain from waging war against the Etruscans. 3 When these envoys, who were more suited to acting than speaking, were on the site and the Gauls and the Etruscans started to fight, they were among the first to fight against the former; so it happened that, since the Gauls recognized them, all the wrath that they felt toward the Etruscans was turned against the Romans. 4 This wrath intensified when the Gauls complained to the Roman Senate through their ambassadors about this outrage and asked that the previously mentioned Fabii be given to them in satisfaction for the insult; not only were they not handed over to them or punished in some other way but, when the electoral assemblies took place, the Fabii were made Tribunes with consular power. 5 So because the Gauls saw those who were supposed to be punished given honors, they considered that it had all been done to disparage and humiliate them and, inflamed with wrath and indignation, they attacked Rome and took it, except for the Capitol. 6 This disaster befell the Romans solely because of their failure to observe justice, for when their envoys had sinned "against the law of nations"[2] and should have been punished for it, they were given honors. 7 Hence it must be considered how every republic and every prince ought to make sure not to commit any such outrage, not only against people in general but even against an individual. 8 Because if a man is deeply

insulted either by the community or by a private citizen and is not avenged to his satisfaction, if he lives in a republic, he seeks revenge, even if it means the latter's downfall; if he lives under a prince and has any greatness of spirit in him, he will never be placated until he has somehow had his revenge on him, even if he should see his own harm in it.

9 To validate this there is no finer or truer example than that of Philip of Macedon, Alexander's father.[3] 10 In his court he had Pausanias, a handsome young Nobleman, with whom Attalus, one of the leading men in Philip's court, was in love; having sought several times to get him to yield to him and finding him averse to such things, Attalus decided to get through deceit and by force[4] what he realized he could not get by other means. 11 He gave a formal banquet to which Pausanias and many other noble barons came. Once everyone was full of food and wine, he had Pausanias seized and brought to him tied up; not only did he satisfy his lust by force but also, humiliating him even more, had many of the others shame him in a like manner. 12 Pausanias complained several times about this outrage to Philip who, after keeping him for a time in hope of being avenged, not only did not avenge him but put Attalus in charge of a province of Greece. Therefore Pausanias, seeing his enemy honored and not punished, turned all his wrath not against the one who had committed the outrage but against Philip, who had not avenged him. 13 One festive morning on the wedding day of Philip's daughter, whom he had married to Alexander of Epirus, as Philip was going to the temple to celebrate it, Pausanius killed him between the two Alexanders, his son-in-law and his son.[5] 14 This example is quite similar to that of the Romans and worthy of note to anyone who governs: he must never have so little consideration for a man as to believe that, if he piles insult upon insult, the one who is insulted will not think of avenging himself no matter what the danger and harm may be to him.

NOTES

1. Livy, 5.35–38; this event occurred during the Gallic invasions in 390 B.C.; but also see Diodorus Siculus, 14, 113–114. The three Fabii were sons of Marcus Fabius Ambustus, sent as envoys to the Gauls who were threatening Rome's allies, the Etruscans of modern-day Chiusi. See above, 1, 39, n.5, for a definition of the "Tribunes with consular power" in sentence 4.

2. Livy, 5.36.6: *"Ibi iam urgentibus Romanam urbem fatis legati contra ius gentium arma capiunt"* (Contrary to the law of nations *[ius gentium],* the envoys took up their weapons, impelled by the fate that was even then urging Rome to its doom). The concept of the "law of nations" has become a standard of international law; ambassadorial neutrality has long been assumed as part of the laws governing commercial relations.

3. This example, which occurred in 336 B.C., is based on Justin, 9.6; but see Martelli, *Storici antichi,* pp. 110–112.

4. Translates *con inganno e per forza,* which is close to the notion of force and fraud in earlier chapters.

5. Alexander I was king of the Molossi, a group of tribes in Epirus, an area of

northwestern Greece, from 342 to 330 B.C. His brother-in-law, Philip II of Macedon (who was married to Alexander's sister, Olympias of Epirus, Alexander the Great's mother) placed him on the throne; Alexander increased the prestige of Epirus and saw his kingdom united with Macedon through his marriage to Cleopatra, Alexander the Great's sister.

~ 29 ~

WHEN FORTUNE DOES NOT WANT MEN TO OPPOSE HER PLANS, SHE BLINDS THEIR MINDS[1]

1 If we consider well the course of human affairs, we shall often see things arise and events come to pass for which heaven[2] did not at all want us to provide for. 2 And when what I am saying occurred in Rome (where there was so much *virtù,* religion, and order), then it is not surprising if it happens much more often in a city or a country lacking the above-mentioned things. 3 And because this passage is quite apt for demonstrating the power of heaven over human affairs, Livy demonstrates it at length and with very effective words.[3] He says that since for some reason heaven wanted the Romans to realize its power, first it caused the Fabii who went as emissaries to the Gauls to make a mistake and, thanks to their actions, provoked them to declare war on Rome. 4 Then it ordained that nothing worthy of the Roman people should be done in Rome to prevent that war by first having ordained that Camillus, who was the one and only person who could remedy such ill,[4] should have been sent into exile in Ardea. 5 Then, as the Gauls came toward Rome, those who had many times named a Dictator to deal with the attack of the Volscians and innumerable other enemies did not name one when Gauls came.[5] 6 Furthermore they drafted their soldiers feebly and without any extraordinary diligence, and they were so slow to take up arms that they were barely in time to engage the Gauls on the Allia River, ten miles from Rome. 7 There the Tribunes made their camp without any of the usual diligence, without scouting the place first and without surrounding themselves with a moat and a palisade, without recourse to any remedy, human or divine. 8 In drawing up their battle order, they formed loose and weak ranks so that neither the soldiers nor the commanders did anything worthy of Roman discipline. 9 Then they fought without any bloodshed, for they fled before they were attacked: the majority ran off to Veii, the rest withdrew to Rome and went into the Capitol without otherwise going to their houses. So the Senate, without thinking of defending Rome, did not even so much as shut the gates; some of them fled and some went with the others to the Capitol. 10 In defending that, however, they did observe some standards that were not disorderly: they did not clutter it with useless men; they stored all the grain that they could in it so that they could withstand a siege; and the majority of the useless throng of old men, women, and children fled into neighboring towns while the rest stayed in

Rome, prey to the Gauls. 11 Consequently, anyone who had read of the deeds accomplished by those people so many years before and then read about later times would not in any way have believed that they were the same people.[6]

12 After Livy has told of all the above-mentioned disorders, he concludes by saying, "To such an extent does Fortune blind men's minds when she does not want her attacking strength to be opposed."[7] 13 Nothing could be truer than this conclusion, so men who live normally, in great adversity or prosperity, deserve less praise or less blame.[8] 14 Because most of the time one can see they have been brought to disaster or to greatness by some great advantage that heaven has granted them, giving or depriving them of the opportunity to be able to act with *virtù*. 15 Fortune is right to do this, for if she wants to bring about great things she selects a man who is of such spirit and such *virtù* that he recognizes the opportunities that she offers him.[9] 16 In the same way, if she wants to bring about great disasters, she elevates men to further such disaster.[10] 17 Were there anyone who might stand in the way, either she kills him or she strips him of all means to be able to accomplish some good.

18 We recognize quite plainly from this text that, in order to make Rome greater and bring it to the greatness it attained, she judged it necessary to defeat it (as we shall discuss at length at the beginning of the next book),[11] but she did not wish indeed to destroy it completely. 19 And we can see that she had Camillus exiled for this but not killed; she had Rome taken, but not the Capitol; she ordained that the Romans would not have any good ideas at all for protecting Rome, but then for defending the Capitol they overlooked no good arrangement at all. 20 In order for Rome to be captured, she had the majority of its soldiers who were defeated at the Allia flee to Veii, and thus she cut off all the ways to defend the city of Rome. 21 In ordaining this she prepared everything for its recovery, since she had brought a whole Roman army to Veii and Camillus to Ardea so as to be able to form a great vanguard under a commander untainted by any shame of defeat and whose reputation was intact for the recovery of his homeland.

22 To confirm the matters discussed, it would be good to cite some modern examples,[12] but because I do not deem them necessary, since this can satisfy anyone, I shall leave them out. 23 I do affirm once again that it is quite true, as all histories show, that men can comply with Fortune but they cannot oppose her; they can weave her warps but cannot break them.[13] 24 Of course they must never give up: since they do not know her purpose and she travels by oblique and unknown paths, they always should have hope and, while hoping, not give up in the face of any Fortune and any travail they find themselves in.[14]

NOTES

1. Compare this title with this chapter's inspiration: the quotation from Livy, 5.37.1, in sentence 12. Compare the sentence following with what Machiavelli says in the first paragraph of his *Life of Castruccio Castracani:* "since Fortune wants to show the world that it is she, and not prudence, who makes men great, she shows her strengths at a time when prudence can play no part, but rather everything must be acknowledged as being from her."

2. Translates *i cieli*. The analogy with *fortuna* is clear in the context of the argument in these chapters, especially when seen in light of "fate" in the quotation from Livy, 5.36.6, quoted in note 2 of the previous chapter.

3. Again, the Livy quotation in sentence 12 below.

4. Marcus Furius Camillus was often considered the savior and second founder of Rome because he drove back attacks from the Etruscans and Gauls. His exile, provoked by a charge from a tribune of the people, is recounted in Livy, 5.32–33. Ardea was the main city of the Rutuli in Latium; it served as Latium's port even though it was three miles from the sea.

5. Livy, 5.37; the rest of this example, with its series of disastrous decisions that clearly upsets both Livy and Machiavelli, closely parallels and often paraphrases chapters 37 to 40.

6. Despite Machiavelli's close paraphrase, this is his conclusion, not Livy's.

7. Quoted in Latin, with two slight alterations, from Livy 5.37.1: *"Adeo obcaecat animos fortuna, cum vim suam ingruentem refringi non vult"*; see Martelli, *Storici antichi,* pp. 113–114. If we were translating this sentence in Machiavelli's terms, we would suggest *virtù* for Livy's *vim*.

8. With this notion that when an individual lives and acts normally within a context that exhibits "great adversity or prosperity" that person is less responsible for the result of what is done, compare Guicciardini's statement: "All cities, all governments, and all kingdoms are mortal; everything, either by nature or by accident, ceases and ends at some point. Therefore a citizen who is alive during his country's final stages should not so much mourn its wretched state and call it misfortunate as mourn himself: what befell his country was bound to happen, but to be born at the moment when such wretchedness had to occur was his misfortune" (*Ricordi,* C. 189). For thoughts similar to Machiavelli's in this sentence, Rinaldi cites a speech by an "older and wiser" man in Lucca; see *Florentine Histories,* 5, 11.

9. As in his *capitolo "Di fortuna,"* Machiavelli emphasizes Fortune's power, "her natural power drives every man and her realm is always violent unless extreme *virtù* extinguishes her" (vv. 13–15). Furthermore, "She arranges time as it suits her: she raises this one up, she pulls that one down—without pity, without law or reason" (vv. 37–39). However, contrasting the careers of Francesco Sforza and Cesare Borgia (*Prince,* chapter 7), he illustrates the "methods of becoming a prince—through *virtù* or Fortune" (p. 157, lines 38–39); whereas in chapter 25 he writes, "the prince who depends completely on Fortune collapses in proportion to her fickleness" (p. 365, lines 49–51).

10. *Prince,* 25, begins: "I am not unaware that many men have been, and still are, convinced that worldly affairs are controlled by Fortune and God so that even prudent men are unable to rule them and have, indeed, no remedy against them. . . . At times . . . I myself am somewhat disposed to such a belief. Nevertheless, since our free will ought not to be destroyed, I think it may well be true that Fortune is the mistress of half of our actions, but that even so she leaves control of the other half—or nearly that much—to us" (pp. 361; 363, lines 1–5, 11–18). There then follows his famous comparison of "Fortune to one of those impetuous rivers," concluding with the assertion that "Fortune . . . shows her power in places where no *virtù* has been marshaled to resist her; she directs her onslaught to those places where embankments and dams have not been constructed to resist her" (p. 363, lines 31–34).

11. Below, 3, 1, in which he interprets the Gauls' invasion as one of the external events that brought Rome back to its original principles (see sentences 9–11).

12. This is what he does in his famous *Ghiribizzi* letter to Giovan Battista Soderini, 13–21 September 1506, important in this context for its discussion of Fortune. "Because it is not customary to bring in the Romans as evidence," he cites examples from recent and contemporary Italian history: Lorenzo de Medici, Giovanni Bentivoglio, the Vitelli, Guidobaldo da Montefeltro, Francesco Sforza, and, obliquely, Pope Julius II; see *Friends,* pp. 134–136.

13. Machiavelli develops an effective metaphor that may reflect a play on the words "good arrangement" *(buono ordine)* of sentence 19 and "warps" *(orditi)* here. Inglese points out that a weaver first stretches the horizontal threads, the warp, and then vertically inserts and intertwines other threads with them, the woof. Thus *fortuna* provides mankind with a basic design that can neither be avoided nor undone at the same time that mankind contributes its actions in completing the final tapestry.

14. As indicated by the number of quotations in the notes above providing comments on *virtù* and Fortune, this chapter is a significant formulation of Machiavelli's position. The issue has been on his mind since the title of 2, 1; for almost thirty chapters his interest has been almost exclusively in *virtù:* that of the Romans clearly overshadows the *virtù* in modern Florence or Italy. Just as in *Prince,* 25, he took care to show that people can control Fortune in some instances, so he emphasizes here that "they must never give up," because they may suddenly find an opportunity for their *virtù* to act effectively. The "good arrangement" of a carefully crafted state is a necessary precondition: it provides the structure within which *virtù* can "oppose" *Fortuna.* See note 18 to the next chapter and Sasso, *Antichi,* 2:280–281.

~ 30 ~

TRULY POWERFUL REPUBLICS AND PRINCES ACQUIRE ALLIANCES NOT WITH MONEY BUT WITH THEIR ARMIES' *VIRTÙ* AND PRESTIGE

1 The Romans were besieged in the Capitol; although they expected help from Veii and from Camillus, because they were driven by hunger they came to terms with the Gauls to ransom themselves for a certain amount of gold.[1] As the gold was already being weighed for this treaty, Camillus arrived with his army; Fortune did this, the historian says, "so that the Romans might not live redeemed by gold."[2] 2 This is noteworthy not only in this respect but also in the ongoing context of the republic's actions, in which we can see that they never acquired towns with money and never made peace with money, but always with their armed forces *virtù*.[3] I do not believe this ever happened in any other republic.

3 Among the other signs by which the power of a strong state can be recognized is to see how it lives with its neighbors. 4 And if it acts in such a way that its neighbors become its tributaries in order to make it their ally, then it is a sure sign that the state is powerful; but if the neighbors, although inferior to it, take money from it, then it is a great sign of its weakness. 5 If you read all the Roman

histories, you[4] will see that the Massaliotes, the Aedui, the inhabitants of Rhodes, Hiero of Syracuse, Kings Eumenes and Masinissa,[5] all of whom were close to the Roman Empire's borders, contributed to expenses and tribute money when Rome needed them in order to have its friendship, seeking from it no other reward than to be defended. 6 The opposite will be seen in weak states.

7 To begin with ours in Florence, in past times when its prestige was greatest[6] there was not a petty lord in Romagna who did not get subsidies from it; in addition, it gave them to the inhabitants of Perugia, Città di Castello, and all its other neighbors.[7] 8 Had the city been armed and strong, everything would have gone the opposite way, because to have its protection many cities would have given it money and sought not to sell their friendship but to buy Florence's. 9 Not only the Florentines but the Venetians and the king of France, who despite so great a kingdom lives as a tributary of the Swiss and the king of England, have lived so basely.[8] 10 All of this results from having their people disarmed and from that king, along with the others mentioned above, having wanted to enjoy an immediate advantage, to be able to plunder the people and avoid an imagined rather than real danger, rather than do things to secure them and make their states happy for all time. 11 If this disorder gives rise to some tranquillity, with time it (of necessity) causes irremediable harm and disaster.

12 It would take too long to tell how many times the Florentines, the Venetians, and that kingdom have ransomed themselves during wartime, and how many times they have submitted to a disgrace to which the Romans were on the point of submitting only once. 13 It would take too long to tell how many towns the Florentines and Venetians have bought; the disorder of this was then evident, and that things acquired with gold cannot be defended with steel. 14 As long as they lived free, the Romans practiced this magnanimity and this way of life; but then when they came under the emperors and the emperors began to be bad and to love shadows more than sunlight, they too began to ransom themselves, first from the Parthians, then from the Germans, and then from other neighboring peoples; and that was the beginning of so great an empire's downfall.[9]

15 Such disadvantages therefore result from having disarmed your people;[10] another greater one results from this: the closer your enemy gets to you, the weaker he finds you. 16 Because anyone who lives in the previously mentioned ways treats the subjects who are within his reign badly and those who are on the borders well in order to have men well inclined to keep his enemies away. 17 From this arises that, in order to keep them farther away, he gives subsidies to the lords and peoples who are close to his borders. 18 Hence it happens that states like these put up a little resistance at the borders, but when the enemy has gotten past them they have no remedy at all. 19 And they do not realize that this way of doing things runs counter to any good order. 20 Because the heart and the vital parts of a body must be kept armored and not its extremities, because it can live without the latter, but if the former is wounded, it dies, these states keep their heart unarmored and its hands and feet armored.

21 What this disorder has done to Florence has been and still is seen every day: once an army crosses its borders and gets close to its heart, it no longer finds any remedy.[11] 22 Not many years ago the same evidence was seen concerning the Venetians; had their city not been surrounded by water, its end

would have been seen.[12] 23 This experience has not been seen so often in France, because it is such a great kingdom that it has few enemies superior to it; nevertheless, when the English attacked the kingdom in 1513, that entire country trembled, and the king himself and everyone else judged that a single defeat could have deprived him of the kingdom and the state.[13]

24 The opposite happened to the Romans, because the closer the enemy came to Rome, the more powerful he found the city in resisting him. 25 When Hannibal invaded Italy, one could see that, after three defeats[14] and the deaths of so many commanders and soldiers, they were able not only to resist the enemy but to win the war. 26 It all resulted from having their heart well armored and taking less account of their extremities. 27 For the foundation of its state was the people of Rome, the Latin nation,[15] the other allied towns in Italy, and their colonies, from which they drew so many soldiers that with them they sufficed to fight and hold onto the world. 28 That this is true can be seen from the question that the Carthaginian Hanno asked Hannibal's emissaries after the defeat at Cannae. After they praised Hannibal's feats, Hanno asked them whether anyone of the Roman people had come to sue for peace and whether any city among the Latin nation or the colonies had rebelled against the Romans; when they answered both these negatively, Hanno replied: "This war is still on as fully as before."[16]

29 From both this discussion and what we have said several times elsewhere, we can therefore see how much difference there is between the way present-day republics act and how the ancients did. 30 We can also see miraculous losses and miraculous gains every day because of this.[17] 31 Because where men have little *virtù* Fortune shows its power greatly; because it is mutable, republics and states are also often mutable and will always be so, until someone emerges who is such an admirer of antiquity that he controls Fortune so that it has no reason to show what it can do at every revolution of the sun.[18]

NOTES

1. Livy, 5.48.8.

2. Machiavelli's Latin, *"ut Romani auro redempti non viverent,"* is adapted from Livy, 5.49.1, which attributes the salvation not to *fortuna* but to the gods and men: *"Sed diique et homines prohibuere redemptos vivere Romanos."* See the discussion in Martelli, *Storici antichi,* pp. 114–116.

3. Livy describes a speech of Camillus that makes this same point in 5.49.3.

4. One of the few instances in the *Discourses* where "you" translates the plural *voi.*

5. See above, 2, 1, nn.27, 29, and 30. The Greek maritime state of Rhodes aided the Roman fleet during Rome's war against Antiochus III, the Great, 192–190 B.C. For Hiero II of Syracuse, see above, the Dedication to the *Discourses,* note 5.

6. Presumably the period when Lorenzo the Magnificent ruled Florence, 1469–1492. In *Florentine Histories,* 8, 36, Machiavelli specifies that the period of Florence's "greatest prosperity" began with its victory over Sarzana in June 1487; Lorenzo died in April 1492. The examples of Perugia and Città di Castello that follow are also mentioned in *Florentine Histories,* 8, 36.

7. The "inhabitants" are not so much the general population as they are the members of the Baglioni family in Perugia and those of the Vitelli in Città di Castello.

8. A reference to various kings of France (Louis XI, Charles VIII, Louis XII, and Francis I) who paid some kind of tribute money. For Francis I and the Swiss in 1515 and 1516, see Guicciardini, *Storia d'Italia,* 12, 18, and for Louis XII and Henry VIII in 1513, see 12, 6; he deals with the earlier French kings in 5, 4. For Machiavelli's analysis of the situation in 1513, see his letter to Vettori of 26 August 1513 (*Friends,* pp. 257–260).

9. In A.D. 217, Emperor Macrinus (Marcus Opellius Severus Macrinus) paid tribute to Artabanus V, king of Parthia, the last of the Arsacids. Members of various Germanic tribes were brought into the Roman army as early as the reign of Augustus; by the time of Caracalla's, A.D. 211–217, government payments to *foederati* were significant enough to be onerous. Eventually, some of the Germanic *foederati* were allowed to occupy outlying areas of the empire. Walker also cites the peace of 348 with the Persians, when part of Armenia was handed over, and the agreements by which various Germanic peoples were allowed to occupy areas of the empire.

10. A constant theme of the *Prince* is a distrust of mercenaries and the need to raise a citizen militia: "Now, at no time has a new prince ever disarmed his subjects. In fact, when he has found them disarmed, he has always armed them: once they have weapons, those weapons become yours. Those men whom you have suspected become loyal, and those who were always loyal remain so: from being subjects, they develop into your supporters" (pp. 317; 319, lines 14–20).

11. Possibly a reference to "the loss of Prato"; see *Discourses,* 2, 27, sentence 12 and note 4.

12. An allusion to Venice's defeat at Vailà (Agnadello) on 14 May 1509; see *Discourses,* 1, 6, n.11 with its cross-references.

13. See *Discourses,* 1, 21, n.4, for the reference to the invasion of Picardy in July 1513 and the Battle of the Spurs on 16 August.

14. Machiavelli here repeats a point, which needs correction, made in *Discourses,* 2, 12, sentence 24; see its note 14.

15. Translates *il nome latino,* which in turn comes from Livy's *socii latini nominis.*

16. Machiavelli recalls an example he used in *Discourses,* 2, 27, sentences 4 to 7; see its note 2. He is paraphrasing, not quoting, Livy, 23.13.2: *"Bellum igitur, inquit, tam integrum habemus, quam habuimus, qua die Hannibal in Italiam est transgressus."*

17. This sentence echoes a phrase from a dispatch to the *Dieci* written 8 February 1508 by Machiavelli, though signed by Vettori, during their mission to the Holy Roman Emperor, Maximilian I, in Germany (*Legazioni e commissarie,* 2:1099); for a similar turn of phrase, see also *Prince,* 12, lines 147–148, p. 229.

18. Inglese reminds us that the relationship between *virtù* and Fortune has shown itself in several guises in Book 2: in chapter 1, *virtù* is a cause of Fortune—see the chapter title and note 21; in chapter 29, sentence 15, Fortune "selects" a person with *virtù,* whereas in chapter 30, sentence 31, it is the man with *virtù* who controls Fortune. See notes 13 and 14 to the previous chapter. Although not in the context of *virtù,* Guicciardini also comments on the power of Fortune: "Whoever thinks it through carefully cannot deny that Fortune has very great power over human affairs. For we constantly see these affairs experiencing very great affects from Fortune's unforeseen circumstances, ones men are powerless to foresee or avoid. Although men's perception and diligence can mitigate many things, nevertheless, they are insufficient by themselves: good Fortune is still needed" (C. 30). See also the quotation from C. 31 below in 3, 9, n.4.

~ 31 ~

HOW DANGEROUS IT IS TO BELIEVE EXILES

1 It does not seem irrelevant to me to discuss among these Discourses how dangerous it is to believe those who have been expelled from their homeland, since those who hold power have to deal with such matters every day—especially since this can be shown with a memorable example that Livy cites in his history, even though it is irrelevant to his main subject.[1] 2 When Alexander the Great crossed into Asia with his army, his brother-in-law and uncle, Alexander of Epirus, came into Italy with troops; he had been sent for by exiled Lucanians, who led him to expect that with their help he might occupy the entire country.[2] 3 So when he came into Italy because of their pledge and expectations, they killed him, because their fellow citizens promised their return to their homeland if they slew him. 4 One should therefore consider how vain are the pledges and promises of those who find themselves deprived of their homeland.[3] 5 Because as far as pledges are concerned it must be realized that any time people can return to their homeland by other means than yours, they will abandon you and join with others, despite any promises they may have made you. 6 As for vain promises and expectations, their desire to return home is so great that they sincerely believe many things that are false and add many things to them cunningly.[4] Consequently, between what they believe and what they say they believe, they fill you with such expectations that, if you rely on them, either you incur futile expenses or you engage in an undertaking that destroys you.

7 I would like the above-mentioned example of Alexander to suffice, along with that of Themistocles of Athens.[5] After he became a rebel, he fled to Darius in Asia, where he promised him so much if he would attack Greece that Darius decided on the undertaking. 8 Later, when Themistocles could not keep these promises, either from shame or from fear of torture, he poisoned himself. 9 And if Themistocles, a most remarkable man, made such a mistake, we must appreciate all the more how much those men who out of less *virtù* allow themselves to be swayed by their will and passion make even more mistakes in these matters. 10 A prince must therefore be slow to undertake things according to the report of a banished man, because most often he is left with either shame or very serious harm. 11 And, because capturing towns by stealth and by intelligence from their inhabitants also seldom succeeds, it does not seem irrelevant to me to discuss it in the next chapter, adding to that in how many ways the Romans acquired them.

NOTES

1. What links Livy's "main subject" to Machiavelli's is the notion of Fortune. Livy ends his account of Alexander of Epirus, which Machiavelli is about to discuss, with the note that it should be included in his history of Rome because of his campaign in Italy, "even though Fortune held him back from attacking the Romans" (*quamquam Romano bello fortuna eum abstinuit* [8.24.18]). See *Discourses,* 2, 28, n.5, for more on Alexander of Epirus.

2. Actually, it was the people of Tarentum (modern Taranto) who asked for his assistance in turning back the threats of neighboring states, chief among which was Lucania. The Lucanians inhabited what today is known as Basilicata, the area north of the Gulf of Taranto between Italy's "toe" and "heel."

3. Livy, 8.24.6, notes that Alexander had a bodyguard of some two hundred Lucanian exiles but that their loyalty was not to be trusted because "their loyalty was likely to change with the change of fortune." Livy then describes how these exiles promised to hand Alexander over dead or alive if the Lucanians would allow the exiles to return home (24.8). See also Thucydides, 6.12, for a reference to exiles interested in successful lies. See the discussion in Martelli, *Storici antichi,* pp. 115–117.

4. Inglese notes that Guicciardini expresses a similar thought in *Storia d'Italia,* 11, 9; but see Martelli, who believes that the political cast given this sentiment is inappropriate for both Machiavelli and Guicciardini (*Storici antichi,* p. 117).

5. For Themistocles, see *Discourses,* 1, 59, n.8. The example following is based on Thucydides, 1.135–138, and Plutarch, *Themistocles,* 23–31. He "became a rebel" when the Athenians persecuted and ostracized him in 471 B.C.; eventually, he went over to the Persian side. The king of Persia to whom he "fled" was not Darius but Artaxerxes I, the son of Xerxes. Ancient accounts are unclear whether he died of sickness or was a suicide and, if the latter, whether because he did not want to betray Athens or because he doubted he could successfully lead a Persian campaign against a revolt in Cyprus. See the discussion of these issues in Martelli, *Storici antichi,* p. 118.

~ 32 ~

IN HOW MANY WAYS THE ROMANS OCCUPIED TOWNS

1 Because the Romans were all prepared for war, they always waged it with every advantage both as to expenditure and as to anything else that is needed for it. 2 This gave rise to their avoidance of taking towns by siege, because they judged this way so expensive and so troublesome that it far surpassed the profit that could be derived from their acquisition. 3 So they thought it was better and more useful to subjugate towns by any other means than besieging them; therefore, in so many wars over so many years, there are very few examples of sieges that they laid.

4 So the ways by which they captured cities were either by storming them or by their surrender. 5 Storming was either by force and open violence or by force mingled with deception. 6 Open violence was either by an attack without knocking down the walls, which they called "attacking the city with a ring"[1] because they surrounded the city with their entire army and attacked it from all sides (and they often succeeded in capturing even a very large city in an attack, as when Scipio took New Carthage in Spain).[2] Or, when the attack was not enough, they addressed themselves to breaking down the walls with battering-rams and other machines of war or they built a mine (in this way they took the city of the Veians).[3] Or, to be even with those who were defending the walls, they built wooden towers or they made earthen embankments against the out-

side of the walls in order to get up to their height on them. 7 In the first case, being attacked on all sides, those who were defending the town against such attacks were in more immediate danger and had more uncertain remedies. For because they needed to have many defenders in every location, either those they had were not enough for them to be able either to manage everywhere or to reinforce one another or, if they could, they were not all of equal courage to resist, and if the tide of battle turned in one place they were all lost. 8 Therefore it turned out, as I have stated, that this method often had a successful outcome. 9 But when it did not succeed right away, they did not often try it again because it was a dangerous method for the army. For extending it over so great an area left it weakened all over, so it was unable to resist a sortie that those within might make, and the soldiers also became disorganized and tired; but for one time and without warning they would try this way. 10 As for breaking down the walls, this was opposed with ramparts, as in modern times. 11 And to resist mines they made a countermine and with this opposed the enemy with either arms or other devices among which was this: they filled vats with feathers, set fire to them, and put them burning in the mine so that their smoke and stench prevented the enemy's entrance. 12 And if they attacked them with towers, they strove to destroy these by fire. 13 As for earthen embankments, they broke the bottom of the wall against which the bank was resting, pulling in the earth that those outside were piling up; so, with the earth being piled up outside and taken away inside, the embankment would not rise. 14 These ways of capturing cannot be tried for a long period, but one must either strike camp or try to win the war by other means (as Scipio did when, going to Africa and having attacked Utica without succeeding in capturing it, he struck camp and tried to defeat the Carthaginian armies)[4] or else resort to a siege, as they did at Veii, Capua, Carthage, and Jerusalem, and towns like those that they took by siege.[5]

15 As for capturing towns by stealthy violence, that occurs as happened at Palaeopolis, which the Romans seized through an agreement with those inside.[6] 16 Many such stormings were attempted by the Romans and others, and few of them succeeded; the reason is that any slightest obstacle breaks down the plan, and obstacles come up easily: 17 either through the plot being uncovered before it is put into action, and it is uncovered with no great difficulty, either through the treachery of those to whom it is communicated, or else through the difficulty of carrying it out, since you have to deal with enemies and people you are not permitted to speak with except under some pretext. 18 But even if the conspiracy were not uncovered in setting it up, innumerable difficulties then arise in putting it into action. 19 Because if you either arrive before the designated time or you arrive later, it ruins everything; if some unexpected noise arises, like the geese of the Capitol,[7] or if the usual routine is broken, the slightest mistake that you make, the smallest failure, ruins the undertaking. 20 Added to this is the darkness of night, which inspires more fear in the people working on those dangerous matters. 21 And because the majority of men who are brought to such undertakings are unfamiliar with the lay of the land and of the places where they have been brought, they get confused, they become cowardly, and they get muddled at the slightest unexpected incident; any trick of their imaginations is

going to make them turn tail. 22 There is no one who has ever been more successful in these fraudulent, nocturnal expeditions than Aratus of Sicyon,[8] who was as good at these as he was cowardly in daytime, open encounters; we can judge this to have been rather because of a hidden *virtù* that he possessed than because these must naturally be more successful. 23 So many of these ways are planned, few of them are brought to a test, and very few of them succeed.

24 As for taking towns by surrender, they give themselves up either willingly or by force. 25 Will arises either from some external necessity that obliges them to seek your protection, as Capua did with the Romans, or from a desire to be well governed, when they are attracted by the good government that a prince exercises over those who have willingly placed themselves in his hands, as did the inhabitants of Rhodes, Massilia, and other such cities that surrendered to the Roman people.[9] 26 As for surrender by force, such force arises either from a long siege, as has been stated above, or from the continual pressure of incursions, pillage, and other bad treatment; wishing to avoid these, a city surrenders. 27 Of all the ways mentioned, the Romans used the last one more than any; and for more than four hundred fifty years[10] they set about exhausting their neighbors with routs and incursions and gaining prestige over them by means of treaties, as we have discussed elsewhere.[11] 28 They always counted on this way, even though they tried them all, but in the others they found either dangerous or useless elements. 29 Because in a siege there is the length and expense; in storming doubt and danger; in conspiracies uncertainty. 30 They saw that they could conquer a kingdom in a single day with the defeat of an enemy army and that they could waste many years capturing a stubborn city by siege.

NOTES

1. Machiavelli's expresses in Latin this method of investing or besieging a city, *aggredi urbem corona;* it is adapted from Livy, 10.43.1: *Prima luce ad moenia omnibus copiis admotis* corona cinxit urbem *subsidiaque firma, ne qua eruptio fieret, portis opposuit* (At dawn he brought all his troops close to the walls and *encircled the city with a ring,* posting a strong group of supporting men to prevent any sally through the gates), and 23.44.3: Itaque coronam oppidum circumdedit, *ut simul in omni parte moenia adgrederetur* (For that reason he surrounded the town with a ring so as to prepare for a simultaneous attack on its fortifications from all sides).

2. Today's Cartagena, a port city in southeastern Spain; Scipio captured it in 210 B.C. See Livy, 26.44–46, as well as a reference to this in *Art of War,* 7, and Martelli, *Storici antichi,* pp. 119–120.

3. As described in Livy, 5.19.9–11, and continued in 21.10–17, when Marcus Furius Camillus ended a ten-year siege of Veii in 396 B.C. This siege was also discussed in *Discourses,* 1, 13; see its note 2.

4. See Livy, 29.34–35; 30.3.5–8. Utica was a north African port northwest of Carthage. Scipio twice failed to capture it toward the end of the Second Punic War: once in 204 and again in 203 B.C.

5. The ten-year siege of Veii lasted from 405–396 B.C.; see note 3 above and cross-reference. The siege of Capua was discussed in *Discourses,* 2, 24; see its note 19. After a lengthy siege, Scipio Aemilianus captured and destroyed Carthage in 146 B.C. at the end

of the Third Punic War. The siege of Jerusalem probably refers to one led by the emperor Vespasian and his son Titus in A.D. 69–70; other commentators suggest a siege in 63 B.C. led by Pompey in an effort to pacify Judea during his reorganization of Asia and Syria.

6. Because the name of the city begins with the Greek root meaning "old," Livy notes that Palaeopolis was the older part of the city of Neapolis, that is, Naples (8.22.5). The siege lasted from 327 to 326 B.C., and the "agreement" is described in Livy, 8.25–26. The syntactical confusion of the next two sentences reflects Machiavelli's own text.

7. See Guicciardini's *Consideration* of *Discourses,* 1, 5, n.2, for this allusion to Manlius Capitolinus and the geese.

8. Aratus of Sicyon (271–213 B.C.) was a general of the Achaean League, a military alliance with Macedonia of twelve towns in the northern Peloponnese. The elements of his character are based on Plutarch, *Aratus,* 10.

9. For Capua, see *Discourses,* 2, 1, n.23; for Rhodes, see *Discourses,* 2, 30, n.5; for Massilia, see *Discourses,* 2, 1, n.30.

10. The 450 years is probably calculated from the traditional date of the establishment of the first republic in 509 B.C. to 59 B.C. when Julius Caesar was first made consul. An alternative would be the period from the traditional founding of Rome by Romulus and Remus in 753 B.C. to 290, the end of the Third Samnite War, when Rome finally controlled the entire Italian peninsula (Vivanti, in his edition of the *Discorsi*). These dates are roughly those of the first ten books of Livy's history.

11. Above, 2, chapters 4 and 6.

~ *33* ~

THE ROMANS GAVE DISCRETIONARY POWERS TO THE COMMANDERS OF THEIR ARMIES

1 When we read this history of Livy's and wish to profit from it, I judge that all the ways of doing things of the Roman people and Senate are to be considered. 2 Among other matters that deserve consideration is to see the authority with which they sent off their Consuls, Dictators, and other army commanders. 3 We can see that their authority was very great and that the Senate reserved nothing to itself but the authority to declare new wars and to confirm peace treaties;[1] everything else was granted to the Consul's judgment and power. 4 For this reason when a war, against the Latins for example, was decided on by the people and the Senate, they granted everything else to the judgment of the Consul, who could either fight a battle or not and attack this or that town as he saw fit.

5 This is confirmed by many examples and in particular by what occurred in an expedition against the Etruscans.[2] 6 For when the consul Fabius had defeated them near Sutrium and intended to pass through the Ciminian forest with the army and enter Etruria, not only did he not consult the Senate but he did not give them any notice of it, even though the war was going to be waged in new, uncertain, and dangerous country. 7 It is confirmed as well by the decisions contrary to this that the Senate made: it learned of the victory

that Fabius had won and feared that he would choose the course of passing through the above-mentioned forest into Etruria; deeming it was a good idea not to attempt such a war and run such a risk, it sent two Legates to Fabius to tell him not to enter Etruria.[3] They arrived after he had already done so and had won a victory, and instead of preventers of the war they returned as emissaries of the conquest and glory that had been achieved.

8 Whoever considers this notion carefully will see it was done very wisely. For if the Senate had wanted a Consul to proceed in a war step-by-step according to what they instructed him, it would have made him less cautious and slower, because it would not have seemed to him that the glory of the victory was entirely his, but [rather] that the Senate took part in it with the advice that he had followed. 9 In addition, the Senate would be obligating itself to try to advise about something that it could not understand, because, despite the fact that in it they were all men with great experience of war, nevertheless, since they were not on the spot and did not know countless particulars that need to be known in order to give proper advice, they would have made countless mistakes in giving it. 10 That is why they wanted the Consul to act on his own and for the glory to be entirely his; they deemed that his love of it would be a check and regulator to make him do the right thing. 11 I have noted this aspect more readily because I see that present-day republics such as Venice and Florence have a different way of thinking; if their commanders, quartermasters, or agents have to set up artillery, they want to be informed and give advice about it. 12 This way deserves the same praise as do the others that, together, have brought these republics to the state in which they currently find themselves.[4]

NOTES

1. This was true from the days of the early kings. Livy, 1.49.7, reports that during his reign, 534–510 B.C., Lucius Tarquinius Superbus broke the custom of consulting the Senate.

2. Quintus Fabius Maximus Rullianus is mentioned in *Discourses,* 1, 31, n.8. The context here, Livy, 9.35–36, is his consulship as commander of the Roman forces advancing to central and northern Etruria through the Ciminian Forest, near modern Viterbo, in 310 B.C. The forest covered a huge "impassable and frightful" area that "hardly anyone except for the general himself was courageous enough to penetrate" *(invia atque horrenda. . . . Eam intrare haud fere quisquam praeter ducem ipsum audebat* [Livy, 9.36.1–2]).

3. Livy, 9.36.14, actually specifies that there were five legates and two tribunes of the plebs; he goes on to note that the emissaries rejoiced *(laetati)* that they were late and so could announce a Roman victory when they returned home.

4. Machiavelli concludes his second book by lashing out at a situation that he personally experienced: the ineffective, inefficient meddling with his plans for a citizen militia by other branches of Florentine government. He also judges the armies of Florence and Venice depleted by prolonged conflict with Emperor Maximilian I, a sentiment Inglese notes Guicciardini echoing in *Storia d'Italia,* 12, 22.

BOOK *Three*

~ 1 ~

IN ORDER FOR A RELIGION[1] OR A REPUBLIC TO ENDURE, IT HAS TO BE TAKEN BACK FREQUENTLY TOWARD ITS ORIGINS[2]

1 That all things in the world have a term to their lives is very true. But the ones that go through the entire cycle that heaven ordains for them are usually those not disordering their body but keeping it so ordered that it either does not change or, if it does change, it is healthy for them and not harmful to them.[3] 2 Because I am speaking of mixed bodies such as republics and religions, I say that those changes taking them back toward their origins are healthy for them. 3 Hence, those that are better ordered and have a longer life can frequently renew themselves through their institutions, or else arrive through some event at such renewal outside of these institutions. 4 And it is plainer than daylight that these bodies do not endure unless they renew themselves.

5 The way to renew them, as has been stated, is to take them back toward their origins. 6 For the origins of all religions, republics, and kingdoms must have some goodness, thanks to which they regain their original prestige and expansiveness. 7 Because this goodness becomes corrupted over the course of time, if nothing happens to take them back to the mark,[4] of necessity it kills off that body. 8 Speaking of human bodies, doctors of medicine say "that every day something gets added that at some point or other requires cure."[5] 9 Speaking of republics, this return toward their origin occurs through either some external event or intrinsic wisdom. 10 As to the former, it can be seen that it was necessary for Rome to be taken by the Gauls in order for it to be reborn and, in being reborn, for it to take on new life and new *virtù,* and for it to take up once again the observance of religion and justice which had begun to become corrupt in it.[6] 11 This can very well be understood from Livy's *History,* where he shows that, when leading the army forth against the Gauls and creating Tribunes with consular power, they observed no religious ceremony.[7] 12 In this same way, not only did they not punish the three Fabii who had fought the Gauls, contrary to the law of nations, but they made them Tribunes.[8] 13 And it can be readily supposed that they began to take less account of the good institutions constituted by Romulus and the other good princes than was reasonable and necessary for maintaining their freedom. 14 This external beating thus occurred so that all the city's institutions might be taken up again and the people might be shown the necessity not only of maintaining religion and justice but also of appreciating their good citizens

and paying more attention to their *virtù* than to the comforts that they thought they lacked because of these good citizens' actions. 15 As we can see, that is exactly what happened: for as soon as Rome was recaptured, they renewed all the institutions of their ancient religion[9] and punished the Fabii who had fought against the law of nations;[10] subsequently they so highly appreciated the *virtù* and goodness of Camillus that the Senate and the others, putting envy aside, placed on him the entire burden of the republic.[11] 16 It is therefore necessary, as has been said, for men who live together under any kind of institution to review themselves often, through either these external events or internal ones. 17 As for the latter, this must arise either from a law, which often calls the men who are in that body to an accounting, or indeed from a good man who arises among them, one who, through his examples and deeds of *virtù*, can have the same effect as an institution.

18 So this good[12] rises up in republics through either the *virtù* of a man or the *virtù* of a law. 19 As for the latter, the institutions that drew the Roman republic back toward its origins were the Tribunes of the people, the Censors, and all the other laws that were passed in opposition to men's ambition and arrogance. 20 These institutions need to be activated by the *virtù* of some citizen who strives courageously to apply them against the power of those who break them. 21 Notable among such actions before the Gauls captured Rome were the deaths of the sons of Brutus, the deaths of the decemvirs, and that of Maelius the Grain Dealer;[13] after the capture of Rome, there was the death of Manlius Capitolinus, the death of the son of Manlius Torquatus, the action of Papirius Cursor against Fabius his Master of the Horse, and the accusation against the Scipios.[14] 22 Because they were exceptional and noteworthy, these things made men be taken back toward the mark whenever one of them occurred; when they began to grow rarer, they also began to give men more room to become corrupt and to cause greater risk and uproar. 23 For there should not elapse more than ten years between one such action and another, because once this time has passed, men start to alter their customs and break the laws; unless something happens to remind them of punishment and rekindle fear in their hearts, there are soon so many delinquents coming together that they can no longer be punished without danger.[15] 24 Those who ruled the Florentine government from 1434 until 1494 used to say in this regard that it was necessary to take back the state every five years, otherwise it was difficult to keep it. They called "taking back the state" putting the terror and fear in men that had been put in them when taking it, since they had at that time punished those who had done wrong, according to that way of life.[16] 25 But because the memory of that beating dies out, men start daring to attempt new things and to speak ill; therefore, it is necessary to provide for this by taking the state back toward its origins.

26 This taking of republics back toward their origin arises also from the simple *virtù* of a man without depending on any law that drives you to any action; nonetheless, they are so prestigious and so exemplary that good men desire to imitate them and bad ones are ashamed of living a life at variance with them. 27 Those in particular who had such good effects in Rome were

Horatius Cocles, Mucius Scaevola, Fabricius, the two Decii, Attilius Regulus, and a few others, who with their rare examples and *virtù* had almost the same effect in Rome as laws and institutions might have.[17] 28 And if the above-mentioned actions, together with these particular examples, had happened at least every ten years in that city, it would of necessity have followed that Rome would never have grown corrupt; but as both of these things began to grow rare, corruption began to multiply. 29 For after Marcus Regulus, no such example was seen there; although the two Catos arose in Rome, there was too great an interval from him to them, and then between the two of them, and they remained so isolated that they could not accomplish any good by their example—especially the last Cato, who, finding the city in great part corrupted, could not make the citizenry improve by his example.[18] 30 And let this suffice as far as republics are concerned.

31 But as to religious organizations, we can see also from the example of our own religion that these renewals are necessary; if Saint Francis and Saint Dominic had not taken it back toward its origin, it would have been completely destroyed.[19] 32 Because through their poverty and exemplification of the life of Christ they brought it back into the minds of men, although it had already died out there. Their new institutions were so powerful that they are the reason that the dishonesty of the prelates and heads of the religion do not cause it to fall. By still living in poverty and enjoying such high standing with the people in the confessional and in their preaching, the prelates make the people understand that it is bad to speak ill of evil, that it is good to live in obedience to them, and that if they do err, to let God punish them. So they do the worst they can, because they do not fear a punishment that they do not see or believe in.[20] 33 This renewal, therefore, has preserved and continues to preserve this religion.

34 Kingdoms also need to renew themselves and bring their laws back to their origins. 35 And what good effect this practice has can be seen in the kingdom of France, a kingdom which lives under laws and institutions more than any other. 36 The *parlements* are what upholds these laws and institutions, especially the one in Paris, which renews them whenever it takes an action against a prince of the realm and condemns the king in its decisions.[21] 37 Up to now it has preserved itself through its steadfast actions against their Nobility; but if at any time it allowed the offenses to go unpunished and they increased, the result would unquestionably be either that they would have to be corrected with great disorder or that the kingdom would dissolve.

38 Therefore it can be concluded that there is nothing more necessary in a society, whether it be a religion, a kingdom, or a republic, than to restore to it the prestige that it had in its beginnings and to strive for this result to be produced either by good institutions or good men and not to have it be produced by an outside force. 39 For although sometimes that is an excellent remedy, as it was in Rome, it is so dangerous that it is in no way to be desired. 40 And in order to demonstrate to anyone how much the actions of individual men made Rome great and produced many good results in that city,[22] I shall proceed to a narration and discussion of them; within their limits this

third book and final part of these first ten books [of Livy] will conclude. 41
Although the actions of the kings were great and noteworthy, nevertheless, since history sets them forth at length, I shall omit them, mentioning only a few things that they did concerning their personal benefit, and we shall begin with Brutus, the father of Roman freedom.[23]

NOTES

1. Translates *sètte.* Rather than specific "sects," Machiavelli means religious institutions with their members; they are analogous here and in sentence 2 to the collectivity of a republic. Rinaldi's notes to this important chapter are particularly helpful in understanding Machiavelli's choice of words and their implications.

2. Translates *ritirarla spesso verso il suo principio.* As Machiavelli's argument unfolds, it becomes clear that he means that the collectivity must from time to time be returned to its original condition with its "original principles," another connotation of *principio.* Because any group risks being corrupted and falling away from the principles that gave it a healthy start, it must be reminded of its origins in order to get it back on its feet again. In sentences 7 and 22 of this chapter he will express a similar thought in a parallel image, *riduca al segno,* to return something to the "mark." In these contexts of health and corruption, the "mark" denotes the standard from which any deviation or degeneration began, and hence would be where a cure should begin. Think of the notational sign § in a musical score that "marks" the beginning or end of a repeated passage.

3. Death is in the nature of things: Machiavelli begins in a vein reminiscent of Lucretius, *De rerum natura,* 2.vv. 1173–1174. The commonplace also exists in Sallust, *Bellum Jugurthinum,* 2.1–2, and Dante, *Paradiso,* 16, vv. 76–80. Machiavelli alludes to it in his *capitolo "Di fortuna,"* v. 121. But not everything lasts the "entire cycle" that heaven has ordained for it, because modifications introduced during adaptation to changing circumstances may have drawn it away from its original—that is, healthy—identity. (Machiavelli provides examples of these modifications above in 1, 17, sentences 12–15, and 1, 37, sentence 5.) Health exists either when the body is ordered so as to preserve its original condition or when some form of direct medical intervention restores it to its original condition. Machiavelli's choice of words drawn from medicine may be designed to reflect his hope that these *Discourses* will help to disclose the laws governing politics just as medicine helps to cure by knowing the laws of health. Both republics and religions ("mixed bodies," *corpi misti*) require intervention. What Machiavelli suggests for Florence parallels what his contemporary, Martin Luther, advocated for the Roman Catholic Church.

4. Translates *segno;* see the discussion in note 2 above. The expression serves an analogous function in Sofronia's resolution of the dilemma in *Clizia,* 5, 3: "I never wanted to make a fool of you. . . . If you make a clean start *[ritornare al segno],* and go back to being the Nicomaco you once were a year ago, we shall all go back too, and nobody will know a thing" (*Comedies of Machiavelli,* pp. 386–387).

5. Based on Galen, this kind of maxim was standard in Renaissance medicine; quoted in Latin: *"quod quotidie aggregatur aliquid, quod quandoque indiget curatione."*

6. Machiavelli has alluded to this topic above, 2, 29, sentence 18. The invasion of the Gauls occurred from 391 to 389 B.C.

7. See 5.38.1. Machiavelli has discussed this episode in 2, 29, sentences 5 through

12; but see 1, 10–14, for more on the function of religion in the state.

8. See 2, 28, nn.1 and 2, for "the law of nations" and Livy, 5.37.1–3.

9. Based on Livy, 5.50–51, especially a sentence in a speech by Camillus before the Roman Senate: "Adversity, then, reminded us of our religion" (51.9).

10. Livy, 6.1.6–7, though only Quintus Fabius is mentioned as having been "punished."

11. Livy, 5.49.8. See 5.43–55 for the career of Camillus after his return from exile; he was made dictator in order to lead the Roman army at Veii.

12. Machiavelli now examines the "good" resulting from a return to the original principles of an institution.

13. For these events occurring prior to the period from 391 to 389 B.C., see above, 1, 16, n.4, and the discussion below, 3, 3, of the sons of Brutus; and 1, 40–45, for Machiavelli's discussion of the decemvirs. Livy points out that aside from two decemvirs who committed suicide in prison, the other eight were in fact exiled (3.58.9); Maelius the Grain Dealer is mentioned below at the beginning of 3.28, where he is referred to as Spurius Maelius, a war profiteer; see Livy, 4.13–16, and Martelli, *Storici antichi,* p. 122. Rinaldi notes that Machiavelli discusses an analogous situation concerning Andrea Strozzi in *Florentine Histories,* 2, 40.

14. For these events after 389 B.C., see below, Guicciardini's *Consideration* of *Discourses,* 1, 5, n.2; and Machiavelli, 1, 24, sentences 10–12, for Manlius Capitolinus; 2, 16, n.4, on the death of the son of Manlius Torquatus; 1, 31, n.8, for Papirius Cursor; and 1, 29, n.10, on the action against the Scipios.

15. A point reminiscent of Machiavelli's thought expressed in the opening sentence of 1, 3 above. As is clear from the next sentence, drawing "back toward the mark" is a constantly repeated process.

16. A reference to the rule of the Medici from Cosimo's return from exile (*Florentine Histories,* 4, 30–33) to Piero's expulsion from Florence after Charles VIII of France invaded Italy. Guicciardini's comments on Cosimo's rule and his "taking back the state" are relevant: "By having a number of citizens given *balìa* for five years, Cosimo secured his power." In other words he made sure that a group of his friends had extraordinary powers; "when the time for the five-year *balìa* was up, he had their authority extended for another five years" (*History of Florence,* 1). Machiavelli deals with the early years of Cosimo's rule in *Florentine Histories,* 5, 1–4. The inference to be drawn here is that the republican government in Florence from 1494 until its overthrow in 1512, which Machiavelli served from 1498 on, exemplifies "taking the state back toward its origins." This may lead to the state's renewal; but see Guicciardini's *Consideration* of *Discourses,* 2, 24, n.1, for the potential implications of "new things" to the immediate audience of the *Discourses.*

17. Horatius Cocles and Mucius Scaevola are discussed above, 1, 24; see notes 2–3. Gaius Fabricius Luscinus was sent to effect the return of prisoners whom Pyrrhus had captured at the Battle of Heraclea in 280 B.C.; Pyrrhus failed in his attempt to bribe Fabricius (see Plutarch, *Pyrrhus,* 20 ff. and below, 3, 20). Publius Decius Mus the Elder and his son, of the same name, both sacrificed their lives to inspire their troops in battle: the former at the Battle of Veseris in 340 B.C. (see Livy, 8.3–11, and above, 2, 16, n.1); the latter at the battle of Sentinum in 295 B.C. (Livy, 10.26–29, and below, 3, 45). For Marcus Atilius Regulus, see above, 2, 18, n.12. After his capture during the First

Punic War, the Carthaginians asked him to negotiate a prisoner exchange. He persuaded the Roman Senate not to agree and returned voluntarily to Carthage where he was cruelly executed. See also Sasso, *Antichi,* 4:214; and Mansfield, *New Modes,* p. 303.

18. For the first Cato, Marcus Porcius Cato the Censor, who died in 149 B.C., see above, 1, 29, n.10; for his great-grandson, the second Cato, see Plutarch, *Cato Minor,* and Dante, *Purgatorio,* 1, vv. 71–72; although he committed suicide rather than live under the rule of Julius Caesar.

19. Again, Dante comes to mind: see his praise of the two saints' taking an institution "back toward its origins" as part of his condemnation of the Church's corruption in *Paradiso,* 11–12.

20. This conclusion is consistent with his remarks above, in 1, 12, sentence 13, and 2, 2, sentences 30–33. It is interesting that the secular Machiavelli sees a pattern of renewal through return to first principles operating in these religious reformers.

21. The eight *parlements* in France had judicial and legislative authority; the one in Paris was the most powerful. Machiavelli greatly respected French political institutions; see his *Ritratto di cose di Francia* (Portrayal of French matters), written after his return from explaining Florence's temporizing policy concerning support of Louis XII against Pope Julius II in 1510. The discussion in *Prince,* 19, also emphasizes the extent to which the *parlements* were an "arbiter that might restrain the nobility and favor the common people without putting any blame on the king"(pp. 293–295, lines 125–127, but see the entire paragraph, lines 108–134).

22. Many readers have found this to be a less than accurate specification of the theme that will unify Book 3, though autobiographical hints abound.

23. Lucius Junius Brutus; the phrase echoes Livy, 8.34.3: *"conditorem Romanae libertatis"* (the founder of Roman liberty).

~ 2 ~

IT IS A VERY WISE THING TO FEIGN MADNESS AT THE RIGHT TIME

1 No one was ever esteemed so prudent or wise for any outstanding action as [Lucius] Junius Brutus deserves to be for feigning idiocy. 2 Although Livy gives just one reason that induced him to such feigning, which was so he could live more safely and preserve his inheritance, nevertheless, considering his actions, we may believe that he also feigned it in order to be watched less closely and to have an easier time attacking the kings and freeing his country whenever he might be granted the opportunity.[1] 3 That he was planning this can be seen, first, in his interpretation of Apollo's oracle, when he pretended to fall down in order to kiss the ground, judging that as a result he would make the gods favorable to his plans, and later, when over the dead Lucretia, among her father, husband, and other relatives, he was the first to draw the knife from her wound and make those present swear that never would they tolerate anyone reigning over Rome in the future.[2]

4 All those who are dissatisfied with a prince must learn from his example:

they must first measure and weigh their forces; if they are powerful enough to reveal themselves as his enemies and wage war upon him openly, they must embark on this path as the less dangerous and more honorable one.[3] 5 But if they are such that their forces are inadequate to declare open war upon him, they must seek energetically to become his ally; to this effect embark upon all those paths that they judge to be necessary, following his wishes and taking delight in all those things that they see him delighting in.[4] 6 First of all, this familiarity lets you live in safety and without incurring any danger and to enjoy the prince's good fortune along with him; it gives you complete ease in satisfying your intent. 7 It is true, some say, that it would be better not to stay so close to princes that their downfall includes you nor so far away that, when their downfall comes, you would not be in time to climb up on their ruins; the middle way would be the truest if it could be followed, but because I believe it is impossible, it is necessary to limit oneself to the two methods mentioned above, that is, either keeping one's distance or drawing close to them. 8 Anyone who does otherwise, if he is a man noteworthy for his accomplishments, lives in continual danger. 9 Nor is it enough to say: "I do not care about anything, I desire neither honors nor profits, I want to live in peace and quiet." Such excuses are heard but not accepted; men of accomplishment cannot choose to stand by, even if they should choose to do so sincerely and without ambition, because no one believes them; so, even if they themselves want to stand by, others will not let them. 10 Therefore it is necessary to act the madman like Brutus, and one is very much acting the madman in praising, speaking, seeing, and doing things contrary to your intent in order to please the prince. 11 And because we have spoken about this man's wisdom in restoring Rome's freedom, we shall now speak of his severity in preserving it.

NOTES

1. Livy, I.56.7–8, says he pretended to be a "dullard" (which is what "Brutus" means) in order not to arouse the enmity of his uncle, Rome's last tyrannical king, Tarquinius Superbus. Machiavelli's link to Livy is based on the latter's assertion that "behind the mask of this opprobrious title, the spirit that gave Rome its freedom might bide its time unseen" *(ut sub eius obtentu cognomen liberator ille populi Romani animus latens opperiretur tempora sua)*.

2. Livy continues by describing how Tarquinius sent his sons to the oracle at Delphi, with their cousin Brutus along "more as a toy than as a comrade," to discover which one would be the next king. The reply was "the first among you to kiss his mother" (1.56.10) Only Brutus understood the true meaning of "mother": "pretending to slip, he fell and touched the earth with his lips" *(velut si prolapsus cecidisset terram osculo contigit)*. The verbal link to Livy is more direct in this episode than in the incident involving the rape of Lucretia, the wife of Lucius Tarquinius Collatinus, by Sextus, a son of Tarquinius Superbus (Livy, 1.58–59). In stressing that Brutus was the first to withdraw the dagger from her body and swear vengeance on the entire Tarquinian line, Machiavelli is closely following 59.1–2.

3. Inglese notes that this sentence may, on the one hand, be directed to "a circle of republican opposition to Lorenzo de' Medici's princedom" and, on the other hand,

be "a sort of 'explanation'—forced and very simplistic, of course—of his own behavior during the years 1513–1515." He suggests another potentially autobiographical reference in sentences 9–10 below; Machiavelli may be referring there to his own ambivalence about active political life and to the contemplative life on his farm at Sant' Andrea in Percussina, near San Casciano.

4. In his *Ricordi* Guicciardini notes: "A tyrant will be as zealous as possible to discover the secrets of your heart, plying you with acts of affection, talking to you at great length, and having you observed by others whom he has ordered to become intimate with you. It is difficult to protect yourself against all these snares. Hence, if you do not want him to understand you, see to it zealously and protect yourself with consummate industry against anything that might give you away, using as much zeal to prevent your being understood as he uses to understand you" (C. 103; see also B. 81).

~ 3 ~

IT IS NECESSARY TO SLAY THE SONS OF BRUTUS IN ORDER TO PRESERVE REGAINED FREEDOM

1 The severity of Brutus was no less necessary than it was useful to preserve the freedom that he had gained for Rome. A father sitting in judgment and not merely condemning his sons to death but also present at their death is a rare example in the annals of history.[1] 2 Those who read ancient history will always recognize that after a change in government, whether from a republic to tyranny or from tyranny to a republic, a memorable action against the enemies of the present circumstances is necessary. 3 Anyone who seizes tyrannical power and does not slay Brutus and anyone who sets a state free and does not slay the sons of Brutus does not stay in power long.[2]

4 And because this topic has been discussed extensively above, I refer you to what was said about it then; here I shall cite only one example, which has been worthy of memory in our time and our country. 5 This is Piero Soderini, who believed that with patience and goodness he could overcome the desire of the sons of Brutus to go back to another form of government, and he was mistaken in that.[3] 6 Although he recognized this necessity in his wisdom, and though fate and the ambition of those who opposed him gave him an opportunity to eliminate them, nevertheless, he never made up his mind to do so. 7 For besides believing he could do away with evil humors[4] through patience and goodness and dissipate men's enmity by handing out rewards, he thought (and often attested to it among his friends)[5] that, in order to strike back boldly at his opponents and defeat his adversaries, it would be necessary for him to seize extraordinary powers and break down civic equality by means of laws. 8 Even if he did not apply it tyrannically later on, this latter means would have so frightened the general public that it would never have agreed after his death to rename a gonfaloniere for life, an institution he deemed it was well to strengthen and maintain.[6] 9 This scruple was wise and

good; nevertheless, an evil should never be allowed to persist out of consideration for a good if that good can easily be overwhelmed by that evil. 10 Because his deeds and intentions must be judged by their outcome, he ought to have believed that if Fortune and life had gone along with him, everyone could realize that what he had done was for the well-being of his native city and not out of his own ambition; and he could have arranged things in such a way that any successor of his could not have done for evil what he had done for good. 11 But he was misled by his initial judgment, since he did not recognize that ill will is neither subdued by time nor placated by any gift. 12 So, because he did not know how to be like Brutus, he lost his government and reputation along with his native city.[7] 13 And just as it is a difficult thing to save a free state, so it is difficult to save a kingdom, as will be shown in the following chapter.

NOTES

1. See above, 1, 16, n.4. Titus and Tiberius, sons of Brutus, formed a conspiracy to restore Tarquinius to the throne. As Livy says, once the plot was exposed, it was the duty of Brutus as consul to sentence the traitors, his sons included: "he who should have been removed as a spectator was the very person Fortune assigned the task of enforcing the punishment" (*qui spectator erat amovendus, eum ipsum fortuna exactorem supplicii dedit* [2.5.5]).

2. "Brutus" as a defender of freedom, "the sons" as those favoring the previous regime. Perhaps here, but certainly in sentence 5, the "sons of Brutus," with respect to Soderini, alludes to the *ottimati,* the aristocratic party in Florence. Inglese notes that Savonarola alludes to Brutus and his sons in a passage, *Sermons on the Psalms,* 11 October 1495.

3. See above, 1, 7, n.7, and 1, 52, nn.4 and 5. Other passages indicating Machiavelli's conflicted, enigmatic judgments about Soderini can be found in the third-to-last paragraph of his 1503 *Parole da dirle sopra la provisione del danaio* (Remarks to be given about the money bill) and *Decennale primo,* vv. 355–381 (1504). Finally, there is an epigram on the death of Soderini—"The night Piero Soderini died / His spirit went to the mouth of Hell. / Pluto yelled: "Why Hell? Silly spirit, / Go up to Limbo with the rest of the babies"—that is balanced by Machiavelli's remarks in *Ricordi ai Palleschi* (Memorandum to Medici supporters, 1512). See also 2, 14, n.4, for the possible connotation of "patience" as "restraint" in this context.

4. Translates *i mali omori,* referring to evil political factions.

5. As one of his "friends," Machiavelli may be speaking from firsthand knowledge.

6. Soderini was elected gonfaloniere for life on 22 September 1502; previously this office (of president of the Signoria) was limited to two months. Machiavelli strongly supported the arrangement as a means of counteracting the power of the *ottimati.* He welcomed Soderini's having this power to exercise on behalf of the republic, not to create a tyranny.

7. After his decade-long association with Soderini and his policies, Machiavelli firmly believed that his fatal flaw was an inability to act decisively. See below, 3, 30, paragraph 2. See also Sasso, *Antichi,* 2:85–89.

~ 4 ~

A PRINCE CANNOT BE SECURE IN A PRINCEDOM WHILE THOSE WHO HAVE BEEN STRIPPED OF IT ARE STILL LIVING

1 The death of Tarquinius Priscus at the hands of the sons of Ancus and that of Servius Tullius at the hands of Tarquinius Superbus show how difficult and dangerous it is to strip someone of a kingdom and leave him alive, even if one tries to win him over by a reward. 2 We can see that Tarquinius Priscus was fooled by believing he possessed the kingdom legally, since it had been given to him by the people and confirmed by the Senate; he did not believe that hatred could be so strong in the sons of Ancus that they would not be satisfied with what satisfied all of Rome. 3 And Servius Tullius was wrong in believing that he could win over the sons of Tarquinius with new rewards.[1] 4 So as to the former, every prince can take notice that he will never be secure in his princedom as long as those who were stripped of it are living. 5 As to the latter, every powerful man may be reminded that new favors never canceled out old injuries; and even less so when the new favor is lesser than the harm was.[2] 6 Servius Tullius was undoubtedly unwise to believe that the sons of Tarquinius would settle for being the sons-in-law of the one over whom they deemed they ought to be king. 7 This desire to reign is so great that it enters the hearts not only of those to whom a kingdom is due but of those to whom it is not due, as was the case with the wife of the young Tarquinius, the daughter of Servius. Driven by this passion and against all things paternal, she drove her husband to deprive her father of his life and his kingdom, so much higher did she value being queen than being a king's daughter. 8 So if Tarquinius Priscus and Servius Tullius lost their kingdom by not knowing how to secure themselves against those from whom they had usurped it,[3] Tarquinius Superbus lost it by not respecting the institutions of the ancient kings, as will be shown in the next chapter.

NOTES

1. Livy narrates the complicated, often grisly events upon which this chapter is based in 1.40–48. He says that the people and the senate elected Tarquinius Priscus, so the sons of Ancus Marcius, Rome's fourth king, did not succeed their father (1.35.6); but see Martelli, *Storici antichi,* p. 123. Livy does say that the sons were angry with their guardian, Tarquinius Priscus, Rome's fifth king, and organized an attempt on his life (40). But at his death, his son-in-law, Servius Tullius, became the sixth king. He, in turn, feared an attempted coup by the sons of Tarquinius Priscus, Lucius Tarquinius and Arruns Tarquinius. To forestall it, he gave each son one of his daughters, both named Tullia, in marriage. After the deaths of both Arruns and the first wife of Lucius Tarquinius, the latter, urged on by Tullia, the widow of Arruns, murdered Servius Tullius and became Rome's next king, Lucius Tarquinius Superbus.

2. Machiavelli may also be reminding us of the epigrammatic way in which he expresses the same thought at the end of *Prince,* 7 (p. 175, lines 302–303), and in a letter to Francesco Vettori dated 29 April 1513 (*Friends,* p. 234). He contradicts this notion

in another letter to Vettori written five months later, 10 August (p. 248). Classical support for the notion expressed in this sentence can be found in the quotation from Tacitus that Machiavelli cited in 1, 29, sentence 4, and in Isocrates, *Philippus,* 37.

3. Although he discusses its drawbacks, one method for securing themselves is to eliminate the previous ruler's family; see *Prince,* 4–5 (p. 131, lines 62–64; p. 133, lines 76–79; and p. 139, lines 41–45).

~ 5 ~

WHAT MAKES A KING WHO INHERITS A KINGDOM LOSE IT

1 After Tarquinius Superbus killed Servius Tullius, who left no heirs, he came into secure possession of the kingdom, since he did not have to fear the things that had hurt his predecessors.[1] 2 And although his way of seizing the kingdom was unusual and despicable, nevertheless, if only he had observed the ancient institutions of the other kings,[2] he would have been accepted and the Senate and the Plebs would not have risen up together against him to take his power away. 3 Thus he was driven out not because his son, Sextus, raped Lucretia but because he broke the laws of the kingdom and governed it tyrannically, since he deprived the Senate of all authority and appropriated it for himself personally.[3] Business that used to be carried out in public to the Roman Senate's satisfaction, he carried out in his palace, receiving blame and hatred for it so that within a short time he stripped Rome of all the freedom that it had retained under the other kings. 4 Nor was it enough for him to make the Fathers[4] his enemies, he also aroused the Plebs against him, tiring them with manual labor that was completely contrary to what his predecessors had employed them for.[5] 5 So by filling Rome with examples of cruelty and arrogance, he had disposed the minds of all the Romans to rebellion whenever they had an opportunity for it. 6 And if the incident with Lucretia had not come along, the first time another one occurred the same result would have been produced. For if Tarquinius had lived like the other kings and his son Sextus had made that mistake, Brutus and Collatinus would have gone to Tarquinius for revenge against Sextus and not to the Roman people.

7 Princes should know, therefore, that they start to lose their state the moment they start to break the laws and those ways and customs that are ancient and under which men have been living for a long time. 8 And if after being deprived of the state they ever become so wise as to recognize how easily princedoms are held onto by those who seek wise counsel, such a loss would pain them far more and they would condemn themselves to greater punishment than they have been condemned to by others. 9 For it is far easier to be loved by the good than by the bad and to obey the laws rather than try to control them. 10 If they want to understand the way they would have to take to do this, they do not have to go to any more trouble than to choose as their mirror the life of good princes, such as Timoleon of Corinth, Aratus of Sicyon, and the like.[6] They[7] would find in their lives such security and

such satisfaction on the part of the ruler and the ruled that they would have to wish to imitate them, since it can easily be done for the reasons mentioned. 11 Because when men are governed well, they do not seek or wish for any other freedom: this is what happened to the peoples governed by the two men just named, whom they compelled to be princes as long as they lived, even though they tried several times to return to private life.[8] 12 And because in this and the two preceding chapters we have discussed the ferment stirred up against princes, and the conspiracies formed by the sons of Brutus against their native land, and those formed against Tarquinius Priscus and Servius Tullius, it does not seem to me to be irrelevant to discuss them extensively in the following chapter, since it is a matter worthy of being noted by princes and private citizens.

NOTES

1. From note 1 to the previous chapter and from this sentence, we can see that Tarquinius Superbus did not "inherit" his kingdom, as this chapter's title states, but usurped it.

2. Advice emphasized by the quotation from Tacitus that Machiavelli cites in 3, 6, sentence 5; see note 4 to that chapter.

3. Livy deals with the rape of Lucretia in 1.58–59; for the tyrannical behavior of Tarquinius Superbus, see 1.49.2–8.

4. Translates *Padri,* referring to the Roman senators, the *patres conscripti* (the enrolled fathers).

5. Tarquinius Superbus ordered the plebeians, in addition to fulfilling their military service obligations, to erect seats in the circus and dig the Cloaca Maxima, the Great Sewer (Livy, 1.56.1–2). Later Livy describes a speech in which Brutus castigates Tarquinius Superbus for "plunging the plebeians as workers into ditches and sewers; men of Rome, victors over all the neighboring peoples, transformed from warriors into artisans and stone cutters" (*labores plebis in fossas cloacasque exhauriendas demersae; Romanos homines, victores omnium circa populorum, opifices ac lapicidas pro bellatoribus factos* [59.9]). See Mansfield, *New Modes,* p. 316, for more on the example of Tarquinius.

6. The "mirror of princes" *(speculum principis)* was a genre of literary and political writing in the Middle Ages and early Renaissance. The *Prince* both belongs to this tradition and breaks new ground. Timoleon is discussed above, 1, 10, n.4, and Plutarch praises him in his *Timoleon* as a patriot who freed Sicily from tyranny; for Aratus of Sicyon, see above, 2, 32, n.8.

7. The sense of "they" as "princes" goes back to sentence 7, but Machiavelli uses the singular *ei* (he).

8. See *Prince,* 24: "[When] the actions of a new prince . . . show *virtù,* they will win men over to his side and commit them to him much more than ancient lineage does. For men are more compelled by concerns of the present than by those of the past. When they deem that the present is good, they enjoy it and seek nothing more" (p. 355, lines 5–13).

~ 6 ~

ON CONSPIRACIES

1 Because conspiracies are such a dangerous thing for princes and private citizens, I did not think a discussion of them should be left out. 2 For we can see that many more princes have lost their lives and their states because of them than because of open warfare, for the ability to wage open war on a prince is granted to few, [but] the ability to conspire against him is granted to anyone.[1] 3 On the other hand, private citizens do not enter upon a more dangerous or rasher undertaking than this, because it is difficult and most dangerous at every one of its stages, and thus many of them are attempted and very few reach the desired outcome.[2] 4 In order, therefore, for princes to learn how to protect themselves against these risks and for private citizens to be more wary of starting them (or rather, learn to be content to live under the power that has been offered them by fate),[3] I shall discuss them at length, not omitting any notable case to document the risk in both kinds. 5 And truly golden is the maxim of Tacitus stating that men should revere things of the past and submit to present ones; they should wish for good princes and accept them no matter what they are like.[4] 6 And in truth, anyone who does otherwise usually ruins himself and his native land.

7 To begin this topic, we must therefore first consider against whom conspiracies are made, and we shall find that they are made either against one's country or against a prince. I would like us to discuss these two at present, because I have spoken enough above[5] about those that are made to hand a town over to the enemy besieging it or about those that resemble them for one reason or another. 8 In this first part we shall deal with those against a prince, and first we shall examine their causes, which are manifold. 9 But one of them is far more important than all the others: being hated by the general public, because it is not surprising for a prince who has stirred up this general hatred against himself to have some private citizens who have been more deeply affronted by him and seek revenge.[6] 10 This desire is intensified in them by the general ill will that they see has been stirred up against him. 11 A prince should therefore avoid these public reproaches (and how he is to avoid them I shall not discuss here, since I have dealt with them elsewhere), because if he protects himself against public hatred, mere private affronts will give him less trouble.[7] 12 First, because rarely will he come across men who care so much about an insult as to endanger themselves in order to avenge it; second, even if they had a mind and the power to do so, they are held back by the general goodwill that they see the prince has.[8] 13 Affronts of necessity are either to property, to life, or to honor.[9] 14 It is more dangerous to make threats against life than to carry them out; rather, threats are very dangerous and there is no risk whatever in carrying them out. For a man who is dead cannot think of vengeance, while those who remain alive usually leave the problem to the dead man. 15 But someone who is threatened and sees himself compelled by a need either to act or to be acted upon becomes a very dangerous man for the prince,[10] as we shall state in detail

in its place.[11] 16 Beyond this need, property and honor are two things that harm men more than any other harm, and a prince must protect himself against them.[12] For he can never dispossess a man of so much that he is left without a dagger to avenge himself; he can never dishonor a man so much that he is left without a mind bent on revenge. 17 Of honors that are taken from men, women's is the most important; after that, an insult to his person. 18 That is what armed Pausanias against Philip of Macedon[13] and has armed many others against many other princes. In our day Giulio Bellanti would not have moved to conspire against Pandolfo, the tyrant of Siena, had not the latter given him one of his daughters as a wife and then taken her away, as we shall discuss in its place.[14] 19 The chief cause that made the Pazzi conspire against the Medici was the inheritance of Giovanni Borromei, which was taken from them by their decree.[15] 20 There is another reason, and a very important one, that makes men conspire against a prince: the desire to free their country, which he has seized. 21 This cause prompted Brutus and Cassius against Caesar; it also prompted many others against the Phalarises, the Dionysiuses, and others who took over their countries.[16] 22 And no tyrant can protect himself against such ferment except by abandoning tyrannical power. 23 And because there is no one who does so, there are few who do not come to ill; from which came the lines of Juvenal: "Few kings descend to the realm of Pluto without slaughter and wounds, / and [few] tyrants do so with a bloodless death."[17]

24 The risks that are taken in conspiracies are great, as I have said above, since they are taken at all stages; because in such cases one runs risks in plotting them, in executing them, and once they are carried out. 25 The conspirators are either one individual or several. 26 We cannot call an individual a conspiracy, but one man who has conceived a firm resolve to murder the prince. 27 Of the three risks that are run in conspiracies, this man avoids the first, because he takes no risk before carrying it out, since no one else knows his secret and he does not take any risk that his plan may reach the prince's ear. 28 Making a decision of this kind can befall any kind of man, great or small, noble or commoner, an intimate of the prince or not, because anyone is entitled to give vent to his own feelings. 29 Pausanias, who already has been spoken of,[18] slew Philip of Macedon, who was on his way to the temple surrounded by a thousand armed men and right between his son and son-in-law. 30 But he was noble and known to the prince. 31 A poor, base-born Spaniard gave a knife-thrust to the neck of King Ferdinand of Spain; the wound was not fatal, but this showed that the man had a mind and the opportunity to do so.[19] 32 A dervish, a Turkish priest, drew a scimitar against Bayazid, the father of the present Turk; he did not wound him, but still he had a mind and the opportunity if he so wanted.[20] 33 I believe that there are many men of such a mind who would like to do so, because there is no punishment or risk in wanting to, but few who do so. But of those who do, there are very few or none who are not slain in the act; so one does not find anybody who wants to go to certain death. 34 But let us set aside these one-man plots and get to conspiracies among several people.

35 I say that all conspiracies found in histories are made by men who are noble or very close to the prince.[21] Because others cannot conspire, unless they

are completely mad, since weak men and those not close to the prince lack all the hopes and opportunities that carrying out a conspiracy requires. 36 First, weak men cannot find like-minded men who will keep their promise, because one cannot yield to their will with any of these hopes that make men undertake great risks; so as soon as they have opened up to two or three persons, they find an informer and fail. 37 But even if they were fortunate enough not to have such an informer, they are surrounded with such difficulty in carrying it out, not having easy access to the prince, that it is impossible for them not to fail in carrying it out. For if noble men, who have easy access, are beset by the difficulties that will be stated below, then the difficulties of weak men must be immensely increased. 38 Consequently (since where life and property are at stake people are not completely insane), when men see they are weak, they are wary of it, and when they are fed up with a prince, they limit themselves to cursing him and wait for those who have a higher rank than they do to avenge them. 39 And if any of these weak men should ever happen to have tried something, they should be praised for their intention, not their prudence. 40 So we can see that those who have conspired were all noble men or the prince's intimates; many of them conspired, impelled as much by too many favors as by too many abuses: as were Perennis against Commodus,[22] Plautianus against Severus,[23] Sejanus against Tiberius.[24] 41 All of them had such riches, honor, and rank conferred on them by their emperors that they lacked only imperial status to complete their power, and since they were unwilling to do without this they were moved to conspire against the prince. 42 And their conspiracies all had the outcome that their ingratitude deserved, though in more recent times some similar ones, like that of Jacopo di Appiano against messer Piero Gambacorti, the prince of Pisa, turned out well; this Jacopo, raised, fostered, and given status by him, then took his power away from him.[25] 43 The conspiracy of Coppola against King Ferdinand of Aragon was among these in our day; Coppola, who had reached such greatness that he did not feel that he lacked anything but the throne, lost his life because he wanted that too.[26] 44 In truth, if any conspiracy against princes formed by noble men ought to have turned out well, it should have been this one, since it was formed by another king, one can say, and by someone who had so great an opportunity to fulfill his desire. 45 But the greed for domination, which blinds them, also blinds them in carrying out this undertaking, because, if they knew how to do this wickedness prudently, it would be impossible for it not to succeed. 46 So a prince who wants to protect himself against conspiracies should fear more those to whom he has done too many favors than those to whom he has done too much harm: the latter lack opportunities; the former abound in them.[27] And the will is similar, because the desire for domination is as great or greater than the desire for revenge. 47 Princes should therefore give enough authority to their friends for there to be some gap between it and the princedom and for there to be something to desire in between; otherwise it will be unusual for what happened to the above-mentioned princes not to happen to them. 48 But let us get back to our topic.

49 I say that, because those who conspire must be Noblemen and have easy access to the prince, we have to discuss how these undertakings of theirs turn

out, such as they have been, and see the cause that made them successful or unsuccessful. 50 And as I said above, risks are to be found within them at three times: before, during, and after. 51 There are few of them that turn out well, because it is almost impossible to get through them all successfully.

52 To begin with discussion of the risks run before, which are the greatest, I say that it is necessary to be very prudent and to have a good deal of luck for a conspiracy not to be revealed during the plotting stage. 53 They are revealed either by denunciation or by deduction. 54 A denunciation arises from finding a lack of loyalty or prudence in the men to whom you communicate it.[28] 55 It is easy to find a lack of loyalty, because you can only communicate it to those whom you trust who would go to their death for you or to men who are dissatisfied with the prince. 56 You might find one or two among those to be trusted, but as you reach out to many, it is impossible for you to find them; then it is necessary for the goodwill they bear you to be great, for the risk and fear of punishment not to seem greater to them. 57 Furthermore, most of the time men are mistaken about the love that you judge a man bears you, and you can never be certain of it unless you test it; and testing it is very dangerous in this context. 58 Even though you may have tested it in some other dangerous matters in which they were loyal to you, you cannot measure this loyalty by that one, since this one far surpasses any other sort of risk. 59 If you measure loyalty by a man's dissatisfaction with his prince, you can easily be mistaken about this, because as soon as you have revealed your intent to that dissatisfied person, you give him the means to get satisfaction and to keep his loyalty either his hatred has to be great or your authority has to be very great.[29] 60 This is why many conspiracies are exposed and crushed in their very initial stages, and when one has been kept secret among many men for a long time it is considered a miracle, as was that of Piso against Nero, and in our own time that of the Pazzi against Lorenzo and Giuliano de' Medici; these were known to more than fifty men, and they got as far as carrying them out before they were exposed.[30]

61 As for being revealed through lack of prudence, that occurs when one of the conspirators talks about it carelessly so that a servant or other third party hears you. That happened to the sons of Brutus, who, while plotting the affair with Tarquin's representatives, were overheard by a slave who denounced them;[31] or else when you happen to communicate it thoughtlessly to a woman or a young boy whom you love or to some such thoughtless person, as did Dymnus, one of the conspirators with Philotas against Alexander the Great, who communicated the conspiracy to Nicomachus, a young boy whom he loved, who told it right away to his brother, Cebalinus, and Cebalinus to the king.[32]

62 As for being revealed by deduction, there is an example of this in Piso's conspiracy against Nero in which Scaevinus, one of the conspirators, the day before he was to assassinate Nero made his will, ordered Milichus, his freed slave, to sharpen an old, rusty dagger of his, freed all his slaves and gave them money, and had bandages ordered for binding up wounds; when Milichus became aware of this affair from these deductions, he denounced him to Nero.[33]

63 Scaevinus was seized and along with him Natalis, another conspirator, since they had been seen talking together at length in secret the day before; and since they did not agree as to the conversation they had had, they were forced to confess the truth so that the conspiracy was exposed to the ruin of all the conspirators.

64 For these reasons, whenever the number of those aware of a conspiracy exceeds three or four, it is impossible to protect oneself against its being revealed through malice, imprudence, or thoughtlessness. 65 When more than one conspirator is captured, it is impossible for it not to be found out, because two people cannot have agreed together about all their conversations. 66 When only one of them is captured, if he is a brave man, he can keep silent about the conspirators through the strength of his courage; but the conspirators have to have no less courage than he does to remain steadfast and not reveal themselves by flight, because the conspiracy is revealed if courage is lacking on one side, whether it is the one who is being held or those who are free. 67 The example that Livy cites of the conspiracy against Hieronymus, the king of Syracuse, is exceptional; when Theodotus, one of the conspirators, was captured, he concealed all the conspirators with great *virtù* and accused the king's friends.[34] On the other hand, the conspirators were so confident of Theodotus's *virtù* that none of them left Syracuse or gave any sign of fear.

68 One therefore goes through all these risks in plotting a conspiracy before one gets to the execution of it; to avoid them, there are the following remedies. 69 The first and truest—or rather, to put it better, the only one—is not to give the conspirators enough time to denounce you and to communicate the affair to them when you want to carry it out, not before. 70 Those who have done so surely avoid the risks there are in discussing it and usually the other risks too; indeed, they have all had a successful outcome, and any prudent man would find it possible to act in this way. I think it is enough for me to cite two examples.

71 Unable to bear the tyranny of Aristotimus, a tyrant of Epirus, Hellanicus assembled many of his relatives and friends in his house; when he urged them to free their country, some of them asked for time to take counsel and organize themselves.[35] So Hellanicus had his servants lock the house, and he said to those he had summoned: "Either you swear now to go and carry out this plan, or I shall hand you all over as prisoners to Aristotimus." 72 Moved by these words, they swore; on leaving, they carried out Hellanicus's orders successfully without losing any time. 73 After a Magus had seized the kingdom of the Persians by subterfuge and Otanes, one of the kingdom's Noblemen, had heard about and revealed the deception, he discussed it with six other princes of that state, saying that the kingdom had to be avenged for the tyranny of the Magus; when some of them asked for time, Darius, one of the six summoned by Otanes, stood up and said: "Either we go now and carry this out or I shall go denounce you all."[36] 74 So they stood up as one without giving anyone time to change his mind and carried out their intentions successfully. 75 The way in which the Aetolians killed Nabis, the tyrant of Sparta, is also similar to these two examples.[37] They sent their fellow citizen, Alexamenes, with thirty

cavalrymen and two hundred foot soldiers to Nabis under the pretext of sending him aid; they communicated the secret only to Alexamenes, and they enjoined the rest, under penalty of exile, to obey him in anything and everything. 76 He went to Sparta and never communicated his mission until he wished to carry it out, so he succeeded in slaying Nabis. 77 In these ways, therefore, these men avoided the risks that are run in plotting conspiracies; whoever imitates them will always avoid these.

78 And to show that anyone can do as they did, I would like to give the example of Piso already cited above. 79 Piso was a great man, of the highest reputation, and an intimate of Nero, who confided in him a great deal.[38] 80 Nero often went to his gardens to eat with him. Piso therefore was able to make friends with men of spirit and courage, who were of a suitable disposition for such an undertaking (which is quite easy for a Nobleman); and if Nero was in his gardens, he could communicate the affair to them and with the proper words stir them to do something they would not have time to reject and could not possibly fail. 81 And, if we examine all the other ones, few that could not be carried out in the same way will be found; but because men generally have little understanding of the actions of the world, they often make very grave errors, all the more so in those that are the most unusual, like this one.

82 Therefore the affair must never be communicated unless it is necessary and at the point of action; and if indeed you want to communicate it, communicate it to one man only of whom you have had very long experience or who is motivated by the same causes as you. 83 It is easier to find one such person than to find several of them, and thus there is less risk. Then, even if he should deceive you, there is some means to protect yourself, which there is not when there are many conspirators. For I have heard it said by some prudent people that one can talk about anything with one man, because the "yes" of one man is worth as much as the "no" of the other, if you do not let yourself be led to write it down in your own hand; everyone should guard against writing as if it were a shoal, because there is nothing that can convict you more easily than something written in your own hand. 84 When Plautianus wanted to have Emperor Severus and his son Antoninus slain, he entrusted the matter to the tribune Saturninus; when the latter tried to denounce him and disobey him, fearing that when it came to a denunciation Plautianus would be believed more than he would, Saturninus asked him for a note in his handwriting to vouch for this order.[39] Blinded by his ambition, Plautianus did it for him, and it then ensued that he was denounced and convicted by the tribune; without that note and some other pieces of evidence, Plautianus would have had the upper hand, so boldly did he deny it. 85 Some remedy can therefore be found for denunciation by one man when you cannot be convicted by writing or some other evidence; one has to watch out for that. 86 In Piso's conspiracy there was a woman named Epicharis who had once been Nero's mistress; judging that it would be a good idea to have among the conspirators the captain of some triremes that Nero kept to guard him, she told him of the conspiracy but not the conspirators.[40] 87 Hence when that captain broke his promise and denounced her to Nero, Epicharis's boldness in denying it was so

great that Nero, since he was uncertain, did not condemn her. 88 So there are two risks in communicating the matter to a single person: first, that he may denounce you in trial; second, that he may denounce you after he is convicted and forced by torture, if he is seized for some suspicion or some information against him. 89 But there is some remedy for either of these risks, since one can be denied on the grounds of the hatred that the man had for you and the other can be denied on the grounds of force that constrained him to tell lies. 90 It is therefore wise not to communicate the matter to anyone but to act according to the examples cited above; or, if you should still communicate it, not to exceed one person, because, if there is some increased risk, it is far less than in communicating it to many.

91 Related to this method is if some need compels you to do to the prince what you realize that the prince would like to do to you, and this is so great that it gives you time to think only of protecting yourself. 92 This need almost always leads the affair to the desired end; I want two examples to suffice in proof. 93 Emperor Commodus held Laetus and Eclectus, leaders of the Praetorian Guards, among his closest friends and intimates; he held Marcia among his principal concubines or mistresses.[41] Because they sometimes berated him for the ways in which he besmirched his person and the empire, he decided to put them to death; he wrote down on a list Marcia, Laetus, Eclectus, and a few others that he wanted to put to death the following night and put it under his pillow. 94 When he went to bathe, one of his favorite young boys, playing in the bedroom and on the bed, came upon this list; as he was going out with it in his hand, he met Marcia, who took it away from him and, upon reading it and seeing its contents, immediately sent for Laetus and Eclectus. When the three of them realized the danger they were in, they decided to act first, and without any delay they slew Commodus the following night.

95 Emperor Antoninus Caracalla was in Mesopotamia with his armies, and he had as his prefect Macrinus, more of a civilian than a soldier. Because it happens that princes who are not good always fear that someone else may do to them what they feel they deserve, Antoninus wrote to his friend Maternianus in Rome, asking him to find out from the astrologers whether there was anyone who aspired to power and to let him know about it.[42] 96 Whereupon Maternianus wrote him that Macrinus was the one aspiring to it; because the letter reached Macrinus's hands before the emperor's and he thereby realized the necessity either to slay Caracalla before another letter arrived from Rome or to die, he commissioned a centurion he trusted, Martialis, one of whose brothers Caracalla had killed a few days before, to slay him, and he carried that out successfully. 97 Thus we see that this necessity that does not allow time has almost the same effect as the way I mentioned above that Hellanicus of Epirus followed.[43] 98 We can also see what I said near the beginning of this discourse:[44] threats do more harm and are the cause of more effective conspiracies to princes than do injuries. A prince should avoid them, because he must either deal with men affectionately or protect himself against them;[45] he should never reduce them to a state where they think that they must either die themselves or put someone else to death.

99 As for the risks that are run while carrying it out, they arise from either a change in plan, a lack of courage in the one who is carrying it out, an error that he makes from a lack of prudence, or a failure to carry the matter out completely with some of those whom one planned to kill surviving. 100 Therefore I say that there is nothing that interferes with or impedes all men's actions more than having to change a plan on the spot without having time and altering it from what had been arranged previously. 101 If such change makes for disorder in anything, it does so in matters of war and matters like the ones we are discussing, because in such actions there is nothing so necessary for men to do as being resolute in carrying out the role assigned to them. 102 If men have turned their imagination for several days to one way and one plan and that is suddenly changed, it is impossible for them not to be all disturbed and for everything not to collapse; so it is far better to carry something out according to the order given, even if one realizes that there are some problems in it, than it is by trying to do away with them to get into countless problems. 103 This happens when there is no time to make new plans; because when there is time, a man acts as he wishes.

104 The conspiracy of the Pazzi against Lorenzo and Giuliano de' Medici is well known.[46] 105 The order given was for them to have a dinner[47] for the cardinal of San Giorgio and to assassinate them at the dinner; who was to assassinate them, who was to take over the palace, and who was to run through the city and summon the people to freedom had been assigned. 106 It so happened that while the Pazzi, the Medici, and the cardinal were at a solemn service in the cathedral in Florence, it was learned that Giuliano would not dine there that day; this made the conspirators meet and decide to do what they were supposed to do in the house of the Medici at a solemn service.[48] 107 That managed to upset the entire plan, because Giovan Battista da Montesecco refused to take part in the murder, saying that he would not do it in church; so they had to settle on new people to be responsible for each action; because they did not have time to set their minds [to it], they made such mistakes that they were crushed while carrying it out.[49]

108 The courage of the man carrying out a conspiracy fails either out of respect or out of the agent's own cowardice. 109 The majesty and respect that a prince's presence entails is so great that it is easy for him either to weaken or to strike fear into an agent. 110 When Marius was captured by the people of Minturnae, a slave was sent to slay him; terrified by Marius's presence and the idea of his name, the man became a coward and lost all strength to kill him.[50] 111 And if this power exists in a man who is in fetters and a prisoner and sunken into ill fortune, how much greater may we consider it to be in an unshackled prince with the majesty of his decorations, his pomp, and his retinue! 112 So this pomp can frighten you, or else, given some agreeable welcome, it can calm you down. 113 Some men conspired against Sitalces, the king of Thrace; after designating the day to carry it out, they assembled at the place agreed upon where the prince was.[51] None of them made a move to attack him, so they departed without having tried anything and without knowing what had kept them from doing so, and each accused the other. 114 They

made the same mistake several times until the conspiracy was revealed and they received punishment for the crime that they were able but unwilling to commit. 115 Two of his brothers conspired against Alfonso, the duke of Ferrara, and as a go-between they used Jean [d'Artiganova], the duke's priest and cantor, who brought the duke to them several times at their request so they had the opportunity to assassinate him.[52] 116 Nevertheless, neither of them ever dared do it, so when they were exposed they received punishment for their wickedness and lack of prudence. 117 This negligence could arise from nothing but either that his presence must have frightened them or some kindness of the prince calmed them down.

118 In executing such plans, problems or mistakes arise out of either a lack of prudence or a lack of courage; for either of these things possesses you and makes you say and do what you should not, carried away by that mental confusion. 119 And the fact that men are possessed and confused cannot be better demonstrated than by Livy when he writes about how the Aetolian Alexamenes tried to assassinate Nabis of Sparta, whom we have mentioned above; when the time came to carry it out, after he revealed to his people what was to be done, Livy says these words: "He, too, had to summon up his courage, troubled by such realization of the matter."[53] 120 For it is impossible for someone, even someone of firm courage, inured to men's deaths and to wielding the sword, not to be troubled. 121 Hence, men who are experienced in such activities must be chosen; trust in no one else, even if he is considered highly courageous. 122 Because no one promises to be a sure thing in important matters unless he has been tested by experience. 123 So this confusion can either make your weapon fall from your hand or make you say things that have the same effect. 124 Lucilla, the sister of Commodus, ordered Quintianus to assassinate him. 125 He waited for Commodus at the entrance to the amphitheater and, accosting him with a naked dagger, shouted: "This the Senate sends you"; these words caused him to be seized before his arm fell to strike.[54] 126 As I stated above, messer Antonio da Volterra was assigned to assassinate Lorenzo de' Medici and accosting him said: "Ah, traitor"; this cry was Lorenzo's salvation and the conspiracy's downfall.[55]

127 For the reasons given, a conspiracy against one leader may not be fully achieved, but it is easy for a conspiracy not to be fully achieved when it is against two leaders; in fact, this is so difficult that it is almost impossible for it to succeed. 128 For it is almost impossible to perform such an action in different places at one and the same time, for it cannot be performed at different times if one is not to spoil the other. 129 Consequently, if conspiring against one prince is a doubtful, dangerous, and not very wise thing, conspiring against two is altogether vain and frivolous. 130 Were it not for my respect for the historian, I would never believe possible what Herodian says of Plautianus when he commissioned the centurion Saturninus for him, alone, to assassinate Severus and Caracalla, who lived in different places, because it is something so far from reason that nothing but this authority would make me believe it.[56] 131 Some Athenian youths conspired against Diocles and Hippias, the tyrants of Athens; they slew Diocles, but Hippias, surviving, avenged him.[57] 132

Chion and Leonidas of Heraclea, disciples of Plato, conspired against the tyrants Clearchus and Satyrus; they slew Clearchus, and Satyrus, who remained alive, avenged him.[58] 133 The Pazzi, whom we have cited several times, succeeded in slaying only Giuliano.[59] 134 Consequently, no one should take part in such conspiracies against several leaders, because they do no good either for oneself or for one's country or for anyone; rather, those who survive become more unbearable and harsher, as Florence, Athens, and Heraclea, which I have already referred to, know.

135 It is true that the conspiracy that Pelopidas made to free his native city, Thebes, had all of these difficulties yet had a very successful outcome. 136 For Pelopidas conspired against not only two tyrants but ten; not only was he not in their confidence and without easy access to the tyrants but he was a rebel; nevertheless, he was able to enter Thebes, slay the tyrants, and free his city.[60] 137 Yet, nonetheless, he did it all with the aid of one Charon, the tyrants' counsellor, from whom he got easy access to carry out his plot. 138 Let there be no one, however, who takes him as an example, because as it was an impossible undertaking and an astounding thing to succeed in, so it was and is considered by the writers, who celebrate it as something rare, almost unparalleled.

139 The execution can be interrupted by a misapprehension or an unforeseen incident that arises at the time of action. 140 The morning Brutus and the other conspirators wished to assassinate Caesar, it happened that he spoke at length with Gnaeus Popilius Laenas, one of the conspirators; when the others saw this long conversation, they were afraid that this Popilius would reveal the conspiracy to Caesar. They were about to try to slay Caesar then and there and not wait for him to get to the Senate; they would have done so except that the discussion ended, and, seeing that Caesar did not make any unusual gesture, they were reassured.[61] 141 Such misapprehensions must be considered with prudent regard, all the more so as it is easy to have them. 142 Because whoever has a troubled conscience easily believes that people are talking about him, a remark made to some other purpose can be heard and trouble your mind and make you believe that it is said about you; it can make you either reveal the conspiracy by your flight or disturb the action by speeding it up ahead of time. 143 This occurs all the more easily when there are many people aware of the conspiracy.

144 Because they are unexpected, accidents can just be shown by examples and men be made cautious by them. 145 Giulio Bellanti from Siena, whom we have mentioned above, in his wrath against Pandolfo, who had taken his daughter away whom he had first betrothed to him, decided to slay him and chose this time.[62] 146 Pandolfo passed by Giulio's houses almost every day on his way to visit a sick relative. 147 Noticing this, therefore, Giulio arranged to have his conspirators in his house under orders to kill Pandolfo as he passed by; posting them in the entrance, armed, he kept one at the window so he would give a signal when Pandolfo, passing by, neared the entrance. 148 It happened that, as Pandolfo arrived and the man had given the signal, he met a friend who stopped him while some of those who were with him went on ahead; seeing them and hearing the sound of weapons, they discovered the

ambush, so Pandolfo was saved and Giulio and his comrades had to flee from Siena. 149 This accidental encounter prevented that deed and caused the failure of Giulio's undertaking. 150 Because such accidents are rare, no remedy can be devised. 151 But it is necessary to investigate all those that can arise and deal with them.

152 There now remains for us only to discuss the risks incurred after a conspiracy is carried out; there is only one: when someone remains alive to avenge the dead prince. 153 Those remaining to take this revenge, therefore, can be his brothers or his sons or other followers who might expect the princedom (they can remain either through your negligence or for the causes stated above).[63] That is what happened to Giovanni Andrea da Lampognano who, along with his fellow conspirators, killed the duke of Milan; one of the duke's sons and two of his brothers who were left alive were in time to avenge the dead man.[64] 154 And truly, in these cases the conspirators are to be forgiven, because they have no remedy for it; but when someone remains alive out of a lack of prudence by their negligence, then they do not deserve forgiveness. 155 Some conspirators from Forlì slew their lord, Count Girolamo, and captured his wife and sons, who were young; because they felt they could not live in safety unless they took over the fortress and the governor of the castle was unwilling to hand it over to them, Madonna Caterina (for that was the countess's name) promised the conspirators, if they allowed her to enter it, to have it turned over to them, and they should keep her sons with them as hostages.[65] 156 Under this promise they let her go in; once she was inside, she berated them from the walls for her husband's death and threatened them with all kinds of revenge. 157 And to prove that she did not care about her children, she showed them her genitalia, announcing that she still had means to make new ones. 158 So, having lacked counsel and realizing their mistake too late, the conspirators paid for their lack of prudence with permanent exile. 159 But of all the risks that can be incurred after a conspiracy is carried out, there is none more certain or more to be feared than when the people are friendly to the prince whom you have killed, because conspirators have no remedy at all for this, because they can never protect themselves against it.[66] 160 As an example there is Caesar who, because he had the people of Rome as his friends, was avenged by them; for after they expelled the conspirators from Rome, they were the cause for all the conspirators being slain at various times and places.[67]

161 Conspiracies that are made against one's country are less dangerous for those who make them than those against princes, because during their planning there are fewer dangers than in the latter; during their carrying out the dangers are the same, and after their carrying out there are none at all. 162 During their planning there are not many dangers, because a citizen can arrange for his rise to power without revealing his thoughts and intentions to anyone, and, if those arrangements of his are not interfered with, he can follow through with his undertaking successfully; if some law does interfere with them, he can bide his time and get there some other way. 163 This assumes a republic in which there is some degree of corruption, because in one that is not corrupt, such ideas cannot occur to one of its citizens, since there is no

place for evil to start there. 164 So citizens may aspire to princedom in many ways and by many means without danger of being suppressed both because republics are slower than a prince, are less afraid, and, consequently, less cautious and because they have more regard for their noble citizens, and, consequently, the latter are bolder and braver in acting against them. 165 Everyone has read of Catiline's conspiracy, written of by Sallust, and knows that when the conspiracy was revealed, Catiline not only stayed in Rome but came to the Senate and insulted the Senate and the Consul, so great was the regard that the city had for its citizens.[68] 166 After Catiline left Rome and was already with his armies, Lentulus and the others would not have been taken prisoner had there not been letters in their handwriting that clearly implicated them. 167 Hanno, a very noble citizen of Carthage who aspired to tyrannical power, had planned to poison the entire Senate at the wedding of one of his daughters and then make himself prince.[69] 168 When this affair became known, so great was the regard that the Senate had for his character that it made no other provision for it than a law setting limits on the cost of banquets and weddings.

169 It is true, of course, that in carrying out conspiracies against one's own country there is more difficulty and greater risk, because your own forces are seldom sufficient to conspire against so many and not everyone is in command of an army, as were Caesar or Agathocles or Cleomenes and the like, who swiftly took over their countries with their own armies.[70] 170 For to men like these the way is very easy and very safe; but the others, who have not amassed so many forces, have to do things either by deception and craft or with foreign troops. 171 As for deception and craft, when the Peisistratus of Athens had defeated the inhabitants of Megara and thereby acquired favor with the people, he went out one morning wounded, saying that the Nobility had injured him out of envy and requesting permission to take armed men along to guard him. 172 From this authority he easily rose to such grandeur that he became the tyrant of Athens.[71] 173 Upon his return to Siena, along with other exiles, Pandolfo Petrucci was given command over the guard of the town square, a thing of little importance that others turned down; nevertheless, these armed men gave him such prestige in time that he soon became its prince.[72] 174 Many others have used different devices and different means and achieved power in the course of time and without risk. 175 Those who have conspired to seize their country with their armed forces or foreign armies have had varying success according to Fortune.[73] 176 Catiline, mentioned above, was overwhelmed by it.[74] 177 When poison failed to bring success for Hanno, whom we have mentioned above, he armed many thousands of people among his followers, and they and he were killed.[75] 178 Some of Thebes's principal citizens called in a Spartan army to help make themselves tyrants, and they took tyrannical power over the city.[76] 179 So, if you examine all the conspiracies made against their country, you will find none, or very few, that are quashed during their planning; but all either succeeded or failed while being carried out. 180 Once carried out, they still do not run any other risks than are involved in the nature of princedom itself, for when one man

has become tyrant, he runs the natural and normal risks that tyranny occasions, for which there are no remedies other than those discussed above.[77]

181 This is all I have to write about conspiracies; if I have discussed those that are made by arms and not by poison, that results from their all following the same pattern. 182 It is true that those with poison are riskier because they are more uncertain, because not everyone has a chance to get it and it is necessary to discuss it with someone who does; this need for discussion puts you in danger. 183 Then for many reasons a poisoned drink may not be fatal, as happened to those who slew Commodus: when he rejected the poison they had given him, they were forced to strangle him if they wanted him to die.[78]

184 Princes thus have no greater enemy than conspiracy, because when one is formed against them, they either get slain or are disgraced. 185 Because if it succeeds, they die; if it is revealed and they slay the conspirators, people always believe that it was an invention of the prince to unleash his greed and his cruelty on the lives and property of those whom he has killed. 186 I do not wish, therefore, to fail to warn a prince or a republic against whom a conspiracy might be made: if ever a conspiracy is revealed to them, seek out and understand its nature very fully before they undertake to avenge it; let them measure fully the conspirators' circumstances and their own. If they find conspiracy widespread and powerful, never reveal it until they have readied themselves with sufficient armed forces to crush it; acting otherwise they would discover their own downfall. 187 Hence, they must conceal it quite assiduously, because once conspirators realize that they are exposed, impelled by necessity, they act without hesitation. 188 For example,[79] when the Romans left two legions of soldiers to defend the Capuans against the Samnites, as we have said elsewhere, the leaders of the legions conspired together to attack the Capuans; when Rome learned of this matter, they commissioned Rutulus, the new Consul, to take care of it; to lull the conspirators to sleep, he announced that the Senate had confirmed the quarters for the Capuan legions.[80] 189 The soldiers believed it, and, thinking they had time to carry out their design, they did not seek to hasten matters; so they remained until they began to see that the Consul was separating them from each other; this aroused their suspicion, causing them to reveal themselves and carry out their plot. 190 And there can be no greater example of both aspects than this: because through it we can see how slow men are in matters where they think they have time and how quick they are when necessity spurs them on. 191 A prince or a republic that wants to postpone revealing a conspiracy to its own advantage cannot use a better approach than craftily offering the conspirators an opportunity near at hand, so, waiting for it or assuming they have time, they give him or it time to punish them. 192 Anyone who has done otherwise has hastened his downfall, as did the duke of Athens and Guglielmo de' Pazzi. 193 When the duke became tyrant of Florence and learned that he had been conspired against, he had one of the conspirators seized without investigating the matter further; that made the others immediately take up arms and wrest the government from him.[81] 194 When Guglielmo was commissioner in Val di Chiana in 1501 and learned that there was a conspiracy on behalf of the Vitelli in Arezzo to take the town

away from the Florentines, he went there right away; without considering either his own or the conspirators' armed forces and without preparing himself with any army, he had one of the conspirators seized on the advice of his son, the bishop. After this capture the others took up arms right away and wrested the city from the Florentines; Guglielmo went from being commissioner to becoming a captive.[82] 195 But when conspiracies are weak, they can and must be crushed without hesitation. 196 Nor should two approaches, more or less the opposite of each other, in any way be imitated: one used by the abovementioned duke of Athens who, in order to show that he thought he had the goodwill of the Florentine citizens, put to death the man who revealed a conspiracy against him;[83] the other used by Dion of Syracuse who, to test the intent of some men whom he held in suspicion, agreed to let Callippus, whom he trusted, pretend to make a conspiracy against him.[84] 197 Both of these ended badly: the first discouraged the accusers and encouraged those who wished to conspire; the other provided an easy way to his death. Indeed, he himself was the leader of his own conspiracy, as he learned by experience; able to plot against Dion without hesitation, Callippus plotted so much that he took away Dion's state and life.

NOTES

1. This sentence may offer the rationale for this chapter's being the longest in the *Discourses.* Although Aristotle briefly discusses conspiracies in *Politics,* 5, Machiavelli's was the first treatise to engage in significant analysis of them. It becomes apparent that fourteenth- and fifteenth-century Italy was rife with such plots. Machiavelli himself was imprisoned and tortured as a result of the Boscoli conspiracy to overthrow the Medici in 1512.

2. Although Guicciardini does not comment on this chapter, he is no more sanguine about the potential for a successful conspiracy; see his *Dialogo del reggimento di Firenze,* Piero Capponi's first speech in Book 2. Several of his *Ricordi* are also relevant. For example, there is the typical stylistic device of expressing his observations as a paradox, namely, that the more precautions one takes for security the more likely one will fail: "Nothing is more at variance with a person's wanting his conspiracies to have a felicitous outcome than seeking to base them on secure foundations and to have almost certain success. Whoever wants to do this must involve many men, much time, and many favorable occasions, all of which create access for discovery. You see, therefore, how dangerous conspiracies are, since things that bring about safety in any other undertaking bring danger in this kind. I believe it also may be because Fortune, who has great strength in these matters, grows angry with anyone who works too diligently to deprive her of power over conspiracies" (C. 20); see B. 55, which adds, "Hence I conclude that it is safer to carry them out at some risk than with too many safety precautions."

3. In *Prince,* 3, Machiavelli notes that "men are willing to change their ruler if they expect improvements. This expectation induces them to take up arms against the prince, but they deceive themselves by so doing because with experience they subsequently realize that matters have become worse" (p. 103, lines 5–11).

4. Loosely translated from *Histories,* 4.8; but, as Martelli points out, there is no sense in Tacitus of "should" (*Storici antichi,* pp. 123–125).

5. In 2, 32, sentences 15–23.

6. As noted below in sentence 11, he discusses this topic "elsewhere": in the longest chapter of the *Prince,* 19, "How To Avoid Contempt and Hatred": "One of the most potent remedies a prince has against conspiracies is not being hated by the people at large [the general public]. For the conspirator always believes that the prince's death will satisfy the people; but when the conspirator believes he might cause the people trouble, he has not the courage to undertake such a project because the obstacles conspirators face are countless" (pp. 289; 291, lines 47–54). *Discourses,* 2, 24, and 28, are also relevant.

7. Translates *guerra.*

8. If a prince has "the goodwill of the people . . . it is impossible for anyone to be so foolhardy as to conspire against him" (*Prince,* 19, p. 291, lines 72–74).

9. In *Prince,* 17, he warns the princes to keep his "hands off the property of his subjects and citizens—and from their women. Yet if he needs to take someone's life, let him take it when there is suitable justification and evident reason" (p. 273, lines 63–66).

10. Machiavelli also discusses the inadvisability of using threats above, in 1, 44, and in 2, 26.

11. Below, sentences 91–98.

12. Machiavelli continues the passage quoted in note 8 by asserting, "But above all he should restrain himself from other people's property: men are quicker to forget the death of a father than the loss of an inheritance" (p. 273, lines 67–69).

13. For this example, see above, 2, 28, sentences 9–14, notes 3 and 5. Because Aristotle uses the same example in a discussion of conspiracies, *Politics,* 5.8.10; 1311b2–3 may be relevant.

14. See sentences 145–149 below, and note 62.

15. See sentences 104–107 for more on the Pazzi conspiracy in 1478. Giovanni Borromei was the father of Giovanni de' Pazzi's wife. The allusion here is to the law that the Medici passed retroactively to prevent him from access to his father-in-law's inheritance. It stated that when there was no will and no male children, a deceased man's inheritance would go to the male grandchildren before the daughters; see Machiavelli, *Florentine Histories,* 8, 2, and Guicciardini, *History of Florence,* chapter 4, which specifies that the law was enacted in 1476.

16. For Phalaris and Dionysius I, the Elder, see above, 1, 10, n.5.

17. Quoted in Latin from Juvenal, *Satires,* 10, vv. 112–113: *"Ad generum Cereris sine caede et vulnere pauci / descendunt reges et sicca morte tiranni."*

18. In sentence 18 above.

19. A sixty-year-old peasant attacked Ferdinand the Catholic on 7 December 1492; the blow glanced off the king's gold chain and his life was spared. One measure of his astuteness was diverting his nobles from thoughts of conspiracy: "he kept the minds of the barons of Castile preoccupied with the campaign [against Granada]; with their thoughts involved in the war, they did not think about sedition" (*Prince,* 21, p. 331, lines 13–16).

20. This attempt also occurred in 1492; see above, 1, 19, n.4, for Bayazid and Selim, "the present Turk."

21. See Aristotle, *Politics,* 5.8.7; 1311a9–21.

22. Perennis, a prefect of the Praetorian Guard, virtually ruled Rome until

Commodus discovered his conspiracy and had him murdered in A.D. 185; see Herodian, *History (De Imperio Romanum Imperatorum post Marcum),* 1.9.

23. See note 39 to this chapter for this event in A.D. 205; based on Herodian, 3.10.6–12.12.

24. As with the two preceding ones, this example is taken from the history of imperial, not republican, Rome. Lucius Aelius Sejanus, the prefect of the Praetorian Guard and after A.D. 23 chief adviser to Emperor Tiberius, reinforced his fear of assassination and urged him to retire to Capreae (Capri) to continue his debaucheries. The power of Sejanus thus became so great that he plotted to seize power, but Tiberius persuaded the Senate to imprison him and sentence him to death in 31. See Tacitus, *Annals,* 5.6–8, and Suetonius, *Tiberius,* 65.

25. At one point Jacopo di Appiano was chancellor to Piero Gambacorti, the ruler of Pisa; but when the latter refused to join his plans to renounce an alliance with Florence in 1392, Jacopo killed him and ruled Pisa until 1398.

26. Francesco Coppola was a rich merchant and adviser to Ferdinand of Aragon, king of Naples, who made him count of Sarno. But in 1485 Coppola joined a group of barons who wanted to overthrow the king. Ferdinand quelled the revolt and promised to pardon the leaders. In 1487, though, he reversed his decision and executed them. Machiavelli refers to this in *Florentine Histories,* 8, 32; in its last sentence he refers to him as "Iacopo."

27. Note that in *Prince,* 17, he says: "friendships acquired through money rather than through greatness and nobility of character may be bought, but they are not owned: they cannot be drawn upon in times of need. Men are less reluctant to cause trouble for someone who makes himself loved than for someone who makes himself feared. For love is supported by a bond of obligation which, since men are evil, they break on any occasion when it is useful for them to do so; but fear is supported by a dread of retribution which can always be counted on" (p. 273, lines 48–58).

28. Guicciardini puts it much more succinctly: "Conspiracies cannot be made without associates and therefore are extremely dangerous; because most men are either imprudent or evil, associating oneself with such people risks too much danger" (*Ricordi,* C. 19). See also B. 158, in which the issue is "changes in governments" and the "associates" are "most of the time mad and wicked men who know neither how to be silent nor how to act."

29. Machiavelli continues the passage from *Prince,* 19, quoted in note 6 above, by pointing out that "a conspirator cannot act alone, and he can find no associates except among those who he thinks are disgruntled. But as soon as you reveal your intention to a disgruntled man, you give him the means to obtain satisfaction, for he can obviously expect every advantage from his knowledge" (p. 291, lines 56–61).

30. For Piso's conspiracy, see note 38 below. Tacitus describes it in *Annals,* 15.48–54; he lists some twenty conspirators and expresses amazement that so many people of different backgrounds could refrain from discussing it. For more on the Pazzi conspiracy, see note 46 below; Machiavelli describes it in detail in *Florentine Histories,* 8, 1–10.

31. Livy, 4.5–7.

32. Based on a life of Alexander the Great by Quintus Curtius Rufus; see 6.7–11. Although the plot was led by the Macedonian general Philotas in 330 B.C., some mod-

ern commentators are skeptical about this account. For a more considered treatment of the sources, even Quintus Curtius Rufus, see Martelli, *Storici antichi,* pp. 126–128.

33. See Tacitus, *Annals,* 15.48; 54–56, for this conspiracy in A.D. 65.

34. See Livy, 24.5, for this conspiracy in 215 B.C. For more on Hieronymus, see above, 2, 2, sentence 20 and note 12.

35. The source for this event occurring in 272 B.C. is the account in Justin, 26.1, and Plutarch, *Moralia, De mulierum virtutibus* (Of virtuous wives), 253.a–b, in which the leader's name is given as Hellanicus, although Machiavelli writes "Nelematus." Aristotimus was tyrant of Elaea, a city of Epirus at the mouth of the Acheron, the river reputed to be the entrance to Hades. For more on the source for this and the next example, see Martelli, *Storici antichi,* pp. 128–130.

36. The Magus was a Zoroastrian priest named Gaumata, who for seven months passed himself off as Smerdis, the brother and heir of King Cambyses, in 521 B.C.; see Herodotus, 3.61–79, in which the cue for the speech quoted is provided but not the words, which Machiavelli invented.

37. See above, 1, 10, n.5, for more on Nabis; see also Book 1, 40, sentence 37. The event referred to here and also in sentence 119 below occurred in 192 B.C.; it is described in Livy, 35.34–36, where the number of foot soldiers is given as one thousand. For more on textual discrepancies, see Martelli, *Storici antichi,* pp. 130–131.

38. Machiavelli alluded to this conspiracy above in sentence 60. After the fire in A.D. 64 that destroyed half of Rome, the city was ready for a conspiracy to assassinate Nero and make Gaius Calpurnius Piso emperor; see Tacitus, *Annals,* 15.48–52. Tacitus refers to Piso's villa at Baiae on the Bay of Naples, but Machiavelli overlooks the point that Tacitus makes: Piso would not murder Nero in his own gardens because that would violate the laws of hospitality.

39. Machiavelli alludes to this event in sentence 40 above; see note 22. Gaius Fulvius Plautianus, a prefect of the Praetorian Guard of Septimus Severus, acquired almost autocratic power and probably would have succeeded the emperor. Dio Cassius, although not the source for this incident, thought that the plot was devised in A.D. 205 by Antoninus, whom we may know better as Caracalla, to eradicate a rival with too much power. But Machiavelli's source, as he acknowledges in sentence 130 below, was Herodian; see 3.10.6–12.12.

40. See Tacitus, *Annals,* 15.51; the trireme captain was Volusius Proculus, who was based at Misenum on the Bay of Naples. But see Martelli, *Storici antichi,* p. 131, for the relevance of Tacitus, *Annals,* 13.12.1, and Suetonius, *Nero,* 26.2.

41. This conspiracy occurred during the last year of Commodus's reign, A.D. 192. For how they "slew Commodus," see note 78, below. For a slight mixup in the source and its relation to Poliziano's translation of Herodian, 1.16.4–17, especially 1.16.5, see Martelli, *Storici antichi,* p. 132. See also *Prince,* 19, pp. 307; 309, lines 318–328.

42. This event occurred in Carrhae in northern Mesopotamia, where Caracalla was fighting the Parthians during the last year of his reign, A.D. 217. Flavius Maternianus was in command of the military in Rome during Caracalla's absence. Macrinus, a man of law, became the next emperor, the first one not to come from the senatorial ranks; he was put to death by his troops the following year. See Herodian, 4.12–13.

43. See note 35 above; strictly speaking, Hellanicus, whom Machiavelli calls Nelematus, was not a leader in Epirus but in a neighboring district of Aetolia.

44. Sentences 14 and 15.

45. An echo of passages in *Prince,* 3, and above, 2, 23, n.8.

46. In *Florentine Histories,* 8, 2–9, Machiavelli discusses this famous conspiracy at the end of April 1478 against Lorenzo de' Medici and his brother Giuliano; it was led by Jacopo and Francesco Pazzi, both members of a banking firm that rivaled the Medici's. They had the support of Pope Sixtus IV, his nephew Girolamo Riario, his kinsman Raffaello Riario, cardinal of the Church of San Giorgio in Velabro, and Francesco Salviati, the archbishop of Pisa. The conspirators believed that the Medici would entertain Cardinal Riario, whom they had sent to Florence expressly in the hopes that the Medici would feel obliged to organize some festivities for him.

47. Translates *desinare,* which refers to the main meal, usually served at midday. In *Florentine Histories,* 8, 5, Machiavelli says, "By means of the cardinal of San Giorgio, Raffaele Riario, the conspirators sought to bring Lorenzo and Giuliano together and, as soon as this happened, to assassinate them. Consequently, the conspirators arranged for the Medici to give a banquet for the cardinal at their villa in Fiesole."

48. The revised plan set the assassination for the Cathedral of Santa Reparata (known today as Santa Maria del Fiore—the Duomo) where the seventeen-year-old cardinal was to celebrate mass on 26 April.

49. The pope's condottiere, Giovan Battista da Montesecco, unfazed by the prospect of murdering the Medici while they ate dinner, balked at doing so in church. The task then fell to Antonio da Volterra and a priest, Stefano di Bagnone, "two men by nature and experience totally inept for so great an exploit" (*Florentine Histories,* 8, 5.) They succeeded in murdering Giuliano, inflicting nineteen wounds, but Lorenzo escaped. The humanist and poet Angelo Poliziano wrote a well-known account of this conspiracy, *Pactianae coniurationis commentarium* (1478); this is translated in Benjamin G. Kohl and Ronald G. Witt, *Earthly Republic,* pp. 305–322.

50. In 88 B.C. the celebrated Roman general and political leader Gaius Marius fled Rome, because his rivalry with the patrician Sulla had led to civil war. He sought refuge in Minturnae, modern-day Minturno, a town near the Gulf of Gaeta south of Rome and north of Naples. None of the people of Minturnae would carry out their magistrates' execution order, but the soldier, or slave, who was sent to kill him was unable to do so because of Marius's "majesty and respect." Although most commentators cite Plutarch, *Marius,* 37–39, as the source, see Martelli, *Storici antichi,* pp. 132–133; for the detail about the slave as the assassin, see Livy, *Epitomae Periochae,* 77, and Valerius Maximus, 2.10.6.

51. Although no writer in antiquity mentions a conspiracy against Sitalces, king of the Odrysians of Thrace from 440 to 424 B.C., several details in Machiavelli's account lead commentators, accepting Walker's hypothesis, to believe that Machiavelli grafted an episode in Herodotus, 5, 92, concerning a tyrant of Corinth, Cypselus, onto the account of Sitalces in Thucydides, 2.29, 95–101. For Martelli's discussion of these sources, see *Storici antichi,* pp. 133–134.

52. Alfonso d'Este, the husband of Lucrezia Borgia, succeeded his father, Ercole I, as duke of Ferrara and ruled from 1505 to 1534. In 1506 a conspiracy was organized against Alfonso that included two brothers, Ferdinando and Giulio, the latter Ercole's illegitimate son and the former, sometimes referred to as Ferrante or Ferrando, a brother of Alfonso and of Giulio; the plot failed and the brothers were condemned to

prison for life. Guicciardini's judgment reads as follows: "many times they had very great opportunity to assassinate him; but held back by a fatal timidity, they always let the opportunity pass by so that, as almost always happens when the execution of conspiracies is put off, once the affair came to light, Ferdinando and the others were imprisoned" (*Storia d'Italia,* 7, 4). This episode is referred to in a letter from Biagio Buonaccorsi to Machiavelli (*Friends,* p. 137, and p. 472, n.4) and in Ariosto, *Orlando Furioso,* 3, 61–62.

53. Machiavelli refers to this above in sentences 75–76; see note 37. He quotes Livy in Latin: *"Collegit et ipse animum, confusum tantae cogitatione rei"* (35.35.18).

54. Anna Lucilla Augusta was accustomed to power because she was the daughter of Emperor Marcus Aurelius and the sister of Commodus, who succeeded his father, Marcus Aurelius, in A.D. 180. Lucilla was first married to the powerful coadjutor of Marcus Aurelius, Lucius Vero. On the latter's death in 169, she was betrothed to Claudius Pompeianus Quintianus, the emperor's chief adviser. When Commodus excluded her from the circles of power, she attempted to organize a conspiracy against him. Machiavelli seems to be following Herodian, 1.8.5–6, because he says the conspirator's name was Quintianus; other authorities state that he was Lucilla's husband, Claudius Pompeianus (see Dio Cassius, 62.4, and Aelius Lampridius, *Scriptores Historia Augusta,* "Commodus," 4). For the use of Poliziano's translation of Herodian, see Martelli, *Storici antichi,* p. 135.

55. See note 49 above. This detail is omitted from Machiavelli's account in *Florentine Histories,* 8, 6, and Guicciardini's *History of Florence,* chapter 4; Piero Parenti (1450–1519) alludes to it in his *Storia fiorentina* but attributes the "cry" to another conspirator, Bernardo Bandini.

56. See note 39 above. Septimius Severus was emperor from A.D. 193 to 211, and his son Antoninus, or Caracalla, reigned from 211 to 217. One textual tradition of the *Discourses* reads "countries" for "places"; because Machiavelli is following Herodian here and the latter uses "places," that seems the safer choice (Inglese). But for more on the use of Poliziano's translation of Herodian, see the discussion in Martelli, *Storici antichi,* pp. 135–140.

57. Based on Justin, 2.9. In 514 B.C. Harmodius and Aristogiton formed a conspiracy against the sons of Pisistratus, Diocles and Hippias (see above, 1, 2, n.17). Walker argues that Justin misread Thucydides, 6.54–59, and Machiavelli follows him in that error: it was Hippias, whose name according to Thucydides should be Hipparchus, and not Diocles, who was murdered.

58. Again, based on Justin, 16.5.1–12. For Clearchus, who was assassinated in 352 or 353 B.C., see above, 1, 16, n.8. He was the brother of Satyrus who, after he "avenged" him, continued to be a tyrant; see Justin 16.5.17–18. See Martelli, *Storici antichi,* pp. 140–141, for discrepancies in the use of Justin.

59. For the death of Giulano only, see Machiavelli, *Florentine Histories,* 8, 6. For life in Florence being, as he says in the next sentence, "more unbearable and harsher," see Guicciardini, *History of Florence,* 4.

60. See Plutarch, *Pelopidas,* 5–13. Machiavelli confuses Charon with Phillidas (7).

61. Plutarch, *Brutus,* 14–16; but see Martelli, *Storici antichi,* pp. 142–143.

62. Machiavelli refers to this conspiracy above in sentence 18. Pandolfo Petrucci seized Siena with his brother Jacopo in 1487 and ruled alone from 1498 to 1512. The

conspiracy occurred in 1508 and, as Inglese notes, is not to be confused with one that Lucio Bellanti led against the Petrucci family in 1495. The Bellanti were a powerful Sienese family who initially supported the Petrucci but later turned against them. Machiavelli discusses Pandolfo Petrucci's career in *Prince,* chapters 20 and 22, and mentions him frequently in his diplomatic correspondence. One context in which Petrucci appears frequently is his masterminding of a conspiracy that Machiavelli curiously omits from this chapter: the one against Cesare Borgia in 1502 known as the *dieta dei falliti* (the assembly of failures). From 1501 to 1505, Machiavelli was involved in three diplomatic missions to Petrucci. A typical assessment occurs in a dispatch dated 18 July 1505, in which he writes of Petrucci's deft maneuvering: "he always kept his feet in thousands of stirrups, and kept them there in such a way that he could withdraw them at will" (*Legazioni e commissarie,* 2:897).

63. In sentence 127–129 above. On this point and the following example, see Mansfield, *New Modes,* pp. 337–338.

64. See Machiavelli's description in *Florentine Histories,* 7, 33–34, of this assassination of Galeazzo Maria Sforza, which occurred in the church of San Stefano on Christmas Day, 1476. In addition to Giovanni, the conspirators were Carlo Visconti and Girolamo Oligato. The revenge was carried out by his son, Gian Galeazzo Sforza, and his two brothers, Ludovico "Il Moro" Sforza and Ascanio Sforza. In *Florentine Histories* Machiavelli does not attribute the conspiracy's failure to the avenging family but rather "these unhappy youths . . . were crushed when those they hoped would have followed and protected them neither protected nor followed." He adds that princes should learn from this failure "to live in such a way and act so as to make themselves revered and loved so that no one, by killing them, can hope to save himself." But Vivanti, in his edition of the *Discorsi,* wonders whether this judgment, written after the *Discourses* at some point between 1520 and 1524, may also reflect the recently thwarted conspiracy against Giulio de' Medici led by several of Machiavelli's "noontime friends" at the Rucellai gardens, including Zanobi Buondelmonti, one of the dedicatees of the *Discourses* (see Dedication, n.1).

65. Machiavelli writes about this conspiracy, which Francesco d'Orso organized on 14 April 1488, in *Florentine Histories,* 8, 34. Count Girolamo Riario was the son of Pope Sixtus IV, and his wife, Caterina Sforza Riario, was the natural daughter of Galeazzo Maria Sforza, mentioned in the previous note. The fortress, Ravaldino, was commanded by Tommaso Feo. Caterina called on her uncle, Ludovico "Il Moro" Sforza, for help and was restored to power in Forlì on 29 April; "having retaken the state, she avenged her husband's death with all manner of cruelty" (*Florentine Histories,* 8, 34). In *Prince,* 20, Machiavelli observes that her fortresses were of little avail against Cesare Borgia, who happily came to the aid of her oppressed subjects in late 1499 and early 1500; in *Art of War,* 7, he cites her fortress as an example of poor construction, though he applauds her "courageous undertaking" in attempting to withstand Cesare Borgia. Guicciardini calls her "an extremely courageous and masculine woman" (*History of Florence,* chapter 19), and in his *Storia d'Italia,* 4, 13, he contrasts her "masculine courage" with the spirit of her "cowardly" and "feminine" troops.

66. A judgment similar to that cited from *Florentine Histories,* 7, 34, quoted in note 64 above, and to the argument of *Prince,* 19.

67. An opinion found in Plutarch's lives of *Brutus,* 18, 20, and *Caesar,* 68–69. In-

glese observes that while at this point Caesar seems to be more of a "civil" prince, a notion Machiavelli fails to develop, his treatment of Caesar above, 1, 10, sentences 11–13, is as the typical Renaissance model of a despicable tyrant. In his *Ricordi* Guicciardini observes: "Do not attempt any changes in government *[novità]* with the expectation that the people will follow you, because that is a dangerous foundation; they may lack the courage to follow and often have a vision different from what you believe. Look at the example of Brutus and Cassius who, after they murdered Caesar, not only lacked the people's support, which they had taken for granted, but also were forced to withdraw to the Capitol out of fear of the people" (C. 121). This notion is expressed in B. 156: "The dispositions and deliberations of the people are so flawed and prompted more often by chance than by reason, that whoever adjusts the progress of his life in no other way than by hoping to become great because of them has little judgment. Figuring them out is more a question of luck than wisdom."

68. For Catiline see above, 1, 10, n.6. The major sources for this and the next sentence are Sallust, *Bellum Catilinae,* 31 and 46–47; Plutarch, *Cicero,* 16–19; and Cicero, *In Catilinam,* 1.1. The conspiracy against Cicero, whom Machiavelli refers to as the Consul, occurred in 63 B.C. Catiline insulted Cicero by reminding the Senate that Cicero was not Roman, because he was born in a Volscian hill town, the present-day Arpino, about sixty-five miles southeast of Rome, near the industrial town of Sora. After Catiline fled to Etruria, one of his co-conspirators, Publius Cornelius Lentulus Sura, wrote him incriminating letters transmitted through envoys in a delegation of Allobrogan Gauls. Their interception led to the arrest of all the conspirators including Lentulus.

69. Occurring around 350 B.C., this conspiracy is described in Justin, 21.4; but see the discussion in Martelli, *Storici antichi,* pp. 142–144. Machiavelli refers to Hanno's death in sentence 177 below.

70. For Julius Caesar see Plutarch, *Caesar,* 32–33; for Agathocles see above, 2, 12, n.3, Justin, 22.1.16, and Plutarch, *Pyrrhus,* 14; for Cleomenes see above, 1, 9, n.11, and Plutarch, *Cleomenes,* 4.

71. This trick is mentioned in Plutarch, *Solon,* 30.1–2 (95), and Herodotus, 1.59.

72. See above, note 62; Petrucci and his brother returned from exile in 1487. Machiavelli says that "Pandolfo and Jacopo seized more power; they became like princes in the city, one through his prudence, the other through his courage" (*Florentine Histories,* 8, 35). It was not until January 1496, however, that Pandolfo was given control over the "guard," a military militia, and it was not until after Jacopo's death in 1497 that Pandolfo had absolute power in Siena; see also Guicciardini, *Storia d'Italia,* 4, 3.

73. One of Machiavelli's premises throughout this chapter is that conspiracies are an aspect of Fortune, not Necessity. Now that this chapter is almost completed, it is clear that his procedure is to illustrate them and devise categories for them. There is only one generalization that he believes can be made about conspiracies: princes are more vulnerable to them than republics, because, as he will argue in the next three chapters, princes are less flexible in dealing with Fortune's shifting times and circumstances. See below, 3, 9, sentence 10.

74. See above, note 68; the sources are Plutarch, *Cicero,* 22, and Sallust, *Bellum Catilinae,* 60.

75. See note 69 above.

76. They formed an oligarchy, which the conspiracy led by Pelopidas tried to overthrow in 382 B.C. Machiavelli refers to this conspiracy above, sentences 135–138, see note 60; the sources are Justin, 3.6.10, and Plutarch, *Pelopidas,* 5.

77. In this and the two preceding chapters.

78. See above, sentences 93 and 94, and note 41, for this conspiracy. They "slew Commodus" by suborning an athlete named Narcissus to strangle him. See Herodian, 1.17.11.

79. For more on the following example, see above, 2, 19, n.12, and 2, 26, sentence 7. The "new Consul" in 342 B.C. was Gaius Marcius Rutulus.

80. This account is based on Livy, 7.38–41; he mentions that they would be wintering in the same towns the next year (38.9).

81. Machiavelli's masterly account of the career of Walter de Brienne, duke of Athens, can be found in *Florentine Histories,* 2, 30; 33–37. After he lost the duchy of Athens, he was sent to govern Florence by Charles, duke of Calabria, whom Florentine Guelphs had asked to govern them in 1325 during their struggle for control of the city with the Ghibellines (see above, 2, 9, n.3). Then in 1342 Florence invited the duke to lead its army, which was losing a war against Pisa. Dealing deftly with various Florentine factions, he had himself appointed the first conservator of the state and then lord for life. Three separate conspiracies were organized against him. The person he "seized" was Antonio Adimari; his arrest led to an insurrection that forced the duke to leave Florence on 26 July 1343.

82. These events occurred in June 1502, not 1501, in the context of Cesare Borgia's third campaign in Romagna (see above, 2, 23, sentences 13–15, and note 9). Guicciardini describes this particular conspiracy, which erupted 4 June, in his *Storia d'Italia,* 5, 8, and *History of Florence,* chapter 22. Guglielmo arrested two conspirators, not one, on the advice of his son, Cosimo de' Pazzi.

83. Machiavelli tells us in *Florentine Histories,* 2, 36, that Matteo di Morozzo exposed the conspiracy.

84. For more on Dion, see above, 1, 10, n.4. The conspiracy in 353/354 B.C. is based on Plutarch, *Dion,* 54–57. Callippus became the next tyrant of Syracuse.

~ 7 ~

WHY PASSING FROM FREEDOM TO SLAVERY AND FROM SLAVERY TO FREEDOM IS SOMETIMES BLOODLESS AND SOMETIMES BLOODY

1 Some may perhaps wonder why it is that of the many changes that are made from a free society to tyranny and the contrary, some are made with bloodshed and others without, for, as one may understand from history, in such alterations countless men have sometimes been killed and sometimes not one of them has been injured. This happened during the change that Rome made from the kings to the Consuls when no one but the Tarquins was expelled without any one else being harmed.[1] 2 It depends on this: whether the government being changed was or was not created by violence. Because if it is

created in violence, it has to bring injury to many people; later, at its downfall, those who were harmed have to want to get revenge, and this desire for revenge brings about bloodshed and the death of men. 3 But if the government is caused by a common consensus of people who have made it great, those people have no reason to harm anyone but the leader later when it falls. 4 The government of Rome and the expulsion of the Tarquins were of this kind, as was also the government of the Medici in Florence so that on their downfall in 1494 no one was harmed but them.[2] 5 Thus, such changes do not turn out to be very dangerous, but those that are made by people who have reason to get revenge are indeed quite dangerous; and these have always been of such a kind as to terrify those who read about them, at the very least. 6 And because history is full of examples of this, I shall leave them out.

NOTES

1. See above, 1, 3, n.2. On the comparison between the Roman and Florentine examples, see Mansfield, *New Modes,* pp. 343–344.

2. Charles VIII invaded Italy 2 September 1494 and on his way to Rome entered Florence on 17 November. Because Florence's ruler, Piero de' Medici, handed over four of Florence's protective strongholds and 200,000 ducats, the Florentines banished him on 9 November along with his brothers Giovanni, the future Pope Leo X, and Giuliano, the future duke of Nemours. Machiavelli deals with this background at the opening of *Decennale* I.

~ *8* ~

ANYONE WHO WISHES TO ALTER A REPUBLIC HAS TO CONSIDER HOW IT IS MADE

1 It has been discussed above how a bad citizen cannot do evil in a republic that is not corrupted;[1] in addition to the reasons that were stated then, the examples of Spurius Cassius and Manlius Capitolinus strengthen that conclusion. 2 Spurius was an ambitious man who wanted to seize extraordinary power in Rome and win over the Plebs by giving them many benefits (such as dividing among them the fields that the Romans had taken from the Hernici).[2] The Patricians discovered this ambition of his, and it was held in such suspicion that when he spoke to the people and offered to give them the money that had been earned from the grain that the treasury had brought from Sicily, they completely rejected it, because they felt that Spurius wanted to give them the price of their freedom. 3 But if the people had been corrupted, they would not have rejected that price, and they would have opened to tyranny the way that they shut off to him. 4 Manlius Capitolinus is a much better example of this, because through him we can see how much an ugly greed for rule later negates *virtù* of mind and body and good deeds done on behalf of one's country.[3] As we can see, this arose in him through the envy that he had at the honors given Camillus; and he came to be so blind mentally that, without thinking

of the city's way of life or examining how it was made, which was not suited yet to receiving an evil form,[4] he began to stir up riots in Rome against the Senate and the city's laws. 5 From this we can see the perfection of the city and the goodness of its matter,[5] for in his case not one of the Nobility, although they were very fierce defenders of each another, made any effort to support him; not one of his relatives undertook any action in his behalf: for other accused men they were wont to appear dressed in black, all in mourning, to beg for mercy for the accused, but not one of them was seen for Manlius. 6 The Tribunes of the Plebs, who were always wont to support things that ostensibly benefited the people and who advanced them the more they were against the Nobles, in this case united with the Nobles to stamp out a common plague. 7 Although the people of Rome, who were very desirous of their own good and fond of things that went against the Nobility, gave much support to Manlius, nevertheless, when the Tribunes summoned him and put his case to the judgment of the people, the people, changing from defender to judge, condemned him to death without any hesitation.[6] 8 Hence I do not believe there is a more appropriate example in Livy's history to show the goodness of all the laws of the republic than this one, seeing that no one in the city acted to defend a citizen full of every *virtù,* who had done very many praiseworthy deeds publicly and privately. 9 Because in all of them love of country was stronger than any other consideration, and they had far more concern for the present dangers that might derive from him than for his past merits; so they were set free with his death. 10 And Livy says: "Such an end had a man who, had he not been born in a free city, would have been memorable."[7]

11 There are two things to consider here: first, that one must seek glory by different means in a corrupted city than in one that still has political life;[8] second (which is almost the same as the first), that men, in their proceedings and particularly in great actions, have to consider the times and adapt to them.[9] 12 And those who through bad choice or natural inclination are not in harmony with their times usually live unhappily and their actions turn out badly, but it is the contrary for those who are in harmony with their times. 13 There is no question that we may conclude from the words of the historian quoted above that if Manlius had been born in the time of Marius and Sulla, when the matter was already corrupted and he would have been able to impress the form of his ambition on it, he would have had the same results and success as Marius and Sulla and the others later who after them aspired to tyrannical power. 14 In the same way, if Sulla and Marius had lived in Manlius's times, they would have been crushed during their first undertakings. 15 For a man can indeed start corrupting a city's people by his ways and his evil expedients, but it is impossible for one man's lifetime to be enough to corrupt it to such a degree that he himself can reap the fruits; and even if it were possible for him to do so over a long period of time, it would be impossible as far as men's way of doing things is concerned, because they are impatient and cannot put off for any length of time something they covet. 16 Furthermore, men deceive themselves about their own affairs and especially what they strongly desire, so either out of lack of patience or through self-deception they would set out on

an undertaking at the wrong time, and it would turn out badly for them. 17 So, in order to seize power in a republic and give it an evil form, one must find its matter put in disarray by time and for it to have been reduced to this disarray little by little from generation to generation;[10] as we have discussed above, this may be brought about of necessity when it has not been often revitalized by good examples or drawn back to its origins by new laws.[11] 18 Manlius would thus have been a rare and memorable man if he had been born in a corrupted city. 19 And therefore citizens who undertake anything in republics in support of either freedom or tyranny must consider the material that they have to deal with and judge the difficulty of their undertakings from it. 20 Because it is as difficult and dangerous to try to make people who wish to live in servitude free as it is to try to enslave people who wish to live free.[12] 21 And because it is stated above that when men act they have to consider the qualities of their times and act according to them, we shall speak at length of this in the next chapter.

NOTES

1. In the previous chapter, sentences 161–164, but see also above, 1, chapters 18, 34, and 55, and 2, chapter 24.

2. This occurred in 485 B.C.; see Livy, 2.41.

3. For more on Manlius Capitolinus, see Guicciardini's *Consideration* of *Discourses,* 1, 5, n.2, and above, 1, 8, n.3, and 1, 24, sentences 10–12. This discussion is based on Livy, 6.14–20.

4. Translates *cattiva forma,* namely, a tyranny.

5. Here and in sentences 13 and 17 below Machiavelli has in mind the notion of the form inherent in the matter; see above, 1, 17, n.2.

6. On the contrary, Livy, 6.20.4–12, indicates some "hesitation": the trial was reconvened the following day.

7. Livy, 6.20.14: *"Hunc exitum habuit vir, nisi in civitate natus esset, memorabilis."*

8. Translates *viva politicamente,* which, as Inglese points out, implies that the city has a rule of law, a just government.

9. Machiavelli anticipates the topic of the next chapter; see its note 1 with quotations of similar expressions of the idea in other writings of his.

10. Guicciardini expresses a similar thought about the length of time such a process might take: "If you see a city starting to decline, a government changing, a new dominion expanding, or other similar activity . . . be careful not to be mistaken about the time involved. Both because of their own nature and because of various obstacles, these activities move far more slowly than men suppose; to be mistaken about this point can cause you a great deal of harm. Be very careful, for it is a step that trips up many people. The same things also happen in private and personal matters, but much more so in public and general matters, since they move much more slowly as a result of their size, and they are also exposed to many more unforeseen events" (*Ricordi,* C. 71; see also B. 140).

11. Machiavelli quite rightly refers us to the opening chapter of this book in the *Discourses;* see especially its note 2.

12. An echo of 1, 55, sentence 28 above; see also the discussion above, 1, 16–17.

~ 9 ~

ADAPT TO THE TIMES IN ORDER ALWAYS TO HAVE GOOD FORTUNE

1 I have considered several times how the cause of mankind's ill or good fortune lies in matching one's course of action with the times.[1] 2 For we can see that some men proceed impetuously in their actions, some with restraint and caution; because the proper limits are exceeded in both of these ways if one cannot observe the right way, one errs in both of them. 3 But, as I have said, a man who matches the times with his course of action and always proceeds as nature obliges you manages to err less and to have a prosperous fortune.

4 Everyone knows that with his army Fabius Maximus used restraint and caution, avoiding all impulsiveness and Roman boldness, and good fortune had it that this way of his matched the times well.[2] 5 Because when Hannibal arrived in Italy as a young man with fresh fortune and had already defeated the Roman people twice, since the republic was almost stripped of its good soldiers and terror-stricken, it could have had no better luck than to get a commander who held the enemy at bay by his delays and caution.[3] 6 Nor could Fabius, either, have encountered times more suited to his ways, and his being victorious derived from this.[4] 7 And that Fabius did this naturally and not by choice was seen, because when Scipio wanted to go over to Africa with the armies to finish up the war, Fabius opposed him strongly,[5] since he was not one who could abandon his ways and habits; so if it had been up to him, Hannibal would still be in Italy, because he did not realize that the times had changed and it was necessary to change his type of warfare. 8 Had Fabius been king of Rome, he could easily have lost the war, because he would not have known how to change his way of doing things as the times changed. 9 But because he was born in a republic, in which there were diverse citizens and diverse feelings, just as it had Fabius, who was very good in proper times for keeping the war going, so it had Scipio later at the right time for winning it.

10 Hence it happens that a republic has a longer life and has good fortune longer than a principality, because, thanks to the diversity of the citizens there are in it, it can adapt better to diversity of circumstances than a prince can.[6] 11 For, as has been stated, a man who is accustomed to proceeding in one way never changes; and when times unsuited to those ways of his change, he must necessarily fail.

12 Piero Soderini, referred to elsewhere, proceeded with kindness and patience in all his affairs.[7] 13 He and his country prospered while the times were in conformity with his way of doing things; but later, as times came when he needed to break with patience and kindness, he was not able to: so he and his country both fell. 14 Throughout his pontificate Pope Julius II acted with impetuousness and haste; because the times went along well with him, all his undertakings succeeded.[8] 15 But if other times had come that required a different idea, he would of necessity have failed, because he would have changed neither his ways nor his rules of behavior.

16 And there are two reasons why we are unable to change: one, we cannot oppose what nature predisposes us to; the other, when someone has prospered greatly from one way of doing things, it is not possible to persuade him that he can do well by acting differently; that is why one man's fortune changes, because it changes the times and he does not change his ways.[9] 17 The downfall of cities also comes about from this, because the institutions of republics do not change with the times, as we discussed at length above. But they take longer, because they have a harder time changing, since times have to come that stir the entire republic; for this a single man, changing his way of doing things, is not enough.[10]

18 And because we have mentioned Fabius Maximus, who kept Hannibal at bay, I think I should discuss in the next chapter whether a commander who wishes to fight a battle with the enemy at all costs can be prevented by one who does not.

NOTES

1. Indeed, this is a favorite point that Machiavelli often makes in the context of Fortune and *virtù*. It is clear from the following contexts that "the times" in this paragraph also include the notion of "circumstances." Machiavelli's 1506 letter to Piero Soderini's nephew, Giovan Battista Soderini, known as the "fantasies" or "speculations" *(ghiribizzi)* letter, contains a passage germane to the rest of this discourse: "The man who matches his way of doing things with the conditions of the time is successful; the man whose actions are at odds with the times and the pattern of events is unsuccessful. . . . But because times and affairs often change—both in general and in particular—and because men change neither their imaginations nor their ways of doing things accordingly, it turns out that a man has good fortune at one time and bad fortune at another. And truly, anyone wise enough to adapt to and understand the times and the pattern of events would always have good fortune or would always keep himself from bad fortune, and it would come to be true that the wise man could control the stars and the Fates. But such wise men do not exist: in the first place, men are shortsighted; in the second place, they are unable to master their own natures; thus it follows that Fortune is fickle, controlling men and keeping them under her yoke" (*Friends,* p. 135). His *capitolo "Di fortuna,"* perhaps written shortly after this letter and dedicated to Giovan Battista Soderini, is also relevant, particularly vv. 100–117: Several passages in the *Prince* deal with this issue: in chapter 18 he writes that a "new prince" needs a flexible mind, altering as the winds of Fortune and changes in affairs require (p. 283, lines 74–76). All of chapter 25 is relevant to this chapter, especially "I also believe that the prince who makes his way of doing things consistent with the condition of the times may be successful. . . . Because Fortune is fickle and men are fixed in their ways, I therefore conclude that men are successful when they act harmoniously with Fortune and unsuccessful when they act inharmoniously with her (pp. 365; 369, lines 51–53; 126–30). Toward the end of his life, he wrote the following to Guicciardini, urging him to persuade Pope Clement VII to stand up to the troops that Charles V, the king of Spain and the Holy Roman Emperor, had sent to sack Lombardy and later Italy: "Now God has brought things to such a pass that, if this moment is not lost, the pope is in time to take the emperor. You are aware of how many opportunities have been lost: do not lose this one or, putting yourself in the hands of

Fortune and Time, put your trust in having it again, because Time does not always bring identical circumstances and Fortune is not always identical. . . . Free Italy from long-lasting anxiety; eradicate those savage brutes, which have nothing human about them save their faces and voices" (*Friends,* p. 387). (The last sentence alludes to Hannibal's dying words as recorded in Livy, 39.51.9.)

2. See above, 1, 53, n.4, and 2, 12, n.14, for the number of Hannibal's victories; Livy discusses the tactics of "the Delayer" in books 22, 23, and 28.

3. See above, 2, 12, n.14; Hannibal was thirty years old. This discussion is reminiscent of the end of *Prince,* 25, where Machiavelli uses his vivid metaphor of Fortune as a woman who "always befriends the young, since they are less circumspect and more brutal: they master her more boldly" (p. 371, lines 136–138).

4. With an eye to Machiavelli's ideas, what Guicciardini has to say about this subject using the same example is worth comparing: "Even those who attribute everything to prudence and *virtù,* and exclude the power of Fortune as much as possible, still must admit that it is very important for you to turn up or be born in a time that highly values those *virtù* or qualities that you value in yourself. We can take the example of Fabius Maximus, whose great reputation rested upon his being temporizing by nature. For he found himself in a type of war in which zeal was destructive, procrastination useful; at another time the opposite might have been the case. Hence his fortune consisted of this: his times required the qualities that were within him. But whoever could change his nature to suit the circumstances of the times, which is difficult and perhaps impossible, that man would be much less dominated by Fortune" (*Ricordi,* C.31; see also B. 52). See also the quotation from *Ricordi,* C. 30 above, 2, 30, n.18.

5. Livy gives the speech in opposition to this campaign in 205 B.C.; see 28.40. On the various uses of Scipio as an example, see Mansfield, *New Modes,* pp. 348–349.

6. Another plus for republics; as was clear from chapter 6, conspiracies are included among "diversity of circumstances" that a republic can rise above more easily than a prince. Inglese believes that the next sentence synthesizes a "doctrine of encounter" whereby rare individuals, when forced by the times and circumstances, can change their nature; he finds this notion, barely hinted at, in Polybius's treatment of Agathocles (9.23).

7. See above, 3, 3, n.3, and cross-references for Machiavelli's varying judgments about Soderini.

8. For Machiavelli's major pronouncements on the career of Julius II, see above, 1, 27, n.2.

9. Inglese draws an important distinction here between fortune as cause and effect: Fortune as cause changes the nature of time and circumstance, hence a person's fortune, the effect of these changes, varies because a person's ways of doing things do not change.

10. As Inglese points out, Machiavelli is extending the notion he articulated above in the first book of this discourse. On the one hand, there is a small cycle of changes in the times and in circumstances that ranges between the poles of impetuosity and restraint; a republic can withstand this kind of cycle if and when the nature of those who govern is equal to the job. On the other hand, there is a large cycle of changes that ranges between the poles of health and corruption; the state is destroyed by this cycle unless someone successfully "draws it back to its origins," the "mark" or "standard" of its "original principles" (3, 1).

~ 10 ~

A COMMANDER CANNOT AVOID BATTLE WHEN AN ADVERSARY WISHES TO FIGHT AT ALL COSTS

1 "The dictator Gaius Sulpicius dragged out the war against the Gauls, as he was unwilling to commit himself to Fortune against an enemy who was daily being weakened by time and his unfavorable position."[1]

2 When an error persists about which all men, or the majority, are deceived, I do not think it is a bad thing to find fault with it again and again. 3 Therefore, although I have several times shown above how much actions concerning important matters diverge from those of ancient times, nevertheless, it does not seem to me superfluous to repeat them at present.[2] 4 Because if there is any way in which people deviate from the ancient customs, they deviate particularly in military actions in which none of those things that the ancients valued highly is practiced at present. 5 This problem has arisen because republics and princes have assigned this responsibility to others, and to avoid danger they have distanced themselves from this exercise.[3] If we occasionally do see a king go in person in our day, we do not, however, believe that his actions will result in other means that might deserve more praise. 6 Because even when they do them, these exercises are done for pomp and not for any other worthwhile reason. 7 However, these kings make less of a mistake than do republics, particularly those in Italy, since they sometimes review their armies personally and they retain the title of commander for themselves; because republics trust in others and do not in any way understand what pertains to war, but on the contrary wish to make decisions about it in order to appear to be the prince, they make countless mistakes in this decision making.[4] 8 Although I have discussed some of them elsewhere,[5] I do not wish to leave out a very important one now.

9 When these lazy princes or effeminate republics send out a commander, the wisest order that they feel they can give him is to insist on his not going to battle for any reason, but rather, above all else, to avoid any skirmish; they think that in so doing they are imitating the prudence of Fabius Maximus, who saved the state for the Romans by delaying combat, but they do not understand that most of the time this order is useless or is harmful. 10 For one must draw this conclusion: a commander who wants to remain in the field cannot avoid battle any time the enemy is set on it at all costs. 11 This order means nothing but: 'wage war on your enemy's terms, not your own.'[6] 12 Because if one wants to remain in the field without doing battle, there is no other sure remedy than to position oneself at least fifty miles away from the enemy and then to keep good spies so that, if he comes toward you, you have time to move away. 13 There is another course of action: barricade oneself in a city; both of these courses of action are quite harmful. 14 In the first, one leaves one's countryside prey to the enemy, and a skillful prince will sooner try the fortune of combat than prolong a war with so great harm to his subjects. 15 In the second course of action the loss is clear, because by withdrawing into a city

with an army you will have to be besieged, and within a short while suffer hunger and surrender. 16 Thus avoiding battle in these two ways is extremely harmful. 17 The method Fabius Maximus used, of staying in strongholds, is good when you have an army of such *virtù* that the enemy does not dare to come after you at your advantage. 18 Nor can one say that Fabius avoided battle, but rather that he wanted it at his advantage; because if Hannibal had gone after him, Fabius would have waited and done battle with him; but Hannibal never dared to fight Fabius on the latter's own terms. 19 So Hannibal avoided battle as much as Fabius; but if one of them had wanted to fight at all costs, the other had only one of three remedies: the two mentioned above or flight.

20 The truth of what I am saying can be clearly seen in countless examples and particularly in the war that the Romans waged against Philip of Macedon, the father of Perseus.[7] For when the Romans attacked Philip, he decided not to get into battle, and to avoid it he tried at first to do as Fabius Maximus had done in Italy; he positioned himself with his army on the summit of a mountain, where he fortified himself considerably, judging that the Romans would not dare to go after him. 21 But going there and fighting him, they drove him from the mountain; and because he was unable to resist, he fled with the majority of his men. 22 What saved him from being completely finished off was the rugged countryside, which made it impossible for the Romans to pursue him. 23 So Philip, who did not want to fight and had positioned himself with his camp near the Romans, had to flee; having learned from this experience that if he did not want to fight, staying up in the mountains was not enough, and not wanting to barricade himself in cities, he decided to choose the other way, staying many miles away from the Roman camp. 24 So if the Romans were in one province, he went off into another; and thus wherever the Romans left, he would go in. 25 Finally, seeing that by prolonging the war in this way his conditions were growing worse and that his subjects were being attacked at times by him, at times by his enemies, he decided to try the fortunes of war and so fought a real battle with the Romans.

26 Therefore it is useful not to fight when armies have the conditions that Fabius's army had and that Gaius Sulpicius's has here;[8] that is, to have such a good army that your enemy does not dare to come after you inside your strongholds and for your enemy to be on your territory without his having gained much of a foothold so that he is suffering from lack of provisions. 27 That is the useful course of action in this case for the reasons that Livy states: "he was unwilling to commit himself to Fortune against an enemy who was daily being weakened by time and his unfavorable position." 28 But in every other situation battle cannot be avoided except to your dishonor and peril. 29 Because to flee as Philip did is like being defeated, and with all the more shame for your not having given any proof of your *virtù*. 30 And if he did manage to escape, it would not have been possible for someone else who was not helped by the terrain as he was.

31 No one will ever say that Hannibal was not a master of warfare. And when he confronted Scipio in Africa,[9] if he had seen some advantage in prolonging the war he would have done so, and perhaps since he was a good

commander and had a good army, he would have been able to, as Fabius was in Italy; but because he did not do so, one must believe that some important reason motivated him. 32 Because if a prince assembles an army and realizes for lack of money or allies that he cannot hold onto such an army for long, he is completely mad if he does not try his fortune before such an army has to be disbanded, for if he waits he loses for sure; if he tries he might win. 33 There is something else that must be considered important: even if one is to lose, one must want to gain glory; there is more glory in being conquered by force than by some other problem that made you lose. 34 So Hannibal must have been constrained by these necessities. 35 On the other hand, if Hannibal had put off the battle and Scipio had lacked the courage to go after him in his strongholds, Scipio would not have suffered, since he had already defeated Syphax and conquered so many cities in Africa that he could remain there as safely and conveniently as in Italy.[10] 36 That did not happen with Hannibal when he opposed Fabius nor with the Gauls who opposed Sulpicius.

37 Still less, even, can battle be avoided by someone who is attacking someone else's country with his army; for if he wants to penetrate the enemy's country, he has to do battle with him whenever his enemy comes to meet him. If he besieges a town, he is even more obliged to fight, as happened in our day with Duke Charles of Burgundy who, when he was besieging Morat, a Swiss town, was attacked and defeated by the Swiss, and as happened with the French army which, besieging Novara, was similarly defeated by the Swiss.[11]

NOTES

1. Quoted in Latin and based loosely on Livy, 7.12.11: *"dictatori neutiquam placebat, quando nulla cogeret res, fortunae se committere adversus hostem."* (But see Ridley, "Edition," p. 334, and Martelli, *Storici antichi,* pp. 144–145, for the question of "based loosely.") The event occurred in 358 B.C. Machiavelli quotes it again in Latin in sentence 27 of this chapter. For a theory about beginning a chapter with a quotation from Livy and Machiavelli's original intention, see above, 2, 3, note 1.

2. The divergence is what sparks the prefaces to Book 1. See also the Preface to Book 2, sentences 22–25, and 2, 4, sentence 35; and for the art of war in particular, see 2, 16–18.

3. The following discussion is often echoed in the *Art of War,* in which military discipline and exercises are examined at length. There is also an interesting connection of ideas between the *ghiribizzi* letter, so fundamental to the previous chapter, and the argument here. That letter was written in 1506 in response to one from Giovan Battista Soderini guardedly praising Machiavelli's efforts to organize a citizen militia, a project that Machiavelli took up zealously in 1506.

4. In *Prince,* 3, Machiavelli reports a conversation at Nantes (during his first legation to Louis XII in November 1500) with Georges d'Amboise, the cardinal of Rouen and the king's finance minister, who asserted that "the Italians had no understanding of warfare" (p. 125, lines 321–322).

5. Above, 2, 12.

6. A solid military tactic reviewed in *Art of War,* 4, based on the examples of Fabius Maximus, Hannibal, and Philip V of Macedon.

7. Philip V of Macedon, not to be confused with the father of Alexander the Great; for Philip see 2, 1, n.19, and for Perseus see Dedicatory Letter, n.5. The following account is based on Livy, 32.9–12. Philip was defeated at the battle of Cynoscephalae in 197/6 B.C.; the Roman army was led by the young Titus Quinctius Flamininus. See also Martelli's discussion of Plutarch, *Flaminius,* 4–5 (*Storici antichi,* pp. 145–147).

8. Referring to the example cited at the beginning of this chapter, occurring in 358 B.C.

9. In 203–202 B.C. during the Second Punic War.

10. Syphax led the Masaesyles, a Numidian tribe, whom Publius Cornelius Scipio Calvus and his brother Gnaeus Cornelius stirred up against the Carthaginians. Carthage defeated Syphax in 212 B.C.

11. See above, 2, 10, n.6, and 2, 17, n.11.

~ 11 ~

ANYONE WHO IS FACING MANY, EVEN THOUGH HE IS WEAKER, WINS SO LONG AS HE CAN WITHSTAND THE INITIAL ASSAULTS

1 The power of the Tribunes of the Plebs was great in the city of Rome, and it was necessary (as has many times been discussed by us),[1] because otherwise it would have been impossible to check the Nobility's ambition, which would have corrupted the republic long before it was corrupted. 2 Nevertheless, as has been stated elsewhere, because in everything some inherent evil lies hidden that makes new incidents emerge,[2] it is necessary to provide against this evil with new institutions. 3 Thus, when the authority of the Tribunes became arrogant and dreaded by the Nobility and by all of Rome, some drawback harmful to Roman freedom would have resulted had Appius Claudius not shown the way in which they should protect themselves against the Tribunes' ambition. This was that they always found someone among the Tribunes who was either afraid or corruptible or a lover of the common good, so they persuaded him to oppose the will of the other ones who wished to favor some proposal contrary to the will of the Senate.[3] 4 This remedy greatly mitigated so much authority and availed Rome for many years.

5 This has made me consider that any time there are many powerful men united against another powerful man, even though all of them together are much more powerful than he is, nonetheless one must always put more hope in the lone, less strong person than in the many, even though they are very strong. 6 Because, aside from all those things by which a lone man can prevail more than many, which are countless, the following will always happen: by using a little effort, he will be able to disunite the many and weaken what was a strong body.[4] 7 I do not want to cite ancient examples of this, of which there would be many, but I would like modern ones that have taken place in our times to suffice.

8 In 1483 all Italy plotted against the Venetians, and when all was completely lost for them and they could no longer stay in the field with their

army, they bribed Lord Luodovico, who governed Milan; with this bribe they made a treaty by which they not only regained the lost cities but usurped part of the state of Ferrara.[5] 9 Thus those who were losing the war came out on top in the peace. 10 A few years ago everyone plotted against France; nevertheless, before the end of the war was seen, Spain rebelled against its confederates and came to terms with France, so the other confederates were obliged also to come to terms a short time later.[6] 11 Without doubt, then, when a war is seen to be waged by many against one individual, we must always judge that the individual is going to come out on top if he is of enough *virtù* as to be able to withstand the initial assaults and to bide his time with delaying tactics. 12 Because if this were not so, he would run a thousand risks, as happened in 1508 to the Venetians, who would have avoided defeat if they had been able to delay with the French army and gain time to win over some of those that were in league against them; but because they did not have an army of *virtù* capable of delaying their enemy and therefore did not have time to separate any of them from the league, they were defeated.[7] 13 Because it was seen that once the pope had regained his possessions he became their ally, and Spain as well, if they had been able to, both of those princes would quite willingly have saved the state of Lombardy for them against France so as not to make it so powerful in Italy.[8] 14 The Venetians would thus have been able to give up a part to save the rest. If they had done this early enough for it not to seem to have been done by necessity and before the war was set in motion, it would have been a very wise course of action; but it would have been shameful once it had been set in motion and perhaps of little advantage. 15 But before it was in motion, few of the citizens in Venice could see the danger, very few could see a remedy, and no one could recommend it.

16 But to return to the beginning of this discourse, I conclude that, just as the Roman Senate had a remedy to save their native city from the ambition of the Tribunes, because they were many, so any prince who is attacked by many will have a remedy any time he can, by prudence, use methods fit to separate them.

NOTES

1. Especially above, Book 1, 3–6; 37; 39, sentences 7–12; 50, sentences 1–6; Book 3, 1, sentences 18–30; 8, sentences 1–10.

2. One of Machiavelli's basic assumptions; see above, 1, 2, sentences 11–12; and 3, 1, sentence 7. The notion expressed in a related passage in 1, 6, sentence 19, is matched in *Prince,* 21: "this is the way things are: whenever we seek to avoid one obstacle, we run into another" (p. 339, lines 121–123).

3. Appius Claudius was a decemvir, but it was his descendent Appius Claudius Crassus who reiterated the proposal discussed (Livy, 4.48.5–7).

4. To illustrate this point, Rinaldi draws attention to Machiavelli's letter to the Ten of 27 October 1502, in which he predicts how Cesare Borgia plans to handle the conspiracy led by the Orsinis and Vitellis: Cesare "will isolate one or two of these confederates; once he has defeated them, he would no longer have anything to fear from them, and he will be able to continue his campaign" (*Legazioni e commissarie,* 1:393).

5. "All Italy" in this case refers to the War between Venice and Ferrara (1482–1484); a league to support Ferrara against Venice was formed in December 1482 by Pope Sixtus IV; Lorenzo de' Medici, the ruler of Florence; Ercole d'Este, the duke of Ferrara; Ferdinand I, the king of Naples; and Ludovico "Il Moro" Sforza, the duke of Milan, who was regent for the young Gian Galeazzo Maria Sforza. In August 1484 Ludovico signed the separate Peace of Bagnolo for which he allegedly received a "bribe." It obliged the signatories of the league to return all Venetian territory taken during the war, and it also gave Venice a "part of the state of Ferrara": the city of Rovigo and the Po delta. See Machiavelli, *Florentine Histories,* 8, 24–26, and Guicciardini, *History of Florence,* chapter 7.

6. Most commentators believe that "a few years ago" refers to the situation in Italy from 1511 to 1513; see the discussion of Pope Julius II and his "Holy League" above, 1, 2, n.6. On 1 April 1513 King Louis XII of France signed the separate Treaty of Orthez with King Ferdinand the Catholic of Spain. Machiavelli discusses the effects of this treaty in a letter to Francesco Vettori, 10 December 1514, in which he refers to England's King Henry VIII's desire "to avenge the insults Spain inflicted upon him" (*Friends,* p. 296). Although it would not alter Machiavelli's argument, "a few years ago" could also refer to events surrounding the League of Venice formed in 1495 against the French King Charles VIII. His invasion of Italy and defeat of the kingdom of Naples prompted the league's formation for the mutual defense of its signatories: Pope Alexander VI, the Holy Roman Emperor Maximilian I, Ferdinand and Isabella of Spain, Venice, and Ludovico "Il Moro" Sforza, the duke of Milan. The treaty was to last twenty-five years in principle, but it was quickly dissolved by various separate treaties: Ludovico Sforza's, signed at Vercelli 9 October 1495, and Ferdinand's, first with Charles VIII on 25 February 1497 and then with Louis XII in August 1498, signed at Marcoussis.

7. A reference to the events surrounding the League of Cambrai; see above, 1, 6, n.11.

8. The Venetians seized Faenza and Rimini, the pope's "possessions," in 1503; Julius II got them back in February 1510 after withdrawing from the League of Cambrai and signing an accord with Venice. The pope could then with Venice's aid turn his attention to Louis XII.

~ 12 ~

A WISE COMMANDER HAS TO IMPOSE EVERY NECESSITY TO FIGHT ON HIS SOLDIERS AND TAKE AWAY THAT OF HIS ENEMIES

1 We have already discussed how useful necessity is to human endeavors, and the glory that it has brought them; and as some moral philosophers have written, men's hands and tongues, two most noble instruments that ennoble him, would not have worked perfectly nor brought human achievements to the high level that we seen them brought to, had they not been driven by necessity.[1] 2 Therefore, because ancient commanders of armies understood the *virtù* of such necessity and how stubborn it made their soldiers' minds to fight, they made every effort so their soldiers would be constrained by it; on the

other hand, they made every effort so their enemies would be freed from it. 3 Because of this they often opened up a route for their enemy that they could have closed off to them, and they closed one off for their own soldiers that they could have left open. 4 Therefore someone who desires either that a city defend itself stubbornly or that an army in the field fight stubbornly must above all strive to instill such necessity in the hearts of those who must fight.

5 Hence a wise commander who has to go and capture a city must gauge the ease or difficulty of capturing it by learning and pondering what necessity constrains its inhabitants to defend themselves; should he find there is a great necessity compelling them to defend themselves, he should judge capture to be hard; otherwise he should judge it to be easy.[2] 6 That is why towns are harder to conquer after a rebellion than they are during the early stages of their conquest, for in the beginning, since they have no reason to fear punishment because they have not committed any offense, they surrender easily; but later, after rebelling, if they think that they have committed an offense and fear punishment for that, they become hard to capture.[3]

7 Such stubbornness also arises from the natural hatreds that neighboring princes and neighboring republics have for each other; this derives from the ambition to dominate and envy for their state, especially if they are republics, as is the case in Tuscany; this rivalry and contention has made and always will make it difficult for one to capture the other. 8 Consequently, anyone who carefully considers the neighbors of the city of Florence and the neighbors of the city of Venice will not be surprised, as are many, that Florence has spent more on wars and conquered less than Venice. 9 For it all results from the Venetians not having neighboring towns as stubborn in their defense as Florence has had, because all the cities bordering Venice were used to living under a prince and not free:[4] those who are used to servitude often have little concern about changing masters; indeed, often they desire it.[5] 10 So although Venice had more powerful neighbors than Florence, finding towns less stubborn, it was able to conquer them more quickly than Florence, which was surrounded only by free cities.[6]

11 Thus, to return to the beginning of this discourse, when attacking a town a commander must strive with all diligence to deprive its defenders of such necessity and, consequently, such determination, by promising pardon if they fear punishment and, if they should fear for their freedom, must show that he is not going against the common good but against a few ambitious men in the city; this has often facilitated campaigns and the capture of towns. 12 Although such pretenses are easily seen through, and especially by wise men, nevertheless, the people have often been fooled by them: desirous of immediate peace, they shut their eyes to any other trap that is set beneath broad promises.[7] 13 In this way countless cities have become subjugated, as happened in Florence very recently, and as happened to Crassus and his army.[8] 14 Although he saw through the Parthians' hollow promises, made to take away his soldiers' necessity to defend themselves, he was still unable to keep them stubborn once they were blinded by the offers of peace that their enemies made them, as one can see in detail when reading of his life.[9]

15 Consequently, I say that when the Samnites, in contravention of their treaty, because of the ambition of a few, overran and pillaged the land of Rome's allies and then sent ambassadors to Rome to sue for peace, offering to restore what they had pillaged and to hand over those responsible for the uprisings and the pillage as prisoners, the Romans rejected them.[10] 16 When they returned to Samnium without hope of a treaty, Claudius Pontius, then commander of the Samnites' army, in a notable oration showed that the Romans wanted war at all cost; although for their part they themselves desired peace, necessity made them pursue war. These were his words: "War is just for those to whom it is necessary, and arms are righteous for those to whom there is no hope except in arms";[11] he and his soldiers based hope of victory on this necessity.

17 And in order not to have to return to this material later, I feel I should cite here the Roman examples that are the most worthy of note. 18 Gaius Manilius was with his army facing the Veians; when part of the Veian army got inside Manilius's palisade, Manilius ran with a detachment to help them; so the Veians could not escape, he blocked every exit to the camp. Hence, because the Veians saw they were closed in, they began to fight with such rage that they slew Manilius and would have crushed all the rest of the Romans if one of the Tribunes had not had the wisdom to open an escape route for them.[12] 19 From this we can see that, as long as necessity constrained the Veians to fight, they fought quite fiercely; but when they saw the way open, they thought more of fleeing than of fighting.

20 The Volscians and the Aequi had penetrated the Roman borders with their armies. 21 The consuls were sent to oppose them.[13] 22 So, as the fighting wore on, the Volscian army, whose leader was Vettius Messius, found itself suddenly hemmed in between its palisade, blocked by the Romans, and the other Roman army; realizing that they had either to die or to make a way for themselves with steel, he said these words to his soldiers: "Go with me; not a wall or a fortification, but armed men resist armed men; equal in *virtù,* you are their superior in necessity, which is the ultimate and greatest weapon."[14] 23 Thus Livy calls this necessity "the ultimate and greatest weapon."

24 Camillus, the wisest of all Rome's commanders, got inside the city of the Veians with his army. In order to facilitate its capture and deprive his enemies of the final necessity to defend themselves, he ordered in such a way that the Veians heard it that no one should harm those who were unarmed; so, throwing their arms down on the ground, he captured the city almost without bloodshed. 25 Many commanders subsequently adopted this method.[15]

NOTES

1. See above, 1, 1, sentence 13; 1, 3, sentence 4. It is unclear who "some moral philosophers" might be; Rinaldi believes the reference is "generic," although he offers Thomas Aquinas, *De regimine principum,* 1, 1, as a possible source, as does Walker.

2. Here is what Guicciardini has to say: "Don't think that an attacker—for example, someone who besieges a town—can foresee all the defense his enemy will put up. Naturally all the usual remedies that the defender will put up will occur to the ex-

pert challenger. But the danger and necessity that the defender is in causes him to come up with extraordinary remedies impossible for someone who is not in those straits to conceive of" (*Ricordi,* C. 166).

3. Here and in the rest of this paragraph Machiavelli may have in mind the protracted campaigns against Pisa, lasting from 1494 to 1509.

4. Although this point is made without reference to Venice in *Prince,* 5, Machiavelli does refer to Pisa in that chapter.

5. In several passages in *Prince,* 3, he notes that "men are willing to change the ruler if they expect improvements" and "the order of things is such that as soon as a strong invader enters a region, all those there who are not so powerful join with him, motivated by their envy of those who have been ruling them" (p. 103, lines 5–7; p. 113, lines 145–149). See also above, 1, 16–17.

6. Again, Guicciardini is relevant: "Many times I have said, and it is quite true, that it has been more difficult for Florentines to attain the small amount of territory that they have to rule than for the Venetians to amass their large one. For the Florentines are in a region where there was a great deal of freedom, something that is very hard to do away with; hence they are extremely hard regions to conquer and, once conquered, are held on to with no less difficulty. . . . The Venetians have conquered towns accustomed to servitude, tenacious neither in their defense nor in their rebellion. And as neighbors the Venetians have had secular princes, whose lives and memories are of short duration" (*Ricordi,* C. 29; see also B. 131).

7. In *Prince,* 24, Machiavelli notes that "men are more compelled by concerns of the present than by those of the past. When they deem that the present is good, they enjoy it and seek nothing more" (p. 355, lines 10–13).

8. Machiavelli refers to the suppression of the Florentine republic under Piero Soderini and the return of the Medici in 1512: they came home at the end of August with the proviso that they would do so as private citizens but had power in their hands by mid-September. For Marcus Licinius Crassus, see above, 2, 18, n.9.

9. Specifically Plutarch, *Crassus,* 26–31; Crassus was defeated in 53 B.C.

10. A reference to the origins of the Second Samnite War, 326–304 B.C. Livy discusses the Samnite decision in 8.39.10–15.

11. Quoted in Latin, with slight changes from Livy, 9.1.10: *"Iustum est bellum quibus necessarium, et pia arma quibus nulla nisi in armis relinquitur spes."* Here Machiavelli omits *nulla,* but he retains it when he uses the same quotation, again with variants, both in *Florentine Histories,* 5, 8, and in *Prince,* 26 (p. 377, lines 51–53); see Martelli, *Storici antichi,* pp. 147–148. The Samnite commander's correct name is Gaius Pontius (Livy, 9.1.2). The "victory" was achieved at the Battle of the Caudine Forks on the Appian Way between Capua and Benevento, northeast of Naples, in the vicinity of Caudium, present-day Arpaia, in 321 B.C.

12. See above, 1, 36, n.1, and 2, 25, n.1, for this situation; rather than "a Tribune," Livy says a lieutenant *(legatus)* opened the "escape route." See the discussion in Martelli, *Storici antichi,* pp. 148–149.

13. These events occurred in 431/430 B.C. and are discussed in Livy, 4.27; the consuls in question were the dictator Aulus Postumius Tubertus and Titus Quinctius Cincinnatus. Livy does not specify that Vettius Messius was the Volscian "leader" (2.48.3).

14. Quoted in Latin in both this and the next sentence from Livy, 4.28.5: *"ite mecum! Non murus nec vallum sed armati armatis obstant. Virtute pares, necessitate, quae ultimum ac maximum telum est, superiores estis."* But Machiavelli's text reads: "*virtute pares,* quae ultimum ac maximum telum est, *necessitate superiores estis.*" Thus, as Ridley, "Edition," p. 330, and Martelli, *Storici antichi,* p. 150, point out, Machiavelli changes Livy's emphasis considerably by changing the position of the relative pronoun *quae,* allowing him to make the "wrong" assertion in sentence 23.

15. Based on Livy, 5.21.13, though Livy says the "order" was given only after the carnage *(sanguinis)* had begun to flag and the Veians had been turned back. Thus the city was not "captured almost without bloodshed."

~ 13 ~

WHICH SHOULD ONE PLACE MORE TRUST IN: A GOOD COMMANDER WHO HAS A WEAK ARMY OR A GOOD ARMY THAT HAS A WEAK COMMANDER?

1 After Coriolanus became an exile from Rome, he went over to the Volscians; hiring an army there to get revenge on his fellow citizens, he returned to Rome, which he left more out of respect for his mother than because of the Romans' forces.[1] 2 Livy says about this passage that it showed how the Roman republic grew more through the *virtù* of its commanders than that of its soldiers, considering that the Volscians had been defeated in the past and had won only when Coriolanus was their commander.[2] 3 Although Livy holds this opinion, it can nevertheless be seen in many passages of his history that the *virtù* of the soldiers had accomplished wonderful feats without a commander and they were more organized and fiercer after their Consuls' death than before they died. 4 That occurred in the army that the Romans had in Spain under the Scipios: after the two commanders died, by its *virtù* it was able not only to save itself but to defeat the enemy and preserve the province for the republic.[3] 5 So, all things considered, many examples will be found in which the *virtù* of the soldiers alone has won the battle and many others in which the *virtù* of the commanders alone has had the same effect; so we may judge that the one needs the other and vice versa.

6 We should indeed consider, first of all, which is more to be feared, a good army badly commanded or a good commander accompanied by a bad army. 7 Following the opinion of Caesar in this, neither of them should be esteemed very highly. 8 Because when he went into Spain against Afranius and Petreius, who had an excellent army, he said that he had little esteem for them, "since he was going against an army without a leader," pointing to the commanders' weakness.[4] 9 On the contrary, when he went into Thessaly against Pompey, he said: "I am going against a leader without an army."

10 Another thing may be considered: is it easier for a good commander to make a good army or for a good army to make a good commander? 11 On this I say that this question seems decided, because it is much easier for many

good men to find or train one man until he becomes good than it is for one man to do so with many. 12 When Lucullus was sent against Mithridates, he was completely inexperienced in warfare; nevertheless, that good army, in which there were many excellent officers, quickly made him a good commander.[5] 13 Because the Romans lacked men, they armed many slaves and gave them to Sempronius Gracchus to train and within a short while he formed a good army.[6] 14 As we have said elsewhere, within a short while after Pelopidas and Epaminondas had freed their native city Thebes from its servitude to the Spartans, they made excellent soldiers of the Theban peasants, able not only to withstand the Spartan army but to defeat it.[7] 15 So the matter is even, because one good one can find the other. 16 Nevertheless, a good army without a good leader usually becomes insolent and dangerous, as the Macedonian army did after the death of Alexander[8] and as the veteran soldiers were in the Civil Wars.[9] 17 So I believe one should put much more trust in a commander who has time to train men and an opportunity to arm them than in an insolent army with an impromptu leader it has created.[10] 18 Therefore, we should have double respect and praise for those commanders who not only have had their enemies to defeat but have had to train their army and make it good before going into combat against them: for they show a double *virtù,* one so rare that, if such a task had been assigned to many, far fewer of them would be esteemed and reputed than there are.

NOTES

1. For Coriolanus see above, 1, 7, n.3. Livy provides a moving speech delivered by his mother, Veturia, who, accompanied by his wife Volumnia and their sons, went to the Volscian camp to persuade Coriolanus not to help the enemy of the Romans (2.40.5–9).

2. Livy, 2.39.2.

3. In 211 B.C. during the Second Punic War, the Carthaginians defeated Publius Cornelius Scipio Calvus and his brother Gnaeus Cornelius in Spain; see Livy, 25.36–39. The Roman army then held an election and chose Lucius Marcius Septimus and Scipio's lieutenant Fonteius as its leaders. Inglese notes that the conclusion Machiavelli draws in the next sentence is one of the rare instances when he goes against Livy, who plays down the plebeians' contribution to Rome's power; but see Martelli, *"Logica provvidenzialistica,"* pp. 341–348, for all the examples used in this chapter.

4. This quotation and the one in the next sentence, both in Latin, are loosely based on Suetonius, *Julius Caesar,* 34; but see Martelli, *Storici antichi,* pp. 151–154. As the First Triumvirate was collapsing and Caesar had taken Rome, he hounded Pompey and defeated his crack troops, led by his lieutenants Lucius Nepos Afranius and Marcus Petreius, at the Battle of Ilerda (modern-day Lerida) on the Ebro River in Spain in 49 B.C. The context for the next quotation is Caesar's victory, still in pursuit of Pompey and his army a year later at the Battle of Pharsalus in Thessaly; Pompey escaped to Egypt.

5. Because commentators cannot make potential sources coincide with Machiavelli's account here, Inglese and Martelli, *Storici antichi,* p. 156, suggest that Machiavelli has misread one of his handwritten notes on the source for this account.

6. On Tiberius Sempronius Gracchus, see above, 2, 26, n.5; see also Livy, 22.57, and 24.14–16.

7. For "elsewhere" see above, Book 2, 21, sentence 8, but see above, 1, 6, n.10, for the defeat at the battle of Leuctra in 371 B.C.

8. Sources for this judgment include Diodorus Siculus, 18.9, Plutarch, *Alexander,* 68, and Justin, 13.2.

9. A reference based on Suetonius, *Caesar,* 69–70, and Livy, *Summaries,* 131.

10. Machiavelli's spokesman in the *Art of War,* Fabrizio Colonna, echoes this belief among his "general rules" in Book 5. The next sentence, too, finds an echo in Book 7.

~ 14 ~

THE EFFECTS THAT ARE CAUSED BY UNUSUAL INVENTIONS THAT APPEAR AND UNUSUAL SOUNDS THAT ARE HEARD IN THE MIDST OF BATTLE

1 How important a new incident may be, resulting from something unusual that is seen or heard in conflicts and fighting, is shown in many passages, especially by an example that occurred during the battle that the Romans waged against the Volscians. Seeing one of the wings of his army giving ground, Quinctius began to shout loudly for them to stand firm, because the other wing of the army was victorious; giving courage to his men and consternation to the enemy with these words, he won.[1] 2 And if such cries have great effect with a well-organized army, they have an even greater one with one that is rowdy and badly organized, because it all gets stirred up by the same wind. 3 I should like to cite a notable example of this that occurred in our day. 4 A few years ago the city of Perugia was divided into two factions, the Oddi and the Baglioni.[2] 5 The latter were in power; the others were in exile. 6 Assembling an army with the aid of their allies and bringing it to a town of theirs near Perugia, one night the Oddi entered the city with the support of their faction and, without being discovered, came to capture the town square. 7 Because the city has chains at every street corner that keep it blocked,[3] the Oddi troops had someone in front of them who broke the fastenings on the chains with an iron sledgehammer so the horses could go through. When the only one left to be broken was the one leading into the square and the call to arms had already been raised, the man who was doing the breaking was hindered by the crowd that was coming behind him, so because of them he could not lift his arms properly to do the breaking. In order for him to maneuver, they were told: "Go back!" That cry, going from rank to rank, saying "back!" started to make the last men run away and little by little the others, too, in such haste that they were put to flight by themselves. Thus the Oddi's plan failed as a result of so a minor an incident.

8 In this we must consider that rules are necessary in an army not so much in order for it to fight in an orderly way as in order for you not to be disrupted by every slightest incident. 9 For just this reason masses of the people are useless for war, because every noise, every cry, every tumult disturbs them and makes them run away.[4] 10 So a good commander, among his other regu-

lations, has to designate those who are to receive his commands and transmit these commands to others, and accustom his soldiers to listen to them alone, and his commanders to say only what he has ordered; because if this aspect is not well observed, it has often been seen to produce widespread disorder.

11 As for seeing new things, every commander must strive to make some of them appear while armies are engaged in combat to give his men courage and take it away from the enemy; for among the incidents that give you victory, this one is very effective. 12 We can cite as evidence for this Gaius Sulpicius, the Roman dictator: when he engaged the Gauls in battle, he armed all the supply-men and lowly people in his camp; when they were mounted on mules and other beasts of burden with arms and banners so they would seem to be troops on horseback, he stationed them behind a hill under his banners and commanded that when a sign was given at the point when the fighting was at its height, they should reveal themselves and show themselves to the enemy.[5] 13 Arranged and done thus, that gave the Gauls such a fright that they lost the battle. 14 Therefore a good commander has to do two things: one, to see if he can frighten the enemy with some of these new inventions; the other, if the enemy uses them against him, be prepared so as to be able to discover them and make them come to naught. 15 That is what the king of India did to Semiramis: noticing that the king had a large number of elephants, she made a lot of them with buffalo and cow hides, put them on camels, and sent them on ahead in order to frighten the king and show him that she, too, was well supplied with them; but when he realized the trick, her plan turned out not only unsuccessful but harmful.[6] 16 When Mamercus was dictator against the people of Fidenae, in order to frighten the Roman army they arranged for a number of soldiers with torches atop their lances to march forth from Fidenae in the heat of the battle so the Romans would break ranks, distracted by the thing's novelty.[7] 17 Concerning this it should be noted that when such inventions contain more truth than fiction, then they can be displayed to men; because they have a good deal of boldness in them, their weakness cannot be discovered so quickly. But when they contain more fiction than truth, it is best either not to do them or, if they are done, to keep them at a distance in such a way that they cannot be discovered so quickly, as Gaius Sulpicius did with the mule-drivers. 18 For whenever there is some weakness in them, it is quickly revealed when they come closer and they do you harm, not good, as the elephants did to Semiramis and the torches to the people of Fidenae. Although in the beginning they disturbed the army slightly, nevertheless, when the Dictator came on the scene, he began to shout at them, saying they should not disgrace themselves by fleeing smoke like bees and they should turn back toward them, crying: "Destroy Fidenae with its own flames, since you could not make it your friend with your kindnesses."[8] This device proved useless to the people of Fidenae, and they were left the losers in the battle.

NOTES

1. A reference to the consul Titus Quinctius Barbatus Capitolinus during a battle with the Volscians in 469 B.C.; see Livy, 2.64.6.

2. The incident occurred in 1495; see Guicciardini, *Storia d'Italia,* 3, 2. The Baglioni, who supported the Guelph faction, ruled Perugia off and on until 1540. The Oddi were Ghibellines; they had support from similar factions in Foligno and Assisi. The town "near Perugia" is Corciano, about six miles due west of Perugia.

3. Guicciardini, *Storia d'Italia,* 3, 2, points out that the chains were put there because Corciano was a "turbulent city."

4. One of the reasons why in all his writings about war, and particularly his citizen militia, Machiavelli emphasized the need for a disciplined army.

5. Gaius Sulpicius Peticus, the man referred to above, Book 3, 10, sentence 1; based on Livy, 7.14–15. Machiavelli also refers to this incident in *Art of War,* 4. For textual discrepancies with Livy, 7.14.7–8, see Ridley, "Roman History," p. 211, and Martelli, *Storici antichi,* p. 157.

6. Based on Diodorus Siculus, 2.16–19. The king of India was Stabrobates; Semiramis was the legendary founder of the Assyrian empire of Nineveh and builder of Babylon. The historical figure around whom this legend grew was Sammuramat, who ruled the Assyrians as regent from 810/809 to 806/805 B.C.

7. See Livy, 4.33, for this account of the dictator and military tribune Mamercus Aemilius and the battle against the people of Fidenae in 426 B.C. Fidenae is the modern Castel Giubileo, northeast of Rome.

8. Quoted in Latin from Livy, 4.33.5: *"suis flammis delete Fidenas, quas vestris beneficiis placare non potuistis."*

~ 15 ~

ONE MAN, NOT MANY, SHOULD HAVE CHARGE OF AN ARMY; MORE THAN ONE COMMANDER CAUSES TROUBLE

1 When the people of Fidenae revolted and massacred the colony that the Romans had sent to there, the Romans created four Tribunes with consular power in order to deal with this outrage. Leaving one of them to protect Rome, they sent three of them against the people of Fidenae and Veii; because the Tribunes were divided and disunited among themselves, they returned with dishonor, but not harm, because they were the reason for the dishonor [but] the *virtù* of the soldiers was the reason for their not being harmed.[1] 2 Seeing this disorder, therefore, the Romans had recourse to the creation of a Dictator so one single man might reorganize what three had disorganized. 3 From this we can understand the uselessness of having many commanders in an army or in a town that must be defended; and Livy cannot say it more clearly than in the following words: "Three Tribunes with consular power revealed clearly how useless the division of command is in war; since each one tended to follow his own opinion, and each one saw things differently, they opened up a place for the enemy's opportunity."[2]

4 Although this is enough of an example to prove the disorder that more than one commander creates in war, I would like to cite a few others, both

modern and ancient, for greater clarification of the matter. 5 In 1500, after King Louis XII of France recaptured Milan, he sent his troops to Pisa to restore it to the Florentines; Giovambattista Ridolfi and Luca di Antonio degli Albizzi were sent there as commissioners.[3] 6 Because Giovambattista was a man of reputation and senior, Luca left everything to be directed completely by him; and if he did not show his ambition by opposing him, he showed it by remaining silent and by neglecting and criticizing everything so that he did not help the actions in the field either by his work or by his counsel, as if he were a man of no consequence. 7 But then quite the opposite was seen when Giovambattista, because of a certain incident that occurred, had to return to Florence; left alone, Luca showed how much he was worth by his courage, diligence, and counsel, all of which were wasted while he had company. 8 In confirmation of this, I would once again like to quote Livy's words; relating how, when the Romans sent Quinctius and his colleague Agrippa against the Aequi, Agrippa insisted that the entire administration of the war be in Quinctius's hands, he says: "In the administration of important matters, it is most advantageous for the highest power to be placed in one man."[4] 9 This is contrary to what our republics and princes do today, sending more than one commissioner or more than one leader to places in order to administer them better; this makes for incalculable confusion. 10 If we were to seek the causes for the downfall of the Italian and French armies in our day, this would be found to be the principal one. 11 And we may truly conclude that it is better to send only one man of ordinary sense on an expedition than two very able men together with the same authority.

NOTES

1. Machiavelli picks up the discussion of Mamercus Aemilius and the battle against the people of Fidenae from the end of the previous chapter. The four tribunes with consular powers were Titus Quinctius Poenus, Gaius Furius, Marcus Postumius, and Aulus Cornelius Cossus (Livy, 4.31.1). The latter named Mamercus Aemilius as dictator (4.31.5).

2. Quoted in Latin, with modifications, from Livy, 4.31.2: *"tres . . . documentoque fuere quam plurium imperium bello inutile esset. Tendendo ad sua quisque consilia, cum aliud alii videretur, aperuerunt ad occasionem locum hosti."* For discrepancies in this account, see Martelli, *Storici antichi*, pp. 158–159.

3. Florence pinned its hopes of regaining Pisa on Louis XII. In June 1500 the king sent a combined force of Swiss and French troops to Pisa, with Florence agreeing to pay their salary. Because the city was in arrears, the army became fractious. (See above, Book 1, 38, n.8.) Machiavelli as well as his friend Biagio Buonaccorsi accompanied the Florentine representatives to Pisa to deal with the situation. The reports sent back to Florence by them provide a personal glimpse of the diplomatic activities, though Denis Fachard, in *Biagio Buonaccorsi: sa vie, son temps, son oeuvre*, notes that they are mostly in Biagio's hand, not Machiavelli's (pp. 74–78). Guicciardini narrates these events in *Florentine History*, 20, and *Storia d'Italia*, 6, though he is silent about the difference of opinion between the two men and Albizzi's actions when he was alone at Pisa.

4. A reference to the consul Titus Quinctius Barbatus Capitolinus, mentioned above, Book 3, 14, n.1, and Agrippa Furius in Rome's war against the Aequi and Volscians in 446 B.C. The passage is freely quoted in Latin from Livy, 3.70.1: *"saluberrimum in administratione magnarum rerum est, summa imperii concedente Agrippa penes collegam erat."*

~ 16 ~

IN HARD TIMES TRUE *VIRTÙ* IS SOUGHT; MEN OF WEALTH OR FAMILY BACKGROUND, NOT THOSE WITH *VIRTÙ*, GET MORE FAVOR IN EASY TIMES

1 It has always been so and always will be: great and rare men are neglected in a republic in peaceful times; out of the envy resulting from the prestige that their *virtù* has given them in such times many citizens wish not only to be their equals but to be their superiors.[1] 2 There is a good passage about this in the Greek historian Thucydides, which shows how when the republic of Athens came out on top in the Peloponnesian War and had checked the pride of the Spartans and subjugated almost all the rest of Greece, it rose to such repute that it decided to conquer Sicily. 3 This campaign came under discussion in Athens. Alcibiades and a few other citizens, intending to be the leaders of such a campaign, recommended that it should be carried out, as men who thought little of the public good but rather of their own honor. 4 But Nicias, whose reputation was the highest among the Athenians, argued against it. In addressing the people, the principal reason he cited so as to gain their trust was the following: that in recommending against waging this war he was recommending something that was not to his advantage. For while Athens remained at peace, he knew that there were innumerable citizens who wanted to get ahead of him; but if war was declared, he knew that no citizen would be superior or equal to him.

5 So we can therefore see that there is this flaw in republics: they have little respect for worthy men in peaceful times. 6 This arouses their indignation in two ways: one, they see themselves lacking their proper rank; the other, they see themselves with men as their associates and superiors who are unworthy and of less competence than they. 7 This flaw in republics has caused many to topple, because those citizens who see themselves undeservedly scorned and realize that the cause of this is times that are easy and free of danger find ways to disturb them, stirring up new wars that put the republic in jeopardy. 8 Considering what the remedies might be, I find two: one, keeping citizens poor so that if they lack *virtù* they cannot corrupt either themselves or others with wealth;[2] the other, organizing for war like the Romans in their early days so that war could always be waged and citizens of repute would always be needed. 9 Because Rome always kept armies outside the city, there was always a place for men's *virtù,* and rank could not be taken from someone who de-

served it and given to someone who did not; if that was still done at times by mistake and as a test, such great disorder and risk for the republic always quickly ensured that it immediately returned to the right path. 10 But other republics that are not organized like it and declare war only when necessity forces them to are unable to avoid such a problem; on the contrary, they will always run up against it and disorder will always arise from it if a neglected citizen of *virtù* is vindictive and has some reputation and following in the city. 11 The city of Rome resisted at one time; but once it had defeated Carthage and Antioch (as has been said elsewhere)[3] and no longer feared wars, it, too, felt it could entrust its armies to anyone it wished, not esteeming *virtù* so much as the other qualities that gave him favor with the people. 12 For this reason, we see that Paulus Aemilius was denied the consulate several times and he was not made consul until the Macedonian War broke out; because it was considered dangerous, by agreement of the entire city it was entrusted to him.[4]

13 When many wars happened one after another in our city of Florence following 1494 and all the Florentine citizens had given bad accounts of themselves, the city happened by chance on one man who showed how armies were to be commanded: that was Antonio Giacomini.[5] 14 While there were dangerous wars to wage, all the ambitions of the rest of the citizens ceased and he did not have any rivals in the choice of the commissioner and leader of the armies; but when there was a war to wage about which there was no uncertainty and much honor and rank [to be gained], he found so many rivals for it that, when three commissioners had to be chosen to lay siege to Pisa, he was passed over.[6] 15 Although it was not obvious what harm to the public resulted from not sending Antonio, it could nevertheless be very readily imagined; for because the Pisans had nothing left to defend themselves or to live, if Antonio had been there, they would have been so hard-pressed before that they would have surrendered unconditionally to the Florentines. 16 But because they were besieged by leaders who knew neither how to press them nor to overcome them, they held out for so long that the city of Florence bought them off, whereas it could have gotten them by force.[7] 17 Such disdain must have had considerable strength for Antonio; and he must have been very patient and good-natured not to wish to avenge himself either by the city's downfall, since he could bring it about, or by harm to some individual citizen.. 18 A republic must guard itself against that, as will be discussed in the following chapter.

NOTES

1. The following account is based on Thucydides, 6.8–24; Machiavelli slants his source to agree with his argument; there is no assertion in Thucydides like the one Machiavelli makes about Nicias in the last sentence of this paragraph. The Sicilian expedition lasted from 415 to 413 B.C., because the people of Segesta sought Athenian help against the towns of Syracuse and Selinunte. Thucydides categorized this second war between Athens and Sparta, the Decelean or Ionian War, which lasted from 414 to 404, as part of the Peloponnesian War, which began in 431. Alcibiades, a friend of Socrates, was an Athenian general and politician whose wealth was as great as his ambition. On

Nicias see above, 1, 53, n.9; but see Martelli, *Storici antichi,* pp. 161–162, for how Machiavelli distorts the example of Nicias to fit the assertion in the chapter's title.

2. On this point see above, 1, 37, n.7, and below, 3, 25.

3. See above, 1, 18, sentences 15–17, and 2, 1, sentences 16–18.

4. Lucius Aemilius Paulus was surnamed Macedonius because his victory at Pydna in 168 B.C. ended the Third Macedonian War (171–168). He first was consul in 182 but was then denied the office until 168. See Plutarch, *Aemilius Paulus,* 6.9–11; but see Martelli, pp. 162–164, for discrepancies and the relevance ofValerius Maximus, 7.5.3.

5. Sometimes referred to as Antonio Giacomini Tebalducci, he was an able condottiere and Florentine commissioner. For two letters that Machiavelli addressed to him, see *Friends,* pp. 113–114, and references to him in that book's Index. Machiavelli's respect for him can be seen in *Decennale Secondo,* vv. 32–45, and in the *Nature di huomini fiorentini* (Types of Florentine men).

6. On several occasions from 1500 to 1505 Giacomini led Florentine forces against Pisa, but the failure of his weeklong attack in mid-September of 1505 led to his resignation in 1506. Machiavelli is now referring to the Pisan situation in 1508 and 1509 when the three commissioners were Alamanno Salviati, Antonio da Filicaia, and Niccolò Capponi (see Guicciardini, *History of Florence,* chapter 30). Although Salviati opposed Machiavelli's efforts to organize a citizen militia, he was a powerful man in Florentine politics, the dedicatee of the *Decennale Primo,* and Francesco Guicciardini's father-in-law. Hence, Machiavelli's remarks about him two sentences later are rather surprising.

7. Although it is not altogether clear that Pisa could have been conquered "by force," it did surrender early in June 1509 after Florence paid 100,000 ducats to Louis XII of France and 50,000 to Ferdinand the Catholic, king of Spain, so they would withdraw their protective armies from the city. As secretary of the Ten of War, Machiavelli was both witness to and participant in the campaign against Pisa.

~ 17 ~

A MAN SHOULD NOT BE OFFENDED THEN ASSIGNED TO AN IMPORTANT ADMINISTRATIVE OR GOVERNMENT MISSION

1 A republic must be very careful not to put someone to whom some noteworthy offense has been done by someone else in charge of some important administration. 2 Claudius Nero left the army with which he was facing Hannibal and went off to the Marches with part of it to meet the other Consul in order to fight Hasdrubal before he joined up with Hannibal.[1] Claudius had been face-to-face with Hasdrubal in Spain. 3 Hemmed with his army into a place where he either had to fight at a disadvantage or starve to death, Claudius was cleverly detained by Hasdrubal with some treaty discussions for so long a time that he got out from under him and took away Claudius's chance to defeat him. 4 When this was learned in Rome, he drew great blame from the Senate and the people; he was talked about disparagingly throughout the city to his great dishonor and contempt. 5 But when he was later made

Consul and sent out against Hannibal, he took the above-mentioned course of action, which was very risky; so Rome remained in great fear and turmoil until the news of Hasdrubal's defeat arrived. 6 And then when Claudius was asked what made him take such a risky course of action, in which without extreme necessity he had more or less gambled Rome's freedom, he answered that he had done it, because he knew that if he succeeded he would regain the glory that he had lost in Spain; and if he did not succeed and his course of action had the opposite result, he knew that he would be getting revenge on the city and the citizens who had so ungratefully and impudently offended him.[2]

7 And when rancors from such offenses can have such an effect on a Roman citizen at a time when Rome was still uncorrupted, we must imagine the effect they can have on a citizen of another city that is not like what it was then. 8 And because no sure remedy can be given for disorders like these that arise in republics, it follows that it is impossible to set up a republic that will last forever, because its downfall can be brought about in a thousand unexpected ways.[3]

NOTES

1. The following examples are based on Livy, 26.17, for the campaign of Claudius Nero in Spain, and 27.44–51; they date from 211 and 207 B.C. during the Second Punic War. In 207 Gaius Claudius Nero headed toward the Marches of Ancona to meet Marcus Livius Salinator, "the other Consul"; they met at Sena Gallica, Machiavelli's Senigallia. Held in check by Claudius Nero, Hannibal was farther south in Apulia, and his brother Hasdrubal had crossed the Alps and was proceeding southeast to meet him. The two armies met at Sena Gallica and fought the bloody battle of the Metaurus River where Hasdrubal was defeated; see above, 2, 10, n.13.

2. This speech is reported in Livy, 27.40, and ascribed to Marcus Livius Salinator. Machiavelli has apparently confused the two consuls, an error that Guicciardini picks up (see his *Consideration* of this chapter, sentence 4). See the discussion in Martelli, *Storici antichi,* pp. 165–167.

3. A basic theme of the *Discourses,* one that Machiavelli asserts above, l, 2, sentence 23, and 3, 1, sentence 1.

~ *18* ~

A COMMANDER CAN DO NOTHING MORE WORTHY THAN PREDICTING HIS ENEMY'S COURSE OF ACTION

1 Epaminondas of Thebes said that nothing was more necessary and more useful for a commander than knowing the enemy's decisions and course of action.[1] 2 Because such knowledge is difficult, the man who acts so as to figure them out deserves even more praise. 3 It is not so difficult to understand the enemy's plans as it is sometimes to understand his actions, and not so much the actions that he carries out far off as those here and now and close at hand. 4 For it has often happened that when a battle has lasted until nightfall,

the winner thinks he has lost and the loser thinks he has won. 5 This error has led to decisions that are contrary to the safety of the man who has made the decision, as happened with Brutus and Cassius, who lost the war because of this error: although Brutus won on his flank, Cassius, who had lost, believed that the entire army had been defeated; this error made him despair for his safety and commit suicide.[2] 6 In our day in the battle that Francis, the king of France, waged against the Swiss at Santa Cecilia in Lombardy, when night fell those of the Swiss who had stayed together believed they had won, since they knew nothing about those who had been defeated and killed. That error kept them from escaping, and they waited until the morning to resume fighting to such great disadvantage for themselves; they also misled the army of the pope and of Spain, and because of this error almost got it destroyed, because after the false news of victory it crossed over the Po, and had it advanced too far it would have been taken prisoner by the victorious French.[3]

7 A similar error occurred in the camps of the Romans and the Volscians[4] when the consul Sempronius marched with his army toward the enemy; once battle was joined, it wore on until evening, with changing fortunes on the two sides. 8 When night fell, since both armies were half-defeated, neither one returned to its encampment; rather, each withdrew into the nearby hills where they thought they would be safer. The Roman army separated into two groups: one went off with the Consul, the other with a certain centurion, Tempanius, thanks to whose *virtù* the Roman army was not completely defeated that day. 9 When morning came, the Roman Consul, without learning anything else about the enemy, withdrew toward Rome; the army of the Volscians did likewise, because each of them believed that the enemy had won, and therefore each withdrew without caring about leaving its encampment as booty. 10 It happened that Tempanius, who was also withdrawing along with the rest of the Roman army, found out from some wounded Volscians that their commanders had left and had abandoned their encampment; at this news he went into the Roman encampments and rescued them, then sacked the Volscians' and returned victorious to Rome. 11 That victory, as we can see, depended solely on which of them heard first about the enemy's disarray. 12 From this we must note that it can often occur that two armies facing one another may be in the same disarray and suffering from the same difficulties and that the one that is the first to learn of the other's difficulties may then remain victorious.

13 I would like to give a domestic, modern example of this.[5] 14 In 1498 the Florentines had a large army in Pisan territory and were strongly threatening the city, whose protection the Venetians had undertaken; because the latter saw no other way to save Pisa, they decided to divert the war by attacking from another side territory held by Florence. Raising a powerful army, they entered through the Val di Lamona, seized the village of Marradi, and besieged the stronghold of Castiglione, which is on the hill above it. 15 When the Florentines heard of this, they decided to relieve Marradi without reducing the forces that they had in Pisan territory; raising new infantry and organizing new cavalry troops, they sent them in that direction under the command of Jacopo IV d'Appiano, the lord of Piombino, and count Rinuccio da Marciano. 16 So when

these troops had been led up onto the hill above Marradi, the enemy took off from around Castiglione and all retreated into the village; after facing each other for a few days, the two armies were suffering a great deal from lack of provisions and every other necessity. 17 Because neither one dared to attack the other and neither knew of the other's disarray, they both decided the same night to strike camp when morning came and retreat, the Venetians toward Brisighella and Faenza, the Florentines toward Casaglia and the Mugello. 18 So when morning came and each of the camps had started to send off its baggage, a woman left the village of Marradi by chance and approached the Florentine camp, counting on old age and poverty and wanting to see some of her relatives who were in the camp. When the commanders of the Florentine troops learned from her that the Venetian camp was breaking up, they were emboldened by the news; changing their plans, they went after them as if they had turned the enemy out of their camp and wrote to Florence that they had repelled them and won the war. 19 This victory arose from nothing but their having learned before the enemy that they were departing: if the news had reached the other side first, it would have had the same result against our people.

NOTES

1. Plutarch, *Apophthegmata regum et imperatorum,* 187 C, has a saying similar to this thought attributed to an Athenian general, Chabrias (c. 420–357/356 B.C.), not to Epaminondas. (Plutarch's authorship of this work is open to question, but it is often attributed to him.) In the context of a comparison with Generals William T. Sherman and George S. Patton, Epaminondas has been hailed as "the real modern military thinker of the ancient world, the sole constitutional general who realized that a democratic nation in arms must make the entire society of the enemy pay for the aggression of its army, must convince his own democratic army that they are morally superior to the enemy" (Victor Davis Hanson, *Soul of Battle,* p. 33).

2. A reference to the battle of Philippi in 42 B.C., in which Mark Antony defeated Cassius; because Cassius was misled and believed Octavius Caesar had defeated Brutus, he committed suicide. Brutus was actually the victor over Octavius, but he was finally defeated twenty days later and had one of his freed slaves kill him; see Plutarch, *Brutus,* 42–43.

3. Santa Cecilia is better known as the location for the Battle of Marignano, where France drove the Swiss out of Italy and defeated the supporting troops of Pope Leo X and Ferdinand the Catholic, king of Spain; see above, 1, 23, n.5, and 2, 22, n.5. Guicciardini, *Storia d'Italia,* 12, 15, mentions that "the army of the Pope and Spain" did cross the Po but withdrew the day before the battle.

4. Throughout this chapter Machiavelli refers to the Aequi; the group in question was really the Volscians. The source for information about the consul Aulus Sempronius Atratinus in 423 B.C. is Livy, 4.37–41. Sextus Tempanius, a cavalry decurion (in charge of ten men), not a centurion, ordered his men to dismount and led them on foot, forcing openings in the enemy lines.

5. Guicciardini describes the situation in his *History of Florence,* chapter 17, and *Storia d'Italia,* 4, 3. Neither of these includes the anecdote about the old woman, but as secretary of the Ten of War, Machiavelli may have heard it in Florence. Marradi,

then a Florentine possession in Romagna, is about forty-two miles northeast of Florence in the valley of the Lamone River. Brisighella and Faenza are about fifty-seven miles and sixty-four miles, respectively, northeast of Florence, Casaglia about thirty-one miles, in the Mugello region. Jacopo IV d'Appiano and Rinuccio da Marciano were Florentine mercenary leaders.

~ 19 ~

WHETHER INDULGENCE, MORE THAN PUNISHMENT, IS NEEDED TO CONTROL THE MASSES

1 The Roman republic was in turmoil because of the enmities between the Nobles and the Plebs; nevertheless, when war threatened them, they sent Quinctius and Appius Claudius out with the armies.[1] 2 Because Appius was cruel and rough as a commander, he was so badly obeyed by his men that, close to defeat, he fled from his sector. 3 Because Quinctius was kindly and of a humane nature, he had obedient soldiers and he carried off victory with them. 4 Thus it seems it is better when controlling masses to be humane rather than haughty, merciful rather than cruel. 5 Nevertheless, Tacitus, with whom many other writers agree,[2] reaches the opposite conclusion in one of his maxims when he says: "For controlling the masses, punishment is worth more than indulgence."[3]

6 And examining how these two opinions can be reconciled, I say: you have to control either men who are normally your associates or men who are always your subjects. 7 When they are your associates, punishment cannot be resorted to entirely, nor the severity that Tacitus is discussing; and because the Roman Plebs had equal power with the Nobility in Rome, someone who became their prince for a time could not handle them with cruelty and roughness. 8 Often one could see that the Roman commanders who made themselves beloved by their armies and dealt with them with indulgence bore better fruit than those who made themselves unusually feared, unless they also had exceeding *virtù* like Manlius Torquatus.[4] 9 But someone who commands subjects, like those Tacitus is discussing, must turn to punishment rather than to indulgence in order for them not to become insolent and trample on you because of your excessive kindness. 10 But this must also be moderated so as to avoid hatred, because making oneself hated has never turned out well for any prince. 11 The way to avoid it is to leave the subjects' property alone; for no prince wants bloodshed unless it conceals his pillage, except when necessity forces him to, and such necessity occurs rarely. But if pillage is mixed in with bloodshed, it always occurs: there is never any lack of reasons and desire for shedding blood, as we have discussed at length in another treatise on this subject.[5] 12 So Quinctius deserved more praise than Appius, and Tacitus's maxim deserves to be approved on his own terms and not in those cases observed by Appius.

13 And because we have spoken of punishment and indulgence, I do not think it is irrelevant to show how an example of human kindness was more effective than arms with the Faliscans.

NOTES

1. Titus Quinctius Capitolinus and Appius Claudius were the consuls for 471 B.C.; see Livy, 2.55–60. This Appius Claudius is not the later Decemvir, whose rape of Virginia is referred to above, 1, 40, n.22.

2. As the relevant classical source, Inglese suggests a passage from Cicero, *De officiis,* 1.88.

3. Machiavelli introduces this quotation with "he says" in Latin and then quotes it in Latin, though commentators have been unable to find it in Tacitus. There is a remark in Tacitus, *Annals,* 3.55.5, about the ineffectiveness of legal punishment and threats, but it contradicts Machiavelli's assertion here. Inglese's explanation for the discrepancy rests on the published critical edition of the *Annals,* which was not available until March 1515, edited by Filippo Beroaldo. Yet the first person to study the manuscript, owned by Pope Leo X, was Cardinal Francesco Soderini in 1509. We have two admiring letters from him to Machiavelli: one in 1502 praising Machiavelli's intellect and one several years later in praise of his work on a citizen's militia (see *Friends,* pp. 31–33; 120–121). Soderini mentions receiving the manuscript from Germany, and we know from a letter that Machiavelli received from Cesare Mauro, whom he met while in Germany in 1508 that this man, a scholar, was on the lookout for classical manuscripts "among the book shops" (p. 167). So Machiavelli may have encountered people who had read the manuscript of the *Annals* before it was printed; thus some of its ideas may have been distorted by hearsay. Walker believes that the publication of the critical edition in 1515 provides a clue about the date of this chapter in the *Discourses,* but, as Inglese notes, there were other opportunities for Machiavelli to have some familiarity with the *Annals,* even if untrustworthy ones. Guicciardini, a careful reader of Machiavelli, does not pick up this error in his *Consideration* of this chapter, as he did above in sentence 4 of his *Consideration* of Machiavelli, 3, 17, sentence 6. Vivanti, in his edition of the *Discorsi,* notes that Guicciardini's brief references to Tacitus in his *Ricordi,* written between 1512 and 1530, do not involve the *Annals:* C 13 and 18 (see also B 78 and 79). Sasso, on the other hand, says Guicciardini may have conflated Tacitus, *Annals,* 1.13.2 with the account of the death of Augustus in Suetonius (*Per Francesco Guicciardini,* pp. 35–37). See also Martelli, *Storici antichi,* pp. 169–171. The emphasis on "indulgence" in this chapter and "humanity" in the next chapter serve to qualify the chapter title above of 2, 13, "that one gets from low to high Fortune more by deceit than by force."

4. See above, 2, 16, n.4, for the "exceeding *virtù*" that Manlius Torquatus displayed in ordering the execution of his own son for disobeying his father's orders.

5. As a gloss on this sentence and sentence 4 of this chapter, see *Prince,* 17, in which he raises the question, Is it better to be loved than feared or to be feared than loved? (p. 271, lines 34–35). His answer is that "men are less reluctant to cause trouble for someone who makes himself loved than for someone who makes himself feared. . . . Nevertheless a prince should make himself feared in such a way that, if he does not gain love, he does avoid hatred" (lines 51–53; 58–60, page 273). See also *Prince,* 19, entitled "how to avoid contempt and hatred." Behind these reference lies Aristotle, *Politics,* 5.9.18; 1315a25–31.

~ 20 ~

AN EXAMPLE OF HUMAN KINDNESS TOWARD THE FALISCANS HAD MORE EFFECT THAN ALL ROMAN MIGHT

1 When Camillus and his army surrounded the Faliscans' city and were besieging it, thinking he would ingratiate himself with Camillus and the Roman people, a schoolteacher to the most noble children of the city left the town with them under the pretext of exercise, led them all into the camp before Camillus, and, presenting them to him, said that through them the town would be given into his hands.[1] 2 Not only did Camillus not accept this gift, but, after having the teacher stripped with his hands tied behind him and putting a rod into the hands of each of those children, he had them accompany him back into town with many beatings. 3 When the citizens heard of this, they were so pleased with Camillus's human kindness and integrity that, no longer wishing to defend themselves, they decided to surrender the town to him. 4 By this authentic example, we should consider how much more effective an act of human kindness, full of charity, may often be in the minds of men than a cruel and violent act and how regions and cities that arms, instruments of war, and every other human force have not been able to open up have often been opened by an example of human kindness and mercy, abstinence, or generosity.

5 There are many other examples of this besides this one in the histories. 6 We see that Roman weapons were unable to drive Pyrrhus out of Italy and Fabricius's generosity managed to, when he showed him the offer that one of his servants had made to the Romans to poison him.[2] 7 We can also see that Scipio Africanus did not gain as much prestige in Spain from the capture of New Carthage as he did from the example of abstinence in which he returned a young, beautiful, intact wife to her husband; the fame of that deed gained him the allegiance of all Spain.[3] 8 We can also see how much the people desire this quality in great men and how much it is praised by writers and those who describe the lives of princes and those who prescribe how they should live.[4] 9 Among these, Xenophon goes to great lengths to show how many honors, how many victories, and how much good reputation his being humane and considerate gained for Cyrus and not giving any example of his being either haughty or cruel, or lustful, or having any other vice that may stain the lives of men.[5] 10 On the other hand, since Hannibal achieved great fame and great victories by ways contrary to these, I think I should discuss in the next chapter how this comes about.

NOTES

1. Based on Livy, 5.27; but see Martelli, *Storici antichi,* pp. 171–172, with his suggestion of the relevance of Valerius Maximus, 6.5.1. The campaign of Marcus Furius Camillus against the Faliscan city of Falerii, modern-day Cività Castellana, about thirty-three miles directly north of Rome, in 394 B.C.

2. This incident is based on Plutarch, *Pyrrhus,* 21, as well as Livy, *Summaries,* 13,

and Cicero, *De officiis,* 1.13. n.40. Pyrrhus's doctor told Gaius Fabricius Luscinus, who was consul in 278 B.C., of the conspiracy against Pyrrhus. The city of Tarentum called on Pyrrhus, the king of Epirus, to fight the Romans in 280 B.C. After a series of costly defeats at Heraclea and Ausculum (what he called his "Pyrrhic victories"), he was defeated at Beneventum in 275. So not until three years later did he withdraw from Italy with but a third of his army remaining. It had nothing to do with "Fabricius's generosity."

3. For the capture in 210 B.C. during the Second Punic War of New Carthage (modern-day Cartagena, a port city in southeastern Spain) by Cornelius Scipio Africanus Major, see Livy, 26.46, and chapter 50 for the return of the hostage promised to the Celtiberian chieftain, Allucius. This example, known as "the continence of Scipio," in which Scipio "sent a daughter back to her father, a wife back to her husband," as Machiavelli puts it below, chapter 34, sentence 21, has been frequently illustrated by artists and described by writers.

4. A reference to the *de regimine principum* tradition, to which the *Prince* belongs, as does Castiglione's *The Courtier,* written in 1514 and published in 1528.

5. In particular, the *Cyropaedeia,* 1.4; 3.1.41–42; 3.3.2; 7.5.72ff.; 8.1–2 and 6. Machiavelli has discussed deception and Cyrus above, 2, 13, sentences 3–5.

~ 21 ~

HOW IT CAME ABOUT THAT HANNIBAL, BEHAVING DIFFERENTLY FROM SCIPIO, GOT THE SAME RESULTS IN ITALY AS THE LATTER DID IN SPAIN

1 I imagine that some people might be surprised to realize that some commanders, despite having acted in completely different ways, have nevertheless achieved results similar to those who have acted in the way described above.[1] So it seems that the reason for their victories does not depend on the causes cited above; it seems rather that these ways do not get you more might or more fortune, since glory and prestige can be acquired in opposing ways. 2 So, not to go beyond the men mentioned above and the better to clarify what I meant, I say that we see Scipio enter Spain and by his human kindness and mercy immediately make that province friendly to him and make himself adored and admired by the people. 3 On the contrary, we see Hannibal enter Italy and, in quite the opposite way—that is to say, by cruelty, violence, and rapine, and every sort of treachery—achieve the same result as Scipio had achieved in Spain: because all the cities of Italy went over to Hannibal, all the people followed him.[2]

4 And if we consider how this may have happened, several causes for it can be seen. 5 The first is that men are desirous of new things,[3] insofar as most of the time those who are well off desire novelty as much as those who are not well off; because, as has been said earlier[4] and it is true, men grow tired of the

good and are troubled at the bad. 6 This desire therefore opens the doors to anyone in a province who makes himself the leader of change: if he is a foreigner, they run after him; if he is from the province, they gather around him, boosting and supporting him so that however he proceeds he succeeds in making great strides in those places.[5] 7 In addition, men are driven by two main things, either by love or by fear; so anyone who makes himself loved commands them just like someone who makes himself feared. Indeed, most often one who makes himself feared is followed and obeyed more than one who makes himself loved.[6]

8 It matters little to a commander, therefore, which of these roads he travels as long as he is a man of *virtù* and that *virtù* lends him prestige among men. 9 For when it is great, as it was in Hannibal and Scipio, it cancels out all the errors that are made by making oneself loved too much or feared too much. 10 For great problems that are likely to cause a prince's downfall can result from either of these ways: because the man who desires too much to be loved becomes contemptible however little he strays from the true path; the other one, who desires too much to be feared, becomes hateful however little he goes beyond the norm. 11 It is impossible to keep to the middle path precisely because our nature does not permit it,[7] but it is necessary to compensate for any excess by exceptional *virtù,* as Hannibal and Scipio did.

12 Nonetheless, we can see that both of them were harmed by their way of living, just as they both were raised up. 13 The height to which both of them were raised has been discussed. 14 The harm in the case of Scipio was that his soldiers in Spain rebelled against him along with part of his allies, and this arose from nothing else than their not fearing him.[8] For men are so restless that however slightly a door is opened to their ambition, they quickly forget any love that they had felt for the prince because of his human kindness, as the soldiers and allies mentioned above did. So to remedy this problem, Scipio was forced to employ some of the cruelty that he had avoided. 15 As for Hannibal, there is no specific example in which that cruelty and faithlessness hurt him, but we may indeed presume that Naples and many other towns that remained faithful to the Roman people did so out of fear of it. 16 This could clearly be seen: his wicked way of life made him more hateful to the Roman people than any other enemy the republic ever had; so, whereas they showed Pyrrhus the man who wanted to poison him while he was with his army in Italy, they never forgave Hannibal, even when he was disarmed and in flight so that they brought about his death.[9] 17 Thus these disadvantages arose for Hannibal from his being considered wicked, a breaker of promises, and cruel; on the other hand, he derived one very great advantage from it, which all writers have admired: no dissension ever arose in his army, either among the soldiers or against him, even though it was made up of different races of men. 18 That can have stemmed only from the terror that his person inspired, which, mixed with the prestige that his *virtù* gave him, was so great that it kept his soldiers calm and united. 19 I therefore conclude that it does not much matter how a commander behaves as long as there is great *virtù* in him that seasons both ways of living. 20 For as has been stated, each

of them has a drawback and a danger when it is not corrected by exceptional *virtù*. 21 And if Hannibal and Scipio achieved the same result, one by praiseworthy things, the other by detestable ones, I do not feel we should leave out further discussion of two Roman citizens who achieved equal glory in different ways but each of them praiseworthy.

NOTES

1. That is, the examples of Camillus and Scipio in the previous chapter. Machiavelli's concern here is one basic to the letter, known as the letter of "fantasies" or "speculations" *(ghiribizzi),* that Machiavelli wrote to Giovan Battista Soderini in 1506. It, too, contrasts the behavior of Scipio and Hannibal as Machiavelli is about to do here: "Cruelty, treachery, and impiety are effective in providing a new ruler with prestige in that region where human kindness, loyalty, and piety have long been common practice, just as human kindness, loyalty, and piety are effective where cruelty, treachery, and impiety reigned for a while; for just as bitter things irritate the taste and sweet things cloy it, so men become impatient with the good and complain about the bad. These causes, among others, opened Italy up to Hannibal and Spain to Scipio, and thus each one made time and affairs consistent with his pattern of doing things" (*Friends,* pp. 136–136). For more on this point, see below, 3, 22, sentence 9.

2. For Livy's assessment of Scipio's policies in Spain, see 27.20.5. His judgment on Hannibal's character can be found in 21.4.6–9, though this may be only a Roman view (see Polybius, 9.22.24–26). In *Prince,* 17, Machiavelli says that Hannibal's "inhuman ruthlessness—together with his extraordinary *virtù*—always made him an object of respect and awe in his soldiers' eyes; without his ruthlessness the rest of his *virtù* would have been inadequate to achieve the same result. Writers who have given this matter cursory attention admire Hannibal's achievements, on the one hand, and on the other hand condemn the primary source of those achievements" (p. 275, lines 87–96). About Scipio he writes: "eventually Scipio's tolerant nature would have damaged his fame and glory, if it had persisted while he exercised supreme command. But because he existed under the senate's control, this harmful characteristic of his was not only hidden, but actually brought him glory" (p. 277, lines 112–117). See also above, 3, 9, n.1. The assertion that "all the cities of Italy went over to Hannibal" is contrary to Livy, 22.54, and distorts historical fact (see Martelli, *Storici antichi,* p. 173).

3. A notion in Machiavelli's *capitolo "Di fortuna,"* vv. 49–51; it is dedicated to Giovan Battista Soderini (see note 1 above).

4. See above, 1, 37, sentences 1–3.

5. A position that Machiavelli also takes in *Prince,* 3.

6. Machiavelli argued these points above, in 3, 19 (see its note 5), as well as in *Prince,* 17 and 19.

7. See the passage from the letter of "fantasies" or "speculations" quoted above, 3, 9, n.1. As Inglese notes, in the 1506 letter the situation in which the leaders find themselves determines their flexible actions. Here the distinction is more between traits of character and how the compensation "for any excess by exceptional *virtù*" is left somewhat in the air.

8. See Livy, 28.24–29; 32–34. Concerning this mutiny Machiavelli remarks in *Prince,* 17: "This insurrection resulted from nothing else than his excessive compassion,

which permitted his soldiers more license than was consonant with military discipline" (p. 275, lines 100–103).

9. See Livy, 39.51, and its discussion of Hannibal's death—a suicide. In his final speech, Hannibal refers to the Romans' warning Pyrrhus of the possibility of someone poisoning him. On this situation see the previous chapter, sentence 6 and note 2.

~ 22 ~

THE HARSHNESS OF MANLIUS TORQUATUS AND THE CIVILITY[1] OF VALERIUS CORVINUS ACHIEVED EQUAL GLORY FOR EACH

1 There lived at the same time in Rome two excellent commanders, Manlius Torquatus and Valerius Corvinus, equal in *virtù,* triumphs, and glory; each of them, insofar as the enemy was concerned, achieved it by equal *virtù,* but, as far as their armies and their treatment of soldiers were concerned, they acted very differently.[2] 2 For Manlius commanded them with every sort of severity without sparing his soldiers either toil or pain; Valerius, on the other hand, treated them with every humane way and means and full of close familiarity. 3 By this it was seen that to get their soldiers' obedience one slew his son and the other never hurt anyone. 4 Nonetheless, despite such different procedures, each bore the same fruit both against the enemy and for the benefit of the republic and himself. 5 For no soldier ever either avoided battle or rebelled against them or went in any way against their will, even though the commands of Manlius were so harsh that all other commands going beyond the norm were called "Manlian commands."[3] 6 So we must consider first how it came about that Manlius was obliged to behave so strictly, then how it happened that Valerius could behave so humanely, then what made these different ways have the same result, and finally which of them it is better and more useful to imitate.

7 If anyone examines carefully the nature of Manlius from the point when Livy begins mentioning him, one will see he was a very strong man devoted to his father and his country and very respectful toward his superiors.[4] 8 These things are known from the death of that Gaul, from the defense of his father against the Tribune, and from his saying to the Consul before he went to fight the Gaul: "Without your orders . . . I will never fight against the enemy, not even if I should see that victory were certain."[5] 9 So once a man like that gets to a rank of commander, he expects to find all men like himself; his strong courage makes him demand strong actions, and this same man, once they have been asked for, wants them to be obeyed. 10 And it is a very sound rule that whenever one gives harsh orders, it takes harshness to have them obeyed, otherwise you would find yourself disappointed in them.

11 Concerning this it should be noted that if one wishes to be obeyed one must know how to command. Those who compare their character with that of the men who are to obey know how to command; when they see conformity, then they command, and when they see nonconformity, they abstain from it. 12

And that is why a wise man said that in order to hold a republic by force there had to be conformity between the man who did the forcing and those who were forced.[6] 13 Whenever there was such conformity, it could be thought that the violence would endure; but if those forced were stronger than the man doing the forcing, it might be feared that the violence would end any day.

14 But to return to our discussion, I say that to ask for hard things one must be strong; and a man who is of such strength and asks for them cannot then get them obeyed by gentleness. 15 But anyone who lacks this strength of mind must shun extraordinary commands, and he can show his human kindness in ordinary ones, because ordinary punishments are ascribed not to the prince but to the laws and institutions. 16 One must therefore believe that Manlius was forced to behave so strictly by his extraordinary commands, which his nature made him prone to; these are useful in a republic, because they bring its laws back toward their origin and into its ancient *virtù*.[7] 17 If a republic were so fortunate as often to have someone who renewed its laws by his example, as we said above, and not only kept it from rushing toward its downfall but pulled it back, it would last forever.[8] 18 So Manlius was one of those who kept up military discipline in Rome by the harshness of their orders, constrained first by his nature and then by his desire that what his natural inclination had made him command should be obeyed.

19 On the other hand, Valerius could act humanely, since he was one for whom it sufficed that things that were customarily obeyed in Roman armies be obeyed. 20 Because this custom was good, it sufficed to bring him honor; it was not difficult to obey and did not require Valerius to punish transgressors, both because there were none and because if there had been any, they would have ascribed their punishment, as has been said,[9] to the rules and not the prince's cruelty. 21 Hence, Valerius could make all human kindness come from him and thereby acquire respect as well as their satisfaction from his soldiers. 22 Thus it occurred that, since both of them got the same obedience, they could get the same result despite acting differently. 23 Those who would wish to imitate them can fall into the vices of contempt and hatred which I mention above concerning Hannibal and Scipio.[10] You avoid this by some exceeding *virtù* that may be in you and not otherwise.

24 Now it remains to consider which of these ways of acting is more praiseworthy. 25 I believe this is open to debate because the writers praise both ways. 26 Nevertheless, those who write about how a prince should behave incline more to Valerius than to Manlius; and Xenophon, whom I have mentioned above, by giving many examples of the human kindness of Cyrus, agrees closely with what Livy says about Valerius.[11] 27 For when he was made Consul against the Samnites and the day came for him to fight, he spoke to his soldiers with the human kindness with which he behaved; and after the speech, Livy writes the following words: "No other commander ever treated his soldiers more familiarly, since he cheerfully shared every duty with the humblest of his soldiers. In military games, too, in which men compete together as equals in speed and strength, he was courteous and easygoing; his countenance remained unchanged whether he won or lost, nor did he spurn anyone who offered

himself as a match. In his deeds he was kind when circumstances permitted; in his speech he was no less mindful of others' freedom and his own dignity; and nothing is more popular than this: he conducted himself in office with the same qualities by which he sought it."[12] 28 Livy also speaks favorably of Manlius, showing that his severity in the death of his son made the army so obedient to the Consul[13] that it was the cause of the Roman people's victory over the Latins. He goes so far in praising him that after this victory, having described the whole order of the battle and shown all the risks that the Roman people ran in it and how hard it was to win it, he draws the following conclusion: that Manlius's *virtù* alone gave the victory to the Romans. 29 Comparing the strength of the two armies, he asserts that whichever side had had Manlius as consul would have won.[14] 30 So considering all that the writers say about it, it would be difficult to make a judgment about this.

31 Nonetheless, so as not to leave this question undecided, I say that I believe Manlius's way is more praiseworthy and less risky for a citizen who lives under the laws of a republic: this way is entirely in favor of the public interest and does not concern private ambition in any respect. For in this way, always showing oneself to be harsh to everybody and loving only the common good, one cannot acquire supporters, because a man who does this does not acquire personal friends that we may call, as was stated above, supporters.[15] 32 So such behavior cannot be more useful or more desirable in a republic, since it does not lack public utility and there can be no suspicion of private power in it. 33 But in Valerius's behavior the contrary holds true, because, although as far as the public interest is concerned it has the same results, nevertheless, because of the personal goodwill that this man acquires with the soldiers, many doubts arise about it so as to have bad effects on freedom over a lengthy command.[16] 34 And if these bad effects do not come about with Publicola, the reason was that the minds of Romans were not yet corrupted and he was not in control of them over a long, continuous period.[17]

35 But if we are considering a prince, as does Xenophon, we will turn completely to Valerius and pass over Manlius, for a prince must seek obedience and love in his soldiers and subjects. 36 Obedience is given to him by his observing the laws and being considered full of *virtù;* love is given him for his courtesy, human kindness, mercy, and the other qualities that characterized Valerius and that Xenophon writes characterized Cyrus.[18] 37 For being a well-loved prince in particular and having one's army as supporters conforms with all the other aspects of his state; but in a citizen who has the army as supporters this does not really conform with his other qualities, which should let him live under the laws and obey the magistrates.

38 One may read among the ancient matters of the Venetian republic that when the Venetian galleys returned to Venice and some dissension arose between those on the galleys and the people, which led to riots and armed combat, and the matter could not be allayed by either the officials' power or the citizens' respect or fear of the magistrates, suddenly a gentleman who had been in command of the sailors the year before appeared before them and they stopped fighting and went away out of love for him.[19] 39 Their obedi-

ence generated so much suspicion in the Senate that shortly thereafter the Venetians took care of him either by prison or by death.

40 Therefore I conclude that Valerius's procedure is useful in a prince and destructive in a citizen not only for one's country but for oneself: for the former because these ways prepare the way to tyranny; for oneself because in making one's city suspicious of one's way of acting it is forced to take precautions, to one's detriment. 41 And on the contrary, I declare Manlius's procedure to be harmful for a prince and useful for a citizen and especially to one's country; also it rarely does harm, at least if the hatred that your severity brings upon you is not increased by any suspicion that your other *virtù* might bring upon you because of your great prestige, as will be discussed below concerning Camillus.[20]

NOTES

1. Translation of a Latinism, *comità,* with a connotation of "humanity" and "humaneness." In the translation of Livy in sentence 27, the phrase *comiter facilis* is translated "courteous and easygoing."

2. On Titus Manlius Torquatus, see above, 2, 16, n.4. For how Marcus Valerius obtained his nickname Corvinus, see above, 1, 60, n.2. The two served Rome both as consul and dictator on several occasions during the fourth century B.C. Ancient authorities credit Valerius with four triumphs and Manlius with only one (Martelli, *Storici antichi,* p. 173).

3. Quoted in Latin from Livy, 8.7.22; see also above, 2, 16, n.4. See the discussion in Martelli, *Storici antichi,* pp. 174–175, and the suggestion of Aulus Gellius, *Noctes Atticae,* 9.13, as a source.

4. See above, 1, 11, n.4.

5. Manlius also killed a huge Gaul in a duel (Livy, 7.10); the quotation is in Latin with a few changes from Livy, 7.10.2; but see the discussion in Martelli, *Storici antichi,* p. 176. Manlius acquired his nickname "Torquatus" from the bloody chain *(torque)* he removed from the Gaul's neck after defeating him. But according to Livy, Manlius's speech was made to the dictator Titus Quinctius Poenus, not to "the Consul" (7.9.3 and 7.10.2).

6. The identity of the "wise man" is unclear. Although Aristotle, *Politics,* 3.10.10; 1286b27–41, has been suggested, there is no notion of "conformity." For it or the idea of balance, see above, 1, 55, sentence 34.

7. An echo of the argument above, 3, 1, sentence 7, and the title of that chapter concerning something "frequently taken back toward its origins." Machiavelli himself draws us back to this discussion, particularly to sentences 17 and 18, at the beginning of his next sentence. It should be noted, too, that Livy, 8.6.14, points out that the capital punishment Titus Manlius meted out to his son was necessary "so that military discipline could brought back to its former ways" *(utique disciplina militaris ad priscos redigeretur mores).*

8. See above, 3, 17, n.3.

9. In sentence 15 of this chapter.

10. In the previous chapter.

11. See above, 3, 20, n.5.

12. Valerius was made consul in 343 B.C., the year the First Samnite War began. The long quotation is from Livy, 7.33.1–3, with slight alterations: *"Non alias militi*

familiarior dux fuit omnia inter infimos militum haud gravate munia obeundo. In ludo praeterea militari, cum velocitatis viriumque inter se aequales certamina ineunt, comiter facilis; vincere ac vinci voltu eodem, nec quemquam aspernari parem qui se offerret; factis benignus pro re, dictis haud minus libertatis alienae quam suae dignitatis memor; et, quo nihil popularius est, quibus artibus petierat magistratus iisdem gerebat."

13. Livy, 8.8.1: "However, the severity of the punishment made the soliders more obedient to their commander" *(Fecit tamen atrocitas poenae oboedientiorem duci militem).*

14. Livy, 8.10.8: "whichever side had been commanded by Titus Manlius would unquestionably have been victorious" *(utrius partis T. Manlius dux fuisset, eius futuram haud dubie fuisse victoriam).*

15. Machiavelli may be referring to 1, 43, sentence 5, in which he discusses the issue of supporters, *partigiani,* having "affection for the person they are fighting for." See also above, 1, 34, sentence 7, and 1, 16, sentences 5–7, where *partigiani* refers to "friendly factions."

16. An issue Machiavelli takes up below, 3, 24.

17. Not all commentators agree on the identification of Publicola, but Inglese's argument is convincing. The context is a discussion of Valerius Corvus. At the end of a long speech he delivers to the troops (as quoted below, 3, 38, sentence 2), he reminds them that, even though the soldiers have given him the surname of Corvinus, "I have not forgotten the ancient surname of our family, the Publicolae" (Livy, 7.32.15). This is a reminder that his surname has a long tradition of support of the people. It means "Friends of the People," as Livy made clear in 2.8.1 when discussing an earlier member of the family, Publius Valerius Publicola, who lived 150 years earlier than Valerius Corvus (see above, 1, 13, sentence 8, and n.7).

18. See *Cyropaedeia,* 4.2 and 5.1, 3; and 8.1–2.

19. Commentators believe the "gentleman" is Vittore Pisani, who saved Venice by defeating the Genoese fleet in 1380 and putting an end to Genoa's status as a naval power. Machiavelli's account is widely at variance with the historical record about Pisani.

20. Friedrich, *Montaigne,* pp. 148–151, makes an interesting comparison between Machiavelli's method in this and the three previous chapters and Montaigne's procedure in his first essay, "By Diverse Means We Arrive at the Same Ends": "One sees how both authors proceed from a *Quod-sic-quod-non* antithesis of abstract maxims to advance to a casuistry which, by observation of individual cases, supports an explanation on the ground of empirical reality. They discover that man is much too variable to be restricted to following a maxim that applies to all cases. Both Machiavelli and Montaigne set aside generality under the pressure of the diversity of history and character. But differences exist. . . . The cleverness of the Italian says excellent things about the paradoxes of human nature. . . . But from all his insights he derives practical conclusions that are intended to serve the politician in his goal-oriented actions. Montaigne draws no conclusion. . . . The puzzle of man emerges from the opposing particular cases and any judgment is denied except the following: one cannot approach man with any uniform judgment. . . . The contemplative Frenchman knows a bit more about man than the practical Florentine who, as all practical people, abbreviates what is infinite" (pp. 149–151).

~ 23 ~

WHY CAMILLUS WAS DRIVEN FROM ROME

1 We have concluded above that if one does as Valerius did, one harms one's country and oneself; doing as Manlius did, one serves one's country and sometimes harms oneself. 2 This can be proved quite readily by the example of Camillus, who resembled Manlius rather than Valerius in his way of doing things. 3 That is why Livy, in speaking of him, says that "the soldiers detested and admired his *virtù*."[1]

4 What made him be considered admirable was his promptness, his prudence, the grandeur of his spirit, the good order that served him in administering and leading armies; what made him hated was being more severe in punishing them than generous in rewarding them. 5 And Livy alleges these reasons for this hatred: first, that he transferred the money drawn from the Veians' property that was sold to the public treasury and did not divide it up with the booty; next, that in the triumph he had his triumphal chariot drawn by four white horses so that people said that out of pride he had wanted to compare himself to the Sun; third, that he made a vow to give Apollo a tenth of the booty from the Veians, and, in order to satisfy the vow, it had to be taken from the hands of the soldiers who had just seized it.[2]

6 In this the things that make a prince hateful to the people can be clearly and easily noted; the principal one is depriving them of property.[3] 7 This is a very important matter, because when a man is deprived of things that have some use in themselves, he never forgets; every slightest need recalls them to you, and, because needs arise every day, you recall them every day. 8 The other thing is appearing to be proud and puffed up; nothing can be more hateful to people and especially free ones. 9 And even if that pride and pomp should cause them no inconvenience, nevertheless, they hate anyone who practices them; a prince must guard himself from this as he would a shoal, for to bringing hatred upon oneself without any advantage is a completely foolhardy and unwise course of action.

NOTES

1. Machiavelli quotes in Latin with alterations from Livy, 5.26.8: *"sed severitate imperii victi eandem virtutem et oderant et mirabantur."* Martelli comments on these alterations, *Storici antichi,* p. 176.

2. The tribunes required Marcus Furius Camillus to account for the spoils taken from the Veians in 391 B.C. He went into exile in the city of Ardea (a town about sixteen miles south of Rome) to avoid sentence, though he did receive a stiff fine (Livy, 5.32.7–9). Livy describes the three reasons for the hatred against him in 5.22–23; 25. On the third reason, see above, 1, 55, sentences 1–5. In general, see Plutarch, *Camillus,* 7.

3. In *Prince,* 17, Machiavelli writes that "above all" a prince "should restrain himself from other people's property: men are quicker to forget the death of a father than the loss of an inheritance" (p. 273, lines 67–69); he repeats the advice in chapter 19:

"what makes" a prince "particularly hated is being predatory and preemptory toward the property and the women of his subjects: he must keep himself away from these" (p. 287, lines 9–12). Behind both works may lie Sallust, *Bellum Jugurthinum,* 3.1–2.

~ 24 ~

LENGTHENING MILITARY COMMANDS ENDED ROME'S FREEDOM

1 If we carefully consider the actions of the Roman republic, we will see that two things were the cause of the dissolution of the republic: one was the disputes that arose from the Lex Agraria; the other was the lengthening of military commands.[1] If these things had been understood clearly at the outset and the correct remedies applied to them, life in freedom would have lasted longer and perhaps been more peaceful.

2 Although as far as the lengthening of command is concerned we cannot see that any rioting ever broke out in Rome, one could nevertheless see how much the power that citizens took on through such decisions harmed the city. 3 If the other citizens whose term in office was lengthened had been as wise and good as Lucius Quinctius, this difficulty would never have been incurred.[2] 4 His goodness is an example worthy of note; because after agreement had been reached between the Plebs and the Senate and the Plebs had lengthened the Tribunes' command to one year, since they judged them likely to be able to resist the Nobles' ambition, the Senate, to vie with the Plebs and not to seem weaker than they, decided to lengthen Lucius Quinctius's consulate.[3] 5 He absolutely rejected this decision, saying that bad examples should be eliminated, not increased by another, worse example, and he asked for new Consuls to be named. 6 If there had been such goodness and prudence in all Roman citizens, they would not have allowed the custom of lengthening terms of office to be introduced; so they would have not come to the lengthening of military commands that in time led to the downfall of the republic.

7 The first man whose command was lengthened was Publilius Philo, when he was encamped by the city of Palaeopolis and the term of his consulate was up; because the Senate felt that he had the victory in hand, they did not send a successor to him but made him Proconsul, so he was the first Proconsul.[4] 8 Although it was promoted for the public good by the Senate, that was what ended Rome's freedom over time. 9 Because the farther away the Romans went with their armies, the more such extension seemed necessary to them and the more they employed it. 10 That created two difficulties: first, a smaller number of men were given experience of command and, because of this, prestige came to be limited to a very few; second, if a citizen remained commander of an army for a long time, he won it over to himself and made it his backer, because the army forgot the Senate over time and recognized him as leader. 11 In this way Sulla and Marius were able to find soldiers who would follow them against the public good; in this way Caesar

was able to take over his country. 12 For if the Romans had not lengthened offices and military commands, although they would not have arrived at so much power so quickly and their conquests would have come later, they would also have become enslaved later.

NOTES

1. Machiavelli examines the Agrarian Law disputes above, in 1, 37, sentences 8–19. Extending the length of time that a leader had military authority is one of the linchpins in Machiavelli's interpretation of Roman history. It is made with particular emphasis in *Art of War,* 1. As he implies above, 3, 22, sentences 33–34, the "bad effects" of lengthening military commands occurred only after Rome was corrupted—a theme basic to Guicciardini's *Consideration* of this chapter (see his sentence 2).

2. For Machiavelli's version of the famous story of how Lucius Quinctius Cincinnatus was called from behind his plow in 456 B.C. and made military tribune and dictator, see the next chapter. Cincinnatus saved the Roman army from the Aequi, then relinquished power to return to the simple life of his farm. For his virtues of frugality, simplicity, and integrity, he became a heroic model of the old Roman Republic.

3. Machiavelli considerably modifies the account in Livy, 3.19–21, to suit his argument (Martelli, *Storici antichi,* pp. 177–181).

4. For the reference to Palaeopolis and this siege at the beginning of the Second Samnite War, see above, 2, 32, n.6. The consul Quintus Publilius Philo commanded the siege, 327–326 B.C. Livy notes that he was the first consul to enjoy two distinctions: having his command lengthened and being granted a triumph after his term expired (8.26.7).

~ 25 ~

ON THE POVERTY OF CINCINNATUS AND MANY ROMAN CITIZENS

1 We have discussed elsewhere how keeping citizens poor is the most useful thing that can be instituted in a free society.[1] 2 Although it is not apparent which institution in Rome was the one that produced this result, particularly since the Agrarian Law met with such opposition, nevertheless, experience showed that four hundred years after Rome had been built there was very great poverty. Nor can it be thought that any other greater institution produced this result than making sure that your path to any rank and any office was not blocked by poverty and that *virtù* was sought out in whatever house it dwelled in. 3 That way of living made riches less desirable.

4 This can be seen clearly, because when the consul Minucius and his army were besieged by the Aequi, Rome was so filled with fear lest that army be lost that they resorted to naming a Dictator, the ultimate remedy for their troubled affairs.[2] 5 They named Lucius Quinctius Cincinnatus, who was then on his little farm, which he tilled with his own hands. 6 This is celebrated by Livy in words of gold when he says: "This is worth listening to for those who despise all human qualities in comparison with riches and believe that there is no room

for great honor or virtue unless lavish wealth abounds."[3] 7 Cincinnatus was plowing his little farm, which did not measure more than four *iugera,*[4] when the Legates of the Senate came from Rome to inform him of his election as Dictator and show him what danger the Roman republic was in. 8 Donning his toga, he went to Rome, and after assembling an army he went off to free Minucius; when he had defeated and plundered the enemy and rescued the latter, he would not let the besieged army have a share in the booty, speaking these words to it: "I do not want you to share in the booty of those whose booty you were about to be."[5] And he stripped Minucius of the consulate and made him a Legate, saying to him: "You will remain in this rank until you have learned how to be a Consul."[6] 9 He had made Lucius Tarquinius, who was serving as a foot soldier because of his poverty, his Master of the Horse.[7] 10 As has been said, we should note the honor that was paid to poverty in Rome and that for a good and brave man such as Cincinnatus four *iugera* of land sufficed to feed him. We can see that there was still such poverty in the times of Marcus Regulus: when he was in Africa with his troops, he requested the Senate's permission to be allowed to return to take care of his farm, which was being ruined by his workers.[8] 11 Two quite noteworthy things can be observed in this: first, poverty and how people were happy in it; gaining honor from war was enough for those citizens, and they left all the profit to the public treasury. 12 Because if Marcus Regulus had thought of enriching himself from war, he would not have been troubled much by his fields' having been ruined. 13 The other thing is to consider the generosity of spirit of those citizens, whose magnanimity rose above that of any prince when they were placed at the head of an army. They did not esteem princes or republics; nothing terrified or frightened them; returning to private life afterward, they became frugal, humble caretakers of their small properties, obedient to the magistrates, respectful of their superiors, so it seems impossible for one and the same spirit to undergo such a change.

14 This poverty lasted until the time of Paulus Aemilius, which was almost the last happy time of the republic, when a citizen whose triumph enriched Rome nevertheless kept himself poor.[9] 15 And poverty was still so much esteemed that Paulus, in honoring those who had behaved well in the war, gave one of his sons-in-law a silver cup that was the first silver there was in his house. 16 Had this subject not been celebrated many times by other men, lengthy discussion could show what better fruits poverty produces than wealth, and how one has honored cities, provinces, religions, and the other has led to their downfall.[10]

NOTES

1. See above, 3, 16, n.2, and especially its cross-reference to 1, 37, sentence 7, and note 7.

2. When the Aequi attacked Rome in 458 B.C., Lucius Minucius led the Roman forces against them. They succeeded in blocking him into his own camp. Hence, when Rome learned of this danger they named Cincinnatus military tribune and dictator.

3. Quoted in Latin from Livy, 3.26.7: *"Operae pretium est audire qui omnia prae divitiis humana spernunt neque honori magno locum neque cirtuti putant esse, nisi ubi effuse afluant opes."* Machiavelli omits the word *ubi* in Livy's final phrase.

4. A little less than three acres.

5. Quoted in Italian based on Livy, 3.29.2, which reads: *"'carebis' inquit 'praedae parte miles, exeo hoste cui prope praedae fuisti.'"*

6. Quoted in Italian based on Livy, 3.29.2, which reads: *"donec consularem animum incipias habere, legatus his legionibus praeeris"* (until you begin to have a consul's spirit, you shall command these legions as a legate); that is, second in command to a general.

7. Livy, 3.27.1, where his name is spelled "Tarquitius"; see Martelli, *Storici antichi,* p. 181.

8. Marcus Atilius Regulus fought Hasdrubal and Hamilcar in 256–255 B.C. during the First Punic War. Concerning his thinking about his fields, see Valerius Maximus, *Factorum ac dictorum memorabilium libri IX,* 4.4.6, "on poverty"; these rhetorical examples also draw on Cincinnatus and Paulus Aemilius.

9. See above, 3, 16, sentence 12, and note 4. The triumph referred to occurred after he defeated the Macedonian king Perseus at the battle of Pydna in 168 B.C. As for the incident with the silver cup and his son-in-law, Aelius Tubero, see Plutarch, *Aemilius Paulus,* 28.

10. The list of "other men" who have written on this theme, one common to both classical and Christian culture, is long; among them, in addition to Valerius Maximus, are Plato, Aristotle, Plutarch, Livy, Sallust, and Dante (*Paradiso,* 15).

~ 26 ~

HOW A STATE MAY FALL THROUGH WOMEN

1 An uprising occurred between the Patricians and the Plebs in the city of Ardea because of a marriage in which, when a rich woman was to be married, a Plebeian and a Nobleman both asked for her hand.[1] Because she did not have a father, her guardians wanted to marry her to the Plebeian, her mother to the Nobleman. 2 This caused such a disturbance that they took up arms, and the entire Nobility armed itself in support of the Nobleman and all the Plebs in support of the Plebeian. 3 So when the Plebeians were defeated, they left Ardea and sent for aid to the Volscians; the Nobles sent to Rome. 4 The Volscians got there first, and when they arrived, they encamped around Ardea. 5 When the Romans came upon the scene, they hemmed the Volscians in between the city and themselves until they forced them to surrender unconditionally, because they were in the grips of hunger. 6 The Romans entered Ardea and killed all the leaders of the insurrection, then settled the city's affairs.[2]

7 There are several things to note in this text. 8 First, we see that women have often been the cause of destruction, have done great harm to those who govern cities, and have caused much discord in them; as we have seen in this history of ours, the outrage done to Lucretia took their state away from the Tarquins, that done to Virginia also deprived the Decemvirs of their power.[3] 9 Among the primary causes for the downfall of tyrants, Aristotle gives the wrongs they have committed against others in respect to women by seducing them or raping them or breaking up marriages, as we discussed at length in this regard in the chapter where we dealt with conspiracies.[4] 10 Therefore I say that

absolute princes and governors of republics should not take this matter lightly, but they must consider the disorders that can arise from such an incident and remedy them in time for the remedy not to bring harm and shame to their state or their republic, as happened to the Ardeans. Because they allowed that rivalry to grow among their citizens, they were led to split into factions; when they wanted to join together, they had to send for outside aid, a great source for imminent servitude. 11 But let us get to the other noteworthy matter, the way to unite cities, concerning which we shall speak in the next chapter.

NOTES

1. For this rebellion in 443 B.C., see Livy, 4.9–10. Livy draws attention to the woman's beauty, not her wealth (4.9.4); but see Martelli's comments on this alteration (*Storici antichi,* p. 182) He also notes Machiavelli's curious use of *femina* (woman) in this sentence (Livy emphasizes her maidenhood *[virgine]* and youth *[puella]*) and compares it to the use of *"la mia donna femmina"* in *Mandragola,* 2, 6, where Nicia refers to "my own wife's whoring" (ed. cit., pp. 196–197). Inglese suggests that Machiavelli's emphasis on the latter may have to do with his warning to princes that what makes them "particularly hated is being predatory and preemptory toward the property and the women of his subjects: he must keep himself away from these"; see the quotation from *Prince,* 19, above, Book 3, 23, n.3.

2. As Livy points out, the Volscian commander was vulnerable because he had not provided his troops with enough food so his men "were in the grips of hunger" (4.10.1). The Romans beheaded "the leaders of the insurrection" (4.10.6). See the discussion in Martelli, *Storici antichi,* pp. 182–183.

3. This "history of ours" is Livy, with reference to the women Machiavelli has already alluded to: Lucretia and the Tarquins, above, Book 3, 2, n.2, and Virginia and the Decemvirs, above, Book 1, 40, n.22.

4. See Aristotle, *Politics,* 5.9.13 (1314b24–25; 5.8.7–17 (1311a9–1312a39); 5.3.1.4 (1303b17–1304a16). For Machiavelli's comments, see above, 3, 6, sentences 17–19 (and nn.12–14). Rinaldi points out that this is the only "accurate" quotation from Aristotle and adds that Martelli, *"Logica provvidenzialistica,"* p. 354, considers it to be "clearly secondhand."

~ 27 ~

UNITING A DIVIDED CITY; AND IT IS NOT TRUE THAT CITIES MUST BE KEPT DIVIDED IN ORDER TO BE HELD

1 From the example of the Roman Consuls who reconciled the Ardeans, we may note the way in which a divided city may be made sound: it is nothing else but slaughtering the leaders of the disturbances; it cannot be cured in any other way. 2 For it is necessary to choose one of three methods: either slaughtering them, as the Romans did, or moving them out of the city, or having them make peace among themselves with the obligation not to attack

one another. 3 Of these three ways, the last one is the most harmful, the least certain, and the most ineffective. 4 For where much blood has flowed or other such injuries, it is impossible for a forced peace to last when people see one another face-to-face every day; and it is difficult for them to refrain from insulting each other, since fresh causes for quarrels can arise among them every day because of their contact.

5 No better example than the city of Pistoia can be given for this. 6 The city was divided between the Panciatichi and the Cancellieri fifteen years ago (as it is still); but then it was up in arms, and today it has laid them down.[1] 7 After many disputes between them, they came to bloodshed, the destruction of houses, looting of property, and every other sort of hostility. 8 The Florentines, who had to bring them together, always used the third method for this; and greater disorders and greater rioting kept breaking out.[2] Finally, worn out, they tried the second method, removing the leaders of the factions, some of whom they put in prison and others they banished to various places until the agreement made could stand, and it has stood until today. 9 But the first method would certainly have been surer. 10 But because such actions have something grand and gallant about them, a weak republic is incapable of performing them and is so far from them that it can barely bring itself to the second remedy.

11 As I said in the beginning,[3] these are the sort of mistakes that princes in our day make when they have to judge serious matters, for they ought to want to hear how those who had to judge similar cases in ancient times behaved. 12 But the weakness of contemporary men, caused by their weak education and their lack of knowledge about such things, makes them judge the judgments of the ancients as being in part inhumane, in part impossible. 13 And they have certain modern opinions completely far from the truth, like the one that the wise men of our city used to utter a while back: that Pistoia had to be held by factions and Pisa by fortresses; and they do not realize how ineffective each of these methods is.

14 I want to leave out fortresses, because we spoke about them at length above,[4] and I want to discuss the ineffectiveness that comes from keeping towns you have under your control divided. 15 First of all, it is impossible for you to keep both factions friendly whether you govern them as a prince or a republic. 16 For nature makes men choose sides in any divided matter and for this side to please them more than that one. 17 So having one faction in a city dissatisfied makes you lose them in the first war that comes along, because it is impossible to guard a city that has enemies outside and in. 18 If it is a republic that governs it, there is no finer way to make your citizens bad and provoke divisions in your city than to have a divided city to govern; for each faction tries to get favors and makes friends for itself by various bribes. So two very serious problems arise from this: first, you never make them friendly because you are unable to govern them well, since the government is often changing with now one tendency, now the other; second, that such concentration on factions necessarily divides your republic. 19 Biondo bears witness to this when he says of the Florentines and Pistoians: "Whereas the Florentines were

intending to reunite Pistoia, they divided themselves."[5] 20 Therefore one can easily imagine the harm that arises from such division.

21 In 1502 when Arezzo was lost along with the entire Tiber Valley and Val di Chiana, taken from us by the Vitelli and Duke Valentino, the king of France sent one Monsieur de Langres to get all the lost cities restored to the Florentines.[6] When Langres found men in every fortified town who, on paying him a call, said that they were of the Marzocco faction,[7] he severely criticized this division, saying that if in France one of the king's subjects said that he was in the king's faction, he would be punished; because saying that would mean no less than that there were people unfriendly to the king in the town: the king wants all the towns to be his friends, united and without factions.

22 But all these methods and opinions that diverge from the truth arise from the weakness of whoever is master; when they see that states cannot be held by force and *virtù,* they resort to devices like these; sometimes in peaceful times they work out to some extent, but when adversity and hard times arrive, they show their deficiencies.

NOTES

1. In late 1500 and then through most of 1501, two rival families in Pistoia—the Cancellieri, who sided with the Florentine republic, and the Panciatichi, who sided with the exiled Medici—tore the city apart with their riots. Because Pistoia was under the dominion of Florence, the republic sent Machiavelli there in February, July, and twice in October 1501. For some of his observations on this situation, see above, Book 2, 25, sentence 10, and also note 4, for the works he published in 1501 and 1502. Guicciardini discusses the situation in *History of Florence,* chapters 20 and 22. He faults the Florentine Signoria for its failure in 1500, "aware of matters deteriorating there," to "provide the necessary measures; it permitted matters to slide along and take their natural effect, which amounted to . . . the rebellion of Pistoia." In *Prince,* 20, Machiavelli notes with some irony, "Our forefathers—those who were thought wise—used to say that Pistoia must be held by factions and Pisa by fortresses" (p. 321, lines 50–52). He will refer to this allusion below in sentence 13.

2. For further comment on this "third method," see *Prince,* 17, in which, on the question of ruthlessness, Machiavelli compares Cesare Borgia and Florence to the latter's disadvantage: "Upon careful reflection, it will be seen that Cesare was much more compassionate than the people of Florence who, in order to avoid the reputation for being ruthless, allowed Pistoia to be destroyed" (p. 269, lines 8–12). Florence "tried the second method" in March 1502.

3. Referring to the Preface of Book 1, sentences 7–8 (and notes 6 and 8).

4. Book 2, 24.

5. A free translation in Italian of Flavio Biondo's Latin: *Historiarum ab inclinatione Romanorum decades,* 2, 9. Biondo (1392–1463) was one of the earliest historiographers in the Italian Renaissance. The pope employed him as a diplomat, but he is better known as a humanist scholar. Breaking ranks with the usual humanist interest solely in ancient history, he discussed European history from the fifth to the fifteenth centuries. Rinaldi adds that Ridolfi says there was a copy of this work in Machiavelli's house (*Vita,* 1978, pp. 5, 7, and 424).

6. For the background on this situation in the valley of the Tiber and Chiana Rivers, see above, Book 1, 38, n.9. Monsieur de Langres is probably Antoine de Torote, the lord of Blacy and Langres (the latter is today in Haute-Marne, and the former is west of Langres in the Yonne); King Louis XII ordered him to go to Arezzo with troop reinforcements of third hundred more lances for Rivoire Imbault; see Machiavelli's letter to the Dieci from Imola, dated 11 October 1502 during his mission to Cesare Borgia (*Legazioni e commissarie,* 1, 344). He is sometimes identified as Philibert de Choiseul, lord of Lanques and governor of Langres. See also Guicciardini, *Storia d'Italia,* 5, 9.

7. That is, Florence; the Marzocco is the lion rampant, the heraldic symbol of Florence.

~ *28* ~

ATTENTION MUST BE PAID TO THE ACTIONS OF CITIZENS, BECAUSE A GOOD ACTION OFTEN MASKS THE BEGINNINGS OF TYRANNY

1 When the city of Rome was in the grips of famine and the public supplies were insufficient to end it, one Spurius Maelius got the idea, since he was quite rich for those times, of privately making a provision of grain and feeding the Plebs with it for his own advantage.[1] 2 For this reason he had so great a number of people supporting him that the Senate, concerned about the problems that might arise from this generosity of his, appointed a Dictator over him and had him put him to death in order to quell it before it gained greater strength.

3 Here it should be noted that often actions which seem good and cannot reasonably be condemned become cruel and are very dangerous to a republic unless they are corrected quickly.[2] 4 And to discuss this matter in greater detail, I say that a republic cannot stand nor govern itself well in any way without citizens of repute. 5 On the other hand, citizens' repute is the cause of republics' tyranny. 6 If one wishes to regulate this matter, one must organize oneself in such a way that citizens are reputed for a reputation that serves and does not harm a city and its freedom. 7 Therefore one must examine the ways in which they gain their reputation, of which there are in reality two: either public or private. 8 Public ways are those by which a man gains a reputation by giving good advice, by acting better for the public welfare. 9 The route to this honor should be opened to citizens, and rewards should be set up for both advice and actions so that they are honored and satisfied by them. 10 If reputations achieved by these routes are genuine and simple, they will never be dangerous; but when they are achieved by private routes, which is the other way mentioned above, they are very dangerous and harmful in every respect. 11 Private routes are doing favors for one or another private citizen by lending them money, marrying off their daughters, defending them from officials, and doing them personal favors of that sort; these make men partisan and encourage the one who is thus favored so he can corrupt the public

sector and break the laws. 12 A well-organized republic must therefore, as has been stated, open the ways to those who seek favors by public routes and close them to those who seek them by private routes. 13 As we can see, that is what Rome did. For to reward those who did good for the public, it instituted triumphs and all the other honors that it gave its citizens; to punish those who sought under various pretexts to become great through private routes, it instituted prosecutions. And if these did not suffice, because the people were blinded by a kind of false good, they instituted the Dictator, who with a royal arm could make anyone who had overstepped the mark return within it, as Rome did to punish Spurius Maelius. 14 For one of these things to go unpunished is likely to cause a republic's downfall, because with such an example for it, it is difficult to be brought back to the true way afterward.[3]

NOTES

1. See above, 3, 1, n.13, for a reference to Spurius Maelius; he hoarded grain during the famine of 439 B.C. By distributing it free to the populace, he gained support for his political advancement. According to Livy, the dictator who put him to death was Lucius Quinctus Cincinnatus (see above, 3, 24, n.2, and 3, 25, n.2); nevertheless, some modern historians challenge the assertion that Cincinnatus served as dictator in 439.

2. See Aristotle, *Politics,* 5.7.7–8; 1308b11–20.

3. In addition to the reference to Aristotle in the previous note, see also two of Machiavelli's treatises written in 1520, *Discursis florentinarum rerum post mortem iunioris Laurentii Medices* (A Commentary on Florentine affairs after the death of Lorenzo de Medici the younger [Lorenzo II]) and *Sommario delle cose della città di Lucca* (A summary of matters in the city of Lucca)—a brief but shrewd piece of political analysis.

~ 29 ~

THE PEOPLE'S MISDEEDS[1] ARISE FROM THEIR PRINCES

1 Princes should not complain about any misdeed that is done by the people they have to govern, because such misdeeds must arise either through his negligence or through his being tainted by similar errors. 2 Anyone who discusses the peoples in our times who have been considered full of thievery and other such misdeeds will see that it all begins with those who govern them, who were of a like nature.

3 Before Pope Alexander VI got rid of the lords who ruled Romagna, it exemplified every sort of quite villainous activity, because there one could see that any slight cause led to extremes of slaughter and pillage.[2] 4 This arose from the wickedness of those princes, not from the wicked nature of men, as they said. 5 Because those princes were poor and wanted to live like rich men, they were obliged to turn to much pillaging and to carry it out in various ways. 6 Among the other dishonest ways they followed, they made laws prohibiting some acts, but then they were the first to give cause for disobeying these laws and never punished those who broke them until they

saw later that many people had fallen into the same crime. Then they turned to punishment not out of zeal for the law they had enacted but out of greed for payment of the fine. 7 From this many problems arose, especially this: the people grew poorer and were not corrected; those who were poorer sought to take advantage of those who were less powerful than themselves. 8 Thus all the evils that were spoken of above erupted, and the prince was the cause of them.

9 Livy shows that this is true when he relates how the Roman Legates, as they were carrying the gift of the Veians' booty to [the Temple of] Apollo, were seized by pirates from Lipari in Sicily and brought to that city.[3] Once their prince, Timasitheus, learned what this gift was, where it was going, and who was sending it, he behaved like a Roman, although he was born in Lipari, and showed the people how impious it was to seize such a gift; so with the agreement of the entire populace he let the Legates go with all their things. 10 The words of the historian are these: "Timasitheus imbued the people, who always resemble their ruler, with religious feeling."[4] 11 In confirmation of this maxim, Lorenzo de' Medici says:

> And what the lord does the many then do,
> for all eyes are turned toward the lord.[5]

NOTES

1. Translates *peccati* here and throughout this chapter, to remove any theological connotation of "sin" and to convey the political sense of the word in this discussion. But see the use of *peccati* (sins) above, Book 2, 18, sentence 11, and note 5, and its echo of *Prince,* 12. The first sentence of this chapter and especially the second one may reflect Cicero, *De legibus,* 3.14.32.

2. The actual "ridding " was done not by Pope Alexander VI but by his son, Cesare Borgia; see above, Book 1, 38, sentences 6–10, and *Prince,* 7 and 17. The "lords" whom Cesare "got rid of" during his first campaign in 1499–1500 were Girolamo Riario and Caterina Sforza in Imola and Forlì; during his second campaign in 1500–1501, Giovanni Sforza in Pesaro, Pandolfo Malatesta in Rimini, Astorre Manfredi in Faenza, and Jacopo Appiano in Piombino; during his third campaign in 1502–1503, Guidobaldo di Montelfeltro in Urbino, Giulio Cesare da Varano in Camerino, Francesco Maria della Rovere in Senigaglia, Vitellozzo Vitelli in Città di Castello, Gian Paolo Baglioni in Perugia, and Pandolfo Petrucci in Siena.

3. The gift was a golden bowl, and the anecdote is given in Livy, 5.28.1–5.

4. Quoted imperfectly in Latin from 5.28.4: *"multitudinem . . . quae semper ferme regenti est similis, religionis iustae implevit"* (Machiavelli's text reads: *"Timasitheus multitudinem religione implevit quae sempre regenti est similis"*). For further commentary on this passage and Machiavelli's next sentence, see Martelli, *Storici antichi,* pp. 183–187.

5. The lines are taken from his *Rappresentazione di San Giovanni e Paolo,* octave 99; the persons in the title are fourth-century martyrs, not Saints John and Paul of the New Testament. The *sacre rappresentazioni* were an early form of drama written in an octave rhymed ABABABCC; they usually were acted by a religious association of men and boys. Lorenzo's play was first performed in 1491; one of the actors was his

twelve-year-old son Giuliano, the future duke of Nemours, the "new prince" to whom Machiavelli originally intended to dedicate the *Prince,* but he died 17 March 1516. Inglese notes that the only Italian poets whom Machiavelli quotes in the vernacular are Dante and Lorenzo de' Medici.

~ 30 ~

FOR A CITIZEN TO DO ANY GOOD ON HIS OWN AUTHORITY IN A REPUBLIC, IT IS FIRST NECESSARY TO ELIMINATE ENVY; AND HOW A CITY'S DEFENSE SHOULD BE ORGANIZED WHEN AN ENEMY COMES

1 When the Roman Senate learned that the entire Etruria had raised a new levy of troops to come and attack Rome and that the Latins and Hernici, who had been allies of the Roman people in the past, had joined with the Volscians, Rome's long-standing enemies, it judged that this war was going to be dangerous.[1] 2 And because Camillus was a tribune with consular power, the Senate believed that it could do without naming a Dictator if the other Tribunes, his colleagues, were willing to yield the supreme command to him.[2] 3 The Tribunes did so willingly, "nor did they believe (says Livy) there was any disparagement of their own dignity in whatever dignity they might concede to him."[3] 4 Hence Camillus, taking this obedience at their word, ordered that three armies be recruited. 5 He wished to be the leader of the first in order to attack the Etruscans. 6 He made Quintus Servilius the leader of the second and ordered him to stay near Rome to oppose the Latins and the Hernici should they make a move. 7 He put Lucius Quinctius at the head of the third army, which he recruited to protect the city and defend the gates and the Curia[4] in any emergency that might arise. 8 In addition, he ordered Horatius, one of his colleagues, to furnish weapons, grain, and other items required during wartime. 9 He put Cornelius, another colleague, in charge of the Senate and public council so he could advise on the actions that had to be taken and carried out daily; thus the tribunes were in place in those times to command and obey for the welfare of their country.

10 From this text we note what a good and wise man may do, and how much good he may cause, and how much use he may be to his country when, as a result of his goodness and *virtù,* he has eliminated envy, which is often the reason why men cannot do good, since envy does not permit them to have the authority necessary for matters of importance. 11 Envy is eliminated in two ways: either through some serious and difficult incident in which each person, seeing himself facing death, puts aside all ambition and willingly hastens to obey the man who he believes can rescue him by his *virtù.* That is what happened with Camillus: because he had given so many signs of his being a most excellent man and had been Dictator three times and

always administered that office in the public interest and not for his own profit, he had made it so that men were not afraid of his greatness; and because he was so great and so highly respected, people did not consider it a disgrace to be subordinate to him (and that is why Livy wisely says the words: "nor did [they] believe" etc.). 12 Another way envy is eliminated is when those who have been your rivals in achieving some reputation and some greatness die either by violence or in the natural order; as long as they see you more respected than they, it is impossible for them ever to accept and yield. 13 And if they are men who are used to living in a corrupted city, where their upbringing has not produced any goodness in them, it is impossible for any incident to change their minds; to fulfill their desire and satisfy their perversity of mind, they would be happy to see the downfall of their country. 14 There is no other remedy for overcoming such envy than the death of those who have it; and when fortune is so favorable to the man of *virtù* that envious men die normally, he becomes glorious without trouble so that he can show his *virtù* without obstacle and without harm. 15 But if he does not have this good fortune, he has to devise any means to get these men out of his way; before he does anything else, he has to find ways to overcome this difficulty.[5]

16 And anyone who reads the Bible with understanding will see that Moses, in order to advance his laws and institutions, was forced to slaughter countless men who were moved to oppose his plans by nothing but envy.[6] 17 Fra Girolamo Savonarola knew this necessity very well; Piero Soderini, the gonfaloniere of Florence, also knew it. 18 One of them[7] could not overcome it, because he lacked the power to enable him to do so and because he was not well understood by those who followed him, who would have had the power. 19 Nevertheless, he did not stop trying, and his sermons are full of accusations and invective against the "wise men of the world," for that was what he called those envious men and those who opposed his institutions. 20 The other one believed that with time, goodness, his good fortune, and benefits to some, he could eliminate envy; seeing himself quite youthful and with his way of doing things gathering so many new favors for him, he believed that he could overcome those remaining men who opposed him out of envy without any disturbances, violence, and uproar.[8] He did not know that the right time cannot be waited for, goodness is not enough, fortune changes, and ill will finds no gift that will placate it. So both of these men fell, and their downfall was caused by their not having known how or been able to overcome envy.

21 The other noteworthy thing is the arrangement that Camillus provided for Rome's internal and external security. 22 Truly, it is not without reason that good historians like ours provide certain detailed and distinct examples so that posterity may learn how to defend itself in similar circumstances. 23 In this text one should note that there is no more dangerous or ineffective defense than one that is made in turmoil and disorder. 24 This is shown by the third army that Camillus recruited to leave behind in Rome to protect the city. For many people then and now would have judged this idea superfluous, since those people were normally armed and warlike, and therefore that it would not be necessary to recruit it otherwise, but it would suffice to arm the

people whenever the need arose. 25 But Camillus and anyone who was wise like him thinks otherwise, because he never allows a multitude to take up arms except with a specific order and method. 26 Therefore, given this example, someone who is put in charge of protecting a city should avoid like a reef arming men in tumult; but he should first recruit and choose those whom he wants armed, whom they must obey, where they should assemble, and where they should go. He should order all those who are not recruited to stay in their houses and protect them. 27 Those who employ this arrangement in an attacked city will easily be able to defend themselves; anyone who does otherwise will not be imitating Camillus and will not defend himself.

NOTES

1. The following is based on Livy, 6.6–7. Contrary to Machiavelli's statement in sentence 5, below Livy says that Camillus first attacked the Volscians in Anzio and only later marched on the Etruscans (6.9). See the discussion in Martelli, *Storici antichi,* pp. 187–188.

2. As Machiavelli notes above, Book 1, 39, sentence 11, consular power was replaced by a group of six military tribunes. In 385 B.C. Furius Camillus was one of the six; the others named in the following sentences (see the speech of Camillus in Livy, 6.6.12–15) are: Servius Cornelius Maluginensis, Quintus Servilius Fidenas, Lucius Quinctius Cincinnatus, Lucius Horatius Pulvillus, and Publius Valerius (6.6.3).

3. Quoted in Latin from Livy, 6.6.7: *"nec quicquam de maiestate sua detractum credebant, quod maiestati eius concessissent"* (with *credebant* for Livy's *credere*).

4. That is, the Senate building.

5. On this topic see also above, Book 1, 16, sentences 9–13, and Book 3, 3–4.

6. See especially Exodus 32:25–28, the death of the idolaters of the golden calf; and also Leviticus 10, and the deaths of Aaron's sons Eleazar and Ithamar; Numbers 12, and the punishment of leprosy meted out to Miriam and Aaron; Numbers 16, and the rebellion of Korah, Dathan, and Abiram, which ended in a slaughter. Machiavelli uses the example of Moses in a political context also in *Prince,* 6.

7. Namely, Savonarola; see above, Book 1, 11, n.12. He "lacked the power" because he could influence only those people in power who adhered to his cause.

8. On Soderini see above, Book 1, 7, n.7; 52, nn.4 and 5, and Book 3, 3, n.3. As for his being "quite youthful," he was born in 1452 and came to power in 1502.

~ 31 ~

STRONG REPUBLICS AND EXCELLENT MEN RETAIN THE SAME SPIRIT AND THEIR SAME DIGNITY IN ANY FORTUNE

1 Among the other magnificent things that our historian has Camillus say and do to show what an excellent man must be like, he puts these words into his mouth: "neither has Dictatorship lifted my spirits nor has exile taken them away."[1] 2 Through these words we see that great men always remain the same in any Fortune; although it varies, at times raising them up, at times oppressing

them, they do not vary but always keep their spirit firm and joined with their way of living in such a way that it is easy to see for each one that Fortune has no power over them. 3 Weak men behave otherwise: they grow vain and intoxicated in good fortune, attributing all the good that they get to a *virtù* which they have never known.[2] 4 That is why they become unbearable and hateful to everyone they have around them. 5 Then from this comes the sudden change in their fate, so when they stare it in the face, they immediately fall into the opposite fault and become cowardly and abject. 6 From this arises the fact that in adversity princes such as these think more of fleeing than of defending themselves, like people who, because they have ill used their good fortune, are unprepared for any sort of defense.[3]

7 This *virtù* and this vice that I say are found in a single man are also found in a republic;[4] the Romans and the Venetians provide examples. 8 No bad fortune ever made the former abject, nor did good fortune ever make them arrogant, as could be seen clearly after their defeat at Cannae or after their victory over Antiochus.[5] For, even though that defeat was quite grave because it was the third one, they never became cowardly, and they sent their armies out; they did not try to ransom their prisoners, contrary to their custom; they did not send to Hannibal or Carthage to sue for peace. Rather, putting aside all such abject measures, they constantly planned on war, arming the elderly and the slaves for lack of men.[6] 9 As was stated above, when Hanno the Carthaginian learned of this, it showed their Senate how little account was to be taken of the defeat at Cannae.[7] 10 And it was seen that hard times did not dismay the Romans or humiliate them. 11 On the other hand, prosperous times did not make them arrogant. For when Antiochus sent emissaries to Scipio to ask for a treaty before they engaged in battle and he lost it, Scipio gave him certain conditions for peace: that he should withdraw into Syria and leave the rest under the control of the Roman people.[8] 12 When Antiochus rejected the agreement, engaged in battle, and lost, he again sent ambassadors to Scipio with the charge that they accept all the conditions that the victor imposed on them; Scipio did not propose to them any other terms than those that had been offered before he won, adding these words: "When Romans are defeated they do not lose courage nor do they grow arrogant when they conquer."[9]

13 We have seen that the Venetians did precisely the opposite of this. In good fortune, since they felt they had earned it for themselves by a *virtù* that they did not have, they became so arrogant that they called the king of France a "son of Saint Mark";[10] they showed no respect for the Church; in no way did they find enough room in Italy; and they had gotten it into their heads that they should set up a monarchy like Rome's.[11] 14 When good fortune later deserted them and they suffered a partial defeat by the king of France at Vailà, they not only lost their entire state by rebellion but they gave a good part of it to the pope and the king of Spain out of cowardice and abjectness of spirit. They became so cowardly that they sent ambassadors to the emperor to become his vassal, and they wrote letters full of cowardice and submission to the pope to move him to pity.[12] 15 They reached this degree of misfortune in four days and after a partial defeat; for

when their army fought while retreating, about half of it actually fought and was defeated so that one of the Proveditors who escaped arrived in Verona with more than twenty-five thousand soldiers, counting infantry and cavalry.[13] 16 So had there been any degree of *virtù* in Venice and its institutions, they could easily have recovered, faced Fortune once again, and managed either to win or to lose more gloriously or to get a more honorable treaty. 17 But the cowardice of their spirit, caused by the quality of their institutions,[14] which were not good for matters of war, made them lose both their state and their courage in one stroke. 18 And it will always happen this way to any that govern themselves as they did. 19 For becoming arrogant in good fortune and abject in bad arises from your way of doing things and from the upbringing that has fostered you. When it is weak and vain it makes you like itself; when it has been otherwise, it also makes you different and, giving you a better understanding of the world, makes you rejoice less at the good and grieve less at the bad. 20 And what is said about an individual may be said about many people who are living in the same republic: they become as perfect as its way of living.

21 Although it has been stated elsewhere that the foundation of all states is a good militia, and where it does not exist there can be neither good laws nor any other good thing, it does not seem superfluous to me to repeat it.[15] For at every point in reading this history we see this need appear, and we see that the militia cannot be good unless it is trained and that it cannot be trained unless it is made up of your subjects. 22 Because one is not always at war nor can one remain at it, so it is necessary to be able to train it in peacetime; and because of the expense this training cannot be done with other than one's subjects. 23 Camillus, as we stated above,[16] had gone against the Etruscans with his army, and when his soldiers saw the size of the enemies' army, they were all frightened, since it seemed to them they were so much fewer that they would be unable to withstand its onslaught. 24 And when this negative disposition in his camp reached Camillus's ears, he appeared in public and, as he went throughout the camp speaking now to some soldiers and now to others, he removed the notion from their minds; finally, without organizing the camp any differently, he said: "what each man has learned or has become accustomed to, he will do."[17]

25 If one carefully considers this situation and the words he said to them to stir up their courage to go against the enemy, one should consider that none of these things could have been said or done to an army that had not been organized and trained in both peace and war. For a commander cannot trust soldiers who have not learned how to do anything or expect them to do anything that holds: even if some new Hannibal commanded them, he would fall under them. 26 For because a commander cannot be everywhere while a battle is being waged, he must of necessity fall unless he has first arranged things on all sides so as to have men who share his spirit and even his organization and ways of doing things. 27 So if a city is armed and organized like Rome, and its citizens, both individually and publicly, are daily expected to test both their *virtù* and the power of Fortune, it will always happen that in every cir-

cumstance they will have the same courage and maintain the same dignity.[18] 28 But when they are unarmed and depend solely on the buffetings of Fortune and not on their own *virtù,* then they will change with its changes, and they will always give the example given by the Venetians.

NOTES

1. A modified quotation in Latin from Livy, 6.7.5: *"neque enim dictatura mihi unquam animose fecit, ut ne exsilium quidem ademit"* (for neither could the dictatorship give me resolution nor could even exile deprive me of it); Machiavelli's text reads: *"Nec mihi dictatura animos fecit, nec exilium ademit."* See Martelli, *Storici antichi,* p. 188.

2. See Machiavelli's *capitolo "Di fortuna,"* ll.71–72.

3. These are the princes he has in mind when he writes in *Prince,* 24, of those who "when periods of adversity came . . . thought of flight, not defense" (p. 359, lines 50–51), and at the end of the *Art of War,* 7, of those who caused "great terrors, sudden flights, and prodigious losses in 1494."

4. See above, Book 3, 9, n.10.

5. For the battle of Cannae, see above Book 2, 12, n.14, and for the background on Antiochus and his defeat in 190 B.C. at Magnesia (ad Sipylum), near Izmir (Smyrna), which opened up Asia for Roman conquest, see above, Book 2, 1, n.19.

6. See above, Book 2, 26, n.5.

7. See above, Book 2, 30, sentence 28, and note 14.

8. The Roman army was commanded by Lucius Cornelius Scipio and his brother Publius Cornelius Africanus; the emissaries were sent to the latter. By "the rest" Machiavelli refers to the territories in Anatolia, the part of present-day Turkey on the Asia Minor peninsula.

9. Machiavelli gives the following quotation: *"Quod Romani si vincuntur, non minuuntur animis; nec, si vincunt, insolescere solent."* Ridley cites Justin, 31.8.8, as the source ("Echoes," pp. 117–118); see also the discussion in Martelli, *Storici antichi,* pp. 189–190. This sentence and the chapter's title might also be an abbreviated version of Scipio's answer to the emissaries of Antiochus in Livy, 37.45.11–12.

10. That is, the French king was subject to the will of Venice (Saint Mark was the patron saint of Venice; the author of the gospel was thought to be buried there).

11. A "monarchy" in the sense of achieving universal power.

12. For the battle of Vailà, see above, 1, 6, n.11. Machiavelli alludes to the battle and its aftermath in *Decennale secondo,* vv. 176–216, but Guicciardini, *Storia d'Italia,* 8, 4–7, provides an excellent account of this situation. The Ghibelline supporters of the League of Cambrai in Bergamo, Brescia, Padua, Verona, and Vicenza opened their gates to the league's armies (8, 4), the "rebellion" Machiavelli mentions. What Venice "gave up" included Romagna, to Pope Julius II, and several port cities in southeastern Italy, to Ferdinand the Catholic, then king of Aragon. Guicciardini uses the same phrase, "abjectness of spirit," to describe the decision of the Venetian senate (8, 6). Thus, Venice sent Antonio Giustiniano to Maximilian "with the utmost speed" to sue for peace (8, 6). Meanwhile, the pope was "wary of the power of [Maximilian I] and [Louis XII]" and wanted to keep them preoccupied so they would not "torment him"; thus he secretly accepted the "letters" from Venice and resolved "with all his might to prevent the misfortunes of the republic from proceeding any further" (8, 7).

13. The reason why it was a "partial defeat" can be found in Guicciardini, *Storia d'Italia,* 8, 5: while Bartolomeo d'Alviano led the majority of Venetian troops defeated at Vailà, another part of the army led by Niccolò Orsini, count of Pitigliano, did not engage the league's army and retreated so that his group remained intact. The *provveditori* were senior Venetian Nobles elected in the Senate, charged with advising army commanders about military matters; the title of *provveditore* was also given to the governor of a Venetian dependency. Before he was elected doge, Andrea Gritti, the *provveditore* in question and the subject of Titian's famous portrait in the National Gallery at Washington, D.C., held various offices in the Venetian republic. (Guicciardini describes the withdrawal to Verona in 8, 7.)

14. For Machiavelli one "institution" that made Venice "not good for matters of war" was their use of mercenaries, which led to "the cowardice of their spirit," because they cared more about their own safety than that of the republic: see the remarks in his letter of 26 August 1513 to Vettori about Venice's use of mercenaries (*Friends,* p. 258). Nevertheless, Venice counted on its own citizens to lead its navy and drew most of its crews from among citizens.

15. This position is expressed above, Book 1, 4, sentence 2; 1, 21, opening paragraph, and Book 2, 1, sentence 6. Furthermore, it is basic to *Prince,* 12: "The essential foundations for every state—whether new, old, or mixed—are good laws and good armies. . . . [T]here cannot be good laws without good armies, and where there are good armies there are good laws" (p. 219, lines 11–15).

16. In the previous chapter, but see also note 1 to that chapter.

17. Livy, 6.7.6: *"Quod quisque didicit, ac consuevit, faciet";* Machiavelli substitutes *aut* (or) for Livy's *ac* (and).

18. The general tenor of this chapter can also be found in Polybius, 6.1.6, and Plutarch, *Demetrius,* 30.

~ 32 ~

THE WAYS THAT SOME HAVE USED TO THWART A PEACE TREATY

1 When Circeii and Velitrae, two of their colonies,[1] rebelled against the Roman people in hope of being defended by the Latins, and the Latins had then been defeated and such hope lost, many citizens advised that emissaries should be sent to Rome to implore the Senate's pardon. That course of action was thwarted by those who had been the fomenters of the rebellion, who were afraid that the entire punishment might come down upon their heads. 2 And to eliminate any discussion of peace, they incited the masses to arm themselves and overrun the Roman borders.

3 It is indeed true that when someone wants either the people or a prince to dismiss an agreement completely from their mind, there is no other truer or more dependable remedy than to have them commit some serious act of villainy against the one with whom you do not want an agreement to be made; because the fear of punishment that he feels he deserves because of the

error committed will always keep him from it. 4 After the first war that the Carthaginians waged against the Romans, the soldiers the Carthaginians had employed for the war in Sicily and Sardinia went off to Africa once peace was made; there, dissatisfied with their wages, they rose up in arms against the Carthaginians; making two of themselves their leaders, Matho and Spendius, they seized many towns from the Carthaginians and sacked many others.[2] 5 At first the Carthaginians tried all other ways than fighting: they sent to them as ambassador their fellow citizen Hasdrubal, who they thought might have some influence on them, since he had been their commander in the past. 6 Upon his arrival Spendius and Matho wanted to obligate all the soldiers never to hope to have peace with the Carthaginians again and thus to obligate them to wage war, so they persuaded them that it was better to slaughter Hasdrubal along with all the Carthaginian citizens who were their prisoners. 7 Consequently, not only did they slaughter them but first they racked them with countless tortures, adding to this act of villainy an edict that all the Carthaginians whom they might capture in the future should be killed in a similar fashion. 8 This decision and its execution made the army cruel and stubborn against the Carthaginians.

NOTES

1. Said to be the home of Circe, near modern San Felice Circeo; Velitrae is the modern Velletri, twenty-five miles southeast of Rome. This incident is based on Livy, 6.21.

2. Although Machiavelli's account contains some discrepancies, the situation, occurring from 241 to 237 B.C., is based on Polybius, 1.65–88. They "sent as ambassador" Gisco, not Hasdrubal (not the Carthaginian general also named thus, Hannibal's brother); see the discussion in Martelli, *Storici antichi,* p. 191. Machiavelli used this same example in *Prince,* 12 (p. 223, lines 73–77), and Fabrizio Colonna refers to it in his sixth speech, *Art of War,* 1. As this book of the *Discourses* comes to a close, there is a great deal of overlap with concerns expressed throughout the *Art of War,* generally thought to have been begun in 1519 and first published in 1521.

~ 33 ~

TO WIN A BATTLE IT IS NECESSARY TO BUILD THE ARMY'S CONFIDENCE BOTH IN ITSELF AND IN ITS COMMANDER

1 For an army to win a battle, it is necessary to build its confidence so that it believes it must win whatever happens. 2 The things that build its confidence are for it to be well-armed and organized and for the men to know one another. 3 And this confidence or organization can only arise in soldiers who were born and raised together. 4 The commander has to be respected so that they have confidence in his wisdom; and they will always have confidence if they see he is organized, diligent, and courageous and that he upholds the dignity of his rank well and with distinction. 5 He will always uphold it if

he punishes them for their errors and does not tire them unnecessarily, keeps his promises to them, shows the road to victory to be easy, and conceals or understates things that from afar could show dangers. 6 When such things are duly observed, they provide a strong cause for the army to be confident and, being confident, for it to win.

7 The Romans used to have their armies acquire such confidence by means of religion; that was why they used auguries and omens when they created Consuls, made troop levies, marched off with their armies, and went into battle.[1] 8 No good, wise commander would ever have attempted any feat of arms without having done any one of these things, realizing that he could lose it easily if his soldiers did not first understand that the gods were on their side. 9 If any Consul or other commander of theirs had fought against the omens, they would have punished him as they punished Claudius Pulcher.[2] 10 And although this point is known in all the Roman histories, nevertheless, it is felt most clearly through the words that Livy puts in the mouth of Appius Claudius. Complaining to the people about the arrogance of the Tribunes of the Plebs and showing that because of them the omens and other matters pertaining to religion were being corrupted, he says as follows: "Nowadays they may be allowed to mock religious worship. 'What difference does it make,' they will say, 'if the sacred chickens do not feed, if they are too slow to come out of their coops, if one of the birds clucks inauspiciously?' These are trivial matters, but by not scorning these trivial matters, our forefathers made this republic the greatest."[3] 11 For in these trivial matters lies the strength to keep the soldiers united and confident, and that is the prime cause of any victory.

12 Nevertheless, such matters must be accompanied by *virtù,* otherwise they are of no avail. 13 When the Praenestines took their army out against the Romans, they went off and set up their camp on the river Allia, the place where the Romans were defeated by the Gauls.[4] 14 They did so to instill confidence in their soldiers and to frighten the Romans by the place's fortune. 15 Although their course of action was plausible for the reasons that have been discussed above, nevertheless, the outcome of the matter showed that true *virtù* has no fear of every slightest incident. 16 The historian states this very well with these words, placed in the mouth of the Dictator, who speaks as follows to his Master of the Horse: "Do you see how, trusting in the fortune of the place, they have taken their stand at the Allia . . . but you, with confidence in your weapons and courage, attack the center of their line."[5] 17 Because true *virtù,* good organization, and assurance gained from so many victories cannot be extinguished by things of little moment, nor does a vain thing frighten them, nor does some disorder harm them. 18 This is made clear, because when two Manlii were consuls fighting against the Volscians, they had rashly sent part of their camp out to pillage with the result that in a short while both those who had gone and those who had remained found themselves besieged; it was not the prudence of the Consuls but the *virtù* of the soldiers themselves that saved them from that danger.[6] 19 Livy says these words at this point: "The soldiers' steadfast valor, even without a leader, saved it."[7] 20 I do not wish to leave out a device that Fabius used to build his army's

confidence when he first entered Etruria, since he judged that such confidence was more necessary because he had brought it into new territory against new enemies.[8] Speaking to the soldiers before the battle, after saying that there were many reasons why they could hope for victory, he said that he could also tell them certain good things from which they would see that victory was assured, if it were not dangerous to let them be known. 21 This method, since it was used wisely, thus deserves therefore to be imitated.

NOTES

1. See above, Book 1, 11–14.

2. See above, Book 1, 14, n.4, for Appius Claudius Pulcher, the man referred to here. The Appius Claudius referred to in the next sentence is Appius Claudius Crassus, a grandson of the decemvir mentioned above, Book 3, 11, sentence 3, note 3; his speech was given in connection with events in 368 B.C.

3. Quoted in Latin with a few changes from Livy, 6.41.8: *"Eludant nunc licet religiones. Quid enim interest* [Livy, *esse*], *si pulli non pascentur, si ex cavea tardius exiverint, si occinuerit avis? Parva sunt haec; sed parva ista non contemnendo, maiores nostri* [Livy, *vestri*] *maximam hanc rempublicam fecerunt."* A note in the Loeb Classical Library edition clarifies the situation, III. p. 344. The Roman practice was determined by "two kinds of omens: (1) the general took with him to the field a coop of chickens, and if these, on being offered corn, came out and devoured it with avidity, the presage was favourable; this kind of divination was called *ex tripudiis,* from the way the corns danced upon the ground as they fell from the beaks of the greedy fowls [a *tripudium* was a religious dance]; (2) the flight of certain birds was observed and any noise—such as the cry of a bird—was held to vitiate the auspice."

4. The Praenestines lived in the modern city of Palestrina, about twenty-four miles east of Rome. The incident is based on Livy, 6.28–29. Machiavelli's expression in the next sentence, "With the place's fortune," echoes *fortunae loci,* Livy, 28.7. The battle against the Gauls occurred in 387 B.C., that against the Praenestines in 380. For it see above, Book 2, 29, sentences 6–9.

5. Quoted in Latin from Livy, 6.29.1–2: *"Vides tu . . . loci fortuna illos fretos ad Alliam constitisse"* [Machiavelli reads *consedisse*] *. . . at tu, fretus armis animisque . . . invade mediam aciem";* see Ridley, "Edition," p. 332, and Martelli, *Storici antichi,* pp. 191–192. The dictator in question was Titus Quinctius Cincinnatus, and his Master of the Horse was Aulus Sempronius Atratinus; the date was 380 B.C.; see Livy, 28.3–4.

6. The patricians Publius and Gaius Manlius were not consuls but military tribunes with consular power for 379 B.C.; see Livy, 6.30.1, and Martelli, *Storici antichi,* pp. 192–193.

7. Quoted in Latin from Livy, 6.30.6: *"Militum, etiam sine rectore, stabilis virtus tutata est."* The "it" in Livy refers to "whatever remained of the Roman People's good fortune" *(quidquid superfuit fortunae populi Romani).* On this truncated quotation, see Martell, *Storici antichi,* pp. 193–194.

8. A reference to Quintus Fabius Maximus Rullianus; for the following speech, see Livy, 9.37.6–7, and above, Book 2, 33, n.2. Fabius refers to a weapon held in secret, but Livy never discloses what it is, so Machiavelli is equally circumspect. Again, there are several discrepancies between Machiavelli's account and Livy's; the most interesting

is that Livy stresses the army's fear of the size of the Etruscan army, not the fact that it is a "new territory." (For some clarification, based on Livy, 9.36.1–8, see Martelli, *Storici antichi,* pp. 195–197.) In 310 B.C. they had crossed a range of volcanic mountains with dense forests separating southern and central Etruria, the Ciminius Mons, south of modern-day Viterbo.

~ *34* ~

WHAT REPUTATION OR RUMOR OR OPINION MAKES THE PEOPLE BEGIN TO FAVOR A CITIZEN; AND WHETHER THEY ASSIGN OFFICES MORE WISELY THAN A PRINCE

1 Elsewhere we have told how Titus Manlius, who was later called Torquatus, saved his father, Lucius Manlius, from an accusation that had been made against him by Marcus Pomponius, a tribune of the Plebs.[1] 2 Although the means of saving him was somewhat violent and unusual, nonetheless, the people so appreciated this filial piety toward his father that not only was he not blamed but, when the Tribunes of the legions were to be chosen, Titus Manlius was the second to be selected. 3 Because of this result, I think it is good to consider the method that the people use to evaluate men for its assignment of offices; so doing, we may see whether what was concluded above is true: that the people are better at assigning them than a prince is.[2]

4 I say, then, that in assigning them the people follow what public rumor and reputation say about someone when it does not know him otherwise by his well-known actions or by a presumption or an opinion they have of him. 5 These two things are caused either by the fathers of such people having been great and worthy men in the city so it is believed that their sons ought resemble them, until they learn the contrary from their actions, or it is caused by the ways employed by the man we are talking about. 6 The best ways that can be employed are keeping company with serious men of good character whom everyone considers wise. 7 Because no greater measure of a man can be had than the company that he keeps, a man who keeps company with decent people deservedly acquires a good name, for it is impossible for him not to bear some resemblance to them. 8 Or else this public reputation is acquired through some unusual, noteworthy action, even a private one, that has turned out honorably for you. 9 Of these three things that give someone a good reputation from the start, none gives a greater one than the latter. 10 Because the first, of relations and forefathers, is so unsure that men are reluctant about it, and it is quickly dissipated unless it is accompanied by the *virtù* of the one man is to be evaluated. 11 The second, which gets you known by way of your relationships,[3] is better than the first; but it is far inferior to the third, because until some sign originating from you is seen, your reputation is based on opinion, which it is very easy to undo. 12 But the

third, since it begins with and is based on fact and your actions, gives you such a reputation from the start that you really have to do many things contrary to it later to undermine it. 13 So men who are born in a republic should choose this tack and strive to begin their rise through some exceptional actions. 14 In Rome many men did this in their youth, either by promulgating a law that acted for the common good, by denouncing some powerful citizen for a transgression of the laws, or by doing some such noteworthy, unusual thing that people would talk about.

15 Such things are necessary not only to begin to make a reputation for oneself but also to maintain and enhance it. 16 And in order to do this, they must be repeated, as Titus Manlius did throughout his life; for after he had defended his father with such great *virtù* and so extraordinarily, and as a result of this deed established his initial reputation, a few years later he fought with that Gaul; and after he killed him, he took from him the golden necklace that gave him the name of Torquatus.[4] 17 This did not suffice; later when he was already at an advanced age, he slew his son for fighting without permission even though he had conquered the enemy.[5] 18 These three actions, then, gave him more of a reputation and have made him more celebrated down through the centuries than any triumphs or any other victories, with which he was as honored as much as any other Roman. 19 And the reason is that in those victories there were very many like Manlius, but in these specific deeds there were either very few or none at all.

20 Scipio the Elder did not derive so much glory from all his triumphs as he got from defending his father while still a youth, on the Ticinus River,[6] and from courageously making several young Romans swear after the battle of Cannae, with his sword drawn, that they would not abandon Italy, as they had already decided to do among themselves.[7] These two actions were the beginning of his reputation and gave him a stepping-stone to his triumphs in Spain and Africa. 21 This opinion of him was further enhanced when he sent a daughter back to her father, a wife back to her husband in Spain.[8] 22 This way of doing things is not necessary only for those citizens who want to acquire a reputation in order to achieve honors from their republic; it is also necessary for princes to sustain their reputations in their princedoms. For nothing brings them so much esteem as giving exceptional examples of themselves by some deed or unusual saying consonant with the common good, which shows the lord to be either magnanimous or generous or just, and which is such as almost to be turned into a proverb among his subjects.

23 But to get back to where we began this discourse, I say that when the people begin to give an office to one of its citizens, basing it on the three reasons mentioned above, they are not doing badly; but later, when extensive evidence of someone's good behavior makes him better known, it is basing it better, because in such a case the people can almost never be mistaken. 24 I am speaking only of those offices that are given to men in the beginning, before they are known by solid experience or before they pass from one activity to another, different one; in such matters and insofar as both wrong opinion and corruption are concerned, the people will always make less important

mistakes than princes do. 25 Because people can be mistaken about a man's reputation, judgment, and actions, evaluating them higher than in truth they are (which would not happen to a prince, because he would be told and would be warned by those who advise him), in order for the people as well not to lack such advice, good organizers of republics have prescribed an order. When a city's offices, in which it might be dangerous to put incompetent men, are to be filled and the people's taste seems to be directed toward naming someone who would be incompetent, any citizen is permitted to disclose the man's flaws in meetings—and he is praised for so doing—in order that the people, not lacking his knowledge, can judge better. 26 The oration of Fabius Maximus attests to this being the practice in Rome. He made it to the people during the Second Punic War when their support during the naming of the Consuls was turning toward Titus Otacilius. Because Fabius judged him incompetent for managing the consulate in those times, he spoke against him, demonstrating his incompetency; thus he deprived him of that office and turned the people's support to someone who deserved it more than he did.[9] 27 In electing officers, therefore, the people judge according to the truest signs they can have about men; and when they can be advised like princes, they make fewer mistakes than princes; and any citizen who wants to begin to have the people's support must win it for himself by some noteworthy deed, as did Titus Manlius.

NOTES

1. See above, Book 1, 11, sentence 5, and the first paragraph of Book 3, 21. The "violent and unusual means of saving him" was the threat of being stabbed to death unless he swore never again to accuse his father (Livy, 7.5.5).

2. See above, Book 1, 47 (and for Guicciardini's position, his *Consideration* of it), and 1, 58.

3. That is, by friendships, as he says above in sentence 6 with "men of good character."

4. See above, Book 3, 22, n.5.

5. See above, Book 2, 16, n.4.

6. The incident from 218 B.C. is based on Livy, 21.46; the phrase "while still a youth, on the Ticinus River" repeats line 79 of Machiavelli's *capitolo "Dell'ingratitudine."* The Ticino is a tributary of the Po.

7. See above, Book 1, 11, sentence 4.

8. See above, Book 3, 20, n.3; the daughter and wife are the same person.

9. See Livy, 24.8. Titus Otacilius had been nominated for the consulship but not elected; the consuls elected were Quintus Fabius Maximus, for the fourth time, and Marcus Marcellus, for the third time (24.9.2).

~ 35 ~

THE RISKS THAT ARE RUN, WHEN BECOMING A PROPONENT, IN COUNSELING SOMETHING; THE MORE UNUSUAL IT IS THE GREATER THE RISKS THAT ARE RUN

1 How dangerous a thing it is to make oneself the proponent of some new idea that relates to many people and how difficult it is to deal with it and to carry it out and, once carried out, to keep it going, would be too long and too deep a matter to discuss. Hence, saving it for a more suitable place,[1] I shall speak only of those risks that are run by citizens or those who advise a prince when they become the proponents in a serious and important decision so that all the advice about it may be attributed to them. 2 For because men judge things by their outcome,[2] any ill that results from it is attributed to the author of the advice; and if good results from it, he is commended for it, but the reward is far from balancing out the harm.

3 When the current Sultan Selim, called the Grand Turk, prepared to undertake the campaigns of Syria and Egypt (according to what some people who come from his lands report), one of his Pashas whom he had on the Persian border urged him to attack the Shah of Persia.[3] 4 Acting on this advice, he embarked on the campaign with a very large army; upon arriving in a very broad region where there are many deserts and few rivers and encountering there the difficulties that once made many Roman armies fail, he was so overwhelmed by them that, even though he won the war, he lost a large part of his troops through famine and plague. So, enraged at the author of the advice, he slew him. 5 One reads that many citizens have urged a campaign, and because it came to a bad end, were sent into exile.[4] 6 Several Roman citizens made themselves the proponents of having a Plebeian Consul in Rome. 7 It happened that the first one who went forth with the armies was defeated; so some harm would have come to those advisers, if the faction in whose interest such a decision had been made had not been so powerful.[5]

8 So it is quite certain that those who advise a republic and those who advise a prince are put in this predicament: if they do not without reservation advise the things that seem useful to them for either the city or the prince, they are failing in their duty: if they do advise them, they endanger their lives and their state, since all men are blind in that they judge good and bad advice by its outcome.[6] 9 Examining how they might avoid either this infamy or this danger, I can see no other way than taking things in moderation and not seizing upon any of them as one's own undertaking and stating one's opinion without passion and defending it without passion, modestly; so if the city or the prince follows it, it is followed voluntarily and it does not seem that he enters upon it drawn by your insistence.[7] 10 If you do this, it is not reasonable for a prince or a people to wish you ill for your advice, since it was not followed against the will of many; for one runs a risk when many people have

been opposed, since they can join together to make you fall if the outcome is unfavorable. 11 And if in this case one lacks the glory that is acquired from being alone against many in advising something when its outcome is favorable, there are, on the other hand, two advantages: first, the lack of danger; second, that, if you advise something modestly and as a result of opposition your advice is not taken and because of someone else's advice some disaster ensues, you receive very great glory from it. 12 Although the glory that is derived from any ills that either your city or your prince has cannot be enjoyed, it is nonetheless to be held in some regard.

13 I do not think any other advice can be given to men on this question, because if one should advise them to be silent and not speak their opinion, it would not be useful for the republic or for their prince and they would not avoid danger, because within a short time they would become suspect. 14 What happened to the friends of Perseus, the king of Macedonia, could also happen to them. After Paulus Aemilius defeated him and he was fleeing with a few friends, it happened that in going over what had happened, one of them began to tell Perseus of many mistakes he had made, which had been the cause of his downfall. Turning to him, Perseus said: "So, traitor, you delayed telling me this until now when I have no further remedy!" With these words he slew him with his own hand.[8] 15 So that man bore the penalty for having kept silent when he ought to have spoken out and for having spoken when he ought to have been silent; he did not avoid the danger by not having given his advice. 16 Hence I believe that the devices mentioned above should be employed and observed.

NOTES

1. It seems that Machiavelli intended to write at least one other chapter to take up this topic in the *Discourses;* he does not. Were it not for the future tense in this chapter, we might assume he was referring to the discussion in *Prince,* chapters 6 through 9.

2. Reminiscent of the wording used in *Prince,* 18: "When there is no court to appeal to, people judge men's actions, and particularly those of a prince, by the final outcome *[si guarda al fine]*" (p. 285, lines 91–93). See below, note 6 to this chapter.

3. For Selim I, see above, Book 1, 19, n.4, especially for how both it and this sentence relate to the dating of the *Discourses.* Other references to him can be found above, Book 1, 1, n.10; Book 3, 6, n.20; and especially Book 2, 17, n.12, for a connection with Ismail I, the Shah of Persia. Who "some people" are is not clear; but see Martelli, *Storici antichi,* p. 197, n.206. The correspondence between Machiavelli and his nephew, Giovanni Vernacci, who lived for a while in Pera, the present-day Beyoglu section of Istanbul, sheds light on the human side of Machiavelli but offers nothing about current events of historical interest; see the Index of *Friends.* A pasha was a military commander or provincial governor.

4. The reference to the Romans concerns the wars against the Parthians in A.D. 113–117. For a historical account of these events in 1516–1517, though without mentioning those who advocated the campaign, see Guicciardini, *Storia d'Italia,* 13, 9: "[Selim] was forced to give up, not because of the enemy's *virtù* (since they lacked confidence in their ability to withstand his army, they had withdrawn into mountainous

and uninhabited regions), but because he had no provisions, for that year had been most unproductive."

5. In 366 B.C., much against the advice of the patricians, the Romans created the first plebeian consul, Lucius Sextius. Then in 362 they put the plebeian Lucius Genucius in command of an expedition against the Hernici, whose capital city was the present-day Anagni, a town midway between Palestrina and Frosinone, southeast of Rome; see Livy, 6.35–41; 7.1. On the inappropriateness of this example to prove Machiavelli's point, see the discussion in Martelli, *Storici antichi,* pp. 197–198.

6. There are several contrasting quotations relevant to this important nexus of Machiavelli's ideas. On the one hand, there is a passage from the 1506 letter to Giovan Batrtista Soderini, the *Ghiribizzi* (Fantasies) letter; referring to Soderini's advice, Machiavelli writes: "This would surprise me if it were not for the fact that my fate has shown me so many and such varied things that I am forced rarely to be surprised. . . . I know you and the compass of your navigation. . . . I think not according to your perspective, wherein nothing but prudence is visible, but to the perspective of the many, which must see the ends, not the means of things" (*Friends,* p. 134). Whether this is written with regret or irony may be judged from the following. First, there is the speech he attributes to Rinaldo degli Albizzi: "he spoke at length pointing out that to judge matters by their outcome was not prudent because often things well advised do not have a good outcome and things ill advised have a good one" (*Florentine Histories,* 4, 7). Second, there is his quiet condemnation of a fickle Florence that "judges matters by their results not by their intentions" (*Florentine Histories,* 8.22). See also above, Book 1, 9, sentences 5–9, and below, 3, 41, sentence 4, note 3. Machiavelli issues a clear warning that "blind" men are prone to judge so; he does not condone man's stupidity to act so.

7. Inglese suggests that this and the following may indicate that Machiavelli harbors some bitterness, remembering the problems he had in getting his idea for a citizen militia off the ground during Soderini's republican regime.

8. This account of an incident during the Battle of Pydna in 168 B.C. is based on Plutarch, *Aemilius Paulus,* 23, where there are not one but two victims; Machiavelli seems to have invented the quotation. The incident is not in Livy's account of the battle, 44.41–46. Martelli suggests that Machiavelli may have consulted some intermediary text (*Storici antichi,* p. 199).

~ *36* ~

WHY THE GAULS[1] WERE, AND STILL ARE, HELD TO BE MORE THAN MEN AT THE START OF A BATTLE AND LESS THAN WOMEN LATER ON

1 The ferocity of the Gaul by the river Anio[2] who defied any Roman to fight him, as well as the combat waged between him and Titus Manlius later, reminds me of what Livy says several times: at the start of a battle the Gauls are more than men, and during the course of fighting they then turn out to be less than women.[3] 2 In examining the reason for this, many believe their nature is like that; I think this is true, but there is no reason why this nature of

theirs, which makes them ferocious at the start, could not be skillfully disciplined to keep them ferocious until the end.[4]

3 To prove this I say that there are three sorts of armies: one in which there is fury and discipline, because out of discipline arise fury and *virtù,* as was the case for the Romans.[5] For one can see in all the histories that in their army there was good discipline, which military training had instilled in it over a long period. 4 Because in a well-ordered army no one ought to carry out any operation except according to regulations. For this reason it will be found that the Roman army, which all other armies ought to take as their example since it conquered the world, did not eat, did not sleep, did not whore, and did not undertake any action, either military or personal, without the consul's order. 5 Because armies that do otherwise are not true armies, and if they accomplish anything, they do so by fury and using force and not by *virtù.* 6 But where well-disciplined *virtù* uses its fury in the right ways and times, no difficulty makes it turn cowardly or makes it lose courage: because good discipline renews the army's courage and fury, fostered by the hope of winning, this is never lacking as long as discipline remains steadfast.[6] 7 The opposite happens in armies in which there is fury and not discipline, like the Gauls'. They nevertheless failed in combat, because when they did not succeed in winning with the first attack and the fury on which they counted was not sustained by any disciplined *virtù* and they had nothing beyond that fury on which to rely, once it cooled off, they failed.[7] 8 On the contrary, the Romans, who feared danger less because of their good discipline and did not lack confidence in victory, fought resolutely and stubbornly with the same courage and the same *virtù* at the end as at the start; in fact, stirred up by the fighting, they would become more and more ardent.[8] 9 The third sort of army is one in which there is neither natural fury nor incidental discipline, like the Italian armies of our day, which are completely ineffective; and unless they fall on an army that is fleeing because of some incident, they will never win. 10 Without citing other examples, one can see every day how they give evidence of not having any *virtù.*

11 So that everyone can learn from Livy's testimony what a good militia should be like and what bad ones are like, I want to cite the words of Papirius Cursor when he wished to punish Fabius, his Master of the Horse. He said: "No one would have respect for men nor for the gods; neither the edicts of generals nor the auspices would be obeyed; without any leave of absence, soldiers would rove throughout hostile as well as peaceful territory; unmindful of their oaths, they would discharge themselves [from the military] on their own authority and whenever it suited them; they would leave their banners almost unprotected, nor would they muster upon command, nor would they distinguish between day or night or between a favorable or unfavorable site; they would fight with or without the general's command and would not pay attention to their banners or formations: like a band of brigands, the military would be blind and haphazard instead of a solemn and sacred service."[9] 12 One can thus easily see from this text

whether the militia of our day is "blind and haphazard" or "solemn and sacred," and how much it lacks to be like what can be called a militia, and how far it is from being furious and disciplined like the Roman one or just furious like the Gallic.

NOTES

1. Translates *Franciosi.* In the context of Roman history we have consistently translated this word as "Gauls," yet it is clear in this chapter that Machiavelli wants us to understand that what was true of the Gauls still is true of the French of his day.

2. It separated the region of the Sabines from Latium. The modern river Aniene joins the Tiber in the north of Rome. During the 1550s Pirro Ligorio constructed an aqueduct so that the river could serve as a source for the fountains of the Villa d'Este, which he designed for Cardinal Ippolito II d'Este.

3. For Titus Manlius see above, Book 3, 22, n.5, and Livy, 7.10. Although he does not quote the passage, the source of this chapter's title, Machiavelli refers to Livy, 10.28.4; Livy "says" it once, not "several times." Inglese notes that Machiavelli quotes this saying in his *Ritratto di cose de Francia* (Portrayal of French matters), which he wrote in 1510; there he erroneously attributes it to Caesar.

4. On this point of skillful discipline tempering nature or the natural, see his *capitolo "Dell'ambizione,"* vv. 109–117. In this chapter "discipline" and its derivatives translate *ordine* and its derivatives.

5. The "fury" or "ferocity" that Machiavelli has in mind in this chapter is that of the Latin *Furor,* an attendant of Mars, hence *furor* as "martial rage."

6. A point similar to the argument above, 3, 33, where "to win a battle it is necessary to build the army's confidence both in itself and in its commander."

7. Machiavelli closes the *Prince* with a quotation from Petrarch's *canzone "Italia mia"* (no. 128, vv. 93–96): "And against their furor / *Virtù* will fight and the battle will be short. / For the ancient valor / Is not yet dead in our Italian heart" (p. 383, lines 154–157). This quotation is a reminder that the *virtù* embodied in one man in the *Prince* is refigured in the *Discourses* in terms of a well-ordered state and its institutions.

8. Livy often contrasts the Romans' "resolute and stubborn" fighting with the cooling of the Gauls' ardor; see 5.39.1; 6.42.7–8; 7.11.1, and 7.12.10. See also Polybius, 2.35.2–4.

9. This is Livy's summary of what Papirius Cursor said, not a direct quotation from his speech. Quoted in Latin with slight changes from Livy, 8.34.8–10: *"Nemo hominum, nemo Deorum verecundiam habeat; non edicta imperatorum, non auspicia observentur; sine commeatu vagi milites in pacato, in hostico errent; immemores sacramenti licentia sola se, ubi velint, exauctorent; infrequentia deserantur signa; neque conveniatur ad edictum; nec discernatur, interdiu nocte, aequo iniquo loco, iussu iniussu imperatoris pugnent; et non signa, non ordines servent; latrocinii modo, caeca et fortuita, pro sollemni et sacrata militia sit."*

~ 37 ~

WHETHER SMALL SKIRMISHES ARE NECESSARY BEFORE A BATTLE; AND IF ONE WANTS TO AVOID THEM WHAT MUST BE DONE TO RECONNOITER AN UNFAMILIAR ENEMY[1]

1 It seems, as we have discussed elsewhere, that in the actions of men, aside from other difficulties, in trying to bring something to its completion there is always some evil close to the good, which can so easily arise along with that good that it seems impossible to avoid one while seeking the other.[2] 2 This is seen in all the things that men undertake. 3 Therefore the good is difficult to achieve unless you are aided by Fortune so it overcomes this common and natural problem by its force.

4 The fight between Manlius and the Gaul has reminded me of this when Livy says: "This combat was of such importance for the outcome of the whole war that the army of the Gauls withdrew from their camp in panic and crossed over into the territory of Tibur and then into Campania."[3] 5 For I consider, on the one hand, that a good commander must at all costs avoid doing anything that although it is of small moment can have a bad effect on his army, because starting a fight in which your entire army is not used and your entire fortune is at risk is a completely rash thing, as I said above when I condemned defending passes.[4]

6 On the other hand, I consider that wise commanders, when they come up against an unfamiliar enemy and he is of some repute, before engaging in battle are obliged to have their soldiers put such enemies to the test in lesser skirmishes so that by getting to know and deal with them their soldiers lose the fear that fame and reputation had given them. 7 This quality is extremely important in a commander, because there is within it a necessity almost that forces you to do so, since you feel you are going toward certain defeat unless you have attempted first by small trials to remove the fear that the enemy's reputation has put in your soldiers' minds.[5]

8 Valerius Corvinus was sent with the armies by the Romans against the Samnites, unfamiliar enemies; in the past they had not tested one another with weapons. Livy says that Valerius had the Romans undertake a few minor skirmishes with the Samnites "so that the soldiers would not be terrified by a new war or a new enemy."[6] 9 Nevertheless, there is a very grave danger that if your soldiers are defeated in those battles, fear and cowardice may grow in them and the opposite effect may result from your plans; that is, that you frighten them whereas you intended to reassure them. So this is one of those things that has its evil so close to its good and they are so closely joined that it is easy to get one when thinking to grasp the other.

10 Concerning this, I say that a good commander must take every precaution so that nothing ever arises that, as a result of some incident, might take

away his army's courage. 11 Beginning to lose is what can take away their courage, and he must therefore stay away from small battles and not allow them unless there is a very great advantage and hope of certain victory. He must not undertake campaigns to defend passes in which his entire army cannot fit; he must not defend fortified towns except the ones that, if he should lose them, would of necessity bring about his downfall. Those he does defend he should organize with both their defenders and his army in such a way that when it comes to their being stormed he can use all his troops; the others he should leave undefended. 12 Because whenever something one abandons is lost and the army is still together, one's reputation in war or one's hope of winning it is not lost. But when you lose something you have intended to protect and everyone believes you will protect it, then there is damage and loss, and like the Gauls, you have almost lost the war for something of little moment.[7]

13 When the Romans were attacking Philip of Macedon, the father of Perseus, a military man of great renown in his time, he abandoned and laid waste to a good number of his towns which he judged he could not defend, just as someone who, to be prudent, judged it more destructive for him to lose his reputation by being unable to protect what he set out to protect than to lose it as something neglected by leaving it as prey to the enemy.[8] 14 When their affairs were in trouble after the defeat at Cannae, the Romans denied assistance to many of their dependents and subjects, telling them to protect themselves as best they could.[9] 15 Such courses of action are much better than taking up defenses and then not protecting them, because in the latter course of action one loses allies and troops, in the former allies only.

16 But to return to small skirmishes, I say that, even if the unfamiliarity of the enemy compels a commander to engage in a few battles, he must do so with such advantage to him that there is no danger of losing it, or else he ought to do as Marius did, which is the best course of action. Going against the Cimbri, a very fierce tribe that came down to plunder Italy, whose coming caused great fear because of their ferocity and great numbers and because they had already defeated a Roman army,[10] Marius judged it necessary before they engaged in battle to do something so that his army might get rid of the terror that fear of the enemy had given it; as a very wise commander, he located his army on several occasions in places where the Cimbri were to pass with theirs. 17 Thus, from within his camp's fortifications, he made sure his soldiers saw them and accustomed their eyes to the sight of the enemy so that when they saw a disorderly throng, laden down with baggage, with useless weapons, and partly unarmed, they would be reassured and grow eager for battle.[11] 18 Just as that course of action was wisely taken by Marius, so it should be diligently imitated by others in order not to run the risks that I state above and not to do like the Gauls, "who, terrified by a matter of little moment, crossed over into the territory of Tibur and Campania."[12] 19 And because we have cited Valerius Corvinus in this discourse, in the next chapter I wish to show what a commander must be like through his own words.

NOTES

1. One of the "general rules" of warfare that Fabrizio discusses at the end of *Art of War,* 7, is: "New and sudden things demoralize armies; they place a low value on things familiar and drawn out. Therefore make your army deal with and learn about a new enemy through minor combats before you do battle with him" (ed. Bertelli, p. 512).

2. For "elsewhere" see above, 1, 2, sentence 11; 1, 6, sentence 19; and 3, 11, sentence 2, note 2. Callimaco also says in his soliloquy, *Mandragola,* 4, 1: "It is true that Nature and Fortune hold all accounts in the balance. You never receive anything good without some evil springing up on the other side" (*Comedies of Machiavelli,* p. 231).

3. Quoted in Latin with some lacunae from Livy, 7.11.1: *"Tanti ea dimicatio ad universi belli eventum momenti fuit, ut Gallorum exercitus, relictis trepide castris, in Tiburtem agrum, mox in Campaniam transierit."* Concerning the accuracy of this citation, see Ridley, "Edition," p. 333, and Martelli, *Storici antichi,* p. 200. Tibur is modern Tivoli, some eighteen miles east-northeast of Rome.

4. See above, 1, 23, sentences 6–10; but see also 2, 12, sentences 15–16.

5. See the argument above in 3, 33.

6. On Valerius Corvinus see above, 1, 60, n.2, and 3, 22, n.2. This incident occurred during the First Samnite War, 343–341 B.C. Machiavelli quotes with some lacunae from Livy, 7.32.6: *"ne eos novum bellum, ne novus hostis terreret."*

7. An allusion to the example of Manlius Torquatus cited in sentence 4 above.

8. A reference to Philip V and his destruction of Athens, and his later retreat from Flamininus in 198 during the Second Macedonian War, 200–197 B.C.; see Livy, 31.14.10 and 32.13.

9. See Livy, 23.5.

10. A reference to Marius fighting against the Cimbri, mentioned above, 2, 8, n.8, and 2, 12, n.17.

11. Based on Plutarch, *Marius,* 13–16.

12. Machiavelli alters the quotation from sentence 4 above by adding in Latin *"qui ob rem parvi ponderis trepidi"* to the phrase *"in Tiburtem agrum et* [deleting *mox*] *in Campaniam transierunt."*

~ 38 ~

WHAT A COMMANDER MUST BE LIKE FOR HIS ARMY TO HAVE CONFIDENCE IN HIM

1 Valerius Corvinus, as we said above,[1] was with his army opposing the Samnites, unfamiliar enemies of the Roman people; hence, to reassure his soldiers and have them know the enemy, he had his men wage a few minor skirmishes. And because this was not enough for him, he decided to speak to them prior to the battle and showed very effectively how little they should regard such enemies, citing his soldiers' and his own *virtù.* 2 From the speech that Livy has him deliver we may observe what a commander must be like for his

army to have confidence in him; these are his words: "Then they also ought to pay attention to whose leadership and auspices they would have to fight under, whether he deserved to be listened to only as a magnificent orator, ferocious only in his words, lacking expertise in military operations, or he was someone who knew himself how to handle weapons, advance before the banners, and be engaged in the heart and storm of battle. Soldiers, it is my deeds, not my words, that I wish you to follow; to seek from me not only discipline but also example, I who with this right hand have won for myself three consulates and the highest praise."[2] 3 These words, if considered well, teach anyone how he must proceed in order to hold the rank of commander; and anyone who acts otherwise will find over time that this rank, whether he is brought to it by fortune or by ambition, will take away reputation and not give it, because it is not titles that make men illustrious but men who make titles illustrious.[3]

4 One must also consider from the start of this discourse that, if great commanders have used extraordinary means to steady the courage of an experienced army when they have to confront unfamiliar enemies, how much greater diligence must be used when one commands a new army that has never seen the enemy face-to-face. 5 Because if the unfamiliar enemy strikes terror in an old army, any enemy must do so even more to a new army. 6 But all these difficulties have often been seen to be overcome by good captains with the utmost prudence, as did Gracchus of Rome and Epaminondas of Thebes, of whom we have spoken elsewhere,[4] who with new armies defeated experienced and very well-trained armies.

7 Here are the methods that they used: training for several months in simulated battles and accustoming them to obedience and discipline; then they employed them with very great confidence in real combat. 8 So no military man should lack confidence he can form good armies if he does not lack men, because a prince who has plenty of men and lacks soldiers must complain not of the cowardice of his men but only of his own laziness and lack of wisdom.[5]

NOTES

1. In the previous chapter, paragraph 3.

2. Quoted in Latin from Livy, 7.32.10–12, with the omission of a clause about his having won all this not by recourse to factions or plots typical of the nobility but "with this right hand": *"Tum etiam intueri, cuius ductu auspicioque ineunda pugna sit; utrum, qui, audiendus dumtaxat, magnificus adhortator sit, verbis tantum ferox operum militarium expers, an qui et ipse tela tractare, procedere ante signa, versari media in mole pugnae sciat. 'Facta mea, non dicta, vos, milites, sequi volo, nec disciplinam modo, sed exemplum etiam a me petere, qui hac dextra mihi tres consulatus, summamque laudem peperi.'"* See Martelli, *Storici antichi,* pp. 201–202, for commentary on the omissions.

3. See Guicciardini's remark: "How appropriate was that saying of the ancients: 'The office reveals the man.' Nothing reveals a man's qualities more than giving him responsibilities and authority. So many men speak well, but do not know how to act; so many on public benches or in the marketplace appear to be worthy men, but once they are employed, they become shadows! (*Ricordi,* C. 163; see also B. 36). He was fond enough of this maxim to incorporate an allusion to it in the final sentence of *Storia d'Italia,* 20, 7.

4. For Gracchus see above, 2, 26, sentence 8; for Epaminondas see above, 1, 21, sentence 8, and 3, 13, sentence 14.

5. Machiavelli opens *Prince,* 14, on a similar note: "A prince, therefore, ought to have no object, thought, or profession but war, its methods, and its discipline; that is the only art expected of one who governs" (p. 247, lines 1–4).

~ 39 ~

A COMMANDER MUST BE KNOWLEDGEABLE ABOUT LOCALES

1 Among the other things that are necessary for a commander of armies is knowledge of locales and countrysides, because without this general and specific knowledge a commander of armies cannot accomplish anything. 2 Just as any science requires experience if one wishes to master it completely, so this one requires a great deal of experience.

3 This experience, or rather this specific knowledge, is acquired by hunting more than by any other exercise.[1] 4 Hence, ancient writers say that the heroes who governed the world in their day were brought up in the woods and on hunts, because in addition to this knowledge hunting teaches us innumerable things that are necessary in warfare. 5 In the life of Cyrus, Xenophon shows that when Cyrus went to attack the king of Armenia, he reminded his men during the planning of that action that this was nothing more than one of those hunts that they had gone on many times with him.[2] 6 He reminded those whom he sent up in the mountains in ambush that they were like those who went to spread nets up on mountain ridges and those who scoured the plains that they were like those who went to flush a wild animal from its lair so that when it was hunted it would run into the nets.

7 This is said to show that hunting, as Xenophon avers, is a metaphor for war, and because of this such activity is honorable and necessary for great men. 8 Nor can this knowledge of the lay of the land also be learned by any convenient means other than by hunting, because hunting makes the one who practices it know in detail what the countryside in which he does it is like. 9 When one has become quite familiar with one region, one then understands all new countrysides with ease; for all countrysides and all parts of them have some similarity to one another so that we may easily pass from knowledge of one to knowledge of another. 10 But a man who has not had real familiarity with one can hardly—or, indeed, can never except over a long period of time—know another one. 11 But a man who has this familiarity knows at a glance how that plain lies, how that mountain rises, where that valley goes, and all the other similar things that he has gotten sound knowledge of in the past.

12 Livy shows us the truth of this by the example of Publius Decius when he was Tribune of the soldiers in the army that Cornelius[3] the consul led against the Samnites; as the Consul had gone into a valley where the Samnites could surround the Roman army and he saw himself in so much danger, Pub-

lius Decius said to the Consul: "Do you see that summit above the enemy, Aulus Cornelius? Because the Samnites have been so blind as to neglect it, it is the citadel of our hope and salvation if we capture it quickly."[4] 13 Before Decius speaks these words, Livy says: "Publius Decius, a tribune of the soldiers, spotted an isolated hill rising above the pass and looming over the enemy's camp; though it was difficult for an army with baggage to approach, it was not very difficult for one lightly equipped."[5] 14 Hence, after the Consul sent him up it with three thousand soldiers and he saved the Roman army and was intending to depart at nightfall and save himself and his soldiers as well, Livy has him say these words: "'Go with me so that while there is still some light we may discover the places where the enemy has posted their guards and where the way out of here lies open.' Wrapped in a small military cloak . . . so that the enemy would not notice the leader walking about, he investigated all these matters."[6] 15 Anyone who examines this entire text, therefore, will see how useful and necessary it is for a commander to know the lay of the land. For if Decius had not known and recognized it, he would not have been able to judge how useful it would be for the Roman army to take that hill, nor would he have been able to recognize from afar whether the hill was accessible or not. And later, when he himself had gone up onto it and with the enemy surrounding him he wanted to leave so as to get back to the Consul, he would not have been able to guess from afar the ways out and the places the enemy guarded. 16 So of necessity Decius had to have such complete understanding: so by taking that hill he saved the Roman army. Later, when he was surrounded, he knew how to find a way to save himself and those who had stayed with him.

NOTES

1. In *Prince,* 14, Machiavelli advises that "in addition to keeping his men well disciplined and trained, [a prince] ought to hunt constantly, and in so doing inure his body to hardships; meanwhile he learns the nature of the terrain, and he comes to understand about the elevation of mountains, the opening out of valleys, the disposition of plains, and the nature of rivers and marshes—matters to which he must devote a great deal of attention" (p. 249, lines 34–42).

2. *Cyropaedeia,* 2.4.22–29. This work about the "education" of Cyrus rather than his "life" is one of the earliest treatises designed to inform readers about what constitutes a wise prince or statesman, the *de regimine principum* tradition. Machiavelli ends *Prince,* 14, with a remark about how much of Scipio Africanus the Elder's "fame is attributable to his emulation of Cyrus and how much—in terms of continence, courtesy, human kindness, and generosity—Scipio conformed to those qualities Xenophon had written about Cyrus" (lines 88–92, p. 253). Rinaldi observes that, because of its similarity to war, hunting is advocated also by Castiglione as training for the courtier (*Courtier,* 1, 22).

3. Aulus Cornelius Cossus was a consul with Valerius Corvinus at the outbreak of the First Samnite War in 343 B.C.

4. Quoted in Latin from Livy, 7.34.4: *"Vides tu, Aule Corneli, cacumen illud supra hostem? arx illa est spei salutisque nostrae, si eam (quoniam caeci reliquere Samnites) impigre capimus."*

5. Quoted in Latin from Livy, 7.34.3: *"Public Decius tribunus militum conspicit*

unum editum in saltu collem, imminentem hostium castris, aditu arduum impedito agmini, expeditis haud difficilem."

6. Quoted in Latin from Livy, 34.7.14–15: *"Ite mecum, ut dum lucis aliquid superest, quibus locis hostes praesidia ponant, qua pateat hinc exitus, exploremus. Haec omnia sagulo militari amictus, ne ducem circumire hostes notarent, perlustravit."* Livy has Publius Decius say "give me no more than the men in the first *(hastati)* and second ranks *(principes)*. Inglese points out that since Machiavelli estimates the size of a Roman legion to be about five thousand foot soldiers (*Art of War,* 3, Fabrizio's third speech) he probably calculated the number of *hastati* and *principes* so as to approximate the size indicated in Polybius, 7.21. See Martelli, *Storici antichi,* pp. 203–205, for commentary on this passage.

~ *40* ~

PRACTICING DECEPTION[1] WHILE WAGING WAR IS A GLORIOUS THING

1 Although practicing deception is detestable in every action, nevertheless, when waging war it is laudable and glorious, and a man who overcomes his enemy by deception is praised in the same way as one who overcomes them with his troops. 2 This is seen in the judgments made on it by those who write the lives of great men; they praise Hannibal and others who were quite noteworthy for doing things in such ways.[2] 3 Because there are many examples of this to be read, I shall not repeat any of them. 4 I shall say only this: I do not mean that deception is glorious if it makes you break a promise and agreements you have made,[3] because, even though this may sometimes gain you a state and a kingdom, as was discussed above,[4] it will never gain you glory. 5 But I am speaking of the deception that is employed against an enemy who does not trust you and which itself consists of carrying on a war, as was that of Hannibal, when along the lake of Perugia he feigned flight in order to surround the Consul and the Roman army, and when, to escape from Fabius Maximus's hands, he set fire to the horns of his cattle.[5]

6 The deception that Pontius, the commander of the Samnites, employed to surround the Roman army at the Caudine Forks was like these: after stationing his army behind the mountains, he sent a number of his soldiers dressed as shepherds across the plain with a large herd of cattle. When the Romans captured them and asked where the Samnites' army was, they all concurred, following the order given by Pontius, in saying that it was at the siege of Nocera.[6] 7 Because the Consuls believed this, it led them to close themselves up within the Caudine defile; once they were inside, they were immediately besieged by the Samnites. 8 This victory, obtained by deception, would have been very glorious for Pontius if he had followed the advice of his father, who said that the Romans should either escape freely or all be slaughtered and the middle way, "which neither gets friends nor eliminates enemies,"[7] should not be taken. 9 As has been discussed earlier in another place, in matters of state that way has always been destructive.

NOTES

1. Translates *fraude,* which Machiavelli defines in sentence 5, below, as "the deception that is employed against an enemy who does not trust you." See above, 1, 18, n.4; 2, 13, n.12; and 2, 18, n.10.

2. Polybius, Plutarch, Cornelius Nepos, *Life of Hannibal,* and Livy are among those with high praise for Hannibal. For Machiavelli's judgments see *Prince,* 17, *Art of War,* 4–7 passim. In *Friends* see the 1506 *Ghiribizzi* (already cited many times) letter to Giovan Battista Soderini (pp. 134; 136); the letter to Francesco Vettori, 26 August 1513 (p. 259); and finally, an allusion to Hannibal's commitment to practical experience and denigration of military theory in a letter to Guicciardini, 4 April 1526 (p. 386 and note).

3. See *Prince,* 18.

4. In 2, 13; see also 1, 59.

5. During the Second Punic War at the battle of Lake Trasimeno, near Perugia, in 217 B.C., Hannibal tricked Fabius Maximus into believing the Carthaginians were retreating even though they were surrounded by mountains; see Livy, 22.4, and Polybius, 3.81–83; Martelli, on the other hand, for the question of "flight" would prefer Frontinus, *Stratagemata,* 2.5.24 (*Storici antichi,* pp. 206–207). Hannibal ordered his troops to set fire to torches and tie them between his cattle's horns. As he drove them through a gap toward the hilltops, Fabius Maximus thought Hannibal was retreating and attacked the cattle. Meanwhile, Hannibal escaped in the opposite direction; see Livy, 22.16–17, Polybius, 3.93, and Plutarch, *Fabius Maximus,* 6; again, Martelli would add Frontinus, *Stratagemata,* 1.5.28 (*Storici antichi,* pp. 207–208 n.216). In Fabrizio's penultimate speech, *Art of War,* 6, this stratagem illustrates the point that Machiavelli discusses above, 3, 14: that a military commander can keep the enemy guessing "by causing some new event whose novelty causes the enemy to wonder and for that reason remain in doubt and stand fast." Frontinus is one of Machiavelli's major sources for *Art of War.*

6. This example occurred in 321 B.C. during the Second Samnite War; see Livy, 9.2–3. The siege was of Lucera, not Nocera, which would have been in the opposite direction (Ridley, also Martelli, *Storici antichi,* p. 208).

7. Quoted in Latin from Livy, 9.3.12: *"quae neque amicos parat, neque inimicos tollit."* For this and the discussion "earlier in another place" in the next sentence, see above, 2, 23, sentence 32 and note 15.

~ 41 ~

THAT ONE'S COUNTRY MUST BE DEFENDED, WITH EITHER DISHONOR OR GLORY, IN ANY WAY THAT IT IS WELL DEFENDED

1 As was said above, the Consul and the Roman army were besieged by the Samnites, who imposed very shameful conditions on the Romans (that is, they wanted to put them under the yoke and send them back to Rome disarmed); because of this the Consuls were as if stunned and the entire army in despair. Lucius Lentulus, a Roman legate, said that it seemed to him that no course of action whatever ought to be forgone to save their country, for since the life of

Rome depended on the life of that army he felt it had to be saved at all costs.[1] 2 And that one's country is well defended however it is defended, whether with dishonor or with glory, because if the army were saved, Rome would have time to cancel out the dishonor; if it were not saved, even though it died gloriously, Rome and its freedom would be lost.[2] 3 So his advice was followed.

4 This deserves to be noted and observed by any citizen who has to advise his country, for where the salvation of one's country is totally at stake, no consideration of whether it is just or unjust, merciful or cruel, praiseworthy or dishonorable, should matter; rather, setting aside any other concern, one should follow absolutely the course of action that saves its life and preserves its freedom.[3] 5 The French imitate this in both word and deed to defend the majesty of their king and the power of their kingdom, so they hear no voice with greater impatience than one that might say, "such a course of action is dishonorable for the king." For they say that their king cannot suffer shame from any of his decisions, whether in good or in adverse fortune, because whether he loses or he wins, they say that it is all the king's affairs.[4]

NOTES

1. Machiavelli continues the example from the preceding chapter. The consuls in question were Titus Veturius Calvinus and Spurius Postumius; Livy, 9.1.1. A "legate" was a superior officer attached to a general or provincial governor.

2. Machiavelli is following his source so closely that he describes the main arguments that Livy attributes to Lucius Lentulus; see 9.4.15. These patriotic thoughts are echoed in Rinaldo degli Albizzi's speech in *Florentine Histories,* 5, 8.

3. An assertion of a maxim, applicable in extreme situations when "the salvation of one's country is totally at stake," mentioned in Cicero, *Laws,* 3.3.8: "the safety of the people is the supreme law" *(salus populi suprema lex esto).* In connection with this sentence, see above, 1, 9, sentences 5–9, and notes, and 3, 35, sentence 8 and note. Inglese remarks of this passage: "This is one of the sharpest presentations of the 'standard' that governs politics in its radical independence from ethics." Walker points out that Machiavelli is on his own in arguing this point: neither Livy, with his notion of *jus gentium* as constituting a higher law than man-made law, nor Cicero supports the idea that "moral obligation is to be subordinated to expediency in affairs of state." To substantiate his assertion, Walker cites Cicero, *De officiis,* 2.3.9 on "expediency" *(utile):* "People have fallen into the habit of using this word corruptedly and pervertedly; it has gradually come about that, distinguishing probity from expediency, it is accepted that something may have probity without being expedient, and be expedient without having probity. No more pernicious doctrine than this could be brought into the life of men" *(In quo verbo lapsa consuetudo deflexit de via sensimque eo deducta est, ut honestatem ab utilitate secernens constitueret esse honestum aliquid, quod utile non esset, et utile, quod non honestum, qua nulla pernicies maior hominum vitae potuit afferri.)* Cicero does not polarize expediency *(utilitas)* and probity or honesty *(honestas).* Machiavelli and Guicciardini, on the other hand, show the way toward a distinction between the realm of absolute morality and pragmatic necessity. Thus the latter principle achieves an autonomy that does not deny the possibility of exercising the former but does not require it. Montaigne, who was familiar with both men's writings and titled one of

his essays "On the Useful and the Honorable," was "clever enough to know that man when he moves into the sphere of political worldliness will have to leave many of his noble scruples at home"; Friedrich, *Montaigne,* p. 184; see his discussion of this issue, pp. 181–188.

4. Machiavelli may have heard some of this type of discussion during his official visits to France in 1500, 1504, and 1510. Walker quotes a passage from Philippe de Commynes, a French chronicler who died in 1511: "I have heard courtiers remark that the king takes what he wills, but I have never heard the king himself say so. No doubt in saying this they showed their devotion to their master, but either they misunderstood his real interests or else they did not know what they were talking about" (*Mémoires,* 5, 19).

~ 42 ~

PROMISES MADE UNDER DURESS DO NOT HAVE TO BE KEPT

1 After the Consuls returned to Rome with their army disarmed and the disgrace they had incurred,[1] the first in the Senate to say that the peace made at Caudium should not be observed was the consul, Spurius Postumius.[2] He said that the Roman people were under no obligation but that he himself was indeed under obligation along with the others who had promised peace; so if the people wanted to free themselves from any obligation, they ought to hand him over as prisoner, and all the others who had so promised, into the hands of the Samnites. 2 He stuck to this conclusion so obstinately that the Senate was content to do so; and sending him and the others as prisoners to Samnium, they protested to the Samnites that the peace treaty was invalid. 3 Fortune was so favorable to Postumius in this instance that the Samnites did not detain him, and when he returned to Rome, Postumius was more glorious in the Romans' eyes for having lost than Pontius was in the Samnites' for having won.[3]

4 Two things are to be noted in this: first, that one can achieve glory in whatever action; because it is achieved normally in victory, in defeat it is achieved either by showing that the loss did not come about as a result of your fault or by immediately doing some action of *virtù* to cancel it out. Second, that it is not shameful not to keep promises that you have been made to promise under duress; and once the duress is gone, promises under duress that concern the commonweal will always be broken, and it will be without any shame for the one who breaks them.[4] 5 Various examples of this may be read in all the histories, and at present some are seen every day.[5] 6 Not only are promises made under duress not kept between princes once the duress is gone but also all other promises are not kept once the reasons that made them be promised are gone. 7 Whether this is praiseworthy or whether such ways ought to be followed by a prince is discussed at length in our treatise *De principe;* so we shall not speak of it at present.[6]

NOTES

1. Namely, Titus Veturius Calvinus and Spurius Postumius; see note 1 to the previous chapter.

2. Based on the speech in Livy, 9.8.3–10. In fact, he no longer was consul, because after the army was defeated at the Caudine Forks (see above, 3, 12, n.11) and the Romans were forced to agree to peace with the Samnites, Quintus Publilius Philo and Lucius Papirius Cursor were elected consuls (Livy, 9.7.15).

3. See Livy, 9.12.3–4.

4. A long-standing principle; see Cicero, *De officiis,* 1.10.32 and Aquinas, *Summa Theologica,* II, II. q.89, a.7, ad. 3.

5. On keeping promises see Machiavelli's judgment of Ferdinand V, the Catholic, king of Spain: "A certain contemporary prince, whom it is better not to name, proclaims nothing but peace and trust, yet he is an extremely dangerous menace to both. Had he respected either, he would have been deprived many times over of either his reputation or his power" (*Prince,* 18, p. 285, lines 100–106). Guicciardini, on the other hand, had a good opportunity to observe Ferdinand; he went to Spain in January 1512, returning in January 1514, as Florence's ambassador. He writes: "Even though a man has got a name for dissimulating and deceiving, still his deceptions will sometimes find believers. It seems a strange thing to say, yet it is very true. I remember that His Catholic Majesty, more than any other man, had a reputation of this sort; and yet in his plots there was never any lack of people who believed him more than was suitable. The latter believe too easily whatever they wish; the former believe out of ignorance" (*Ricordi,* C. 105). A judgment mirrored in Guicciardini's *Storia d'Italia,* 5, 5, concerning Ferdinand's treatment of Frederick of Aragon, king of Naples, in 1501: "But it was universally considered that Ferdinand's integrity and faithfulness were no less lacking. Everybody marveled that, because of his greed to obtain some area of the kingdom of Naples, he should have conspired against a king of his own blood; and in order to overthrow him more easily, he had always fed him with false promises of help."

6. Machiavelli is using the Latin title to refer to his discussion in *Prince,* 18, "How Princes Should Keep Their Word."

~ 43 ~

MEN WHO ARE BORN IN A COUNTRY CONFORM MORE OR LESS TO THE SAME NATURE FOR ALL TIME

1 Wise men are wont to say, and not by chance or without reason, that anyone who wants to see what is to be should consider what has been: for every thing in the world at every time has its own analogue in ancient times.[1] 2 This happens because, since these things are done by men, who have and always did have the same passions, they must of necessity produce the same result. 3 It is true that their actions are more full of *virtù* at times in this country than in that one, at times in that one more than this, according to the form of the upbringing from which those peoples have derived their way of life. 4 Knowing future

matters through those of the past is also facilitated by seeing a nation retain the same customs over a long time, it being either continuously greedy or continuously deceitful or having some other such vice or virtue.[2]

5 Anyone who reads about the past affairs of our city of Florence and examines those that have occurred in recent times will find the French and German people full of greed, arrogance, ferocity, and untrustworthiness, because all four of these things have at various times harmed our city deeply. 6 As for a lack of trustworthiness, everyone knows how many times money was given to King Charles VIII, how he promised to return the fortresses of Pisa, and how he never did return them.[3] 7 In this the king showed his untrustworthiness and his great greed. 8 But let us set these recent matters aside. 9 Everyone may have heard what happened in the war that the Florentine people waged against the Visconti, dukes of Milan; because Florence lacked other expedients, it decided to bring the emperor into Italy so that he would attack Lombardy with his reputation and troops.[4] 10 The emperor promised to come with many troops and wage war against the Visconti and defend Florence from their power if the Florentines gave him a hundred thousand ducats to set out and a hundred thousand once he was in Italy. 11 The Florentines agreed to these conditions; after they paid him the first sum and then the second, he arrived at Verona and turned back without accomplishing anything, claiming it was the result of their not having complied with the agreements that existed between them. 12 So that if Florence had not been either constrained by necessity or overcome by passion and had read and been familiar with the ancient customs of the barbarians, it would not have been deceived by them either this time[5] or many others, since they have always acted one way and have always used the same methods everywhere and with everyone. 13 As it can be seen that they did in ancient times to the Etruscans who, being attacked by the Romans, because they had been put to flight and defeated by them several times, and realizing that they could not resist their attack with their own troops, made an agreement with the Gauls who lived on this side of the Alps in Italy to give them a sum of money so they would be obligated to join their armies with them and go against the Romans.[6] The outcome was that the Gauls, after taking the money, then did not want to take up arms on their side, claiming that they had gotten it not to wage war against their enemies but so they would refrain from pillaging Etruscan territory. 14 Thus, because of the Gauls' greed and untrustworthiness, the Etruscan people were left at once without their money and without the aid that they were hoping for from them. 15 So we can see from this example of the ancient Etruscans and that of the Florentines that the French[7] have used the same methods, and because of this, one can easily imagine how much princes can trust in them.

NOTES

1. Machiavelli returns to a theme enunciated in Preface A to Book 1, sentence 8. It is a time-honored theme with biblical antecedents in Ecclesiastes ("The thing that hath been, it is that which shall be; and that which is done is that which

shall be done; and there is no new thing under the sun" [1:9] and "That which hath been . . . hath already been" [3:15]), and common in the Renaissance, especially important to the philosopher Giordano Bruno (1548–1600). Compare the quotation from Guicciardini, *Ricordi,* C. 76, in Preface A to Book 1, n.9, with C. 117, quoted above, 1, 39, n.1.

2. Translates *virtù.*

3. Machiavelli refers to events in November 1494, after Charles VIII forced Piero de' Medici to hand him the fortresses at Pisa in return for sparing a French attack on Florence, and again during the summer of 1495; see Guicciardini, *History of Florence,* chapters 12–13; see also *Storia d'Italia,* 1, 14; 2, 1. When Charles VIII left Pisa in June 1495, he put Robert de Balzac, sieur d'Entraigues, in command of the Pisan fortresses. D'Entraigues promptly turned them over to the Pisans; Walker points out that Commynes considered this act a flagrant breach of trust (*Memoirs,* 8, 21).

4. See Machiavelli, *Florentine Histories,* 3, 25, for the war between Florence and Gian Galeazzo Visconti; it lasted from 1390 until the duke's death in 1402. Florence appealed to Rupert III of the Palatinate (1352–1410), king of Germany from 1400 to 1410. He invaded Italy in 1401 but was defeated by the Visconti in October; thus he "turned back" as a result of this defeat, not because Florence reneged on its agreement (Inglese).

5. Referring to the period of Charles VIII.

6. In 10.10.8–12, Livy discusses this treaty, traditionally assigned to the year 300 B.C., with the Cisalpine Gauls, those on the south side of the Alps.

7. Machiavelli means that from the time of the Gauls to the present day the French "have used the same methods." All too often, in Machiavelli's experience, Florence had to appeal to France for help and was obliged to pay heavily for it—often for services not rendered. Nevertheless, throughout most of his diplomatic career, Machiavelli strongly advised Florence to side with the French. Hence this chapter ends on an atypical note. Oddly enough, he does not cite Livy's opinion of the Gauls, which Machiavelli's remarks would suggest might be held by some of his contemporary Florentines. Livy says that the Etruscans objected to the Gauls because "everyone dreaded having men of so savage a race for neighbors" (*tam efferatae gentis homines horrebat* [10.10.11]).

~ 44 ~

WHAT COULD NEVER BE ACHIEVED BY NORMAL MEANS OFTEN IS ACHIEVED BY ENERGY AND DARING

1 When the Samnites were attacked by the Roman army and were unable to stand up to the Romans with their army face-to-face in the field, they decided to leave their cities in Samnium guarded and go with all their army into Etruria, which had a truce with the Romans, and see by going there whether they might induce the Etruscans through the presence of their army to take up arms again, which they had refused the Samnite ambassadors.[1] 2 In the talks that the Samnites had with the Etruscans, particularly in showing them

what cause had induced them to take up arms, they used a notable expression when they said "they had rebelled because peace was more oppressive for slaves than war for the free."[2] 3 So partly by persuasion, partly through the presence of their army, they induced the Etruscans to take up arms again. 4 In this it should be noted that when a prince wishes to obtain something from someone else, he must not give him room to deliberate, if the occasion permits it, and act in such a way that he sees the need for quick decision, which is when the one who is asked sees that sudden, dangerous indignation will result from refusal or delay.

5 In our day this device can be seen to have been well employed by Pope Julius with the French and by Monsieur de Foix, the king of France's general, with the marquess of Mantua.[3] Because Pope Julius wanted to drive the Bentivoglios out of Bologna and he deemed that he needed French troops and Venetian neutrality to do so, when he asked both of them and received an equivocal and vacillating reply from them, he decided to make both of them come to agreement with him by not giving them time. 6 Leaving Rome with all the troops that he could throw together, he set off toward Bologna; he sent a message to the Venetians to remain neutral and one to the king of France to send him troops. 7 Thus, because the lack of time limited both of them and they saw that it would stir the pope's clear indignation if they delayed or refused, they gave in to his wishes: the king sent him aid and the Venetians remained neutral.

8 Again, when Monsieur de Foix was with his army in Bologna, he learned of the revolt of Brescia and wanted to go and recapture it; he had two routes: one, a long and tiring one through the king's domain, and the other a short one through the domain of Mantua. Not only did he need to pass through the marquess's domain but he had to go in through some locks between swamps and lakes, which that region is full of, that were closed off by fortresses and other means and guarded by him.[4] 9 So, deciding to go by the shorter route and in order to overcome every difficulty and not give the marquess time to deliberate, all at once Foix moved his army by that route and told the marquess to send him the keys to that passage.[5] 10 So the marquess, troubled by the sudden decision, sent him the keys; if Foix had behaved with more hesitation, he would never have sent them to him, because the marquess was in league with the pope and the Venetians and one of his sons was in the pope's hands: matters that gave him many suitable excuses for refusing the key.[6] 11 But overwhelmed by the sudden course of action for the reasons stated above, he handed them over. 12 The Etruscans did the same with the Samnites when, because of the presence of the Samnite army, they took up arms that they had refused to take up in other times.

NOTES

1. A reference to an episode in 297 B.C. during the Third Samnite War, 298–290.

2. Quoted in Latin from Livy, 10.16.5: *"rebellasse, quod pax servientibus gravior, quam liberis bellum esset."*

3. For background on Julius II and France, see above, 1, 27, n.2; it is also

alluded to in 2, 24, n.11. For background on Louis XII, Gaston de Foix, and Francesco II Gonzaga (1466–1519), the fourth marquess of Mantua, see above, 2, 16, n.9, and 2, 17, n.3.

4. At that point Louis XII controlled the duchy of Milan and Francesco Gonzaga controlled the system of defensive locks and canals in Mantuan territory known as the Serraglio.

5. Guicciardini, *Storia d'Italia,* 10, 10, provides a detailed account of de Foix's tactical decision to cut through the Mantuan territory without giving Gonzaga time to deny him permission. He notes that the "passage" in question was over the Pontemulino bridge on the Mincio River. Because Guicciardini writes of Gaston de Foix that "almost at the same time as he crossed [the river], he sent a request to the marquess of Mantua for permission to cross . . . in order not to allow time, given the sudden request, for the marquess to take precautions," he seems to be following closely Machiavelli's description in this discourse of how to "achieve by energy and daring what could never be achieved by normal means," as in the chapter's title.

6. Gonzaga was a standard-bearer of the Church and part of Pope Julius II's Holy League against France, as was Venice. As proof of his loyalty to Julius II, Francesco had handed over his ten-year-old son, Federico, as hostage. Federico remained in Rome from 1510 to 1513; he succeeded his father as marquess of Mantua in 1519.

~ 45 ~

WHICH IS THE BETTER COURSE OF ACTION IN BATTLE: TO STAND UP TO THE ENEMY'S ONRUSH AND THEN FIGHT BACK OR TO ATTACK THEM FURIOUSLY FIRST?

1 The Roman consuls Decius and Fabius were confronting the Samnite and Etuscan armies with two armies, and since they happened to fight a skirmish and a battle at the same time, it may be noted which of the two different procedures the two Consuls used in that action is better.[1] 2 For Decius attacked the enemy with all his might and effort; Fabius only stood up to it, deeming a slow attack to be more effective and reserving his onrush for the end when the enemy had lost its initial ardor for fighting and, as we say, his dash. 3 From the outcome of the affair we can see that Fabius's plan succeeded much better than Decius's: the latter wore himself out in the first onrushes so that, seeing his detachment turning back rather than the contrary, in imitation of his father he sacrificed himself for the Roman legions in order by his death to earn the glory that he had not been able to achieve by victory.[2] 4 When Fabius learned of that, in order not to achieve less honor in living than his colleague had achieved in death, he drove forward all the troops that he had saved for this need; as a result he gained a most happy victory. 5 From this we can see that Fabius's procedure is surer and more to be imitated.[3]

NOTES

1. Machiavelli continues to take his examples from events of the Third Samnite War. In 295 B.C. Publius Decius Mus the Younger and Quintus Fabius Maximus Rullianus were consuls. See Livy, 10.27–29. The "action" referred to was a battle near Sentinum (modern Sassoferrato) on the eastern slopes of the Appenines, about 130 miles west of Ancona. The Roman victory against the combined forces of Gauls, Samnites, Etruscans, and Umbrians (Livy, 10.27.3) was significant in establishing Rome's supremacy in Italy.

2. For the self-sacrifice of Publius Decius Mus the Elder at the battles of Veseris and Trifanum in 340 B.C., see above, 2, 16, sentences 1–7 and notes.

3. Fabrizio refers to this comparison in his third speech from the end of *Art of War,* 4.

~ *46* ~

HOW IT HAPPENS THAT A FAMILY IN A CITY RETAINS THE SAME CUSTOMS FOR SOME TIME

1 It seems not only that one city has certain different ways and institutions from another and brings forth men who are either tougher or more effeminate but also that in the same city such a difference can be seen to exist between one family and another.[1] 2 This can be found to be true in every city, and in the city of Rome we may read about a great many examples of it. For we see that the Manlii were tough and stubborn, the Publicoli kindly and friendly to the people, the Appii ambitious and enemies of the Plebs, and similarly many other families each had qualities distinct from the others.[2] 3 This cannot arise solely from their blood, because that would have to change according to changing intermarriages, but it must of necessity derive from different upbringing from one family to another. 4 For it is very important for a young boy to start at an early age to hear good or ill of something, because he must needs be impressed by it, and then afterward throughout all periods of his life he regulates his way of doing things from that. 5 If this were not so, it would be impossible for all the Appii to have had the same desire and for them to have been stirred by the same passions, as Livy notes in many of them. When one of them finally had been made Censor and his colleague gave up the office at the end of eighteen months as the law required, Appius refused to give it up, saying that he could keep it for five years according to the first law established by the Censors.[3] 6 Although a great many meetings were held concerning this and a good number of riots generated, nonetheless, there was never any way to get him to give it up despite the will of both the people[4] and the majority of the Senate. 7 If one reads the speech that Publius Sempronius, a tribune of the Plebs,[5] made against him, one will note in it all the arrogance of the Appii and all the goodness and kindness observed by countless citizens to obey the laws and the prophecies of their country.

NOTES

1. Although based on Livy, 9.33–34, the argument of this discourse follows from above, 3, 43, especially sentence 4.

2. Vivanti suggests in his edition of the *Discorsi* that this reflection may be sparked by Machiavelli's source in the previous discourse. It is a speech that Livy assigns to Publius Decius Mus the Younger; as he plunged into the enemy's forces and sure death, he invoked the name of his father: "why should I delay the destiny of our house any longer? The privilege of being sacrificed to avert our country's perils is a privilege granted our family" (*Quid ultra moror . . . familiare fatum? Datum hoc nostro generi est ut luendis periculis publicis piacula simus* [10.28.13]).

3. Appius Claudius Caecus was censor in 310 B.C.; his "colleague" was Gaius Plautus (Livy, 9.29.5). It was the *lex Aemilia* of 434 B.C. (Livy, 4.24.5) that reduced the term of office of censor from five years to a year and a half.

4. Livy, 9.34.26, points out that Appius was dependent on the support of three plebeian tribunes for his success in remaining in office.

5. See Livy, 9.34.1–25.

~ 47 ~

FOR LOVE OF HIS COUNTRY, A GOOD CITIZEN SHOULD FORGET PERSONAL AFFRONTS

1 The consul Marcius was with his army against the Samnites, and when he was wounded in a fight so that his troops were in danger, the Senate deemed it necessary to send Papirius Cursor there as dictator to make up for the the consul's disability.[1] 2 Because it was necessary for the Dictator to be named by Fabius, who was consul with the armies in Etruria, the Senators, fearing that Fabius would refuse to name him since they were enemies,[2] sent two ambassadors to him to beg him to set aside his personal hatreds and name him for the public well-being. 3 Fabius did so, moved by love of his country, even though by his silence and many other means[3] he indicated that this nomination troubled him. 4 All those who seek to be considered good citizens should take this as an example.

NOTES

1. See Livy, 9.38, for this incident in 310 B.C. The consul was Gaius Marcius Rutulus; the consul in Etruria was Quintus Fabius Maximus Rullianus. It was his duty to name a dictator because Marcius could not be consulted.

2. The enmity resulted from an episode in 325 B.C. at the Battle of Imbrinium; see above, 1, 31, n.8. Livy, 9.38.11, does not specify that there were "two ambassadors" (Ridley, "Roman History," pp. 212–213; Martelli, *Storici antichi,* pp. 208–209).

3. Machiavelli follows Livy, 9.38.14, closely.

~ *48* ~

WHEN ONE SEES ONE'S ENEMY MAKE A GRAVE ERROR, ONE SHOULD BELIEVE THERE IS A RUSE BEHIND IT

1 As the Consul had gone to Rome for some ceremonies, Fulvius was left as legate in the army that the Romans had in Etruria; to see whether they could catch him in their snares, the Etruscans set up an ambush near the Roman camps and sent some soldiers dressed as shepherds with a large herd of cattle and had them come into the view of the Roman army. Disguised in this way, they drew near to the camp's palisade, whereupon the Legate, astonished at their presumption, which seemed improbable to him, found a way to discover the deception: so the Etruscans' plan was spoiled.[1] 2 Here one can conveniently note that an army commander must not give credence to an error that he clearly sees the enemy make, for there will always be trickery behind it, since it is unlikely for men to be so careless. 3 But often the desire for victory blinds men's minds: they see nothing but what seems to be in their interest.

4 When the Gauls had defeated the Romans at the Allia and found the gates open and unprotected upon their arrival in Rome, they stayed an entire day and night without going in, since they were afraid of trickery and could not believe that there was so much cowardice and so little good sense in Roman breasts that they would abandon their country.[2] 5 When the Florentines were encamped at Pisa in 1508, Alfonso del Mutolo, a Pisan citizen, happened to be a prisoner of the Florentines; he promised that if he were freed he would hand over one of Pisa's gates to the Florentine army.[3] 6 He was freed; then to discuss the matter he came many times to speak with the legates of the commissioners, and he came not secretly but openly and accompanied by Pisans, whom he left to the side when he was speaking with the Florentines. 7 So one could have inferred his double-dealing mind, because it was unlikely if the discussion had been in good faith that he would have dealt with it so openly. 8 But the Florentines were so blinded by their desire to take Pisa that, going on his orders to the Lucca gate, they left several of their leaders and other soldiers behind there[4] to their dishonor because of this Alfonso's double betrayal.

NOTES

1. Here Machiavelli follows his sources less closely, confusing two separate ambushes; see Livy, 10.3–4. Livy mentions an earlier incident when Marcus Valerius Maximus, the dictator, not a consul, had returned to Rome for the ritual of renewing the auspices. During his absence his Master of the Horse, Marcus Aemilius Paulus, fell into a trap and was ambushed by the Etruscans. After the dictator's return to his troops, the incident with Gnaeus Fulvius occurred. But because the legate's scouting patrol was too small to cope, it was actually Marcus Valerius Maximus who won the day. See Martelli, *Storici antichi,* p. 209.

2. Based on Livy, 5.39.1–3; see Martelli, *Storici antichi,* pp. 209–210. Machiavelli has dealt with this episode and the fall of Rome to the Gauls in 390 B.C.: see above, 2, 29, sentences 5–10.

3. Because the Florentine calendar is calculated *ab Incarnatione Christi* (from the Incarnation of Christ), this episode occurred in March 1509. Guicciardini discusses it in *History of Florence,* chapter 31, and *Storia d'Italia,* 8, 8.

4. Guicciardini says, "the Pisans gained nothing from this deception except the death of a few men who had approached the area adjacent to the outside gate so that they could enter the city once the signal was given; among those killed were Canaccio da Pratovecchio (as he who was Alfonso del Mutolo's captor was called), in whom those who were responsible for the ruse had confided. Also killed there was Paolo da Parrano, the captain of a Florentine company of light horse" (*Storia d'Italia,* 8, 8). And "everyone was amazed that Alfonso had concocted such a ruse for so small a gain" (*History of Florence,* chapter 31).

~ 49 ~

TO KEEP A REPUBLIC FREE, IT NEEDS FRESH PROVISIONS[1] EVERY DAY; AND WHY QUINTUS FABIUS DESERVED TO BE CALLED MAXIMUS

1 As has been said elsewhere,[2] every day in a great city incidents necessarily arise that require a doctor; and the more important they are, the wiser the doctor who has to be found. 2 If such incidents ever arose in any city, they arose in Rome, both strange and unexpected ones. This was the case when it seemed that all the Roman women had conspired against their husbands to slaughter them: there were so many women who had poisoned them and so many who had prepared poison to poison them with.[3] 3 This was also the case in the conspiracy of the Bacchanals which was discovered at the time of the Macedonian war, in which many thousands of men and women were already involved.[4] It would have posed a threat to the city had it not been discovered, or else if the Romans had not been accustomed to punishing great numbers of people who had done wrong. For if the grandeur of the republic and the power of its actions were not seen by countless other signs, it is seen by the nature of the penalties that it imposed on those who did wrong. 4 Nor was it afraid to put to death by way of justice an entire legion at a time and a city, and to banish eight or ten thousand men under extraordinary conditions that were to be observed not by a single man but by so many, as happened to the soldiers who had fought unsuccessfully at Cannae. It banished them to Sicily and enjoined them not to live in a city and to eat standing up.[5]

5 But of all the other actions, decimating the armies was [the most] terrifying, when one man out of every ten in an entire army was slain by lots.[6] 6 Nor could a more frightening punishment than this be found to punish great numbers. For when great numbers do wrong and it is unclear who is

responsible, all cannot be punished because there are too many; punishing some of them and leaving some of them unpunished would be an injustice to those who are punished, and the unpunished would be encouraged to do wrong another time. 7 But if you slaughter a tenth of them by lots when they all deserve it, whoever is punished complains of his lot; the unpunished are afraid lest it be their turn another time, and they refrain from doing wrong.

8 So the poisoners and the Bacchanals were punished for their sins as they deserved. 9 Although such diseases have bad effects in a republic, they are not fatal, because there is almost always time to correct them; but there is no time for those that concern the state which, if they are not corrected by a wise man, bring about a city's downfall. 10 As a result of the Romans' generosity in giving citizenship to foreigners, so many new people were born in Rome and they began to play so great a part in elections that the government began to change and departed from the ways and the men that it had been accustomed to follow. 11 Noting this, Quintus Fabius, who was a Censor, put all the new people from whom this disorder derived in four Tribes so that, restricted to such small areas, they could not corrupt all of Rome.[7] 12 Fabius understood this matter well, and he applied a suitable remedy to it without any upheaval; this was so acceptable to the citizenry that he deserved the name of "Maximus."

NOTES

1. Translates *provvedimenti,* but Machiavelli is being metaphorical here. What he means are "new precautions," "new measures." It could be argued that Machiavelli closes the third book of his discourse on the same note as he began it: with a call for a republic's renewal, "fresh provisions," by being brought "back toward their origins." The "doctors of medicine" who daily must provide a "cure" (above, 3, 1, sentence 8) are needed "every day" in this final chapter as well. Indeed, it could also be argued that the "lawgivers" of the first sentence of the first chapter in Book 1 who helped to found Rome and establish its *virtù* were the inspiration for their descendants who sustained it through "fresh provisions."

2. Above, 1, 33–34, 49; Rinaldi adds, to expand on the "provisions" of the chapter title, the "actions" exemplified above, 3, 1, sentences 21–23 and 26–28.

3. See Livy, 8.18; he notes that 179 women were found guilty of poisoning (8.18.10).

4. In 186 B.C. the Roman Senate ordered an investigation of the spread of a mystic cult of Dionysus (Latin, Bacchus) that was practiced in Rome by the Bacchanals, or followers of Bacchus; it was more of a semi-secret society than a conspiracy (see Livy, 39.8–18). Nevertheless, the results of the four-month investigation horrified the Senate and resulted in executions, demolitions of their meeting places, and prohibition of the rites; "more than seven thousand men and women were involved in the conspiracy" (Livy, 39.17).

5. Livy discusses sending legions in disgrace to Sicily in 23.25; but neither there nor in the moving speech he quotes in 25.5.5–7 does he mention the restrictions that Machiavelli lists.

6. Livy first mentions in 2.59.11 the punishment of *decimatio,* on the orders of Appius Claudius Sabinus, against his troops who threw away their weapons and fled during a battle against the Aequi and Volscians in 471 B.C. See also Polybius, 6.38, and *Art of War,* Fabrizio's third speech in Book 6.

7. This is Quintus Fabius Maximus Rullianus, mentioned above, chapter 47. According to Livy, in 303 B.C., "partly to cause harmony, partly to prevent the elections from being in the hands of people of the lowest class, he separated out all the mob of the Forum marketplace and threw them together into four tribes, to which he gave the name of 'urban' tribes. This arrangement is said to have been so gratefully received that by his settlement of the orders he won the surname of 'the Great,' which all his victories had not brought him" (*simul concordiae causa, simul ne humillimorum in manu comitia essent, omnen forensem turbam excretam in quattuor tribus coniecit urbanasque eas appellavit. Adeoque eam rem acceptam gratis animis ferunt ut Maximi cognomen, quod tot victoriis non pepererat, hac ordinum temperatione pareret* [9.46.14–15]). Following Rubinstein's lead, Rinaldi observes that the patricians' loss of control over elections in ancient Rome was analogous to the Medici's loss of control over local elections in Florence. See also Martelli, *Storici antichi,* pp. 210–213.

Considerations

of the Discourses *of Niccolò Machiavelli*

FRANCESCO

GUICCIARDINI

Contents

· *Considerations* of BOOK ONE ·

~ 1:1 ~

[WHAT THE ORIGINS OF CITIES HAVE USUALLY BEEN AND WHAT WERE ROME'S ORIGINS]

1 In the first Discourse, the distinction that is made that all cities are built either by outsiders or by indigenous men is right. Venice and Athens fall into the second category, as does Rome—but differently from Athens and Venice; the latter were built by indigenous people because they needed either secure shelter or shared government. But Rome, with none of these requirements, was built rather as a colony of Alba,[1] that is, either by Albans or by subjects of Alban power out of love for the places where they had been raised or their aspiration for self-rule. And because of Aeneas, Rome cannot be grouped with cities built by outsiders, because that would be seeking its origins too far back and they are not to be related to the earliest ancestors of the builders.

2 As for the category of cities built by outsiders, it is not true simply that the colonies sent out to ease the region's population are always dependent on others, because many nations, for example the Gauls, the Cimbri, etc., sent out a part of their population to seek new homes for the above-mentioned reason.[2] Once these colonies were founded, they had no dependency upon or recognition from their native land at all. Hence it is a truer and fuller distinction to say that those cities built by outsiders are either built so that they have to stand on their own and not depend for anything *even* on those responsible for their origin or they are built so they must acknowledge those in their native land as rulers. In this second type, it is true that they cannot initially get very far, but as time goes on many incidents can occur to free them from that subjection; then it may happen that they achieve notable growth. 3 Florence and all Rome's colonies were of this type, because after the fall of Rome many of them became magnificent and powerful cities. Perhaps if one were to consider them individually, one would not discover that fewer colonial cities had risen to memorable power than did cities with their origins in freedom. They grew or did not grow depending upon the location, constitution, and fortune that they had. 4 It is true that colonial cities generally have taken longer to begin growing, since they were initially subject to others. But if meanwhile they have had an opportunity to increase in wealth and population thanks to the advantage of their location, their good constitution, or some other reason, then later on they have found it possible to grow powerful.

5 A large population is a city's primary basis for power and wealth. It is hard for a city located in a barren area to increase in population, unless it possesses a

salubrious climate like Florence or the convenience of the sea like Venice. Therefore it is better to settle in a fertile country, because inhabitants congregate there more readily. But were it possible to keep a large number of people at one location—I do not mean a totally unproductive location but not a rich one—undoubtedly the need to provide for themselves would contribute more to making it *virtuoso*[3] than good laws: the latter can be altered by the will of men, but necessity is a constant law and stimulus. 6 This step certainly was one that governed Rome. Although located in a fertile region, it nevertheless possessed no rural hinterlands and was surrounded by powerful neighbors; Rome was forced to expand by *virtù* of arms and treaties. This point is being made in connection not with a city that seeks to live according to philosophy,[4] but with those cities that seek to conduct themselves according to the usual ways of the world—as they must act. Otherwise, being weak, they would be crushed and trampled by their neighbors.

NOTES

1. Alba Longa was an ancient city in central Italy, about twelve miles from Rome, the present-day Castel Gandolfo. Because legend declared it to have been founded by Ascanius, the son of Aeneas, and it was the birthplace of Romulus and Remus, it had special status in discussions of Rome's origin.

2. The Cimbri were a Germanic tribe that settled in Noricum (roughly speaking, modern Austria) where they were defeated by Rome in 113 B.C. They joined with the Helvetii in modern Switzerland as independent units and migrated into Roman territory where they were defeated by Marius in 101 B.C. at Vercelli in Piedmont.

3. Translates *farlo virtuoso,* with *virtù* signifying the location's being "productive" for a large number of people living in one spot.

4. Living "according to philosophy" means living according to a system of abstract principles. Guicciardini's implied judgment is that this is an unwise, if not unrealistic, policy.

~ *1:2* ~

[HOW MANY KINDS OF REPUBLICS THERE ARE AND WHAT KIND THE ROMAN REPUBLIC WAS]

1 There is no doubt that a mixed government of three types—a prince, the aristocracy, and the people—is better and more stable than a simple government of any one of the three types, particularly when it is mixed so that the good characteristics of any one form are chosen and the bad left out.[1] This is the essential point to consider and the point which those who set it up may fail to note. 2 To discuss this subject in detail, I state that in royal government[2] public affairs are run much better with more order, more swiftness, more discretion, and more resoluteness when they depend on the will of only one man rather than when they are in the hands of many. 3 Its disadvantage is that if it falls into the hands of a wicked man with free rein to do evil all the

power given him to perform good deeds he will use for quite bad ones. Similarly, if he is good but ineffective, countless disorders result from his inaction. 4 And even if the king is chosen by election and not by succession, there is no absolute insurance against these dangers, because the electors may often be deceived, considering someone to be good and prudent who is the opposite. The magnitude of his power and freedom of action frequently alters the character of the one elected, and in particular if he has children it is difficult for him not to want them to be his successors. Once the king has absolute power, it is difficult to prevent this, even if it goes against the constitution of the kingdom, but he can bring it about only through guile and unsavory means.

5 So if one seeks to establish a government that receives as much as possible of the good of royal government and not the ill, it is impossible for it to receive all the benefits and to avoid all the ills; one must be content with less of the benefits rather than, by trying to gain more advantages, receive the ills as well. Hence it is necessary to make him king for life but to limit his power by ensuring that the king cannot decide anything entirely on his own—or at least only things of lesser importance. Setting it up in this way, the benefit of having an eye constantly watching over public affairs would be gained: a chief to whom matters could be referred, an administrator who could propose, request, and record them. 6 One would lose the advantage of having a single person with the power to deliberate and execute matters, but since it is impossible to have this without the danger of his having power to turn the kingdom into a tyranny, it is a lesser evil to have fewer benefits in safety than many benefits with such grave risk. 7 Therefore let the king, that is, the leader who represents this prince, have power limited so that he alone cannot decide important matters; let him be king by election, not by succession. If it is arranged this way, it is better that he be king for life than for a limited period, but, if he is king for a limited period, it is better to be for a long term than a short one. 8 The Venetians have done better in this than the Romans or the Spartans, because the Spartan kings always came from the same family and by succession, while the Roman kings, although they had a senate and some semblance of a republic, nevertheless had so much power that it was easy for them to turn their kingdom into a tyranny, the elements of which were visible under Servius Tullius and then evident under Tarquinius Superbus.[3] 9 And if we wish to call the power of the consuls royal, then it was not for life but for a year, whereas the Venetian prince rules for life, he is elected, and his power is quite limited.

10 In a government of aristocrats, there is this advantage: because there are many of them, they cannot establish a tyranny so easily as one man. Because they are the most qualified men in the city, they govern it with greater intelligence and wisdom than the masses. Because they are respected, they have less cause to afflict it, as they could easily do if they were discontented. 11 The disadvantage is that finding themselves with great power they may promote matters that are useful to them and oppress the people; because there are no limits to men's ambitions for self-aggrandizement, they may turn on one another and foment sedition. That causes the city's downfall through

either tyranny or some other means. If they are aristocrats by succession and not by election, matters soon pass from the hands of prudent and good men into those of imprudent and wicked ones.

12 In order to derive all possible good from this form of government and to avoid evil, the aristocrats must not always be of the same lineage and families, but a senate must be elected from the entire body of the city to handle perplexing matters, that is, from everybody legally eligible to take part in public officialdom.[4] In other words, they should be the pick of the city's prudent, noble, and rich men; they should be a permanent body or at least last for a very long term. They should be numerous so they are more readily tolerated by others; the latter will constantly expect that they or their family will take the place of those who might be absent on a given day. Also, with a large number in the Senate, one may hope that each man who deserves it may enter; even if a few who are less than ideal enter, that is less troublesome than if some capable person were excluded. They should not have absolute power over all public affairs so they do not arrogate too much power to themselves, particularly that of naming public officials, especially those who have simple or mixed powers[5] or deal in public finances.[6] They should not have power to make laws without the consent of the people so they will be unable either to alter the form of government or to modify the institutions[7] of the city for the benefit of the powerful and to the detriment of the minority. They should, however, have power to debate and decide matters for which men's wisdom is most indispensable: war, peace, negotiations with princes, and all matters essential to the preservation and expansion of dominion. 13 The Spartans had aristocrats of this kind, namely, from the entire body of the city, not those from a particular class; the Romans had them, but with one distinction: in this case the Patricians were the aristocrats from the outset, the remainder were Plebeians, the cause of all their sedition.

14 A good point about government of the people is that while it lasts there is no tyranny; laws are more powerful than men, and the aim of every deliberation is to seek the universal good. The bad thing is that because of their ignorance the people are not capable of discussing significant matters—and that is why a republic that submits matters to the people's deliberation soon declines.[8] They are unstable and always seeking innovation; therefore, they are readily stirred up and deceived by ambitious and seditious men; they often persecute qualified citizens because of their need to seek novelty and excitement. 15 To avoid these things one must not entrust any significant matter to the people except those that would threaten freedom were they in the hands of others: for example, electing public officials and creating laws. These matters ought not to come before the people until they have first been digested and approved by the highest officials and the Senate. But those they initiate should indeed not take effect unless they are confirmed by the people. Free debate ought not to be permitted, for that is a great tool of sedition. In the council of the people only those designated by public officials should be able to speak, and only on topics that the officials have designated. 16 By setting up government in this fashion, one will have the mixture described in the Discourse.

NOTES

1. Although Guicciardini agrees with Machiavelli that a mixed government is the best form, he sets out to prove that Venice is a better example to follow than either Rome or Sparta, which Machiavelli favors.

2. Translates *governo regio;* for the next two paragraphs Guicciardini alters Machiavelli's terms, based on the root *principe,* which Guicciardini used in the first sentence, for ones based on the root *regio.*

3. Although Machiavelli does not refer to Venice in 1, 2, it will be a frequent point of comparison for both him and Guicciardini. Servius Tullius was Rome's sixth king (traditionally from 578 to 535 B.C.), and Tarquinus Superbus was Rome's seventh and last (traditionally from 534 to 510 B.C.).

4. With his remarks in this paragraph directed to the situation in Florence, Guicciardini favors an elected ruler and elected officials serving for a lifetime, but neither the ruler nor the magistracy is to be hereditary.

5. Vivanti glosses this phrase in his edition of the *Discorsi* as referring to the power to adjudicate civil and criminal cases.

6. Translates *che sono magistrati di utilità.*

7. Translates *ordini.*

8. This will be a consistent point of contention between Guicciardini and Machiavelli. In *Prince,* 9, Machiavelli dismisses "that trite adage, 'Whoever builds upon the people builds upon mud'" (p. 197, lines 105–106). Guicciardini's notion of a mixed republic centers power in a consultative senate composed of members from the nobility and aristocracy; see also Book II of his *Dialogo del reggimento di Firenze,* written between 1519 and 1524. For the suggestion that Guicciardini may have read Machiavelli's chapter in manuscript form, see Introduction, n.1.

~ *1:3* ~

[THE EVENTS THAT LED TO THE CREATION OF TRIBUNES OF THE PEOPLE IN ROME, MAKING THE REPUBLIC MORE PERFECT]

1 It is propounded too absolutely that "men never do any good except out of necessity" and that whoever organizes a republic should presume everyone to be bad, because there are many who, even when they have the power to do evil, do good, and all men are not bad. 2 It is true, both in establishing a republic and in all other activities, that matters should be arranged in such a way that anyone who wishes to do evil is unable to, not because all men are always bad but in order to provide for those who may be bad. In this context one should consider that men are all inclined by nature toward good; all things being equal, they prefer good to evil. If some have a different inclination, that is so contrary both to the custom of others and to the prime object that nature sets before us that they should be called monsters rather than men. 3 So everyone is inclined by nature toward good,

but because our nature is weak and at each step in the lives of men we encounter opportunities that may turn us away from the good, such as sensual pleasure, ambition, and greed, whenever wise men, providing for this danger, have been able to save men from the power to do evil, they have done so. And whenever they have been unable to do so absolutely because it cannot always be accomplished, indeed rarely, they have added another remedy: enticing mankind to good with rewards and frightening them from evil with punishments.[1]

4 The reason for the election of Tribunes was that mentioned in the Discourse; i.e., to provide protection for the Plebs against the Nobility, i.e. the Patricians. This happened in four ways. First, because the Plebs had their own official, they came to have a public leader with whom they could consult and deal with their needs; when the Plebs appealed to him, they were no longer scorned as a body without a head. Second, because they had such power of intercession, no public decision could be taken in Rome against the will of even a single one of the Tribunes. Third, the Tribunes could submit new laws to the people. Fourth, they could summon before the judgment of the people the citizens that any of the Tribunes might wish. 5 When the Tribunes were first created, these powers were not intended, but in the course of time they were either taken on or expanded by interpretation of the law creating them. These powers did not do what the Discourse states; namely, that the Tribunes formed a magistracy between the Senate and the Plebs. Although the Tribunes did mitigate the powers of the Nobles, they did not, conversely, temper the unruliness of the Plebs.[2]

NOTES

1. Guicciardini states this point more broadly in his *Ricordi:* "All men are by nature inclined more toward the good than toward evil; nor is there anyone who would not more willingly do good rather than evil, unless other considerations sway him toward the contrary. But human nature is so frail, and opportunities inviting evil occur so frequently in the world, that men let themselves be easily turned away from the good. Hence wise legislators discovered rewards and punishments, which are nothing more than a desire to hold men firm in their natural inclination by hope and fear" (C. 134; see also B. 3, in which it is clear that is self-interest that turns men "away from the good," and Q-2. 4).

2. Guicciardini is clearly uncomfortable with Machiavelli's argument in these early chapters. Stating at the end of his second chapter (sentence 36) that by "continuing its mixed form of government, Rome created a perfect republic. It attained this perfection on account of the dissension between the Plebs and the Senate," Machiavelli asserted a causal relationship that was a new way of thinking about a republican form of government. Guicciardini betrays his assumptions here, because Machiavelli does not refer to "the unruliness of the Plebs" in 1, 3.

~ *1:4* ~

[THE DISCORD BETWEEN THE PLEBS AND THE ROMAN SENATE MADE THAT REPUBLIC FREE AND POWERFUL]

1 I have written more extensively [on this topic][1] elsewhere, so I shall now dispense with it briefly, but I conclude that the cause of the discord between Patricians and Plebeians in Rome was that the city's orders were divided; that is, one segment were Patricians, the other Plebeians. And all the magistrates were Patricians, and Plebeians were excluded, so any hope of attaining that status was denied to the Plebeians. 2 If there had not been this distinction at the outset between Patricians and Plebeians, or at least if half the public offices had been given to the Plebs, as was done later, those divisions would not have arisen. They cannot be worthy of praise, and it cannot be denied that they were harmful, although perhaps in some other republic, with less *virtù,* they might have done more harm. The Plebeians would not have desired the creation of Tribunes and that office would not have been necessary, because with public offices shared they would have shared power; freedom would have involved no more danger for the Patricians than it did for the Plebeians. 3 And it is certain that once public offices were shared, that office did more harm than good, and by the end at least they were an instrument and a cover for those who wished to overthrow the republic. And particularly, in my opinion, they cannot be praised for their authority either to propose new laws or to intercede.

4 So it was not the discord between the Plebeians and the Senate that made Rome free and powerful, because it would have been better had there not been any causes for discord. Nor were the rebellions useful, though they certainly did less harm than in other cities, and it would have been very useful for Rome's greatness had the Patricians yielded sooner to the will of the Plebeians rather than thought up ways to avoid needing the Plebeians. But praising discord is like praising a sick man's illness, because the remedy that has been used on him is the right one. 5 This discord started with the origins of Rome, because from its beginnings there was a distinction between Patricians and Plebeians, but under the kings it did no harm, because, since the kings held the power, the Senate could not oppress the Plebeians by itself. Whatever the Senate did not accomplish to advance the Plebeians' interests, the kings did, sometimes even more ambitiously than they should have, as we read of Servius Tullius.[2] They were also sometimes wont to elect Plebeians into the Patrician class, which made the others more readily tolerate that rank, which they, too, might hope to attain. 6 These reasons all vanished once the kings were driven out, because the Patricians became masters of the city and arbiters of everything; the Plebs had no one to turn to or who took care of their interests, and their leaders no longer had any hope of being elected to the rank of Patrician, because the Patricians disdained them as commoners and foreigners like Appius Claudius were more likely to be elected.[3] 7 No one noted this discord when the kings were driven out, since men were

thinking more of the present evil, namely, that of the kings, and those who do not have great skill in public matters can understand them only by experience. Hence rarely, perhaps never, has it turned out that a republic has had perfect organization from the beginning. 8 Therefore the remedy that was found for rebellion was useful, but not eliminating the causes that gave rise to it at the outset certainly was not useful.

9 As for the other aspects of Roman government, I mean those laws respecting the form of government of the republic, I do not wish to discuss them in detail now, but I do not think that they were such that anyone wishing to establish a republic should take them as an example. 10 Military discipline was quite exceptional, and its *virtù* compensated for the other flaws of government, which are less important in a city that endures through its armed might than in those that are governed by industry, evasive tactics,[4] and the arts of peace.

NOTES

1. See the discussion in Book 2 of his *Dialogo del reggimento di Firenze,* pp. 143–153.

2. The sixth king of Rome (traditionally from 578 to 535 B.C.), whose reforms brought more plebeians into an active military and political role; Livy notes in 1.46.1 that he divided conquered territory among the people, thereby gaining their favor.

3. Originally a Sabine, Appius Claudius settled in Rome and became a patrician (451 B.C.); he was interested in bettering the plebeians' standard of living—see Livy, 2.16.4–7.

4. Translates *girandole* ("whirligigs," "artifice," or "whim"); Vivanti suggests *intrighi* ("intrigues," "entanglements," or "plots"). Guicciardini's emphasis on "the arts of peace" may be due in part to his experience with diplomacy as Florentine ambassador to the court of Ferdinand the Catholic of Spain from 1512 to 1514.

~ *1:5* ~

[SHOULD THE GUARDING OF FREEDOM BE ENTRUSTED TO THE PEOPLE OR THE NOBLES;[1] AND WHICH HAS GREATER CAUSE TO CREATE DISTURBANCES: THOSE WHO SEEK TO ACQUIRE OR THOSE WHO SEEK TO CONSERVE?]

1 I do not understand the chapter title, that is, what it means to entrust the guarding of freedom either to the people or to the Nobility. For it is one thing to say who should have the governing power, the Nobility or the Plebs, and Venice is an example of that point, because the upper classes have it to such an extent that the Plebs are entirely excluded from it. It is another to say, when everybody participates in the government, who should be invested with a particular authority or concern for the defense of freedom,

whether Plebeian officials or noble ones. Rome can serve as an example for this point, since both the Nobles and the Plebs took part in governing, [yet] the office of the Tribunes, which ostensibly was particularly charged with guarding freedom, was plebeian. 2 However, to put it better, the Patricians were no less responsible than the Plebeians for guarding freedom in Rome, because both the Consuls and the Dictators had the duty and authority to defend freedom. We can see this with both Spurius Melius and Manlius Capitolinus, one of whom was assassinated and the other imprisoned by dictators because they plotted against freedom; and at a later date the sedition of the Gracchi and the conspiracy of Catiline were crushed by the consuls.[2] 3 In addition, authority to indict was common to both Patricians and Plebeians and both other officials and tribunes could summon people to court; the Tribunes were not created to defend freedom against those who sought to tyrannize the entire republic but solely to defend the Plebs against those who sought to tyrannize them. Although the Tribunes summoned citizens to court more frequently, they did so because, since it was a plebeian office, they had more credit with the Plebs, and in a certain sense this function appeared to be specifically theirs. 4 But as for the title of the chapter, I shall always praise a mixed government, as described above, above all others, and in such a government I prefer that the guarding of freedom against those who seek to oppress the republic belong to everybody, always avoiding as much as possible the distinction between Nobles and Plebs. A mixed government is of necessity so balanced that one class is a guard against the other in defense of freedom.

5 But if it should ever be necessary to set up either a government purely of Nobles or of Plebs in a city, I think it would be less a mistake to make it a government of the Nobility. Because, since they have more wisdom and more quality, one may have a greater expectation that they might put themselves into some reasonable form, whereas with the Plebs, since they are full of ignorance, confusion, and many bad qualities, one may only expect them to ruin and wreck everything. 6 I shall not go further with this distinction: you wish to form either a republic that acquires or one that preserves, for a government by the Plebs is neither for acquiring nor for preserving, and the government of Rome was mixed, not plebeian. 7 This conclusion agrees with the opinion of all who have written about republics, who prefer a government of the elite to one of the masses.

NOTES

1. Translates *grandi;* see above, *Discourses,* 1, 5, n.1.

2. During the famine in Rome in 440–439 B.C., Spurius Maelius profited by purchasing grain, withholding it from the market, then selling it when he could win support for his political aspirations. When Rome realized that he sought to become king, Cincinnatus was appointed dictator. He ordered a trial, but C. Servilius, the Master of the Horse who was sent to bring in Melius, murdered him first (Livy, 4.13–14). Manlius Capitolinus received his surname from saving the Capitol during

the invasion of the Gauls in 387 B.C. The traditional story had it that he was awakened by the cackling of Juno's sacred geese and hence beat off a nocturnal raiding party (Livy, 5.47). Although a patrician, he defended plebeians who were in debt to patricians and was impeached for treason (Livy, 6.15–20). Livy notes (in 6.20.12) that tribunes hurled Manlius to his death from the Tarpeian Rock. Tiberius Sempronius Gracchus and his younger brother Gaius were distressed by the conditions of the Roman poor. They became tribunes of the people and introduced radical agrarian reform measures. Tiberius wanted to increase the number of small, independent farmers and to restrict the amount of public land that could be privately held. He thus angered the patricians and the ruling oligarchy; he was killed by a mob of senators in 133 B.C. From 123 to 121, Gaius continued to sponsor agrarian reform, advocated a more democratic government, and sought citizenship for the Latins; he died in a riot in 121. Catiline was a patrician demagogue who conspired against the consuls; he aroused the wrath of Cicero, who denounced his conspiracies in the Roman senate in 62 B.C.

~ 1:6 ~

[WHETHER SOME FORM OF GOVERNMENT COULD HAVE BEEN DEVISED IN ROME THAT MIGHT HAVE AVOIDED HOSTILITY BETWEEN THE PEOPLE AND THE SENATE]

1 I believe it is true that once the Romans wanted to use the common people for military service, as they were obliged to do by the small number of Patricians, and since they wanted to use their own armed forces, it was necessary to keep them satisfied. The Patricians' unwillingness to do so caused many uprisings and much turbulence, for they neither would admit them into the government nor refrain from the abuses that gave the Plebeians cause to desire participation in it. For the Patricians had possession of public properties and were very strict about collecting debts, and we can assume that in all other matters justice was not equal, that it was partial to the group that had all the authority in its hands. 2 But I do say that if in the early stages of freedom there had not been a distinction between Patricians and Plebs, as the Fourth Discourse mentions, or if at the outset they had shared public offices, as was later done of necessity, then there would not have been the uprisings and the turbulence among them, which ceased as soon as the Plebeians got a share in government until the time of the Gracchi. Then, when the city was already corrupt, turbulence broke out because of new feelings and causes that no longer involved the Plebeians' being against the Patricians, but the lower class against the richer and more powerful, among whom were numbered many Plebeian families who had earlier been raised by public office to the rank of Patricians. 3 I say further that had the Patricians, without entirely sharing the government with the Plebeians, been able to deal with the abuses, and had they opened the way for Ple-

beian leaders to become Patricians at certain times, perhaps there would not have been uprisings. For experience showed that in the laws proposed by Publius Sextius, the Plebeians were satisfied by provisions concerning debts and property and they did not care about public office.[1] The Plebeians' leaders who longed to govern but could not get it by other means, however, denied the Plebeians any hope of obtaining one without the other. 4 Therefore I do not see why it was impossible for the Romans to organize their government for there not to be these uprisings and this turbulence between the Senate and the Plebeians. On the contrary, I deem it would have been quite easy and, since it could have been done, we cannot praise those defects in government that caused the city to remain filled with uprisings and turbulence and to create the Tribunes. Once peace was restored to the city, that office, armed with so many powers, did more harm than good.

NOTES

1. See note 5 to Machiavelli, 1, 5; the consul in question is Lucius, not Publius, Sextius.

~ *1:7* ~

[HOW ESSENTIAL INDICTMENTS ARE TO MAINTAINING FREEDOM IN A REPUBLIC]

1 It is very true that it is quite useful, indeed almost essential, for there to be easy ways in a city to prosecute bad citizens legally and judicially, particularly any who plot against the government. But it is also necessary to be careful that they are set up in such a way that innocent people are not easily bothered or punished. 2 For aside from being unjust, it is also destructive to the city, since if this danger goes against Nobility and the upper classes and they live under this continual suspicion, they necessarily become discontented. Discontentment among the most powerful becomes dangerous to republics in many ways. Although wrongful accusation of a citizen is in itself insignificant, it gains significance because of the fear it inspires in others, as was seen with Alcibiades and was almost seen when Themistocles was unjustly expelled from Athens; and Rome felt this with Coriolanus.[1]

3 It is therefore necessary to be quite cautious on this point; in my opinion it is too dangerous to let the people be the judge of indictments; they do not understand or investigate matters well, and they are easily stirred up by false rumors and slander. 4 It is also inappropriate for such authority to rest with a few citizens, because if they are elected by a small group, they become too powerful; if they are elected by greater numbers, they act too circumspectly. In fact, the judges should be numerous, that is to say, more than fifty. 5 And certainly the model of the Florentine *Quarantia* was not ill-considered if many of its poorly designed features had been modified.[2] 6 To

see that it is not good to make the people the judges for indictments, aside from the reasons cited above, one must consider that often citizens who wish to aggrandize their position make their way by means of the people; that is, they propose things to please the masses. Because the latter consider surface and rank, not the end being sought, they are led into servitude before they notice where they have been taken, so it is impossible to prosecute such men by means of the people. The Gracchi are an example: they were authors of seditious laws and, making their way toward stripping the Senate of its authority, they could be prosecuted only against the will of the people. Similarly with Manlius Capitolinus, against whom a Dictator had to be appointed because, until his intrigue to make himself king was revealed, the people followed him.[3]

7 Therefore a republic must be so constituted that either indictments are adjudicated by different men in accordance with the differing laws and feelings within a city, or the men assigned to adjudicate are commingled so as to have a mixture suitable for every type of crime. I would caution against restricting their number to too few, while selecting them as carefully as possible and drawing them from the middle rather than either extreme.

NOTES

1. Alcibiades (c. 450–404 B.C.) was an Athenian general and statesman and friend of Socrates; he was accused of religious profanation, but later restored his good name. Themistocles (c. 528–462 B.C.) was an Athenian statesman who led the democratic faction; he lost his support during the struggles with Sparta and was accused of involvement in the treason of Pausanias; around 471 he was banished from Athens for a ten-year period. See *Discourses,* 1, 7, n.3, for Coriolanus.

2. Piero Soderini, taking his cue from a Venetian institution, established the *Quarantia,* a board of forty judges convened on an *ad hoc* basis to hear cases of alleged serious crimes against the government, ones not under the purview of *Otto di guardia e di balìa* (Council of Eight of Guard).

3. See note 2 to Guicciardini's *Consideration* of *Discourses,* 1, 5, for the Gracchi and Manlius Capitolinus.

~ *1:8* ~

[SLANDER IS AS HARMFUL TO A REPUBLIC AS INDICTMENTS ARE USEFUL]

1 The conclusion that slanders are despicable is correct, but they are so natural in a free city that it is difficult and perhaps impossible to eliminate them. For when a false charge arises against a citizen, as it can both through the malice of its authors and by error, how can we prevent it from spreading through the masses, which are more disposed to believe evil than good? 2 Besides, there is no lack of people to fan the flames of rumors through

either hatred or envy. So in Rome, where the route to indictment was so easy and broad, how many false charges were made against citizens? 3 As an example there was Fabius Maximus along with many others.[1] Neither can those who wrongly slander always be indicted or punished, nor can a form of republic be created otherwise than on paper that so promptly thwarts all illegal acts. 4 Hence among all free peoples there have been and always will be no lack of slanderers; it suffices that false slanders often die out by themselves with time and the truth. 5 Nor will indignation at being slandered ever move a serious citizen to cause an uprising against a republic. Though he may be indignant against someone who he thinks was the author of the slander, he is also indignant, and even more so against anyone who has wrongfully indicted him. 6 But private indignations never cause significant disorders in a city that is well governed in other respects. Nor do slanders which are put down when they are scandalous, like that of Manlius Capitolinus, who sought to arouse the Plebs against the Senate; if they are not scandalous they can be ignored, because they die out of their own accord. 7 And the example of Cosimo de' Medici, who figures without being named in his Discourse, is nonsense. The road to power was opened for him not by slanders but by his shrewdness[2] and principally his immense wealth; because the government of Florence was highly disorganized and full of sedition by its own nature, it was easy for Cosimo to bribe citizens and to proceed toward tyranny by fomenting divisions in the city and becoming the leader of one faction. 8 And because there is not adequate material to prove the conclusion of the Discourse, the example of messer Giovanni Guicciardini was trumped up. It is true that he was unjustly slandered and that, since the courts were in a state of confusion, he had no way to prove his innocence through them, though he did everything in his power, to the point even of voluntarily incarcerating himself. Yet the divisions within the city did not originate in this slander of him, nor were they increased by it. On the contrary, dissension among the citizens fanned the flames of his case and made it more significant than it would have been normally.[3]

NOTES

1. Based on an incident in Plutarch, *Fabius Maximus,* 7: because of slanders against Fabius Maximus, Hannibal called off a plundering raid on the territory of the Roman dictator in Campania.

2. Translates *prudenza* because here the context requires something other than "prudence" or "wisdom."

3. In his *Oratio defensoria,* written in 1527 as a response to an imaginary accuser, Guicciardini points out that his ancestor was acquitted of all charges; see also Machiavelli, *Florentine Histories,* 4, 25, cited above in 1, 8, n.9.

~ *1:9* ~

[IT TAKES ONE SINGLE MAN TO ORGANIZE A REPUBLIC AFRESH OR TO REFORM IT COMPLETELY, DISREGARDING ITS FORMER INSTITUTIONS]

1 There is no doubt that one single man can organize matters better than many and that in a disordered city a man deserves praise if, when he is unable to reorganize it in any other way, he does so by violence or deception and extreme means. 2 But pray God there should be no need to restore republics in such a way because, aside from the fact that men's minds are false (and a man might become a tyrant under the guise of honesty), there is also danger that an intention that was good at the outset can become evil. Because someone who does this cannot relinquish his authority as soon as the laws have been formulated, since once laws are ushered in violently they would immediately be annulled. Therefore he has to stay in power long enough for the passage of time and experience to stabilize them, and during this period it is possible for the sweetness of power and the unbridled power to rule to change his initial good intentions into evil ones.[1] 3 This sort of medicine is desirable, therefore, only if there is no other hope for cure, but it is dangerous and sets a bad example. And a man who does not retain authority for himself, except as long as it is necessary for stabilizing what he has organized (like Lycurgus or anyone else who might be cited as an example), is most highly worthy of praise. 4 But I do not know how much someone who retains power as long as he lives, even if he governs uprightly and leaves a good form of government as his legacy, should be praised, because he can be considered only as one motivated by personal ambition. Although what he has achieved may be useful to the city and he is not to be despised, like someone who misuses the power he has seized, still even he is worthy of every reproach. 5 As for what the Discourse states about Romulus, that since he formed a senate he acted for the common good and not out of personal ambition, I shall say nothing else for now, because it is necessary first to read and consider the life of Romulus, who, if I recall correctly, feared that he would be slain by the Senate for taking too much power for himself: that must be considered carefully.[2]

NOTES

1. An assertion similar to Lord Acton's: "Power tends to corrupt and absolute power corrupts absolutely"; see his letter to Bishop Mandell Creighton, 5 April 1887. In his *Ricordi* Guicciardini elaborates on this point: "Were all men good and prudent, it would be appropriate for those in legitimate power over others to be gentle rather than severe. But because most men are either none too good or none too prudent, one needs to rely more on severity. Whoever thinks otherwise deceives himself. I readily grant that whoever can successfully mix and blend one with the other would create a wondrous accord and harmony than which nothing could be sweeter. But heaven allots these boons to few—perhaps to no one" (C. 41). Man's evil nature is a theme in Q-2. 15, and B. 12, 85, 119, 120, and 150.

2. Guicciardini is probably referring to Plutarch, *Romulus,* 26.3–8, but Livy, 1.8.7, mentions that Romulus appointed one hundred senators. The traditional story of his death, which Plutarch also gives, involves an apotheosis: Romulus vanished mysteriously during a storm after reigning for forty years (Livy, 1.16.1–2) and ascended to heaven, where he became the god Quirinus, part of a ruling triumvirate with Mars and Jupiter.

~ *1:10* ~

[THE FOUNDERS OF A REPUBLIC OR A KINGDOM ARE WORTHY OF PRAISE, BUT THOSE OF A TYRANNY ARE WORTHY OF SHAME]

1 The title of this Discourse is quite right, for the founders of kingdoms and republics deserve the highest praise and the founders of tyrannies the highest blame. 2 But because cases vary and the author mixes examples together, we must consider that it rarely happens that a man who seizes tyrannical power in a free country does so out of such need; if he does, it is rare for him not have some responsibility for it, so he remains tinged with some sort of justification. 3 And this kind of man, one of whom was Caesar, full of many other kinds of *virtù* but driven by ambition for complete control, is certainly quite monstrous and despicable. 4 It is true that sometimes the forms of freedom are so disorganized and cities so rife with civil unrest that necessity leads some citizens, who are unable to save themselves otherwise, either to seek tyrannical power or to side with someone else who does. 5 In this case anyone who put love of country before his personal safety would be worthy of great praise. But because this love or strength is more often wished for than to be found in men, one can readily excuse someone who is inspired by such a motive; the more so if the government he opposes is disorganized, because many things called freedom often are not. 6 One might cite the example of our city in which, after the change of government in '26,[1] several good and well-qualified citizens were persecuted and oppressed and finally, upon the arrival of the prince of Orange,[2] required either to disobey orders given by the Eight, to remain in Florence under penalty of sedition, or to stay there at the risk of being slaughtered or at least with the certainty of being detained as suspects. 7 Necessity led them either to wish for the change of a government that under the name of freedom is tyrannical and destructive of their city or to let themselves be deprived of their city and their possessions in silence and with the greatest injustice. 8 Consequently, anyone who is the author of tyranny in a free city and does so out of a desire for complete control, deserves the deepest censure. Caesar, Phalaris, Pisistratus, and others like them were such men: one more infamous than the next, as they used their tyrannical power more or less ruthlessly and as they were graced more or less with other kinds of *virtù*.

9 The other case is when men inherit tyrannical power: they deserve less blame for remaining in power than those who have founded it from the outset.

And if they renounced it, they would deserve all the more praise, since they are less obligated to undo the sin of usurping it. 10 There are very few, perhaps none, who have relinquished a tyranny without being forced to, nor is that surprising, since a man who is brought up under tyranny has no eyes to recognize what glory can be gained by liberating one's native land. He does not consider this possibility with the same enthusiasm as private citizens because, accustomed to that way of life, he judges that the highest good lies in power; because he is unaware of the fruits of glory, no other reason can convince him to renounce tyranny. 11 Aside from that, danger may stop him even if he were willing, since it is difficult for tyrannical power to have been acquired and retained without many enemies and without harming many people; hence, retiring to private life or leaving one's sons as private citizens seems dangerous, especially since people are ungrateful and new freedoms are generally full of disorder. 12 And if Sulla did so, that is a very rare example.[3] He was able to act more with greater security, because the government remained in the hands of men from his faction so that not only was he secure while he lived but also, once he died, his acts were preserved and his memory revered.

13 The case of those who are kings and princes, whether created legitimately as were the kings of Sparta and the first Roman kings or considered legitimate through the passage of time, is different. 14 Among them, if they have absolute authority, a few can be found who govern justly, so they deserve to be called good princes, but I know of none who created such perfect laws in their kingdom as there deservedly ought to be, that is, who organized it in such a way that neither their children nor their next of kin inherited the rule, but succession was by election. 15 And if any kingdom ever had this institution, I believe that it was kept there more by some necessity than by the will of the ruler, because the love that fathers bear their children is too great and that which leads people to bequeath an illustrious reputation for their house is of no small account, either.

16 Hence these ideas, that tyrants should give up their power and kings should organize their kingdoms carefully, denying succession to their posterity, are more easily depicted in books and in men's imaginations than carried out in fact. Indeed, though private citizens have often discussed these ideas, actual examples of them are rare; hence, those who do not do such things deserve less censure, since there are very few, perhaps none, who have done so.[4]

NOTES

1. Guicciardini refers to the events in Florence of May 1527; he dates events according to the old calendar and hence says 1526. Once the news that the imperial army of Charles V had sacked Rome reached Florence, Silvio Passerini, the cardinal of Cortona, Pope Clement VII's governor in Florence, fled the city along with the teenage representatives of Medici power, Alessandro and Ippolito de' Medici. Thus control of the city reverted to the anti-Medici faction led by Niccolò Capponi and

Filippo Strozzi; they were behind the Last Republic in power from 1527 to 1530 in Florence. See above, 1, 7, n.8 concerning the Eight.

2. In 1529 Pope Clement VII shifted his allegiance to Charles V and concluded the Treaty of Barcelona, one of whose provisions turned control of the cities of Italy, including Florence, over to Philibert de Chalon (1502–1530), prince of Orange, one of the emperor's most distinguished commanders. Attempting to assert imperial control of Florence in 1529, Philibert laid siege to the city on 24 October. The siege was not lifted until August 1530, but Philibert was killed earlier that summer. Thus, we have a *terminus a quo* for these "Considerations." Because they were probably written in 1530, there may be some reason to believe that self-justification motivates the conclusion Guicciardini draws in the next sentence. Fearing confiscation of his "possessions," Guicciardini went into voluntary exile, because he had sided with the "tyrannnical and destructive" Medici and rejected the "freedom" of the short-lived Florentine republic.

3. Sulla, often cited as a typical example of a Roman dictator, ruled Rome from 82 to 79 B.C. He frequently used cruel, extralegal means; he proscribed many of his opponents, most of whom were killed, after he initiated a policy of using military force against the state during a civil war. He relinquished his powers, retired to private life in 79, and died the following year.

4. Guicciardini's concluding paragraph typifies his stance with respect to Machiavelli. His is a realistic assessment of Machiavelli's conclusion, especially his penultimate sentence, to which Guicciardini directly alludes in his own penultimate sentence.

~ 1:11 ~

[ON THE RELIGION OF THE ROMANS]

1 It is certain that arms and religion are the principal foundations of republics and kingdoms and so necessary that if either is missing one can say that vital, substantial parts are missing; but I do not really know if it is true that if we had to argue which prince Rome was most indebted to, Romulus or Numa, Numa would deserve the higher praise or that Numa's difficulties were greater. Rather, I would incline toward the opposite view, and it seems to me that can be shown by a quite compelling reason. If the first king of Rome had been Numa and not Romulus, certainly the city would have been threatened in its beginnings by its neighbors and Numa would not have left room for Romulus to put armies in, as Romulus allowed Numa to put religion in. 2 Therefore Romulus was more essential to Rome's beginnings than Numa. 3 Furthermore, as the writer also says, those were times when religious feeling was high in Rome's neighboring cities too; consequently, with them as example and analogy, it was easy to dispose the Roman people to it. 4 The truth of this is shown by the fact that after Romulus's death the still very savage and warlike people willingly elected as king not a bellicose man or one used to commanding armies; they wanted instead to have a king venerated for

justice, religion, and the arts of peace: because they had nobody like that in Rome, they went and got him from the neighboring cities. This clearly demonstrates that the Romans themselves tended to want to organize their religion and good laws dealing with the arts of peace so that Numa found men already disposed to accept good laws. 5 And certainly either the wisdom or the fortune of the Romans, or both together, were admirable, because their first two kings were quite outstanding, one in the arts of war, the other in those of peace, and because their first one was warlike, since through arms he endowed the new city with such life, it could await Numa and someone to organize it with religion.

~ 1:12 ~

[HOW IMPORTANT IT IS TO TAKE RELIGION INTO ACCOUNT; AND SINCE, THANKS TO THE ROMAN CHURCH, ITALY HAS LACKED IT, SHE IS IN SHAMBLES]

1 It is impossible to speak so much ill of the papal court that it does not deserve worse: it is a disgrace, an example of all the ignominy and opprobrium in the world.[1] 2 And I also believe it is true that the Church's greatness, that is, the power that religion has given it, has been the reason why Italy has not fallen into a monarchy, because on the one hand it has had such influence that it has been able to become the leader and summon foreign princes when necessary against those who were going to attack Italy, and on the other hand, since the Church lacked its own armies, it did not have enough forces to enable it to establish temporal dominion aside from what others were willing to grant it. 3 But I do not really know whether Italy's not coming under a monarchy has been fortunate or unfortunate for this land. For if this might have brought glory to the name of Italy and good fortune to the city that dominated, it would have been disastrous for all the others: oppressed by the shadow of one, they would have had no means of achieving any greatness whatever, since it is the custom of republics not to share the fruits of their freedom and power with any but their own citizens.

4 Even if an Italy divided into many dominions has at various times suffered many calamities that she might not have suffered under a single dominion, although barbarian invasions were more frequent during the Roman Empire than at any time,[2] nevertheless, during every one of these periods Italy has had so many flourishing cities that she would not have had under one republic that I deem a monarchy would have been more unfortunate than fortunate for her. 5 This reason does not hold for a kingdom that is more common to all its subjects; thus we see France and many other countries living happily under one king. However, as a result either of some destiny of Italy or the nature of its people, having such a temper that they are intelligent and warlike, this country has never been easy to bring under one power, even

when the Church was not there. Rather, it has always naturally desired freedom,[3] and I do not believe a record exists of any other power having been able to possess it entirely except the Romans, who subjugated it through great *virtù* and violence, and when the republic died and the emperors lacked *virtù*, they easily lost power over Italy. 6 Therefore, if the church of Rome has been opposed to monarchy, I do not readily concur that was unfortunate for this country, since it has preserved her in a way of life that is most harmonious with her very ancient customs and tendencies.

NOTES

1. Guicciardini can be strongly anticlerical: "I do not know who can loathe the ambition, avarice, and sensuality of the clergy more than I do," though, alluding to Popes Leo X and Clement VII, he does note that "the position I have had under several popes has obliged me, in my own interest, to take pleasure in their greatness." Otherwise, "I should have loved Martin Luther as myself" and rejoiced "to see this bunch of villains get their just deserts, that is, to be either without vices or without power." (*Ricordi,* C. 28; see also B. 124). It was the arrival of the Dominican preacher Johann Tetzel in Saxony during the fall of 1517 to proclaim Pope Leo X's indulgence for the construction of Saint Peter's Church in Rome that goaded Martin Luther into posting his ninety-five theses on the doors of the castle church in Wittemberg. Although calls for the reform of the Roman Catholic Church were widespread before 1517, Machiavelli was certainly working on *The Discourses* then and Guicciardini's *ricordo* was written within a decade of this event too.

2. Vivanti points out in his edition of the *Discorsi* that the barbarian invasions occurred principally at the end of the Roman Empire before Italy was divided into smaller states and kingdoms

3. One of Guicciardini's basic assumptions, reiterated in the last sentence and again in the third paragraph of his comment on 1, 16, is this natural desire for freedom among the Italian peoples, inherited from their Roman ancestors.

~ 1:14 ~

[THE ROMANS INTERPRETED OMENS ACCORDING TO NEED AND PRUDENTLY MADE A PRACTICE OF OBSERVING RELIGION, BUT THEY DID NOT OBSERVE IT IF NECESSARY; AND IF ANYONE RASHLY DISPARAGED IT THEY PUNISHED HIM]

1 I am not sure that military commanders used the authority of omens and auguries shrewdly, but I do believe that their minds were filled with religion, especially during the early periods. And I am not troubled by the example of Papirius, since, after receiving the report from the *pullarii* who were responsible for it, he did not have to pay any attention to what was reported to him by a third party.

~ 1:16 ~

[PEOPLE WHO ARE ACCUSTOMED TO LIVING UNDER A PRINCE FIND IT DIFFICULT TO HOLD ONTO THEIR FREEDOM IF THEY ARE SET FREE BY SOME EVENT]

1 I make a very great distinction in this Discourse between people who have never known freedom and those who have been free at some point but have lost their freedom through some event. For in that case the institutions of freedom can be recovered more easily if someone who has experienced them is still alive and many reminders of the former republic remain. 2 The desire for freedom burns all the more brightly in the hearts of men when they have experienced the evils of tyranny, and even more if it did not fall into their hands because the line of tyrants died out but because, impelled by the bitterness of servitude, they have regained it by dint of arms. 3 These love freedom more than people who have never known it and also are more likely to take up a republic's institutions again, and the body[1] is also readier for it, since in a city that has always had a prince there is great inequality between one citizen and another, which is completely opposed to the freedoms under which men are quite equal. 4 But in a princedom some men are very great, others small, because the prince, out of either need or similarity of spirit, has a circle of men who are almost closer to the prince than they are to ordinary citizens.

5 This inequality is therefore quite unconducive to freedom in people who have always had a princedom; it cannot exist in a city that has not known very lengthy servitude. For generally a man who usurps freedoms in order to make people less desperate and to cause less upheaval retains the appearance of freedom as much as he can and, on the surface, devises a way to govern a tyranny in the manner of a republic; thus the equality of citizens is not eliminated entirely. 6 Do not bring up as evidence to the contrary the Romans, who adapted very well to freedom even though they had never known it, because they changed nothing of the institutions that existed under the kings, aside from transferring the kings' power to the consuls; if the institutions were good, that came not so much from wisdom as from good fortune, because the monarchical institutions were such as to serve freedom too; and the creation of the consuls is not believed to have been their invention but one learned from commentaries by Servius Tullius.[2] 7 This is shown to be true, because as time went on, constrained by necessity and instructed by experience, they created the other institutions necessary for the preservation of freedom and order in the city. 8 And the Romans did not lack that other spur to the desire for freedom, namely, having endured the outrages of tyranny, because they were stirred up by no other occasion or event than having experienced very bitter servitude under Tarquin. 9 And it is even less surprising for them to have been disposed to freedom because in those days almost all the neighboring peoples were free; these examples move and inflame men a great deal.

10 Thus it is difficult to preserve newly acquired freedom and far more difficult for people who have been in continuous servitude than for those who have at some point been free. There is no better remedy for preserving it than organizing a government so balanced that, on the one hand, it is swift to crush those who plot against freedom and, on the other, it is safe for those who wish to live properly. It should not be inclined to persecute the rich and powerful when they give no cause for it or averse to welcoming those citizens who have been friends to tyranny, if either their behavior or the rank they have offers hope that they will not be enemies of freedom. 11 Because it often happens, as we in Florence have seen from experience,[3] that when the government succeeding a tyranny is reasonable, well organized, and safe for everyone, those who were able to be happy under the tyrants are happy under it, especially in those cities that naturally have an appetite for freedom. For those who have been favored, if they find they have fair opportunities, as they most often do, and perhaps have recognized the annoyances of servitude more closely than other people, are happy to rest and enjoy what is theirs once they find security and equal rank with the other citizens. 12 And assuring men in this way pacifies and unites the city, whereas if they are kept under suspicion and harassed it cannot enjoy peace and quiet whether they remain inside it or are driven out.

13 So a republic should be organized in such a way as to be prompt in punishing those who plot against the state; it should be strict and inexorable in this, reprimanding as quite serious offenses even those that seem slight. But it should hound no one out of mere suspicion nor hold suspect either those men who have held rank under the tyrant or those who are naturally restless, those who have fallen on hard times, or those who are so constituted that they cannot hope for any rank except under the tyrant. 14 It should especially make certain that discord does not develop in the city, as it does every time a government is not well organized, because when there is discord the party that has less power rushes over to the tyrant even if it was his enemy. 15 Those were the reasons that brought the Medici back to Florence in '12, not through their former friends but through many who had been their enemies, and the bitter, indiscriminate persecution after '26 of those who had been their friends made many people wish for the Medici's return, which they would otherwise have abhorred no less than the rest of the people. 16 The new freedom should not want there to be sons of Brutus, that is, men who plot against the state so as to have a reason for developing prestige and terror through its severity. For although it is necessary to dip one's hands in blood in such cases, it would have been better not to have had to and for Brutus not to have sons than to have them only to be slaughtered. 17 It should not consider as sons of Brutus any but those who are naturally restless and rapacious and who are unable by nature to find a place in freedom, because these are the ones who are dangerous, not those who are naturally adaptable in mind and rank, who can hope to savor the fruits of freedom along with others.

18 As for a prince who has the people as his enemy, since he, too, is referred to in this Discourse, I say that if they are enemies because of the harshness and bitterness of servitude then it is easy to deal with them by doing away with abuses and governing justly and humanely. But if the root of enmity is the desire for freedom—as we have seen our Florentines, who wanted to be free in order to have a share of the public offices, to have a hand in the government—then no kindness, no gentleness, no good treatment from the tyrant is likely to eradicate this desire, and the tyrant can never trust them no matter how well he treats them. 19 It is indeed true that when men in addition to being deprived of freedom are also mistreated they fall into despair, and a desperate man does not wait for opportunities but seeks them out; he will put himself at any risk to gain his freedom. Whereas those who have no other anguish than the desire for freedom do not hasten but wait for opportunities, and when they come, it is of no use to the tyrant to him to have behaved well and governed kindly and acted like Clearchus. It is naive to believe that he slaughtered the aristocrats in order to satisfy the people, because had they been his friends little would have been gained; but because he was suspicious of them and wanted to crush them, he acted as if he were doing it to please the people. 20 Therefore a prince's remedy is either to get the kind of partisans for himself who are powerful enough to crush the people or to subdue and destroy the people so that they cannot rise up and bring in new inhabitants such as have no reason to desire freedom.

NOTES

1. In his edition of the *Discorsi,* Vivanti glosses "body" *(materia)* as "human material," i.e., "the social structure," "the body politic"; see above, 1, 17, n.2.

2. Servius Tullius is credited with a series of constitutional reforms, though some argue that even these are trumped-up precedents for reforms granted the plebs in the fourth century B.C. Following a tradition established by Plutarch, *Moralia, de fortuna Romanorum,* Guicciardini frequently credits "good fortune" and chance as significant components of Rome's success. Machiavelli discusses this issue in *Discourses,* 2, 1, though Guicciardini writes no *Consideration* of it.

3. Guicciardini refers to the expulsion of the Medici in 1526.

~ *1:23* ~

[ONE SHOULD NEVER RISK ONE'S ENTIRE FORTUNE AND NOT ONE'S ENTIRE ARMY, SO DEFENDING PASSES IS OFTEN HARMFUL]

1 From the conclusion drawn by the Discourse, although it is quite true, I do not believe that we can criticize the course of action that the Albans and the Romans agreed to take. For although both of them risked their entire fortune and not their entire army, we must consider that what each of them reduced for himself was also taken from his partner so that the loss and gain were equal; when the stakes are even, they are hard to criticize. 2 For instance, had the Ro-

mans fought with part of their army against the entire Alban army, it would have been unwise, but because they had reduced the Albans' army equally, they remained just as powerful fighting with part of their army against an equal part of the enemy's army as if they had fought each other with their entire army. 3 And it must be considered that although the blood relationship that was alleged between the two peoples[1] led them to contend for power in such a peaceful way so as not to destroy each other completely and because neither expected mischief from the other, still it is believable that the principal reason was their recognition that their armies were equal so that it was difficult to judge which side was more likely to win if they had fought normally. 4 If one of them had thought it had an advantage, it seems likely that it would have been neither so good-hearted nor so unwise as to accept that course of action. And, assuming such equality, I do not see how this decision, not merely between related peoples but even between alien peoples—namely, to try and find which side ought to have dominion without all the killing and destruction that wars produce—can be blamed. 5 And although putting oneself in such imminent jeopardy by depriving oneself of the power to recover, to vie with fortune, may seem too bold, still there is the compensation that the exact same conditions are on the other side; so if it makes it easier for you to lose, it also makes it easier for you to win.

6 As for not opposing an enemy in Alpine passes, I think it is a matter that needs sound consideration and a good eye. For the site can be such that one may reasonably hope to hold the pass or at least lose it with little harm to yourself and great harm to your enemies. The enemy can also be in such a situation that robbing him of time is quite important and opposing him in a mountain pass has the effect of at least forcing him to stay there for many days, as we read about Titus Quinctius in Macedonia[2] and other commanders. 6 And in each of these cases I think the one who attempted this defense was worthy of praise. We read that great men have done this in the mountains and along rivers, which is almost the same thing. In our day Gonzalo Fernandez defeated the French by placing himself at a ford on the Garigliano;[3] in Livy, Scipio criticized Antiochus for not trying to prevent the Romans from crossing the Hellespont.[4] 7 The commander must be experienced and has to consider carefully the site and the nature of both the enemy and his own army. To be sure, it is easy for him to determine whether the place is such that one can be attacked there and whether it is suitable for large offensive and defensive forces, because the same difficulties, both that many cannot stay in narrow places and the lack of food supplies, may militate against those trying to pass as well as those trying to prevent it. 8 And even if they should pass through at other locations, as the French did in 1515,[5] it does the defender no harm because he does not come in contact with the enemy and because he is not deprived of the opportunity to carry out the same defenses in the plains that he could have carried out to begin with, as the Swiss did. And it was not this problem, which has little effect on military men, nor demoralization, which does not move anyone who has not pinned all his hopes on mountains, but other disorders, disorders among themselves, that made not all but only part of them do battle with the king at Marignano. Had they all fought there, perhaps they would not have been the losers.

9 So a commander should see whether he has means enough to hope to be able to hold a pass against the enemy, because being able to block the entire opposing army with part of your own is a very safe course of action. 10 Let him see whether at least it is important to make the enemy lose time. If he hopes for one or the other, as can easily occur and I believe examples may be found everywhere, the commander will be praised for opposing the enemy in mountain passes. 11 He should also consider whether he has more confidence in his own army than he has fear of his enemies' in the open field. He should reach his decision according to these considerations; he should not take any account of the example of the Romans cited in this Discourse. In addition to other reasons that may perhaps have made them decide not to attempt such a defense, the impossibility of doing so also contributed to it, because they were not masters either of the Alps that Hannibal crossed over or of a wide area of the surrounding plains. It would have been a very unwise course of action to lead the army into a place where they would have had to fight the local inhabitants as well as the enemy, where they would lack food supplies and where all the other difficulties were still left. 12 Indeed, this example can be turned around: because during his crossing of the Alps Hannibal had suffered so much harm as a result of the local inhabitants' raids, how much more would he probably have suffered had he encountered the Romans' resistance there as well!

13 The reason why few commanders have stationed themselves to block the crossing of mountain passes is not that they did not want to risk their entire fortune with part of their army, which should not be avoided when so many other advantages combine to compensate for the army they lack, but because it is difficult to do so.

NOTES

1. Livy alludes to the Trojan War background of the early history of Rome in 1.3. Ascanius, the son of the Trojan hero Aeneas, accompanied his father on their escape from Troy. Once they landed in Italy, Ascanius founded the city of Alba Longa. Legend had it that the last Alban king, Numitor, had a daughter, the vestal Rhea Silvia, who had twin sons, Romulus and Remus, fathered by Mars. After the brothers decided to found a city on the Tiber, which eventually became Rome, they fought and Remus was killed. To obtain women for the city, the Albans carried off the Sabine women and fought a war with the Sabines. Eventually the two peoples were joined and formed Rome's early population.

2. During the Second Macedonian War (200–197 B.C.) Philip V briefly hemmed in a Roman army led by Titus Quinctius Flamininus in the mountains of Epirus.

3. Similarly, during the disputes between King Louis XII of France and Ferdinand of Aragon, the king of Spain, over conflicting claims on the kingdom of Naples, the great Spanish general Gonzalo Fernández de Córdoba hemmed the French in at Montecassino and won decisively at the Battle of the Garigliano, 28 December 1503.

4. Livy, 37.36.

5. See Machiavelli, 1, 23, n.5; Guicciardini deals with this material in his *Storia d'Italia,* 13. 12.

~ 1:24 ~

[WELL-ORGANIZED REPUBLICS ESTABLISH REWARDS ANDPUNISHMENTS FOR THEIR CITIZENS AND NEVER OFFSET ONE WITH THE OTHER]

1 It can perhaps be said of Horatius that he was acquitted not so much out of consideration for his merits as because it did not seem wrong to slay a sister who complained about something that brought the country salvation and freedom and insulted her brother who was the author of so much good. If we understand it that way, it is not surprising that he was brought to trial, since murder required acquittal by the public, not by private citizens. 2 Nevertheless, the truth appears to be that slaying her was a crime, because if she had done wrong it was not up to private citizens but to the magistrates to punish her, and the memory of his merits brought about the acquittal of Horatius, especially considering that she had given him some cause for it by spoiling such a fine victory for him with her tears and complaints. 3 And in this case there were all these factors coming into play: that the murder was not premeditated but was done in very justifiably provoked anger by a youth angered during the celebration of so fine a victory, that it had outraged only her father and themselves, that since the merits of Horatius were so great and so recent, it would have been more reprehensible for the Roman people to condemn him than it was to acquit him. 4 Not because it is good to make it a rule to compensate evil with good, which, as the Discourse states, would be destructive, but because where there are so many contributing factors, it is quite proper to depart from the rule and set an example, not for someone who wants indiscriminately to balance merits with sins, but for someone who has to judge, so he can balance them when there are as many contributing factors as there were in the case of Horatius.

~ 1:25 ~

[ANYONE WHO WANTS TO REFORM AN OUTMODED GOVERNMENT IN A FREE CITY SHOULD RETAIN AT LEAST THE GHOST OF FORMER WAYS]

1 This Discourse's conclusion is more essential for someone who does not change the type of government but reforms it, for example, someone who wants to introduce new institutions in a free city, than it is for someone who changes the type of government. Because if I introduce freedom after monarchy as the Romans did, and men have already come to the opinion that the society is not good, then there is no need to preserve the former institutions so exactly. 2 And the examples of the lictors and the "king for sacrifices" are of no great significance, because in one case there was respect for a superstition that

men might have in their religion, and in the other case it would have been intolerable for them to provide the Consuls with the regalia of greater power after they changed the royal power because it was excessive.[1]

NOTES

1. Guicciardini, on the origin of political power, notes that "states cannot be held according to good conscience because, if you consider their origin, they all originate in violence—except for republics within, but not beyond, their own lands. I do not exempt the emperor from this rule or even less priests, whose violence is twofold: the force they use against us consists of both temporal and spiritual weapons" (C. 48; see also B. 95). Guicciardini's word for "states" is *stati,* which may convey in this context the sense of political power, government—even territory.

~ *1:26* ~

[A NEW PRINCE IN A CITY OR A REGION THAT HE HAS TAKEN MUST MAKE EVERYTHING NEW]

1 There are some cities or monarchies that take little account of the changing of their princes: they are also not accustomed to being governed so legitimately that they cannot tolerate a prince who rules with little concern for politics.[1] 2 In places of this kind, strong measures for founding a princedom are unnecessary; if there are some individuals unhappy with the change, a wise prince has many ways to win them over, as long as this dissatisfaction is based on concern for their self-interest, because he has plenty of means—favors and public offices—to satisfy men. 3 But the difficulty arises where the people's inclination is totally against the new government, as it is in cities accustomed to freedom when they come under a tyrant and as in kingdoms that have been under one dynasty for a very long time and have general respect for that family's name and memory. Of course, one can hope to win these over with good treatment and eventually make them forget the memory of their previous rulers. 4 But treating well those who have an inclination toward freedom is not an adequate measure, because no gentleness can eradicate from their breasts the desire to govern and [not][2] to acknowledge a superior. Therefore a prince must use strong measures in such cases, keeping in mind, however, that he should win over the part that one may hope to win over with benefits, because if, on the one hand, violent measures give you security, on the other, they make for weakness in a thousand ways, especially for a prince who is not based on his own military power. 5 Hence a prince must have the courage to use these extraordinary means whenever it is necessary; nevertheless, he must be so prudent as not to let pass any opportunity that presents itself to stabilize his affairs with kindness and favors. He should thus not take what the writer says as an absolute rule, since he always shows excessive fondness for extraordinary and violent measures.[3]

NOTES

1. Translates *uno principe che domini poco politicamente.*

2. The editors of most Italian editions supply this "not."

3. Guicciardini's caveat may be sparked by one of Machiavelli's sentences (see above, 1, 26, n.5) or by remarks about Cesare Borgia in both *Prince* and *Descrizione del modo tenuto dal duca Valentino nello ammazzare Vitellozzo Vitelli, Oliverotto da Fermo, il signor Paolo e il duca di Gravina Orsini.* Despite his judgment here, Guicciardini seems willing to accept Machiavelli's argument while trying to restrict it to specific situations.

~ *1:28* ~

[HOW THE ROMANS WERE LESS UNGRATEFUL TOWARD THEIR CITIZENS THAN WERE THE ATHENIANS]

1 If Rome had never lost its freedom after the expulsion of the kings, we could perhaps agree with the reason considered in the Discourse for the Athenians' having been readier to attack their citizens than the Romans were. But if one considers that the Decemvirs[1] seized tyrannical power and held on to it until necessity forced them to give it up, one will say that this difference arose from some other basis, and especially if we remember that even during the period of recovery, in which the memory of injuries usually has a more terrible effect because it is still fresh, Rome acted quite humanely and with the greatest circumspection against the Decemvirs and their adherents. 2 So we must say that this either arose from the nature of the Romans, who did not have the fickleness characteristic of the Athenians, in common with the other Greeks; or else, as I believe, the cause was a difference in government. The Athenian government was totally popular, and public assemblies dealt with declarations of war, peace treaties, and other important decisions. But in Rome, although the people played their part, the Senate's power was great and the Plebeians were counterbalanced by the power of the Nobility; normally, apart from the naming of magistrates and the creation of new laws, the Senate dealt with serious matters and, although the Tribunes had power to bring them before the people, nevertheless, it was not exercised except when there was either great boldness or urgent reason.

3 Hence citizens in Athens could become powerful[2] through their skills[3] with the populace much more easily than in Rome, and in a totally popular government they could come under suspicion more easily and they could be attacked more easily and with less cause. 4 But in Rome the power of citizens was checked, since in order to maintain it they needed not only popular favor but also the Senate's consent; when citizens have less power there is less reason to suspect them. And when a government is mixed there is neither so much inclination nor such ease of attacking the powerful; although one Tribune could denounce them to the people in Rome, another Tribune could also oppose the denunciation and would perhaps do so if he saw it was slanderous. 5 Therefore

the character of the Roman government, more serious by nature, more temperate and more prudent than the Athenians', was the reason why citizens had a less open path to tyranny; consequently, there was less reason to suspect them, and also there could not be such means for attacking the powerful.

NOTES

1. The *Decemviri legibus scribundis* were ten patricians charged with preparing a new legal code when the Roman constitution was suspended, traditionally in 451 B.C. During their one-year tenure, the Decemvirate ruled Rome and revised its laws. The following year ten new Decemvirs were elected, of whom Appius Claudius is the best known. So as not to confuse Guicciardini's and Machiavelli's use of "the Ten" to refer to a Florentine council in later chapters, we translate "the Ten" in the context of Roman history as "Decemvirs" or "Decemvirate."

2. Translates *farsi grandi*.

3. Translates *arte*.

~ 1:29 ~

[WHICH IS MORE UNGRATEFUL, THE PEOPLE OR A PRINCE?]

1 Although ingratitude is sometimes shown out of avarice and sometimes out of suspicion, it can also be shown for other reasons, such as ignorance, and malice, which has its root in envy; and if we carefully consider all these sources, I do not think one is more foreign to the people than a prince. Quite the contrary. 2 Let us speak, as the writer says, of the ingratitude that is shown toward those who have taken care of public business. It is of two sorts: either not rewarding them according to their deserts or offending instead of remunerating them; the latter is more pernicious, the former is more common, and in neither will anyone who examines them carefully find the people less at fault than a prince but rather more in my opinion. 3 And first, concerning avarice, which very rarely causes ingratitude in anything other than reward, I think that if the people, who by instinct reward seldom and very little, are not very guilty of it princes are not very guilty of it either, because they have innumerable opportunities to reward men without dipping into their purses and also with things that they do not keep for themselves but are wont to give others. 4 Undoubtedly princes often neglect to reward someone who has served well out of avarice or an ungrateful nature (which is another cause that can be added to the above-mentioned ones). In comparison with rewards given by the people, the examples of princes who have rewarded are innumerable. 5 And the fact that the people often successively give public offices to their citizens when they have acted well should not be advanced in this respect, because it is done more out of a belief in or expectation of being well served by them than out of gratitude for the services rendered.[1]

6 As for suspicion, I think that the people normally grow suspicious much more easily and with less foundation than a prince, because they show less care and have fewer means to oppose a false slander. When they do start to grow suspicious, they dishonor without regard for the one they suspect, without the slightest craft or circumspection. Whereas a prince who is not completely injudicious sometimes goes on pretending, and if he avoids trusting in someone for those things that might harm him, he does not abstain from others,[2] taking care not to make him lose all hope. 7 There are certainly innumerable examples of both republics and princes that have shown ingratitude out of suspicion; and if Rome[3] erred less in this than other republics, it erred much more than the Discourse says, as will be stated below. The examples of Camillus and Scipio are not excusable on those grounds. 8 I do confess that in this case princes bite back harder because they resort to the knife and to forceful actions much more readily than the people do.

9 As for the other two headings, ignorance and malice based on envy, I think that the people are incomparably more ungrateful: both because they are distracted by various activities and for other reasons, they have less understanding, discrimination, and knowledge than does a prince. As for envy, it occurs more easily among the people, who generally are bothered by the least sign of outstanding greatness, be it birth, riches, *virtù,* or reputation. Nothing displeases them [more] than seeing other citizens have greater standing than they do, and they always desire to humble them. 10 It does not happen this way to a prince, for it does not happen that he shall envy someone who is inferior to him; therefore, if the greatness of others is not such as to breed suspicion in him, it will not bother him and he will not attack it out of such malice.

11 There remain the examples cited in the Discourse. What Mucianus did against Antonius Primus is not an example of a prince's ingratitude toward a subject but of two men who lived under a prince, each of whom seeks to get for himself the credit for what has been accomplished. That Vespasian made no arrangements did not arise from any suspicion that he had of Antonius Primus but from the fact that he did not like Antonius's insolent nature, and much more from the great regard that he had for Mucianus.[4] 12 Nor is the example of Gonzalo Fernández of any use to our discussion, because King Ferdinand could not be called ungrateful toward him, since he so rewarded him that from being a poor knight he came to have estates worth thirty thousand crowns.[5] If the king deprived him of rule over the kingdom, it was because he had many reasons to suspect Gonzalo justly because of the arguments that could arise between him and the heirs of King Philip[6] over the kingdom's succession; moreover, it is certain that Gonzalo governed the kingdom with such power that nothing remained to the king but the royal name. 13 Thus a prince may not be called ungrateful if he makes arrangements so the person who has benefited him cannot offend him and so he may take pleasure in what he has gained through that person, if he does it in the way that King Ferdinand did; because Gonzalo lived forever after in Spain with riches and great honor among the other grandees.

14 As for the examples of Rome's ingratitude: if fewer examples exist there than in other republics, the reason is that its government was better organized than many others. Though even Rome does not lack for examples: as in the case of Camillus, whose exile is hard to justify; of Fabius Maximus, who, although he had chosen the right means to defend Rome against Hannibal, was made equal to a Master of the Horse with such dishonor;[7] of Cicero, who quelled the Cataline conspiracy;[8] and of Metellus, Publius Rutilius,[9] and many other well-known and innocent men who at various times were condemned or sent into exile. 15 And I am amazed that this Discourse justifies the case of Scipio by seeking to attribute to suspicion what arose purely from envy and ignorance, because in his time Rome was governed in such a way as to have nothing to fear from any citizen and Scipio's greatness was not to be feared, since it was not based on factions or a following of men but on the power that his *virtù* and his merits gave him in the city. 16 It was never such, either, that he had mastery over public decisions or that officials were named at his will. Consequently, his advancement never displeased men of wisdom, and if Cato opposed him, that arose either from personal enmity or from the leanings that Cato always had against the Nobility, not from the public welfare. His "righteousness"[10] does not justify this ingratitude because, although Cato's habits were "righteous," since he was full of that ancient gravity and austerity, he did not lack a reputation for ambition, for persecution of the Nobility, for immoderate speech, and for a bitter nature. He showed these qualities in this manner: after Scipio's death and thus the cessation of any pretext for claiming suspicion, he was even more bitter toward his brother, Asiaticus.

17 Because it is quite far from the truth, I do not wish to neglect what the Discourse says about it being to freedom's advantage in a republic that has not yet been corrupted for the people sometimes to offend those whom they ought to reward and sometimes to suspect those whom they ought to trust. Any ingratitude, any injustice is always harmful, and the republic must be so governed that the good are always rewarded and the innocent are not frightened. 18 I readily admit that sometimes refraining from trusting good men out of suspicion is less of an error than putting oneself in the hands of bad ones, but this reason does not make the lesser evil good when it is not necessary to choose between one or the other.

NOTES

1. Guicciardini also advises: "Don't let the ingratitude of the many intimidate you from conferring favors on men. For conferring favors without an ulterior motive is per se something generous, almost divine; moreover, sometimes while conferring benefits on someone you may find the person so grateful that he offsets all the ingratitude of others" (C. 11; see also B. 43). See also the quotation from C. 24 quoted below in Guicciardini's *Consideration* of 1, 32, n.1.

2. An editorial emendation in the Italian text.

3. An editorial emendation in the Italian text.

4. See above, 1, 29, n.3.

5. See above, 1, 29, n.4. Guicciardini's discussion here is consistent with what he writes in his *Storia d'Italia,* 7, 2 and 8; 12, 19.

6. Ferdinand's father-in-law Philip I, "the Handsome," (1478–1506). He was the son of Maximilian I, the Holy Roman Emperor. Through his marriage to Ferdinand's daughter Juana he established the Hapsburg dynasty in Spain. Their children were Charles V (1500–1558), Holy Roman Emperor (1519–1556) and king of Spain as Charles I (1516–1556); and Ferdinand I (1503–1564), Holy Roman Emperor from 1556 to 1564.

7. Quintus Fabius Maximus, known as *Cunctator* (the Delayer) because he advised Rome to avoid direct contact with Hannibal during the Second Punic War, 218–201 B.C. A tribune of the people proposed that even as Master of the Horse he should lead with powers equivalent to the dictator (Plutarch, *Fabius Maximus,* 9).

8. In 58 B.C. Cicero was exiled because a tribune of the people, Publius Clodius Pulcher, accused him of executing a Roman citizen without trial.

9. In 100 B.C. the demagogic tribune of the people, Lucius Appuleius Saturninus, allied with Marius, passed an Agrarian Law opposed by his rival, Quintus Caecilius Metellus, and his enemy, Publius Rutilius Rufus; Saturninus forced them both into exile.

10. Translates *santità.*

~ 1:30 ~

[THE MEANS A PRINCE OR A REPUBLIC SHOULD USE TO AVOID THIS VICE OF INGRATITUDE, AND THE ONES COMMANDERS OR CITIZENS SHOULD USE SO AS NOT TO BE TROUBLED BY IT]

1 I laud a prince's going on campaigns in person, because they gain a different kind of prestige and all his men serve him differently than when he conducts them through commanders. And I think that it is perhaps necessary for a tyrant or someone who does not have a firm hold on his state to remember this Discourse, but it is of little benefit to a great and natural king. 2 We see the example of our princes every day in this regard: although they generally make war by using commanders, still rarely if ever does one of these disasters befall them.

~ 1:32 ~

[A REPUBLIC OR A PRINCE SHOULD NOT POSTPONE CONFERRING FAVORS ON MEN UNTIL HE NEEDS THEM]

1 It is one thing to buy new favors to make someone who is normally your friend more friendly to you when you need him, and quite another to try to win over someone who is utterly unfriendly to you. 2 The first, as happened with the Romans, is much easier, the second is exceedingly difficult; nevertheless, it is also far more useful in the first case to have done so before it was necessary. 3 But in

either case, I do not blame anyone who has been so imprudent as not to make provision beforehand if, driven by necessity, he tries a remedy that, even if it has little hope of working, does not involve any risk of doing harm.[1]

NOTES

1. In another context Guicciardini notes: "Nothing is more ephemeral than the memory of benefits received. So, rely more on people whose situation is such that they cannot let you down than on people on whom you have conferred favors, because the latter often do not remember the favors, or they take for granted that they are smaller than they are, or they consider them done almost as if you were obliged to confer them" (B. 24; see also C. 42). But see the quotation from C. 11 quoted above in Guicciardini's *Consideration* of 1, 29, n.1.

~ *1:39* ~

[THE SAME EVENTS ARE OFTEN TO BE SEEN AMONG DIFFERENT PEOPLES]

1 I do not think that the Florentines' quarrel with the Council of Ten was altogether baseless, because according to the city's age-old institutions, introduced under various forms of government, that council had more power than well-constituted freedom should allow. They had the authority without anyone else's participation to make peace, war, truces, and alliances, to hire any and as many generals as they wanted, and to spend all money without any appropriations or limits; in general, they had as much power in matters pertaining to war as did the Florentine people. 2 There arose in great part from that too-absolute power the people's feeling that they would no longer obey the council. But experience showed that even if too much power was harmful it was also extremely harmful during periods of difficulty for the city to lack a council of wise men to supervise and take charge of matters. So, learning by hard knocks what they were not able to by reason, they once again established the Council of Ten for war, limiting its power in matters that were judged dangerous; for these they decreed that the participation of the eighty was required.[1] 3 So with this decision, even in peacetime, they never again made any problems about appointing the council; it was called the Ten of Liberty and Peace, not, as before, the Ten of Power, which had absolute authority.[2]

4 The example of Terentillus is not similar, because when they were not on a military campaign, the consuls' power was in no way absolute. It was subject to the people's approval and limited by the Tribunes' right to intervene; in every serious matter they were executors of the Senate's will rather than its masters. Hence there was less reason to curb it. In fact, it was a completely seditious movement; it aimed at introducing a purely popular and licentious government. 5 Hence, even though at that time the Plebs were quite powerful and very much inclined to attack the patrician officers, it

turned out that it was easier for consular power to be defended, since its power was not excessive but temperate and appropriate.

NOTES

1. The *Ottanta,* or Council of Eighty, modeled on Venice's Senate, played a legislative role and appointed ambassadors and military commissioners.

2. See note 3 to Machiavelli, 1, 39.

~ *1:40* ~

[THE ESTABLISHMENT OF THE DECEMVIRATE IN ROME AND WHAT SHOULD BE NOTED ABOUT IT, IN WHICH WILL BE CONSIDERED AMONG MANY OTHER THINGS HOW A REPUBLIC CAN BE EITHER SAVED OR CONQUERED BY SUCH AN EVENT]

1 I am convinced that the principal mistake made by Appius and his associates was to be convinced that they could set up a tyranny in the city of Rome in those days when it was organized by excellent laws, imbued with very sacred customs and quite ardent in its desire for freedom, and it was too difficult to take by force because its population was warlike. Therefore that tyranny endured so long as they could claim with some justification—that is, having to finish the laws—that their office should last. But once this ruse was exposed, the first incident, though a minor one, brought down their tyranny, which I do not believe would have been more stable even if they had resorted to attacking the Nobility with the Plebs' support, because the people were far too enamored of the idea of freedom. 2 And we can see the example of Manlius Capitolinus who, although he acted against the Senate and used purely popular means, was attacked by the people themselves as soon as they were made aware that he was seeking to seize their freedom.

3 As for the general question of whether it is better for someone who wants to seize tyrannical power either to act with the support of the people or to make friends of the Nobility, differing examples can be found. For Sulla took over a tyranny in Rome and strengthened it with the backing of the Nobility, but the duke of Athens, on the other hand, was made tyrant in Florence with the Nobles' support, which he was unable to retain because of his imprudent and frivolous behavior, which led to his rapid downfall.[1] 4 Thus many examples can be found on both sides, and each side also has its reasons. For he who has the people on his side has a larger number of followers, and the people tolerate greatness more easily than do the Nobles; nevertheless, he who has the Nobility on his side has a more vigorous, effective, and valiant base, one that does not change its mind so easily and often for frivolous reasons, as do the people. 5 These are actions that cannot be taken according to a fixed rule, but the conclusion must be drawn from

the moods of the city, from the essence of things, which varies according to the conditions of the times and other situations that are in flux.

NOTES

1. The Florentine Signoria called in the Frenchman Walter of Brienne, known as the duke of Athens, to lead their army after Pisa defeated it in 1342. Today we would call such a person a "soldier of fortune." With the aid of some nobles, he shortly established a tyranny, which in turn was attacked by three conspiracies; the duke was eventually ousted in 1343. See Machiavelli, *Florentine Histories,* 2, 33–38.

~ *1:47* ~

[EVEN THOUGH MEN MAY BE MISTAKEN IN GENERAL MATTERS, THEY ARE NOT MISTAKEN IN PARTICULARS]

1 What the Discourse says as to men's being more easily mistaken in general matters than in particulars can be stated in another way: experience often disabuses men about what they had supposed before they got their hands dirty. For it is not surprising if someone ignorant of the particulars of matters should change his mind after he has known and seen them at first hand; the example of the Florentines is relevant: because they did not have that information in the piazzas and they did not see the reports that they later saw in the palace, they could readily have an idea at variance with the truth. 2 We may also consider in the example of the Romans that the people felt it was scandalous and contemptible for everyone as a whole not to be qualified for office. It seemed to them that they had gained a good deal of ground when they succeeded in being qualified for an office with consular power, so to some extent they felt relieved and abstained from electing unsuitable people, as if they had not fought out of any particular ambition to attain that rank but only to remove the opprobrium of the Plebs as a whole being prohibited by law from holding public offices. Therefore Livy puts it well: "The people were satisfied now that Plebeians were permitted to run for office."[1]

3 The other conclusion of the Discourse, that the people are mistaken less in the distribution of offices and positions than in other matters, I believe to be true. The reason is simply that the subject is more easily understood. In this case the people's judgment is based not on its own information about a citizen's merit but on the full complement of views that has arisen about the citizen over time and from the experience that this or that individual has had with him. 5 I do not accept, however, that the people are not mistaken about this, or at least less often than are the few. For the people are guided in this judgment not by particular information but by general opinion; they do not examine or distinguish subtly, so they are often mistaken, especially in those elections for which few are eligible: they believe false rumors and are influenced by frivolous causes. In fact, because of their ignorance, they are much more dangerous than is the judgment of the few.

NOTES

1. Quoted in Latin from Livy, 4.6.11: *"contentus eo quod ratio habita plebeiorum esset."*

~ *1:49* ~

[CITIES WITH FREE ORIGINS LIKE ROME HAVE DIFFICULTY FINDING LAWS TO SUSTAIN THEM, BUT FOR CITIES THAT HAVE BEEN ENSLAVED FROM THE START IT IS VIRTUALLY IMPOSSIBLE]

1 Both this discourse and many others demonstrate what I have said elsewhere[1] against the author's ideas: aside from military discipline, the Roman government was defective in many respects. What is more absurd than empowering one lone man to stop public actions or to prevent a decision made by the city from taking effect, as those Consuls did?[2] 2 Although checking them with the Tribunes was good, nevertheless, there was no recourse at all for a Tribune who wished to cause disorders of this kind. 3 It was also a mistake for it to be in the power of the two Censors for such good works to bar from the Senate Mamercus Æmilius, a highly honored citizen and one to whom the republic owed so much. Indeed, just a single man had the power to do so. 4 I do not believe that he had any other recourse than either a law made by the people to restore him to the Senate, which we do not read was done, or for the next Censors when they selected the Senate to restore him to it. I am not certain they could do that, either, though I believe so.

NOTES

1. In the last paragraph of his *Considerations,* 1, 4, and Bernardo's third speech from the end of *Dialogo del reggimento di Firenze,* Book 2, pp. 145–154.

2. Machiavelli actually discusses this issue in his next discourse; in the rest of this *Consideration,* Guicciardini focuses on Machiavelli's chapter 49.

~ *1:58* ~

[THE MASSES ARE WISER AND MORE CONSTANT THAN A PRINCE]

1 Whoever attributes constancy and wisdom to the people and sets them above princes for these two qualities is no doubt taking on a difficult task, one quite at variance with men's opinion. When princes are regulated by laws, no one who has written on political matters has ever doubted that the government of one man was better than that of the masses,[1] even when regulated by laws, or that not only government by a prince but even that of an aristocracy[2] is preferable to it. 2 For where the number is smaller, *virtù* is

more unified and is better able to produce its effects; there is more order in things, more thought and reflection in negotiations, more resolve. But where there are masses, there is confusion; in such disharmony of minds where there are differing judgments, differing ideas, and differing ends, there can be no rational discussion, no sound resolve, and no firm action. 3 Men act frivolously on any vain suspicion or any vain rumor; they do not discern, they do not distinguish, and they revert with the same frivolousness to decisions that they had previously condemned: to hating those they loved, to loving those they hated. Hence it is not without reason that the masses are compared to the waves of the sea which, depending upon which way the winds blow, roll now this way, now that way, without any rule, without any stability. 4 In sum, it cannot be denied that on their own the people are a vessel of ignorance and confusion. Therefore purely popular governments have everywhere been short-lived, and, in addition to the countless riots and disorders that they have been filled with as long as they have endured, they have given birth to either tyranny or the final downfall of their city.

5 There are so many and such well-known examples that there is no need repeating them; they have deservedly given birth to the very ancient and common opinion among all writers that there is neither wisdom nor constancy in the masses. 6 If we consider it carefully, this is not inconsistent with either reason or the examples that the author of the Discourse cited. For insofar as he alleges that a people regulated by laws is no less lacking in *virtù* or wisdom than a prince regulated by laws and cites the Roman people as an example, my main point is that neither his reason nor his example is relevant to the case. For it is one thing to consider the masses[3] making decisions on their own and another to consider a popular government established so that weighty and significant decisions have to be made by the wisest men. 7 In the first case there will often be fickleness, ignorance, and confusion, though the masses be regulated by laws as much as one wishes; in the second case, if matters are decided wisely and regularly, that is not because the masses lack those defects but because they do not exist in the wisest men. 8 Such were the Roman people: the Senate, the Consuls, and the principal officials decided the most important matters. Even though they were regulated by good laws, imbued with sacred customs and extremely devoted to their freedom, if the masses had had to make decisions, in their decisions there would frequently have appeared the imprudence and fickleness that writers criticize in other masses with very grave harm to their republic.

9 Furthermore, even if we were to describe the decision making of the Romans as decisions made by the masses, one should select for comparison a prince who, relative to other princes, had the same degree of *virtù* as the people of Rome had among other peoples. I believe without any doubt that he will act in all his affairs with greater wisdom and greater constancy than the Roman people did because, for the reasons cited above, all things being equal there is more order, more discrimination, more resolve, more firmness

in one man than in many. 10 Conversely, if we take a people untrammeled by laws and a free and untrammeled prince, as they almost all are (even those of France, whom the author calls "bound" [by law], who have it in their power to do as they please within their realm), I say that we may perhaps find in a prince more of the other vices than in the people and greater readiness to carry them out than the people have. In discussing these matters the author departs from the terms of his argument, but generally one will find more wisdom and constancy, which is specifically the author's topic, than one will find among the masses.[4] When they are unregulated, one will never see anything but imprudence and inconstancy, the desire for innovation, unmoderated suspicion, perpetual envy of those having authority or rank. 11 Although some quite imprudent princes are to be found, and their imprudence, when it is of this last sort, is perhaps more destructive than that of the masses, I say that if, for example, we pick two hundred years of a kingdom, we will find wise and unwise kings; but if we pick two hundred years ruled by the masses,[5] we will find uninterrupted imprudence and fickleness.

12 The examples showing that there are many more defects in a prince than in the people are irrelevant,[6] because the thesis is not a discussion of other vices, but simply whether there is more imprudence and inconstancy in the people than in princes. 13 So it is not pertinent to say that a city makes more progress under a popular government than under a prince, because that arises from other causes; but if you gave me fifty years of a good popular government and as many of an equally good prince, I do not doubt that greater progress would be made under a prince. 14 But because a prince's successors are not always like him, progress under a popular government is going to be more continuous than under a prince. Both may very well go together: that it may be better fortune for a city to fall under a popular government than under princes, a consideration which is outside of our discussion, and yet that usually there is more imprudence and inconstancy in the people than in a prince.

NOTES

1. Translates *una moltitudine.* Guicciardini uses *una moltitudine,* implying government by the populace; Machiavelli uses *la moltitudine,* implying government of a republic with some participation of the masses. Guicciardini's uses of *una* will be noted in subsequent notes; this is the first of four in this *Consideration.* As for attributing "wisdom to the people," in his *Ricordi* he comments, "Whoever speaks about the people is truly speaking about an insane animal smothered in a thousand and one errors and confusions, devoid of judgment, discernment, and stability" (C. 140; see also B. 123).

2. Translates *ottimati.*

3. Translates *una moltitudine.*

4. Translates *una moltitudine.*

5. Translates *una moltitudine.*

6. It is unclear to which examples in Machiavelli's chapter 58 Guicciardini refers.

~ 1:60 ~

[THE CONSULATE AND ALL OTHER OFFICES IN ROME WERE GIVEN WITHOUT REGARD TO AGE]

1 The Discourse does not recall that Scipio Africanus the Younger could not be made consul until the prohibition of age was first removed for him by a special law, and that Cicero says in the . . .[1] that a thirty-three-year-old man needs ten more years in order to be consul. If it was otherwise with Valerius Corvinus, it must be said, to tell the truth, that the institutions were those at the beginning of the republic and others arose over the course of time. 2 And such was also the case with the term of office, because in the beginning there was no prohibition against prolonging the consulate; at least someone who was Consul then could after a short while be elected Consul once again. But later a law was made that there had to be an interval of at least ten years between one consulate and another. 3 Whether these two laws, that is, the prohibition of age and the time limit, are useful for republics will be treated elsewhere, because it is not under our consideration here, since they are not treated in the Discourse.

NOTES

1. Part of Guicciardini's text is missing here; Scarano suggests *Orationes Philippicae,* 5.48, and *De officiis,* 2.59; *Brutus (De claris oratoribus),* 323; *De lege agraria,* 2.3. See also Ciccro, *De legibus,* 3.3.

· *Considerations* of BOOK TWO ·

[PREFACE]

1 The conclusion that ancient times are often praised more than is due is quite valid and the author considers the reasons very well; a few others could be added, but I shall pass over them. 2 But I am not in agreement with him when he says that there always has been as much good in the world in one age as in another although the places may vary. We can see that it is quite true, as a result either of the influence of the heavens or of some other hidden explanation,[1] that sometimes there occurs during certain ages, not only in one region but throughout the whole world, more *virtù* or more vice than there was in another age, or at least one art or one discipline flourishes more than it had flourished in any part of the world at another time. 3 And to begin with the technical arts that the writer mentions: who does not know how excellent painting and sculpture were in the time of the Greeks and then the Romans; how they later remained in obscurity throughout the world; and how, after being buried for many centuries, they have returned to light in the past hundred fifty or two hundred years?[2] 4 Our own times and those of our fathers and grandfathers in whatever part of the world have witnessed only minimal and dim vestiges of military discipline, but who does not know how it flourished in ancient times not only among the Romans but in many regions? 5 The same can be said about literature and religion, which doubtless have been completely buried during some ages, and during others have been excellent in many places and held in highest esteem. 6 The world has seen some ages filled with wars; others have experienced and enjoyed peace. As a result of these variations in the arts and religion and changes in human affairs, it is no wonder that men's customs, too, have varied; they often take their impetus from an institution, from opportunity, or from necessity. 7 That ancient times are not always to be preferred to present ones is therefore a valid conclusion, but it is not really valid to deny that one age is sometimes more corrupt or has more *virtù* than others.

NOTES

1. As for there being "as much good in the world," see Guicciardini's letter to Machiavelli, quoted above, Preface to Book 2, n.3. There are two sides to Guicciardini's conviction that "the influence of the heavens" or a "hidden explanation" can be readily explained. On the one hand, he writes: "That spirits do exist may, I believe, be affirmed. I am talking about what we call spirits, i.e., those airy ones who speak familiarly

with people. For I have had the sort of experience with them that makes me think that I can be most certain about them. But what they are, what their nature is, I believe to be as little understood by the person who persuades himself that he understands as by the person who never gives it a thought. This understanding and the prediction of the future, which we sometimes see people make either through craft or frenzy, are occult potencies of Nature—or rather, of that higher *virtù* that sets everything in motion: manifest to him, hidden from us; the minds of men cannot attain them" (*Ricordi,* C. 211). On the other hand, his skepticism about those who interpret such "influence" is clear: "Philosophers, theologians, and everyone else who inquire into the supernatural and the invisible say thousands of inanities; for the fact is that mankind is in the dark about such matters, and their inquiries into them has served and serves more to exercise their intellect than to discover truth" (*Ricordi,* C. 125), and "How much luckier astrologers are than the rest of mankind! If they tell one truth among a hundred lies they obtain so much trust that even their falsehoods are believed. The rest, telling one lie among much truth lose trust, and no one believes them even when they speak the truth. This is a result of mankind's inquisitiveness: desiring to know the future, and without any other means, they are prone to race after anyone who promises enlightenment" (*Ricordi,* C. 57; see also B. 145).

2. Guicciardini expresses a characteristic notion of sixteenth-century thought: its awareness of and pride in the rebirth of the arts in a particular country. Although Machiavelli grants the arts their distinction (see Preface A to Book 1, sentence 3; Preface to Book 2, sentence 6; and the very end of Fabrizio's final speech, *Art of War,* 7), he does not, unlike Guicciardini, emphasize their rebirth in Italy.

~ 2:10 ~

[THE SINEWS OF WAR ARE NOT MONEY, AS COMMON OPINION WOULD HAVE IT]

1 Whoever was the author of the maxim that the sinews of war are money and those who later repeated it did not mean that money alone was enough to wage war, or that it was more necessary than soldiers, for that would have been not only a false belief but also a quite ridiculous one. It meant that those who waged war had a very great need of money and that without money it was impossible to keep it going, because it is necessary not only for paying soldiers but for providing weapons, provisions, spies, ammunition, and much equipment used in warfare. These things are required in such superabundance that it is impossible for those who have not experienced it to imagine it.[1] 2 Although an army lacking in money sometimes provides it by its *virtù* and with the aid of victories, nevertheless, such examples are extremely rare, especially in our day; in every case and at all times money does not run after armies until after they have won. 3 I grant that those who have their own soldiers wage war with less money than those who have mercenaries; nevertheless, those who wage war with their own soldiers also need money, and not

everyone has his own soldiers; it is much easier to get soldiers with money than to get money with soldiers. 4 So anyone who construes the maxim according to the meaning of the one who said it, and according to how it is commonly understood, will not be surprised by it or in any way condemn it.

NOTES

1. Guicciardini had in fact "experienced" it and Machiavelli had not. In Machiavelli's letter to Guicciardini, written after 21 October 1525, he refers to the fact that his friend "has striven for ten years to earn honor and profit . . . though with the greatest deprivation and peril" (*Friends,* p. 370). Machiavelli is commenting on Guicciardini's service to two Medici popes, Leo X and Clement VII, as governor in Modena, Reggio, and Parma. During his defense of Parma against the invading forces of Francis I in 1521, he persuaded the mercenaries not to desert. He was also made commissioner general and later lieutenant general of the papal armies.

~ 2:12 ~

[WHETHER IT IS BETTER WHEN ONE FEARS ATTACK TO LAUNCH A WAR OR TO WAIT FOR IT]

1 If one finds many examples for both sides in the present Discourse, there are also many reasons that make the case so uncertain that it is not easy to resolve it; if we are to consider it thoroughly, one needs many considerations that the author has omitted. 2 For to make just the one distinction—either my subjects are armed or they are unarmed—is not enough.[1] It is necessary to think further: whether my people are loyal or they are inclined to rebellion; whether the towns are strong or they are weak; as far as money is concerned, whether I can endure a long war, even if it is on my own soil so that it eats up my revenues, or I could not sustain one. 3 Because the enemy's nature and progress must always determine the direction and all the acts of war, one must also consider the enemy's circumstances; that is, what kind of army he has, what lands, what revenues, what means for keeping a war going on his own soil, what means for waging one abroad. 4 When I am expecting war by someone else, there is also a difference between saying: I am carrying it onto his soil, and saying: I am leaving my country and meeting the enemy outside his country (that is the case with King Ferdinand). 5 There is a difference between saying: I am starting a war on his soil before he has started one against me, and saying: I already have war on my own soil, but to force my enemy to withdraw I am also starting one on his soil; that is what Scipio did when Hannibal was in Italy, what Agathocles did when the Carthaginians besieged him, and what the Florentines did so often during the wars the Visconti fought against them. 6 As for this last instance, I shall always deem that anyone who has war on his own soil, if he has an opportunity at the same time to start one on his enemy's, should do so. Because it is an unexpected thing, it

upsets all the enemy's plans, and any slight success that you have there forces him to withdraw with all or part of his army to defend his soil; it is like what happens with the remedies physicians use to cure illnesses: they always consider diversion to be a potent and highly appropriate remedy.[2]

7 There remains the resolution of the other cases. Drawing distinctions, I state that when the enemy from whom you fear war has a larger army and more power than you, you cannot think of waging war against him on his soil, because carrying war to someone else's soil takes large forces and many opportunities. These are not so necessary for someone who wages war on his own soil, because he makes use of the advantages of his land, his subjects, and his enemy's difficulties; with such remedies he can go along biding his time. King Ferdinand, who could not put an army in the field equal to his enemies', was in this category. 8 But when you feel equal to the enemy in men, money, and other advantages for war and organized with the forces that are necessary for waging war on his soil, I should be inclined to advise not waiting for war on one's own soil. If you win, the prize is greater, because the victory can easily bring you the acquisition of someone else's kingdom, whereas victory on your own soil brings you nothing but the freeing of your state. If you lose, there is less harm, because you lose nothing but that army and you have more time to regroup, whereas if you lose at home, if your enemy gathers speed with his victory—as Hannibal was able to do at Cannae and as Paolo Orsini did to Ladislas,[3] and Duke Giovanni did to King Ferdinand[4] in modern times—one battle is enough to make you lose your power in modern times.

9 If you carry the war to your enemy's soil, you have already spoiled his plan to make war on yours and you have hindered the preparations necessary for that purpose so that, even if he defeats you, he needs time and new arrangements in order to come and fight against you on your soil; this gives you space to reorganize and regroup. 10 And I should uphold this conclusion all the more readily if I saw that the enemy did not have a strong country or did not have loyal subjects or that his government was in such a state that his revenues could easily be upset or, if he suffered defeat, that it would be hard for him to regroup in a short space of time. 11 I see that the Romans, whenever they were able, always stole a march by fighting on their enemies' soil: against King Philip of Macedon, against Antiochus, and against the Carthaginians; when they did not do so, they were sorry not to have. 12 I am not convinced by the writer saying that if the Romans had in the same space of time suffered the three defeats in Gaul that they suffered from Hannibal in Italy they undoubtedly would have been done for, because that is positing an impossible case: that someone who suffers a defeat on someone else's soil, especially in a distant place, can so suddenly after the first defeat send two new armies there, one after the other. 13 Anyone who does decide on the course of avoiding war at home by carrying it onto someone else's soil does so with the justification that he can just as well hope to defeat the enemy as fear being defeated; otherwise he should await it on his own soil, as the Romans did with Hannibal. As Livy says,[5] if they were conquered on their own soil, hav-

ing been inexperienced in war for many years and having to fight a very experienced commander and soldiers, the Romans would perhaps have been far more easily defeated by him at the start of the war in Spain or Africa.

NOTES

1. Rinaldi, 1:802, n.6, points out that several commentators have remarked that beginning with the end of Machiavelli's opening sentence, "I have heard reasons cited on each side," this chapter of his *Discourses,* as well as both 2, 18 and 27, proceed like parodies of a Scholastic disputation. So it is as if Guicciardini's tactic in this *Consideration* is to draw attention to the lack of subtlety in Machiavelli's Scholastic parody, despite the distinction that Machiavelli makes in sentence 17; Guicciardini does not, however, "consider" either 2, 18 or 27.

2. The notion of "remedy" here is aided by the medical connotation of "diversion." According to the Renaissance notion of humours, "diversion" was a process of drawing harmful humours to a part of the body where they could be extracted, as with leeches.

3. Ladislas, who was king of Naples from 1386 to 1414, attempted numerous conquests in central Italy from 1400 until his death. In 1409 Paolo Orsino, a member of a powerful Roman family and a general who switched allegiances easily, sided with Florence and forced the king to give up what he had won in Florentine territory.

4. John of Anjou, the son of Réné of Anjou, was the duke of Calabria. Attempting to assert the Neapolitan barons' power against that of the king of Aragon, Ferdinand I, he defeated the latter at the battle of Sarno, 7 July 1460. By 1462 Ferdinand had restored himself to power in Naples.

5. Livy, 21.16.

~ 2:13 ~

[ONE GETS FROM LOW TO HIGH FORTUNE MORE BY DECEIT THAN BY FORCE]

1 If the writer calls "deceit" any shrewd action or dissimulation that is done even without fraud, his conclusion may be true: that force alone very rarely (I do not say never, which is too absolute a word) leads men from low to high fortune. 2 But if he calls "deceit" what really is deceit, that is to say, not keeping one's word or other fraudulent acts, I believe it may be found that many have acquired kingdoms and vast empires without deceit. 3 One of these was Alexander the Great, another was Caesar, who from a private citizen brought himself to so much greatness with skills other than deceit, always revealing his ambition or appetite for dominion. 4 Xenophon is not fresh in my memory right now, but I believe that he teaches Cyrus not deceit but prudence, diligence, and fair pretense or dissimulation. 5 I do not call it deceit if the Romans made such treaties with the Latins that they were able to tolerate Roman dominion with patience. Even at the outset it was not so that the

Latins would be unaware that under the semblance of an equal confederation there was servitude. But finding themselves powerless and not being treated in such a way as to give them cause for despair made them wait: I do not say until they had discovered the Romans' aim, which they would have been quite stupid not to have recognized from the start, but until they had a large enough number of men and were experienced enough in military discipline to hope to be able to vie as equals with the Roman people. 6 So it was wisdom, not deceit, for the Romans to treat the Latins well, and I believe it is quite true that without such efforts and wise ruling methods not only does one rarely rise from low to high fortune but also one has difficulty retaining greatness. 7 But as to deceit, it is debatable whether it is always a good instrument for attaining greatness. Although one may often do many fine deeds with deception, often having a reputation for deceit also robs one of the opportunity to pursue one's intentions.

~ 2:14 ~

[MEN OFTEN DECEIVE THEMSELVES BY BELIEVING THAT HUMILITY CAN OVERCOME PRIDE]

1 The conclusion of the Discourse contradicts in part what he said elsewhere, namely, that in dangerous cases there is greater wisdom in delaying than in meeting them head-on.[1] Hence one must make the distinction that when your army is not equal to your enemy's it is better to reach an agreement, even relinquishing some things, than to bring destruction immediately down upon oneself, because with time may come events that suffice to deal with your future danger. 2 But when your forces are equal or almost equal to the enemy's, even if entering into war is dangerous and difficult, starting it is so important that you should not be willing to give it up so as not to diminish your prestige and make you cowardly and your enemy arrogant. 3 Thucydides discusses this reason at length through the persona of Pericles[2] when he advised the Athenians to choose war with the Lacedaemonians, although [it was] difficult and dangerous, rather than to accept the conditions they proposed, even though they seemed in themselves of little consequence.

NOTES

1. Guicciardini is probably thinking of *Discourses,* 2, 12, although his choice of words echoes the title of *Discourses,* 1, 33, a chapter Guicciardini does not "consider."

2. See above, 2, 10, n.14.

~ *2:15* ~

[WEAK STATES WILL ALWAYS BE HESITANT TO MAKE UP THEIR MINDS, AND LENGTHY DECISIONS ARE ALWAYS HARMFUL]

1 Hesitations in decision making proceed from two causes: one, from weakness in those who have to decide; I do not mean weakness in armed forces and power but weakness in wisdom and intelligence. This cause may befall a prince just as well as a republic; I believe that when the Discourse says "weak governments," it means weak in wisdom, although weakness in armed forces may in part increase irresolution, because usually the courses of actions that weak states have to choose are more fraught with difficulties and dangers. 2 The other cause, which is characteristic of republics, exists when there are several men who must decide and their opinions differ; this can arise either from ill will, because they have different aims, or else with no ill will, because men's judgments do not coincide, as is often the case even among wise men. 3 And it is true that these hesitations are usually harmful, because while you are hesitant you cannot take care of either one case or the other. If they are sometimes useful, as would have happened to the Lavinians, who would not have suffered grief from that brief march had they delayed making up their minds three or four days longer, nevertheless, this is a usefulness that comes about by chance rather than otherwise. 4 Thus indecisiveness is to be abhorred, decisiveness very greatly to be admired; but one must note that remaining neutral can also proceed from decisiveness, not from indecisiveness. In the second case neutrality is reprehensible; in the first it can be both useful and harmful according to the nature of the cases; dealing with them is not our present subject. 5 I say the same thing about postponing some other actions or operations, for if the delay comes about through irresoluteness, it is always worthy of condemnation, but if it is done deliberately, it may be worthy of praise.

~ *2:19* ~

[THAT CONQUESTS BY POORLY CONSTITUTED REPUBLICS THAT DO NOT ACT IN ACCORDANCE WITH ROMAN *VIRTÙ* LEAD TO THEIR DOWNFALL, NOT THEIR RISE]

1 Who doubts that the city of Florence and the republic of Venice would be weaker and less powerful than they are had they enclosed their territory within narrow limits? 2 Because they have subdued the neighboring cities and broadened their jurisdiction, it is not easy for any neighbor to attack them. They are not troubled by every minor incident. Unless there is some great

upheaval, they keep their enemy outside the heart of their state. War does not easily approach their walls. Having many subjects gives them many ways of increasing public revenues and makes the dominant city richer in the private sector. 3 By these means, even if they are not armed with their own soldiers, they hire foreign ones, and being defended by them is better than not being defended by anyone. 4 I concede that a republic that has its own arms is more powerful and profits more from its conquests, but I shall not concede that an unarmed republic becomes weaker the more it conquers, or that Venice, which now fears neither kings nor emperors, would be safer than it is now were it to be without dominion over land and sea. 5 If that were true, I do not know why the Discourse limits itself only to republics, because for the same reasons a prince without his own arms would end up weaker, not stronger, from conquests and enlargement of his dominion. Both reason and experience amply show this to be quite false.

~ *2:24* ~

[FORTRESSES GENERALLY DO FAR MORE HARM THAN GOOD]

1 Antiquity should not be praised so much that a man blames all modern institutions that were not in use among the Romans; because experience has revealed many things that the ancients did not consider, and, furthermore, because origins are different, certain things that were not suitable or unnecessary to some are suitable or necessary to others. 2 Therefore, if the Romans were not wont to construct fortresses in subjugated cities, that is not a reason for anyone who constructs them today to be wrong, because many instances occur for which it is very useful to have fortresses both to a prince or a tyrant with his own citizens and to a lord with his subjects, and to a ruler with foreigners.

3 The reasons seem so obvious to me that I am amazed that this opinion should have its contradictors, principally because, if subjects were always completely in accordance with their rulers, that is, that when they are well treated they would love their prince, I admit that as far as they are concerned, fortresses would be useless to any prince who governed well, because the love of his people would be sufficient to defend him from his citizens and subjects. 4 But considering how many times people, even well treated, often are not very reasonable, how desirous of new things, how much the memory of the former prince means for them if they are now under a new rule, how strong the desire for freedom if they are used to having it, and how often for this and other considerations a prince or tyrant is obliged to govern his citizens or subjects with some abuse, I say that it is necessary for both those who may have a friendly people and those who

cannot hope to achieve such goodwill to rely to some extent on force, on keeping their people in some fear.[1] Otherwise they would too often be prey to the fickleness, the malevolence, the just hatred of their subjects. 5 The reason that is cited in the Discourse, that fortresses encourage princes to be insolent and behave badly, is quite frivolous, because if we were to consider this, a prince would have to go without guards, without arms, and without armies, for the more he had to seek to live in such a way as to be liked by the people, the more he would find himself at their mercy. 6 Then, too, things that are useful in themselves should not be avoided, even if the security that you derive from them may encourage you to be bad.[2] For example, is medicine to be blamed because men who trust in it may protect themselves less from the disorders and causes that occasion illness? 7 That is neither good reasoning nor a cause for rejecting the good, since the evil that may develop from it is in your power to act on or not.

8 To come to particulars based on the Discourse's organization, I say that fortresses in a city are quite useful to a tyrant and to any prince in it because, knowing that the prince is secure in his fortress, neither the people nor his individual enemies can cause an uprising at any slight opportunity, for it is difficult to do so in such a way that the prince is slaughtered with all his offspring. Nor is it easy to have forces and reinforcements prepared in such a way that the fortress can be closed off or taken so swiftly that the prince does not have time to recapture the town with new troops brought in through the fortress. 9 I say the same about a subjugated city, which, because of the obstacle of the fortress, cannot think of revolting unless it sees a foreign army, hostile to the prince, in the region. 10 The example of Milan and the others that he cites, which lost states although they had fortresses, are not good: [it was] not because of only the people's revolt but because of the opportunity for a powerful war; it could be said that if they had not had them they would perhaps have lost them much earlier, even in peacetime. 11 And if by means of[3] the fortress a lost town is not always recaptured, sometimes some have also been seen to be recaptured, as happened to Monsieur de Foix at Brescia; although he was there with a powerful army, had he not been brought in through the fortress, it would not have been enough to recapture Brescia. 12 And when one does not recover a town by means of a fortress, the fear of the fortress is sufficient to keep the enemy engaged without making any other attack until it has been captured; such a lapse of time can be the source of great benefit to those who find themselves attacked.

13 And as for the example of the Romans that is cited, setting aside the examples of Duke Guido, Ottaviano, and the others, whose authority is not enough to confound the authority of so many others who have constructed fortresses, I say that if the Romans did not use fortresses there could be two causes. First, as the author has said elsewhere,[4] during the early stages of their power they were not wont to reduce cities to open servitude but to hold them under an appearance of freedom and an alliance of equals; that policy did not allow for building fortresses. Second, because they always found

themselves with well-organized and very powerful armies and in many places with colonies, they figured that they had less need of fortresses, especially since they were accustomed rather to destroy cities that they considered very hostile. Nevertheless, if they had judged them useless, they would have destroyed Tarentum's and the others that they found [already] constructed, because a fortress constructed by others would be as useless as one that was constructed by you. 14 I therefore admit that in many cases and on many occasions fortresses are of no avail, that there are other remedies for the security of your state perhaps at times more useful and stronger than fortresses. But fortresses are often useful to those who hold them to protect themselves against conspiracies, to escape from revolt, and to recover lost towns. 15 Therefore we do not make use of them in our day without cause: they were in use among the ancients, and the Romans did not demolish them at Tarentum and the other places where they found them built.

NOTES

1. In contradistinction to Machiavelli's belief that the peoples' desire to protect their freedom is an element of stability in the body politic, Guicciardini sees being "desirous . . . of new things" as potentially destabilizing. Behind this appetite for "new things" lies Guicciardini's fear that the people may revolt. Indeed, he may be relying on his reader's awareness that in classical Latin *res novae* (new things) connoted "revolt" or "revolution."

2. Guicciardini's argument here seems at variance with his remarks in his *Consideration* of *Discourses,* 2, 13.

3. Translates *per virtù.*

4. Above, 2, 1, a chapter for which Guicciardini wrote no *Consideration.*

~ 3:17 ~

[A MAN SHOULD NOT BE OFFENDED THEN ASSIGNED TO AN IMPORTANT ADMINISTRATIVE OR GOVERNMENT MISSION]

1 A prince has to be much more careful than a republic not to put his trust in someone he has offended, because a man offended by a prince recognizes the offense [as coming] entirely from him, but a man offended by a republic recognizes the offense [as coming] more from some private individual who has harassed him or has been in office than in the name of the city; therefore, he does not feel he is getting revenge by harming the city. 2 Moreover, someone who seeks the downfall of his own country hurts his family, his friends, all his own interests, and himself, and to his own shame; this does not happen to someone who acts against a prince. 3 It is also easier to do away with a prince than a republic, and for this reason someone who has been offended may more readily conceive such an idea. 4 Therefore I would not be quick to avoid a citizen offended by his republic, especially when the offense has not been very egregious, in which case consideration could be had for him. But Claudius Nero's offense cited in the Discourse is too absurd to be believed: that because he had been slandered during the time he was in Spain, and with some reason too, he had been so contemptuous that he might desire to be defeated. And the words that the writer says that he used were not his own but those of [Marcus Livius] Salinator, who had been condemned by the people after his consulate, and after receiving such disgrace, it is no wonder if he had more resentment over it. 5 Although he may have spoken thus either out of contempt or because of certain natures or fancies that men have, it is to be believed that in fact he meant otherwise. This is shown by his actions, first before his election to the consulate, which he rejected stubbornly until he was almost forced by the principal citizens, an office he would have wanted if he had had any desire for vengeance, and then when he was elected Consul, he did his best to win, and he went very reluctantly into battle with Hasdrubal, although he had at first said he wanted to provoke it.

~ 3:19 ~

[WHETHER INDULGENCE, MORE THAN PUNISHMENT, IS NEEDED TO CONTROL THE MASSES]

1 Severity stripped of all human kindness, or let us say courtesy, is useless to someone who controls others, and human kindness or graciousness unaccompanied by some degree of severity is the same; one equally seasoned with the other would be most precious and would make for a tempered harmony that is very sweet and admirable. 2 But because such seasoning is rarely or never found in any man (the order of nature being such that all our affairs have some imperfection), it appears rather that every man either has more severity than graciousness or more graciousness than severity. It is not without reason that we are unsure which is more suitable: whether someone who, partaking of both, has more severity, or else someone who has more human kindness; meaning, therefore, as for those who have as much of one as of the other, that where fear abounds, love should not be lacking, and where love abounds, fear should not be lacking. 3 Concerning this, the first distinction that occurs to me is to consider the nature of those whom you control. For some are of so noble and generous a disposition that they go along with graciousness more readily than with fear; others, on the contrary, are imbued with a certain hardness and cannot bow to gentleness, but must be subdued and broken by harshness. 4 Unquestionably one must adjust to people such as these according to their condition. On this subject Frederick Barbarossa, a most excellent prince and one who, [though] born in Germany had a long experience with Italy, said that the two principal nations of the world, and with respect to the others full of much *virtù,* were the Germans and the Italians.[1] But they had to be ruled in different ways: the Germans were arrogant, insolent, and of such a nature that any gentleness you showed them they attributed rather to fear than to human kindness; on the other hand, the Italians [were] more pliant, more courteous, and of such a nature that harshness irritated them rather than frightened them. Hence with the latter it was sometimes necessary to excuse misdeeds and to act with clemency; with the former, to punish them severely because otherwise they would become more insolent.

5 The other distinction that occurs to me is that one must differentiate between one who rules as a prince and on his own authority and one who rules as a minister and in another's name, because I believe that a prince must be deeply concerned with seeking the goodwill of the people, since many cases can occur when he has need of his people's special affection to hold onto power. 6 But I would make a distinction among those who command in another's name. If it is an army, then it would be necessary to emphasize love rather than fear, because if one has to lead them into actions that endanger their lives they are best brought to it by love. But for someone who governs a city or a province in another's name, if nothing else is

required of him but temporary responsibility and he is not the supreme lord for whom the people have to be motivated to more than they are normally expected to do, I believe he conducts his affairs better with somewhat more terror than ordinary princes. For because the people know that favors come from someone else and that after a certain time he will no longer be in office, the goodwill that they bear him cannot provide a significant foundation for those purposes for which love of the prince is so highly desired. 7 I say therefore that since we are speaking of good and legitimate governments, it can hardly be taken for granted that where there is fear there is not also love, because severity of justice, which is what produces fear, can be only loved by those who want to live well, and vice versa, the love that arises from human kindness, from easygoingness of character, and from the inclination to do favors, accompanied by justice, as must be taken for granted in a good government, cannot help being feared.

NOTES

1. Frederick I, called Barbarossa, was king of Germany from 1152 to 1190 and king of Italy from 1155 to 1190. He was Holy Roman Emperor from 1152 until 1190, though he was crowned in 1155. His conflict with the cities of northern Italy and with the Church resulted from Pope Adrian IV's claim that Germany was a papal fief, which Frederick quickly denied. Guicciardini may be indulging in some irony here, too, because his quick denial took the form of a "long experience with Italy," one that involved six invasions between 1154 and 1184 during the struggles between Guelphs and Ghibellines.

~ *3:24* ~

[LENGTHENING MILITARY COMMANDS ENDED ROME'S FREEDOM]

1 Extending the term of military commands was unquestionably a great opportunity for anyone who wanted to seize control of the republic. For it was an instrument for winning over one's soldiers and gaining a following among kings and in foreign countries and provinces, and it increased the commanders' wealth so that they could corrupt men, as Caesar's long command in Gaul did for him.[1] 2 But the principal basis for the city's ills was its corruption: devoting itself to greed and to pleasure, it had so degenerated from its ancient customs that the city's bloody divisions were the result; among a free people tyranny always arises from these. 3 That was why it was easy to corrupt citizens and soldiers, and someone like Catiline,[2] without military authority and without troops, might hope to seize control of the republic; from this arose a conspiracy of the more powerful men to divide up the military commands and the armies among themselves and with these forces to keep the others down. Hence the extraordinary extensions of military

commands like that of Caesar, who was given a ten-year command not because of some advantage to the republic or the needs of war or admiration for his *virtù* but because of his conspiracy with Crassus and Pompey to seize control of the republic.[3] 4 The military command had not been extended for Sulla when he first began to struggle with Marius, but the reason for it was the division between the Nobility and the Plebs;[4] and because the Plebs had Marius as their leader, the Nobility was forced to get a leader for itself. 5 I conclude therefore that when Rome was not corrupted the extension of military commands and the continuation of the consulate, which they often practiced in difficult times, were a useful and venerable measure; but once the city was corrupted, civil strife and the seeds of tyranny were sown even without the extension of military command. 6 And therefore we may conclude that even if there had not been extensions as well neither Caesar nor the others who seized control of the republic would have lacked either the idea or the ability to disturb it some other way.

NOTES

1. Guicciardini would reduce the period when the lengthening of military command had any real influence on Caesar's career to the period from his conquest of Gaul beginning in 58 B.C. and his victory over the Helvetii at Bibracte until he crossed the Rubicon in 49.

2. A reference to the conspiracy of Catiline in 63 B.C.

3. I.e., the formation of the First Triumvirate in 60 B.C.

4. Thus Guicciardini takes issue with Machiavelli's example of Sulla by arguing that it was class conflict that led to his victory in 88 B.C.

Works Consulted

Ascoli, A. R., and Victoria Kahn, eds. *Machiavelli and the Discourse of Literature.* Ithaca: Cornell University Press, 1993.

Bandello, Matteo. *Le Novelle.* Edited by Gioachino Brognoligo. Bari: Laterza *(Scrittori d'Italia),* 1928.

Baron, Hans. *The Crisis of the Early Italian Renaissance.* Princeton: Princeton University Press, 1966.

———. "Machiavelli the Republican Citizen and Author of *The Prince.*" In his *In Search of Florentine Civic Humanism: Essays on the Transition from Medieval to Modern Thought,* 2: 101–151. Princeton: Princeton University Press, 1988.

Berlin, Isaiah. "The Originality of Machiavelli." In his *Against the Current: Essays in the History of Ideas,* 25–79. New York: Viking, 1980.

Bondanella, Peter. *Machiavelli and the Art of Renaissance History.* Detroit: Wayne State University Press, 1973.

Butters, H. C. *Governors and Government in Early Sixteenth-Century Florence.* Oxford: Clarendon Press, 1985.

Celse, Mireille. "La *beffa* chez Machiavel, dramaturge et conteur." In *Formes et significations de la "beffa" dans la littérature italienne de la Renaissance,* edited by André Rochon, 1, 99–110. Paris: Université de la Sorbonne nouvelle, 1972.

Chabod, Federico. *Machiavelli and the Renaissance.* Translated by David Moore. London: Bowes and Bowes, 1960.

Colish, Marcia. "The Idea of Liberty in Machiavelli." *Journal of the History of Ideas* 32 (1971): 323–351.

———. "Machiavelli's Art of War: A Reconsideration," *Renaissance Quarterly* 51 (winter 1998): 1151–1168.

Curtius, Ernst Robert. *European Literature and the Latin Middle Ages.* Translated by Willard R. Trask. New York: Pantheon (Bollingen Series 36), 1963.

De Grazia, Sebastian. *Machiavelli in Hell.* Princeton: Princeton University Press, 1989.

Dionisotti, Carlo. *Machiavellerie: Storia e fortune di Machiavelli.* Turin: Einaudi, 1980.

Dorey, T. A., ed. *Livy.* London: Routledge and Kegan Paul; Toronto: University of Toronto Press, 1971.

A Florentine Diary from 1450 to 1516 by Luca Landucci Continued by an Anonymous Writer 'Till 1542 with Notes by Iodoco del Badia. Translated by Alice de Rosen Jervis. London: Dent; New York: Dutton, 1927.

Friedrich, Hugo. *Montaigne.* Berkeley and Los Angeles: University of California Press, 1991.

Gagneux, Marcel. *"Une tentative de démythification de l'idéologie républicaine: les* Considérations *sur les* Discours *de Machiavel de François Guichardin."* In *Culture et société en Italie du moyen âge à la renaissance: hommage à André Rochon. Centre interuniversitaire de recherche sur la Renaissance italienne,* no. 13: 199–217. Paris: Université de la Sorbonne nouvelle, 1985.

Garin, Eugenio. *Machiavelli fra politica e storia.* Turin: Einaudi, 1993.

Gilbert, Felix. "Bernardo Rucellai and the *Orti Oricellari.*" *Journal of the Warburg and Courtauld Institutes* 12 (1949): 101–131. Reprint, Felix Gilbert, *History: Choice and Commitment,* 215–246. Cambridge: Harvard University Press, 1977.

———."The Composition and Structure of Machiavelli's *Discorsi.*" *Journal of the History of Ideas* 14 (1953): 135–156. Reprint, Felix Gilbert, *History: Choice and Commitment,* 115–133. Cambridge: Harvard University Press, 1977.

———."Florentine Political Assumptions in the Period of Savonarola and Soderini." *Journal of the Warburg and Courtauld Institutes* 20 (1957): 187–214.

———. *Machiavelli and Guicciardini: Politics and History in Sixteenth-Century Florence.* Princeton: Princeton University Press, 1965.

Godman, Peter. *From Poliziano to Machiavelli: Florentine Humanism in the High Renaissance.* Princeton: Princeton University Press, 1998.

Guicciardini, Francesco. *Le cose fiorentine.* Edited by Roberto Ridolfi. Florence: Leo Olschki, 1945.

———. *Dialogo del reggimento di Firenze.* Edited by Mario Anselmi and Carlo Varotti. Turin: Bollati Boringhiere, 1994.

———. *Dialogue on the Government of Florence.* Edited by Alison Brown. Cambridge: Cambridge University Press, 1994.

———. *The History of Florence.* Translated by Mario Domandi. New York: Harper Torchbooks, 1970.

———. *The History of Italy.* Edited and translated by Sidney Alexander. New York: Macmillan; London: Collier-Macmillan, 1969.

———. *Maxims and Reflections of a Renaissance Statesman (Ricordi),* Translated by Mario Domandi. New York: Harper Torchbooks, 1965.

———. *Opere (Storie fiorentine, Dialogo del reggimento di Firenze, Ricordi, e Altri Scritti).* Edited by Emanuella Scarano. Turin: Unione tipografico-editrice torinese, 1970.

———. *Ricordi.* Edited by Mario Fubini and Ettore Barelli. Milan: Biblioteca Universale Rizzoli, 1984.

———. *Scritti politici e ricordi.* Edited by Roberto Palmarocchi. Bari: Laterza *(Scrittori d'Italia),* 1933.

———. *Selected Writings.* Edited and Translated by Cecil and Margaret Grayson. London: Oxford University Press, 1965.

———. *Storie fiorentine dal 1378 al 1509.* Edited by Roberto Palmarocchi. Bari: Laterza *(Scrittori d'Italia),* 1931.

———. *Storia d'Italia (I–IX),* vol. 2, and *Storia d'Italia (XI–XX),* vol. 3. Edited by Emanuella Scarano. Turin: Unione tipografico-editrice torinese, 1981; reprint, 1987.

Hale, J. R. "Armies, Navies, and the Art of War." In *The New Cambridge Modern History,* 2: 481–509. Cambridge: Cambridge University Press, 1968.

———. *Artists and Warfare in the Renaissance.* New Haven: Yale University Press, 1990.

———. *The Literary Works of Machiavelli.* London: Oxford University Press, 1961.

Hanson, Victor Davis. *The Soul of Battle: From Ancient Times to the Present Day, How Three Great Liberators Vanquished Tyranny.* New York: Free Press, 1999.

Hulliung, Mark. *Citizen Machiavelli.* Princeton: Princeton University Press, 1983.

Kahn, Victoria. *Machiavellian Rhetoric: From the Counter-Reformation to Milton.* Princeton: Princeton University Press, 1994.

Kohl, Benjamin G., and Ronald G. Witt, ed. and trans. With Elizabeth B. Welles. *The Earthly Republic: Italian Humanists on Government and Society.* Philadelphia: University of Pennsylvania Press, 1978.

Machiavelli, Bernardo. *Libro di ricordi.* Edited by C. Olschki. Florence: F. Le Monnier, 1954.

Machiavelli, Niccolò. *Arte della guerra e scritti politici minori.* Edited by Sergio Bertelli. Milan: Feltrinelli, 1961.

———. *The Chief Works and Others.* Translated by Allan Gilbert. 3 vols. Durham, N.C.: Duke University Press, 1965.

———. *The Comedies of Machiavelli.* Edited and translated by David Sices and James B. Atkinson. Hanover, N.H.: University Press of New England, 1985.

———. *Discorsi sopra la prima deca di Tito Livio.* Edited by Gian Mario Anselmi and Carlo Varotti with Paolo Fazion and Elisabetta Menetti. Torino: Bollati Boringhieri, 1993.

———. *Discorsi sopra la prima deca di Tito Livio.* Edited by Giorgio Inglese. With an introduction by Gennaro Sasso. Milan: Biblioteca universale Rizzoli, 1984.

———. *Discorsi sopra la prima deca di Tito Livio seguiti dalle Considerazioni ai Discorsi del Machiavelli di Francesco Guicciardini.* Edited by Corrado Vivanti. Torino: Giulio Einaudi, 1983.

———. *Discourses on Livy.* Translated by Julia Conaway Bondanella and Peter Bondanella. Oxford: Oxford University Press, 1997.

———. *Discourses on Livy.* Translated by Harvey C. Mansfield and Nathan Tarcov. Chicago: University of Chicago Press, 1996.

———. *The Discourses.* Translated by Leslie J. Walker, S.J. London: Routledge and Kegan Paul, 1950. Reprint, revised by Brian Richardson, edited by Bernard Crick. New York: Penguin, 1970.

———. *Florentine Histories.* Translated by Laura F. Banfield and Harvey C. Mansfield, Jr. Princeton: Princeton University Press, 1988.

———. *Legazioni e commissarie.* Edited by Sergio Bertelli. 3 vols. Milan: Feltrinelli, 1964.

———. *Machiavelli and His Friends: Their Personal Correspondence.* Edited and translated by James B. Atkinson and David Sices. DeKalb: Northern Illinois University Press, 1996.

———. *Opere.* Edited by Ezio Raimondi. Milan: Ugo Mursia, 1971; 7th ed., 1976.

———. *Opere.* Vols. 1 and 2. Edited by Rinaldo Rinaldi. Turin: Unione tipografico-editrice torinese, 1999.

———. *Opere.* Vol. 1. Edited by Corrado Vivanti. Turin: Einaudi-Gallimard, 1997.

———. *Opere: Istorie fiorentine e altre opere storiche e politiche.* Vol. 2. Edited by Alessandro Montevecchi. Turin: Unione tipografico-editrice torinese, 1971.

———. *The Prince.* Edited and translated by James B. Atkinson. New York: Macmillan, 1985.

———. *Il Principe.* Edited by L. Arthur Burd. Oxford: Clarendon Press, 1891. Reprint, 1968.

———. *Il Teatro e gli scritti letterari.* Edited by Franco Gaeta. Milan: Feltrinelli, 1965.

———. *Tutte le opere.* Edited by Mario Martelli. Florence: Sansoni, 1971.

Mansfield, Harvey C., Jr. *Machiavelli's New Modes and Orders: A Study of the Discourses on Livy.* Ithaca: Cornell University Press, 1979.

———. *Machiavelli's Virtue.* Chicago: University of Chicago Press, 1996.

Martelli, Mario. "La Logica provvidenzialistica e il capitolo XXVI del *Principe.*" *Interpres* 4 (1981–1982): 262–384.

———. *Machiavelli e gli storici antichi.* Rome: Salerno, 1998.

———. *"Schede sulla cultura di Machiavelli." Interpres* 6 (1985–1986): 283–330.

Najemy, John M. *Between Friends: Discourses of Power and Desire in the Machiavelli-Vettori Letters of 1513–1515.* Princeton: Princeton University Press, 1993.

Niccoli, Ottavia. *Prophecy and People in Renaissance Italy.* Translated by Lydia G. Cochrane. Princeton: Princeton University Press, 1990.

Pacini, Marcello, ed. *La virtù e la libertà: Ideali e civiltà nella formazione degli Stati Uniti.* Turin: Edizioni della fondazione Giovanni Agnelli, 1995.

Parel, Anthony J. *The Machiavellian Cosmos.* New Haven: Yale University Press, 1992.

Petrarca, Francesco. *Le Familiari.* Vol. 4. Edited by Vittorio Rossi and Umberto Bosco. Florence: Sansoni, 1942.

Phillips, Mark. *Francesco Guicciardini: The Historian's Craft.* Toronto: University of Toronto Press, 1977.

Pincin, Carlo. *"Osservazioni sul modo di procedere di Machiavelli nei Discorsi."* In *Renaissance Studies in Honor of Hans Baron,* edited by Anthony Molho and John A. Tedeschi, 385–408. DeKalb: Northern Illinois University Press, 1971.

———. *"La prefazione e la dedicatoria dei* Discorsi *di Machiavelli." Giornale storico della letteratura italiana* 143 (1978): 72–83.

———."*Sul testo di Machiavelli: I* 'Discorsi sopra la prima deca de Tito Livio.'" *Atti dell' Accademia delle Scienze di Torino* 94 (1959–1960): 506–518.

Pitkin, Hanna Fenichel. *Fortune is a Woman: Gender and Politics in the Thought of Niccolò Machiavelli.* Berkeley and Los Angeles: University of California Press, 1984.

Pocock, J. G. A. *The Machiavellian Moment: Florentine Political Thought and the Atlantic Republican Tradition.* Princeton: Princeton University Press, 1975.

Rebhorn, Wayne A. *Foxes and Lions: Machiavelli's Confidence Men.* Ithaca: Cornell University Press, 1988.

Ridley, R. T. "Echoes of Justin in Machiavelli's *Discorsi.*" *Critica Storica* 25 (1988): 113–118.

———."Machiavelli and Roman History." *Quaderni di Storia* 18 (1983): 197–219.

———."Machiavelli's Edition of Livy." *Rinascimento,* 2d ser., 27 (1987): 327–341.

Ridolfi, Roberto. *The Life of Francesco Guicciardini.* Translated by Cecil Grayson. New York: Knopf, 1968.

———. *The Life of Niccolò Machiavelli.* Translated by Cecil Grayson. London: Routledge and Kegan Paul, 1963.

———. *Vita di Niccolò Machiavelli (settima edizione italiana accresciuta e riveduta).* Florence: Sansoni, 1978.

Rubinstein, Nicolai. "Florentine Constitutionalism and Medici Ascendancy in the Fifteenth Century." In *Florentine Studies: Politics and Society in Renaissance Florence,* edited by Nicolai Rubinstein, 442–462. London: Faber and Faber; Evanston, Ill.: Northwestern University Press, 1968.

———. *"Il Poliziano e la Questione delle Origini di Firenze,"* in *Il Poliziano e il Suo Tempo: Atti del IV Convegno Internazionale di Studi sul Rinascimento,* 104–107. Florence: Sansoni, 1957.

———."Politics and Constitution in Florence at the End of the Fifteenth Century." In *Italian Renaissance Studies: A Tribute to the Late Cecelia M. Ady,* edited by E. F. Jacob, 148–183. London: Faber and Faber; New York: Barnes and Noble, 1960.

Sasso, Gennaro. "Intorno alla composizione dei *Discorsi.*" *Giornale storico della letteratura italiana* 134 (1957): 514ff.

———. *Machiavelli e gli antichi e altri saggi.* Milan and Naples: Riccardo Ricciardi Editore. Vol. 1, 1987; vol. 2, 1988; vol. 3, 1988; vol. 4, 1997.

———. *Niccolò Machiavelli: Storia del suo pensiero politico.* Bologna: Società Editrice Il Mulino, 1980.

———. *Per Francesco Guicciardini: Quattro Studi.* Rome: Istituto storico per il medio evo, 1984.

Skinner, Quentin. *The Foundations of Modern Political Thought.* 2 vols. Cambridge: Cambridge University Press, 1978.

Stephens, J. N. *The Fall of the Florentine Republic, 1512–1530.* Oxford: Clarendon Press, 1983.

Strauss, Leo. *Thoughts on Machiavelli.* Seattle: University of Washington Press, 1969.

Sullivan, Vickie B. *Machiavelli's Three Romes: Religion, Human Liberty, and Politics Reformed.* DeKalb: Northern Illinois University Press, 1996.

———, ed. *The Comedy and Tragedy of Machiavelli.* New Haven: Yale University Press, 2000.

Viroli, Maurizio. "Machiavelli and the Republican Idea of Politics." In *Machiavelli and Republicanism,* edited by Gisela Bock, Quentin Skinner, and Maurizio Viroli, 143–171. Cambridge: Cambridge University Press, 1990.

———. *Machiavelli.* New York: Oxford University Press, 1998.

———. *Niccolò's Smile: A Biography of Machiavelli.* New York: Farrar, Straus, and Giroux, 2000.

Weinstein, Donald. *Savonarola and Florence: Prophecy and Patriotism in the Renaissance.* Princeton: Princeton University Press, 1970.

Whitfield, J. H. *Discourses on Machiavelli.* Cambridge: W. Heffer, 1969.

———. *Machiavelli.* Oxford: Basil Blackwell, 1947. Reprint, New York: Russell and Russell, 1966.

Index of Names & Places